UNIVERSAL HISTORY.

UNIVERSAL HISTORY,

FROM THE

CREATION OF THE WORLD

TO THE

BEGINNING OF THE EIGHTEENTH CENTURY.

BY THE LATE

HON. ALEXANDER FRASER TYTLER,

LORD WOODHOUSELEE,

SENATOR OF THE COLLEGE OF JUSTICE, AND LORD COMMISSIONER OF JUSTICIARY IN SCOTLAND, AND FORMERLY PROFESSOR OF CIVIL HISTORY, AND GREEK AND ROMAN ANTIQUITIES, IN THE UNIVERSITY OF EDINBURGH.

IN TWO VOLUMES.

VOL. II.

BOSTON:

FETRIDGE AND COMPANY.

1854.

CONTENTS.

BOOK THE FIFTH.

CHAPTER IV.

CHAPTER V.

CHAPTER VI.

CHAPTER VII.

BOOK THE SIXTH.

CHAPTER I.

CHAPTER II.

CHAPTER III.

CHAPTER IV.

CHAPTER V.

CHAPTER VI.

CHAPTER VII.

CHAPTER VIII.

CHAPTER IX.

CHAPTER X.

CHAPTER XI.

CHAPTER XII.

CHAPTER XIII.

CHAPTER XIV.

CHAPTER XV.

CHAPTER XVI.

CHAPTER XVII.

CHAPTER XVIII.

CHAPTER XIX.

CHAPTER XX.

CHAPTER XXI.

CHAPTER XXII.

CHAPTER XXIII.

CHAPTER XXIV.

CHAPTER XXV.

CHAPTER XXVI.

CHAPTER XXVII.

CHAPTER XXVIII.

CHAPTER XXIX.

CHAPTER XXX.

CHAPTER XXXI.

CHAPTER XXXII.

CHAPTER XXXIII.

CHAPTER XXXIV.

CHAPTER XXXV.

CHAPTER XXXVI.

UNIVERSAL HISTORY.

BOOK THE FIFTH.

CHAPTER IV.

Establishment of Christianity in the Empire.

A THOROUGH acquaintance with the history of the world and the state of mankind at the time of our Savior's birth has led the wisest and most enlightened inquirers to conclude, that the Almighty having designed to illuminate the world by a revelation, there was no period at which it was more certainly required than that in which it was actually sent; nor could any concurrence of circumstances have been more favorable for its extensive dissemination, than that which took place at the time of our Savior's mission. A great part of the known world was at this time under the dominion of the Romans, and subject to all those grievances which are the inevitable result of a system of arbitrary power. Yet this circumstance of the union of so many nations into one great Empire was of considerable advantage for the propagation and advancement of Christianity: for that spirit of civilization which nations, hitherto sunk in barbarism, derived from an intercourse with a refined and liberal people, was favorable to the diffusion of a religion which was founded in an extension of the social feelings; that is to say, in universal charity and benevolence. These nations were, previous to this, sunk in the grossest superstition. The pagan religion had no influence towards refining or improving the morals of mankind. The only attributes which distinguished the heathen gods from the race of ordinary men were their power and their immortality. They were endowed with the same passions as human creatures, and those distinguishing attributes of power and immortality served, in general, only to extend the measure and the enormity of their vices. The example of their gods was, therefore, an incentive to *vice* instead of *virtue*; and those rites with which many of them were worshipped, and which were conceived to be peculiarly acceptable to them, were often the grossest violations not only of *decency* but of *humanity*.

The *philosophy* too of the pagan world was but ill calculated to supply the place of religion in the refinement of morals. The doctrines of Epicurus, which were highly prevalent at the time of the birth of Christ, by representing pleasure as the chief good, by imposing no restraint on the indulgence of the passions, and limiting all happiness to the enjoyments of the present life, tended to corrupt and degrade human nature to a rank little superior to that of the brutes. Next to the Epicurean system, the doctrines most prevalent at that time were those of the new Academy, very different from those of the old Academy, founded by Plato. The new *Academics* asserted the impossibility of arriving at truth, and held it entirely a matter of doubt whether vice or virtue were preferable. These opinions evidently struck at the foundation not only of religion, but of morality: and as to the other sects, although the *Platonists*, the *Stoics*, and the disciples of *Aristotle*, made the belief of a God a part of their philosophy, and some of them—as, for example, the *Stoics*—entertained sublime ideas with regard to the nature of virtue and the dignity of man, yet the austerity of their doctrines, and indeed the incomprehensibility of many of their tenets, gave them but few followers in comparison with the popular sects of the *Epicureans* and new *Academics*.*

At no period, therefore, of the history of the world, did mankind stand more in need of a superior light to dispel the mists of error, and to point out the path of true religion and of virtue, than at that great era when the *Messiah* appeared upon earth. The propagation of a new religion, which thus strongly opposed itself, not only to the prevailing passions and habits of mankind, but to established and revered systems of philosophy, could not fail to encounter a violent and obstinate opposition. Let us take a short progressive view of the state of the church in the four first centuries from its institution.

The severe persecutions which the first Christians underwent from the Romans, who had then acquired the sovereignty of the greatest part of the known world, have been reckoned a singular exception to that spirit of toleration which this enlightened people showed for the various systems of idolatrous worship, different

* Not only was this the situation of the pagan world, but even the Jews themselves at this period were a most corrupted and degenerate people. That law which they had received from God they had vitiated by the intermixture of heathen doctrines, and ceremonies borrowed from the pagans; while their doctors dissented from the opinions of each other in the most essential articles, such as the literal or figurative interpretation of the Scripture, the temporal or the spiritual authority of the promised Messiah, the materiality or spirituality of the soul; in short, Judaism itself was so much corrupted or disguised, that it had become a source of national discord and division among its own votaries, as well as the object of abhorrence and contempt to the pagan world.

from their own, which they found prevailing in the countries which they conquered; but this may be very easily accounted for: the Romans showed a spirit of toleration to the religious opinions of other nations, because they found nothing in these which aimed at the subversion of their own religion, nor any thing of that zeal of making converts which so remarkably distinguished the votaries of Christianity. The religion of the Romans was inseparably interwoven with their system of government. The Christians, by exposing the absurdities of their system of worship, in effect undermined the fabric of their political constitution; and hence they were not without reason considered by the Romans as a dangerous body of men, whom it became the interest of the empire to suppress and exterminate. Hence those opprobrious epithets with which they have been stigmatized by the Roman writers, and hence those cruel persecutions which they underwent from the emperors and their deputies in the provinces.

In the first century after the death of Christ, the emperors Nero and Domitian exercised against the Christians all that sanguinary cruelty which preëminently distinguished their characters; and the number of martyrs whose names are recorded to have suffered in those persecutions, though suspected to be exaggerated much beyond the truth, was yet extremely great. These were, no doubt, chiefly men of some eminence, whose consideration and authority with the lower ranks of people made them to be regarded as peculiarly dangerous, or whose wealth offered a tempting object to the avarice of the Roman governors.

But, under all these discouragements, Christianity made a most rapid and wonderful progress, through the power and efficacy of its first teachers, those holy men to whom the *Messiah* himself had given in charge the enunciation of his religion to mankind.

There is no subject which has afforded greater controversy than the ascertainment of that external form which our Savior is supposed to have given to the primitive church, or that method which was instituted for its government. While the supporters of the Roman Catholic Faith maintain, that is was our Savior's intention that the whole Christian church should form one body, which was to be governed by St. Peter and his successors—the doctors of the church of England deny the evidence of any divine institution of a supreme perpetual head ; but refer to the *Apostles* the nomination of *Bishops*, or *Ministers*, presiding over a certain district, whom the civil authority, and regulations of good policy, afterwards subjected to a *Metropolitan*, a *Patriarch*, or an *Archbishop*. The Presbyterians again affirm, that it was the intention of the Great Author of Christianity that all ministers and teachers of the Gospel should be upon a level of perfect equality. To these three opinions a fourth may be added, which, perhaps, comes nearer the truth than any of them, and this is, that neither Christ nor his Apostles have laid down *any certain or precise system of church government;* but, confining their precepts to the pure doctrines of religion, have, with admirable wisdom, left all Christian associations to regulate the government of their churches in that manner which is best adapted to the spirit of their political constitutions, and to the varying state of mankind in different ages or periods of society.

It is certain that, during the first century from the death of Christ, the several churches which had been instituted by the Apostles, or their successors, were entirely independent of each other; and the bishops, or presbyters, who governed them, acknowledged no sort of subjection to any common head; not till the *second* century, was there such a thing known as a general council of the church.

About the middle of the second century, we find that the books of the New Testament had been collected into one volume, and were received as a canon of faith in all the Christian churches. This selection of the inspired books from the compositions of many ministers, or teachers of Christianity, who had written in imitation of their style and had recorded the acts of our Savior and his Apostles, is supposed to have been made by some of the early Fathers of the church. The four Gospels, it is generally believed, had been collected during the lifetime of St. John. The books of the Old Testament had been translated from the Hebrew into Greek by the orders of Ptolemy Philadelphus, in the year 285 before Christ.*

---

* The most ancient account we have of this Septuagint translation of the Bible is from Aristeas, an officer in the guards of Ptolemy Philadelphus, at the time when it was completed. He informs us that Ptolemy, being desirous of forming a very great library at Alexandria, employed Demetrius Phalereus, a noble Athenian, to procure from different nations all books of any reputation that were among them. Demetrius informed him that the Jews were possessed of a most extraordinary volume, containing the ancient history of that people, and the ordinances of their lawgiver Moses, which he represented as a singular curiosity. Ptolemy immediately sent to Jerusalem to procure this volume, and being desirous of understanding its contents, he requested of Eleazer the High Priest to send him six elders of each of the tribes, men of fidelity and ability, to translate it into the Greek language; in consideration of which favor, he agreed to set at liberty all the Jewish captives, to the amount of a hundred and twenty thousand, whom his father Ptolemy Soter had reduced to slavery. The request was granted; a magnificent copy of the Old Testament, written in letters of gold, and *seventy-two* learned men, were sent from Jerusalem to Alexandria, where they were received with the utmost respect, and lodged in a palace prepared for their reception.

In modern times, Dupin, Prideaux, and others, have endeavored to discredit many of the circumstances enumerated by Aristeas; but all agree in the main fact, that a translation of the books of the Old Testament was made into Greek under Ptolemy Philadelphus, and lodged in the Alexandrine library.

For four hundred years this translation was in high estimation with the Jews; it was read in their synagogues in preference to the Hebrew, and that even in Jerusalem and Judea. But when they saw that it was equally valued by the Christians, they became jealous of it, and employed Aquila, a heathen proselyte o the Jewish religion, to make a new translation, which he completed about A. D. 128. In this work Aquila took care to give such a turn to all the ancient prophecies relating to the Messiah, that they should not apply to Jesus Christ;

As the Christian religion was received, at first, by many, from the conviction of its truth from external evidence, and without a due examination of its doctrines, it was not surprising that many who called themselves Christians should retain the doctrines of a prevailing philosophy to which they had been accustomed, and endeavor to accommodate these to the system of revelation, which they found in the sacred volumes. Such, for example, were the Christian Gnostics, who intermixed the doctrines of the oriental philosophy concerning the two separate principles, a good and an evil, with the precepts of Christianity, and admitted the authority of Zoroaster, as an inspired personage, equally with that of Jesus Christ. Such likewise were the sect of the Ammonians, who vainly endeavored to reconcile together the opinions of all the different schools of the pagan philosophy, and attempted, with yet greater absurdity, to accommodate all these to the doctrines of Christianity. From this confusion of the pagan philosophy with the plain and simple doctrines of the Christian religion, the church, in this period of its infant state, suffered in a most essential manner. The Christian doctors began now to introduce that subtle and obscure erudition which tends to perplex and bewilder, instead of enlightening the understanding. The effect of this in involving religion in all the perplexity of the scholastic philosophy, and thus removing its doctrines beyond the comprehension of the mass of mankind, was, with great justice, condemned by many of the wisest fathers of the church; and hence sprung those inveterate and endless controversies between faith and reason, religion and philosophy, which began at that early period, and have, unfortunately, continued to the present day.

We have remarked, that hitherto the Christian churches were entirely independent of each other. About the middle of the second century, the Greek churches began to unite into general associations; the whole churches of a province forming one body, and agreeing to be governed by general rules of discipline, which were concerted and framed by a council of the elders, or deputies from each particular church. These assemblies the Greeks termed Synods, and the Latin churches, following the same example, termed these general meetings Concilia; and the rules of discipline there enacted were called Canons. As it was necessary for the maintenance of order in these assemblies that some person of authority should preside, the right of presiding was conferred, by an election of the several bishops, either upon some one of themselves possessing eminent virtue or abilities, or, not improbably, on the

---

and other translations on the same insidious principle were made by Symmachus and Theodotion.

Those who desire more particular accounts of the Septuagint translation may consult Prideaux' Connections, part 2. b. i.; Hody de Bibliorum Textibus; Owen's Inquiry into the Septuagint versions; Blair's Lectures on the Canon; and Michaelis's Introduction to the New Testament.

person who had the most extensive church or diocese ; and hence arose the right of the Metropolitans. A short time after, we find a superior order in the church, who regulated ecclesiastical matters over a whole kingdom, or rather a district, of the Christian world : these were styled Patriarchs ; and by and by, in the ordinary course of policy, a subordination took place even among these, and the Bishop of Rome was generally acknowledged, in the right of his predecessor, St. Peter, as the head, or chief of the Patriarchs. We shall see afterwards how this Patriarch, by adding temporal power and authority to spiritual, contrived to maintain a supreme ascendency, not only over all ecclesiastical persons, but civil governors and sovereign princes.

In the meantime, however, the Christian church was stilll considered, by the Roman emperors, in a hostile point of view. Even Trajan forgot, at times, the humanity of his character ; and numbers of the Christians, in his reign and in that of his successor Adrian, were, under the pretence of a political necessity, subjected to all the rage of sanguinary persecution : nor was this intolerant zeal abated under those excellent princes the Antonines ; and, in the succeeding reign of Severus, the whole provinces of the empire were stained with the blood of the Christian martyrs.

In the third century, the Christian church enjoyed greater tranquillity ; but this was owing less to a spirit of humanity in the Roman emperors, than to particular political circumstances, and chiefly to the short, violent, and turbulent reigns of many of those who swayed the sceptre.

The Christian doctrines were not more vigorously combated by the *secular* arm, than by the pens of the heathen philosophers. Porphyry, a Syrian by birth, and a man of great abilities, wrote a long and most laborious work against Christianity ; and Philostratus, one of the most eminent rhetoricians of that age, contrived a new method of attack, which was by drawing artful comparisons between the life and doctrines of Christ and those of the ancient philosophers. These attacks, however, were, on the whole, rather serviceable than dangerous to the cause of Christianity, since they excited the zeal and abilities of many of the ablest Fathers of the church to defend its doctrines, and oppose, by their writings, the malevolent efforts of its enemies. The works of Origen—of Dionysius, bishop of Alexandria—and of Cyprian, bishop of Carthage—are read at this day with much pleasure and profit ; and, at the time they were written, contributed, in a most eminent degree, to the advancement of religion. It must, however, be observed, with regard to the works of Origen, that from one idea of his, regarding the interpretation of the Scriptures, he exposes the Christian religion to be contaminated by every extravagance of the human brain. It was his notion that the Scriptures ought not always to be literally interpreted ; and even where the literal sense was to be received, as in historical facts, that there was always a mystical and hidden meaning which these were intended to convey. It is easy to perceive, that as this leaves room for the utmost latitude of conjecture with regard to these hidden meanings, nothing could be more dangerous than the allowance of such mode of interpretation, and accordingly, it was productive of innumerable errors and dissensions. Christianity, however, on the whole, made the most rapid progress in the third century. A great part of the Gauls, of Germany and of Britain had now received the light of the Gospel.

In the fourth century, the Christian religion was alternately persecuted and cherished by the Roman emperors. Under Diocletian, there was, for many years, a most sanguinary persecution, which arose less from a spirit of cruelty in that emperor than from the easiness of his temper in giving way to the persuasions of his son-in-law Galerius, and the remonstrances of the heathen priests.

The church, we have seen, was restored to tranquillity by the accession of Constantine the Great, whose zeal for the propagation of Christianity, in the latter part of his reign, was as ardent —and, as some have thought, as intemperate—as that of its enemies for its destruction. His three sons, Constantine, Constantius, and Constans, without the genius of their father, inherited his religious principles, and were active in the extirpation of paganism and the promotion of Christianity.

We have seen how great was the reverse under the succeeding reign of Julian: genius, learning, philosophic moderation, heroic valor on the one hand, superstitious credulity, bigotry, and hypocrisy on the other, composed this singularly inconsistent character. The methods, which he took to undermine the Christian religion, we have observed, were dictated by the most consummate policy and artifice. His attempts to reform the pagan worship, and his depriving the Christians of the common privileges of citizens and of the benefit of the laws, were more fatal to the cause of religion than any other species of persecution. The succeeding emperors, Valentinian I., Valens, Gratian, and Valentinian II., contributed in a great degree to heal those wounds which Christianity had suffered from the attacks of Julian; but it was reserved for Theodosius to put a final period to the pagan superstition in the Roman empire.

In the history of the human mind there are no events more deserving of attention than the rise and fall of popular superstitions. As the polytheism, which had so long maintained its authority over the Roman empire, came to a final period at the time of which we now treat, it is worth our while to bestow some consideration upon an event of that magnitude and importance. The structure of the pagan religion in the Roman empire was so interwoven with its political constitution, as to possess a very strong hold on the minds of the people.

From the age of Numa to the reign of Gratian, the Romans preserved the regular succession of the several colleges of the sacerdotal order.* Fifteen pontiffs exercised supreme jurisdiction over all things and persons that were consecrated to the service of the gods, and determined all questions with regard to religion. Fifteen augurs observed the face of the heavens, and determined the success of the most important enterprises according to the flight of birds. Fifteen keepers of the Sibylline books consulted the records of future events. Six vestals guarded the sacred fire. Seven epulos prepared the table of the gods, conducted the solemn processions, and regulated the ceremonies of the annual festivals. The *flamens* of Jupiter, of Mars, and Quirinus were considered as the ministers of the tutelar gods of Rome. The *king* of the sacrifices represented the person of Numa and of his successors in the religious functions, which could be performed only by royal hands. The confraternities of the Salians and the Lupercals practised the most ridiculous rites, by way of recommending themselves to the favor of the gods. The authority which the Roman priests had formerly obtained in the councils of the republic was gradually weakened by the establishment of the imperial dignity, and by the removal of the seat of the empire; but the veneration of their sacred character was still protected by the laws and manners of their country, and they still continued, more especially the college of pontiffs, to exercise in the capital, and sometimes in the provinces, the rights of their ecclesiastical and civil jurisdiction. They received from the public revenue an ample salary, which liberally supplied the splendor of the priesthood, and the expenses of the religious worship of the state; as the service of the altar was not incompatible with the command of armies, the offices of pontiff or of augur were aspired to by the most illustrious of the Romans. Cicero, as well as Pliny, acknowledge that the office of augur was the height of their ambition. Even the Christian emperors did not refuse this ancient office of the highest dignity, but accepted, like their predecessors, of the robe and ensigns of *Pontifex maximus*. Gratian was the first who rejected those profane *insignia*. He applied to the service of the state or of the church the revenues of the priests and vestals, abolished their honors and immunities, and thus undermined the ancient fabric of Roman superstition, which had subsisted for eleven hundred years. Paganism was still, however, the constitutional religion of the senate. The temple in which they assembled was adorned by the statue and altar of Victory—a majestic female standing on a globe, with flowing garments, expanded wings, and in her hand a crown of laurel. The senators continued to take their solemn initiatory oaths upon the altar of the goddess, till this ancient monument was removed from its

* Gibbon's Roman History, ch. 28

pedestal by the emperor Constantius. Julian had restored the altar of Victory; and Gratian once more abolished it, though he spared the public statues of the gods which were in the temples of the city. In the time of Theodosius, a majority of the senate voted an application to the emperor to restore the altar and statue of Victory; and the cause of paganism was artfully and eloquently pleaded by the senator Symmachus, as that of Christianity by the celebrated Ambrose, archbishop of Milan.

The dispute was managed on both sides with great ability. The argument of Symmachus was certainly the best that could be brought in support of his cause; he balances the certain effects of an adherence to ancient customs with the uncertain consequences of innovation. If, says he, the past ages of the Roman state have been crowned with glory and prosperity—if the devout people have obtained the blessings they solicited at the altars of the gods—is it not advisable to persevere in the same salutary practices, rather than risk the unknown dangers that may attend rash innovations? The reasoning was plausible. But the arguments of Ambrose had a more solid foundation; he exposed the futility of that blind and indolent maxim that *all* innovations are dangerous; he reprobated that absurd veneration for antiquity, which would not only maintain mankind in childhood and ignorance, but discourage every improvement of science, and replunge the human race into their original barbarism. After removing that veil which shut out the light, he displayed the beauty and excellence of the Christian system, and finally prevailed, to the conviction of the senators, against the able advocate of paganism. In a full meeting of that order, the question was solemnly proposed by Theodosius, whether the worship of Jesus Christ or of Jupiter should be the religion of the Romans. Jupiter was degraded and condemned by a large majority. The decrees of the senate, which proscribed the worship of idols, were ratified by the general consent of the people. The citizens flocked to the churches to receive the sacrament of baptism, and the temples of the pagan deities were abandoned to ruin and contempt.

The downfall of paganism in the capital was soon followed by its extirpation in the provinces. Theodosius began by prohibiting sacrifices; and lest the temples should incite to the celebration of ancient ceremonies, he ordered them to be shut. But the zeal of the bishops and fathers of the church exceeded their commission: they marched at the head of numerous bands of their new proselytes, and determined to abolish every remnant of idolatry by levelling the temples with the ground. Happily, the skill and solidity with which many of those ancient buildings had been constructed preserved them from absolute ruin; a few likewise were saved by being converted into Christian churches. The temple of Serapis, at Alexandria, in a part of which was the celebrated library of the Ptolemies, was one of the most magnificent structures of the East.

Theophilus, the bishop of Alexandria, had determined its downfall. The priests took arms in defence of their god, but were finally overpowered by the strength of numbers; the temple was ransacked, the library pillaged and destroyed, and the awful statue of the god himself underwent the general fate. The catastrophe of Serapis is eloquently described by Gibbon. A great number of plates of different metals, artificially joined together, composed the majestic figure of the deity, who touched on either side the walls of the sanctuary. The aspect of Serapis, his sitting posture, and the sceptre which he bore in his left hand, were extremely similar to the ordinary representations of Jupiter. It was confidently reported, that if any impious hand should dare to violate the majesty of the god, the heavens and the earth would instantly return to their original chaos. An intrepid soldier, animated by zeal, and armed with a weighty battle-axe, ascended the ladder—and even the Christian multitude expected with some anxiety the event of the combat. He aimed a vigorous stroke against the cheek of Serapis; the cheek fell to the ground; the thunder was still silent, and both the heavens and the earth continued to preserve their accustomed order and tranquillity. The victorious soldier repeated his blows; the huge idol was overthrown and broken in pieces, and the limbs of Serapis were ignominiously dragged through the streets of Alexandria. His mangled carcass was burnt in the amphitheatre, amid the shouts of the populace; and many persons attributed their conversion to this discovery of the impotence of the tutelar deity. After the fall of Serapis, some hopes were entertained by the pagans that the indignation of the gods would be expressed by the refusal of the Nile's annual inundation; but the waters began to swell with most unusual rapidity. They now comforted themselves that the same indignation was to be expressed by a deluge; but were mortified to find at last that the inundation brought with it no other than its usual salutary and fertilizing effects.*

Theodosius was too good a politician to adopt a persecuting system. The temples, it is true, were shut up, sacrifices prohibited, and idols destroyed; but still the ancient opinions were entertained and tolerated: no universal conformity was requisite, and the civil and military honors of the empire were bestowed without distinction on Christians and on pagans. The utmost freedom was allowed in speech and in writing on the subject of religion, as is evident by what remains of the works of Zozimus, Eunapius, and other teachers of the Platonic school, who attacked Christianity with the utmost virulence. There was great wisdom in this conduct of Theodosius. Paganism fell by a rapid, yet by

* The Egyptians remarked, that when the Nile did not rise to the height of 12 cubits, a famine was generally the consequence—as was likewise the case when it rose above 16 cubits. **The register of the river was a well within the temple of Serapis, at Memphis.**

a gentle decline; and twenty-eight years after the death of Theodosius, the vestiges of the ancient religion were scarcely discernible in the Roman empire.

A superstition, in many respects as absurd and irrational, began to pollute the Christian church in those ages, and still continues to maintain a very extensive influence. This was the worship of saints and relics. At Rome, the bones of St. Peter and St. Paul —or rather what they believed to be such—were removed from their graves one hundred and fifty years after their death, and deposited in magnificent shrines. In the following ages, Constantinople, which could boast no treasures of that kind within her own walls, had recourse to the provinces, and acquired from them the supposed bodies of St. Andrew, St. Luke, and St. Timothy, after these had been dead for three hundred years. But these sacred treasures were appropriated solely to the churches of the capitals of the empire; other cities and their churches borrowed portions of these older relics; and where they had not interest to procure these, their priests had dexterity to discover relics of their own. The possession of these bones was found to conduce very much to the acquisition of more substantial treasures. It was easy to find skeletons, and to give them names; but it was necessary to prove their authenticity and virtue, by making these bones perform miracles. Artifice and roguery had a powerful assistant here in popular credulity; and even natural events, when ascribed to the mediation of saints and martyrs, became proofs of their divine and supernatural power. It was easier for the vulgar mind to approach in prayer the image, or simply the idea of a holy man—one who had been on earth subject to like passions with themselves—than to raise their imaginations to the tremendous and incomprehensible nature of the Supreme Power: hence the prayers to saints, and the peculiar devotion to one out of many,—as he to whom most frequent court was paid, would be naturally held to take the greatest interest in the welfare of his votary.

As the objects of religion were become more familiar to the imagination, it was not wonderful that such rites and ceremonies should be introduced as were best fitted to affect the senses of the vulgar. The pompous pageantry of the pagan superstition was soon rivalled by that of the Christian; and as the polytheism of the former found a parallel in the numerous train of saints and martyrs of the latter, the superstitions and absurd ceremonies of both came very soon to have a near resemblance.

The attachment to the pagan systems of philosophy, particularly the Platonic, which found its votaries among many of the Christian doctors at this period, led to a variety of innovations in point of doctrine, which in a little time acquired so deep a root as to be considered as essential parts of the Christian system. Such, for example, was the notion of an intermediate state, in which the soul was to be purified by fire from the corruptions and vices of the flesh: hence also the celibacy of the priests, and various other notions, which yet prevail in the church of Rome, and have in the minds of the people acquired from time an equal authority with the express institutions of the gospel.

With regard to the celibacy of the priests, we know that in the *primitive* church all the orders of the clergy were allowed to marry.* It was, however, thought, that as abstinence and mortification was a Christian duty, there was more sanctity and virtue in celibacy than in wedlock.

Monastic institutions had likewise their origin in the fourth century, the most destructive species of superstition that ever took hold of the minds of mankind. But of these and of their progress—of the diversities of their orders, and of their rapid increase over all the Christian kingdoms, we shall afterwards treat more at large, in our account of the state of the church in the age of Charlemagne.

In our next chapter we shall pursue the outlines of the history of the Romans, to the entire extinction of the empire of the West—a period which furnishes the delineation of ancient history.

CHAPTER V.

Last Period of the Roman History—Arcadius and Honorius—Theodosius II.—His Code of Laws—Attila—Progress of the Goths—Gothic Kingdom of Italy.

We have now arrived at the last period of the empire in the West, when every thing tending irresistibly to decline, prognosticated a speedy and absolute extinction of the Roman name in those regions where it first was known.

The barbarous nations, we had observed, from frequent inroads, though most commonly repulsed, had yet gradually begun to establish themselves in the frontier provinces: we had remarked the progress they made in the reigns of Valentinian, Valens, Gratian, and Theodosius; but at this period our attention was solicited to the consideration of an object of peculiar importance, the extinction of paganism in the Roman empire, and the full establishment of the Christian religion. This great event naturally led to a brief retrospective view of the progress of Christianity during the four preceding centuries. We now proceed to a

* 1st Epistle to Timothy, ch. iii.

rapid delineation of this last period of the history of the Romans, —from the end of the reign of Theodosius, to the fall of the Western empire.

Theodosius the Great, who, by the death of Valentinian II., enjoyed the undivided sovereignty of the empires of the East and West, made a partition upon his death-bed between his two sons, Arcadius and Honorius, assigned the Eastern empire to the former, and the Western to the latter.* At the time of the accession of these princes, Arcadius was seventeen, and Honorius ten years of age. Their ministers were *Rufinus* and *Stilicho*, to whom Theodosius had intrusted the government during the nonage of his sons. Rufinus, a man of no principle, but of great ambition, soon became jealous of an associate in power ; and in order to gratify his mean ambition, he considered it a small matter to make a sacrifice of his country. Courting his own elevation in the public ruin, he invited the barbarian nations to invade the empire.† The Huns were not slow in obeying the summons. They poured down from Caucasus, and overspread in an instant Armenia, Cappadocia, Cilicia, and Syria. A band of the Goths at the same time, under the command of Alaric, made dreadful havoc in the provinces between the Adriatic and Constantinople. Stilicho, the emperor's chief general, who was possessed of excellent military abilities, made head against these barbarians with considerable success ; until, by the infamous machination of his rival Rufinus, the greater part of his troops were compelled to leave their commander, and purposely called off upon another service, at the very eve of an engagement with Alaric, which, in all probability, would have given the Romans a decisive victory. Stilicho was obliged to retreat with precipitation ; but this involuntary dishonor was amply revenged by his troops, who no sooner returned to the Eastern capital, than, with furious indignation, they massacred Rufinus in the presence of the emperor Arcadius.‡

Alaric the Goth, in the meantime, ravaged Greece, took the city of Athens, and, pouring down on the Peloponnesus, laid waste the whole country. He was again opposed by Stilicho, whose success was a second time disappointed by the eunuch Eutropius, who had succeeded Rufinus in his influence over the weak and dissolute Arcadius. This abandoned minion made a

* The following was the division of the empire between these princes. Honorius had the sovereignty of Italy, Gaul, Spain, and Britain ; with the provinces of Noricum, Pannonia, and Dalmatia. Arcadius governed Thrace, Asia Minor, Syria, and Egypt, and the whole country, from the lower Danube to the confines of Persia and Æthiopia. Illyrium was divided between the two princes.—Gibbon, *Decline and Fall*, ch. 29.

† That Rufinus carried on a treasonable correspondence with the barbarians has not, I believe, been directly proved, but his frequent visits to the camp of the Goths, and the circumstance of their sparing his estates amidst the general devastation, were considered as strong presumptive evidence of his treason.

‡ A scene which is described by the poet Claudian (lib. ii. in Rufin.) in strong, but horrid colors.

peace with Alaric, and even bestowed upon the Goth the government of eastern Illyria, under which denomination was at that time comprehended the whole of Greece. How miserable must have been the abasement of the Eastern empire at this time, when the Goths had thus established themselves under the very walls of the capital!

The influence of the eunuch Eutropius was unbounded with his sovereign; but though courted, as we may suppose, like all other ministers, by the parasites of the court, he was deservedly detested by the people. A striking monument of his fears from the popular odium, and the apprehension of undergoing that fate which he merited, appears in that most sanguinary of the Roman statutes, the law of Arcadius and Honorius for the punishment of those who should conspire the death of the emperor's ministers. A capital punishment was inflicted on the offender himself; it is declared that his children shall be perpetually infamous, incapable of all inheritance, of all office or employment; that they shall languish in want and misery, so that life itself shall be a punishment to them, and death a consolation.* Amid the other laws of Arcadius and Honorius, many of which are remarkable for their clemency and moderation, this sanguinary statute would strike us with just surprise, were it not known to have been framed by the infamous Eutropius for the security of his own precarious authority, and as a shelter for himself against the public odium.

Secure as he now imagined himself in the favor of his sovereign, and defended by the terror of his own uncontrolled authority, this base eunuch endeavored to engross the whole power of the government. He caused the weak Arcadius to create him a Patrician, to honor him with the title of *father to the emperor*, and at length to confer on him the consulship. His image, preceded by the fasces, was carried in triumph through all the cities of the East, but was more generally saluted with hissing than with applause. At length that insolence, which, in mean souls, is the usual attendant of undeserved elevation, so far transported him beyond the bounds of decorum, that having affronted the empress Eudoxia, a high spirited princess, she painted his character in such colors to her husband Arcadius, that he dismissed him from all his dignities, gave him up to the cries of the people, who demanded justice upon him as a traitor, and caused him to be publicly beheaded.

Arcadius, however, was not emancipated from his bondage; he only changed his governor: for Gainas, a Goth, the rival of Eutropius, and who had been instrumental in accelerating his downfall, succeeded to his whole power and influence. He would have proved a dangerous minister, as he aimed at nothing less than

* Ut his denique perpetua egestate sordentibus, sit et mors solatium et vita supplicium.—Codex. Just. l. 9. tit. 8. l. 5.

a declared share of the empire ; but his ambition was checked in the beginning of his career, for he lost his life in an attack made by the Huns, in the neighborhood of the Danube.

Alaric, we observed, had obtained from Arcadius the sovereignty of Illyria. This ambitious prince was not so to be satisfied. His army proclaimed him king of the Visigoths, and he prepared to penetrate into Italy, and take possession of Rome. He passed the Alps, and Rome trembled for her safety, but was preserved by the policy, or rather treachery of Stilicho, who commanded the armies of Honorius. He drew Alaric into a negotiation, under the notion of giving him a settlement beyond the Alps, and then suddenly fell upon his army, while unsuspicious of an attack; Alaric was forced to return to Illyria, but meditated a full and terrible revenge.

On this occasion, Honorius celebrated at Rome a splendid triumph, and a monument was erected, recording, in the proudest terms, the eternal defeat of the Goths, *Gætarum nationem in omne ævum domitam.** But this vain *eternity* was bounded by the revolution of a very few months.

The Gothic prince, at the head of an immense army, appeared again in Italy, and determined to overthrow the capital of Honorius. Rome was panic-struck ; — resistance appeared fruitless ; and Stilicho exerted his political talents in negotiating a truce with Alaric, for the payment of an immense sum of money. 4000 pounds' weight of gold was the sum stipulated, on promise of which, Alaric returned again into Illyria. This was the last public service of Stilicho ;—the man who had repeatedly saved his country from destruction, fell a victim at last to the jealousy of his contemptible sovereign, and to the machinations of a rival, Olympius, who wished to supplant him in his power. He was beheaded by the mandate of Honorius. The character and talents of Stilicho are recorded in the poems of Claudian, whose genius deserved to have been the ornament of a better age. Alaric, soon after, made his demand for the promised tribute. It was contemptuously refused by Honorius, and the incensed Goth again entered Italy, and with amazing celerity penetrated to the gates of Rome : he made himself master of the Tiber, cut off the city from all supply, both by land and water, and reduced it to such extremity, that deputies were sent by Honorius, who again purchased a cessation of hostilities for 5000 pounds' weight of gold and 30,000 of silver ; but to secure its payment, the Goth insisted that several of the principal citizens should put their children into his hands as hostages. On these terms Alaric again returned.

The Alani, Suevi, and Vandals taking advantage of these disorders in the Western empire, passed the Pyrenean mountains, and desolated all Spain. Their ravages were beyond imagination

---

* Mascou, Hist. of Anc. Germ., viii. 12.

dreadful, and these calamities were aggravated by a pestilence and famine, which then raged with fury in that unhappy country. The barbarians divided the kingdom, and were no sooner settled in their possessions than, by a wonderful reverse of character, they became a mild, humane, and industrious people. They were now known under the general denomination of Vandals. The Romans kept possession of that part of Spain now called New Castile, and the Vandals had all the rest of the kingdom.

Alaric now renewed his demand on Honorius for the stipulated sum; still it was refused, with equal perfidy and imprudence. The Goth had been too forbearing; his patience was at length exhausted, and he laid siege to Rome for the third time, took the city, and abandoned it to be pillaged by his troops.* Still, however, he was humane in his revenge; he ordered his soldiers to be sparing of blood; he commanded that no senator should be put to death; that the honor of the women should remain inviolate; that the churches should be sanctuaries to all who betook themselves to them for shelter,—and that the public edifices should be preserved from destruction; and these orders were faithfully obeyed. Alaric might have reigned in Italy, but his views extended now to Sicily, and to the conquest of Africa. For these great enterprises he was busied in preparation when he died suddenly, leaving for his successor, his brother Ataulphus. The Goths had a custom of concealing the burying-place of their great men. They turned aside the current of a small river, and dug a grave in the bed, there burying Alaric, and then returning the water to its course.

Honorius, equally indolent and despicable as his brother Arcadius, was so far from seizing the opportunity of Alaric's death, to regain the lost provinces of the empire, that he made a treaty with Ataulphus, and having broke it with his usual perfidy, the Goth was naturally provoked to further encroachments. Honorius was glad to purchase a peace by giving him some of those provinces which still remained to the Romans in Spain, together with his sister Placidia in marriage. Thus we see the Goths gradually uniting themselves with the empire, and acquiring a connection by the rights of blood with those dominions of which they aspired at the possession. Honorius, much about the same time, allowed to the Burgundians, another tribe of northern barbarians, a just title to their conquests in Gaul. Ataulphus the Goth died soon after, recommending to his brother and successor to preserve the friendly alliance they had formed with the Romans.

Meantime, Arcadius, in the East, was wholly governed by his empress Eudoxia. This weak and dissolute prince died in the

* See a very minute and curious picture of the state of Rome, and the manners of the Romans at this period, drawn by Mr. Gibbon chiefly from Ammianus Marcellinus (lib. xiv. c. 6, and lib. xxviii. c. 4.)—Gibbon's Rom. Hist. ch. 31

year 408, leaving the Eastern empire to his son Theodosius II., a child of seven years of age.

Pulcheria, the elder sister of Theodosius, on the death of her father, took the sole government of the empire, in the name of her infant brother. She was a prudent and intelligent princess. The Eastern empire enjoyed under her administration, which the weakness of her brother allowed to be of forty years' continuance, all the blessings of good order and tranquillity.*

At this time (the beginning of the fifth century) in the west of Europe, is supposed to have been laid the foundation of the French monarchy by Pharamond. But of this, and the doubts attending the existence of this prince, we shall afterwards treat more particularly under the first period of modern history. Honorius died in the year 423. The death of a weak and of a vicious prince would, in former times, have been accounted a blessing, but the empire was now laboring under that universal decay which was beyond a remedy. It has been justly remarked that, notwithstanding the despicable character of both these emperors, Arcadius and Honorius, their laws, with few exceptions, breathe often the most admirable sentiments, and the wisest political principles: but this proves no more than that there were some men of abilities who were employed in framing them; it was another thing to enforce their observance, and while that was neglected, as the deplorable situation of the empire too well declares, they were words without meaning, empty sounds, to which the public administration of government was a daily contradiction.

Theodosius II. is famous in history for the celebrated code of laws which bears his name. In the view of reforming the complicated system of jurisprudence, of which the multiplicity of contradictory statutes formed a most inconsistent mass, he caused a code to be composed solely of the laws of the Christian emperors, which from that time he declared should be the only statutes in force. The new laws added from time to time to this collection were called *Novellæ*, and this code was enforced by Valentinian III., the successor of Honorius in the Western empire, as it was by Theodosius in the East.† It is curious to remark that this

* "Pulcheria," says Mr. Gibbon, "alone discharged the important task of instructing her brother in the arts of government, but her precepts may countenance some suspicion of her capacity, or of the purity of her intentions. She taught him to maintain a grave and majestic deportment, to walk, to hold his robes, to seat himself on his throne in a manner worthy of a great prince; to abstain from laughter; to listen with condescension; to return suitable answers; to assume by turns a serious or a placid countenance; in a word, to represent with grace and dignity the external figure of a Roman emperor. But Theodosius was never excited to support the weight and glory of an illustrious name.' Gibbon, Decl. and Fall, ch. xxxii.

† It is not a little extraordinary that Mr. Gibbon, in the whole of his account of the reign of Theodosius II., has never once mentioned this celebrated code of laws, which is certainly not the least remarkable circumstance relative to the life and character of this insignificant emperor.

code of laws subsisted only for ninety years in the East, though in the West it remained in force after the destruction of the empire, and was partly adopted by the Visigoths. Genseric, king of the Vandals, in the meantime established a formidable power in Africa; he soon made himself master of the Roman province,* and while Theodosius was obliged to employ his whole force against the Huns, that barbarian procured himself to be acknowledged for an independent sovereign, who had a just title to his conquests.

The Huns were at this time governed by two brothers, Attila and Bleda. Attila joined to great courage and excellent political talents an unbounded ambition. The two brothers, after overrunning Tartary to the borders of China, had crossed the Danube, and laid waste the Roman provinces of Mœsia and Thrace. Attila, impatient of a divided power, murdered his brother, and proceeded to extend his conquests from the Eastern ocean to the *Sinus Codanus*, or the Baltic. Theodosius attempted to soothe him by conferring on him the title of general of the Romans, but was soon glad to purchase a peace of his general at the price of 6000 pounds' weight of gold, and a tribute besides of 2000 pounds, to be paid annually in all time to come. Theodosius became more despicable in the eyes of Attila by an unsuccessful attempt to procure his assassination, which Attila pardoned, though at the same time with this severe reproach, that he considered him as a vile and perfidious slave, who had traitorously conspired to murder his master.† Theodosius II. died soon after, having reigned ingloriously for forty-two years. He left an only daughter, who was married to Valentinian III., emperor of the West, but the imbecility of this prince prevented him from availing himself of that title to both empires. Pulcheria, the sister of Theodosius, who had in reality governed the empire during the whole reign of her weak and insignificant brother, now boldly placed herself on the throne, and at the same time married Marcianus, a soldier of fortune, and their joint title was acknowledged by the Eastern empire. The West was in the lowest state of imbecility. Rome, unable to defend her provinces, allowed them to drop off without an attempt to retain them. It was at this time that the Britons, by a very melancholy deputation, implored the Romans to protect them against the Picts and Scots.‡ "We are (said they) in the

---

* In this barbarian war, Carthage, which, in the course of five hundred and eighty-five years from the time of its destruction by the younger Scipio, had risen to the rank of a splendid and opulent city, under the government of a Roman proconsul, was taken by Genseric, the inhabitants completely stripped of their wealth, and all the lands of the proconsular province divided by the conqueror amongst his Vandal officers.—Procop. de Bello Vandal. l. i. c. v. Gibbon chap. xxxiii.

† See Gibbon, chap. xxxiv., for a detail of this transaction, curiously descriptive of the character and mode of life of the Huns.

‡ The feeble and distracted state of the empire had now for a long course of years allowed no attention to be given to this distant province. The legions had

utmost misery, nor have we any refuge left us; the barbarians drive us to the sea, the sea drives us back upon the barbarians." In return to this miserable supplication, the Romans gave them to understand that their own situation was such that they could now afford them nothing but compassion. The Britons, therefore, in despair, made an application to the Saxons, a people settled at the mouth of the river Elbe. These, with the Angles from Jutland, made themselves masters of the country which they were invited to protect, and established by degrees the Heptarchy, or seven distinct kingdoms, which subsisted till the age of Charlemagne, when they were united into one monarchy by Egbert. But of these transactions we shall treat more particularly in our account of the first period of the history of Britain.

Attila in the meantime meditated the total destruction of the empire. He hesitated at first whether to turn his arms towards the East or the West.* Genseric, king of the Vandals, ambitious of a share in the general devastation, invited the Hun to begin his attack upon Gaul. Attila begun his progress at the head of 500,000 men, the Gepidæ, Rugii, Turcilingi, and Ostrogoths, each led by their own prince, though all under the banners of Attila.

Ætius, at that time general of the Romans, and a man of remarkable abilities, had the address to render Genseric the Vandal apprehensive of his own safety, and to persuade him to join the Romans against the invaders. The Visigoths, too, took part with the empire, and the army of Ætius was likewise increased by the Franks, Burgundians, and several other nations, from the universal dread of the arms of Attila. The hostile powers came to a decisive engagement in the plains of Champagne. 162,000 men are supposed to have fallen in this battle.† Attila was overpowered by the superior military skill of Ætius, and obliged to make a precipitate retreat. Theodoric, king of the Visigoths, was killed in the engagement.

But Attila, though foiled in this attempt, returned in the following year with fresh forces. The Romans had not as yet had time to recruit; they retreated before the barbarians, and left the country

been gradually withdrawn, and about forty years before this period, under the reign of Honorius, the Romans had entirely left the island, and Britain was regarded even by the empire as an independent country.—See Procop. de Bello Vandal. l. i. c. 2.—Bede, Hist. Gent. Anglican. lib. i. c. 12.—Gibbon's Rom. Hist. chap. xxxi. The nature of the government that subsisted in Britain, and the state of that country during this interval of forty years, till the Saxon invasion, can only be conjectured. Mr. Gibbon has given a fanciful picture of it, towards the end of the chapter above quoted. According to his idea, the country was ruled by the authority of the clergy, the nobles, and the municipal towns.

* Previous to his determination, he sent a defiance to both the courts, and his ambassadors saluted both the emperors in the same tone of authority. "Attila, *my* lord and *thy* lord, commands thee to provide a palace for his immediate reception."—Gibbon, chap. xxxv.

† "Bellum atrox," says Jornandes, "multiplex, immane, pertinax, cui simile nulla usquam narrat antiquitas: ubi talia gesta referuntur ut nihil esset quod in vitâ suâ conspicere potuisset egregius, qui hujus miraculi privaretur aspectu

without defence. The districts of Venetia and Liguria being evacuated by their inhabitants, part of these betook themselves for shelter to the islands in the Adriatic gulf, where they built huts, and laid the first foundation of the illustrious city and state of Venice.

Valentinian III., shut up in Rome, sent to Attila to sue for peace, and promised an immense tribute. On these terms the Hun withdrew, and the Romans were soon after delivered by his death from the terror of his name and arms. He was known in the empire by the epithet of the Scourge of God.

His dominions were ruined by the dissensions of his sons, among whom they were divided. They formed distinct settlements in Illyria, Mœsia, Dacia, and at the mouth of the Danube, and several of them became the allies of the empire. The Ostrogoths received from Marcian all Pannonia, from upper Mœsia to Noricum, and from Dalmatia to the Danube.

Valentinian, sunk in debaucheries, and the dupe of his parasites, was persuaded by false insinuations to destroy his general Ætius, the man who had saved the empire from absolute destruction, but the abandoned prince himself was soon after assassinated by one of his favorites.

A minute detail of the transactions of the times at which we are now arrived would be equally tedious and unimportant. We shall content ourselves with the leading facts. Marcian was succeeded in the Eastern empire by Leo, who, upon his death, bequeathed the empire to Zeno, a weak, wicked, and profligate man. The empire of the West, after Valentinian III., had for some time a succession of princes, or rather of names, for history records of them no transactions which merit the smallest notice. The Gothic nations continued their progress. Euric, king of the Visigoths, had subdued almost the whole of Spain as well as the southern part of Gaul. Nepos, who then held the empire of the West, sent his general Orestes to oppose the conquests of Euric, but the general turned his arms against his prince, and dethroning Nepos, raised to the empire his own son Romulus, surnamed Augustus, or *Augustulus*. In him the empire of the West was doomed to come to a final period.

Odoacer, a prince of the Heruli, with a formidable army, had found his way into Italy. He attacked Pavia, where Orestes had fled for security, and having taken that city, and put to death Orestes, he consented to give Augustulus his life, on his resigning the throne. The terms were complied with, and Odoacer was now in reality what he styled himself, *king of Italy*. Thus ended the Western empire of the Romans, having subsisted, from the building of Rome, 1224 years.*

* In a fragment of a poem of Gray's, which has been preserved by Mr Mason, a very fine passage occurs, painting, in all the force of his splendid

Ingenious men may point out a variety of internal as well as external circumstances, which had their operation in producing the decline, and at length the ruin of this immense fabric; but they may be all reduced to one single head. The fall of the Roman empire was the inevitable effect of its overgrown extension. The commonwealth subsisted by the virtuous and patriotic ardor of the citizens; but the passion for conquest, which at first found sufficient scope in the domestic wars among the Italian states, was, after their reduction, necessarily extended to a distance. Remote dominion relaxed the patriotic affection, which of necessity grew the weaker, the more extensive were its objects. The vices of the conquered nations infected the victorious legions, and foreign luxuries corrupted their commanders. Selfish interest took the place of public virtue; the people were enslaved by despots, who, regarding as the first object the security of their own power, found it often their wisest policy to abase that martial spirit which was no less formidable to the master of the state than to its foreign enemies. Thus the military character of the Romans went gradually to decay, because it was purposely depressed by the emperors; and thus their extensive dominions, wanting their necessary support of brave, of virtuous, and of disciplined troops, fell an easy prey to that torrent of barbarians which overwhelmed them.

Historians universally agree that the Romans gained by their change of masters. Odoacer retained the imperial laws, the officers, and the form of government; and he diminished the taxes. He, with an affected show of moderation, sent to Zeno the imperial ornaments, and requested for himself only the dignity of patrician, which Zeno had the prudence not to refuse. This spiritless emperor was now embroiled with the Ostrogoths, who were settled in Pannonia and Thrace, and were governed by two kings of the name of Theodoric; the younger had been educated at Constantinople, and loaded with honors by Zeno. At the request of Theodoric, Zeno granted him permission to attempt the conquest of Italy, transferring it to him as a kingdom in case he should succeed in wresting it from Odoacer. Zeno died soon

---

style of poetic description, the irruption of the barbarous nations into Italy:—

Oft o'er the trembling nations, from afar,
Has Scythia breathed the living cloud of war;
And where the deluge burst, with sweeping sway,
Their arms, their kings, their gods were rolled away.
As oft have issued, host impelling host,
The blue-eyed myriads of the Baltic coast;—
The prostrate south to the destroyer yields
Her boasted titles and her golden fields;
With grim delight, the brood of winter view
A brighter day, and heavens of azure hue,
Scent the new fragrance of the blushing rose,
And quaff the pendent vintage as it grows.

Mason's Life of Gray, p 196.

after. Theodoric, followed by the whole nation of the Ostrogoths, broke into Italy with impetuous fury. Odoacer met him between Aquileia and the Julian Alps, but was defeated. A second engagement ensued at Verona, and a third on the banks of the river Addua, in all of which Theodoric was successful. Odoacer was forced to shut himself up in Ravenna, where for two years and a half he sustained an obstinate siege. At length, compelled by famine, he was driven to a negotiation, by which he surrendered all Italy to Theodoric, reserving to himself the titles of royalty. What the motive was is now uncertain, but Theodoric, a few days after, put him to death with his own hand—a deed which, considering the excellent and generous character of that prince, there is every reason to presume had a just cause.

Italy had begun to taste of happiness under Odoacer; it was still increased by the new monarch. Theodoric showed what profound political talents are capable of effecting even in the most unpromising situation, and how much public happiness is dependent on the virtues and talents of the sovereign. I shall afterwards have occasion pretty fully to describe the administration, and illustrate the character, of this excellent prince. Without drawing a sword after the death of Odoacer, he enjoyed the kingdom of Italy as if it had been his natural inheritance. He allied himself with the barbarous nations around him. He married the daughter of Clovis, king of the Franks, who, in the year 486, had annihilated the Roman power in Gaul; he gave one of his daughters to Alaric, king of the Visigoths; another to Gondebald, king of the Burgundians; and his sister to Thrasamond, king of the Vandals; thus establishing a bond of union and harmony among the neighboring princes, but where it was not observed, enforcing it by his arms.

In the latter part of his life, having his temper imbittered by suspicions of treasonable conspiracies, he became for a while severe, and even cruel, in his administration. The learned Boetius, who had formerly been high in his favor, falling under these suspicions, was put to death. During the confinement preceding his death, he composed that excellent treatise "De Consolatione Philosophiæ." The heart of Theodoric awaking afterwards to that humanity of disposition which was natural to him, he sunk into deep remorse and melancholy, and died at the age of seventy-four. He was succeeded by his grandson Athalaric; during whose infancy his mother Amalasonta held the reins of government with such admirable political wisdom and moderation, that the people were not sensible of the loss of her father.

While such was the state of Italy under its Gothic sovereigns, the empire of the East was under the government of Justinian. This prince began his reign with no favorable dispositions towards him on the part of his subjects, as it was known that he had countenanced the commission of great enormities, and been concerned in several assassinations of those whom he either feared or hated. The truth is, that if the Roman name seems to rise from its abasement for a while during the reign of this prince, it was less from the virtues, talents, or abilities of the emperor, than from the uncommon merit of his generals; yet to these generals he behaved with the most shameful ingratitude. He was in his own character a weak, vain, and despotic man; but he was fond of study; and if he had any talent, it was in jurisprudence. He was a rancorous enemy to the ancient Greek philosophy, and he abolished by an edict the schools of Athens, which had produced a constant succession of teachers from the days of Socrates, during a period of nine centuries.* Justinian wished to bring about a league of amity with the Persians, who were dangerous enemies to the empire; but Cabades, their sovereign, treating his embassy with contempt, Justinian sent against them his general Belisarius, who had already signalized himself by his services. He defeated them at Dara; they revenged their disgrace, however, in the following year, by gaining a victory over Belisarius at Callinicum, who was prompted to engage at a disadvantage, from the intemperate ardor of his troops. This want of success Justinian thought proper to punish by recalling Belisarius, who was doomed to be often the sport of fortune, and the victim of weakness, caprice, and ingratitude. Cabades the Persian dying at this time, was succeeded by Chosroes, an able prince, to whom Justinian meanly a second time proffered terms of accommodation. Chosroes granted him a peace, but upon the most humiliating conditions. He received 11,000 pounds' weight of gold, and several important fortresses.

The city of Constantinople had been harassed, during the two last reigns, with violent popular factions, which had arisen from the intemperate fondness of the people for the diversions of the circus—a striking indication of the most irretrievable degeneracy of national character. The factions took the names of the green, the blue, and the red, from the dresses worn by the charioteers of the different parties. Justinian espoused with zeal the faction of the blue, while his queen Theodora, with equal intemperance, took part with the green. Her party proceeded so far as publicly to insult the emperor; and, upon the punishment of some of their ringleaders, took up arms to avenge their cause, and proclaimed Hypatius, a man allied to the blood-royal, for their monarch. Justinian appeared and offered indemnity, on condition of their returning to their duty but they compelled him to retreat for safety to his palace. The injured Belisarius, who had not forgot his allegiance or his affection for his country, shocked at these proceedings, speedily assembled the troops, and attacking the rebels with a dreadful slaughter, at length brought all into submis-

* See Gibbon, vol. iv. p. 112, et seq.

sion. Justinian meanly proclaimed this deplorable victory over the whole empire.

Belisarius was now again to be employed in more glorious services. Gelimer, king of the Vandals in Africa, having mounted the throne by deposing Hilderic the lawful monarch, Justinian sent a remonstrance in favor of Hilderic, which Gelimer treated with contempt. He resolved to carry war into Africa, and the conduct of it was committed to Belisarius, who in a few months routed Gelimer, abolished entirely the monarchy of the Vandals, and completed the conquest of Africa. Ungenerous suspicions again influenced the weak Justinian against this man, who was the support and honor of his empire ; and Belisarius was obliged to return to Constantinople, to vindicate his injured reputation. He came off with glory, and a triumph was decreed him, which was adorned by the captive Gelimer.

It is not a little surprising to see enterprises of the highest importance begun and carried through by a weak and imprudent monarch ; but Justinian was fortunate in his generals, though never prince was less worthy of being so.

Athalaric, the Goth, a weak and debauched prince, had died in Italy, of which the government was still in the hands of his mother, Amalasonta. After the death of her son, she had raised to the throne her cousin Theodatus, who infamously repaid that service by putting her to death. Justinian, who considered himself as the protector of the Gothic monarchy, in order to avenge this atrocious deed, sent Belisarius into Italy with an army. He marched to the gates of Rome, which surrendered without an attack ; he possessed himself of the city, and with 5000 men undertook to defend it against 100,000 of the rebel Ostrogoths, who sat down to besiege him. The particulars of this war it is not to our purpose minutely to trace. It is sufficient to say, that after various successes, the Goths themselves, filled with admiration at the character of Belisarius, requested him to accept of the crown of Italy ; but that generous and heroic man refused the offer of a kingdom, incapable of betraying the interests of his sovereign, although he had repeatedly experienced his ingratitude. He declared that he had sufficient glory in reducing the capital of the Western empire to submission to its ancient masters.

Italy again attempted to withdraw herself from the newly imposed yoke of the empire. Totila, the present viceroy, inherited the courage and the virtues of Theodoric ; he raised a considerable army, and defeating the Romans, made himself master of Lucania, Apulia, Calabria, and Naples. Belisarius was sent a second time into Italy, but with so inconsiderable a body of troops that he was obliged to shut himself up in Ravenna. Rome, holding out for the emperor, was in the meantime besieged and taken by Totila, who generously spared the inhabitants ; and, convoking the senate drew a striking picture of the difference between the gentle government of Theodoric and Amalasonta, and their late oppressions; and concluded with a severe reproach for their treachery to a nation to whom they were so highly indebted. Totila had resolved to destroy Rome; but the city was saved by a remonstrance from Belisarius, who convinced the Goth, that to save that capital, the glory of the world, would contribute more to his honor than to destroy it. Totila contented himself with dispersing its inhabitants; but in this he acted imprudently, for Belisarius immediately took possession, and defended it with vigor and success. At length, the weakness of his army, and the increasing strength of the Goths, obliged that able general entirely to evacuate Italy, and to return to Constantinople, where the wealth, which he had accumulated, threw an unfavorable stain upon his character, which it is not easy to remove. Totila retook Rome, which he rebuilt and new peopled; afterwards, however, the imperial arms meeting with some success in Italy, he became desirous of coming to an accommodation with Justinian. The Goth offered large concessions and an annual tribute, and obliged himself to serve the emperor in all his wars. These terms, however, were obstinately and haughtily refused. Such is the character of a little mind, mean, servile, and submissive under the pressure of adversity; imperious, domineering, and inflexible upon the smallest glimpse of prosperous fortune. Contemning the offers of allegiance from Totila, he sent a more powerful army against him than he had ever sent into Italy. Narses, an eunuch, but an able general, commanded; and in a decisive engagement in the duchy of Urbino, the Goths were defeated, and the gallant Totila slain in battle. In a second engagement his successor, Theia, met with a similar fate; all Italy, in fine, was reconquered; and the Gothic monarchy, founded by Theodoric, was now extinguished. Theodoric and Totila may be compared with the greatest men of antiquity; and the Gothic nation, and particularly the Ostrogoths, who settled in Italy, instead of that contempt, with which they have been treated by Procopius and some other writers, deserve, in many respects, the greatest regard and veneration.

Narses, who had destroyed the Gothic monarchy, and completed the conquest of Italy, governed that kingdom with great ability for thirteen years, when he was recalled, and ignominiously treated by Justin, successor to Justinian, a weak, imprudent, and voluptuous prince. It is said, that in revenge he invited the Lombards into Italy; a fact, which is not at all improbable. These were one of the many nations from Scandinavia, but whose distinct origin is very uncertain; they overrun, and made themselves masters of the greatest part of the country in the year 568.

The final and irretrievable loss of Italy was not the only misfortune with which Justin had to struggle. Chosroes, that scourge of the empire, broke the fifty years' truce which he had concluded with Justinian; and the Romans were now again involved in a Persian war, which was not terminated til several years afterwards, under the reign of Heraclius, in the 626th year of the Christian era.

A remarkable revolution now awaited the empire, which, from a slender beginning, effected a surprising change on the great theatre of human affairs. This was the rise of Mahomet and his *religion.* But here we fix the termination of ancient history, and the commencement of the modern. Previous, however, to our entering upon this second and most important part of our work, we shall consider, with some attention, the *manners*, *genius*, *laws*, *and policy of those Gothic nations* who subverted the Roman empire in the West, and, establishing themselves in every quarter of Europe, are justly considered, at this day, as the parent stock of most of the modern European nations.

CHAPTER VI.

Genius and Character of the Gothic Nations.

THE ancient nations of Scandinavia have been compared to an mmense tree, full of sap and vigor, which, while its root and stem were fostered in the hardy regions of the North, extended, by degrees, its wide branches over all Europe. To drop the language of metaphor, we know that the present European nations are, in fact, a mixed race, compounded of the *Scandinavians*, who, at different periods, invaded every quarter of this Western continent, and of the nations whom they subdued in their progress. As this is certainly the case, we have little room to doubt that the laws, manners, and customs of the modern nations of Europe are the result of this conjunction; and that, in so far as these are different from the civil and political usages which prevailed before this intermixture, the difference is to be sought in the original manners and institutions of these Northern nations.

This consideration, as it has led to much research into the history and antiquities of the nations of Scandinavian origin, has opened up to us a variety of curious particulars, of equal importance to the historian and to the philosopher. It will, therefore, be an employment neither unpleasing nor unprofitable, if we attempt to give a view of the most interesting particulars of the history, manners, and usages of the Scandinavians, such as we have reason to believe them to have been before their intermixture with the nations of the South; and after thus endeavoring to obtain an acquaintance with the original character of this people, I shall consider the change which that character underwent when they became sovereigns of the greatest part of the Roman empire in Europe.

It is very evident that if we can at all attain to a knowledge of the character of this remarkable people antecedently to their intercourse with the southern kingdoms, it must be from the most ancient chronicles now existing among the present Scandinavian nations. For this source of information is infinitely more to be relied on than the accounts of Roman writers, who, although well qualified to describe them after their migration and establishment in the South, had no knowledge of their character while in their original seats.

The most ancient Scandinavian Chronicles attribute to all the northern European nations an *Asiatic origin.* These Chronicles give strong grounds for conjecturing that the Goths of Scandinavia were a colony of Scythians, from the borders of the Black Sea and the Caspian; that this migration was performed about seventy years before the Christian era—though, according to some authors, not less than one thousand years before this period; and that the Cimbri, the inhabitants of the Chersonesus Cimbrica, or Denmark, were the descendants of the Cimmerian Scythians. All the ancient writers of the North make mention of an invasion of Scandinavia by a colony of Asiatics; of bloody wars on that account; and of the original inhabitants being expelled, or driven very far to the North, by these invaders. Odin, who afterwards came to be regarded as the chief deity of the Scandinavians, was formerly the principal god of the Scythians who inhabited the country about Mount Taurus.

The Northern Chronicles say that a Scythian prince of the name of *Sigga,* who, according to the custom of his country, was chief priest of the god, having raised a large band of followers, set out upon a warlike expedition to the northwest of the Black Sea; that having subdued several of the Sarmatian or Russian tribes, he penetrated into the country of the Saxones, which he conquered, and divided among his children. The Icelandic Chronicles record the names of these children; and it is remarkable that, at this day, the sovereign princes of Westphalia, of East Saxony, and of Franconia, pretend to derive their origin from princes bearing these names.

Sigga afterwards entered Scandinavia by the country of Holstein and of Jutland; and taking possession of the island of Funen, he built there the city of Odenzee, so called after the Scythian god, whose name he from that time assumed to himself, and dropping his name of Sigga, took that of Odin. Extending his conquests, he made himself master of all Denmark, of which he gave the sovereignty to his son Sciold, who, in the Icelandic Chronicle, stands the first of the princes who took the title of king of Denmark. The same Chronicle informs us that Sigga (now called Odin) continued his progress, and entering Sweden, was received by the inhabitants, and even by the prince, with divine honors; that, upon the death of this prince, the Swedes made him offer of the sovereignty; and that, penetrating from thence into Norway, he forced all the Scandinavian princes, one after another, to submit to his authority.

But Odin distinguished himself not only as a conqueror, but as a legislator and consummate politician. Under this character of divinity, while his immense conquests gave credit to his pretensions, he found the imposture highly advantageous in procuring an easy submission to all his laws and regulations. These, if we may believe the ancient chronicles, were extremely wise and salutary, and gave to those barbarous nations a species of civilization to which hitherto they had been entirely strangers. The historical evidence arising from these Scandinavian Chronicles, of an Eastern people migrating to the northwest, and spreading themselves over all the northern kingdoms, is much confirmed when we attend to the perfect coincidence that appears between the manners of the ancient Scandinavians, and those of the ancient Scythians.

The religion of the ancient Scandinavians forms a very curious object of inquiry, and is the more worthy of attention that it was most intimately connected with their manners. Three great moral principles were the foundation of their religion, and influenced their whole conduct. These were, "to serve the Supreme Being with prayer and sacrifice; to do no wrong or unjust actions; and to be valiant and intrepid in fight." These were the principles of the ancient religion, which, although accompanied by a most wild and extravagant mythology, yet resting on this pure and simple basis, had a wonderful effect upon the character and manners of the people. Keeping in view these principles, if we peruse the *Edda*, or sacred book of the Scandinavians, we shall see amidst all its absurdities the traces of a luminous and rational system of religion, which does no dishonor to the people who professed it.

Mallet, who, in his Introduction to the history of Denmark, has given an abridgment of this sacred book, has clearly shown, that although it contains the substance of a very ancient religion, it is not itself a work of very high antiquity. The Edda, according to his account, was compiled by an Icelandic author a short time after the introduction of Christianity into that island, with the sole purpose of preserving the memory of the ancient poetry of the Scandinavians, which was inseparably connected with the ancient mythology. The compiler, who endeavored to collect the best specimens of this ancient national poetry, was obliged, in order to render these intelligible, to explain that mythology on which they were founded, and thus, in fact, to unfold the whole doctrines of that ancient religion. Snorro Sturleson, the Icelandic writer who compiled the Edda as it is in its present form, lived in the beginning of the thirteenth century, and was supreme judge of Iceland. The work, besides the specimens of ancient poetry, consists of certain dialogues on the subject of mythology, which proceed on this fiction, that a king of Sweden, named Gulphus, being at a loss to comprehend the origin of those notions of theology which prevailed in his country, and which tradition reported to have been originally derived from the Asiatics, undertook a journey in disguise to Asgard, a city of Asia, in order to be instructed in the genuine principles of that religion. He had several conversations with three princes, or rather priests, who answered all his questions, and fully explained to him the whole of the Celtic mythology. These dialogues compose the greatest part of the Edda; and from them it is easy to deduce a short account of the religion of the Scandinavians.

Odin, as we have before said, was their principal divinity; and it is very remarkable, that to him they attributed every character that could inspire fear and horror, without any mixture of the amiable or merciful. He is called in the Edda, the terrible and severe God, the father of carnage, the avenger, the deity who marks out those who are destined to be slain. This terrible God was held to be the Creator and Father of the Universe. The next in power to Odin, was Friga or Frea, his wife. The God of heaven, says the Edda, united himself with the goddess of the earth; and from this conjunction sprang all the race of subordinate deities. This Frea, or the heavenly mother, came naturally to be considered as the goddess of love and of pleasure.

The third divinity in power and in authority was Thor, the son of Odin and of Frea, who was supposed to partake of the terrible attributes of his father, and was believed to be constantly occupied in warring against Loke, the father of treachery, and the rest of those giants and evil spirits who envied the power and meditated the destruction of Odin. The Edda enumerates likewise a great train of inferior deities, male and female, among the last of whom are the virgins of the Valhalla, or Hall of Odin, whose office was to mark out those whom Odin destines to be slain in battle, and to minister to the deceased heroes in Paradise.

The creation of the world, as described in the Edda, is full of those wild and extravagant ideas which an ignorant and rude people must of necessity form, when left to their own conjectures on matters beyond the reach of human intellect.

I have observed that the religion of the Scandinavians had the greatest influence on their conduct and character. They were convinced that as this world was the work of some superior intelligences, so these presided continually over all nature, which they supposed to be of itself perfectly inanimate, and requiring *constantly* the interposition of deity to direct and regulate its motions. All the actions of men they believed therefore to proceed from this continual interposition of a deity, without whose aid they could no more move their limbs, or perform any vital function, than a stone could change its place. They therefore believed implicitly in fate or predestination, and in the absolute impossibility of a man's avoiding that course or destiny which was prescribed for him.

But while this was their firm persuasion, they allowed likewise the moral agency of man, and the possibility of his deserving rewards and punishments for his actions; a difficulty which more enlightened people have long labored to reconcile. The favorites of Odin were all those who had died a violent death, either by the hand of an enemy, or, what was equally meritorious, by their own. These went directly after their death to Valhalla, or the palace of Odin. The wretch who had the pusillanimity to allow himself to be cut off by disease was unworthy of the favor of the gods, and was doomed to a state of punishment in the next world, and to the perpetual sufferance of anguish, remorse, and famine.

The way in which the departed heroes pass their time in Valhalla, or in the palace of Odin, is described in several places of the Edda. They have every day the pleasure of arming themselves, marshalling themselves in military order, engaging in battle, and being all cut to pieces; but when the stated hour of repast arrives, their bodies are reunited, and they return on horseback safe to the hall of banquet, where they feed heartily on the flesh of a boar, and drink beer out of the skulls of their enemies, till they are in a state of intoxication. Odin sits by himself at a particular table. The heroes are served by the beautiful virgins, named Valkirie, who officiate as their cup-bearers; but the pleasures of love do not enter at all into the joys of this extraordinary Paradise.

These notions of religious belief among the Scandinavians, arising from a native ferocity of character, had a strong effect on their national manners and on the conduct of individuals. Placing their sole delight in war, and in the slaughter of their enemies, they had an absolute contempt of danger and of bodily pain. It was not enough that they exposed themselves without fear to the greatest perils—they courted death with avidity. Several most remarkable instances of this intrepidity of character we find in the Icelandic Chronicle. Harald with the blue teeth, king of Denmark, who lived about the middle of the tenth century, founded on the coast of Pomerania a city which he named Julin or Jomsburg. He had sent thither a colony of young Danes, under the command of a famous leader named Palnatoko. This man's ambition was to form a nation of heroes. All his institutions tended to instil into his subjects the contempt of life. It was disgraceful for a citizen of Jomsburg to hesitate to engage in an enterprise where the event was inevitably fatal: on the other hand, it was glorious to seek for every opportunity of encountering death.

The Chronicle of Iceland records some instances of this savage heroism which almost exceed belief. In an irruption made by the Jomsburgers into the territories of Haquin, a Norwegian chief, the invaders were defeated, and a few had the misfortune to escape death in the field, and to be taken in arms. They were condemned to be beheaded, and this intelligence was received by them with every demonstration of joy. When the spectators of their fate expressed their astonishment at this conduct, "Why should you wonder," said one, "that I should rejoice to follow where my father is gone before?" Another thus addressed his executioner: "I suffer death," said he, "with the highest pleasure: I only request that you will cut off my head as quickly as possible. We have often disputed," said he, "at Jomsburg, whether life remained for any time after the head was cut off: now I shall decide the question. If any life remains, I shall aim a blow at you with this knife which I hold in my hand. Dispatch," said he, "but don't abuse my hair, for it is very beautiful." Whether these instances are real or fabulous, even the fabrication of such facts by a very ancient author shows that they were consentaneous to the spirit of his country: but, in truth, the manners of other savage tribes who are in a similar state of society, furnish proofs even at this day that such a character as that of the Jomsburgers is not out of nature.

Among these nations, this characteristic of an absolute contempt of death was not peculiar to the Jomsburgers. It was common to all the branches of that great parent stock. The poet Lucan has taken notice of this singular feature, and assigns its true cause—the belief of a future state, where rewards were to be bestowed solely on the brave.* To avoid the disgrace of dying a natural death, and thus forfeiting the joys of Paradise, the ferocious Scandinavian had often recourse to self-destruction. An Icelandic author mentions a rock in Sweden from which the old men frequently precipitated themselves into the sea, in order that they might go directly to the hall of Odin.

In the Paradise of the Valhalla, the heroes ranked around the table according to the degree of favor they had obtained in the sight of Odin, from the slaughter they had committed on earth. He who had killed, with his own hand, the greatest number of enemies, was seated in the highest place: the heavenly virgins paid him peculiar attention, and most frequently presented to him the enlivening draught from the human skull into which they poured it.

That fine remnant of ancient poetry, which is entitled the

---

* "——Certe populi quos despicit Arctos
Felices errore suo! quos ille timorum
Maximus haud urget lethi metus; inde ruendi
In ferrum mens prona viris, animæque capaces
Mortis et ignavum est rediture parcere vitæ.

Death-song of King Regner Lodbrog, affords full confirmation of all we have said on this ferocity of character of the Scandinavians. This prince, who was king of Denmark, flourished about the end of the eighth, or beginning of the ninth century. After a life of great military glory, he was at last made prisoner by Ælla, a Northumbrian prince, and condemned to die by the poison of vipers. Lodbrog died with the usual intrepidity of his countrymen. He drowned the acute feelings of his sufferings by singing this chronicle of his exploits, while his attendants, who stood around him, joined at stated intervals in a sort of chorus, "We hewed with our swords." In this death-song, Lodbrog seems to derive the highest pleasure from recounting all the acts of slaughter and carnage that he had committed in his lifetime. These were his only consolation: they were, in his idea, a certain passport to the joys of Paradise, and insured for him a distinguished place at the banquet of Odin. After enumerating a series of heroic deeds, but all of a most atrocious and sanguinary nature, he thus concludes: "What is more beautiful than to see the heroes pushing on through the battle, though fainting with their wounds! What boots it that the timid youth flies from the combat? he shall not escape from misery;—who can avoid the fate which is ordained for him? I did not dream that I should have fallen a sacrifice to Ælla, whose shores I have covered with heaps of the slain. But there is a never-failing consolation for my spirit,—the table of Odin is prepared for the brave. There the hero shall know no grief. There we shall quaff the amber liquor from the capacious skulls. I will not tremble when I approach the hall of the god of death. Now the serpents gnaw my vitals; but it is a cordial to my soul that my enemy shall quickly follow me, for my sons will revenge my death. War was my delight from my youth, and from my childhood I was pleased with the bloody spear. No sigh shall disgrace my last moments. The immortals will not disdain to admit me into their presence. Here let me end my song—the heavenly virgins summon me away—the hours of my life are at an end—I exult and smile at death!"

We have given some idea of the religious belief among these nations. It is proper that we should say something of their mode of worship.

Tacitus, in speaking of the religious worship of the ancient Germans, remarks, that they had neither temples nor idols; that they thought it impious to suppose that the Divinity could be contained within the walls of a building raised by man; and that it was degrading to the dignity of the Supreme Being to represent him in the human figure.* Such, likewise, were originally the notions of all the Celtic tribes. The open air was the temple of

* "Cæterum nec cohibere parietibus Deos, neque in ullam humani oris speciem assimilare, ex magnitudine cœlestium arbitrantur."

the Divinity; and a forest, or grove of oaks whose venerable gloom was suited to the solemnity of the occasion, was the place where it was usual to worship by prayer and sacrifice. The altar was composed of one immense stone, or of three placed together, forming a base for one of a larger size laid at top, to serve as a table. A single, a double, and sometimes a triple row of stones, fixed in the ground in a circular form, surrounded the altar. Of these, which are called *Druidical* circles, there are vast numbers to be found through all the northern kingdoms of Europe, and no where more frequently than in Britain.* The most remarkable monument of this kind at present existing is that prodigious circle upon Salisbury Plain, which is known by the name of Stonehenge.† In the northern counties of Scotland, we every where meet with smaller circles of the same kind, which there seems no reason to doubt were devoted to religious purposes. In these groves, and upon these altars, the Druids offered sacrifices of various kinds, the most acceptable of which were human victims. This was not to be wondered at, considering that it was their opinion, that the Supreme Deity placed his chief delight in blood and slaughter. With these barbarous people the number nine was supposed to have something in it of peculiar sanctity. Every ninth month there was a sacrifice offered up to the gods of nine human victims: and in the first month of every ninth year was held an extraordinary solemnity, which was marked with dreadful slaughter. Dithmar, an historian of the eleventh century, has the following passage: "There is," says he, "in Zeeland, a place named Lederun, where every ninth year, in the month of January, the Danes assemble in great multitudes; and upon that occasion they sacrifice ninety-nine men, and the same number of horses, dogs, and cocks, in the firm assurance of thus obtaining the favor and protection of their gods."

The victims, upon those occasions, were commonly captives

* There are two of these monuments, of a very large size, near Stromness, in the Orkney Islands, one of a semicircular form of thirty-two feet radius, consisting of seven stones, from fourteen to eighteen feet in height, and the other a circle of 336 feet diameter, consisting of sixteen stones, from nine to fourteen feet in height. Round this ditch, at unequal distances from each other, are eight small artificial eminences. The altar stood without the circle, to the south-east. At some distance from the semicircle there is a stone eight feet high, with a round hole or perforation in it; and it is customary at this day, among the country people, when a solemn promise is made (for example of marriage) for the contracting parties to join their hands through this hole. This is called the promise of Odin, and is held to be particularly inviolable.—Memoirs of the Soc. of Scott. Antiq., vol. i. p. 263.

† Stonehenge consists of two concentric circles, of which the outer is 180 feet in diameter. The upright stones of which these circles are composed, are placed at the distance of three and a half feet from each other, and joined two and two at the top by stones laid across, with tenons fitted to the mortises in the uprights, for keeping the transverse stones in their place. The size of these stones is various, from four to seven yards in height, and generally of the breadth of two yards, and thickness of one. The walk between the circles is three hundred feet in circumference.

taken in war; and such were the honors paid to them, and the flattering prospects set before them by the Druids, of the great rewards awaiting them in a future state, that these deluded creatures went exulting to the altar, esteeming it the highest honor to be thus peculiarly set apart for the service of the great *Odin*. Lucan, in the third book of his "Pharsalia," has a very fine passage, in which he has touched several of the most striking peculiarities of the druidical superstition, a passage in which there is a wonderful assemblage of those circumstances which strike the mind with horror.

"There is," says he, "without the walls of Marseilles a sacred grove, which had never been touched by axe since the creation. The trees of it grew so thick, and were so interwoven, that they suffered not the rays of the sun to pierce through their branches; but a dreary damp and perfect darkness reigned through the place. Neither nymphs nor sylvan gods could inhabit this recess, it being destined for the most inhuman mysteries. There was nothing to be seen there but a multitude of altars, upon which they sacrificed human victims, whose blood dyed the trees with horrid crimson. If ancient tradition may be credited, no bird ever perched upon their boughs, no beast ever trod under them, no wind ever blew through them, nor thunderbolt did ever touch them. These tall oaks, as well as the black water that winds in different channels through the place, fill the mind with dread and horror. The figures of the god of the grove are a kind of rude and shapeless trunks, covered over with a dismal yellow moss. It is the genius of the Gauls," continues he, "thus to reverence gods of whom they know not the figure; and their ignorance of the *object of their worship* increases their veneration.* There is a report that this grove is often shaken and strangely agitated; and that dreadful sounds are heard from its deep recesses; that the trees, if destroyed or thrown down, arise again of themselves; that the forest is sometimes seen to be on fire, without being consumed, and that the oaks are twined about with monstrous serpents. The Gauls dare not live in it, from the awe of the divinity that inhabits it, and to whom they entirely abandon it. Only at noon and at midnight a priest goes trembling into it, to celebrate its dreadful mysteries; and is in continual fear lest the deity to whom it is consecrated should appear to him."

From this description, we may perceive with what artful policy the Druids had heightened the sanctity of their own character, by concealing the mysteries of their worship, and pervading the minds of the people with the deepest awe and reverence for every thing that regarded that religion of which they were the guardians. No

* Similar to this is the fine expression of Tacitus, in describing the secret worship of the goddess Hertha, or Earth, by the Angles and some other of the Germanic nations: "Arcanus hinc terror, sanctaque ignorantia, quid sit Illud quod tantum perituri vident." Tacit. de Mor. Germ. cap. 40.

vulgar step durst enter the sacred grove, and the priest himself feigned to approach it with fear and trembling. It was by these arts that the Druids, as all historians agree, had an influence and ascendency over the minds of the people, far exceeding that of the priests under any other system of pagan worship. Armed with this influence, they did not confine themselves to the duties of the priesthood, but exercised in fact, many of the most important offices of the civil magistrate.* And so very powerful was the hold which this order of men had upon the minds of the people, that it became a necessary policy with the Romans to depart in this instance from their accustomed spirit of toleration; since they found it impossible to preserve their conquests over any of the nations of Celtic origin, till they had utterly exterminated the Druids, and abolished every vestige of that potent superstition. This was the policy of the Romans in Gaul, as well as in Britain; and in those provinces it was successful. But, in the meantime, the Hydra wounded in one quarter was daily increasing in the strength and vigor of its principal members. And the primitive tribes of Scandinavia amply revenged the injuries of their brethren of Gaul and of Britain.

Thus, from the preceding review of the principal features which composed the character of the ancient nations from whose blood we are sprung, it may be inferred, that nature, education, and prevailing habits, all concurred to form them for an intrepid and conquering people. Their bodily frame invigorated by the climate in which they inhabited—inured from infancy to dangers and to difficulties—war their constant occupation—believing in a fixed and inevitable destiny—and taught by their religion that an heroic sacrifice of life was a certain assurance of the enjoyment of eternal happiness;—how could a race of men, under these circumstances, fail to be the conquerors of the world?

In this short dissertation on the manners of the North, I have endeavored to give some idea of the original character and genius of those branches of that great family which were destined to overrun and subdue the fairest regions of Europe. It remains now to exhibit this people in a different point of view, and to mark the character which they assumed in their new establishments. Vulgar prejudice has long annexed the idea of barbarian to the name of Goth, and it has been rashly and erroneously imagined, that the same rudeness and ferocity of manners which it is acknowledged distinguished these northern heroes in their native seats, attended their successors while settled in the polished provinces of the Roman empire. We shall see them, on the contrary, when sovereigns of imperial Rome, superior in many respects to

* This Tacitus plainly informs us of: "Cæterum neque animadvertere, neque vincire, neque verberare quidem, nisi sacerdotibus permissum, non quasi in pœnam nec ducis jussu, sed velut Deo imperante."

their immediate predecessors, and aspiring at a character of refinement, moderation, and humanity, which would have done no dishonor to the better times and more fortunate periods of that declining state.

CHAPTER VII.

Character of the Gothic Nations after the Conquest of Italy

It has been usual to consider the Gothic nations as a savage and barbarous race, pouring down from the inclement and uncultivated regions of the North, marking their course with bloodshed and devastation, and, like hungry wolves, falling upon the provinces of the empire, and involving all in undistinguished ruin. It is certainly not surprising that the name of Goth should to the ears of the moderns convey the idea of ferocity and barbarism, when we find popular writers, and those even of no limited degree of information, promoting this false and erroneous opinion, by holding forth a few instances of brutality and ignorance among some of the princes of the Gothic nations, as characteristic of the manners and genius of the whole. Voltaire, in his *Essai sur les Mœurs et l'Esprit des Nations* (chap. xvii.), after recapitulating some examples of the cruelty of Clovis and his successors in the monarchy of the Franks (and among the rest, the monstrous fiction of the atrocious murders said to be committed by Queen Brunehilda), concludes with this observation, that besides the foundation of some religious houses, there is no trace remaining of those frightful ages but a confused tradition of misery and devastation :—"Il ne reste de monumens de ces âges affreux que des fondations de monastères et un confus souvenir de misère et de brigandage. Figurez-vous des déserts, où les loups, les tigres, et les renards égorgent un bétail épars et timide ; c'est le portrait de l'Europe pendant tant de siècles." That this portrait of Europe, as M. Voltaire terms it, was a very false and exaggerated one, we shall now proceed to show.

What were the manners of those Gothic nations before they left their seats in the North, we have already seen, and must acknowledge that, at this period, their character, if not marked by absolute barbarism, was at least distinguished by a most sanguinary and ferocious spirit. This, however, is not absolutely inconsistent with a species of humanity, and is frequently allied to great generosity of mind. Though bloody and implacable in war, they were not strangers to the virtues of peace;—hospitality and kindness to strangers, which are the common virtues of rude nations, they possessed in a high degree. The respect, likewise, which the Scandinavians entertained for the female sex was a striking feature in their character, and could not fail, in many respects, to humanize their dispositions.

The Goths, in their progress southwards, subduing nations more refined than themselves, would naturally make proportional advances in civilization; and therefore it is not surprising that, by the time they had attained a footing in the empire, we find them in many respects a humane, and even a cultivated and enlightened people. Before their settlement in the Roman provinces, they had laid aside their idolatrous superstitions for the Christian religion. To their notions of morality, we have the most honorable testimonies from various authors. Grotius, in his preface to his publication of Procopius and Jornandes, has collected many of these testimonies. Salvianus, the bishop of Marseilles, who lived about the middle of the fifth century, has drawn a parallel between the manners of the Romans and those nations whom they still affected to term barbarous—which is as much to the honor of the latter, as it is to the disgrace of the former. "Omnes fere barbari," says he, "qui modo sunt unius gentis ac regis se mutuò amant; omnes pæne Romani se mutuò persequuntur. Vastantur pauperes, viduæ gemunt, orphani proculcantur; in tantum, ut multi eorum et non obscuris natalibus editi et liberaliter instituti, ad hostes fugiant—quærentes scilicet apud barbaros Romanam humanitatem, quia apud Romanos barbaram immanitatem ferre non possunt."*

From this honorable character as a nation, from their integrity, love of justice, and good faith, "we may remark," says Grotius, "that in the whole course of those wars carried on in Italy under the generals of Justinian, no province or district ever voluntarily departed from their allegiance to the Gothic government." In fact, it is not possible to produce a more beautiful picture of an excellent administration than that of the Gothic monarchy under Theodoric the Great, in Italy. Of this the letters of Cassiodorus, his secretary, a man of eminent learning and abilities, give a very complete idea. We find in these the political constitutions of a prince who seems to have continually employed his thoughts on what might equally aggrandize his empire and promote the happiness of his subjects. It is a high pleasure to set in a conspicuous light the almost forgotten merits of one of the most illustrious characters that ever adorned the annals of history; I shall therefore,

* "The barbarians, if of the same nation and under the same sovereign, entertain for each other the most kindly feelings of regard. The Romans as universally persecute each other: so much so, that many of them, and these of no low degree, fly for protection to the enemy; exposed to barbarian cruelty among the Romans, they seek Roman hospitality from the barbarians."

while on this subject of the genius and character of the Gothic nations, throw together some particulars descriptive of the excellent administration of this truly great and excellent monarch.*

In a former chapter we have seen Theodoric derive his right to the kingdom of Italy from the gift of the emperor Zeno, after he had subdued the country. He was received by the Romans with the submission due to a conqueror, which his humane policy soon changed into the affection due to a native prince. Where laws and customs were good, he attempted no innovations; he retained the Roman laws, the Roman magistrates, the same internal police, and the same distribution of the provinces. The Goths, as conquerors, were naturally entitled to the chief military honors and commands; but the Romans alone were preferred to all civil employments. He seems from the first to have adopted the spirit of a Roman, in the most enthusiastic regard for every remain of the ancient grandeur of the empire. Instead of that savage spirit which pleases itself often in effacing those remnants of antiquity, which are too strong a contrast to modern barbarism, it was the regret of Theodoric to find such noble works in ruins,—his highest pleasure to preserve and to imitate them.†

As Theodoric made no alteration in the laws, superior magistrates, or forms of government, so he contented himself with the same tributes and taxes which had been levied by the emperors. These, however, he collected in the manner the least possibly oppressive; and he was ever ready to abate, and even remit them entirely, on occasions of public scarcity or calamity. Of this humane indulgence we have many beautiful instances. He remitted to the inhabitants of Campania the taxes of a year, in consideration of what they had suffered from an eruption of Mount Vesuvius. In his letter on that occasion to the governor of Campania, he tells him that the inhabitants of the province had petitioned him for relief; that to grant their request he wished only to be rightly informed of the extent of their sufferings; he required him, therefore, to send some person of character and integrity into the territory of Nola and Naples to view the lands, that he might proportion his relief to their misfortunes. The citizens of Naples, in gratitude for their sovereign's benevolence, erected in the forum his statue, in mosaic work—a specimen of art which attracted the admiration of all Italy. In the same humane and liberal spirit he exempted the inhabitants of Lipontum, in Apulia, from all taxes for the space of two years, in consideration of their lands being laid waste by the Vandals, in a descent from the coast of Africa. It was a maxim of his which he often

---

* A very curious picture of the ordinary mode of life of Theodoric is contained in an epistle of Sidonius Apollinaris (l. i., ep. 2.), of which Mr. Gibbon, in the 36th chapter of his History, has given an elegant translation.

† Acerbum nimis est (Theod. loq.) nostrum temporibus antiquorum facta decrescere qui ornatum urbium quotidie desideramus augere.—Cass. Var. Q. 35.

exemplified: "Sola virtus est misericordia, cui omnes virtutes cedere honorabiliter non recusant." (Cass. Var. Q. 9.) A most beautiful instance of his clemency—nay, something beyond it—is preserved in one of his letters to the Roman senate. Liberius had been an active minister under Odoacer, whom Theodoric had stripped of the kingdom of Italy. Theodoric acquainted the senate, by letter, that he had bestowed rewards and honors on Liberius and on his son, for the very reason that *he* had meritoriously and faithfully served Odoacer, though his enemy; that to him whom fortune had now made his sovereign he had not fled as a base refugee, nor courted his favor by vilifying his former master.*

One of the first actions which signalized the reign of this illustrious prince is an example equally of the most judicious policy and of singular humanity. In the reign of Odoacer, in a predatory expedition of the Burgundians, under Gondebald, into Italy, the whole province of Liguria was desolated, and a great number of the inhabitants carried into captivity. Theodoric undertook to repair this misfortune; he sent Epiphanius, a bishop of great eloquence as well as sanctity of character, to Lyons, which was the court of Gondebald, with an offer of ransom from Theodoric for all the Ligurian captives. The Burgundian prince, won by the eloquence of the prelate to emulate the generosity of his brother sovereign, gratuitously discharged all who had not been taken in arms, and required for the rest a very moderate ransom. The return of these captives, to the amount of many thousands, into Italy, exhibited a spectacle which drew tears from the eyes of all the beholders, and contributed equally (as Muratori remarks) to the glory of religion, and to the honor of that humane prince by whose means so unexpected a blessing was derived to his subjects. The religion of Theodoric (as that of all the Gothic nations after their conversion from idolatry) was Arianism, or that system which professes the Unity of the Godhead, and holds the Son only to be the first and most excellent of created beings, whom God has chosen to be his instrument in the redemption of mankind: a doctrine which is commonly supposed to have been first openly professed and vindicated by Arius, a presbyter of Alexandria, in the fourth century. It was, however, condemned by the council of Nice, summoned by Constantine the Great; and as the Gothic nations paid no regard to this ecclesiastical decree, but adhered to those opinions which their own bishops had taught

* "Et ideo," says he, "sic factum est ut ei libenter daremus præmium quia nostrum fideliter juvabat inimicum." In another of the letters of Theodoric to the senate he has these fine expressions: "Benigni principis est non tam delicta velle punire, quam tollere, ne aut acriter vindicando, æstimetur nimius, aut leviter agendo putetur improvidus. At vos quos semper gravitas decet, nolite truculenter insequi inania verba populorum. Quid enim discrepit a peccante, qui se per excessum nititur vindicare?"

them, they were treated by the Catholics as little better than heathens. Even the excellent Theodoric has been loaded with calumnies by some of the most bigoted fathers of the church, while those of a more truly Christian spirit have done ample justice to his merits. Partial as he was to the tenets of Arius, yet, after his establishment in Italy, he attempted no reformation of the prevailing religion of the country. The Catholics were not only unmolested in the exercise of their religion, but, by the excellent ecclesiastical regulations for the maintenance of peace and good order, and by the care shown in the appointment of prelates of known probity of character, it is acknowledged by the Catholics themselves, that at no period did the church enjoy greater harmony or prosperity. The humane toleration of Theodoric extended not only to different sects of Christians, but even to those who, as inveterate enemies of the Christian faith, are generally regarded with a degree of abhorrence. The Synagogue of the Jews at Genoa had fallen to ruin; Theodoric allowed them to rebuild it. "Religionem," says he, "imperare non possumus; quia nemo cogitur ut credat invitus." This truly laudable spirit of toleration was common, as Grotius remarks, to all the Gothic nations.

Such was the character of Theodoric the Great, a prince, whom it is certainly no exaggeration to term, in the words of Sidonius Apollinaris, "Romanæ decus columenque gentis." It may, perhaps, be remarked, that one extraordinary example of this kind, which might have arisen in any age or nation, is not sufficient to warrant any general inference with regard to the manners of a whole people; and had this example been singular in the annals of the Gothic nations in Europe, we must have admitted the force of the objection. It was not, however, singular, as may be proved by the example of many of the Gothic princes, whose characters, if not attaining on all points to the striking eminence of Theodoric, were yet such as justly entitle them to the admiration and respect of posterity. I shall instance Alaric, Amalasonta, the daughter of Theodoric, and Totila. We have seen, in the course of our historical detail, the progress of the conquests of Alaric upon the Western empire, and the perfidious conduct of Honorius, who, under the direction of his ministers Stilicho and Olympius, compelled the generous Goth to extremities. In revenge of their repeated acts of treachery and perjury, wearied out at length, and highly exasperated by their perfidy, Alaric revenged himself by the sack of Rome, which he had twice before spared on the faith of a treaty which Honorius had violated. Yet such was the humanity of this barbarian captain, that he gave the most express orders for restraining all effusion of blood, unless in case of obstinate resistance. He particularly enjoined that the churches should be held as an inviolable asylum for all who fled thither for shelter, and that the treasures and jewels which they contained (strong temptations to armed troops in the tumult of victory!) should not be touched under the severest penalties. His orders were religiously obeyed ; aud so remarkable was the moderation and singular clemency of this Gothic and heretic conqueror, that the Catholic fathers themselves have transmitted to posterity the most honorable testimonies of his virtues.

Amalasonta, the daughter of Theodoric, governed Italy during the minority of her son Athalaric. Such was the political wisdom, the equity and lenity of her administration, that the loss of Theodoric, beloved, or rather adored, as he was by his subjects, was scarcely felt. By the counsels and under the direction of his excellent minister, Cassiodorus, she pursued the same plan of government, directing, at the same time, her utmost attention to the proper education of her son, whom she wished to train up in every great and useful accomplishment. The passion of this princess for the cultivation of literature was so strong, as to draw upon her the reproach of some of the more illiterate of her subjects, who blamed her, in the education of her son, for bestowing more attention on the study of letters than on martial and athletic exercises. But she rightly conceived that the ferocious spirit of the times required rather to be softened than fostered and encouraged.

We have seen the conduct of Totila when, like Alaric, twice master of Rome, (which he won by force of arms, after an obstinate resistance,) he imitated the conduct of that conqueror, not only in his clemency to the vanquished, and in his care to preserve the city from destruction, but even in rebuilding, with the utmost magnificence, what, in the fury of a siege, it had proved impossible to preserve from violence. On his first taking possession of the city, he assembled the senate, and, with great eloquence, recapitulating the favors they had received from the Gothic sovereigns, Theodoric and Amalasonta, and contrasting their mild and equitable administration with the severities they had experienced under the emperors and their officers, he bitterly reproached them with their base servility as well as ingratitude to their benefactors. Being now, however, master of Italy, the Romans experienced under his government every happiness which a nation can derive from the virtues of a prince. "Habitavit cum Romanis," says Paulus Diaconus, a contemporary author, "tanquam pater cum filiis." He restored the senate to rank and splendor. He adorned the city with many costly structures, made the most salutary regulations for its being constantly supplied with provisions, regulated the rates at which they were to be sold, and gratified the Romans by restoring the ancient Circensian games, which he exhibited with a magnificence rivalling that of the most illustrious of the emperors: in fine, he made the Gothic government as respectable as it had been under Theodoric ; so that with truth it might be said of the administration of those princes, that they made good the promise of that great man upon his accession to the throne of Italy:—"that the only regret of the people would be not to have come at an earlier period under the sway of the Goths."

The stream of Gothic inundation, in its first irruption upon the provinces of the empire, had divided itself into two great branches upon the death of Hermaneric. One branch of the nation, remaining at Pannonia, and choosing for themselves a chief or king, were termed Ostrogoths, in opposition to the other branch, which, choosing a different sovereign, separated themselves and migrated to the westward, whence they were termed Westrogoths or Visigoths. These last, under Alaric, after some successful inroads upon the exterior provinces, we have seen, penetrated into Italy, and carrying every thing before them, were for some time masters of the capital of the Western empire. Upon the death of Alaric, Italy was for awhile free from the dominion of the Goths, till the period when Theodoric the Ostrogoth acquired a gift of the sovereignty from Zeno, in reward of his delivering that kingdom from the usurpation of Odoacer and the Heruli. The Western or Visigoths, in the meantime, after the death of Alaric, had withdrawn into Gaul. Honorius assigned to them the province of Aquitaine, and their prince Ataulphus fixed his residence at Thoulouse, which continued for some time to be the capital of the empire of the Visigoths, till Clovis and his Franks, from zeal to the Catholic religion and detestation of the heretical opinions of these Arians, drove them out of Gaul: when they took their way across the Pyrenees, and, settling in Spain, made Toledo the capital of their kingdom. The race of the Visigoth princes in Spain was termed the race of the *Balti*, as that of the Ostrogoths was the *Amali*—ancient names of the chiefs, or heads of the two distinct families, from which these sovereigns were descended. It was remarkable that the Ostrogoth princes of the race of the Amali—for instance, Theodoric, Amalasonta, and Totila—had a predilection for the laws of the Romans, and enforced the universal observance of them in their dominions; while the Visigoth princes, of the race of the Balti, almost all of them rejected the Roman jurisprudence, and adhered to a code of their own, formed from the ancient laws and customs of the Gothic nations. The reason, I apprehend, was this. The Ostrogoth princes, taking possession of Italy, not as invaders, but rather as recovering it from the usurpation of the Heruli, and holding it as a gift from the lawful proprietors, the emperors of the East, were received by the Italians as friends, protectors, and lawful sovereigns. They found there an excellent system of laws, and a people living under them disposed to every duty of allegiance. To have changed these laws would have been the height of imprudence. The Visigoths, on the contrary, wherever they came, were invaders. They had often laid waste the provinces of the empire, and particularly Italy, by their incursions; they were regarded as enemies by the Romans, and both nations looked upon each other with an eye of jealousy. It would therefore have been extremely unnatural in them to have adopted the laws of a people with whom they were constantly at variance; they therefore kept to their own laws and ancient usages, which, as soon as they had obtained a fixed residence, it was the care of their sovereigns to compile and digest into a regular code. It is therefore from this collection of the laws of the Visigoths, that we may naturally expect to derive the most certain information, that we can now attain, of the genius and spirit of this ancient people. In the preface to these laws of the Visigoths, we are informed that they were first begun to be digested into a code by king Evaricus or Euric, who reigned about the year 470 of the Christian era. They were corrected and augmented by Leovigildus, who died in 586, and enlarged likewise by some succeeding monarchs, the last of whom was Ervigius, who died in 687. Thus, the first formation of this code of the laws of the Visigoths was prior, by fifty years, to the date of the compilation of the pandects or digests of the Roman laws made by the command of Justinian, who, it is not improbable, adopted from this code of the barbarians the idea of collecting the substance of that immense mass of the Roman laws into one body, which we are informed, before his time, lay scattered in two thousand volumes.

The learned and ingenious author of the History of Charles the Fifth has, in his preliminary discourse, in treating of the pernicious consequences of the feudal system, certainly greatly overcharged the picture, when he represents the state of the Gothic governments to be a scene of tumult and dissension, where there was no common or connecting interest to promote a tranquil and regular administration. That this was not the case, these Gothic laws afford the fullest proof; for, it is impossible that such laws should have been the fruit of dissension, or of an impotent administration. That historian indeed tells us that these laws fell soon into disuse, and that customs, vague and capricious, were substituted in their place. But that this was not the case among the Visigoths, at least till the Saracen invasion of Spain, I believe is incontrovertible; and that they never were in oblivion is evident from this fact, that the *Forum Judicum* or *Fuero Juzgo*, which is acknowledged to be the fountain of the Spanish law, is in reality, at this day, in great part composed of these ancient laws of the Visigoths. From this code (of the Leges Visigothorum), which is extremely worthy of the perusal both of the lawyer and the student of history, I shall make a short abstract of a few of the statutes, which will fully evince what the reader may already be disposed to believe, that these nations, at the period of which we now treat, were in a state of society very remote from barbarism; perhaps even further advanced in civilization and refinement, than any contemporary people of the west of Europe.

In order that all judges might have a certain fixed and immutable rule, ascertaining the extent of their jurisdiction, it is declared by these laws, that no judge shall presume to decide in any lawsuit unless he finds in this book a statute precisely applicable to it. Such causes as fell not under any of those statutes are declared to be reserved for the jurisdiction of the prince. Lib. ii., tit. i., l. xii.

Although there seems to reign in many of the penal laws of the Visigoths a considerable degree of severity, it is tempered at the same time with great equity. One excellent law, which was applicable to all prosecutions for crimes, was that which limited the punishment of all offences to the offender himself, without affecting his children or heirs. While the Roman emperors were enacting such sanguinary statutes, as that of Arcadius and Honorius, which declares that the children of those convicted of treason shall be perpetually infamous, incapable of all inheritance, of all office or employment; that they shall languish in want and misery, "so that life shall be to them a burden, and death a comfort" —while such was the spirit of the laws of the enlightened Romans, let us remark the complexion of those of the barbarian Goths: "Omnia crimina suos sequantur auctores. Nec pater pro filio, nec filius pro patre, nec uxor pro marito, nec maritus pro uxore, nec frater pro fratre, nec vicinus pro vicino, nec propinquus pro propinquo, ullam calamitatem pertimescat. Sed ille *solus* judicetur culpabilis qui culpanda commiserit, et crimen cum illo qui *fecerit moriatur:* nec successores aut hæredes, pro factis parentum, ullum periculum pertimescant." (Lib. vi., tit. i., l. viii.*) It were to the honor of us moderns, that the penal laws of the most civilized nations in Europe were dictated in the same spirit of humanity.

The laws against murder were uncommonly rigid. If the friends of the deceased neglected to prosecute for the crime, any other peron whatever might bring the murderer to justice. (Lib. vi., t. i., . xv.) If a man, by pure accident, should put another to death, he was guilty of no crime; yet, if intending but the smallest injury to another, such as a blow with the hand or foot, he should accidentally put him to death, he was guilty of homicide. (Lib.vi., ibid.) If a man, aiming a blow at one person, should kill another; if the murderer began the quarrel, he was punished with death. If it was begun by the person at whom the blow was aimed, that person paid a heavy fine to the relations of the deceased—100 solidi of gold—and the murderer half the sum. (Ibid., l. iv.) It was death to give a woman drugs to procure abortion, and equally criminal if that effect should follow from a stroke or any wilful

* "Let all crimes be visited on the perpetrator alone. Let no father for a son nor son for a father, no husband for a wife, or wife for a husband, &c., dread any responsibility. Let the crime die with him who has committed it, and let not the heir dread any danger from the deeds of his predecessor."

injury. Child-murder was punished with the death of the parent. (Lib. vi., tit. iii.) If a master, even upon the highest provocation, should put his slave to death, he was fined in a pound of gold, became perpetually infamous, and was deprived of the power of making a testament. (Lib. vi., t. v., l. xii.) If a master maimed his servant of a hand, foot, ear, nose, lip, or eye, he was condemned to three years' banishment from the province in which he resided. (Lib. vi., t. v., l. xiii.) The *lex talionis* was in great observance among the Gothic nations. The Visigoth code provides, that for every offence for which there is not a special statutory punishment, the *pœna talionis* should take place. It was a very ample extension of this retaliation, that he who wilfully set fire to a house was burnt himself. If a judge, corrupted by bribery, condemned an innocent man to punishment, he suffered the like punishment himself.

It is remarkable that we find in these laws of the Visigoths no traces of those singular and barbarous modes of trial, which were in use among most of the other Gothic nations, even at a period posterior, by several ages, to the code of which we now treat. I mean what was termed the judgment of God—the trial of crimes by judicial combat between the accuser and accused, and the ordeal or trial by fire and water. These customs, we know, continued long to prevail among the Franks and Normans ; but there is no evidence that they were ever in use either among the Visigoths or Ostrogoths ; I therefore omit any further mention of them in this place, but shall take particular notice of them in treating afterwards of the European manners in the age of Charlemagne. It is asserted by Montesquieu, in his Spirit of Laws, b. xxviii., l. ii., that the distinguishing character of these laws of the barbarous nations was, that they were not confined to a certain district; but that in every Gothic nation it was usual to apply that law which was peculiar to the country of the litigants. The Frank, says he, was tried by the law of the Franks ; the Aleman by the law of the Alemans ; the Burgundian by that of the Burgundians ; the Roman by the Roman law ; and he seeks for some ingenious reasons to account for this peculiarity, which reasons he finds in the manners of the German nations, as described by Cæsar and Tacitus, of their living in distinct provinces, free and independent of each other, united only when there was a common enemy, but each retaining their own established laws and customs. This certainly held true with regard to some of those tribes which Montesquieu has enumerated, but is not true with regard to all the Gothic nations. The Visigoths, of whose laws we have been treating, are a direct proof of the contrary. So far from allowing those of different nations who were under the monarchy of the Visigoths to be judged by the laws of the country to which by birth they belonged, a Frank by the law of the Franks, and a Roman by that of the Romans, these laws expressly declare that in their dominions no other code shall have the smallest force, but that of the Visigoths. They observe, with regard to the laws of other nations, that though abundantly eloquent, they are involved in perplexities,* and a penalty of thirty pounds of gold is imposed on any person who shall cite in judgment any code of laws belonging to other nations. (Lib. x., ibid.)

In treating of the laws of the Gothic nations, I have taken this example of the laws of the Visigoths, not from any opinion of their superior excellence to those of the other nations whom we, after the example of the Romans, have chosen to term barbarous. By any person who attentively examines the laws of the other Gothic nations, the laws of the Visigoths will not be found by any means to merit a superior regard. Montesquieu even affects to depreciate them as often vague and declamatory—a censure which will, in particular instances, apply to every compilation of the laws of different monarchs. But judicious and respectable as we have seen them to be, they must, in point of more extended policy, yield to the laws of the Franks and of the Lombards. Of the excellence of the former, M. Montesquieu has collected some striking proofs in the 28th book of his Spirit of Laws; and whoever wishes to see a very judicious estimate of the merits of the latter, viz., the laws of the Lombards, may find it in the fifth book of Giannoni's History of Naples.

The government of the Goths, as we find them after their settlement in the provinces of the empire, was monarchical. This form had its rise, as it has in all barbarous nations, from the choice of a military chief to command them in their expeditions. The throne, among the Goths, continued to be elective long after they had obtained fixed settlements. It was natural, when time had rooted them in their possessions, that a sort of mixed elective and hereditary monarchy should take place. The powerful lords and barons would not easily part with their right of election, but the choice would come to be confined to the family of the last sovereign, or he upon his death-bed, with the advice of these lords, would nominate his successor. Such, in fact, we find to have been the case both in the kingdom of the Ostrogoths and Visigoths. The choice did not necessarily fall upon the eldest son; brothers, and even bastards, were frequently called to the throne. Torrismond, the Visigoth, was succeeded by his brother, Theodoric II. Alaric II., the Visigoth, who was killed by Clovis, the king of the Franks, left a legitimate son, Amalaric; he was, however, succeeded by his bastard son, Gesalaric, upon whose death, Amalaric came to the throne. These facts prove two things, first, that the throne was elective, and secondly, that the election was

---

* Quamvis eloquiis polleant, tamen difficultatibus hærent. Ideo nolumus sive Romanis legibus, sive alienis institutionibus amplius convexari. Lib. ii., tit ', l. ix.

confined to the family, though not limited to the eldest child, or even to legitimate children. Upon the failure of the blood royal, the election was free.

The chief officers in the administration of the Gothic government were the dukes and counts. These officers, we have seen, were known in the Roman empire before the time of Constantine. The former were the highest in military command, and the latter the first among the civil dignities. The duke, as his name imported, *dux exercitus*, was the commander-in-chief of the troops of the province over which he presided. There is, however, reason to believe that his office was not confined to a military command alone. He even appears to have had sometimes the supreme civil as well as military government in the province. Pantinus, in his treatise on the Gothic dignities, gives an instance from which it appears that even the higher clergy were subject to his jurisdiction.

As the office of the duke was, however, chiefly confined to military affairs, that of the *comes*, or count, was principally exercised in the civil. He was the highest civil judge in the province, with power of reviewing the decrees of all inferior jurisdictions. He had the power of suspending from office and punishing his subordinate judges for negligence or misdemeanor. In the absence of the count from the town or district where he presided, he named a *præpositus* or *vicarius*, to decide in ordinary matters, but with instruction to report to him all cases of difficulty. As the office of the duke infringed sometimes on that of the count in his civil power, so did that of the count upon the duke's in military; for it appears that, on sudden emergencies, the *comes* could summon out all the military force. This was probably when, from the distance of the residence of the duke from the extremities of the provinces, or his being engaged in the exercise of his duty in a remote quarter, there was a necessity for another to act in his place. In general, however, the office of count was that of the supreme civil judge, and that of the duke the chief military dignity; at least, it appears to have been such in Italy under the Ostrogoth princes.

The Gothic government seems then, upon the whole, to have been an absolute monarchy, of a mixed hereditary and elective nature. The nobles, it is plain, if they did not determine the succession of the crown, at least ratified it. Of this convocation of the *proceres*, for that purpose, we have frequent mention in the Gothic historians. These *proceres* were probably the body of the dukes and counts. The monarch, once elected, was absolute in the most ample sense. We do not find any laws limiting or even prescribing his powers; and it is certain that the nomination of all dignities, offices, and magistracies, was in the sovereign. He imposed tributes and taxes at his discretion; and could condemn capitally without form of trial. Of this we have a strong instance in Theodoric the Great, which is the only stain upon his memory —the condemnation of the philosopher Boetius and the senator Symmachus, on slight suspicions of treasonable designs—a procedure which only an absolute and despotic power in the sovereign could have warranted.

Here we close our review of what may properly be called *Ancient History*.

BOOK THE SIXTH.

CHAPTER I.

Arabia—Ancient Manners and Religion—Rise of Mahomet—His Doctrines—Conquests—Death—Causes which contributed to the rapid progress of his Religion—Conquests of the Successors of Mahomet—change in the National Character after the removal of the Seat of Empire to Bagdad—Learning of the Arabians.

At the period of the extinction of the Roman power in the West, the Eastern empire was in a state of weakness, apparently fast verging to a fate similar to that which the Western had undergone; but its catastrophe was not yet at hand, and was to come from a different quarter. A small spark of superstition, kindling, in the meantime, in the heart of Arabia, produced a new religion, and a new empire which arose to a very high degree of splendor. To that quarter, therefore, we now turn our attention, to mark the rise of the Mahometan superstition, and the foundation of the empire of the Saracens.

Arabia is a large peninsula, divided in the middle by the tropic of Cancer. It is bounded on the north by Syria and Palestine; on the south, by the Indian Ocean; on the east, by the Gulfs of Bassora and Ormuz; and on the west, by the Red Sea, which separates it from Egypt. It is divided into three parts: Arabia Petræa, which, as its name implies, is a barren and rocky country, bordering on the Red Sea; Arabia Deserta, so named from the sandy deserts with which it abounds, is adjacent to the Gulf of Ormuz; and Arabia Felix, a comparatively fertile and delightful clime, forms the southern part of the Peninsula.

Before the period of which we now treat, the Arabians had lived chiefly in independent tribes, and were almost unknown to other nations. The inhabitants of the interior part of the country were mostly shepherds; and those of the coasts and frontiers, pirates and plunderers. They lived in tents, and occasionally migrated from one country to another, without laws or any established police, and acknowledging no superior but the head of their tribe. Their manners are described as being, beyond measure, barbarous; their religion an incoherent assemblage of all the superstitions with which the neighboring countries abounded. They had a confused tradition, that they were descended from the Patriarch Abraham; and they retained, of the Jewish religion, the ceremony of circumcision, ablutions, and the horror for certain meats, which they regarded as unclean. With these rites, they combined the worship of idols, and the belief of three goddesses of equal power and wisdom, and co-existent with the Supreme Being.

The city of Mecca was the residence of the chief of these idols. A small square edifice, or temple, called the Cāābba, was held throughout all Arabia to be a place of the most supreme sanctity. Within this temple was a stone, which was the peculiar object of veneration, and was said to have descended from Heaven, in those days of innocence when man was free from guilt as he came from the hands of his Creator. The stone was then white, but gradually became sullied, as man became more wicked, till at last it grew entirely black. From the pilgrimages which it was customary to make to this temple, and the riches it brought thither, Mecca became the most considerable city of Arabia.

The wandering tribes had a sort of rank, or settled preëminence among themselves, though we know of no head whom they all obeyed. One of the principal of these tribes was that of Koreish; yet it does not appear to have been remarkably flourishing at the time of the appearance of Mahomet; for he, though a prince of that race, was born to no ampler inheritance than an Æthiopian slave and five camels.

This extraordinary person was born in the year 571 of the Christian era.* His father died before his birth, his mother when he was but a few years old; and his relations put him into the service of a woman of the name of Cadigha, who traded into Syria. In his intercourse with this country, he had opportunities of observing the manners of a nation more polished than his own, and felt the defects of his own education, for as yet he could neither read nor write. Syria was at this time a Roman province. He was struck with the manners of the people, their laws, their government and policy. His mind was of that reflecting turn which profits by every observation. It is probable that in this country, where he found a mixture of Jews and Christians, his thoughts first turned upon religion; and finding that the gross superstition and idolatry of his own country offered ample room for a reformation, which presented the most flattering objects to an ambitious mind, he began to conceive the project of establishing a new religion. Christianity presented a system of the most beautiful morality; but, the religious notions of his countrymen inclining to Judaism, he thought it advisable to retain some great

* The precise era of his birth has been much disputed, and has been fixed, by different authors, at various periods from the year 560 to the year 620 of the Christian era. The date given in the text is that now most commonly adopted.

features likewise of that ceremonial, as well as certain idle customs and ceremonies to which the Arabians had long been addicted ; such as the pilgrimage to the temple of Mecca, and the adoration of the black-stone. His most politic idea was the thought of attracting proselytes to his new religion, by accommodating it, as much as possible, to the voluptuous spirit of his countrymen. But as yet the whole system was, probably, only a dream, which the poverty and obscurity of its author could give him very little prospect of ever realizing.

Mahomet, however, was fortunate enough to insinuate himself into the good graces of his mistress, Cadigha, and, marrying her, he saw himself raised to a situation which made him one of the most considerable men of his country. Instead of abandoning his former project, he considered his new situation as only a stronger incentive to the prosecution of his plan, which his influence and fortune promised materially to facilitate. He began, therefore, to put his scheme in practice. He endeavored to remedy the defects of his education, by acquiring some knowledge of letters. He affected a solitary life ; bestowed a great deal in charity ; retired, at times, to the desert, and pretended that he held conferences with the angel Gabriel. The epilepsy, a disease to which he was subject, was, he pretended, a divine ecstasy, or rapture, in which he was admitted to the contemplation of Paradise. He made his wife an accomplice in the cheat, and she published his visions and reveries to all the neighborhood. In a short time the whole city of Mecca talked of nothing but Mahomet. He began to harangue in public ; and his natural eloquence, which was wonderfully animated, joined with a noble, commanding, and majestic figure, gained him many proselytes.

This was the substance of the religion, which he held forth as a new revelation.* He taught that mankind should acknowledge one God, without division of substance, or of persons ; an eternal and all-powerful being, Creator of the universe ;—That the laws of this being, whose beneficence is equal to his power, are such as tend universally to the happiness of his creatures ;—That the duty which man owes to God is to pray seven times a day ; to honor him by such ceremonies as are figurative of his bounties ; to love all mankind, as members of one family ; to assist the poor and protect the injured ; and to show kindness even to inferior animals. To these precepts, which it must be owned are excellent, Mahomet joined others, which recommended his doctrine to the passions of his followers. He was himself of an amorous and voluptuous constitution. The pleasures of love were, by the religion of Mahomet, held forth as a duty in this life, and the highest reward for the good Mussulman in a future state. He permitted his followers to have four wives, and as many slaves for their concubines as they

---

* See Sale's Koran, Preliminary Discourse, Section 4th.

pleased. He himself, as a prophet, arrogated a superior privilege, and had fifteen wives.

He taught that God Almighty had engraven these laws in the hearts of the first race of men ; but that vice and iniquity gradually prevailing, and wearing out their impression, he had sent, from time to time, his prophets upon earth, to revive his holy precepts by their doctrines and example. The most eminent of these prophets, he affirmed, were Abraham, Moses, Jesus Christ—and Mahomet, the last, the greatest of all—who was destined to extend the know ledge of the true religion over all the earth.

The ceremonies of circumcision, ablution, and the pilgrimage to Mecca, he recommended as exterior and visible signs, by which God desired that man should signify his belief of the more speculative tenets of his religion. These laws he pretended to have received from God Almighty, by the hands of the angel Gabriel, who presented him, from time to time, with parcels of that book, or Koran, in which they were contained. The fundamental doctrines of the Koran are such as have been enumerated. They are, it is true, intermixed with a variety of absurdities—errors in history, chronology, and philosophy; but these the countrymen of Mahomet, in his time, may well be supposed to have overlooked ; and the learned Mussulman, at this day, will probably consider them as corruptions and interpolations of the original text. It must be acknowledged, that the work itself is full of fine conceptions, and abounds with that brilliant and figurative eloquence which is characteristic of oriental writing. In many places, when the majesty and attributes of God are described, the style is most sublime and magnificent, and nearly resembles that of the Sacred Scriptures—from which, indeed, it is quite obvious that the composer of the Koran drew many of its most shining ornaments.

The illiterate character and ignorance of Mahomet, in his younger days, leaves no doubt that, in the composition of this work, he must have had able assistants ; but as he was possessed of strong natural talents, and a brilliant imagination, the chief merit was, in all probability, his own. The production of the work in small and detached parcels was a highly politic measure ; for by leaving it in his power to add to it from time to time, according as he was favored with new revelations, he had it in his power to remove or explain any errors or inconsistencies, the detection of which might otherwise have been fatal to his imposture.

The disciples of Mahomet daily increased, and among these were the most respectable of the citizens of Mecca. Tumults, however, arising, and frequent disputes between the Believers and Infidels, the magistrates of the city thought it necessary to remove the cause of the disorder, and Mahomet was banished. His flight, which was termed the Hegira, was the era of his glory ; his disciples followed him, and he now became sensible of his own strength. He began from that moment to be fired with the ideas of conquest; he betook himself to Medina, and there, with the sword in one hand and the Koran in the other, he preached to his votaries—empire and dominion in this world, and eternal happiness in the next. He now determined to take vengeance on the people of Mecca, for their blind ingratitude to the prophet of God; and marching against them, as it is said, with only 113 men, he attacked and took the city. Omar, one of the bravest of the Arabians, had joined him at Medina. His followers, after this first success, which was regarded as miraculous, increased prodigiously. In a few years, he had subdued to his empire and religion all Arabia. With a mixture of strange presumption and enthusiasm, he now wrote to Cosrhoes, king of Persia, and others of the neighboring princes, that they should embrace his religion; and, what is yet more surprising, two of these princes actually became Mahometans. He now turned his arms against the Eastern empire, and marching into Syria, took several of the towns belonging to the Romans; but in the middle of his conquests, Mahomet, at the age of sixty-three, was seized with a mortal disease, the effect, it was said, of poison. The conclusion of his life was admirable. Let him, said he, to whom I have done violence or injustice now appear, and I am ready to make him reparation. For several days preceding his death, he ordered himself to be carried to the mosque, and there harangued the people with wonderful eloquence, which, from a dying man, had a powerful effect. It is by no means improbable that he believed himself inspired—as the singular success of all his enterprises might have persuaded a mind of that enthusiastic turn, of a divine interposition in his favor. It is certain, that with his latest breath he continued to inculcate the doctrines of his new religion. He recommended to his followers to keep the sword unsheathed till they had driven all infidels out of Arabia; and in the agonies of death he declared to Ayesha, the best beloved of his wives, that God, by the mouth of the angel Gabriel, had given him the choice of life or death, and that he had preferred the latter.

The rapid success which attended the propagation of the religion of Mahomet may be accounted for from a few natural and simple causes. The first of these was certainly that signal favor which attended his arms, and, as we shall immediately see, those of his successors. The martial spirit, when inflamed by the enthusiasm of religion, is irresistible: and while repeated victories persuaded many of a divine interposition in favor of the prophet and his law, the terror of his arms inclined others submissively to receive that religion which was propagated by the sword. Neither was it surprising that a religion which adapted itself so entirely to the passions of men should find a number of willing votaries among the luxurious nations of the East. The gross ignorance, too, of many of those nations might readily have rendered them the dupes of a less artful system of imposture than the fable of Mahomet; and to add to all, it must be owned with regret, that the shameful animosities and dissensions which then prevailed among the different sects of the Christian church had too much contributed to bring the true religion into disesteem and contempt.

Mahomet, by his last will, had nominated Ali, his son-in-law, and Fatima, his daughter, to succeed him; but Abubeker, his father-in-law, had the address to secure the soldiery: he pretended a prior nomination, and bringing Ayesha and Omar over to his interest, he secured the succession.

As disputes began to arise among the believers, Abubeker collected and published the scattered books of the Koran, which, it is probable, had never till that time been united; and prosecuting the conquests of Mahomet, he made an inroad into Palestine, defeated the army of Heraclius, the emperor, and took Jerusalem, subjecting the whole country between Mount Libanus and the Mediterranean. Abubeker died in the midst of his conquests, and Omar, by the unanimous voice of the army, was called to the throne. He prosecuted the conquests of his predecessors, and in one campaign deprived the Romans of Syria, Phenicia, Mesopotamia, and Chaldea; then turning his arms against Persia, this rapid conqueror, in the space of two years, brought that immense and magnificent empire under the dominion of the Saracens,* and extinguished the ancient religion of Zoroaster, of which no trace remains, but what is preserved by the inconsiderable sect of the Guebres. In the meantime, the lieutenants of Omar were extending the conquests of the Saracens in other quarters: they subdued all Egypt, Libya, and Numidia. In this conquest was burnt the celebrated library founded at Alexandria, by Ptolemy Philadelphus, and augmented by succeeding princes. The Saracens argued that all the knowledge which was there treasured up was either contained in the Koran, and therefore superfluous—or not contained in it, and therefore unnecessary to salvation.

Amid these extensive conquests, Omar was killed by a Persian slave. His successor, Otman, followed the steps of his predecessors, and added to the dominion of the caliphs Bactriana and part of Tartary; while one of his lieutenants ravaged the islands of the Archipelago, took Rhodes, where he destroyed the celebrated Colossus; and passing into Sicily, threw consternation into the heart of the Italian states. Otman was succeeded by Ali, the son-in-law of Mahomet. This prince, whose name is to this

* The Arabians, who were, in fact, Ishmaelites, or descendants of Abraham by his concubine Hagar, are supposed to have assumed the name of Saracens, to induce the belief of their being the legitimate descendants of Abraham, by Sarah his wife.—Howel, part iii., chap. iii.

day revered by the Mahometans, inherited, in many respects, the genius of his father-in-law; but he was cut off by treason in the midst of his conquests, after a reign of four or five years. He transferred the seat of the caliphs from Mecca to a city called Couffa, on the banks of the Euphrates; from whence it was afterwards removed to Bagdad.

The genius of the Arabians, fired by enthusiasm and invigorated by conquest, seemed now in the train of carrying every thing before it. It is wonderful what may be achieved by a people who are once in the track of glory. Nations, in fact, seem to have their ages of brilliancy, when all is life, and vigor, and enterprise; and these perhaps preceded, and again to be followed by, an era of inanimation, weakness, and degeneracy.

In this splendid period of the history of the Saracens, their conquests were incredible. Within half a century from the first opening of the career of Mahomet, they had raised an empire more extensive than what remained, at this time, of the dominion of the Romans.

There was a succession of nineteen caliphs of the race of Omar, or, as they are termed, the Ommiades; after which began the dynasty of the Abassidæ, who were descended directly, by the male line, from Mahomet. Almanzor, the second caliph of this race, changed the seat of the Saracen empire to Bagdad; and from that period the Mahometans assumed a character to which they had hitherto been strangers. Almanzor had genius and taste for literary pursuits; the sciences began to be cultivated at Bagdad; and the learning of the Romans was transplanted thither from Constantinople. The philosophers and *literati* of the East flocked to that capital, where their talents attracted both respect and reward. The successors of Almanzor, educated in the school of the sciences, showed them the same favorable attention; and under Haroun Alraschid, who was himself a most accomplished literary character, learning, and all the arts of utility, as well as elegance, rose to a pitch of splendor which they had not known since the reign of Augustus. Alraschid flourished in the middle of the ninth century, and was contemporary with Charlemagne.

The sciences for which the Arabians were most distinguished at this time were medicine and astronomy. They had made no inconsiderable progress in mechanics; geometry they had brought to a very considerable height; and they were, if not the inventors of algebra the first who adopted that science from the farther East. Their poetry was singularly beautiful: they added a regularity to the oriental verse, retaining at the same time all its luxuriant imagery. Haroun Alraschid himself composed very beautiful verses.

The manners of the Arabians in this period of the splendor of their empire are better learned from some of their romantic compositions, than from any accounts of historians. That book which is familiar to every one, "The Arabian Nights' Entertainments," is not only a most pleasing composition in point of imagination, but contains, as an original work, a genuine picture of oriental manners, and conveys very high ideas of the police and splendor of the empire of the caliphs, in the time of Alraschid.

CHAPTER II.

MONARCHY OF THE FRANKS.

Uncertainty of the early History of the Franks—Merovingian Period—Mayors of the Palace—Change in the Dynasty effected by Pepin—Manners and Customs—Form of Government and Laws of the Franks—Feudal System.

LEAVING at present the history of the Eastern nations, we turn our view to the Western part of Europe, to take a short survey of the origin of the monarchy of the Franks, who, in the course of a few ages, raised, on the ruins of the Roman power, a great and flourishing empire. The rise of a new dominion is also, at the same period, to be traced in Italy:—the church, which had hitherto been confined to an authority in spiritual matters, exalting herself into a temporal sovereignty; and, under the title of a charter from Heaven, arrogating a supreme control over all the princes of the earth.

The history of the origin of the Franks is in no degree more certain than that of any of the other barbarous nations, who overran the Western empire. The most probable opinion is, that they were, originally, those tribes of German nations, inhabiting the districts that lie on the Lower Rhine and the Weser, who in the time of Tacitus passed under the names of Chauci, Cherusci, Catti, Sicambri. These, and some other petty nations around them, forming a league for mutual defence against the Roman power, termed themselves Franks, or Freemen.*

The first who is mentioned in history as the sovereign of this united people is Pharamond, and he seems to possess but a doubtful or legendary xistence.† His successor and kinsman Merovius, who is the head of the first race of the French monarchs known by the name of the Merovingian, is a personage whose history

---

* Gibbon, vol. i., c. x. Howel, part iii., book ii., c. 5.

† Mezeray has, notwithstanding, bestowed four books of his great History of France on the establishment of the Franks in Gaul, preceding the reign of Pharamond.

is fully as doubtful as that of his predecessors. His grandson was the famous Clovis, who succeeded to the monarchy of the Franks in the year 482. He was a prince of intrepid spirit, who from the beginning of his reign, and while yet in the twentieth year of his age, projected the conquest of all Gaul.

The Romans at this time maintained a very feeble authority in that country; and Syagrius, governor of the province, was quite unable to make head against this enterprising prince. The conquest was soon achieved.* Clovis next threw his eyes upon the kingdom of Burgundy. Gondebald had usurped the throne of Burgundy, by the murder of his father Chilperic. Clovis married Clotilda, the daughter of Chilperic, and on pretence of avenging his murder, dethroned Gondebald, but allowed him afterwards to hold his dominions as his ally and tributary.

Clotilda had great influence over her husband. The Franks had not yet embraced the Christian religion, but adhered to their ancient idolatry. Clotilda converted Clovis ;† in all probability, by persuading him that this measure was the most effectual means of conciliating the affection of all the Gallic nations. Clovis, accordingly, was baptized, and most of the Franks followed his example.‡

The politic and ambitious genius of Clovis derived from his conversion to Christianity a new pretext for extending his empire. The Visigoths, who, as has already been observed, were all of the Arian persuasion, possessed Languedoc and Aquitaine. Clovis now pretended that his conscience would not allow him to rest while a nation of heretics remained in any part of Gaul. With the assistance of his tributary, Gondebald, he immediately invaded the territory of the Visigoths, and in a short time deprived them of their whole dominions. The Visigoths retired into Spain, and made Toledo the seat of their kingdom. Theodoric the Great, who had been prevented from affording aid to his Gothic brethren by a war in which he was then engaged with the emperor Anastasius, was resolved as soon as possible to avenge their quarrel. He hastened across the Alps into Aquitaine, and there, in a decisive engagement near the city of Arles, he entirely defeated and dispersed the armies of Clovis and Gondebald; and retook from them the whole territory of the Visigoths, which he added to his own dominions. This was the period of the glory of

* Gibbon, c. 38.

† Mezeray, tom. i., p. 320. Gibbon, vol. vi., c. 28.

‡ The generous enthusiasm and barbarian magnanimity of Clovis is well characterized by the following anecdote. Soon after his conversion, while he was hearing a sermon, preached by the bishop of Rheims, in which the preacher gave an impassioned description of the sufferings and death of Christ, Clovis suddenly started up in the assembly, and seizing his spear, exclaimed in a loud voice, "Would to God that I had been there with my valiant Franks, I would soon have redressed his wrongs!"—Fredegarii Epitome, cap. 21.

Clovis. He died soon after, in the 511th year of the Christian era.*

France, which during the reign of Clovis had become an extensive and powerful monarchy, was in a short time thrown back into a state of weakness and division, almost equal to that from which it had so recently emerged.

Clovis left four sons, who divided the monarchy among them, and were continually at war with each other. Their short and distracted reigns, the mischiefs arising from a divided empire, the miserable anarchy which prevailed through every part of the kingdom, and the deplorable weakness of the whole of the princes of the Merovingian race, render the history of France, at this period, a most disgusting as well as uninstructive picture; nor is it till the rise of the *Maires du Palais*, when a degree of order arose under the usurpation of those officers, that the transactions of those dark ages become at all interesting. On the death of Dagobert the First, who left two infant sons, Sigibert and Clovis the Second, the government fell into the hands of their chief officers, the Majores Palatii, or Mayors of the Palace. These officers founded a new power, which, for some generations, held the French monarchs in the most absolute subjection, and left them little else than the name of king.

The proper kingdom of the Franks was at this time divided into two distinct provinces, of which the line of separation ran from north to south. The eastern part was called Austrasia; the western, Neustria. Pepin, surnamed Heristel, Mayor of the Palace, and Governor of Austrasia, made war against the impotent monarch of Neustria, drove him into Paris, took the city, and thus became master of the whole kingdom. He was generous enough to spare the life of his sovereign. He allowed him the rents of some inconsiderable territories, and continued himself to govern France, with admirable wisdom and moderation, during a period of twenty-seven years. He never affected the title of King, but contented himself with that of Duke of Austrasia, and Mayor of the Palace of Neustria. The only weak and impolitic action of his life was the last, the appointment of his infant grandson Theobald to succeed him in his dignities, while at the same time he left a son Charles, surnamed Martel, in every respect worthy of those honors, and capable of asserting and vindicating with spirit what he might, with justice, esteem his right.

Austrasia declared for Charles, who immediately assumed the title of Duke, to which, as by hereditary right, he added that of Mayor of the Palace. The young Chilperic, the nominal monarch, had a degree of spirit beyond that of his predecessors; and

* The name Clovis, which is the same as Lewis, is variously given by different ancient authors; we find it Chlodovæus, Hludowicus, Chlodvig, Ludvich, &c.—Howel, part. iii., ch. i., sect. 3.

endeavored to emancipate himself from that bondage to which they had patiently submitted. He treated the Mayor of the Palace as a rebel and usurper, and sought by force of arms to reduce him to subjection. A civil war took place, which ended fatally for Chilperic. Charles Martel was victorious, but allowed the monarch to retain, like his ancestors, the royal name and insignia, while he himself possessed the whole power and authority. Charles Martel governed France for about thirty years with great wisdom, spirit, and ability. He was victorious over all his intestine foes; he kept in awe the neighboring nations; he delivered his country from the ravages of the Saracens, whom he entirely defeated between Tours and Poictiers—thus averting the imminent danger of Mahometanism overspreading Western Europe; and he died honored and lamented, bequeathing, in presence of his officers, the kingdom of France, as an undisputed inheritance, to his two sons, Pepin and Carloman.

Charles Martel had now assumed the name of king. His sons at first followed their father's example, and were styled, like him, dukes and mayors of the palace, the one of Austrasia, the other of Neustria and Burgundy; Childeric III., a son of the last nominal prince, being permitted, in the meantime, to hold the insignia of royalty. But Carloman, the younger son of Charles, inspired with a devout apathy for the empty honors of this world, thought proper to retire into a cloister; and Pepin, the elder, now possessed of the entire administration, determined to assume the name, as he possessed the power of king.

The means which Pepin adopted to secure to himself an undivided sovereignty are characteristic of the spirit of the times. He could have deposed his weak and nominal sovereign, and put him to death. His power was equal to any attempt, of which the measures he followed afford perhaps a stronger proof than if he had resorted to force to compass his ends. He sent an embassy to Rome to Zachary the pope, proposing it as a question to his holiness, whether he, or Childeric, had the best title to the throne. Zachary had formed the scheme of erecting a temporal dominion in Italy, and wished, for that purpose, to employ the arms of France to wrest the kingdom from the Lombards. An opportunity now offered of securing the friendship of Pepin, which the designing pontiff, on due consideration of its advantages, scrupled not to embrace. He decided the question by declaring that it was conducive to the honor of God, and the interests of the church, that Pepin, who already exercised the office of king, should possess the title also. Thus have the holy fathers often chosen to veil their schemes of avarice or ambition, confounding their own temporal views with the sacred interests of religion.

The kings of the Franks had hitherto been inaugurated by a ceremony peculiar to the Gothic nation. Seated on a shield, they were carried through the ranks and received the homage of the army. Pepin, aware of the violence he had done to human institutions, was anxious to impress the belief that his right to the crown was of heavenly origin. He adopted from Scripture the ceremony of consecration by holy oil, and was anointed by the hands of Boniface, archbishop of Mentz; * and this ceremony became ever after an established usage in the coronation of Christian princes. The church, for very obvious reasons, annexed to this ceremony a very high degree of importance. The hierarchy thus assumed a supremacy over temporal governments; and hence, in after times, has the Head of the Church arrogated to himself the right of disposing of kingdoms, as an inherent branch of his spiritual sovereignty and jurisdiction.

The first or Merovingian race of kings thus came to an end in the person of Childeric III., who, with an infant son, was conducted to the monastery of St. Bertin, where they passed the remainder of their days. This dynasty of weak and insignificant princes had filled the throne of France for three hundred and thirty-four years.† There reigned at Paris alone twenty-one princes of this race; but including the various divisions into which the kingdom of the Franks was split, we have to reckon about forty princes of the family of Merovius.

In the person of Pepin, son of Charles Martel, commenced the second, or Carlovingian race of the monarchs of France, perpetuating in their name the illustrious foundation of a family which, to this day, gives princes to a great part of Europe. Pepin prepared to discharge his obligations to the see of Rome, of which he was reminded by a most extraordinary *letter from heaven*, written by pope Stephen III., the successor of Zachary, *in the character of St. Peter!* Urged by this invocation, he passed the Alps, and compelled the king of the Lombards to evacuate the greater part of his territories. His conquests put him in possession of a great part of Italy, and enabled him, as is said, to bestow upon the pope the territories of Ravenna, Bologna, and several other states, the first temporal possessions of the see of Rome. This gift, it must be owned, has been called in question, as the zealous advocates for the temporal sovereignty of the popes maintain that their right, in the Italian territory, was of a much more ancient date; while those who dispute that sovereignty assert that they never had any other title than a gradual usurpation of a temporal

* Bonifacius was an Englishman, who, professing no other end than the propagation of Christianity, migrated from his own country into Germany and France, and ingratiated himself so highly with Charles Martel and Pepin, as to regulate all the affairs of the church within their dominions. He founded many bishoprics, and at last fixed his own residence at Mentz, which for many subsequent ages continued the see of the first archbishop of Germany.

† It is a remarkable circumstance in the history of the Merovingian period, and goes far to account for the weakness and misery of the kingdom, that almost all the princes of this race ascended the throne while yet infants.—Mezeray, in his Abrege Chronologique, has attached to the name of each prince, as it occurs, the age at which he began to reign :—vide p. 323, et seq.

interest, from what was originally only a spiritual jurisdiction. What appears most probable is, that Pepin actually made gifts to the see of Rome of some of those territories from which he expelled the Lombards, to be held by the church as a patrimony, but of which he himself meant to retain, or whenever it should suit him, to assume the sovereignty.

Pepin, with all those precautions to color his usurpation of the crown of France, endeavored to establish his security on a more effectual basis, by diligently courting the affection of his subjects. From the beginning of the French monarchy the supreme legislative power was understood to reside in the general assemblies of the people, called the *Champs de Mars*. When the feudal system became prevalent, a great weight of authority was added to the nobles from their beneficia, or fiefs, which, in a short time, inclined the government to a sort of aristocracy. The kings, as we have seen, became absolute ciphers. Pepin, however, when he ascended the throne, changed entirely the face of affairs; yet as it would have been dangerous, with his defective title, to have exasperated the nobles, by encroaching greatly on those powers to which they had been accustomed, he very politically consulted them in all matters of importance. When on his death-bed, he summoned a general council of the grandees, and asked their consent to a division of his kingdom between his sons Charles and Carloman; which was, in fact, an acknowledgment of a right in the nobility of the kingdom to dispose of the crown. Pepin died at the age of fifty-three, having reigned sixteen years from his coronation, and having governed France for twenty-seven years from the death of his father Charles Martel.

The manners of the Franks during this period of their history form an interesting subject of inquiry. It is natural to believe that, at this remote period, slight diversities only would prevail between the manners of neighboring tribes; and the accounts, which Tacitus has given of the habits, customs, and laws of the ancient Germans, may be considered as the best record we possess of the manners of the ancient Franks. Every man was a soldier, because the tribe was constantly in a state of war. The kings, who commanded these tribes, had a very limited authority. In all matters of consequence, the business was deliberated in the assembly; that is to say, in the camp. The government, in short, was democratical.

From the time of the establishment of the Franks in Gaul, we find the most evident traces of the same constitution. The king had no legislative authority, and a very limited judicative power All right of legislation resided in the general assembly of the people, called the Champs de Mars, from being held annually on the first day of March. In these assemblies, the king had no more than a single suffrage, equally with the meanest soldier; and it was only when actually in the field, or when it was necessary to enforce military discipline, that he ventured to exercise any thing like authority. This is strongly exemplified in a story which is recorded of Clovis I. After the battle of Soissons, a large vessel of silver was part of the booty: Clovis, being informed that it had been carried off from the church of Rheims, asked permission of the army to take it, that he might restore it to the church. A soldier, standing by, struck the vessel with his battle-axe, and with great rudeness desired the king to rest satisfied with the share that should fall to his lot. Clovis durst not, at the time, resent this insolence, for all were then upon an equal footing; but he knew the privilege which he had when military discipline was to be enforced, and took advantage of it; for some time afterwards, observing the same soldier to be negligent in the care of his arms, he called him out of his rank, and charging him with his offence, cut him down with his battle-axe.* There was not a murmur heard, for Clovis had not exceeded the limits of his authority.

This story conveys a very distinct idea of the degree of power possessed by the first kings among the Franks. The people knew no subordination but a military one. In every other respect they held themselves to be on a footing of equality and independence.

After the establishment of the Franks in Gaul, things necessarily altered, by degrees, from the new situation in which they were placed. The Gauls, the conquered people, were exposed to all the brutality of their conquerors; they were treated in every respect as slaves: of this the Salic laws, the most ancient code existing among the Franks, furnish a strong proof. The murderer of a Frank paid 200 solidi, while the murderer of a Gaul paid only 100. The Gauls, notwithstanding these degrading distinctions, preserved a part of their possessions, because their conquerors found more than they had occasion for. They even, at first, enjoyed their lands without paying any taxes; but were subjected, in common with the Franks, to the obligation of making war at their own charge, and of furnishing lodging and conveyance to officers travelling on the service of the state.

Clovis allowed the Gauls to retain their own laws; either from policy, or because he could not give them a new code. As these laws were unknown to the Franks, it was of consequence also necessary that the Gauls should choose their own judges.

The Franks, on the other hand, were governed by the Salic and Ripuarian laws, distinctions of the different tribes or nations of Franks before they left Germany. Nothing can convey a stronger picture of the detached and independent character which these tribes still maintained after their settlement in Gaul, and

* "Coup bien hardi," says Mezeray, "et qui le fit extrêmement redouter des François." Tom. i., p. 311.—Gibbon (ch. 38.) alludes to this singular and characteristic story, but does not tell it.

their union under one prince, than their retaining their different codes of laws. It is true that these laws were new modelled, in many respects, by Clovis, and by succeeding sovereigns; for, being framed while these German nations were heathens and idolaters, it was necessary to adapt them to the spirit of Christianity.

This diversity of laws among the Gauls and the different tribes of Franks was attended with much inconvenience; and numberless disadvantages, arising from this source, were felt in the civil policy of France down to the revolutionary period at the close of the eighteenth century. The manners of the Gauls, which, under the Roman governors, had attained a high degree of polish, were entirely opposite to the rude barbarity of their conquerors. To form a code of laws which would have united both nations was an absolute impossibility: there arose, therefore, as necessary a distinction of laws as of manners; and even when time had nearly annihilated the latter distinction, it was not to be expected that the laws should approach to any common standard, for those derived, on the other hand, additional force from the operation of the same cause, and the revolution of time only riveted their observance.

The ancient Germans had the highest veneration for their priests. It was, therefore, natural for the Franks, after their conversion, to preserve the same reverence for the ministers of their new religion. We find that the bishops held the first place in the national assemblies. They were employed under Clotarius I. to correct the Salic and Ripuarian laws, and they had a sort of superintendence over the judicial tribunals. In the absence of the king, it was competent to appeal to the bishops from the sentences of the dukes and counts.

The Franks, owing their conversion to Christianity to their recent connection with the Gauls, very naturally chose their first bishops from that nation. This was an important advantage to the conquered people, for it was most natural that those bishops should employ the influence they obtained from their ecclesiastical functions, as well as the respect which they attracted from their superiority in literature and acquirements, to better the condition of their own countrymen, and to raise them from that state of servility and abasement to which the Franks were at first disposed to confine them. Such was, in fact, the case; for, in a very few generations, the condition of the Gauls was so much changed, that, provided they chose to live under the Salic and Ripuarian laws instead of the Roman, they became entitled to all the privileges of the Franks. They had their seat in the Champ de Mars, and their vote in all public deliberations. They seemed even to be regarded with more peculiar favor by the sovereigns, several of whom, from political motives, chose to attach the leading men among the Gauls to their service, by bestowing on them considerable offices of dignity in the state.

The Franks thus incorporated with the Gauls, a new system of policy was visible in this united monarchy, which by degrees pervaded most of the European kingdoms. The rise of this singular fabric, the feudal system, has given occasion to much curious speculation; and as opinions extremely various and contradictory have been expressed by eminent writers, the subject merits a full investigation.

By the feudal system is properly meant that tenure or condition on which the proprietors of land in most of the countries of Europe for so many ages held their possession; viz., an obligation to perform military service whenever required by the sovereign or the overlord, who originally gave them a grant of that possession.

In the infancy of the Roman state, among other institutions which historians have been fond of attributing to the political sagacity of Romulus, was the connection between patron and client. Occasions have frequently occurred of remarking the error of referring to a particular author, whether politician or lawgiver, such institutions as are the natural result of the state of society in which we find them. Of this the *Clientela* and *Jus patronatus* of the Romans is an example. It is evident that this connection of patron and client is nothing more than a species of the same clanship which subsists in all barbarous nations, where war is the chief occupation; and which naturally continues to subsist, even when the state has acquired that degree of political stability in which war becomes a frequent accident instead of a constant employment. This *Clientela* was strongly in observance among the ancient Gauls, and no less so among their conquerors the Franks, as well as among all the other Germanic nations.

Among the ancient Gauls, all military power being lodged in their chiefs or kings, as their civil, juridical, and ecclesiastica power was monopolized by the Druids, it was customary for the people to devote themselves with the most absolute submission to their chiefs, who formed a barrier for them against the tyranny of the Druids, which was severely felt and complained of. This attachment to the chief they ratified by an oath of allegiance, which bound them to participate his fortune in every thing. Thus Cæsar tells us, that there were few of those men who would not rush on to death when their leader had fallen, and count it the highest dishonor to survive him.

In Gaul, this *Clientela* subsisted not only between the different ranks of persons, but even between cities and provinces, with their inferior districts and villages. These last owed to the canton, province, or city the obligation of taking up arms whenever necessity required, in return for the defence and protection afforded them.

In all the feudal governments it was customary for the sovereign, whenever occasion required, to summon his vassals, by public proclamation, to repair to the standard of their lord. In the same manner, we find in ancient Gaul, as described by Cæsar, that, on urgent occasions, a general summons was issued by the chief for all to attend who were capable of bearing arms; and to enforce the more prompt obedience, it was customary to put to death the man who came last to the assembly.

It is evident that, in this ancient policy of the Gauls, there was a great affinity with the clanship or vassalage in the fiefs or *feus*. Yet it is to be observed, that in this species of clientela we have mentioned as in use both among the Romans and Gauls, we see nothing as yet of an assignment or gift of land, which afterwards in the *feus* became the subject of the contract; and in consideration of which all the services of vassalage were performed. The origin of these, therefore, yet remains to be investigated.

When Rome became subject to the emperors, they established garrisons upon the frontiers, both for keeping the provinces in subjection, and preventing inroads from neighboring unconquered nations. Thus there were several legions stationed along the Rhine, which was then the boundary between the Gauls and Germany. To conciliate the affections of the soldiery was a very material object with the first emperors; and for this purpose no policy seemed more proper than to assign to them gifts of portions of land in the provinces where they were stationed. This, we find, was the case even in Italy, as we may learn from the first and ninth eclogues of Virgil.

Of these distributions of land we find frequent mention among the ancient Roman lawyers. They became more frequent among the latter emperors, who found it necessary to court the favor and support of the army, now become the disposers of the imperial diadem. These distributions of land were at first only for life. The first who allowed them to descend to the heirs of the grantees was Alexander Severus, who, as Lampridius informs us, permitted the heirs of the grantees to enjoy their possessions, on the express condition of their following the profession of arms. Constantine the Great in like manner made gifts of land to his principal officers, perpetual and hereditary.

In the decline of the empire there were two classes of soldiers principally distinguished, of whom mention is frequently made by Ammianus Marcellinus and Procopius. These were the Gentiles and Scutarii. They were esteemed the flower of the imperial armies, and on them it is probable that the largest beneficia, or gifts of land, would be bestowed; and consequently that these were the *beneficiarii* so frequently mentioned in the Roman authors.

Such, then, we find to have been the state of Gaul at the time of the invasion of the Franks. These conquerors, possessing themselves of a province, which they found in a great measure parcelled out into *benifices* or gifts to the soldiery who had been its former conquerors, and adopting the very judicious policy of allowing the privileges of Franks to all who chose to live under the Salic and Ripuarian laws, made very little change in the property or possessions of those who chose to conform to that condition. It was only changing the superior or overlord, and exacting from the beneficiaries the same oath of allegiance and military service to their new conquerors which they had sworn to their former superiors, the emperors or governors. The Gentiles and Scutarii now became *gentilshommes* and *ecuyers;* the names by which we know the ancient beneficiaries to have been distinguished in the French monarchy.

This hypothesis appears to afford a solution to all those difficulties which attend the history generally given of the origin of the feudal system. When we examine the accounts given by Pasquier, Mably, Condillac, and Robertson, we find the main difficulty to lie in this circumstance. The beneficia or feus are said, by these authors, to have been granted by the king or chief out of the conquered lands, to his chief captains or officers, as a reward of their services, and a tie to secure their aid and assistance when necessary in military expeditions. Yet it is at the same time allowed, and history will not permit the fact to be controverted, that these chiefs or kings had no land to bestow; for nothing is more certain than that, whatever conquest was made, whatever booty was gained, or lands acquired, the share of the chief was assigned to him by lot as well as that of the private men. Of this the anecdote of Clovis at the battle of Soissons furnishes a sufficient proof. The Abbé Mably, indeed, although he takes notice of this fact, and says at the same time that the first kings among the Franks had nothing to distinguish them from their subjects, unless the privilege of commanding the army, yet, when he comes to account for the origin of the *beneficia*, is forced to give them a portion of land, which he calls their *domaine*, and out of which, he says, they made gifts to such of the grandees as they wanted to secure to their interest. What this *domaine* was, however, he does not attempt to inform us. In fact, we have the best authority to say, that the lands which, during the Merovingian race, belonged to the king in patrimony, were a mere trifle, and could by no means be the subject of those gifts or benefices. Eginhart, in his Life of Charlemagne, speaking of the successors of Clovis, at the time when the mayors of the palace had begun to assume an ascendant, has these remarkable words:—"Regi, nihil aliud relinquebatur, quam ut, regio tantum nomine contentus, crine profuso, barbâ submissâ, solio resideret, ac speciem dominantis effingeret: cum præter inutile regis nomen, et precarium vitæ stipendium, quod ei præfectus aulæ, prout videbatur, exhibebat, nihil aliud proprii possideret quam unam, et eam perparvi redditus, villam, in qua domum, et ex quâ famulos sibi necessaria ministrantes, atque obsequium exhibentes paucæ numerositatis habebat."*

This passage gives a very complete idea of what was the extent of the king's domain: at least, at the time when the mayors of the palace came to have authority, and we have no ground from history to presume that, before that period, it had ever been much more extensive. It seems, therefore, in every respect, a reasonable hypothesis, that the *beneficia*, which could not have been created by the kings of the Franks out of their own property, were, in fact, not created by them at all, but subsisted in Gaul at the time of the invasion of the Franks. These conquerors, no doubt, dispossessed many of the Gauls of their lands, but they did not dispossess all. The Salic and Ripuarian laws establish many regulations with regard to the Romans and Gauls who possessed lands, subjecting them to the same burdens as the Franks, of furnishing horses, provisions, and carriages in time of war. The Roman taxes and census being entirely abolished on the coming in of the Franks, the great ease which the Gauls found in being delivered from those burdens, to which their new services were comparatively light, very soon reconciled them to their new masters, and made them the most faithful of their subjects.

The authors who, according to the common supposition, hold these *beneficia* to have been granted by the kings of France out of their domain, involve themselves in another difficulty, for which they give but a very lame solution. The king, as may be supposed, being very soon divested of all his property, by the creation of a very few *beneficia*, it remains still to be accounted for, how these feudal tenures came to be universally prevalent, so that the whole property of the kingdom was held in that way: for the fees created out of the domain could be divided only among a small number of the grandees; and the rest of the kingdom would be held as absolute and unlimited property. To account, therefore, for these tenures becoming universal, a very unnatural hypothesis is resorted to. Such of the subjects as held their lands in free property are supposed to have become sensible that it would be more for their advantage to hold them as *beneficia*, and to have surrendered them into the hands of the king, becoming bound to serve him in war, as the condition on which he was to restore them their property. The motive for this extraordinary

---

* "The king had no other marks of royalty than long hair and a long beard. He sat on his throne and mimicked the airs of a sovereign, but in reality he had nothing else but the name. His revenue, except a small country-seat and a few servants, was no more than the precarious bounty that was allowed him by the mayor of the palace."—Eginhart, Vit. Car. Magni.

"The domain of the Frank monarchs became afterwards more extensive, and their residences in different provinces of the kingdom more numerous; but we cannot attach any great ideas of magnificence to these establishments, when we find Charlemagne regulating the number of hens and geese which each is to maintain."—Gibbon, cap. 59, note 88.

proceeding is said to have been, that they found it necessary to have a powerful protection in the king or chief. But what protection could this king or chief afford them, who was a man, perhaps, poorer than themselves ; and who, according to this notion, had no other certain dependence for assistance from his grandees, than from the few to whom he had granted benefices out of his domains? Had not these unlimited proprietors a much more powerful incitement to preserve their independence, which made each a sovereign within his own territory ; and were they not better protected by that general equality which subsisted among them, as well as by that natural jealousy, which, being felt alike by *all*, would incite them to combine in preventing any *one* from attempting unjust encroachments?

When we further take into view, that these *beneficia* were, originally, only grants for life, and held to be revocable, at all times, at the will of the grantor, the supposition of any free and unlimited proprietor surrendering his possessions, to be held by such a tenure, is wholly incredible. The exchange would have been that of liberty for dependence; absolute property for precarious possession.

This power of disposing of the fortunes of their subjects, by the revocation of their benefices, could not long continue under such weak princes as those of the Merovingian race. The more powerful of the *beneficiarii* soon determined to render their situation more secure. A measure of this kind could not, it may be presumed, have been attempted, if all the *beneficiarii* had been, as at first, Romans and Gauls ; but at this time, by the changes made by the sovereigns, a great part of the benefices must have come into the hands of Franks. These, taking advantage of the weakness of the monarchy, and of the disorders which occupied the kingdom, during the contests between Gontran and Childebert, determined to seize that opportunity of establishing themselves in their possessions. In a council held to treat of a peace between these princes, the *beneficiarii* obliged them to consent in a treaty, that the king should no longer be at liberty to revoke benefices once conferred. This innovation, however agreeable to the greater part of the beneficiaries, was a check to the ambition of such men as either had no land, or thought they had too little ; and these discontents afforded a pretext to succeeding princes for resuming their power of revocation. The treaty in question, however, was soon after solemnly confirmed in an assembly held at Paris.

Such was the state of the lands in France about the middle of the Merovingian period ; part possessed in *beneficia*, or fiefs, which were now become hereditary, and part occupied by allodial, or absolute proprietors, the descendants of those Franks who received shares of land at the conquest. In that state of fluctuation, in which property of the former description remained, till it became irrevocable in the manner mentioned, it is easy to perceive that allodial property was a much more valuable possession. Many of the allodial proprietors, during the perpetual civil wars of the Merovingian princes, found means greatly to increase the opulence and the extent of their territories. In those disorders, the castles and places of strength, where the more powerful lords resided, were naturally resorted to by the inhabitants of the territory. They were continually filled with retainers and dependents, who sought the protection of the lord or seigneur; which being of consequence in securing their possessions from invasion, they courted by making him annual presents, either of money or of the fruits of their lands. This connection became, in a very short time, that of vassal and superior; a tacit contract, by which the vassal was understood to hold his lands, upon the condition of paying homage to the superior, and military service when required—the symbol of which vassalage was a small annual present.

It was equally natural for the superior or seigneur to acquire a civil and criminal jurisdiction over his vassals. In those disorderly times, the dukes and counts, who were the judges in the provinces and districts, occupied with their own schemes of ambition, paid very little attention to the duties of their office. Many of them made a scandalous traffic of justice, oppressing the poor, and regulating their sentences according to the price paid for them. In this situation, the inferior ranks of the people naturally chose, instead of seeking justice through this corrupt channel, to submit their differences to the arbitration of their seigneurs, to whom they had sworn allegiance. By degrees, the vassals came to acknowledge no other judge than their superior; and, in the territory of these seigneurs, the public magistrates soon ceased to have any kind of jurisdiction.

The seigneurs were now the sole judges, as well as the commanders or military leaders, of all who resided within their territories. Even bishops and abbots who possessed seigneuries exercised these powers, and led their men out to war. The whole kingdom was now divided between these seigneurs and the *beneficiarii*—that is to say, all lands were held in feu either of the prince or of subject superiors.

CHAPTER III.

Charlemagne—The new Empire of the West—Manners, Government, and Customs of the Age—Retrospective View of the Affairs of the Church—Arian and Pelagian Heresies—Origin of Monastic Orders—Pillar-Saints—Auricular Confession.

THE Merovingian race of the kings of France having come to an end by the usurpation of Pepin, and the deposition of Childeric III., a new series of princes, the descendants of the illustrious Charles Martel, filled the throne of France for a period of 253 years.

The injudicious policy of Pepin in dividing between two ambitious princes, his sons, a kingdom already filled with intestine disorder, must soon have involved France in all the miseries of civil war, had not the fortunate death of Carloman averted this calamity. Charles was now acknowledged monarch of all France; and in the course of a glorious reign of forty-five years, this prince, who, in more respects than as a conqueror, deserved the surname of Great, extended the limits of his empire beyond the Danube, subdued Dacia, Dalmatia, and Istria; conquered, and rendered tributary to his crown, all the barbarous nations as far as the Vistula or Weser; made himself master of the greatest part of Italy, and alarmed the fears of the empire of the Saracens. The longest of his wars was that with the Saxons. It was thirty years before he reduced to subjection this ferocious and warlike people.

The motive of this obstinate war, on the part of Charlemagne, against a people who possessed nothing alluring to the avarice of a conqueror, was ambition alone; unless we shall suppose that the ardor for making proselytes had its weight with a prince, whose zeal for the propagation of Christianity was a remarkable feature in his character,—a zeal, however, which carried him far beyond the bounds which humanity ought to have assigned to it. Charlemagne left the Saxons but the alternative of being baptized or drowned in the Weser. Impartial history records with regret, that this conquest of the Saxons was stained with many instances of sanguinary ferocity on the part of the victor.

But the talents of Charlemagne were yet more distinguished in the civil and political regulation of his empire than in his extensive conquests. It was the misfortune of France, at this period, to be equally oppressed by the nobility and the clergy,—two powers equally jealous of each other, and equally ambitious of uncontrolled authority. Pepin, who was an able politician, had endeavored to mitigate the disorders arising from this source, by the system of parliaments or annual assemblies in the month of May, * to which the bishops and abbots, together with the chief of the nobility, were summoned by the sovereign to deliberate on the situation of the state, the necessities of government, and the wants of the people. Charlemagne ordered these assemblies to be held twice in the year, in spring and in autumn. It was the business of the assemblies, in autumn, to deliberate only and examine. The interests of the kingdom relative to foreign princes, the causes of grievances and the sources of abuse, were investigated; and prepared for the consideration of the assembly in spring, the Champs de Mai, which had the sole power of enacting laws. This last assembly was not composed alone of the clergy and grandees. Charlemagne gave the people, likewise, a share in the system of legislation, by admitting from each county twelve deputies or representatives. These, with the nobility and clergy, formed three separate chambers, who each discussed, apart, the affairs which concerned their own order, and afterwards united to communicate their resolutions, or to deliberate on their common interests. The sovereign was never present, unless when called upon to ratify and confirm the decrees of the assembly, or to serve as a mediator, when the different branches could not come to an agreement.

Still further to harmonize the discordant parts of his empire, Charlemagne divided the provinces into different districts, each of which contained several counties. He abolished the ancient custom of governing them by dukes; and in their place he appointed three or four royal envoys, called *Missi Dominici*, to govern each province or *Missaticum*, obliging them to an exact visitation of it every three months. These envoys held four courts in the year for the administration of justice; and the arrangement in which the business of these courts was conducted reflects the highest honor on the character of Charlemagne. The causes of the poor were first heard, next those of the king, then the causes of the clergy, and lastly those of the people at large. Yearly conventions were also held by the royal envoys, where all the bishops and abbots, the barons and the deputies of the counts were obliged to attend personally, or by their representatives. At these conventions, the particular affairs of the province were treated of; the conduct of the counts and other magistrates examined, and the wants of individuals considered and redressed. At the general assembly or parliament, these envoys made their

* The president Henault assigns as the reason for changing the time of meeting from March to May, that cavalry being introduced into the army under Pepin the former season of assembling was too early to allow them to obtain subsistence for their horses.

report to the king, and to the states, of the situation of their district, and thus the public attention was constantly and equally directed to all the parts of the empire. All the ranks of magistrates were kept in their duty by this public and frequent scrutiny into their conduct; and the people, secured from oppression, began to taste the sweets of genuine liberty, in the subjection to equal, wise, and salutary laws.

This propitious change, reflecting the highest honor on the talents and virtues of Charlemagne, was but a temporary blessing to his subjects. His successors had not, like him, the wisdom to perceive that moderation in authority is the surest foundation of the power of a sovereign.

The most important transactions in the reign of Charlemagne are those which regard Italy. The extirpation of the Lombards, whose dominion had been greatly abridged by his father Pepin, was proposed to Charlemagne by Pope Adrian I. The French monarch had formed an alliance with Didier, the last king of the Lombards, and had married his daughter; but the contending interests of the two sovereigns soon interrupted the amity between them. The queen was sent back to her father's court; and Charlemagne, in obedience to the summons of the Pope, prepared for the conquest of Italy. He passed the Alps, subdued all Lombardy, forced Didier to surrender himself at discretion, and thus put a final period to the government of the Lombards, which had subsisted above two hundred years.

Charlemagne made his entry into Rome at the festival of Easter, amid the acclamations of the people. He was saluted king of France and of the Lombards; and at this time he is said to have confirmed the donation made to the popes by his father Pepin.

The empire of the East was at this time ruled by the empress Irene. On the death of Constantine surnamed Copronymus, his son Leo Chazares succeeded to the throne. In the first years of his reign he procured his son Constantine, an infant, to be associated with him in the empire; and dying left this prince, then nine years old, to the government of his mother Irene, who ruled the empire rather as a sovereign than as a regent. She was an able woman, and foresaw the danger to the empire from the ambition and power of Charlemagne. To avert any hostile purposes, till she should be in a condition to oppose them with effect, she brought about a negotiation for the marriage of her son with the daughter of Charlemagne; but it was far from her intention that this match should ever be accomplished. Irene, on the contrary, was too fond of power herself to consent to any thing that might deprive her of the reins of government. She kept the young Constantine in the most absolute dependence and submission; and when at last he endeavored to assume that dignity which belonged to him, she, on pretence of treasonable designs, threw him into prison, deprived him of his eyes, and put him to death. She afterwards, with the same insincerity as before, proposed an alliance with Charlemagne herself, and offered him her hand in marriage; but while the negotiation was in progress, a revolution took place in the empire, and the ambitious empress was driven from her throne, and died an exile in the island of Lesbos.

Charlemagne found himself obliged frequently to visit Italy, both to establish his own power in that country, which was endangered by the partisans of the descendants of the Lombard kings, and to defend the authority of the popedom, which was now firmly devoted to his interests. In the last of his expeditions to that country he underwent the ceremony of inaugural consecration by the hands of Leo III., and in the church of St. Peter was solemnly crowned emperor of the Romans,—a title which, three hundred years before, had expired in the person of Augustulus. It is not improbable, that, had Charlemagne chosen Rome for his residence, that great, but fallen empire might have once more revived, perhaps recovered its ancient lustre; if at the same time he had himself abolished, and his successors discontinued, that mischievous policy of the early French monarchs, of dividing their dominions among their children. But Charlemagne had no capital of his empire; his chief residence, indeed, was at Aix-la-Chapelle; but his constant and distant wars allowed him no permanent seat of empire; and he, like his predecessors, divided, even in his lifetime, his dominions among his children.

This great prince was no less respectable in his private than in his public character. He was a man of the most amiable dispositions, and there never was a sovereign to whom his subjects were more attached from considerations of personal regard. His secretary and historian, Eginhart, gives a beautiful picture of his domestic life, and the economy of his family, which is characteristic of an age of great simplicity. He never rode abroad without being attended by his sons and daughters; the former he instructed in all manly exercises, in which he himself was particularly skilled; and his daughters, according to the simple manners of the times, were assiduously employed in the various labors of housewifery, particularly in spinning wool with the distaff. For his children he indulged in all the affection of the fondest parent, and he bore the premature loss of some of them with less magnanimity than might have been expected from so heroic a mind.*

* There are some minds of so malignant a temperament as to derive the highest gratification from the discovering, or, failing discovery, from the invention of materials to degrade any character of acknowledged excellence. To Voltaire and Gibbon we willingly consign the merit of those detestable calumnies with which they have endeavored to reduce the character of Charlemagne to the standard of their own creed. An infamous perversion of the meaning of a single passage in Eginhart's "Life of Charlemagne" has, by these authors, been made the groundwork of a charge of the deepest criminality; and the worthy secretary is thus made to calumniate his master, for whom, in every line, he expresses

Charlemagne died in the year 814, in the seventy-second year of his age. Contemporary with him was the illustrious Caliph of the Saracens, Haroun Alraschid, whose conquests, excellent policy, wisdom, and humanity, entitle him to be ranked among the greatest of princes. He expressed a peculiar admiration for the virtues and character of Charlemagne, and cultivated his friendship by embassies and presents.

Of all the lawful children of Charlemagne, Lewis, surnamed the Débonnaire, was the only one who survived him. He succeeded without dispute to the dominions of Charlemagne, with the exception of Italy, which that monarch had settled upon his grandson Bernard, the son of Pepin.

Of the manners, customs, and government of the age of Charlemagne many particulars have been touched upon with much nicety and penetration by Voltaire in his *Essai sur les Mœurs et l' Esprit des Nations.* Other particulars, however, appear to demand rather a more minute consideration than that lively and ingenious writer has thought proper to bestow on them.

We have seen in what manner Charlemagne new modelled the government of the provinces by the excellent system which he introduced into the provincial conventions under the royal envoys.

It does not, however, appear that the ancient chief magistrates, the dukes and counts, lost entirely their authority. They continued to have the military command of the troops of the canton, and the charge of procuring levies from each, according to its strength and the measure of its population. Cavalry came now into general use, but their numbers must have been very inconsiderable, for twelve farms were taxed to furnish only one horseman. The province furnished six months' provisions to its complement of soldiers, and the king provided for them during the remainder of the campaign.

The engines used in the attack and defence of towns were the same that were in use among the Romans, for the Franks had no other masters in fortification than they. The battering ram, the ballista, the catapulta, and testudo, were accordingly employed in all their sieges.

Charlemagne was very attentive to the increase and management of his navy. To protect his trade and secure his provinces from invasion, he stationed ships of war in the mouths of all the large rivers, from the Mediterranean to the Baltic. The nobility of his kingdom were obliged to personal service in his fleets as

---

the utmost esteem and veneration. Sensible of the inconsistency of charging Charlemagne with criminality with his own daughters, (which Eginhart is supposed to have done,) and the fact of the secretary having married one of these princesses, Gibbon disposes of this difficulty by arguing, that the suspicion under which these fair damsels labored, " without excepting his own wife," disproved the fact of the marriage! How much more natural the conclusion, that the fact of the marriage disproved the suspicion!—See Gibbon, ch. xlix., note 97.

well as in his armies. He made Boulogne one of the chief stations for his navy, and restored the ancient pharos of that town, which had been destroyed by time. He bestowed the utmost attention on the encouragement of commerce. The merchants of Tuscany and Marseilles traded to Constantinople and Alexandria, and interchanged the commodities of Europe and Asia. He projected, and partly carried into execution, the splendid design of uniting the Rhine and the Danube by a canal, and thus forming a communication between the Western Ocean and the Black Sea. Venice, which, at the time of Attila's depredations in the north of Italy, had arisen from a few inconsiderable huts, where the inhabitants of the country had sheltered themselves from their invaders the Huns, was now a considerable commercial state. Genoa was likewise enterprising and industrious; and the cities of Rome, Ravenna, Milan, Arles, Lyons, and Tours, became noted for the manufacture of woollen stuffs, glass, and iron work; but silk was not yet wove in any city in the Western empire, nor for 400 years afterwards. A taste for the more luxurious articles of Eastern magnificence was repressed by Charlemagne, by sumptuary laws, and still more powerfully restrained by the extreme simplicity of his own manners and dress.* The value of money at this time was nearly the same as in the Roman empire at the time of Constantine. The golden *sous* of the Franks was the *solidus Romanus*, which was worth about twelve shillings and sixpence sterling; the silver *denarius*, worth about fifteen pence. Besides these, which were actual coins, there were other fictitious or numerary denominations of money. The numerary *liber* (livre) of the age of Charlemagne was supposed to be a pound or twelve ounces of silver, which was divided into twenty parts, each of which was a *solidum* or *sous* of silver. The variation of the money of France under the same denominations has from that time to the present been prodigious. The livre, instead of a pound of silver, which is worth about three pounds sterling, is now nearly of the value of tenpence.

The *Capitularia*, or laws of Charlemagne, were compiled and reduced into one volume as early as the year 827. They remained afterwards for many centuries in oblivion; but were at last rescued from obscurity in 1531 and 1545, by the care of some learned men of Germany, and since that time there have been several very elegant editions of them published in France. These capitularies present a variety of incidental circumstances, from which we learn the manners and customs of the times. Unless in the great cities, there were not, in any of the European kingdoms, inns for the accommodation of travellers; they repaired, according to the

* "He wore in winter," says Eginhart, "a plain doublet, made of an otter's skin, woollen tunic, fringed with silk, and a blue coat; his hose consisted of transverse bands of different colors."—Eginhart, Vit Car. Mag.

custom of the times, to any house they chose, and it was reckoned the highest breach of civil and religious duty to deny accommodation to any traveller.*

The state of the arts and sciences under Charlemagne was very low. The towns were small, thinly scattered, built of wood, and perhaps even the walls were of that material. The mechanic arts were much more cultivated in Arabia at this time, than in the Western empire. The caliph Alraschid sent a present to Charlemagne of a clock which struck the hours by a bell, the first that had been seen in Europe, and which at that time was admired as a miracle of art.†

Where the state of the useful arts was so low, it is not to be supposed that the fine arts could have been successfully cultivated. Indeed in those unfavorable periods, had not a spark been kept alive by the existing monuments of ancient taste and genius, the arts of painting and sculpture must have been totally extinguished.‡ As to music, we have authorities for knowing that it was frequently practised in those ages, but probably with no higher claim to excellence than their painting or sculpture. The monk of Ingelheim, in his Life of Charlemagne, informs us, that while the emperor was at Rome, there was a contest of skill between the French and Roman musicians, and that the latter instructed the former in the art of playing on the organ.

Architecture, though totally changed in its style, from what is properly termed the Grecian, attained, nevertheless, a much higher degree of eminence in those barbarous times, than any other of the fine or useful arts. That style of architecture termed the Gothic, though, by some fastidious critics, most absurdly treated with contempt, has its positive merit and excellence, as well as the Grecian; its character as strongly marked, and its proportions as certainly defined. There is a melancholy majesty, a powerful ingredient of the sublime, which it is the exclusive privilege of this species of architecture to produce.

In those times, the knowledge of letters was confined to a few of the ecclesiastics. Charlemagne himself, however, was by no means illiterate. He spoke Latin with great fluency. Eginhart informs us, that he was curious in the knowledge of the motions of the stars; and that he even tried to write, but this, says the secretary, was a preposterous labor, and too late begun. But the

---

* "Præcipimus ut in omni regno nostro, neque dives neque pauper peregrinis hospitia denegare audeant: id est sive peregrinis propter Deum ambulantibus per terram, sive cuilibet itineranti. Propter amorem Dei, et propter salutem animæ suæ, tectum et focum et aquam nemo illi deneget."—Capit. Car. Mag. a Baluzio.

† Alraschid sent also a natural wonder which would excite no less the curiosity and admiration of a barbarous age,—a large elephant.—Mezeray, tom. i., p. 474.

‡ "Nulla tempora fuere," says Muratori, "quibus pictores desiderati fuerunt Sed qui, qualesve pictores, bone Deus!"—Muratori, Dissertationes, Diss. 24.

encouragement which Charlemagne gave to literature, and the honors he bestowed on those who successfully cultivated letters, marked a genius beyond the age in which he lived. He was at great pains in inviting learned men from all quarters to reside in his dominions of France. Italy, where letters were not yet totally extinguished, furnished some men of abilities whom he employed in teaching the sciences to the Franks. His care extended to that country as well as to France, for the monk of St. Gall informs us, that two Irish priests (Scoti de Hibernia), having come to France, men eminent for literature, Charlemagne received them with the greatest kindness, and kept one of them in France, while he sent the other to teach the sciences in Italy.* Nothing is more certain, than that the Britannic Isles in those ages of darkness preserved more of the light of learning than the rest of the European kingdoms. *Alcuinus*, whom Charlemagne employed as his preceptor, and honored with several important embassies—and *Dungallus*, who was likewise in high estimation with that prince for his learning—were both from Britain. Among those most eminent for their abilities in the age of Charlemagne, was likewise our countryman the Venerable Bede, who in a variety of works, ecclesiastical, historical, and poetical, showed an extent of learning singular, indeed, for the age in which he lived.†

But, after all, the low state of literature may be figured from the extreme scarcity of books, the subjects on which they were written, and the very high estimation which was put upon them by those who possessed them. The gift of a trifling manuscript to a monastery, of the Life of a Saint, was sufficient to entitle the donor to the perpetual prayers of the brotherhood, and a mass to

* On the authority of the monk of St. Gall, the following anecdote is related of Charlemagne, which marks the strong interest which he took in disseminating among his subjects the advantages of education, and the attention which he personally bestowed on those seminaries of learning which he founded. In an examination of one of these institutions in which were a number of boys, sons of the nobility, as well as of the lowest class of the people, it happened that the latter acquitted themselves very much to the satisfaction of the monarch, while the young noblemen, on the other hand, made a very inferior appearance. Charlemagne, observing this, placed the poor boys on his right hand, and thanked them for their obedience to his orders, and their attention to their studies: "Continue to improve yourselves, my children," said he, "and you shall be well rewarded with bishoprics and abbeys. I will raise you to honor and consequence. But for you," said he, turning to his left, and frowning on the nobles, "you delicate, handsome creatures, you are of high birth and rich, you did not think it necessary to regard my orders, or your own future reputation; you have despised knowledge and given yourselves up to play and laziness, wasting your time in useless amusements; but know," said he, with a tremendous look, as he raised that arm that had won so many victories, "that neither your birth nor beauty shall be of any avail with me, whatever they may with others; for from Charles you have nothing to expect, unless you speedily recover your lost time, and make up for your former idleness by diligence in future."—Pulter's Historical Developement of the Political State of the German Empire, book i. c. 6.

† "Neque enim silenda laus Britanniæ, Scotiæ et Hiberniæ, quæ, studio liberalium artium, eo tempore antecellebant reliquis occidentalibus regris; et cura monachorum, qui literarum gloriam alibi aut languentem aut depressam in iis regionibus impigre suscitarunt et tuebantur."—Muratori, Diss. 43.

be celebrated for ever for the salvation of his sou.. A complete copy of the sacred Scriptures given to a city or state was esteemed a princely donation. The reputation of learning was then acquired at a very easy rate. Extracts from the different works of the Fathers literally transcribed, and often patched together without order or connection, composed the valuable works of those luminaries and instructers of the age: nothing was more common than those commentaries called *Catenæ*, which were illustrations of some of the books of Scripture, by borrowing sentences successively from half-a-dozen of the Fathers, making each to illustrate a verse in his turn.

In treating of the manners, jurisprudence, and policy of the Goths, some account has already been given of those systems of laws which, by the barbarian tribes, were not injudiciously preferred to the jurisprudence of the more polished nations whom they subdued. Some particulars which distinguished the laws of the northern nations, and especially of the Franks, deserve to be more attentively considered. These are the peculiar fines for homicide, the judgments of God, and the judicial combat.

Among all barbarous nations, the right of private revenge is allowed; which is not only expedient in such a state of society, but absolutely necessary, where there is neither sufficient amplitude in the penal laws to apply to the variety of criminal acts, nor coercive force in any branch of the state to carry such laws into execution. Among the ancient Germans, revenge was always honorable—often meritorious. The independent warrior chastised or vindicated with his own hand the injuries he had received or given; and he had nothing more to dread than the resentment of the sons or kinsmen of the enemy he sacrificed. The magistrate, conscious of his weakness, interposed, not to punish, but to reconcile; and he was satisfied if he could persuade the aggressor to pay, and the injured party to accept the moderate fine imposed as the price of blood.

When a government has attained to such stability as to allow the improvement of jurisprudence, the quality of persons enters but in very few instances into the consideration of the measure of crimes. The life of the meanest citizen as well as of the highest is under the equal protection of the law. But barbarians cannot reason as wise politicians; and in a state where men are, in a great measure, their own judges and avengers, the most unjust distinctions cannot fail to take place. It was no wonder that the life of a Roman should have been appreciated at a trifle by their barbarian conquerors, who established such distinctions among the ranks of their own citizens, that while some illustrious murders would cost the perpetrator six hundred pieces of gold, others might be expiated for a fine of fifty pieces.

The Visigoths and the Burgundians were the first among the Gothic nations who showed a spirit of equity and impartiality, as well as judicious policy, in deviating from those barbarous distinctions in the laws of their northern brethren. We have noticed the equal severity of the law of the Visigoths, both in the crime of murder and robbery; and the Burgundian code was, in that respect, alike remarkable. So likewise, as the manners of the Franks grew more civilized, their laws became proportionally equitable; and under the reign of Charlemagne, murder was universally punished with death.

The ignorance of the judges, as well as the weakness of their authority in those rude ages, laid a natural foundation for another singularity in their legal forms, which was, the judgment of God. A party accused of a crime was allowed to produce a certain number of witnesses, more or fewer according to the measure of the offence; and if these declared upon oath their belief in the innocence of the accused, it was accounted a sufficient justification. Seventy-two compurgators were required to absolve an incendiary or murderer;* and Gregory of Tours relates, that when the chastity of a queen of France was suspected, three hundred nobles swore, without hesitation, that the infant prince had been actually begotten by her deceased husband.

It is not improbable that the notorious perjuries occasioned by this absurd practice gave rise to another equally preposterous, and much more dangerous to the unhappy criminal. It was in the option of the judge to condemn the party accused to undergo the trial of cold water, of boiling water, or of red-hot iron. They began with the performance of the mass, and the accused person solemnly took the sacrament. If the trial was by cold water, the priest gave his benediction to the water, and performed exorcism, to expel evil spirits. The culprit, tied hand and foot, was then thrown into a pool of water; where, if he sank to the bottom, and probably was drowned, it was a proof of his innocence: but if he swam above, he was accounted certainly guilty, and condemned to death accordingly. The trial by hot water was performed by making the accused person plunge his naked arm into a vessel of boiling water, and fetch from the bottom a consecrated ring. The arm was immediately put into a bag, and sealed up by the judge, to be opened after three days; when, if there were no marks of burning, the culprit was declared innocent.† It is well known that there are compositions which powerfully resist the immediate effects of fire; and which, in all probability, were not unknown in those days when there was so much occasion for them.

---

* "Si quis ingenuus ingenuum castraverit, vel hominem Ripuarium interfecerit, ducentis solidis culpabilis judicetur; aut si negaverit cum duodecim juret.—Si quis eum interfecerit qui in truste regia est, sexcentis solidis culpabilis udicetur; vel si negaverit, cum septuaginta duobus juret.——Si quis ingenuum Ripuarium interfecerit, et eum cum ramo cooperuit, vel in puteo seu in quocunque libet loco celare voluerit, quod dicitur *Mordridus*, sexcentis solidis culpabilis iudicetur, aut cum septuaginta duobus juret."—Leg. Ripuar., cap. vi., vii., et. xi.

† Capitularia Regum Francorum, a Baluzio, tom, ii., p. 639 et seq.

The third proof was by holding in the hand, for a certain space of time, a red-hot iron; or by walking barefooted over several burning ploughshares, or bars of iron. Perhaps it might be possible to elude even the dangers of this experiment, though certainly more difficult than the last. Another ordeal was of a gentler sort; it was performed by consecrating a piece of barley-bread and cheese, and giving it to the accused to eat, who, if he was not choked by it, was declared innocent.*

Among the most inveterate and longest established of these ancient customs was that of judicial combat. Both in civil and in criminal proceedings, the accuser and the accused were under the necessity of answering a mortal challenge from the antagonist who was destitute of legal proof either to establish or refute a charge. This sanguinary and most iniquitous proceeding, which was calculated to redouble oppression, and add strength to the strong against the weak, continued, for many ages, to be allowed in all the kingdoms of Europe. So rooted has the custom been, that even the wisdom of more polished ages, and the prohibitory and penal enactments of councils of the church, and of sovereign princes, have been found quite inadequate to restrain it.†

In treating of the genius and character of the middle ages, it is necessary, without attempting to give a connected view of ecclesiastical history, to consider the state of the church as connected with the illustration of manners or of national policy. Before the age of Charlemagne, and during that period, the Christian church was rent into numberless divisions, arising both from disputed points of doctrine, and from less essential matters of forms and ceremonies. The Arian and Pelagian heresies, with the numberless sects which sprung from these as from a parent stem,

* Similar modes of trial appear to have formed a part of the jurisprudence of many ancient nations. The law of Moses prescribes an ordeal for the trial of the chastity of married women, viz. that the husband who suspected the fidelity of his wife should bring her to the priest with an offering in her hand, of a certain quantity of barley-meal; and the priest, after administering a certain form of execration to a cup of water, shall make the woman drink it; under the assurance that, if guilty, the water shall cause her belly to swell, and her thigh to rot.—Numbers, ch. v. The anxiety of conscious guilt is to this day appealed to in a similar method by the Brahmins of India.

† By a decree of the Council of Trent, the practice of judicial combat is described as a cunning invention of the devil, that, by the death of their bodies, he may get immediate possession of the souls of the combatants; and is prohibited under the highest penalty—any Christian prince permitting the practice within his dominions was to be excommunicated. The combatants themselves were condemned to excommunication, forfeiture of their property, and the person who fell in combat was denied Christian burial. The instigator of a duel, and even the spectators, were condemned to perpetual excommunication.—Concil. Trident. Sess. 9. sub Pont. Pio. A. D. 1563.

The learned Mr. Harris has, in his Philosophical Inquiries, shown that the custom of the ordeal may be traced up to the time of Eteocles and Polynices, that is, before the Trojan war. The ordeal by red-hot iron is particularly mentioned in the Antigone of Sophocles. Harris's Phil. Inquiries, part 3, chap. 1.

For much fanciful reasoning, and misapplied ingenuity, on the subject of these ancient customs, see Montesquieu, Esprit des Loix, liv. 28., ch. 17.

continued for many years to embroil the church, and to occasion the most violent contentions. We have already observed that Arius, a presbyter of Alexandria, who lived in the fourth century, maintained that Christ, the second person of the godhead, was totally distinct from the first person, or God the Father: that Christ was the first, and the noblest of those beings whom God had created out of nothing: that He was the instrument by whose subordinate operation the Almighty Being had formed the universe; and was therefore inferior to him both in nature and dignity. The opinions of Arius, with regard to the third person of the Trinity, are not so well known. His doctrine, concerning the inferior nature of the Son of God, was examined, and solemnly debated in the council of Nice, which was assembled by Constantine, and it was there condemned by a plurality of suffrages. The Nicene creed declared Christ to be consubstantial with the Father, and pronounced a sentence of deposition and banishment on Arius. His doctrines, however, continued to find many zealous supporters, and the emperor Constantine himself, becoming at length a convert to his opinions, recalled Arius from banishment, and ordered the patriarch of Constantinople to restore him to his ecclesiastical functions and dignities. This, however, was prevented by the sudden death of Arius, an event which his enemies interpreted as a judgment of heaven to punish his heresy and impiety; but which his disciples and partisans attributed to the intolerant zeal of some of his adversaries.

In the fifth century arose the Pelagian heresy. The authors of it were Pelagius and Cælestius, the former a native of Britain, the latter of Ireland. These men looked upon the doctrines commonly received concerning the original corruption of human nature, and the necessity of divine grace to enlighten the understanding and purify the heart, as prejudicial to the progress both of religion and virtue, and tending to lull mankind into a presumptuous and fatal security. They maintained that these doctrines were equally false and pernicious; that the sins of our first parents were imputed to them alone, and not to their posterity; that we derive no corruption from their fall; but are born as pure and unspotted as Adam came from the hands of his Maker: that mankind, therefore, are capable of repentance and amendment, and of arriving at the highest degree of piety and virtue, by the use of their own natural faculties and powers. These doctrines, which struck deep at the very root and foundation of Christianity, gave a great alarm to the church. They were very ably combated by St. Augustin; and this sect was condemned by an ecclesiastical council almost as soon as heard of: but its votaries propagated their opinions in secret, and continued to be numerous for several ages.

But not only was the church rent in pieces by these disputes on essential articles of faith, other matters, comparatively of much less importance, excited the most violent commotions One great article of dissension in those times was the worship of images, which had been gradually gaining ground for some centuries. It arose first from the custom of having crucifixes in private houses, and portraits of our Saviour and his apostles, which sometimes being of considerable value, were, among other religious donations, bequeathed by dying persons to the church, where they were displayed on solemn festivals. The clergy at first took pains to repress that superstition. In the year 393 we find St. Epiphanius pulled down an image in a Church of Syria, before which he found an ignorant person saying prayers. Others, however, of his brethren were not so circumspect or scrupulous, and in time the priests even found their interest in encouraging the practice: for particular images in particular churches, acquiring a higher degree of celebrity than others, and getting the reputation of performing miraculous cures, the grateful donations that were made to the church were a very considerable emolument to the ecclesiastics.

In the year 727, the emperor Leo, the Isaurian, was desirous of extirpating this idolatry, which he very justly considered as disgraceful to Christianity; but his measures were too violent; he burnt and destroyed all the paintings in the churches, and broke to pieces the statues. The people were highly exasperated; and he attempted to enforce his reformation by punishment and persecution, which had no beneficial effect. His son, Constantine Copronymus, took a wiser method by procuring a general sentence of the clergy, condemning the practice as impious and idolatrous. This prince had a genius for reformation. He wished to abolish the monks, who had greatly increased, and at this time engrossed prodigious wealth; but this evil had taken too deep a root. The origin of these associations merits more particular inquiry.

In treating of the earliest age of the Christian church, it has already been remarked that one great source of the corruption of its doctrines, was an attempt to reconcile them to, or intermingle them with, the notions of the heathen philosophers. This intermixture is the true source from whence the impolitic and destructive system of monachism took its rise. It was a doctrine, both of the Stoic and Platonic philosophy, that in order to raise the soul to its highest enjoyment, and to a communion with superior intelligences, it was necessary to separate it from the body, by mortifying and entirely disregarding that earthly vehicle, which checked its flight, and chained it to the mean and sordid enjoyments of the senses. These prevailing notions of the heathen philosophy, joined to a mistaken interpretation put upon some of the precepts of the gospel, contributed to inspire some enthusiastic Christians with the same ideas. The first of these who thought of separating themselves from society were a few, who, after Constantine had restored peace to the church, being now free from persecution, began to conceive that since they were no longer exposed to the persecutions of temporal power, they ought to procure for themselves voluntary grievances and afflictions. In that view they betook themselves to wilds and solitudes, where they spent their time in caves and hermitages in alternate exercises of devotion, and in rigorous acts of penance and mortification. Some of them loaded their limbs with heavy irons ; others walked naked till their bodies acquired a covering of hair like the wild beasts ; and others chose still more nearly to ally themselves to the brute creation, by actually grazing with them in the fields. One father, called a *saint*, has actually left a panegyric on these *Βοσκοι*, or grazing saints. A certain class, however, of a more rational spirit of devotion, employed themselves occasionally in manual labor, the price of which afforded them a frugal subsistence, and enabled them to bestow alms on the poor who visited their cells.

Egypt is allowed to have shown the first example of the monastic life. A young fanatic, of the name of Antony, retired about the year 302 to the desert bordering the Red Sea, where his austerities first attracted admiration and respect, and afterwards procured him numberless imitators. He lived to the age of 105, and had the satisfaction of seeing before his death the whole country swarming with madmen like himself.

The reputation which these persons acquired for superior sanctity, and the extraordinary blessings which were believed to attend their pious vows and prayers, naturally procured them many remuneratory donations from those who believed they had profited by their intercessions. Some of the holy men began to lead a very comfortable life ; and still pretending to bestow all their superfluities in alms and charitable donations, they retained as much as to enable them to pass their time with much ease and satisfaction. Towards the end of the fourth century, these monks or hermits had multiplied in such a manner, that there was not a province in the East that was not full of them. They spread themselves likewise over a great part of Africa ; and in the West, they penetrated within the limits of the bishopric of Rome, and soon became very numerous over all Italy.

It would seem that these holy fathers did not always confine themselves to their cells ; but profiting by the great veneration which they had acquired for superior sanctity, they frequently found their way to cities, and took an active part in secular affairs. Under Theodosius the Great, some of these meddling priests had occasioned such disturbances in the empire, that that prince, on a complaint from the judges and magistrates of the provinces, issued an edict prohibiting them to quit their solitudes, or appear in the cities ; but they had art or influence enough with this same prince to prevail on him, very soon after, to revoke this edict.

About this time many of these devotees began to form themselves into societies, and prescribed to themselves certain observances and common rules, to which they bound themselves by oath: these were obedience to their superior, strict chastity, and poverty. These societies were called *Cœnobia;* and the persons who composed them Cœnobitæ, from their living together in common. But they took different denominations, from the names of those holy persons who associated them together, or were the first superiors of their order. Thus St. Benedict, who introduced monachism into Italy, was the founder of that particular order called Benedictine, which has distinguished itself in most of the countries of Europe, by the ambition of many of the brotherhood, as well as by the enormous wealth which they found means to accumulate; and, we ought to add, by the laborious learning which some of them displayed.

Benedict was an Italian by birth; he had studied at Rome, and soon distinguished himself by his talents as well as superior sanctity. An affectation of singularity, probably, made him retire, when a very young man, to a cave at Subiaco, where he remained for some years. Some neighboring hermits chose him for their head, or superior; and the donations which they received from the devout and charitable very soon enabled them to build a large monastery. The reputation of Benedict increased daily, and he began to perform miracles, which attracted the notice of Totila, the Gothic king of Italy. The number of his fraternity was daily augmented, and it became customary for the rich to make large donations. We may judge of the reputation which Benedict's institution had acquired, even in his own lifetime, from this fact—that the celebrated Cassiodorus, who had long and ably discharged the office of first minister to the Gothic kings of Italy, in the decline of his life, took the vows of the Benedictine order, and founded a monastery on his own estate; where, in the exercises of devotion, in the enjoyment of the tranquillity of the country, and in the composition of those excellent works which he has left to posterity, he passed the remainder of his days.

Benedict, finding his fraternity grow extremely numerous, sent colonies into Sicily and into France, where they throve amazingly. Hence they transported themselves into England; and, in a very little time, there was not a kingdom of Europe where the Benedictines had not obtained a footing.

In the East, the first who associated the *monachi solitarii* into a *cœnobium*, was Basil, the bishop of Cæsarea, in Cappadocia, in the middle of the fourth century. From thence they spread themselves into Greece, and overran the Eastern empire, as the Benedictines had done in the West. Monasteries for women were in the same age founded in Egypt by St. Pacomo, whose sister became the abbess of the first female convent. These females, after a certain time of probation, received the veil, and took the vows of perpetual virginity, obedience, and poverty

From the Cœnobia, founded by Basil, Benedict, and Pacomo, there sprung in the following age an infinite number of other orders, under different rules. St. Augustin, in Africa established the *Canons Regular*, whose order, we are told, was framed in imitation of the apostolic life; whence, we may suppose, they followed in their cells different occupations as artisans. Afterwards the Mendicants arose, who, to the three vows of chastity, obedience, and poverty, added that of living by begging charity.

It was not for some centuries after the period of which we now treat, that the military religious orders took their rise, such as the Knights of St. John of Jerusalem, the Teutonic Knights, and the Templars.

What contributed very much, however, to increase the reputation of the monastic fraternities, in those unenlightened periods, was that portion of scholastic learning which was almost peculiar to them; and moderate as that degree of knowledge was, it certainly prevented the entire extinction of ancient literature, and preserved some feeble sparks, which the care of a happier age afterwards cherished and raised up to warm and enlighten the world.

As the affectation of superior sanctity, and the pride of being singular, gave rise to many of the austerities of the monastic life, the same motive led some men to seclude themselves from social life in a still more extraordinary manner than that practised by any of the religious orders. These men were termed *Stylites*, or Pillar Saints. They mounted themselves on the tops of stone pillars, and stood there immovable for many years. One Simeon, a native of Syria, gave the first example of this most amazing folly, and passed thirty-seven years of his life upon pillars of various heights, beginning with one of nine feet, and, increasing from year to year, till he died on a pillar of forty cubits. Another saint, of the same name, lived sixty-eight years in the same manner. The veneration which these holy men acquired excited a number of imitators, and their degrees of sanctity were always estimated according to the height of their pillars, and the number of years they had passed upon them. For above six centuries this superstitious frenzy prevailed in the East, nor was the practice altogether abolished till the twelfth century.

In the age of Charlemagne, according to the received opinion of Protestants, auricular confession began first to be used. The bishops commenced the practice, by requiring that the canons should confess to them. The abbots obliged their monks to the same submission; and these again required it of the laity. Public confession was now in use in the West; for when the Goths embraced Christianity, their instructers from the East had seen it abolished there under the patriarch Nectarius, at the end of the fourth century.

The canonization of saints was practised by every bishop for twelve centuries : at length, the number growing out of all bounds, the popes thought it necessary to assume the exclusive right of canonization. Pope Alexander III., one of the most profligate of men, was the first who issued a solemn decree reserving to himself the sole right of making saints.

Christianity was carried northward by the conquests of Charlemagne ; but all beyond the limits of his conquests was in a state of idolatry. All Scandinavia was idolatrous. Poland was in the same state ; and the whole inhabitants of that immense tract of country which is now the empire of Russia were pagans, like their neighbors of Tartary. The British and Irish, according to the most probable accounts, had, long before this period, received the first rays of Christianity; but in Britain it was almost totally extinguished, till it was revived under the Saxon heptarchy by the wife of one of the princes; as the Franks, in like manner owed to the wife of Clovis their conversion from idolatry.

CHAPTER IV.

Successors of Charlemagne—Their Weakness and Dissensions—Rise of the Feudal Aristocracy—First Incursions of the Normans—Their Settlement in Normandy—State of the Eastern Empire—Of Italy and the Church—Rise of the Secular Power of the Popedom—Schism of the Greek and Latin Churches—The Saracens conquer Spain—Extinction of the Empire of Charlemagne—Empire of Germany—Otho the Great.

Lewis, surnamed the Débonnaire, was the only one of the lawful sons of Charlemagne who survived him. He had been before his father's death associated with him in the empire, and was now hailed emperor and king of France by the nobles assembled at Aix-a-Chapelle. He was afterwards inaugurated by Pope Stephen IV. It has already been noticed that Charlemagne, on the death of his son Pepin, bestowed on his grandson Bernard the kingdom of Italy. Lewis commenced his reign by making a partition of his dominions. He associated his eldest son Lotharius as his colleague in the principal part of his kingdom. He gave Aquitaine, or that part of the southern provinces of France which forms about a third part of the whole kingdom, to his second son Pepin, and assigned Bavaria to Lewis the youngest. The three princes were solemnly crowned, and the two youngest immediately put in possession of their kingdoms. This procedure alarmed the jealousy and indignation of Bernard, king of Italy, who, as son of the elder brother of Lewis, thought he had a preferable title to the empire of his grandfather Charlemagne. The archbishops of Milan and Cremona espoused his cause; but the unhappy prince was too weak to make his pretensions effectual: abandoned by his troops, he was forced to throw himself on the mercy of his uncle, who inhumanly ordered his eyes to be put out, which occasioned his death.

In the partition of his empire, Lewis had shown the height of imprudence. He had given the whole to his three sons, Lotharius, Pepin, and Lewis. A fourth son was born to him of a second marriage, Charles, afterwards surnamed the Bald, for whom it became necessary to provide a patrimony. This could not be done without giving umbrage to the three elder brothers, who were in fact now independent sovereigns. Each had his party who espoused his interest; and the kingdom was a scene of turbulence and anarchy. Complaints were heard in every quarter of the most outrageous abuses; and Lewis, seriously wishing to redress the grievances of his subjects, called a general assembly, or *champ de mai*, at Aix-la-Chapelle. Here an arrogant monk, named Valla, either instigated by a party, or by the insolent rancor of his own disposition, took upon him to accuse the emperor publicly as being the author of the general calamities; he reproached him with his design of providing for his youngest son, whom he stigmatized as a bastard, at the expense of the elder, who, he said, had as good a right to their crowns as Lewis to his own. The pusillanimous Lewis patiently heard these invectives; and, instead of inflicting on their author that punishment which he so amply deserved, he contented himself with dismissing the factious monk to his convent, where he remained no longer than till by his incendiary machinations he had brought the three brothers openly to declare war against their father. It was in vain that Lewis proposed terms of accommodation—that he set forth the equity and probity of his intentions, and summoned assemblies of the states to devise the most probable means of securing the peace of the empire. The princes were exasperated; the ecclesiastic had gained to his party several bishops and abbots; and Gregory IV., as the popes now saw it was for their interest to humble the emperors, took a decided part with the rebels. Gregory came to France, and threatened the emperor with excommunication. The French bishops, on the emperor's side, showed a becoming spirit. They threatened the pope, in their turn, with excommunication—*Si excommunicaturus veniet, excommunicatus abibit.* But Gregory had both resolution and artifice. While a negotiation was on foot, the pope was admitted into Lewis's camp; he corrupted one half of his army, and on the night of his departure they abandoned their sovereign, and repaired to the standard of Lotharius. The unhappy Lewis surrendered himself a prisoner to his rebellious children, and delivered up the empress, with his son Charles—the innocent cause of the war. The empress, as the highest mark of indignity that could be offered to her, had her head shaved, and was thrown into prison; and Charles, then a boy of ten years of age, was confined in a convent. Valla, the monk, now proclaimed the throne vacated by Lewis, and Lotharius was declared emperor. The first step of his administration was infamous and detestable. He compelled his father—whose paternal affection, weak indeed and imprudent, had associated him in the imperial dignity—to do public penance in the church of Notre Dame at Soissons, and to read with a loud voice a list which was given him of his crimes, among which appeared impiety, sacrilege, and murder. He was then conducted to a monastery, where he was confined for a year, till the dissensions of his children again replaced him on the throne. Lewis and Pepin, quarrelling with their elder brother Lotharius, restored Lewis le Débonnaire to his kingdom, and brought the empress and her son from banishment; but he did not long enjoy his change of fortune; for his son Lewis again commencing a rebellion, the weak and unfortunate father died of a broken heart.

The ruinous policy of this unhappy and despicable prince had introduced irrecoverable weakness and disorder into the empire. Lotharius, now emperor, and Pepin, his brother's son, took up arms against the two other sons of Lewis le Débonnaire, Lewis of Bavaria, and Charles the Bald. A battle ensued at Fontenai, in the territory of Auxerre, where it is said there perished 100,000 men. Lotharius and his nephew were vanquished. Charlemagne had compelled the nations whom he subdued to embrace Christianity; Lotharius, to acquire popularity and strengthen his arms, declared an entire liberty of conscience throughout the empire, and many thousands reverted to their ancient idolatry. In punishment of this impiety, Lotharius was now solemnly deposed by a council of bishops, who took upon them to show their authority no less over the victorious than over the vanquished princes. They put this question to Charles the Bald and to Lewis of Bavaria—"Do you promise to govern better than Lotharius has done?" "We do," said the obsequious monarchs. "Then," returned the bishops, "we, by divine authority, permit and ordain you to reign in his stead"—a proceeding in which it is difficult to say whether the arrogance of the clergy most excites our indignation, or the pusillanimity of the monarchs our contempt.

Lotharius, though excommunicated and deprived of his imperial dignity by these overbearing ecclesiastics, found means, at last, to accommodate matters so with his brothers, that they agreed to a new partition of the empire. By the treaty of Verdun, concluded between the brothers, it was settled that the western Frankish empire, or the country now called France, which was to be the share of Charles the Bald, should have for its boundaries the four great rivers, the Rhone, the Saone, the

Maese, and the Scheldt. Lotharius, together with the *title* of emperor, was to possess the kingdom—which was in fact little more than a nominal sovereignty; but to which was added, of real territory, those provinces which lay immediately adjoining to the eastern boundary of France, viz. that which from him took the name of Lotharingia, now Lorraine, Franche Comté, Hainault, and the Cambresis. The share of Lewis of Bavaria was the kingdom of Germany.

Thus Germany was finally separated from the empire of the Franks. The shadow of the Roman empire founded by Charlemagne still subsisted. Lotharius, after procuring his son Lewis to be consecrated King of Lombardy by Pope Sergius II., being attacked by a mortal distemper, chose to die in the habit of a monk, which he thought a sure passport to heaven. He was succeeded in the empire and kingdom by his eldest son Lewis. He had assigned Lorraine to his second son Lotharius, and Burgundy to his youngest son Charles. Among these princes and their uncles, Lewis of Bavaria and Charles the Bald, endless contentions arose; and the vast empire of Charlemagne, the scene of perpetual war and disorders, was fast sinking into contempt. On the death of Lewis II., Charles the Bald attempted, but without success, to wrest from the sons of Lewis of Bavaria the empire of Germany. His own kingdom of France was at this time visited by the inroads of his Norman neighbors, and groaned under all the calamities of war at home as well as abroad. The Saracens attacked him on the side of Italy; his nephew Carloman, son of Lewis of Bavaria, had invaded his dominions; and a conspiracy of his nobles threatened both his crown and life. He is said to have fallen a victim to this conspiracy, and to have died by poison.

Charles the Bald was the first of the French monarchs who made dignities and titles hereditary—a policy which gave a severe blow to the regal authority. It was indeed under the reigns of these weak princes of the posterity of Charlemagne that the feudal aristocracy first began to strengthen itself against the power of the crown. Walled castles and fortresses were erected by the nobility throughout France and Germany, from which they sallied out at the head of their armed vassals to plunder and lay waste the possessions of their rivals. We find in the capitularies of Charles the Bald a royal ordonnance prohibiting the erection of such castles, but the edict was contemned, and the sovereign had no power to enforce his prohibition. From this period, the barbarous custom of private war prevailed in all the kingdoms of Europe, and marked alike the weakness of the sovereign power and the general ferocity of manners of the middle ages.

The Normans, a new race of invaders from Scandinavia, began, under the reign of Charles the Bald, to attract the attention and alarm the fears of most of the European nations. The kingdoms of Scandinavia, which have been termed *officina humani generis*, seem to have resembled a beehive, of which the stock multiplies so fast, that it is necessary to send off immense swarms from time to time, to seek new establishments for themselves, and to leave a sufficiency of subsistence for those that remain behind. The Normans, or *Northernmen*, were a new race of Goths, who poured down in a torrent upon the countries to the south of them. They had begun their depredations towards the end of the reign of Charlemagne; but the terror of his arms prevented them from making any considerable encroachment on his empire. Under Lewis the Débonnaire they made further advances. They were expert at ship-building, and at that time constructed vessels capable of containing about one hundred men. In the year 843 they sailed up the Seine, and plundered the city of Rouen. Another fleet sailed up the Loire, and laid waste the whole country as far as Touraine. They did not confine their depredations to cattle, goods, provisions, or money, but carried off men, women, and children into captivity. Emboldened by the little resistance they met with under a weak and impotent administration, they in the following year covered the sea with their fleets, and landed almost at the same time in England, France, and Spain. Spain, then under a vigorous Mahometan government, took measures to repel the invaders, and succeeded; but in France and England, the state of the country was highly favorable to the success of their enterprise.

In the year 845, the Normans sailed up the Elbe, plundered Hamburgh, and penetrated into Germany. They had at this time a fleet of 600 ships, with Eric, king of Denmark, at their head. He detached Regnier, one of his admirals, with 420 vessels up the Seine; Rouen was plundered a second time, and the corsairs proceeded along the river to Paris. The Parisians took to flight, and, abandoning the city, it was burnt down by the Normans. The city was at that time entirely built of wood. Charles the Bald, too weak to make head against the invaders with his forces, gave them 14,000 marks of silver on condition of their evacuating France—the most effectual means to secure their return. Accordingly, they quitted the Seine, but sailed up the Garonne, and plundered Bourdeaux. Pepin, then king of Aquitaine, conducted himself yet worse than Charles the Bald; for, being unable to resist the invaders, he shamefully joined them, and united his forces to assist them in ravaging the whole kingdom of France. Germany, Flanders, and England shared the miseries of this confederacy. Charles, surnamed the Gross, equally pusillanimous with his predecessors of the blood of Charlemagne, yielded a part of Holland to the Normans, in the view of pacifying them; the consequence was, that they seized upon Flanders, passed without resistance from the Somme to the river Oise, burnt the town of Pontoise, and proceeded a second time with great alacrity to Paris. The Parisians, however, were now better prepared for their reception. Count Odo, or Eudes, whose valor afterwards raised him to the throne of France, was determined that his countrymen should not basely abandon their capital as before. He made every preparation for defence and for vigorous resistance. The Normans applied the battering ram to the walls, and effected a breach, but were bravely beat off by the besieged. The venerable Bishop Gosselin, an honor to his character and profession, repaired every day to the ramparts, set up there the standard of the cross, and, after bestowing his benedictions on the people, fought gallantly at their head, armed with his battle-axe and cuirass; but the worthy prelate died of fatigue in the midst of the siege. The memory of this good man, although the scruples of pious Catholics have denied him canonization, is more precious, more truly respectable, than half their calendar.

The Normans blocked up the city for eighteen months, during which time the miserable Parisians suffered all tho horrors of famine and pestilence. At length, another shameful truce was concluded between the barbarians and Charles the Gross, which, like the former, served only to make them change the scene of their devastations. They laid siege to the town of Sens, and plundered Burgundy, while Charles assembled a parliament at Mentz, which, with great propriety, deprived this pitiful monarch of a throne which he was unworthy to fill. This assembly called to the empire Arnold, a bastard, of the blood of Charlemagne; while Eudes, count of Paris, was elected king of France.

Raoul, or Rollo, the most distinguished of the Scandinavian leaders, having assembled an immense body of troops, made a landing in England in the year 885. After some successes in that quarter, he steered his course to France, where he began to think of forming a fixed establishment. His son, the second Rollo, repaired the city of Rouen, which he determined to make his capital; and, marrying the daughter of Charles the Simple, to whom Eudes had ceded the crown and part of the dominions of France, Rollo acquired the provinces of Normandy and Britany as her portion. He embraced the Christian faith, and turned his thoughts to the improvement of his provinces and the happiness of his subjects. The Danes and Scandinavians, now settled in Normandy, and uniting with the Franks, produced that race of warriors whom we shall presently see the conquerors of England and of Sicily.

While the empire of Charlemagne was thus hastening to its downfall under his degenerate successors, that of Constantinople exhibited an appearance in some respects still venerable and respectable. It has been compared by the fanciful Voltaire to an immense tree, still vigorous, though old and stripped of some of its roots, and assailed on every side by violent storms. This empire had nothing left in Africa, and had lost Syria, with part of

Asia Minor. It still defended its frontiers against the Mahometans towards the eastern coast of the Black Sea, but it was ravaged by other enemies towards the western coast and towards the Danube. The Abari and Bulgarians, both tribes of Scythian extraction, laid waste all the fine province of Romania, which Trajan and Adrian had adorned with splendid cities; and growing more adventurous by their successes, they alternately committed ravages on the empires of the East and West.

While the frontiers of the Eastern empire were thus attacked by the barbarians, Constantinople itself was for some ages the theatre of disgraceful revolutions, achieved by the most atrocious crimes. The attention dwells with horror on the bloody tragedies of this period :—one emperor assassinated in revenge of murder and incest; another poisoned by his own wife; a third stabbed in the bath by his servants; a fourth plucking out the eyes of his brothers; a mother the murderer of her own son, that she might herself enjoy his throne. Of such complexion was that series of sovereigns who swayed the empire of the East for nearly two hundred years.

To increase the misfortunes of the empire, the Russians, in the tenth century, embarking on the *Palus Mœotis*, or Sea of Asoph, sailed through the Cimmerian Bosphorus, and ravaged the whole coasts of the Euxine Sea; while the Turks, a new race of barbarians of Scythian or Tartarian extraction, began also to make inroads on the Eastern empire. But of the first migration of these invaders we have hardly any authentic account.

Under all these misfortunes, Constantinople still remained the most populous, the most opulent, and the most polished city of Christendom. It was probably indebted for its welfare, amid all these distresses, to its extensive commerce, the consequence of its situation, which gives it the command of two seas.

At this period, the affairs of Italy and the church form an important feature in the history of Europe. We have seen with what consummate art the popes laid the foundation of their temporal authority under Pepin and Charlemagne, the donations from these princes conferring on them their first territorial possessions, which were part of the dominions of the Lombard kings. The popes now began to consider themselves as sovereigns, in every sense of the word, and to take all prudent measures for the security of that power which they had acquired. Gregory IV. repaired the harbor of Ostia, at the mouth of the Tyber; and Leo IV. fortified the city of Rome. It was somewhat singular that there was still in Rome a vestige remaining of the ancient form of the republican constitution. Two consuls were elected every year; and a prefect was created, who was a kind of tribune of the people. Over these magistrates, however, the popes extended an absolute control and jurisdiction, and became soon the temporal sovereigns of Italy.

As the spiritual heads of the church, and the representatives and successors of St. Peter, the jurisdiction claimed by these ambitious men was not confined to the kingdom of Italy. They held forth, as a consequence of being the vicars of Christ upon earth, that they were vested with a supreme jurisdiction, in matters ecclesiastical, in all the Christian kingdoms of Europe. Pope Nicholas I., in his apostolical bulls and letters, published to all Christendom that a right of appeal lay to the holy see from the sentences of all church judicatures whatever; that it was therefore necessary and proper that the pope should have his legates in all Christian countries, to preserve the rights of the church; that it belonged to the pope alone to call the general councils, and that the canons or regulations of these councils were of much higher authority than any civil laws; that it was proper for subjects to give due obedience to their temporal sovereigns while *they* conducted themselves dutifully to the holy church, but otherwise they were tyrants, to whom the people owed no allegiance. It is easy to see the tendency of these maxims, to which it is not a little surprising that the princes of Europe for many ages should have paid the most implicit deference.

A literary forgery of a very extraordinary nature was called in, to give authority to these assumed powers. About the middle of the ninth century a book appeared, under the name of Isidorus, bishop of Seville, alleged to have been compiled by that prelate about the year 630, which contained a set of fabricated letters of the bishops of Rome, as far back as the year 93—together with fictitious, or at least mutilated and interpolated, decrees of councils; the scope of all which was to prove that the bishop of Rome was the direct successor of St. Peter, and inherited his apostolical character, and that the foundations of the church rested on him; that all bishops and ministers should be independent of the secular powers, and exempted from taxes; that the church was paramount in authority over all the princes and sovereigns of the earth; that the head of the church could excommunicate and depose them, and absolve all subjects from their allegiance. This precious code, of which the forgery was not fully exposed till the sixteenth century, had a most powerful effect in those ages of ignorance and superstition, as it appeared to contain the clear sense of the Christian church on those most material articles, transmitted down from the earliest periods, and acknowledged without the smallest dispute.*

Yet, in the middle of the ninth century, and at a time when the papal authority was at its height, one circumstance of a very extraordinary nature is said to have occurred, which, with evil-

* On this curious subject see Putter. Hist. Develop. of the German Empire, b. i., ch. 7; Cosin's Scholastical Hist. of the Canons of Scripture, ch. vi., § 83; Mosheim's Ecclesiast. Hist., cent ix., part ii., ch. ii., § 8.

disposed men, threw much ridicule upon the clergy, and particularly on the holy see—as, if true, it certainly interrupted that so much vaunted succession of regular bishops which is said to have followed from the days of St. Peter to the present. This was no less than the election of a woman to the dignity of the popedom. Between the pontificate of Leo IV., who died in the year 855, and that of Benedict III., who was elected in 858, a certain woman, who had the address to disguise her sex for a considerable time, is said, by learning, genius, and great address, to have made her way to the papal chair, and to have governed the church for two years, till her holiness was unfortunately detected by bearing a child in the midst of a religious procession. This real or fabulous personage is known by the title of Pope Joan. During five centuries this event was generally believed, and a vast number of writers bore testimony to its truth; nor until the period of the reformation of Luther was it considered by any as either incredible in itself or ignominious to the church. But in the seventeenth century, the existence of this female pontiff became the subject of a keen and learned controversy between the Protestants and the Catholics; the former supporting the truth of the fact, and the latter endeavoring to invalidate the evidence on which it rests. Mosheim, a very learned and acute writer, steers a middle course; and though he is disposed to doubt the many absurd and ridiculous circumstances with which the story has been embellished, for the purpose of throwing ridicule on the head of the Romish church, yet is inclined to think that it is not wholly without foundation. Gibbon treats the story as a mere fable.*

It is curious to remark that while the clergy were steadily aiming at temporal power, secular princes, as if interchanging character with them, seem to have fixed their chief attention on spiritual concerns. The monastic life was now universally in the highest esteem, and nothing could equal the veneration that was paid to such as devoted themselves to the sacred gloom and indolence of a convent. The Greeks and orientals had long been accustomed to regard the monkish discipline with the greatest veneration, but at this time the same folly had infected the whole of Europe. Kings, dukes, and counts, regarding their secular duties as mean and sordid, beheld with contempt every thing that regarded this world, and, abandoning their thrones and temporal honors, shut themselves up in monasteries, and devoted themselves entirely to the exercises of prayer and mortification. Others, whose zeal had not led them quite so far, showed their reverence for the church by employing ecclesiastics in every department of secular government. At this time all embassies, negotiations, and treaties of state, were conducted by monks and abbots, who most naturally

* For an ingenious statement of the whole controversy, see Bayle's Dict., art. Papesse Jeanne

contrived that all public measures should contribute to the great end of advancing the sovereign and paramount jurisdiction of the pope and the ecclesiastical councils.

At this period, however, when every thing seemed to concur in increasing the power of the popedom, that remarkable schism took place which separated the Greek from the Latin church. The patriarchal see of Constantinople was the object of ambitious contention, as well as the imperial throne. The emperor, dissatisfied with the patriarch Ignatius, deposed him from his office, and put Photius, eunuch of the palace, a man of great talents and abilities, in his place. Pope Nicholas, jealous of his authority, which he had some reason to think was encroached on by the patriarchs of Constantinople, who had withdrawn the provinces of Illyrium, Macedonia, Achaia, Thessaly, and Sicily, from their dependence on the holy see, sent a solemn embassy to Constantinople to reclaim those provinces. His demand was treated with contempt, and the patriarch of Constantinople avowed openly his pretensions to an equality of power with the Roman pontiff. Pope Nicholas determined to vindicate his authority against this formidable usurpation, and for this reason took the part of Ignatius, the deposed patriarch, against Photius, who had been raised to that dignity by the emperor. He thundered out a sentence of excommunication against Photius, deposing him from his sacerdotal function; to which Photius replied by excommunicating the Pope, and deposing him from the apostolical chair. He then assumed the title of *Œcumenical* or General Patriarch, and accused all the western bishops of heresy, not only for adhering to the Roman pontiff, but for various heterodox articles of doctrine, and unchristian practices: such, for example, as using unleavened bread in the sacrament; eating cheese and eggs in Lent; shaving their beards; and lastly, that they prohibited priests to marry, and separated from their wives such married men as chose to go into orders. The last of these articles, he alleged, gave rise to the most scandalous immoralities. During the dependence of this dispute between the pontiffs, Michael, the emperor who had raised Photius to the patriarchal chair, was murdered by his rival Basileas, who, immediately on his mounting the imperial throne, deposed the patriarch in the midst of his triumph; and a council of the church being called at this time, at Rome, Photius was unanimously condemned to do penance for his usurpations and heresies. Soon after, however, Photius, who was a man of consummate ability, prevailed on the emperor to reinstate him as patriarch, and he was now declared innocent by four hundred bishops, three hundred of whom were the same men who had before signed his condemnation. This is a disgraceful picture of depravity; but conscience and religion are too weak to combat against state policy.

While the Pope found it for his interest to be on good terms with the emperor of the East, there was great peace and harmony in the general councils, and no controversies arose on disputed articles of faith or discipline. Pope John VIII. was a good politician; but his successors, having quarrelled with the Greek empire, adopted the decrees of that council which had condemned Photius, and rejected those of the last council which had acquitted him. Photius, on his part, immediately resumed the accusation of heretical tenets, the celibacy of the clergy, shaving the beard, and eating eggs in Lent; and, at once, contended for the supremacy of the see of Constantinople over all the bishops in Christendom. Photius, whose life was strangely checkered with good and evil fortune, was deposed, and died in disgrace; but his successors adhered to his pretensions and supported them with vigor, so that, for many ages, the dispute continued with great animosity.*

During these perpetual contests for ecclesiastical power and preëminence, the Christian religion itself was debased both by the practice and the principles of its teachers. The sole object of the clergy was to accumulate wealth and temporal distinctions. While they indulged in every species of voluptuousness and debauchery, they were so deplorably ignorant, that it is confidently asserted there were many bishops who could not repeat the Apostles' Creed, nor read the Sacred Scriptures. This indeed was a necessary consequence of the iniquitous distribution of ecclesiastical preferments. These were either sold to the highest bidder, or were bestowed as bribes by the sovereigns and superior pontiffs, to attach the most artful and often the most worthless to their interest. Hence it was that the most flagitious and ignorant wretches were frequently advanced to the highest stations in the church; and that upon several occasions civil magistrates, artificers, and even soldiers, were by a strange metamorphosis converted into bishops and abbots.

While the Constantinopolitan empire was thus entirely occupied with theological dissensions, which produced no other fruit than intestine division and weakness, the Saracens, equally zealous in propagating the doctrines of their false prophet, studied, at the same time, the aggrandizement of their empire, and were making rapid encroachments on the territories of the Christian princes. In the beginning of the eighth century, they subverted the dominion of the Visigoths in Spain; and, with very little difficulty, achieved the conquest of the whole of that peninsula.

---

* Photius was in all respects a remarkable man. During a life almost constantly embroiled in political intrigues, he yet found time to cultivate letters with high success; and there are several of his works remaining which evince a great depth of erudition, a surprising diversity of knowledge, and much critical judgment. Of these the most remarkable is his "Bibliotheca," which contains an analytical account of about two hundred and eighty of the most celebrated of the ancient Greek writers, the greatest part of whose works have perished; so that this analysis of Photius, which is most minute and accurate, and in many instances an abridgment of the original works, is, on that account, an invaluable composition.

The caliphs, as already observed, had in a very few years from the first foundation of their empire by Mahomet, reared up a most extensive dominion in Asia, Africa, and Europe. In Africa they were masters of all that had formerly been subject to the Roman power; and, at the time of which we now treat, they had lately founded the city of Morocco, in the neighborhood of Mount Atlas. The caliph, Valid Almanzor, had given the government of his African states to his viceroy Muza, who, projecting the conquest of Spain, sent thither his lieutenant Tariffe with a very considerable army. The situation of the country was at the time extremely favorable for such an enterprise. Witiza, the Gothic prince, was one of the weakest of men, and his successor Rodrigo one of the most wicked and profligate. The Goths were attached by no affection to their governors, and it was with difficulty that an armed force was collected sufficient to take the field against the invaders. In one memorable engagement Rodrigo lost his life, and the Saracens, in the year 713, became masters of the whole country. The conquerors did not abuse their success; they left the vanquished Goths in possession of their property, their laws, and their religion. Abdallah, the Moor, married the widow of Rodrigo, and the two nations formed a perfect coalition. In the space of thirty months all Spain had been joined to the empire of the caliphs, except the Rocks of Asturias, where Pelayo, a relation of the last king Rodrigo, preserved his liberty, kept a sort of court, and, as the Spanish historians say, transmitted his crown to his son Favila, who maintained for several years this little remnant of a Christian monarchy in the midst of the conquerors of his country. The Moors, for some time, carried every thing before them, and pushed their conquests beyond the Pyrenees into Gaul; but a spirit of division arising among their emirs, or governors, some of whom aimed at independent power, Lewis the Débonnaire took advantage of these disturbances, sent an army into Spain, and invested Barcelona which he took after a siege of two years.

From this period the Moorish power in the north of Spain began to decline; they had shaken off the dependence of their caliphs, and they were no longer supported by their countrymen of Africa. The Christian monarchy in the heart of the Asturias began at this time to recover vigor. Alphonso the Chaste, who was of the race of Pelayo, refused any longer to pay the annual tribute which the Moors had exacted. The Christians of Navarre followed the example of their brethren of the Asturias, and chose for themselves a king, as did likewise those of the province of Arragon; and in a few years neither the Mahometans nor the French were in possession of any part of the northern provinces. It was at this time that the Normans invaded Spain; but, meeting with a repulse which they did not expect, they turned back and plundered France and England.

While the Moors were thus losing ground in the north of Spain, their countrymen had established a very flourishing monarchy in the southern part of the Peninsula. Abdalrahman, the last heir of the family of the Ommiades, the caliphate being now possessed by the Abassidæ, betook himself to Spain, where, being recognised by a great part of the Saracens in that country as the representative of their ancient caliphs, he encountered and defeated the viceroy of the rival caliph, and was acknowledged sovereign of all the Moorish possessions in the south of Spain. He fixed the seat of his residence at Cordova, which from that time, and for two centuries after, was distinguished as the capital of a very splendid monarchy. It is this period, from the middle of the eighth to the middle of the tenth century, which is to be accounted the most flourishing age of Arabian magnificence. While Haroun Alraschid made Bagdad the seat of a great and polished empire, and cultivated the arts and sciences with high success, the Moors of Cordova, under Abdalrahman and his successors, vied with their Asiatic brethren in the same honorable pursuits, and were, unquestionably, the most enlightened of the states of Europe at this period. The empire of the Franks indeed, under Charlemagne, exhibited a beautiful picture of order, sprung from confusion and weakness, but terminating with the reign of this illustrious monarch, and leaving no time for the arts introduced by him to make any approach to perfection. The Moors of Spain, under a series of princes, who gave every encouragement to genius and industry, though fond at the same time of military glory, gained the reputation of superiority both in arts and arms to all the nations of the West. The Moorish structures in Spain, which were reared during the eighth, ninth, and tenth centuries, many of which yet remain, convey an idea of opulence and grandeur which almost exceeds belief. The Mosque of Cordova, begun by Abdalrahman the First, and finished about the year 800, is still almost entire, and countenances every notion which historians have given of the splendor and magnificence of the Moorish monarchy of Spain.

The Saracens were at this time extending their conquests in almost every quarter of the world. The Mahometan religion was now embraced over the most of India, and all along the Eastern and Mediterranean coast of Africa. Some of the African Saracens invaded Sicily, as they had done Spain, and the arms neither of the eastern nor of the western emperors were able to drive them out of it. From Sicily they began to meditate the conquest of Italy; they sailed up the Tyber, ravaged the country, and laid siege to Rome. A French army, under one of Lotharius's generals, advancing to its relief, was beaten; but the city, in the meantime, being supplied with provisions, the Saracens thought fit to desist for awhile until they should increase their forces. On this occasion Pope Leo IV. showed himself worthy of being a sovereign. He employed the treasures of the church in fortifying the city, stretching iron chains across the Tyber, and making every preparation for a vigorous defence. The spirit of an ancient Roman seemed revived in this venerable pontiff; he infused courage and resolution into all around him. The Saracens, on attempting to land, were furiously driven back and cut to pieces: a storm had dispersed one half of their ships; and the invaders, unable to retreat, were either slaughtered or made prisoners.

The Saracens might have reared an immense empire, had they, like the Romans, acknowledged only one head; but their generals always affected independence. Egypt shook off the yoke of the caliphs, and became the residence of an independent Sultan. Mauritania followed the same example, and became the empire of Morocco, under its absolute prince. Spain, or at least the kingdom of Cordova, had thrown off its dependence on the caliphs of the race of Abassidæ, and obeyed a race of princes of the ancient family of the Ommiades. In this state of division, the Saracen power had ceased to be considered as one empire; yet it is to be observed, that all these separate sovereigns continued to respect the Caliph of the East as the successor of Mahomet, though they acknowledged to him no temporal subjection.

After the deposition of Charles the Gross, the empire of Charlemagne subsisted only in name. Arnold, or Arnulph, a bastard son of Charlemagne, made himself master of Germany. Italy was divided between Guy, duke of Spoleto, and Berengarius, duke of Friuli, who had received these duchies from Charles the Bald. Arnold considered France to be his property as emperor, but in the meantime it was possessed by Eudes and Charles the Simple. The dukes of Spoleto and Friuli had their pretensions to the empire as well as Arnold: they were both of the blood of Charlemagne. Formosus, who was pope at this time, complaisantly invested them all three in succession with imperial dignity; in fact, the Roman empire no longer subsisted. The country which obeyed the nominal emperors was but a part of Germany; while France, Italy, Spain, Burgundy, and the countries between the Maese and the Rhine, were possessed by different independent princes. The emperors were tumultuously elected by the bishops, and such of the grandees as were most in power, who were become hereditary princes, and who, in reality, were more independent than their sovereign.

In speaking of the election of emperors at this period, it is not to be supposed that there was any limited number of electors, as came afterwards to be the case. A century after the period of which we now treat, we have historical evidence that the election of the emperor was in the people at large; but by what means the sentiments of the people were taken, it is not easy to conceive. Probably each duke, or count, was considered as the organ of the district over which he presided.

After the death of Arnold, his son Lewis was chosen emperor

of the Romans. He was the last of the blood of Charlemagne, and upon his death, Otho, duke of Saxony, by his influence and credit, put the crown upon the head of Conrad, duke of Franconia; on whose death Henry, surnamed "The Fowler," son of the same duke Otho of Saxony, was elected emperor, in the year 918.

The incapacity of preceding emperors, and the disorders occasioned by the vast number of petty princes, who all exercised sovereign authority in their own states, had reduced the empire to extreme weakness. The Hungarians, descendants of the ferocious Huns, committed such depredations, that the emperor Conrad was content to pay an annual tribute to keep them quiet. Henry the Fowler, who was a prince of great abilities and excellent endowments, changed the face of affairs much for the better. His good policy united the disorderly nobles; he vanquished the Hungarians, and freed the empire from the disgraceful tribute which was imposed during the reign of his predecessor. To this prince Germany owes the foundation of her cities; for before this period, excepting the castles on the mountains, the seats of the barbarous nobility who lived by plunder, and the convents, filled with an useless herd of ecclesiastics, the bulk of the people lived dispersed in lonely farms and villages. The towns built by Henry were surrounded with walls, and regularly fortified; they were capable of containing a considerable number of inhabitants; and, in order that they might be speedily peopled, it was enjoined by the sovereign that every ninth man should remove himself, with his whole effects, from the country, and settle in the nearest town. In the same spirit of judicious policy, Henry subjected the tilts and tournaments to proper regulations: thus preserving and encouraging an institution which kept alive among his subjects the martial spirit, and that high sense of honor which prompts to deeds of heroism; while he restrained every thing in the practice which savored of barbarism, or tended to insubordination, by rendering ndividuals the judges and avengers in their own quarrels. This prince held no correspondence with the see of Rome; he had been consecrated by his own bishops, and during his whole reign Germany seemed to have lost sight of Italy.

Henry the Fowler was succeeded by his son Otho the Great, who again united Italy to the empire, and kept the aspiring popedom in subjection. Otho was, in every respect, the character of the greatest celebrity at this time in Europe. He increased the imperial dominions by the addition of the kingdom of Denmark, or at least rendered that nation for a considerable time tributary to the imperial crown. He annexed Bohemia likewise to the empire; and seems to have assumed to himself a jurisdiction paramount in authority over all the sovereigns of Europe.

Italy, at the accession of Otho the Great, was the scene of crimes equally detestable, and murders as atrocious, as those which stained the annals of the Constantinopolitan empire at the same period. Formosus had been bishop of Porto before he arrived at the popedom, and in that station he had been twice excommunicated by Pope John VIII. for rebellion and misdemeanor. Stephen, who succeeded Formosus in the see of Rome, caused his body to be dug up: the corpse was convicted of various crimes, beheaded, and flung into the Tyber. The friends of Formosus, however, conspired against and deposed Stephen, who was afterwards strangled in prison, while the body of Formosus was recovered, embalmed, and interred with all pontifical honors. Sergius III., who, before he arrived at the popedom, had been banished by John IX., a friend of Formosus, no sooner attained the pontifical chair, than he caused this abused carcass to be dug out of the grave a second time, and thrown into the Tyber.

Marozia, the mistress of Sergius III., and her sister Theodora, two women of the most abandoned and flagitious character, now ruled every thing in Rome; and maintaining their ascendency by the most detestable crimes, and murders without end, they filled the pontifical chair in rapid and monstrous succession with their paramours or their adulterous offspring.

While Rome and the church were thus rent in pieces, Berengarius, duke of Friuli, disputed with Hugh of Arles the sovereignty of Italy. Such was the situation of things when, at the solicitation of most of the Italian cities, and even of the pope himself, Otho the Great was called to the aid of this unfortunate country. He entered Italy, overcame the duke of Friuli, and was consecrated by the pope emperor of the Romans, with the titles of Cæsar and Augustus, his Holiness himself taking the oath of allegiance to him. Otho hereupon confirmed the donations made to the holy see by Pepin, Charlemagne, and Lewis the Débonnaire. John XII. was not long faithful to his engagement of alliance. He entered into a confederacy with the duke of Friuli, invited his son to Rome, and solicited the Hungarians to invade Germany. Otho hastened back to Rome, which he had but recently quitted, called a council, and brought the pope to trial. John was deposed, and Otho again left Rome; but hardly had he taken his departure when John had the address to excite an insurrection of the people, who dethroned his rival Leo VIII., and reinstated him in the pontifical chair. But John did not live to enjoy his triumph: three days after his reinstatement he met the reward of his crimes, and perished by the hand of an indignant husband, who detected him in the arms of his wife. These dissensions again recalled Otho to Rome, where he took an exemplary vengeance on his enemies by hanging half the senate. Such was the state of Rome under Otho the Great; and it continued with little variation under Otho II. and III., under Henry II., and Conrad, surnamed the Salic. Amid these contentions of parties it became a usual practice to adjust the difference by setting the popedom up to public sale, and disposing of it to the highest bidder, and bishoprics and inferior benefices were filled in the same manner. Benedict VIII. and John XIX., two brothers, publicly bought the popedom one after another, and on the death of the latter it was purchased in a similar manner for a child of ten years of age, Benedict IX. The emperor, Henry III., who was a prince of abilities and authority, resumed to himself the right of filling the pontifical chair, and nominated successively three popes without any opposition on the part of the church or people of Rome.

CHAPTER V.

HISTORY OF BRITAIN — Earliest State — Landing of Julius Cæsar—Conquest by the Romans—Abandonment of Britain on the Gothic Invasion of Italy—Irruptions of the Picts and Caledonians—Saxon Invasion—Heptarchy—Union under Egbert—Danish Invasions—Alfred the Great—His Institutions—His Successors—Norman Conquest.

THE history of the British Isles has hitherto been postponed, till we should be enabled to consider it in one connected view, from its rudest stage to the end of the Anglo-Saxon government, and the conquest of England by the Normans, which properly constitutes the first period of British history.

The origin of the population of kingdoms is always uncertain. Arguments derived either from a similarity of manners among ancient nations, or from the etymology of local names, and designations of provinces and their inhabitants, are extremely fallacious and inconclusive. Nations the most unconnected, when examined in the same state of society, or at the same period of their progress from barbarism to civilization, will always exhibit a similarity of manners; which, therefore, can never be considered as a proof of their relation to each other: and there is no opinion of the origin of nations, however whimsical or ridiculous, that may not find its support from the versatile and pliable etymology of words. Such speculations fall not within the province of the general historian.

All ancient writers agree in representing the first inhabitants of Britain as a tribe of Gauls; the Romans found among them the same monarchical government, the same religion and language, as among the Celtæ on the continent. They were divided into many small nations or tribes, unconnected with and independent of each other. Tacitus mentions a spirit of independence to have prevailed even among the individuals of each state or nation, which, while it excited frequent factions, prevented the chief or prince from ever attaining the absolute authority of a despot. Their religion was that of the Druids; the uncertainty regarding whose particular tenets is universally acknowledged. It is, however, generally agreed that they taught the belief of one God, Creator of the universe; of the limited duration of the world, and its destruction by fire; of the immortality of the human soul, and its transmigration through different bodies, in which the just and the wicked met with a retribution for their conduct in the present state: but on these doctrines, as general principles, tney seem to have reared an immense superstructure of fable. Their worship was polluted by the horrid practice of human sacrifice; and the chief office of their priests was to divine future events from the flowing of the blood of the victim, or the posture in which he fell after receiving the fatal blow. The influence of this religion was so great as to extend over every department of the government of the Britons. The Druids were not only the priests, but the judges, civil and criminal; and the bondage in which they held the minds of the people was so strict as to supply the place of laws. The Romans, after the conquest of Gaul, found it impossible to reconcile to their laws and institutions the nations whom they had subdued, while this religion subsisted, and in this instance were obliged to depart from their usual principles of toleration. They abolished the religion of the Druids by the severest penal enactments.*

In this situation were the inhabitants of Britain when Julius Cæsar, after having overcome the Gauls, began to look to the conquest of this island. The natives, conscious of their inability long to resist the Roman arms, endeavored, before his arrival, to appease him by submissions, which had no effect in altering his purpose. He landed, as is supposed, near to Deal; and, contrary to his expectation, found himself opposed, not by a tumultuous troop of barbarians, but by a regular and well-disciplined army, who attacked him with the most determined courage. Though repulsed, they persevered in repeated attacks on the legions, and, availing themselves of all their local advantages, spun out the campaign till the approach of winter, with very little loss to themselves. Cæsar was soon equally disposed as they to an accommodation; and after some weeks spent in ineffectual operations, he reëmbarked his troops, determined to return with a much greater force. In his second invasion, he brought with him five legions, making at least 20,000 foot, a competent body of horse, and a fleet of 800 sail.

To resist so formidable an army, the Britons, hitherto disunited

---

* A most elaborate account of the history, manners, learning, and religion of the Druids, is to be found in Henry's History of Britain, b. i., ch. 4.

under their different princes, entered into a confederacy, appointing Cassibellanus, king of the Trinobantes,* their commander-in-chief. They now made a most desperate resistance, and showed all the ability of practised warriors. The contest, however, was in vain; Cæsar gained several advantages; he penetrated into the country, burned the capital of Cassibellanus, the present St. Alban's, or Verulamium; deposed that prince, and established his own ally, Mandubratius, upon the throne; and, finally, after compelling the country to articles of submission, he returned again into Gaul.

Britain was for some time rescued from the yoke of the Romans by the civil wars in Italy, which gave sufficient employment at home; and, after the fall of the commonwealth, the first emperors were satisfied with the conquests they had obtained over the liberties of their country: so that the Britons for near a century enjoyed their freedom unmolested.† But in the reign of Claudius the conquest of Britain was seriously determined. Claudius, after paving the way by Plautius, one of his generals, arrived himself in the island, and received the submission of the southeast provinces. The rest, under Caractacus, or Caratach, made an obstinate resistance; but were at length subdued by Ostorius Scapula; and Caractacus, as has been already noticed, was defeated, and sent prisoner to Rome; where his magnanimous behavior procured him a very respectful treatment.‡

Yet the island was not subdued. Suetonius Paulinus, under the emperor Nero, was invested with the chief command. He directed his first attempts against the island of Mona, now Anglesey, upon the coast of Wales, which was the centre of the Druidical superstition; and expelling the Britons from the island, who made a most frantic resistance, he burned many of the Druids, and destroyed their consecrated groves and altars. Having thus triumphed over the religion of the Britons, he thought his future progress would be easy; but he was disappointed in his expectations. The Britons, more exasperated than intimidated, were all in arms, and headed by Boadicea, queen of the Iceni, had attacked several of the Roman settlements. Suetonius hastened to the protection of London. The Britons, however, reduced it to ashes, massacred the inhabitants that remained in it, putting to death 70,000 of the Romans and their allies. Suetonius revenged these losses by a decisive victory, in which 80,000 Britons fell in the field. Boadicea, to escape slavery, or

* The country of the Trinobantes comprehended Middlesex and Essex.—Camden.

† The Britons conciliated the favor of Augustus by sending ambassadors to Rome, from time to time, with presents. These consisted of works in *ivory* (query, whence the material?) bridles, chains, amber, and glass-vessels.—Strabo, lib. iv.

‡ For a brief narrative of the Roman transactions in Britain prior to the time of Agricola, see Tacitus, vit. Agr., cap. xiii. &c.

an ignominious death, put an end to her own life by poison. Still this success was not attended with the reduction of the island, which was not accomplished till Julius Agricola received the command, and formed a regular plan for the subjugation of Britain. He secured every advantage which he obtained by proper garrisons; and, pushing northward beyond the centre of the island, he fixed a chain of forts between the Friths of Clyde and Forth, which secured the Roman provinces from the incursions of the barbarous inhabitants from the north. He cultivated very successfully, likewise, the arts of peace; and, by degrees, reconciled the southern Britons to the laws and government ot the Romans. The Caledonians still defended their barren mountains, which, happily for them, the Romans did not think worth much pains to subdue. Adrian visited Britain, and built a new rampart between the Tyne and the Frith of Solway. The Roman province was consequently, at this time, somewhat retrenched in its limits. It was afterwards extended by the conquests of Antoninus Pius, and Severus, who carried his arms very far into the north. The details of these expeditions, however important to a Briton, exceed the circumscription of general history.*

By the decline and fall of the Roman empire, Britain again recovered her liberty. The legions which defended the island were carried over to the protection of Italy and Gaul against the Gothic invaders. The southern Britons did not regain peace by this change, for they were invaded by the Picts and Caledonians, and so degraded and abased was the national spirit by its subjection to the Roman yoke, that the Britons solicited the protection of Rome against their unconquered neighbors. A trifling assistance was all that the state of the empire could afford. The Romans, as a last good office, assisted them in rebuilding the wall erected by Severus, and counselling them to arm manfully in their own defence, they bade a final adieu to Britain about the year 448, after having been masters of a considerable part of the island for nearly four centuries.

The legions had been entirely withdrawn about forty years before this period; and, under the reign of Honorius, Britain was considered an independent country. From that period till the descent of the Saxons in 449, the state of the country, and the nature of the government, can only be matter of conjecture.†

The character of the southern inhabitants of the island appears at this period to have been extremely despicable; they could not avail themselves of the liberty they had gained by the

* The reader will find this first period of British history fully and ably illustrated by Camden, "Romans in Britain;" and Chalmers in his Caledonia, b. i., the Roman Period.

† See a fine visionary picture of it (acknowledged to be such by the historian himself) in Gibbon, c. xxxi Decl. and Fall of Rom. Emp.

departure of the Romans. The Picts and Caledonians considered the southern Britons as a people fitted for slavery. They broke down from their mountains with unresisted fury, and carried havoc and devastation along with them. The Britons, instead of vindicating their rights by a magnanimous opposition, again renewed their abject solicitations to the Romans; but the Goths had given to them too much employment at home to permit their sending aid to a distant and useless province. In this extremity, numbers of the Britons fled across the sea into Gaul, and settled in the province of *Armorica*, which from that time became known by the name of Brittany. It was happy for those who remained, that their enemies, the Picts and Caledonians, had too much of the predatory disposition to think of making complete conquests, or securing what they had won. They were satisfied with ravaging a part of the country, and retired again to their mountains. The Britons, in this interval of peace, behaved as if secure of its continuance. They made no preparations for resisting an enemy, whom they might easily have foreseen they would often have to cope with. A new irruption of the Picts and Caledonians totally disheartened them; and, to complete their shame, they sent a deputation into Germany, to invite the Saxons to come to their assistance and protection.

The Saxons were at this time regarded as one of the most warlike tribes of the ancient Germans. They occupied the sea-coast from the mouth of the Rhine to Jutland; and had made themselves known to the Britons by piratical expeditions on their coasts. They received this embassy with great satisfaction, and under the command of two brothers, Hengist and Horsa, they landed in the year 450 on the island of Thanet, and immediately marched to the defence of the Britons. The Scots and Picts, unable to resist the valor of these foreigners, were defeated and compelled to retire to the north. The Saxons, as might have been expected, next turned their thoughts to the entire reduction of the Britons. After various and alternate changes of success, the Saxons, having brought over large reinforcements of their countrymen, finally accomplished the reduction of South Britain. Different parts of the country having been subdued by different leaders, who were each ambitious of independence and absolute authority, the country, even after its final reduction, which was not till above a century and a half* after the first landing of the Saxons, exhibited a broken and divided appearance. Seven distinct provinces were formed into independent kingdoms!

The history of the SAXON HEPTARCHY is extremely obscure. The duration of the several kingdoms till their union under Eg-

---

*It is in this period that is placed the reign of king Arthur, prince of the Silures, who achieved many victories over the Saxons, and having signally routed them in the battle of Badenhill, fought A. D. 520, secured the tranquillity of his people for above forty years.

bert is almost all that can be noted with any approach to historical certainty.

The kingdom of Kent began in the year 455, under Escus the son of Hengist, and during the reigns of seventeen princes lasted till the year 827, when it was subdued by the West Saxons. Under Ethelbert, one of the Kentish kings, the Saxons were converted to Christianity. Pope Gregory the Great sent over into Britain the monk Augustine, with forty associates, who very effectually propagated the doctrines of Christianity by their eloquence and the exemplary purity of their morals.

The second kingdom of the Heptarchy is that of Northumberland, which began in the year 547, and lasted, under twenty-three princes, till the year 926. The third was that of East Anglia, which began A. D. 575, and in which, before its union in 928, there reigned fifteen successive princes. The fourth, Mercia, the largest and most powerful of the Heptarchy, comprehended all the middle counties of England. It subsisted from the year 582 to the year 827. The fifth kingdom of the Heptarchy was that of Essex, of which, before its union, there were fourteen princes. Of Sussex, which was the sixth kingdom of the Heptarchy, there were only five princes before it was finally reduced. The seventh, which ultimately subdued and united the whole kingdoms of the Heptarchy, was that of Wessex, or the West Saxons. It began in the year 519, and had not subsisted above eighty years, when one of its princes conquered the kingdom of Sussex and annexed it to his dominions.

In the kingdoms of the Heptarchy there was no exact rule or order of succession; and the reigning chief, considering all the princes of his family as his rivals, was seldom at ease till he had secured himself by putting them to death; hence, and from another cause, which was the passion for a monastic life, the royal families were entirely extinguished in all the kingdoms of the Heptarchy, and Egbert, prince of the West Saxons, remained at last the sole surviving descendant of the Saxon conquerors who subdued Britain. These were favorable circumstances for the ambition of Egbert, and naturally incited him to attempt the conquest of the whole Heptarchy. The Mercians were at that time the greatest and most powerful of these petty kingdoms, and held Kent and East Anglia as tributary states. Some intestine differences facilitated the conquest, and Egbert, after several desperate engagements, reduced them entirely under his authority. Essex was subdued with equal facility. Sussex, we have before remarked, had been very early added to the dominion of the West Saxons. The East Angles submitted of themselves, and craved the protection of the victorious Egbert; and the Northumbrians soon after followed their example.

Thus the whole kingdoms of the Saxon Heptarchy were united into one great state, nearly 400 years after the arrival of the

Saxons in Britain, by the victorious arms and judicious policy of Egbert. This great event, which is properly the foundation of the kingdom of England, took place in the year 827.

England, thus united, was soothing herself with the prospect of peace and tranquillity, which during the contentions of the Heptarchy she had never enjoyed; but this happiness was yet at a distance. The Normans, whose devastations had rendered them formidable to the continental kingdoms, now began to show themselves on the coast of England, where they were known by the name of Danes. Their first landing had taken place in the year 787, in the kingdom of Wessex. From that time, for several centuries, England was never free from the ravages of these barbarians; whose invasions became from time to time more formidable, according as resistance exasperated them, or the hopes of plunder allured fresh bands of their countrymen to join in their expeditions.

Under Alfred, the grandson of Egbert, England, from this source alone, was reduced to the lowest extremity. This prince, whose singular endowments of mind were united to great heroism and courage, had for some years, with various success, made the most vigorous efforts to free his country from the scourge of the Danes. In one year he engaged them in eight battles; and while he flattered himself that he had reduced them to extremity, a new torrent poured in upon the coast, which obliged him to offer proposals of peace. These, though agreed to by the Danes, were not fulfilled; they still continued their depredations, and the Saxons were reduced to such despair, that many left their country, fled into the mountains of Wales, or escaped beyond sea. Alfred himself was obliged to relinquish his crown. He concealed himself in the habit of a peasant, and lived for some time in the house of a neatherd. Collecting afterwards a few followers, he betook himself to a small retreat in Somersetshire, surrounded by forests and morasses; where he lay concealed for the space of a year, till the news of a prosperous event called him again into the field.

A chief of Devonshire, a man of great spirit and valor, had, with a handful of his followers, routed a large party of Danes, and taken a consecrated or enchanted standard, in which they reposed the utmost confidence. Alfred, observing this symptom of reviving spirit in his subjects, left his retreat; but before having recourse to arms, he resolved to inspect himself the situation of the enemy. Assuming the disguise of a harper, he passed without suspicion into the Danish camp, where his music and drollery obtained him so favorable a reception that he was kept there for several days, and even lodged in the tent of their prince. Here, having remarked their careless security, their contempt of the English, and their own real weakness, he immediately, by private emissaries, summoned a rendezvous of the bravest of the Saxon nobles, inviting them to appear at Bricton, on the borders of Selwood forest, attended by all their followers. Thither they accordingly resorted in very great numbers. The English beheld with rapture their beloved monarch, whom, from his long absence, they had accounted dead. They were impatient to march under his banner, and Alfred led them immediately to the attack. Their enemies, the Danes, surprised at the sight of a foe whom they looked upon as entirely subdued, made a very feeble resistance, and were put to flight with great slaughter. The English might have entirely cut them to pieces; but the generosity of Alfred inclined him rather to spare and incorporate them with his subjects. He allowed them to settle in the provinces of East Anglia and Northumberland, which the late ravages had almost depopulated, and the Danes, embracing the Christian religion, were united with the English. The more turbulent of them found opportunity to escape beyond the sea, where, under the command of Hastings, a notorious plunderer, they prepared themselves for fresh depredations.

Alfred employed this interval of tranquillity in restoring order to the state: in establishing civil and military institutions, and chiefly in equipping a respectable fleet, which had been hitherto totally neglected by the English. These precautions were extremely necessary, for the Danes attempted more than once a new invasion, and committed the most destructive ravages. At length, after a very complete defeat, and a most exemplary severity, which Alfred now found it necessary to adopt with those whom he took prisoners, these northern pirates suspended for several years their predatory visits to Britain.

England now enjoyed full tranquillity under this excellent prince; and Alfred saw his kingdom in the possession of every happiness which could flow from the salutary laws and institutions which he had established; when he died in the vigor of his age, after a glorious reign of nearly thirty years.

Alfred, whether we view him in his public or private character, deserves to be esteemed one of the best and greatest of princes. He united the most enterprising and heroic spirit with the greatest prudence and moderation; the utmost vigor of authority with perfect affability and a most winning deportment; the most exemplary justice with the greatest lenity. His civil talents were in every respect equal to his military virtues. He found the kingdom in the most miserable condition to which anarchy, domestic barbarism, and foreign hostility could reduce it: by the valor of his arms, and by his abilities as a politician and lawgiver, he brought it to a pitch of eminence and glory, which, till then, England had never attained. The outlines of his admirable plan of political economy merit particular attention, as being, in fact, the foundation of the venerable system of the British Constitution.

Alfred divided all England into counties; these he subdivided into hundreds; and the hundreds again into tithings. Ten neighboring householders formed a tithing, a fribourg, or decennary, over which one man was appointed to preside, called a tithingman or borgholder.* Every householder was answerable for the conduct of his family, and the borgholder for the conduct of all within his district. Every man was punished as an outlaw who did not register himself in some tithing; and none could change their habitation without a warrant from the tithingman or borgholder. When any person was accused of a crime, the borgholder was summoned to answer for him; if he declined to become his security, the criminal was committed to prison till trial. If he escaped before trial, the borgholder was subjected to a penalty.

The borgholder, in deciding disputes or small lawsuits, summoned his whole decennary or tithing to assist him. In matters of greater importance, in appeals from the decennary, or in controversies arising between members of different decennaries, the cause was brought before the hundred, which consisted of ten decennaries, or one hundred families of freemen; and which was regularly assembled every four weeks for the deciding of causes. Their method of deciding deserves particularly to be noticed as being the origin of juries, that inestimable privilege of Britons. Twelve freeholders were chosen, who, having sworn, together with the presiding magistrate of the hundred, to administer impartial justice, proceeded to the determination of the cause. Besides those monthly meetings of the hundred, there was an annual meeting appointed for the regulation of the police of the district, and for the correction of abuses in magistrates. The people, like their ancestors, the ancient Germans, assembled in arms, whence the hundred was sometimes called a *wapentake;* and these meetings thus served both for the support of military discipline, and for the administration of justice.

Superior to the court of the hundred was the County Court, which met twice a year, after Michaelmas and Easter, and consisted of all the freeholders of the county. The bishop and aldermen presided in this court, and their business was to receive appeals from the hundreds and decennaries, and decide disputes between the inhabitants of different hundreds. The alderman formerly possessed both the civil and military authority; but Alfred, judging properly that this gave too much power to the nobility, appointed a sheriff in each county, who enjoyed a like authority with the alderman in his judicial powers. His office

---

* Borgh, in the Saxon language, according to Spelman, signifies a pledge or security. In these small communities or neighborhoods, every man was security for the conduct of his neighbor, and hence the origin of the word *neighbor*, quasi Nigh Borgh, or near pledge. Jamieson assigns a different etymology, viz , *Nahgibür*, Germ. from *nach*, near, and *gibur*, inhabitant.—Etymol. Dict. voce *Nichbour*

was likewise to guard the rights of the crown, and to levy the fines imposed, which at that time formed a very considerable part of the public revenue.

An appeal lay from all these courts to the king himself, in council; and Alfred, in whom his subjects deservedly placed the highest confidence, was overwhelmed with appeals from all parts of the kingdom. The only remedy for this was to reform the ignorance and restrain the corruption of the inferior magistrates, from whence it arose. Alfred, therefore, was solicitous to appoint the ablest and the most upright of his nobility to exercise the office of sheriffs and earls. He punished many for malversation, and he took care to enforce the study of letters, and particularly of the laws, as indispensable to their continuing in office.

Alfred likewise framed a body of laws, which, though now lost, is generally supposed to be the origin of what is termed the common law of England. The institutions of this prince will bring to mind many of the political regulations of Charlemagne, which have been described at some length, and to which those of The Great Alfred bear a very near resemblance.

This excellent prince wisely considered the cultivation of letters as the most effectual means of thoroughly eradicating barbarous dispositions. The ravages of the Danes had totally extinguished any small sparks of learning, by the dispersion of the monks, and the burning their monasteries and libraries. To repair these misfortunes, Alfred, like Charlemagne, invited learned men from all quarters of Europe to reside in his dominions. He established schools, and enjoined every freeholder possessed of two ploughs to send his children there for instruction. He is said to have founded, or, at least, to have liberally endowed the illustrious seminary afterwards known as the University of Oxford.

His own example was the most effectual encouragement to the promotion of a literary spirit. Alfred was himself, for that age, a most accomplished scholar, and considering the necessary toils and constant active employment, it is surprising how much he employed himself in the pursuits of literature. He is said to have divided his time into three equal parts:—one was allotted to the despatch of the business of government; another to diet, exercise, and sleep; and a third to study and devotion.* By this admirable regularity of life, he found means, notwithstanding his constant wars, and the care of entirely new modelling and civilizing his kingdom, to compose a variety of ingenious and learned works. He wrote many beautiful apologues and stories in poetry of a moral tendency. He translated the histories of Bede and Orozius, with the treatise of Boethius, De Consolatione Philosophiæ

* Leland, in his Collectan. (cura Hearne, tom. i., 259,) mentions his manner of reckoning time by a candle marked with twenty-four divisions, which always burnt in his study.

Alfred, in short, in every view of his character, must be regarded as one of the wisest and best of men that ever occupied the throne of any nation.*

The most complete system of policy which human wisdom can devise must be ineffectual under weak governors and magistrates. The admirable institutions of Alfred were but partially and feebly enforced under his successors; and England, still a prey to the ravages of the Danes, and to intestine disorders, relapsed again into confusion and barbarism.

Edward, the son and successor of Alfred, whose military talents bore some resemblance to those of his father, had no share of his political genius. He fought his battles with intrepidity; but unable to take advantage of circumstances, or to secure the order and force of government by a well-regulated administration, his reign was one continued scene of war and tumult, as were those of his successors, Athelstan, Edmund, and Edred. In the reign of the latter prince, the priesthood began first to extend its influence over the minds of the English monarchs, and to concern itself no less in temporal affairs than in spiritual. Dunstan, a fanatical bigot, but sufficiently awake to his own interest and that of the church, ruled every thing under Edred, and under his successors Edwy, Edgar, and Edward the Martyr.

Under Ethelred, the successor of Edward, a youth of despicable talents, the Danes began seriously to project the conquest of England. Conducted by Sweyn, king of Denmark, and Olaus, king of Norway, they made a formidable descent upon the island, and, after various successes, compelled the dastardly Ethelred repeatedly to purchase a peace, which they as constantly violated. Ethelred indeed furnished them with strong causes. In the spirit of the weakest and most treacherous policy, he attempted to cut off, by a general massacre, all the Danes that had established themselves in the island. This produced, as might have been anticipated, the redoubled vengeance of their countrymen. At length the English nobility, ashamed of their prince, and seeing no other relief to the kingdom from its miseries, swore allegiance to Sweyn the Danish monarch; and Ethelred fled into Normandy, where he found protection from Richard, the grandson of the great Rollo, who, as we have already seen, first established his northern followers in that part of France.

Ethelred, upon the death of Sweyn, who did not long enjoy his new dominions, endeavored to regain his kingdom; but he found in Canute, the son of Sweyn, a prince determined to make good his father's rights. The inglorious Ethelred died soon after, and left his empty title to his son Edmund, surnamed *Ironside;* who possessed indeed courage and ability to have preserved his

---

*The character of Alfred is admirably described by Carte—Hist. of Eng., vol i., b. 4., § 18.

country from sinking into such calamities, but wanted talents to raise it from that abyss into which it had already fallen. After several desperate but unsuccessful engagements, he was compelled by his nobility, who urged it as the only means of saving the kingdom, to come to an accommodation with Canute, and to divide the dominions of England by treaty. The Danish prince got Mercia, East Anglia, and Northumberland; and the southern provinces were left to Edmund. But this prince survived the treaty only a few months. He was murdered at Oxford, by a conspiracy of the Danes, who thus made way for the succession of their monarch Canute to the throne of all England.

Edmund Ironside had left two sons, Edwin and Edward; the first measure of Canute was to seize these two princes, whom he sent abroad, to his ally the king of Sweden, with request that, as soon as they arrived at his court, they might be put to death. Humanity induced the Swedish monarch to spare their lives; he sent them into Hungary, where Solyman, the Hungarian king, gave his sister in marriage to Edwin the elder prince, and his sister in-law to Edward. Of this last marriage were born two children, Edgar Atheling, and Margaret, afterwards spouse to Malcolm Canmore, king of Scotland.

Canute, from the extent of his dominions, was one of the greatest monarchs of the age. He was sovereign of Denmark, Norway, and England. His character, as king of England, was not uniform. He was, in the first years of his reign, detested by his subjects, whom he loaded with the heaviest taxes, and exasperated by numberless acts of violence and oppression. In his latter years, his administration was mild and equitable, and he courted, in a particular manner, the favor of the church by munificent donations and endowments of monasteries.* He sustained the glory of his kingdom by compelling Malcolm Canmore to do homage for his possession of Cumberland, which that high-spirited prince had refused to submit to.

Canute left three sons:—the eldest, Sweyn, was crowned king of Norway; the youngest, Hardiknute, was in possession of Denmark, and claimed right to England, in virtue of a prior destination of his father, who afterwards altered his will, and left that kingdom to his immediate elder brother, Harold. A civil war would have ensued between these princes had not the English nobility interfered, and prompted a division of the kingdom. Harold, it was agreed, should have all the provinces north of the Thames, while Hardiknute should possess all to the south.† Emma, widow of

* "In the latter part of his life, to atone for his many acts of violence, he built churches, endowed monasteries, and imported relics; and had, indeed, a much better title to saintship than many of those who adorn the Roman calendar. He commissioned an agent at Rome to purchase St. Augustin's arm for one hundred talents of silver, a much greater sum than the finest statue of antiquity would then have sold for."—Grainger's Biog. Hist., Class i.

† Carte, Hist. of Eng., vol. i., b. iv., § 31.

Canute, and mother of Hardiknute, had two sons by her former marriage with Ethelred. These princes, Edward and Alfred, had been brought up in Normandy, where their uncle, Robert, duke of Normandy, protected them against the resentment and jealousy of Canute. Harold wished to prosecute his father's purpose of extinguishing the Saxon blood in the posterity of Ethelred. Alfred, one of the princes, was invited to London, with many professions of regard. But Harold had given orders to surprise and murder his attendants, and the prince was led prisoner to a monastery, where he soon after died. Edward, hearing of his brother's fate, fled back into Normandy. Harold did not long enjoy the fruits of his crime, for he died in the fourth year of his reign; and Hardiknute, king of Denmark, betaking himself to England, was acknowledged sovereign of the whole kingdom without opposition. After a violent administration of two years he died, to the great comfort of his subjects, who now seized the opportunity of entirely shaking off the Danish yoke. The posterity of Edmund Ironside, Edgar Atheling and his sister Margaret, were the true heirs of the Saxon family; but their absence in Hungary appeared to the English a sufficient reason for giving a preference to Edward, the son of Ethelred, who was fortunately in the kingdom, and the Danes made no attempt to resist the voice of the nation.

Edward, surnamed the Confessor, mounted the throne with the affections of his subjects. He was a mild, but a weak and pusillanimous prince. From his education in Normandy he had contracted a strong relish for the manners of that people, many of whom attended him into England, and were his particular favorites. His reign was embroiled by the turbulent and factious spirit of Godwin, earl of Wessex, and governor of Kent and Sussex. This nobleman, grounding his hopes upon his extensive authority and wealth, and the imbecility of his sovereign, very early conceived a plan for subverting the government, and assuming absolute power. He attempted an open rebellion in the kingdom, which Edward found no other means of quelling than by coming to an accommodation with the traitor. Godwin died in the interim, and his son Harold, an enterprising youth, while he affected a modest and complying disposition to his sovereign, concealed the same ambitious views. He secured the affections of the nobility, united them to his interests, and succeeding to the immense possessions of his father, he was soon in a condition to make his pretensions formidable to Edward. This prince, then in the decline of life, would willingly have settled his dominions on his nephew, Edgar Atheling, the only remaining branch of the Saxon line, but the imbecility of this young man, he foresaw, would never make good his right against the pretensions of one so popular as Harold, whose views clearly aimed at sovereign power. It appeared to Edward more advisable to nominate for his successor William, duke of Normandy, a prince whose power reputation, and great abilities, were sufficient to support any destination which he might make in his favor.*

This celebrated prince was the natural son of Robert, duke of Normandy, by the daughter of a furrier of Falaise. Illegitimacy, in those days, was accounted no stain, and his father left him, while yet a minor, heir to his whole dominions. He had to struggle with an arrogant nobility, several of whom even advanced claims to his crown; but he very early showed a genius capable of asserting and vindicating his rights, and soon became the terror both of his rebellious subjects and of foreign invaders. He reduced his patrimonial dominions to the most implicit obedience: and through the whole of his life he seems to have regarded it as a fixed maxim, that inflexible rigor of conduct was the first duty and the wisest policy of a sovereign.

William paid a visit to England; and Edward, receiving him with all the regard due to the relationship that subsisted between them, and to the character of so celebrated a prince, gave him to understand that he intended him for his successor. His return to Normandy, however, gave the ambitious Harold an opportunity for the prosecution of his schemes. He continued to extend his influence among the nobility, by the most insinuating address, and it is not improbable that the rigid severity of the character of William, to which the manners of Harold formed so strong a contrast, contributed to the success of his pretensions.

Edward died in the twenty-fifth year of his reign, and Harold had so well prepared matters, that he took possession of the throne with as little disturbance as if he had succeeded by the most undisputed title.

Thus ended the line of the Saxon monarchs in England. The duke of Normandy, on receiving intelligence of the accession of Harold, resolved to assert his claims in the most effectual manner. He used the formality of first summoning that prince to resign his possession of the kingdom; but his summons was answered by a spirited declaration from Harold, that he would defend his right with the last drop of his blood. The preparations made by William for an invasion of England occupied a considerable length of time, and were proportionally formidable. The fame of so great an enterprise, in an age of adventure, excited many of the nobility throughout the different kingdoms of Europe to repair with their followers to his standard. The counts of Anjou and Flanders encouraged their subjects to engage in the expedition, and even the court of France, though evidently contrary to its interest to contribute to the aggrandizement of so dangerous a vassal, increased the levies of William with many of the chief nobility of the kingdom. Harold Halfager, king of Norway, undertook to favor the expedition, by making a landing with a

* Carte, vol. i., b iv., § 39.

formidable army in one quarter, while William invaded the island in another. The emperor, Henry IV., of Germany engaged to protect the dominions of Normandy in the absence of its prince; and the pope, Alexander II., gave his sanction to the enterprise, by pronouncing Harold an usurper, and directing a sentence of excommunication against all who should adhere to his interest.

William had now assembled an army of 60,000 men, of whom 50,000 were cavalry; and a fleet amounting, it is said, to 3000 vessels great and small. The attack was begun by the Norwegian army under Halfager, who entered the Humber with 300 sail. The Norwegians, in the first engagement, defeated and put to flight an English army under Morcar, earl of Northumberland, and Edwin, earl of Mercia, the brothers-in-law of Harold, who, in the meantime, collecting a formidable force, revenged this loss by the total rout and dispersion of the army of Halfager. This victory, though honorable to Harold, was the immediate cause of his ruin; he lost many of his bravest officers in the action, and disgusted the rest by refusing to distribute the Norwegian spoils among them.

William the Norman had, in the meantime, landed at Pevensey on the coast of Sussex. The best politicians of the court of Harold endeavored to dissuade that prince from hazarding an immediate action. It would have been unquestionably his wisest plan to have waited the relaxation of the first ardor of the Normans; to have harassed them by skirmishes, and cut off their provisions, which, in the end, must, in all probability, have given the English a complete victory. But the ardor of Harold could not brook delay; he hastened with impetuosity to a general engagement, on which depended the fate of his kingdom; and in the memorable battle of Hastings, which was fought (October 14, 1066) on both sides with desperate courage from the morning till the setting of the sun, the death of Harold, and the total discomfiture of his army, after some ineffectual struggles of further resistance, placed William, duke of Normandy, in possession of the throne of England.

CHAPTER VI.

On the Government, Laws, and Manners of the Anglo-Saxons.

THE period of British history to which we are now arrived may be properly concluded by some reflections on the government and manners of the Anglo-Saxons, as there are several particulars in the structure of that government, and in the policy of this ancient people, which are supposed to have had their influence on the British constitution, such as we find it at present, and are topics from which speculative men and political writers have not unfrequently drawn conclusions applicable to our own times, and the present system of government.

The Saxons, who enjoyed the same liberty with all the ancient Germans, retained that political freedom in their new settlements to which they had been accustomed in their own country. Their kings, who were no more than the *chiefs* of a clan or tribe, possessed no greater authority than what is commonly annexed to that character in all barbarous nations. The chief, or king, was the first among the citizens, but his authority depended more on his personal abilities than on his rank. "He was even so far considered as on a level with the people, that a stated price was fixed on his head, and a legal fine was levied on his murderer; which, although proportioned to his station, and superior to that paid for the life of a subject, was a sensible mark of his subordination to the community." *

A people, in this period of society, it is not to be imagined would be very strict in maintaining a regular succession of their princes. Although the family of the prince had its respect and acknowledged superiority, there was no rule steadily observed with regard to succession to the throne, which was generally regulated by present convenience, always paying the first attention to the progeny of the last monarch, if any of them was of age and capacity for government. In the case of minors, the succession generally took a collateral turn: an uncle was promoted to the government, and having children himself, the sceptre, at his demise, often went to his descendants, to the exclusion of the elder line. All these changes, however, required the concurrence, or,

* Hume, Appendix I, of which the following account of the Anglo-Saxon government is an abridgment.

at least, the tacit acquiescence of the people. Thus the monarchies were not, strictly speaking, either *elective* or *hereditary;* and though, in some instances, the decree of a prince was followed in the choice of his successor, they can as little be regarded as properly testamentary. The suffrages of the states sometimes conferred the crown, but they more frequently recognised the person whom they found established, provided he was of the blood royal. Our knowledge of the *Anglo-Saxon* history and antiquities, though much the subject of research, disquisition, and controversy, is, after all, too imperfect to afford us means of determining, with any certainty, the prerogatives of the crown and privileges of the people, or of giving any accurate delineation of their government. This uncertainty must result, in a great measure, from their political system being actually various in the different kingdoms of the Heptarchy; and, likewise, from its undergoing changes and alterations during the course of six centuries, from the *Saxon invasion* to the *Norman conquest.*

One great feature, common to all the kingdoms of the *Heptarchy,* we know, was the *national* council, called the *Wittenagemot,* or assembly of the wise men, whose consent was requisite for enacting laws, and for ratifying the chief acts of public administration. The preambles to all the laws of the Saxon monarchs still remaining, leave no doubt as to the existence of this council; but who were its constituent members is a matter of considerable uncertainty. The *bishops* and *abbots* were unquestionably an essential part; and it is as certain that this supreme court regulated both ecclesiastical and civil matters. It likewise appears that the *aldermen,* or (what was a synonymous term) the *earls* and governors of counties, had a seat in this assembly; but the doubt is whether the commons had any place there, or who were those *wites,* or wise men, who are mentioned as discriminated from the prelates and from the nobility. This is a point which the factions of modern times have chosen to take up and dispute with as much acrimony as if it materially interested us under the present constitution to settle with precision what it was a thousand years ago. The monarchical party affirm that these *wites,* or wise men, were judges, or men learned in the laws. The advocates for the rights of the people hold them to have been the representatives of boroughs, or what we now call commons. Perhaps the truth lies between these opinions. As the idea of representation is too refined for a very rude system of government, the most rational opinion seems to be, that the *wites,* or *sapientes,* were such men of fortune, landholders, as fell neither under the denomination of clergy nor nobility, but whose weight and consequence was such as to entitle them, without any election, to compeer at the assembly of the states, and to assist in their deliberations. Whether there was any requisite extent of land, that was understood to bestow this qualification, is altogether uncertain.

One thing undoubted, with regard to the Anglo-Saxon government, is, that it was extremely aristocratical. The royal authority was very limited; the people as a body were of little weight or consideration. After the abolition of the Heptarchy, the noblemen, who resided at a distance in the provinces, where the inspection and influence of the king would but very improperly extend itself, must naturally have acquired almost the whole power and authority. The great offices, too, which they enjoyed, became, in a manner, hereditary in their families; and the command of the military force of the province, which it was necessary to give them from the continual danger of foreign invasion from the Danes, would naturally very much increase the power of the nobles. Another circumstance, productive of the same consequence, was the imperfection of the administration under a ferocious and military people, which contributed much to introduce that strong connection of clientship which we find subsisting in all nations in a similar state of society. Even the inhabitants of towns placed themselves under the protection of some particular nobleman, and feeling the ties of that connection more strongly than any other, were accustomed to look up to his patronage as that of a sovereign. The laws even favored these ideas. A client, though a freeman, was supposed so much to belong to his patron, that his murderer was obliged to pay a fine to the latter, as a compensation for his loss, in like manner as he paid a fine to the master for the murder of a slave. Many of the inferior rank of citizens entered into associations, and subscribed a bond, obliging themselves to be faithful to each other in all cases of danger to any one of the confederates; to protect his person, to revenge his wrongs, to pay the fines which he might incur through accident, and to contribute to his funeral charges. This last practice, as well as the connection of client and patron, are strong proof of the imperfection of laws, and of a weak administration. Only to remedy such evils would men have recurred to these connections and associations.

The Saxons were divided, as all the other German nations, into *three* ranks of men, the *noble*, the *free*, and the *slaves*. The nobles were called *thanes*, and these were of two kinds—the *king's thanes* and the *lesser thanes*. The latter seem to have been dependent on the former, and to have received lands, for which they either paid rent or military services. There were two laws of the Anglo-Saxons, which breathe a spirit very differ ent from what one would naturally expect from the character of the age, when the distinction of superior and inferior is commonly very strongly marked. One of the laws of Athelstan declared, that a merchant who had made three long sea voyages on his own account was entitled to the quality of thane; and another declared that a *ceorle*, or husbandman, who had been able to purchase five hides of land, or five plough-gates, and who had a chapel, a kitchen, a hall, and a bell, was entitled to the same rank. The freemen of the lower rank, who were denominated *ceorles*, cultivated the farms of the thanes for which they paid rent, and they appear to have been removable at the pleasure of the thane.

The lowest and most numerous of the orders was that of the slaves or *villains*; of these slaves there were two kinds, the household slaves, and those employed in the cultivation of the lands: of the latter species are the serfs, which we find at this day in Poland, in Russia, and in others of the northern states. A master had not, among the Anglo-Saxons, an unlimited power over his slaves. He was fined for the murder of a slave, and if he mutilated one, the slave recovered his liberty.

The laws of Edgar inform us that slavery was the lot of all prisoners taken in war. From the continual wars that subsisted, first between the Saxons and Britons, and afterwards between the several kingdoms of the Heptarchy, this class of men could not have failed to be numerous.

Though the Anglo-Saxon government seems, upon the whole, to have been extremely aristocratical, there were still some considerable remains of the ancient democracy of the Germans. The courts of the Decennary, the Hundred, and the County, were well calculated to defend general liberty, and to restrain the power of the nobility. In the country courts, or *shire-motes*, the freeholders were convened twice a year, and received appeals from the inferior courts. The cause was determined by a majority of voices; and the bishop and alderman, who sat as presidents, had no more to do, than to collect the suffrages and deliver their own opinion. An appeal lay from all the courts to the king, but this was not practised unless in matters of importance. The alderman received a third of the fines that were levied in these courts, and the remaining two-thirds went to the king, which formed no inconsiderable part of the crown's revenue. As writing was little practised in those ages, the most remarkable civil transactions were finished in presence of these courts, such as the promulgation of testaments, the manumission of slaves, and the concluding of all important bargains and contracts.

The punishments inflicted by the Anglo-Saxon courts of judicature, and the methods of proof employed in causes, were much the same as we have remarked among the other barbarous nations of northern origin. The pecuniary fines for every species of crime, and the modes of proof by the judgment of God, by the ordeal of fire or water, by single combat, or by producing a certain number of evidences, named *compurgators*, who swore that they believed the person spoke the truth;—all these we have observed to have been common to the Germanic nations, and to those of Scandinavian origin, except, as we have before remarked, the Visigoths and Ostrogoths.

As to the military force of the nation during the government of the Saxons, we know that the expense and burden of defending the state lay equally upon all the land; and it was usual for every five hides, or ploughs, to furnish one man for the service.* The ceorles, or husbandmen, were provided with arms, and obliged to take their turn in military duty. There were computed to be 243,600 hides in England: consequently the military force of the kingdom consisted of 48,720 men, though, upon extraordinary occasions, there is no doubt that a greater number might be assembled.

The king's revenue consisted partly in his *demesnes*—which were entensive—partly in the tolls and imposts on boroughs and seaports, and a share of the fines imposed by the courts of judicature. The *Dane-gelt*, which is often mentioned, was a land-tax imposed by the state, either for the payment of sums exacted by the Danes, or for the defence of the kingdom against them.

The law of succession among the Anglo-Saxons was, that the land was equally divided among all the male children of the deceased, which was called the custom of *Gavel-kind*. Lands were chiefly of two kinds, *Book land*—or what was held by charter or book, which was regarded complete property; or *Folk land*—what was held by tenants removable at the pleasure of the proprietors.

Upon the whole, the Anglo-Saxons seem to have been a rude, unlettered, uncivilized people, among whom laws, of themselves imperfect, had yet more imperfect and limited influence. Their national character merits little other praise than that of hardiness and courage, which too often degenerated into ferocity. They were unquestionably behind the *Normans* in every point of civilization, and the conquest was to them a real advantage, as it put them in a situation to receive slowly the seeds of cultivation, and some knowledge in the arts and sciences, of which, till then, they were almost totally ignorant.

---

* The hide of land has been generally supposed equal to two hundred acres; but, from the use of the word in Doomsday book, there is reason to believe that the hide was no certain measure of land, but as much land as, according to its quality, was supposed to be of a certain value. This value, there is room to think, was about twenty Norman shillings.

CHAPTER VII.

State of Europe during the Tenth, Eleventh, and Twelfth Centuries.

FRANCE, which, under the splendid dominion of Charlemagne, had revived the western empire of the Romans, and rivalled, in extent of territory and power, the proudest times of ancient Rome, had dwindled down, under the weak posterity of this prince, even to the point of sustaining a diminution of her proper territory. At the time of the elevation of Hugh Capet, the founder of the third race of her kings, France comprehended neither Normandy, Dauphiny, nor Provence. On the death of Lewis V., surnamed Fainéant, or the Idle, his uncle Charles, duke of Brabant and Hainault, if the rules of succession to the throne had been observed, or the posterity of Charlemagne respected, ought to have succeeded to the crown of France; but Hugh Capet, count of Paris and lord of Picardy and Champagne, the most powerful and the most ambitious of the French nobles, whose greatgrandfather Eudes, or Odo, and grandfather Robert the Strong, both sat on the throne of France, by usurping the right of Charles the Simple, availing himself of these pretensions, and assembling his forces, dispersed a parliament summoned for investing his rival, the duke of Brabant, with the ensigns of royalty and was elected sovereign of the kingdom by the voice of his brother peers. Charles of Brabant was betrayed by the bishop of Laon, and given up to Hugh Capet, who allowed him to die in prison.

Thus the posterity of Charlemagne being utterly extinct, Hugh Capet is the founder of the third, or Capetian race of monarchs, who, from the year 987 down to the present age, have swayed the sceptre of France for more than eight hundred years: an instance of uninterrupted succession in a royal family which is unexampled in the history of mankind. France, divided into parties, continued in a state of weakness and domestic misery during the reign of Hugh Capet and his successor Robert, whose reign affords no event worthy of record, unless a most audacious exertion of the authority of the pope over the sovereign of France. King Robert had married Bertha, his cousin in the fourth degree —a marriage which, though within the prohibitions of the Canon law, was, in every respect, a wise and politic connection, as it united the contending factions in the kingdom. Although in Catholic countries, even at this day, private persons can easily purchase a dispensation from the pope for such matches, the French king met with no such indulgence. Gregory V., in the most insolent manner, dared to impose on king Robert a penance of seven years, ordered him to quit his wife, and excommunicated him in case of refusal. The emperor Otho III., who was Robert's enemy, gave this decree sanction by his presence at the council where it was pronounced, which makes it probable that this shameful procedure had its origin more in political reasons than in a religious motive. Be that as it may, the effect of this sentence of excommunication was very serious to Robert; the unhappy prince was abandoned by all his courtiers, and even his domestics. Historians inform us, that two only of his servants remained with him, whose care was to throw into the fire what he left at his meals, from the horror they felt at what had been touched by an excommunicated person. This absurdity is scarcely credible, and ought perhaps to be ranked along with another circumstance, likewise recorded of this event — which is, that the queen, in punishment of this pretended incest, was brought to bed of a monster. Voltaire well remarks, that there was nothing monstrous in this whole affair, except the bold assurance of the pope, and the weakness of the king, who, to obey him, separated from his wife. The piety of king Robert's character was signalized by his laying the foundation of that superb structure, the church of Notre Dame at Paris, one of the noblest Gothic edifices in the world.*

The subserviency of this monarch to the domineering spirit of the popedom had its natural effect in exciting the holy fathers to further exercises of authority. Robert had been excommunicated for marrying his relation; and his grandson, Philip I., was excommunicated for divorcing a lady who was his relation, to make way for a mistress. Of all the superstitions of these times, it was not the least prejudicial to the welfare of states, that the marriage of relations, even to the seventh degree, was prohibited by the church. Henry, the father of Philip I. of France, to whom almost all the sovereigns of Europe were related, was obliged to seek a wife from the barbarous empire of Russia.

The prevailing passion of the times of which we now treat was a taste for pilgrimages and adventures. Some Normans, having been in Palestine about the year 983, passed at their return, by the sea of Naples, into the principality of Salerno, in Italy, which had been usurped by the lords of this small territory from

---

* The president Hénault informs us that this church was built on the foundation of an ancient temple of Jupiter. If this is true, it has been the peculiar lot of this edifice to have seen, in modern times, the revival of its ancient worship, and to have been dedicated once more, in the course of a mad revolution to the gods and goddesses of paganism.

the emperors of Constantinople. The Normans found the prince of Salerno besieged by the Mahometans, and relieved him by raising the siege. They were dismissed loaded with presents, which encouraged others of their countrymen to go in quest of similar adventures. A troop of Normans went, in the year 1016. to offer their services to Benedict VIII., against the Mahometans; others went to Apulia, to serve the duke of Capua; a third band armed first against the Greeks, and then against the popes, always selling their services to those that best paid for them. William, surnamed Fier-a-bras, or strong-arm, with his brothers Humphry, Robert, and Richard, defeated the army of pope Leo IX., besieged him in his castle at Benevento, and kept him there for a year a prisoner; and the court of Rome was obliged to yield to these Normans a very considerable portion of the patrimonies of the holy see. Pope Nicholas II. gave up the principality of Capua to Richard; and to Robert he gave Apulia, Calabria, and the investiture of Sicily, provided he could wrest it by his arms out of the hands of the Saracens, who were at that time in possession of most of the country. Robert, on his part, agreed to pay annual tribute, and to do homage to the pope. He immediately prepared to extirpate the Saracens from Sicily; and in the year 1101, Roger the Norman completed the conquest of the island, of which the popes have to the present age remained the lords paramount.

The state of the northern kingdoms of Europe was at this time extremely barbarous. Russia, like France, owed its conversion to Christianity to its queen or empress, who was the daughter of Basilius, the emperor of Constantinople, and married the czar of Tsaraslow, in the eighth century. The Swedes, after their first conversion, relapsed again into idolatry, and appear, during the eighth, ninth, tenth, and eleventh centuries, to have sunk into the most absolute barbarism. Poland, down to the thirteenth century, was in no better situation. The empire of Constantinople still existing, maintained a struggle against the Bulgarians in the west, and the Turks and Arabians on the east and north. In Italy, the nobility, or independent lords, possessed all the country from Rome to the Calabrian Sea; and most of the rest was in the hands of the Normans.

The dukes of Savoy, who are now the kings of Sardinia, began at this time to make a figure. They possessed, by inheritance, the country of Savoy and Maurienne, as a fief of the empire. The Swiss and the Grisons were under the government of viceroys, whom the emperor appointed. Venice and Genoa were rising gradually into consequence, from the wealth which they acquired by a pretty extensive Mediterranean commerce. The first doge of Venice, who was created in 709, was only a tribune of the people elected by the citizens. The families who gave their voices in this election are many of them still in existence, and are unquestionably the oldest nobility in Europe. The city of Venice, however, had not obtained its name for near two centuries after this period. The doges at first resided at Heraclea; they paid homage to the emperors, and sent annually, as a petty kind of tribute, a mantle of cloth of gold. But these marks of vassalage did not diminish their real power, for they acquired by conquest all the opposite side of Dalmatia, the province of Istria, with Spalatro, Ragusa, and Narenza; and about the middle of the tenth century the doge assumed the title of duke of Dalmatia; the republic increased in riches and in power; and, prosecuting trade with great spirit, they soon became the commercial agents of the European princes for all the produce and manufactures of the East.*

Spain was at this time chiefly possessed by the Moors. The Christians occupied about a fourth part of the country, and that the most barren of the whole. Their dominions were Asturia, the princes of which took the title of king of Leon; and part of Old Castile, which was governed by counts, as was Barcelona and a part of Catalonia. Navarre and Arragon had likewise a Christian sovereign. The Moors possessed the rest of the country, comprehending Portugal. Their capital, as we have before observed, was the city of Cordova, a most delightful residence, which they had adorned with every embellishment of art and magnificence. These Arabians were at this time, perhaps, the most refined and polished people in the world. Luxury and pleasure at length corrupted the princes of the Moors, and their dominions, in the tenth century, were split among a number of petty sovereigns. Had the Christians been more united than they, they might, perhaps, at this time have shaken off the Moorish yoke and regained the sovereignty of the whole kingdom; but they were divided among themselves, continually at war, and even formed alliances with the Moors against each other. Yet the Christian princes possessed, at this time, a very considerable proportion of the territory of Spain; and at a period when the feudal oppression was at its height, and the condition of the commonalty, through the greater part of Europe, was in the lowest stage of degradation, one of these small Christian kingdoms exhibited the example of a people who shared the sovereignty with the prince, and wisely limited his arbitrary government by constitutional restraints. This was the kingdom of Arragon, in which not only the representatives of the towns had a seat in the Cortes, or national assemblies, but an officer was elected by the people, termed a Justiza, who was the supreme interpreter of the law, and whose *recognised duty* it was to protect the rights of the people against the encroachments of the crown. This officer, whose person was sacred, was chosen from among the commoners;

* Voltaire sur les Mœurs, ch. xliii.

he had a right to judge whether the royal edicts were agreeable to law, before they could be carried into effect; and while the king's ministers were answerable to him for their conduct, he was responsible to the Cortes alone. This great officer had likewise the privilege of receiving, in the name of the people, the king's oath of coronation; and during this ceremony he held a naked sword, pointed at the breast of the sovereign, whom he thus addressed:—"We, your equals, constitute you our sovereign, and we solemnly engage to obey your mandates on condition that you protect us in the enjoyment of our rights: if otherwise, not." The kingdom of Arragon was, therefore, at this time a singular example of a limited monarchy, and of a people enjoying a high portion of civil liberty, at a time when the condition of the inferior ranks, in all the surrounding nations, was that of the severest servitude.

In the year 1035, one of these Christian princes, Ferdinand, the son of Sancho, king of Arragon and Navarre, united Old Castile with the kingdom of Leon, which he usurped by the murder of his brother-in-law. Castile henceforth gave name to a kingdom, of which Leon was only a province. In the reign of this Ferdinand lived Rodrigo, surnamed the Cid, the hero of the great tragedy of Corneille and of many of the noblest of the old Spanish romances and ballads. The most famous of his real exploits was the assisting Sancho, the eldest son of Ferdinand, to deprive his brothers and sisters of the inheritance left them by their father. There were at that time near twenty kings in Spain, Christians and Mahometans, besides a great many independent nobility--lords, who came in complete armor, with their attendants, to offer their services to the princes when at war. This custom was common at that time over all Europe, but more particularly among the Spaniards, who were a most romantic people; and in his age, Rodrigo of Bivar, or the Cid, distinguished himself above all other Christian knights. Many others, from his high reputation and prowess, ranged themselves under his banner, and with these having formed a considerable troop armed *cap-a-pie*, both man and horse, he subdued some of the Moorish princes, and established for himself a small sovereignty in the city of Alcasar. He undertook for his sovereign, Alphonso, king of Old Castile, to conquer the kingdom of New Castile, and achieved it with success; to which he added, some time after, the kingdom of Valencia. Thus Alphonso became, by the arms of his champion the Cid, the most powerful of those petty sovereigns who divided the kingdom of Spain.*

In those ages of discord and darkness, the contentions between the imperial and the papal power make the most conspicuous figure.

---

* Voltaire sur les Mœurs, ch. xliv. *Cid* is merely the Moorish or Arabic for *Lord.*

The right of the emperors of Germany to nominate the popes had undergone many changes. Henry III., who was a prince of great abilities, resumed this right, which his predecessors had neglected, and named successively three popes, by his own sovereign will, and without the intervention of a council of the church. From his time, however, the imperial authority began to decline in Italy; and during the minority of his son, Henry IV., several of the popes obtained the chair of St. Peter by bribery and intrigue. Alexander II. was chosen pope in the year 1054, without consulting the imperial court, and maintained his seat, though the emperor actually nominated another. It was the lot of this emperor, Henry IV., who was not deficient in spirit, to have to do with a continued series of the most domineering and insolent pontiffs that ever filled the papal chair. Alexander II., instigated by Hildebrand, one of his cardinals, excommunicated Henry on the pretence of his having sold ecclesiastical benefices, and frequented the company of lewd women; and the effect of this arrogant procedure was, that the people of Italy began to spurn at the imperial authority. On Alexander's death, this same daring Hildebrand had interest to procure himself to be elected pope, without waiting for the emperor's permission. He took the title of Gregory VII., and meditating to shake off at once all dependence on the empire, his first step was to denounce excommunication against all those who received benefices from the hands of laymen, and against all who conferred them. This was a measure that struck not only against the right of the emperor, but against the privilege of all sovereigns, who, in their dominions at least, were in constant use of conferring benefices. Henry, the emperor, happened to be at war with the Saxons when he received a summons by two of his holiness's legates to come in person to Rome, and answer to the charge of his having granted the investiture of benefices. He treated this insolent message with proper contempt. Gregory had, at the same time, denounced a sentence of excommunication against Philip I. of France, and had likewise expelled from the pale of the church the Norman princes of Apulia and Calabria. What gave weight to sentences of this kind, which would otherwise have been held in derision, was that policy of the popes by which they took care to level their ecclesiastical thunder against those who had enemies powerful enough to avail themselves of the advantages which such sentences gave them against the party excommunicated. Henry, it must be owned, thought of rather a mean revenge against the pontiff. By his orders, a ruffian seized the pope while he was performing divine service, and after bruising and maltreating him, confined him to prison. The pontiff, however, soon recovered his liberty, and assembling a council at Rome pronounced a formal sentence of deposition against the emperor. This awful sentence ran in the following erms:—"In the name of Almighty God, and by *our* authority,

I prohibit Henry, the son of our emperor Henry, from governing the Teutonic kingdom and Italy. I release all Christians from their oaths of allegiance to him, and I strictly charge every person whomsoever never to serve or to attend him as king." What gave the whole force to this sentence of deposition and excommunication was the disaffection of most of the German princes to the person and interest of Henry. Taking advantage of the pope's bull, they assembled an army, surrounded the emperor at Spires, made him prisoner, and released him only on condition, that he should abdicate the throne and live as a private person till the event of a general diet at Augsburg, where the pope was to preside, and where he was to be solemnly tried for his crimes.

Henry, now reduced to extremity, was forced to deprecate the wrath of that power which he had formerly so much despised. Attended by a few domestics, he passed the Alps, and finding the pope at Canosa, he presented himself at his holiness's gate, without either guards or attendants. This insolent man ordered him to be stripped of his clothes, which were exchanged for a haircloth; and, after making him fast for three days, condescended to allow him to kiss his feet, where he obtained absolution, on condition of awaiting and conforming himself to the sentence of the diet of Augsburg. The people of Lombardy, however, still adhered to the interest of the emperor. Though they were provoked at his mean submission, they were enraged at the insolence of the pope, and rose up in arms to maintain the right of their sovereign, while Gregory was inciting a rebellion against him in Germany. A considerable party, however, of his subjects still favored the cause of Henry, while the rest, considering their sovereign as justly deposed for his contumacy against the holy church, elected Rodolph, duke of Suabia, for their emperor.

Henry, reassuming a proper spirit, resolved to depose the pope, and to make a vigorous effort for the recovery of his crown, by giving battle to his rival Rodolph. He accordingly assembled a council of bishops in the Tirolese, who solemnly excommunicated and deposed the pope, Gregory VII. The sentence bore that he was a favorer of tyrants, a man guilty of simoniacal practices, of sacrilege, and of magic. The last accusation was founded on his having predicted, in the most positive terms, that Henry, in the first engagement against Rodolph, would fall in battle. The event gave the lie to his prophecy, for Rodolph was the victim, and was killed in battle by the celebrated Godfrey of Boulogne, who afterwards conquered Jerusalem. Gregory, however, kept his seat in the chair of St. Peter, and still persevered in his audacity. Henry was determined to punish him in the most exemplary manner, and laid siege to Rome, which he took by storm, while Gregory, blocked up in the castle of St. Angelo, continued still to threaten excommunication and vengeance. This pontiff, whose insolent, tyrannical, and inflexible character involved him in perpetual faction and war, was allowed at length to die quietly in his bed. Henry was obliged to repair to Germany; the Neapolitans came to the relief of Rome; and Gregory in the meantime died at Salerno. The Catholic church has devoutly placed this venerable pontiff among the number of her saints.

His successors in the popedom continued to act upon the same principles, and it was the fate of Henry IV. to be constantly excommunicated and persecuted by every pope in his time. Urban II. instigated Conrad, the son of Henry, to rebel against his father; and after Conrad's death, his brother, afterwards Henry V., followed the same unnatural example. The miseries of this unfortunate prince were now drawing to a period. He was confined by his rebellious subjects in Mentz, where he was again solemnly deposed by the pope's legates, and stripped of his imperial robes by the deputies of his own son. He made his escape from prison, and after wandering for some time in want, he died at Liege.

The emperor Henry V., who had joined with the pope in all the measures against his father, had taken that part only to accomplish his own purposes of ambition. No sooner had he obtained the sovereignty, than he maintained the same pretensions to humiliate the popes. He obliged Paschal II. to allow the emperors to have the right of conferring benefices—a prerogative for which his father had paid so dear; but after many disputes and a great deal of bloodshed, he was in the end compelled, like his father, to yield to the terms prescribed to him, and to renounce this right for himself and his successors. Things went on much in the same way, during a succession of popes and a succession of emperors; there was a constant struggle, which in general terminated in favor of the holy see.

Frederic I., surnamed Barbarossa, a prince of great talents and of high spirit, was summoned to go to Rome to receive the imperial crown from Adrian IV.* It was customary at this time, from the ambiguous relation in which the popes and emperors stood to each other, for the pope to intrench himself upon the emperor's approach, and for all Italy to be in arms. The emperor promised that he would make no attempt against the life, the person, nor the honor of the pope, the cardinals, and the magistrates. A knight, completely armed, made this oath, in the name of Frederic Barbarossa; but the ceremonial required, that when the pope came out to meet him, the emperor should prostrate himself on the ground, kiss his feet, hold the stirrup of his horse while he mount-

* This pope was an Englishman, of the name of Nicholas Breakspear; the only Englishman that ever sat in the chair of St. Peter. His learning and abilities raised him from poverty and obscurity, first to the dignity of abbot of St. Rufus in Provence, next to that of cardinal, (in 1146,) and lastly to the papacy, (in 1154.) He said of himself, that "he had been strained through the limbec of affliction; but that all the hardships of his life were nothing in comparison with the burden of the papal crown."

ed, and lead him by the bridle for nine paces. Frederic refused at first these humiliating marks of submission: the cardinals looked upon it as the signal of a civil war, and betook themselves to flight; but Frederic was reasoned into compliance with a ceremony which he was determined to hold for nothing more than a piece of form. His indignation broke out immediately in the plainest terms, when the deputies of the people of Rome informed him that they had chosen him, though a foreigner, to be their sovereign. "It is false," said he, "you have not chosen me to be your sovereign: my predecessors, Charlemagne and Otho, conquered you by the strength of their arms; and I am, by established possession, your lawful sovereign." But the spirit of this prince and his intrepid activity were not equal to the extreme difficulties with which he had to struggle; the popes, who disputed his right to the empire; the Romans, who refused to submit to his authority; and all the cities of Italy, which wanted to vindicate their liberty. Poland, too, and Bohemia, were at war with him, and gave him constant occupation. The troubles of Italy at last compelled him to measures, which his haughty spirit could very ill brook. He acknowledged the supremacy of Alexander III., he condescended to kiss his feet, and to hold the stirrup, and to restore what he possessed which had at any time belonged to the holy see. On these terms he gave peace to Italy, embarked on an expedition to the holy wars, and died in Asia, by bathing himself, while overheated, in the Cydnus—the same river which, in a similar manner, had almost occasioned the death of Alexander the Great.

Under his son, Henry VI., the spirit of the popedom and of the emperors continued still the same. Pope Celestinus, while Henry VI. was kneeling to kiss his feet, took that opportunity of kicking off his crown.* He made amends to him, however, for this insolence, by making him a gift of Naples and Sicily, from which Henry had extirpated the last of the Norman princes. Thus Naples and Sicily were transferred to the Germans, and became an appanage of the empire. Each succeeding pope seemed to rise upon the pretensions of his predecessor; till at length Innocent III., in the beginning of the thirteenth century, established the temporal power (for which his predecessors had been so long struggling) upon a solid basis. Taking advantage of the divisions of Germany, where opposite factions had chosen two emperors, Frederic II. and Otho of Saxony, Innocent, by espousing the party of Otho, obtained for the popedom the absolute possession of Italy, from the one sea to the other. He had

---

* Voltaire doubts, as most of his readers will do, the literal truth of this story, but allows that the very fabrication of such a story marks the inveterate animosity which subsisted between the emperors and the popes, as much as if it had been true.—Voltaire sur les Mœurs, ch. xlix.

the sovereignty of Rome, where he abolished the name of consul, which had subsisted to this time; and Innocent found himself possessed of a power which was supreme in every sense of the word

---

CHAPTER VIII.

HISTORY OF ENGLAND during the Eleventh, Twelfth, and part of the Thirteenth Centuries:—Reign and Character of William the Conqueror—Doomsday book—William Rufus—Henry I.—Stephen—Henry II. (Plantagenet) Richard Cœur de Lion—King John—MAGNA CHARTA.

THE consequence of the battle of Hastings, which was fought on the 14th of October, 1066, was the submission of all England to William the Conqueror. William advanced by rapid marches to London, and before he had come within sight of the city, he received the submission of the clergy and the chief nobility, among whom was Edgar Atheling, the nephew of Edward the Confessor, and the last male of the Saxon line. This prince had just before been acknowledged as king upon the intelligence of the death of Harold, but he wanted both spirit and abilities to make good his title. William accepted the crown upon the same terms on which it was usually conferred on the Saxon monarchs; which were, that he should govern according to the established customs of the kingdom: for this politic prince, who might have ruled upon any conditions, was pleased that his usurpation should receive the sanction of something like a free consent of his subjects. From the beginning of his reign, however, his partiality to his countrymen, the Normans, was abundantly conspicuous. They were promoted to all offices of honor and emolument, and he gave extreme disgust to the English by the partition which he made among these foreigners of the lands of the most illustrious nobility of the kingdom, as a punishment for having adhered to the defence of their king and country. A visit which William paid to his Norman dominions gave these discontents time to ripen and break out, and a conspiracy is said to have been secretly formed for destroying at once all the Normans by a general massacre, upon Ash Wednesday, 1068. The return, however, of William soon silenced these discontents; the chief persons accused of promoting this conspiracy fled over sea, and the body of the people were intimidated into tranquillity.

From that time forward William lost all confidence in his subjects of England. He determined to treat them as a conquered nation, and to secure his power by humbling all who were able to make resistance. This policy, however, embroiled him in perpetual commotions. Malcolm Canmore, king of Scotland, and Sweyn, king of Denmark, with the chief of the old Saxon nobility, excited a most formidable insurrection in the north. The activity of William, however, disconcerted their measures before they were ripe for execution; he made peace with the Scottish king, and showed an unusual instance of clemency, in accepting the submission of his rebellious subjects. These instances of rebellion must have sufficiently informed him of their disposition; but they did not alter the general tenor of his conduct; he continued to treat the English with distance, reserve, and severity. New vexations and impositions brought on new insurrections, and William was obliged in person to make several progresses through the kingdom, which generally reduced matters only to a temporary tranquillity. In short, he had no great reason to love his subjects of England, and he was heartily detested by them. He was a prince to whom nature had denied the requisites of making himself beloved, and who, therefore, made it his first object to render himself feared. Even the Normans, instigated probably by the French, endeavored to withdraw themselves from his yoke. To establish order in that country, he carried over an army of Englishmen; thus, by a capricious vicissitude of fortune, we see the Normans brought over for the conquest of the English, and the English sent back to conquer the Normans. With these troops he reduced the rebels to submission, and returned to England to be again embroiled in conspiracies and rebellion. The last and severest of his troubles arose from his own children. His eldest son, Robert, had been promised by his father the sovereignty of Maine, a province of France, which had submitted to William; he claimed the performance in his father's lifetime, who contemptuously told him, he thought it was time enough to throw off his clothes when he went to bed. Robert, who was of a most violent temper, instantly withdrew to Normandy, when in a short time he engaged all the young nobility to espouse his quarrel. Brittany, Anjou, and Maine likewise took part against William, who brought over another army of the English to subdue the rebellion. The father and son met in fight, and being clad in armor did not know each other, till Robert, having wounded his father and thrown him from his horse, his voice (calling out for assistance) discovered him to his antagonist. Stung with consciousness of the crime, Robert fell at his feet, and in the most submissive manner entreated his forgiveness. The indignation of William was not to be appeased: he gave his son his malediction instead of his pardon; and though he afterwards employed him in his service and left him heir to his Norman dominions, it does not appear that the prince was ever received into favor.

The last of the enterprises of William was against France, to which he had been excited by some railleries which Philip I. had vented on occasion of his personal infirmities. William, to convince him that he could yet make himself formidable, entered that province of the kingdom called *the Isle of France* with an immense army, and destroyed, burnt, and plundered all that lay in his way. An accident, however, put an end to his life. He was thrown from his horse, and carried to a small village near Rouen, where he died. He bequeathed the kingdom of England to his youngest son, William, who had always been his favorite. This bequest would have availed little, but for a concurrence of favorable circumstances. The English people hated Robert, the eldest son, who had lived little among them, and whose rebellion they disapproved. Lanfranc, archbishop of Canterbury, was the friend of William Rufus, and the principal nobility of the kingdom were attached to his interest. To Robert he left Normandy; and to Henry, his second son, he left the effects of his mother Matilda, without any inheritance in territory.

William the Conqueror, though not an amiable, was certainly a great prince. He possessed extreme vigor of mind, and a bold and enterprising spirit, which was always regulated by prudence. The maxims of his administration were severe, but enforced with consummate policy. He introduced into England the feudal law, which he had found established in France, and which, during that age, was the foundation both of the stability and of the disorders in most of the monarchical governments of Europe. He divided all the lands of England, with a very few exceptions besides the royal demesnes, into baronies; and he bestowed these, with the reservation of stated services and payments, on his Norman followers. From these Norman barons are descended some of the most ancient and noble families of England. William, in short, through the whole of his reign, considered the English as a conquered nation. Under the Anglo-Saxon government the people had enjoyed a very considerable portion of freedom. The greater barons, perhaps even some of the landholders, had their share in the government, by their place in the Wittenagemot, or assembly of the states. Under William, the rights and privileges of all the orders of the state seem to have been annihilated and overpowered by the weight of the crown ; but this very circumstance, unfavorable as it may appear to the people's liberties, was, in fact, the very cause of the subsequent freedom of the English constitution. It was the excessive power of the crown that gave rise to a spirit of union among the people in all their efforts to resist it ; and from the want of that spirit of union in the other feudal kingdoms of the continent,—a spirit which was not excited in them by a total extinction of their liberties as it was in England by the whole career of William the Conqueror,—we can easily account for the great difference at this day between their constitutions and ours, with respect to political freedom.

One of the most oppressive measures of William the Conqueror was the enactment of the forest laws. He reserved to himself the exclusive privilege of killing game throughout all England, and enacted the most severe penalties on all who should attempt it without his permission. Not satisfied with this severe and most impolitic measure, William, to gratify his passion for the chase, laid waste a country of about fifty miles in circuit, drove out all the inhabitants, and threw down the villages, and even churches, to make the New Forest in Hampshire; thus exterminating at once above 100,000 inhabitants, many of whom perished from famine. It is not, therefore, without reason that Lord Lyttelton remarks, "that Attila himself did not more justly deserve to be named the *Scourge of God*, than this merciless Norman." It was this severe restriction of the forest laws—this mark of servitude—that, above every other circumstance, lay heavy on the English, and, in the reign of the succeeding prince, excited at length those vigorous efforts which produced the most favorable concessions for the general liberty.

Preparatory to William's plan of reducing England entirely under the feudal government, he found it necessary to engage in and complete a very great undertaking. This was a general survey of all the kingdom, an account of its extent, its proprietors, their tenures, and their values; the quantity of meadow, pasture, wood, and arable land which they contained; the number of tenants, cottagers, and servants of all denominations who lived upon then. Commissioners were appointed for this purpose, who, after six years employed in the survey, brought him an exact account of the whole property in the kingdom. This monument, called *Doomsday book*, the most valuable piece of antiquity possessed by any nation, is at this day in existence, and is preserved in the English Exchequer. It was, in the year 1782, printed by an order of parliament. It may easily be conceived how much it must tend to illustrate the ancient state of the kingdom.

William II., surnamed Rufus, had all his father's vices without his good qualities. No action of importance signalized his reign, which was of thirteen years' duration. The *red* king was a violent and tyrannical prince; arbitrary and overbearing to his subjects, and unkind to his relations. The despotism of his authority, however, kept the kingdom in peaceable submission. He indulged without reserve that domineering policy which suited his temper; and which, if supported, as it was in him, with courage and vigor, proves often more successful in disorderly times than the deepest foresight and the most refined political wisdom. He left some laudable memorials of a truly royal spirit in the building of the Tower of London, Westminster Hall, and London Bridge.

While hunting the stag, he was killed by a random shot of an arrow, and leaving no legitimate issue, the succession devolved, of course, on Robert of Normandy, his elder brother; but he was then too distant to assert his pretensions. This valiant prince was at that time distinguishing himself by his heroism in the first crusade against the infidels in Palestine, and the throne of England was, in the meantime, occupied by Henry, his younger brother, without opposition. The circumstances in which Henry I. had acquired the crown had their influence upon the whole tenor of his life; so true it is, that fortune and accident often decide what shall be a man's character. Had Henry I. mounted the throne, as the nearest heir to the preceding monarch, it is not to be doubted, that from the dispositions which he certainly possessed, he would have been a great, perhaps a good and virtuous prince; but his cause was a bad one, and was not easily to be supported with a good conscience and a virtuous character. Not satisfied with the usurpation of the crown of England, he determined to strip his elder brother, likewise, of his dominions of Normandy. Robert returned with all speed from his Eastern expedition, but his army was defeated, and he himself taken prisoner. Henry carried him in triumph to England, where he ungenerously detained him in close confinement in Wales during the remainder of his life.

An usurper must secure his power by acts of popularity. Henry, soon after his accession to the throne, granted a charter,* extremely favorable to the liberties of the people, and which has been justly regarded as the groundwork of the claim of privileges made by the English barons in the reign of king John, which he confirmed by Magna Charta. These privileges, it is even contended by the zealous advocates for the rights of the people, were of a much more ancient date. "Henry I.," says Lord Lyttelton, "by this charter restored the Saxon laws which were in use under Edward the Confessor;" but with such alterations, or, as he styled them, emendations, as had been made by his father, with the advice of his parliament; at the same time, annulling all civil customs and illegal exactions, by which the realm had been unjustly oppressed. The charter also contained very considerable mitigations of those feudal rights claimed by the king over his tenants, and by them over theirs, which either were the most burdensome in their own nature, or had been made so by an abusive extension. In short, all the liberty that could well be consistent with the safety and interest of the lord in his fief was allowed to the vassal by this charter, and the profits due to the former were settled according to a determined and moderate rule of law. "It was," says Sir Henry Spelman, "the original of king John's Magna Charta, containing most of the

* For the provisions of this charter, see Carte's History of England, b. v., § 48.

articles of it, either particularly expressed, or, in general, under the confirmation it gives to the laws of Edward the Confessor."

Henry was now absolutely master of England and Normandy. Fortune seemed to smile upon him, and to promise a reign of uninterrupted tranquillity; but his life was near a period, and even that short interval was overcast with calamity. His only son, William, a youth of great promise, in whom all his hopes were centred, and whom he loved with an excess of tenderness, was drowned in his voyage from Normandy, whither his father had carried him, that he might be recognised as his successor in his foreign dominions. Henry from that moment lost all relish for life; the remaining years of his reign were occupied chiefly in opposing the pretensions of his nephew, the son of his elder brother Robert; who, with the aid of France, sought to make good his title to the throne of his grandfather, William the Conqueror. The death of this prince, however, relieved him of his fears from that quarter. His daughter, Matilda, he had first given in marriage to the emperor, Henry V. of Germany. On his demise she had married Geoffry Plantagenet, eldest son of the count of Anjou. She was destined by Henry to be his successor in the dominions of England and of Normandy. But he had imprudently taken a measure which defeated these intentions. He had invited to his court his nephew, Stephen, son of the count of Blois. Stephen, who was grandson to William the Conqueror, by Adela, his fourth daughter, was a young man of talents and ambition; he saw the success of his uncle's usurpation, and meditated to run the same career. He used every art to gain popularity; and, by his bravery, generosity, and familiar address, he acquired the esteem both of the nobility and the people. Henry, his uncle, died in Normandy, after a reign of thirty-five years, and left, by his will, his daughter Matilda heiress of all his dominions. Stephen was at that time likewise in Normandy, but hastening immediately to England, he found the body of the nation disposed to acknowledge his pretensions. Hugh Bigod, earl of Norfolk, and steward of the household, having averred upon oath, that the late king had expressed his intentions to make Stephen his heir, the archbishop of Canterbury anointed him king without further scruple. The chief pretext on which the partisans of Stephen grounded their denial of the right of Henry's daughter, Matilda, to the crown, was her illegitimacy. Her mother Matilda, it was alleged, had in her youth taken the veil, and consequently Henry's marriage with her was illegal and impious. The pretext had no solid foundation, for it was clearly proved that the queen had never taken the vows, though, while living in a convent, she had worn the habit of a nun. The party of Stephen, however, had such influence at Rome, that the pope (Innocent II.) declared his title good on the above ground.

Stephen was an *usurper*, and therefore began his reign with many acts of popularity. It is indeed difficult to say, whether complaisence might not have been his real character; for his turbulent and checkered reign afforded no opportunity for a display of the milder virtues, even if he possessed them. His competitor, Matilda, was extremely formidable, not only from foreign connections, but from a numerous party of the English, who were devoted to her interest. David, king of Scotland, a prince of great valor and prowess, whose father, Malcolm Canmore, had married the sister of Henry I., espoused the cause of his niece Matilda, and made a formidable incursion into the heart of England, but sustained a signal defeat in the great battle of the Standard.* Robert, the earl of Gloucester, a natural brother of Matilda, escorted her into England, with a numerous army, to vindicate her right to her father's kingdom. They engaged Stephen near to the city of Lincoln, defeated his army, and took him prisoner. Matilda, was acknowledged immediately for lawful sovereign of the kingdom, and the unfortunate Stephen thrown into a dungeon. But mark the caprice of fortune—the conduct of Matilda, haughty, insolent, and severe, became immediately disgustful to her subjects; an insurrection was formed, which, before she was apprized of her danger, drove her from her throne. Stephen was taken from his prison, and again recognised as sovereign. Matilda fled the kingdom, and the death of her partisan, the earl of Gloucester, put an end to all her prospects of ambition.

Stephen was, however, now to compete with a new rival, more formidable than any that had yet opposed him. This was Henry, the son of Matilda, a youth of the most promising abilities, and of great personal promise. While in the sixteenth year of his age, impatient of signalizing himself in a field where he had so glorious an interest to contend for, he solicited his great-uncle, David, king of Scotland, to confer on him the order of knighthood, a ceremony considered as essential, in those days of chivalry, to the practice of arms. His mother invested him with the possession of Normandy. He succeeded to his father's inheritance of Anjou; he married Eleanor, heiress of Guienne and Poitou, the divorced wife of Lewis VII. of France; and, possessed of these extensive domains, he now resolved to reclaim his hereditary dominions of England. He landed in England with a considerable force, and after taking several towns that refused to acknowledge his title and pretensions, he prepared to terminate his dispute with Stephen in a decisive engagement. Fortunately for all parties, Eustace, the eldest son and heir of Stephen, a weak prince, died at this critical juncture. This event opened the way for an accommodation, of which these were the

* So called from the English standard being mounted on a mast, fixed in a large chariot.—See an account of this battle in Carte, b. v., § 77.

terms:—that Stephen should enjoy the crown during his life, which should devolve at his death to Henry, while William, the only surviving son of Stephen, should inherit Boulogne and his patrimonial estate. This treaty gave great joy to the kingdom, and passed into effect soon after by the death of Stephen, and the peaceable accession of Henry Plantagenet to the throne of England.

Henry II. succeeded to the kingdom, of which he was in every sense most deserving, with the unanimous approbation of his subjects. Conscious of his own powers, he employed himself without reserve in the reformation of abuses, which under his predecessors had acquired such root and strength as to have become part of the constitution; he dismissed immediately all the mercenary troops, who had committed great disorders in the kingdom.

To secure upon a firm foundation the liberties of the people, as well as his own prerogatives, he gave charters to many of the principal towns, by which the citizens claimed their freedom and privileges independent of all subject superiors. These charters are the groundwork of the English liberty, and the first shock which weakened the feudal government established by William the Conqueror.

Henry's authority at home seemed to be fixed on the securest basis, and his power abroad was very extensive. In right of his father, he was master of Anjou, Touraine, and Maine; in that of his mother, of Normandy; and in that of his wife Eleanor, of Guienne, Poitou, St. Onge, Auvergne, Perigord, Angoumois, and the Limosin; to which he soon after added Brittany, by marrying his son, who was yet a child, to the infant heiress of that dukedom. Thus he was possessed of more than a third of France; and, enjoying the affection of his subjects with a well-established authority in his kingdom of England—every thing seemed to promise that he would be one of the happiest, as well as one of the most powerful of the European monarchs; but a gloomy cloud was gathering apace, which soon overwhelmed all these prospects of happiness. The clergy of his kingdom, headed by one of the most ambitious and daring of men, abridged his power, embroiled his dominions, and entirely destroyed his peace. This man was Thomas à Becket, whom Henry had raised from meanness and obscurity to the highest offices of the state, and dignities in the church. From a menial office in the law, he became ecclesiastic, archdeacon of Canterbury, constable of the Tower, and chancellor of England. His revenues were immense, his expenses incredible; he lived with a pomp and retinue equal to that of his sovereign, with whom he was on a footing of the most familiar intimacy and friendship. On the death of the archbishop of Canterbury, the king, who had in view to reform ecclesiastical as well as civil abuses, conferred the primacy of England on his favorite Becket, as he expected that, from grat:

tude and affection to his benefactor, he would the more readily coöperate in his measures; but he was miserably disappointed. Becket's promotion to the archbishopric of Canterbury, which made him for life the second person in the kingdom, produced a total change in his conduct and demeanor. He resigned immediately the office of chancellor, and affected in his own person the most mortified appearance of rigorous sanctity. He soon manifested the motive of this surprising change. A clergyman had debauched the daughter of a gentleman, and murdered the father to prevent the effects of his resentment. The king insisted that this atrocious villain should be tried by the civil magistrate; Becket stood up for the privileges of the church, and refused to deliver him up. He appealed to the see of Rome. This was the time for Henry to make his decisive attack against the immunities claimed by the church, when, to defend these, it must vindicate the foulest of crimes. He summoned a general council of the nobility and prelates at Clarendon, where the following regulations were enacted: that churchmen when accused of crimes should be tried in the civil courts; that the king should ultimately judge in ecclesiastical and spiritual appeals; that the prelates should furnish the public supplies as barons; that forfeited goods should not be protected in churches. These, with several other regulations, were subscribed by all the bishops present, and Becket, with much reluctance, was obliged to add his name to the number. It remained that the pope should ratify these regulations, which was to expect that he would abridge his own authority. Alexander III. peremptorily refused it, and Becket, pretending the deepest remorse for his rash acquiescence in such impious concessions, prevailed on his holiness to absolve him from the offence. Henry now perceived that he had no alternative but to take the strongest measures. He summoned a council at Northampton, where Becket defended his cause in person, but was condemned as guilty of contempt of the king's authority, and as wanting in that allegiance he had sworn to his sovereign. His whole estates and property were confiscated, and three several prosecutions immediately brought against him, to account for sums he had received and improperly expended during his several offices. The courage of the prelate seemed to grow from his misfortunes: arrayed in his episcopal garments, and with the cross in his hand, he repaired to the palace, entered the royal apartments, and boldly declared that he put himself under the protection of the supreme pontiff of the Christian church. He then took his leave, and embarked immediately for the continent, where Lewis, king of France, who was Henry's mortal enemy, gave him a most cordial reception, and on his arrival at Rome, the pope honored him with the highest marks of distinction. Henry, exasperated at these favors shown to an exile and a traitor, resolved at once to throw off all dependence on the see of Rome. He immediately issued orders to his justiciaries, prohibiting, under the severest penalties, all appeals to the pope or archbishop of Canterbury; and he declared it treason to bring from him any mandate into the kingdom. Becket, in his turn, issued from Rome a sentence of excommunication against all the king's ministry, and threatened the same sentence against Henry himself, if he did not immediately repent and atone for his past conduct.

The consequences of papal excommunications were, in those days, (as we have seen,) extremely fatal. Henry was aware of his danger, and began to fear that he had carried his resentment too far. It is probable that he found his subjects disapproved of his procedure; and he now seemed inclined to bring matters to an accommodation. Becket, who regretted his substantial losses, was equally disposed to a reconciliation; the prelate was allowed to return, and had an interview with his sovereign, whose generosity agreed to restore him and his adherents to all their benefices, and to allow matters to remain on the footing they had been before their differences.

Becket gloried in his heart at this triumph, which served only to increase his ambition, insolence, and presumption. The condescension of Henry convinced him of his own superiority, and of his sovereign's weakness. He began to make triumphal processions through the kingdom, and to exercise his spiritual and judicial powers with the most arbitrary increase of authority. The archbishop of York, who, in his absence, crowned the king's eldest son, was suspended from his function, as were several other prelates who had officiated at the solemnity. Deposition and excommunication were daily occurrences, and Henry, who was then in Normandy, heard with surprise and indignation, that his whole kingdom was in a flame, from the turbulent and tyrannical conduct of the primate. A few hasty words which he uttered upon the first intelligence of these disorders, were interpreted by some of his servants into a mandate. Four of them immediately embarked for England, where they arrived next day, and finding Becket in the act of celebrating vespers in the cathedral church of Canterbury, they beat out his brains before the altar. Thus the man, who ought to have fallen by public justice as a traitor, was, from the mode of his death, considered as a saint and martyr.

The murder of Becket gave the king unfeigned concern; he saw that his death would produce those very effects with regard to the church, which he most wished to prevent; and that the bulk of his subjects, blinded by the influence of their priests and confessors, would consider him as his murderer. He made the most ample submissions to the pope, who pardoned him on assurance of sincere repentance.

The minds of the people were withdrawn from these disquieting topics, by an object of no less importance. The Irish, an ancient and early civilized people, who for some time after their first conversion to Christianity, are said to have outshone all the nations of the West in learning and the knowledge of the arts and sciences, were replunged into barbarism by the invasion of the Danes, who overran the whole country, and kept the natives in the most oppressive state of dependence and servitude. In the period of which we now treat, the country was divided into five principalities, Ulster, Leinster, Munster, Meath, and Connaught; each of which was governed by a prince of its own; but these five principalities were subdivided among a number of petty chiefs, who acknowledged very little subordination to the prince. Dermot M'Morroch, a weak, licentious tyrant, who was king of Leinster, had ravished the daughter of the king of Meath, who, in revenge for the injury, with the aid of a neighboring prince, expelled him from his kingdom. The ravisher sought protection of Henry, and offered to hold his crown tributary to that of England in case he should recover it by his assistance. Henry empowered his subjects, by letters patent, to arm in defence of the exile. Several of the nobility, particularly the earl of Pembroke, surnamed Strongbow, raised troops for the purpose of an invasion. They landed in Ireland, and were laying waste the country, and reducing every thing to subjection, when Henry himself, jealous of their success, in case they should achieve the conquest without his personal assistance, landed in that kingdom in the year 1172, with a few troops, and took possession of the country with very little opposition. He proceeded from Waterford to Dublin, and received the submission of all the chiefs of Leinster and Meath. Many of the chiefs, likewise, of Munster and of Connaught, followed the same example. But Roderic O'Connor, the prince of Connaught, and nominal monarch of Ireland, still refused to submit. It was not till three years afterwards that he acknowledged the sovereignty of Henry, which acknowledgment he signified by sending deputies to the king at Windsor, who received this flattering embassy with great solemnity in full council. The record of this transaction has been preserved, and fully explains the nature of the submission demanded from the Irish. Henry considered himself as the feudal monarch of Ireland; and Roderic, in his own name, and in the name of all his vassals, was required to do him homage and pay him tribute. The tribute stipulated was every tenth hide of land, to be applied to the use of the public, and a proper provision of hawks and hounds to be furnished annually for the king's pleasures. All Ireland was to be subjected to these stipulations, except those parts of the country which the earl of Pembroke and his followers had conquered before the arrival of Henry, which were left in the absolute possession of the Welsh and English barons. These were the territories of Meath, Wexford, Dublin, and Waterford, which were denominated the English *pale*. Henry divided Ireland into counties, and appointed vicecomites, or sheriffs, to preserve the peace: he erected courts of justice, and introduced the laws of England; but he took no steps to establish or secure his authority in Ireland; and no sooner had he crossed the channel, than the Irish chiefs renounced their allegiance, and the English and Welsh barons were left to defend their possessions of the pale in the middle of a hostile country in the best way they could. Henry seemed now increasing in power and glory, and in every happiness that could flow from the affection of his subjects. He had caused his eldest son, Henry, to be anointed king, and acknowledged for his successor. His second son, Richard, was invested with the sovereignty of Guienne and Poitou. His third, Geoffrey, had, in the right of his wife, the duchy of Brittany; and John, the youngest, was destined to be monarch of Ireland. This exaltation of his children was the source of calamities and disquiets, which imbittered the life of this excellent prince, and at length brought him to an untimely grave.

The story of Rosamond Clifford is familiar to all who, at any time, have amused themselves with ballad and romance. The jealousy which this beautiful favorite occasioned in the breast of Eleanor, the consort of Henry, and the disquiets which that monarch sustained from her haughty and disgusting temper, are no fiction, though, perhaps, the barbarous revenge by the murder of Rosamond, in the bower of Woodstock, may be accounted such.*

Prince Henry, a proud and ambitious youth, was not satisfied with the honors paid him by his father, without receiving a present share in the administration. Geoffrey and Richard, of the same disposition with their brother, were persuaded by the queen to assert their title to their several territories, and on refusal of their demands they betook themselves to the court of France, where they received protection and assurances of assistance from Lewis. They drew to their interest many of the greater barons of England, and these unnatural children prepared, with the aid of a powerful army, to invade and dispossess their father of his dominions. The heroism of Henry's mind got the better of his feelings as a parent. He flew to the continent, opposed them with spirit in every quarter, and had speedily reduced the confederated rebels, with their foreign ally, to propose terms of reconciliation, when he was alarmed by an irruption from William, king of Scotland. Returning to England, he found the ancient leaven of disaffection, on account of Becket's murder, revived, and violently fermenting in the breasts of his subjects. To con-

* Carte vindicates Henry from this stain on his character, by endeavoring to prove that his connection with Rosamond ceased on his marriage with queen Eleanor; but a register of the birth of Geoffrey Plantagenet, Rosamond's youngest son, which exists in the Cotton Library, disproves this.—See Percy's Reliques of Ancient Poetry, vol. ii.—Introduction to the Ballad of Fair Rosamond.

ciliate their minds, he resolved on expiating his alleged guilt, by the most solemn penance and humiliation. He walked barefooted through the city of Canterbury, and, on arriving at the cathedral, prostrated himself on the ground before the tomb of the martyr, and passed a day and night in fasting and prayer: not satisfied with this mortification, he submitted his bare shoulders to be scourged by the monks of the chapter. Absolved now from all his offences, reconciled to the church and to his subjects, he prepared to revenge the depredations of the Scots, which he did in the most effectual manner by a decisive victory, in which William their king became his prisoner. The foreign rebels, finding all disturbances quieted at home, abandoned their enterprise; but the turbulent and ambitious spirit of the princes was not quieted. Jealous of each other, they concurred in no measures except those of resistance and opposition to their father. Two of them, indeed, expiated their crime by an early death. Geoffrey, who was stigmatized in England by the name of the *child of perdition*, was killed in a tournament at Paris; and Henry, the eldest, died of a fever, lamenting on his death-bed his unnatural conduct with the deepest remorse.

The afflictions of Henry were not at an end. Philip, now king of France, disputed his title to the guardianship of Geoffrey's son, Arthur, prince of Brittany, and threatened a formal invasion. Richard was again seduced from his duty, and openly ranged himself on the side of the king of France; and Henry saw his continental dominions invaded, plundered, and possessed by the confederates. A treaty, however, was set on foot, in which, after many mortifying concessions, Henry agreed to defray the charges of the war to the king of France, and to give a free pardon to all his rebellious lords and their vassals. A list was presented to him of their names, among whom he saw that of his son John, his favorite child, whom he had till that moment believed faithful to his duty. The unhappy father broke out into expressions of the utmost despair; cursed the day on which he had received his miserable being, and bestowed on his ungrateful children a malediction, which he never could be prevailed on to retract: a lingering fever, caused by a broken heart, soon after terminated his life. Richard, it is said, came to view the body of his father, and, struck with remorse, accused himself in the deepest terms with having contributed by his unnatural conduct to bring his parent to the grave. Thus died Henry, in the fifty-eighth year of his age, an ornament to the English throne, and a monarch surpassing all his contemporaries in the valuable qualities of a sovereign. During his reign, all foreign improvements in literature and politeness, in the laws and the arts, seem to have been, in a good measure, transplanted into England; and that kingdom was become little inferior in those respects to any of its continental neighbors. Henry's attention to the administration of justice had gained him so great a reputation, that even foreign and distant princes made him the umpire of their differences: he determined a dispute regarding some controverted territory between the kings of Navarre and Castile. The reign of Henry was remarkable for an innovation which was afterwards carried further by his successors, and was attended by the most important consequences to the government. He abolished that military force which was established by the feudal institutions, by exchanging the military services of the crown's vassals for money. These payments were termed *scutage*, and they were employed by the sovereign in levying troops from abroad. Whether this policy was beneficial, or otherwise, is disputable: one good consequence, at least, was, that it weakened the strict bonds of the feudal system, which was a fertile source both of despotism in the prince, and anarchy and disorder among the vassals.

Richard I., surnamed Cœur de Lion, had all those qualities which gain the admiration of a romantic age, but few that could conduce to the happiness of his subjects or command the approbation of posterity. The whole of his reign was a tale of romance, intrepid valor, imprudence, and misfortune. All Europe was at that time infected with the enthusiasm of the holy wars, and Richard, immediately upon his accession, prepared to signalize himself in an expedition to Palestine, which his conscience, or rather his romantic turn of mind, represented to him as the only field of real glory for a Christian prince. Little regardful of the interests of his people, he raised an immense sum of money, by all the various methods of arbitrary enforcement, and forming a league with Philip Augustus, king of France, who possessed somewhat of his own disposition though with less generosity, the two sovereigns agreed to join their forces in an expedition against the Infidels. Many were the mistrusts and mutual reconciliations between these two monarchs: at length, after the taking of Acre, and a few other successful exploits jointly performed, Philip thought proper to return to France, and left the field of glory to Richard without a rival. The English monarch went on from victory to victory. The most remarkable of his battles was that near to Ascalon, where he engaged and defeated Saladin, the most renowned of the Saracen monarchs, and left 40,000 of the enemy dead upon the field. Ascalon surrendered, as did several other cities, to the victorious Richard, who now prepared for the siege of Jerusalem; but at the most important crisis, which, if fortunate, as every thing seemed to promise, would have terminated the expedition in the most glorious manner, the king of England, on a review of his army, found them so wasted with famine, with fatigue, and even with victory, that, with the utmost mortification of heart, he was obliged entirely to abandon the enterprise. The war was finished by a truce with Saladin, in which it was agreed that the Christian pilgrims should pass to

Jerusalem in perfect security. Richard now thought of returning to his dominions, but unwilling to put himself in the power of his rival Philip, by traversing the kingdom of France, he sailed with a single ship to Italy, and was wrecked near Aquileia. Thence proceeding to Ragusa, and putting on a pilgrim's disguise, he resolved to make his way, on foot, through Germany. He was discovered, however, at Vienna, by Leopold, duke of Austria, and thrown into prison by the command of the emperor, Henry VI. No sooner was Richard's situation known to his subjects, than they vied with each other in contributions for his ransom, which was fixed at an exorbitant sum by the emperor, and opposed with every artifice of the meanest policy by the king of France. His brother John, likewise, who in his absence had endeavored to usurp the government of England, is said to have had a conference with Philip, in which the perpetual captivity of Richard was agreed upon, while he himself was to be secured upon the English throne. These cabals, however, were unsuccessful. Richard obtained his liberty on payment of a ransom equal to about £300,000 sterling, which his subjects levied by the cheerful contributions of all ranks of the state. On his return to his dominions, he was received with the utmost transports of delight and satisfaction. Richard had given his subjects no real cause of affection towards him; during a reign of ten years he was but four months in the kingdom; but it is the disposition of the English to revere heroism, and to commiserate misfortune. His traitorous brother, after some submission, was received into favor; and Richard, during the residue of his reign, employed himself in a spirited revenge against the perfidious Philip, whose dominions he harassed by a war, which he carried into the heart of France. A treaty, however, was brought about by the pope's legate, and the contest was terminated soon after by the death of Richard, who, in an assault upon the castle of one of his rebellious vassals in the Limosin, was killed by an arrow. He died in the tenth year of his reign, and forty-second of his age.

His brother John, surnamed *Sans terre*, or Lackland, who was then in England, succeeded to the throne without opposition. There was, however, a claimant alive, whom John, by every means, wished to get rid of; this was prince Arthur, the son of his brother Geoffrey, who, at this time, under the protection, and with the aid of Philip, king of France, had secured to his interest the continental provinces. The war, therefore, which Richard had waged with France, was renewed with great animosity, but was of short continuance, for Arthur, on whose account it had been raised, together with his mother Constance, suspecting treachery from the French monarch, threw themselves on the clemency of John. A suspicion better founded, of the more treacherous designs of his uncle, soon after compelled Arthur again to fly to Philip his former protector; hostilities were renewed between France and England, and the brave youth, who ventured to head a little army of his own countrymen, fell once more into the hands of John, who determined to rid himself of all further vexation on that score. The fate of Arthur is uncertain : he was never heard of from the moment of his confinement. The most probable account is, that he was poniarded by John himself, who found in those servants to whom he gave the murder in charge, a reluctance to execute their horrid commission.* John, whose character had always been disgusting to the English, was now completely detested; and conscious of the estimation in which he was held by his subjects, he regulated himself, through the whole course of his reign, by those tyrannical maxims of policy, which hold the principle of fear in the subject to be equivalent to affection. Philip, his active rival, in a few successful inroads entirely despoiled him of his continental dominions. He made some pitiful efforts to regain them, which exposed him to the contempt of Europe. In this situation, detested and despised, a controversy with his clergy with regard to the supplying of the vacant see of Canterbury embroiled him with the church, and drew on him the indignation and censure of the pope, who, degrading the prelate whom he had chosen, named another in his place.

John, unwilling to submit to the first stretch of ecclesiastical authority, refused to acquiesce in the pope's nomination, and, with the most impolitic violence, sent some of his knights to expel the Augustin monks of Canterbury from their convent, and to take possession of their treasures. Innocent III., who knew his own powers and the weakness of the person with whom he had to contend, sent three English prelates to inform him, that if he persevered in these injurious and undutiful measures, he would put his dominions under the sentence of an interdict. The threat was disregarded, and the interdict pronounced. By that formidable sentence, a stop was immediately put to divine service through the whole kingdom, and to the administration of all the sacraments, except baptism. The church doors were shut, and the statues of the saints laid upon the ground; the dead were refused burial, and were thrown into the ditches and on the highways. The people were prohibited the use of animal food, and debarred from shaving their beards, or giving any attention to their apparel. Every circumstance, in short, seemed calculated to inspire religious terror. It was in vain that John opposed his temporal power to this proof of ecclesiastical authority: the pope seconded his blow by the sentence of excommunication, which absolved the people from all allegiance to his government, and declared him impious and unfit for human society. John, however, despised,

* Hume directly charges John with stabbing Arthur with his own hands.—Hume, ch. x. As also Carte, though he disbelieves some of the particulars, to which Hume attaches credit —Carte, b. vi., 70.

detested, and excommunicated, continued still refractory; he endeavored to maintain his authority by the most cruel acts of tyranny and violence. The pope, to finish his part, pronounced a sentence of deposition; and, at the same time, made a donation of the kingdom of England to Philip of France, who prepared immediately an immense land and naval armament to take possession of his new territories. But the scheme of the pope was deeper laid: it was by no means his intention that Philip should join England to the dominions of France; his view was to intimidate John into an absolute submission to his authority from the terror of the dangers that hung over him. At the same time that he made this donation to Philip, he sent his legate into England, who acquainted John, that it was still in his power to prevent the impending ruin by putting himself and his kingdom implicitly under the protection of the holy see. John eagerly grasped at the offered condition, and, in a solemn convocation of the nobles and people, took an oath, upon his knees, by which, for the expiation of his sins, he surrendered to pope Innocent, and his successors, all his dominions, and every prerogative of his crown, and engaged to hold them as his holiness's vassal for a yearly tribute of a thousand marks.

Philip, incensed at the intelligence of this negotiation, by which he saw the pope had plainly overreached him, determined, notwithstanding, to prosecute the war. An insurrection, however, in his own territories, and a successful attack made upon his fleet by the English admiral, in which four hundred of his ships were taken and destroyed, obliged him entirely to abandon the enterprise.

John was now at ease from foreign hostilities, but he had too plainly manifested his mean and odious character to hope for the allegiance or quiet submission of his subjects. Langton, archbishop of Canterbury, who had been installed, in consequence of the pope's nomination, against the will of the king, and who was his inveterate enemy, had formed a plan for the reformation of the government. A charter, very favorable to the liberties of the people, and tending to abridge the power of the sovereign in many capital articles, had been granted by Henry I. A copy of this charter, which had never been followed by any substantial effect, came into the possession of Langton, who, in a conference with some of the principal barons, proposed that, on the ground of these concessions from his predecessor, they should insist, that John should grant a solemn confirmation and ratification of their liberties and privileges. The barons bound themselves with an oath to support their claims by a vigorous and steady perseverance. An application was drawn up and presented to the sovereign, who, unwilling to yield and yet unable to refuse, appealed to the holy see. The pope had now an interest to support his vassal, and he wrote instantly to England, requiring by his supreme authority, that all confederacies among the barons, which tended to disturb the peace of the kingdom, should be immediately put an end to. This requisition met with its just disregard. The associated barons had taken the most effectual measures to enforce their claims. They had assembled an army of two thousand knights, and a very numerous body of foot. With these forces they surrounded the residence of the court, which was then at Oxford, and transmitting to the king a scroll of the chief articles of their demand, they were answered, that he had solemnly sworn never to comply with any one of them. They proceeded immediately to hostilities, laid siege to Northampton, took the town of Bedford, and marched to London, where they were received with the acclamations of all ranks of the people. The king, who found his partisans daily abandoning him, began now to talk in a more submissive strain. He offered, first to submit all differences to the pope, and this being peremptorily refused, he at length acquainted the confederates, that it was his supreme pleasure to grant all their demands. At Runnymede, between Staines and Windsor, a spot which will be deemed sacred to the latest posterity, a solemn conference was held between John and the assembled barons of England, when, after a very short debate, the king signed and sealed that great charter, which is at this day the foundation and bulwark of English liberty,—MAGNA CHARTA.

The substance of this important charter is as follows. The clergy were allowed a free election to all vacant church preferments, the king renouncing his power of presentation. Every person aggrieved in ecclesiastical matters was allowed a freedom of appeal to the pope, and for that purpose allowance was given to every man to go out of the kingdom at pleasure. The fines upon churchmen for any offence were ordained to be proportional to their temporal, not their ecclesiastical, possessions. The barons were secured in the custody of the vacant abbeys and their dependent convents. The reliefs or duties to be paid for earldoms, baronies, and knights' fees, were fixed at a rated sum, according to their value, whereas before they had been arbitrary. It was decreed that barons should recover the lands of their vassals forfeited for felony, after being a year and a day in possession of the crown; that they should enjoy the wardships of their military tenants, who held other lands of the crown by a different tenure; that a person knighted by the king, though a minor, should enjoy the privileges of a man come of age, provided he was a ward of the crown. It was enacted, that heirs should marry without any disparagement, that is, that no sum should be demanded by the superior or overlord upon the marriage of his vassal. No scutage or tax was to be imposed upon the people, but by the great council of the nation, except in three particular cases,—the king's captivity, the knighting his eldest son, and the marriage of his eldest daughter. When the great council was to be assembled, the prelates, earls, and great barons were to be called to it by a particular writ, the lesser barons by a summons from the sheriff. It was ordained that the king should not seize any baron's lands for a debt to the crown, if the baron possessed personal property sufficient to discharge the debt. No vassal was allowed to sell so much of his land as to incapacitate him from performing the necessary service to his lord.

With respect to the people, the following were the principal clauses calculated for their benefit. It was ordained that all the privileges and immunities granted by the king to his barons should be also granted by the barons to their vassals. That one *weight* and one *measure* should be observed throughout the kingdom. That merchants should be allowed to transact all business without being exposed to any arbitrary tolls or impositions; that they, and all freemen, should be allowed to go out of the kingdom and return to it at pleasure. London, and all cities and boroughs, shall preserve their ancient liberties, immunities, and free customs. Aids or taxes shall not be required of them, except by the consent of the great council. No towns or individuals shall be obliged to make or support bridges, unless it has been the immemorial custom. The goods of every freeman shall be disposed of according to his will or testament; if he die intestate, his heirs at law shall succeed to them. The king's courts of justice shall be stationary, and shall no longer follow his person; they shall be open to every one, and justice shall no longer be bought, refused, or delayed by them. The sheriffs shall be incapacitated to determine pleas of the crown, and shall not put any person upon his trial from rumor or suspicion alone, but upon the evidence of lawful witnesses. No freeman shall be taken or imprisoned, or dispossessed of his free tenements or liberties, or outlawed or banished, or any way hurt or injured, *unless by the legal judgment of his peers*, or by the *law of the land*; and all who suffered otherwise in this and the former reigns, shall be restored to their rights and possessions. Every freeman shall be fined in proportion to his fault, and no fine shall be levied on him to his utter ruin.

Such were the stipulations in favor of the higher orders of the state, the barons, the clergy, the landholders, and freemen. But that part of the people who tilled the ground, who constituted in all probability the majority of the nation, seem to have been very lightly considered in this great charter of freedom. They had but one single clause in their favor, which stipulated that no vallain or rustic should by any fine be bereaved of his carts, his ploughs, and instruments of husbandry; in other respects they were considered as a part of a property belonging to an estate, and were transferable along with the horses, cows, and other movables, at the will of the owner. John, at the same time that he signed the Magna Charta, was compelled by the barons to sign the Charta de Foresta, a deed of a most important nature to the liberties of the subject. William the Conqueror, we have remarked, had reserved to himself the exclusive privilege of killing game over all England, and the penalties on any subject encroaching upon this right of the sovereign were most oppressive and tyrannical. The most rigorous of these penalties were abolished by the Charta de Foresta; pecuniary fines were substituted for death and demembration. Those woods and forests that had been taken from their proprietors in the former reigns were now restored to them, and every man was left at liberty to enclose his woods, or to convert them into arable land at his pleasure.

The barons, in order to secure the observance of these important charters, prevailed likewise on John, who was ready to grant every thing, that twenty-five of their own number should be appointed conservators of the public liberty. The ease with which John had made all these concessions was entirely a piece of simulation on the part of that treacherous prince. The barons were lulled into security, and had disbanded their forces, without taking any measures for reassembling them, while John, in the meantime, had privately enlisted a large body of foreign troops, Germans, Brabantines, and Flemings, who, landing in the kingdom, immediately commenced hostilities. An English army, headed by the earl of Salisbury, was likewise in the king's interest; and by these acting in different parts at the same time, storming every citadel which refused to acknowledge the king's absolute authority, and burning, massacring, and plundering in every quarter, the whole kingdom was a scene of horror and devastation.

The barons, unable to act in concert or to raise an army that could stand before these ravagers, were reduced to the desperate measure of entreating aid from France. Philip immediately despatched his eldest son Lewis, at the head of an army of 7000 men. The barons became bound to acknowledge him as their lawful sovereign; and the first effect of his appearance in the kingdom was the desertion of a very large part of John's foreign troops, who refused to serve against the heir of their master. Lewis advanced to London, where he received the submissions of the people, who took the oath of fealty; but discoveries were soon made that tended at once to withdraw the English from all allegiance to their foreign master. One of the French courtiers (the Viscount de Melun) had declared upon his death bed that he knew, from the mouth of Lewis, that it was his intention to exterminate entirely the English barons, and to bestow their estates and dignities upon his own French subjects. This, though a most improbable scheme, received some confirmation from the visible partiality that Lewis already showed to his foreign subjects. The most powerful of the nobility took the alarm immediately; they even chose to join their unworthy sovereign, rather than be the dupes and victims of a treacherous foreigner. John, with these aids, was resolved to make a vigorous effort for the preservation of his crown. But this vicious tyrant, from whom England could in no situation have ever received benefit, was cut off by a fever at Newark. Henry III., his son, a boy of nine years of age, was immediately crowned at Bristol, under the auspices of the earl of Pembroke, Mareschal of England, who was at the same time appointed guardian of the king and protector of the realm. The disaffected barons, whose object of hatred and enmity was now removed, returned cheerfully to their allegiance. Lewis found himself deserted by all his partisans among the English; an engagement ensued, in which the French troops were defeated; and their prince, finding his cause to be daily declining, was glad at last to conclude a peace with the protector, and entirely to evacuate the kingdom.

CHAPTER IX.

State of Europe in the Thirteenth Century—The Crusades.

WHILE these eventful transactions were carrying on in Englanu, and John, by compulsion, was making those concessions to his barons, which a wise and a good prince would not have thought it injurious to regal dignity to have voluntarily granted, a young emperor had been elected in Germany, and enjoyed the throne which Otho IV. had resigned before his death; this was Frederick II., son of the emperor Henry VI. The emperors, at this time, were much more powerful than their neighboring monarchs of France; for, besides Suabia, and the other extensive territories which Frederick had in Germany, he likewise possessed Naples and Sicily by inheritance; and Lombardy, though sometimes struggling for independence, had long been considered as an appanage of the empire.

The pope reigned absolute at Rome, where all the municipal magistrates were subject to his control and authority. Milan, Brescia, Nantua, Vicenza, Padua, Ferrara, and almost all the cities of Romagna, had, under the pope's protection, entered into a confederacy against the emperor. Cremona, Bergamo, Modena, Parma, Reggio, and Trent were of the imperial party. These opposite interests produced the factions of Guelph and Ghibelline, which for a length of time embroiled all Italy in divisions, and split towns and even families into parties. The Guelphs stood up for the supremacy of the pope, the Ghibellines for that of the emperor.

Frederick II., by his policy and his arms, carried on a vigorous contest with four popes successively without bringing any of them to submission. By two of these popes, Gregory IX. and Innocent IV., he was excommunicated and solemnly deposed; but Frederick kept possession of his throne and maintained his independence. In consequence of the last sentence of deposition, he wrote, in the most spirited manner, to all the princes of Germany, "I am not the first," says he, "whom the clergy have treated so unworthily, and I shall not be the last. But you are the cause of it, by obeying those hypocrites, whose ambition, you are sensible, is carried beyond all bounds. How many infamous actions may you not discover in the court of Rome! While those pontiffs are abandoned to the vices of the age, and intoxicated with pleasure, the greatness of their wealth extinguishes in their minds all sense of religion. It is, therefore, a work of charity to deprive them of those pernicious treasures which are their ruin; and in this cause you ought all to cooperate with me."

Innocent IV. endeavored by every engine in his power to excite the Germans to rebel against this spirited emperor. Conspiracies were formed against his life—assassins hired to murder him—and several attempts made to cut him off by poison. Of all these iniquitous proceedings he made loud complaints, which the pope never gave himself the trouble of answering. Whether these machinations were in the end effectual is not certainly known; but Frederick, after a life of much disquiet, died at Naples in the fifty-second year of his age, and thirty-eighth of his reign.

For eighteen years after the death of Frederick II., the Germanic empire was without a sovereign, and was rent by incessant factions and divisions. Yet, distracted as they were among themselves, the Germans allowed the pope to gain nothing by their situation. Italy, indeed, was equally a prey to factions, which gave the popes too much to do at home to think of meddling with the affairs of a distant kingdom. France was still weak, and Spain was divided between the Christians and Mahometans. England, as we have seen, was a miserable theatre of civil war and anarchy. Yet, at this period, distracted as appears to have been the face of all Europe, one great scheme or project seems to have given a species of union to this discordant mass; a project, from the issue of which arose new kingdoms, new establishments, and a new system of manners. This was the crusades, or holy wars, of which we now proceed to give a short account.

We have mentioned the irruption of the Turks, or Turcomans upon the empire of the Caliphs. The manners of these Turcomans were like those of most of the other tribes from the north of Asia; that is to say, they were freebooters, who lived by plunder, and had no strong attachment to any country. The Turks, it is probable, came from those regions beyond Mount Taurus and Imaus, and were, therefore, a race of Tartars. About the eleventh century they made an irruption upon Muscovy, and came down upon the banks of the Caspian Sea. The imprudent policy of the Arabians themselves first introduced these strangers into their empire, who were destined to overthrow it. One of the caliphs, grandson of Haroun Alraschid, hired a body of Turks to be his life-guards; this gave them some name and reputation they gradually increased in number, and acquired influence in the civil wars, which took place on occasion of the succession to the caliphate. The caliphs of the race of the Abassidæ were deprived by the caliphs of the race of Fatima of Syria, Egypt, and Africa; and the Turks subdued at last, and stripped of their dominions, both the Abassidæ and the Fatimites.

Bagdad, the seat of the empire of the caliphs, was taken by the Turks in the year 1055, and these conquerors followed the same commendable policy with the Franks, the Goths, and Normans, in accommodating themselves to the laws and manners of the conquered people. From this period, the caliphs, from being temporal monarchs, became only the heads or supreme pontiffs of the Mahometan religion, as the popes of the Christian; but the difference was, that the caliphs were sinking from their ancient dignity, while the popes were daily advancing in power and splendor. At the time of the first crusade, Arabia was under a Turkish sultan, though the caliph still retained his rank and nominal importance. Persia and Asia Minor were likewise governed by Turkish usurpers; the empire of Constantinople had been in some degree of lustre under Constantine Porphyrogenitus, and under Nicephorus Phocas; but the succeeding princes weakened and reduced it to a shadow. Michael Paphlagonatus lost Sicily, and Romanus Diogenes almost all that remained in the East, except the kingdom of Pontus; and that province, which is now called Turcomania, fell soon after into the hands of Solyman the Turk, who being now master of the greatest part of Asia Minor, established the seat of his empire at Nicæa, and began to threaten Constantinople at the time of the commencement of the first crusade.

The Greek empire, thus circumscribed in Asia, comprehended, however, or the European side, all Greece, Macedonia, Thrace, Epirus, and Illyria, and the Isle of Crete, now Candia. The city of Constantinople itself was populous, opulent, and voluptuous. Its inhabitants styled themselves not Greeks, but Romans, and the people of Rome, whom they termed Latins, were, in their opinion, a set of barbarians, who had revolted from them and shaken off their authority.

The territory of Palestine, or the Holy Land, appears to have been over-stocked with inhabitants, great numbers of whom had dispersed themselves into different parts of Asia and Africa, where they applied to traffic with uncommon spirit for those rude ages.

When Omar, the successor of Mahomet, seized on the fertile country of Syria, he took possession of Palestine, and as the Mahometans esteemed Jerusalem a holy city, Omar built there a magnificent mosque. Jerusalem at this time contained about seven or eight thousand inhabitants, whose chief wealth arose from the charitable donations of pilgrims, both Christians and Mahometans for the latter paid a degree of veneration to the mosque of Omar, as well as the Christians to the holy sepulchre.

A pilgrim, to whom history has given the name of Peter the Hermit, first raised up that spirit of THE CRUSADES which inflamed all Europe. This man, who was a native of Amiens, had travelled into the Holy Land, where he had suffered much oppression from the Turks. At his return to Rome, he complained in such high terms of the grievances to which the Christian pilgrims were subjected, that Urban II. thought him a very fit person to set on foot the grand design which the popes had long entertained of arming the whole Christian world against the infidels; and Urban himself convoked a general council at Placentia, where the project was proposed and highly approved of; but from the occupation which the Italian nobility found at that time at home, no active measure followed this approbation. The French possessed more of the spirit of adventure than the Italians. The design was no sooner proposed in a council, held at Clermont, in Auvergne, than they took up arms with the most enthusiastic emulation. The principal nobles immediately sold their lands to raise money for the expedition, and the church bought them at an easy rate, and thus acquired immense territorial possessions: even the poorest barons set out upon their own charges, and the vassals attended the standard of their lords. Besides these, whom we may suppose to have been influenced by the piety of the design, an innumerable multitude, a motley assemblage of beggars, slaves, malefactors, strumpets, debauchees, and profligates of all kinds, joined the throng, and hoped to find in those scenes of holy carnage and desolation, means of making their fortune by plunder.* A general rendezvous was appointed at Constantinople. Godfrey of Bouillon, duke of Brabant, a lineal descendant of Charlemagne, was, from his great military character, chosen to command an army of seventy thousand foot, and ten thousand horse, all armed completely in steel. Above eighty thousand ranged themselves under the banner of Peter the Hermit, who walked at their head

---

* Many even of these miscreants had their own motives of piety. Mr. Gibbon's observation has both truth and wit in it. "At the voice of their pastor, the robber, the incendiary, the homicide arose by thousands to redeem their souls, by repeating on the infidels the same deeds which they had exercised against their Christian brethren."—Gibbon, ch. lxviii.

with a rope about his waist, and sandals on his feet. Peter's lieutenant was Walter the Pennyless, and in the van of his troop were carried a sacred goose, and a goat, which (monstrous to believe!) were said to be filled with the Holy Ghost. This immense and disorderly multitude began their march towards the East in the year 1095. They made the first essay of their arms, not upon the unbelievers, but on their fellow Christians. The first exploit which signalized the expedition was the taking of a small Christian city in Hungary, which had refused to starve its own inhabitants by supplying such a tribe of hungry locusts with provisions. This impious city was stormed and pillaged, and the inhabitants massacred. Another band of these adventurers were employed, in the meantime, in putting to death all the Jews wherever they could find them. The consequence of these abominable proceedings was, that the crusaders were considered as enemies wherever they passed, and most of the countries rose in arms to oppose their progress. No less than three different armies were cut to pieces in Hungary. Peter the Hermit, however, found his way to Constantinople, where Alexius Commenus was at that time emperor, a prince of great wisdom and moderation, which he clearly manifested by his conduct to the crusaders Dreading the consequences of that spirit of enthusiasm which haa put in motion such immense multitudes, Alexius, though with much reluctance, thought it his wisest policy to put on the appearance of friendship, and to allow them a free passage through the imperial dominions into Asia. Anna Commena, the daughter of Alexius, an accomplished princess, who has excellently written the history of her own time, relates many circumstances which strongly mark the rude, uncivilized, and brutal spirit of those heroes or chieftains who figured in those romantic expeditions; among the rest is one anecdote extremely characteristical. The chiefs of the crusade being admitted to an audience of the emperor who was seated on his throne, amidst all the pomp of Eastern magnificence, one of these captains, a Frank count, stepping up to the throne, seated himself by the emperor's side, saying, in the Frank language, "What a pretty fellow of an emperor is this who places himself above such men as we are!" Earl Baldwin, one of the crusaders, ashamed of this unmannerly insolence of his countryman, rose immediately, and pulling him from his seat, thrust him out of the assembly. Alexius, with much prudence, expressed no resentment at daily instances of similar brutality; he took a wiser course, he hastened to get rid of his troublesome guests by furnishing them with every necessary aid; and he fitted out his vessels immediately to transport them across the Bosphorus. They landed in Asia, and marched on with the utmost alacrity to meet the infidels: but Solyman, the sultan of Nicæa, gave them a very fatal check. The greatest part of those immense numbers, which had ranged themselves under the Hermit's standard, were cut to pieces. The Turks preserved all the women for their seraglios;—for men, women, and children had taken up the cross and embarked in the expedition. In the meantime, a new swarm of crusaders, to the amount of several hundred thousands, had arrived at Constantinople. These were commanded by Godfrey of Bouillon, by Raymond, count of Thoulouse, by Hugh, brother of Philip I. of France, by Robert, duke of Normandy, eldest son of William the Conqueror, and several of the most considerable princes of Europe, most of whom had mortgaged and even sold their territories to supply themselves with money for the expedition. It was otherwise with the brave Bohemond, son of Robert Guiscard, the conqueror of Sicily; he had no estates, for his father had disinherited him. It was, therefore, an expedition in which he had nothing to lose, and might possibly gain; he had formerly fought with success against the empire of Constantinople, and was more dreaded by the Greeks than all the rest of these adventurers. Bohemond was attended by his cousin, the gallant and accomplished Tancred, whose merits, amplified by fiction, make a conspicuous figure in the fine poem of Tasso, the *Gierusalemme Liberata.*

Such immense and seemingly inexhaustible torrents pouring down upon Constantinople, gave, as we may naturally suppose, very great uneasiness to the emperor Alexius. Excellent politician as he was, he found it impossible to prevent continual differences and a great deal of bloodshed. The crusaders imagined that the piety and merit of the undertaking gave them a just claim to be maintained and supported gratuitously by all who professed themselves to be Christians. They behaved with insufferable insolence and folly; and matters came at length to that extremity, that it was seriously proposed by these new crusaders to begin operations against the infidels by the destruction of Constantinople, the capital of the Christian world in the East. This storm, however, was averted by the emperor Alexius. He once more furnished the crusaders with all they wanted, loaded them even with presents, and transported them into Asia. The army was reviewed near to Nicæa, where it was found to consist of 600,000 foot, including women, and 100,000 horse. We have no accounts transmitted to us how such multitudes procured subsistence when once they had come into a hostile country. It is difficult to conceive that they could have procured it by plunder without such a total dispersion as must have rendered all their enterprises ineffectual against such a formidable enemy as the Mahometans. The Venetians refused to send their vessels to supply them with provisions, because they made very great profits at this time by trading with the Mahometans. The merchants of Genoa and Pisa indeed sent their ships, laden with stores, to the coasts of Asia Minor, where they made immense profits by selling them to the crusaders; and to this cause has been attributed the first rise of the Genoese wealth and splendor. But after all, these resources were extremely inadequate, and it is highly probable that the greatest part of the calamities and misfortunes which the crusaders underwent must have arisen from a scarcity of provisions.

The Turks and Arabians were at first unable to stand the shock of such prodigious multitudes, whose armor gave them likewise a very great advantage; for at this time it was customary not only for the horseman, but his horse, to be clothed entirely in iron. The Turks were twice defeated, and Bohemond made himself master of the country of Antioch. Baldwin, the brother of Godfrey of Bouillon, penetrated into Mesopotamia, and took the city of Edessa. At length they appeared before Jerusalem; and though famine, sickness, and great losses, even by their victories, had reduced their immense army to twenty thousand men, they resolutely attacked a garrison of forty thousand, and after a siege of five weeks took the city by storm. The whole inhabitants, soldiers and citizens, men, women, and children, who were either Mahometans or Jews, were put to the sword. It is affirmed by all the historians that, after this inhuman massacre, the Christians went in solemn procession to the place where they were told was the sepulchre of our Savior, and there burst into a flood of tears.* This mixture of barbarity and cruelty with the tender feelings, is derided by some authors, and especially Voltaire, as something out of nature, and scarcely possible; but when it is considered what was the motive of many of these men, the enthusiasm which animated them in a cause which they were persuaded was to conduct them to heaven, the contending feelings with which they were agitated, detestation for those infi-

---

* The effect produced on the mind by the first view of those most venerable monuments of the origin of our holy religion is well described by the Abbé Marita, in his travels through Cyrus, Syria, and Palestine. "The sepulchre of Christ, which is open only on solemn days, is in the church of the Resurrection. All pilgrims and devotees come hither to celebrate the holy mysteries, under the protection of the governor, who sends a party of soldiers to escort them, and they enter the church in procession, with the sound of plaintive music. On this occasion I think it would be difficult for any person, of whatever religion, not to be inspired with sentiments of reverence and awe on the sight of this most august temple. Gloomy, and of an immense size, it is lighted principally by the lamps which are suspended from its roof. The pilasters are become black by length of years, and no ornaments are to be seen on its walls. The altars and statues of the saints are of coarse stone, and the chandeliers of wood. Every thing used here for religious service is in the simplest and plainest taste. In a word, this church is poor, but it is what a church ought to be. The Deity requires only from man purity of heart and an exemplary life. The company of devotees bend before the stone of unction, which served for embalming the body of Christ when it was brought down from Mount Calvary, and repeat a prayer; after which the priests and assistants worship the cross. Near this is the chapel of the Annunciation, where the officiating priest sits down, and presents his hand to be kissed, while different hymns are chanted before the altars which bear the names of the different mysteries of the Catholic church. The air of humility and attention with which this service is performed is truly affecting."

dels who, as they imagined, had polluted by their impious worship the most sacred monuments of their religion, and joy and gratitude for the recovery and vindication of those venerable remains, we shall find nothing in the deportment of these crusaders but what is natural and consistent with their situation. The only just reflection that can arise from this fact is, the conviction that there is no engine so powerful in its operation on the human mind as religion, which can reconcile the same man to what are seemingly the most opposite extremes.

The Holy Land was thus recovered by the Christians, and Godfrey of Bouillon obtained the title of king of Jerusalem; but it was only a title, for a papal legate arriving in the meantime, claimed the city as the property of God, and took possession of it as such. Godfrey reserved the port of Joppa, and some privileges in Jerusalem.

The crusaders began now to be divided among themselves. They had formed three petty states in Asia, Antioch, Jerusalem, and Edessa; and some years after, a fourth, which was that of Tripoli in Syria, in the conquest of which the Venetians had some share; they lent their ships, and stipulated in return for a part of the conquered territory. Even these little states were divided, and almost every small town had a lord or a count for its sovereign. There were counts of Joppa, and marquises of Galilee, Sidon, Acra, and Cesarea.

The Turks, in the meantime, were not exterminated from the Holy Land; on the contrary, they possessed many considerable garrisons, and were continually annoying the Christians, whose strength and numbers were daily diminishing. A new swarm of adventurers, however, set out from the West in the year 1146; that is, about fifty years from the period of the departure of the first crusade. Their numbers are computed to have been about two hundred thousand. This immense body, consisting of Italians, Germans, and French, marched under the command of Hugh, brother to Philip I. of France. These met with the same fate which we have seen attended the army of Peter the Hermit. The Turks cut them entirely to pieces, and Hugh, their leader, died helpless and abandoned in Asia. The situation of Jerusalem at this time was extremely weak; the numbers of the garrison were greatly reduced. Even the monks, who were at first instituted to serve the sick and wounded, were obliged to arm in the common defence, and they associated themselves into a military society, called Templars and Hospitallers. This was the origin of these two orders of knights, who afterwards signalized themselves by their exploits, and becoming rivals, fought *against each other* with as much keenness as ever they had done against the infidels.

In the meantime Pope Eugenius III. despatched St. Bernard, a furious and enthusiastic monk, to preach a new crusade in France, which kindled up a flame through the whole kingdom. Lewis VII. surnamed *the Young*, who was then on the throne, set the example himself by taking the cross, and, in conjunction with Conrad III., emperor of Germany, appeared at the head of three hundred thousand men. The Germans set out first, and jealous of the French sharing in their glory, had no sooner arrived in Asia than they began hostilities; but the sultan of Iconium, a very able prince, drew them artfully into disadvantageous ground, and with very little trouble cut them all to pieces. Conrad, in the disguise of a pilgrim, fled to Antioch; the enterprise of Lewis the Young met with the same fate. Rashness, and an absurd contempt of their enemies, joined to a total ignorance of the country in which they fought, exposed the French army to innumerable hardships, and they were at length totally defeated among the rocks of Laodicea. Lewis, who had carried his young wife, Eleanor of Guienne, along with him, had the addition of domestic distress to his misfortunes. That lady's gallantries were so notorious, that Lewis thought it necessary to divorce her. Thus, his expedition to the Holy Land cost him not only his great army, but the loss of Poitou, the patrimonial inheritance of his queen, and one of the finest provinces of his dominions. Conrad returned alone to Germany, and thus ended the second crusade, yet more disastrous than the first. It is computed that the number of Europeans who, in both these expeditions, left their country and perished in the East, amounted to one million six hundred thousand.

The Turks and Christians in Palestine were, in the meantime, mutually exterminating and destroying each other, when a new character appeared on the stage, who, in all respects, was one of the greatest men who have adorned the annals of the world; this was Saladin, the nephew of Noureddin, the sultan of Egypt. In a very short space of time he had overrun Syria, Arabia, Persia, and Mesopotamia, and now formed the design of the conquest of Jerusalem, then under the dominion of the Christian prince, Guy of Lusignan.

Lusignan, with what slender forces he could assemble, made the best resistance possible; but his army was defeated, Jerusalem taken, and he himself made prisoner. Saladin treated him with the utmost humanity and generosity. An incident is recorded of this hero which is extremely characteristic. He invited his royal prisoner to a banquet, and with his own hand presented him a cup of liquor, which Lusignan, after having drank, offered to Rainauld de Chatillon, one of his captains. While Chatillon was raising the cup to his lips, Saladin, immediately rising from his seat, struck off his head with the sabre. When Lusignan expressed his horror and astonishment at this action, he was told that it was an ancient custom of the Arabians never to put to death those prisoners to whom they had once given meat or drink;

but that Chatillon was a perjured wretch, unworthy of clemency, whom Saladin had devoted to punishment.

On Saladin's making his entry into Jerusalem, the women, who hoped to move him to compassion, threw themselves at his feet, entreating for mercy to their captive fathers, husbands, and children, but the generous nature of this conqueror needed no entreaty to prompt to an exertion of humanity; he spared the lives of all his prisoners; he restored to the Christians the church of the Holy Sepulchre; and, though attached himself to the faith of Mahomet, he permitted no injury to be offered to the vanquished in the exercise of their religion. He even granted Lusignan his liberty, on his swearing never to take up arms against his deliverer; but Lusignan shamefully violated his oath, and prepared himself for a new attack upon his conqueror. The Christians, in the meantime, lost almost all their possessions in Asia; and pope Clement III., alarmed at the victories of Saladin, began to rouse up a new crusade for the Holy Land from France, Germany, and England,—while another was destined to extirpate the pagans from the North of Europe. This northern crusade, it is supposed, consumed about one hundred thousand Christians, besides the infidels they destroyed.

Philip Augustus, then king of France; Frederic Barbarossa, emperor of Germany; and Richard Cœur de Lion, king of England, took up the cross at the same time, and armed prodigious multitudes from their several dominions. Frederic lost his life in Asia by bathing, while heated, in the Cydnus; his army, which amounted to 150,000 men, by frequent losses was so reduced that his son, the duke of Suabia, could collect no more than seven or eight thousand, with whom he joined himself to Lusignan. Richard and Philip, on reviewing their forces at Ptolemais in Syria, where they joined the nominal king of Jerusalem and the duke of Suabia, found the total amount of their army to be above 300,000 men. Ptolemais was taken; but the duke of Suabia died, and Philip and Richard, mutually jealous of each other's glory, and ever at variance, could do nothing effective while united. Their disgust rose to such a height, that Philip, over whom Richard, on all occasions, had assumed a superiority, thought proper to return to his own dominions.

Richard was now left sole competitor with the illustrious Saladin, and had the honor of defeating him in battle and dismounting him from his horse; but his victories were without effect; his army was reduced by famine, sickness, and fatigues, and on arriving at Jerusalem, which he flattered himself with recovering from the infidels, he found his force so inferior, that he was obliged to abandon the enterprise, and to make his escape from Palestine in a single vessel. What was his fate in Germany, and the misfortunes that succeeded, have been already related in treating of the English history during the reign of this romantic monarch. Soon after died the illustrious Saladin, leaving behind him the character not only of one of the most heroic, but of one of the best of princes. In his last illness, instead o the imperial ensigns which used to adorn the gates of his palace, he ordered a winding sheet to be hung up, while a slave proclaimed, with a loud voice,—"This is all that Saladin, the conqueror of the East, has obtained by his victories!" He bequeathed, by his last will, a large sum of money to be distributed equally among the poor, whether they were Mahometans, Christians, or Jews, intending, as Voltaire well remarks, to teach, by his bequest, that all men are brethren, and that when we assist them we ought not to inquire what they *believe*, but what they *feel*.

This great prince died in the year 1195. The passion for religious warfare was not yet extinguished in Europe; a new expedition was fitted out in the year 1202, under Baldwin, count of Flanders, consisting of about 40,000 men. The object of this crusade was different from all the rest, and its leaders, under the cloak of a holy war, proposed, instead of extirpating the infidels, to dethrone the emperor of Constantinople, and put an end to the empire of the East. Isaac Angelus, the emperor, had been deprived of his liberty by his brother Alexius; but his son maintained a considerable party in his interest, and the crusaders offered him their assistance to regain the empire. The prince disgusted both parties of his countrymen by accepting the aid of foreigners, and the consequence was that he was strangled by one of his own relations. Baldwin and his army, on pretence of revenging his death, laid siege to Constantinople: he took it almost without resistance. The crusaders put all that opposed them to the sword; and it is remarked, as strongly characteristic of a spirit of national levity, that the French, immediately after a scene of massacre and pillage, celebrated a splendid ball, and danced with the ladies of Constantinople, in the sanctuary of the church of St. Sophia. Thus Constantinople was taken for the first time, sacked, and plundered by the Christians. Baldwin was elected emperor, and the imperial dominions were divided between him and the other leaders of the crusade. The Venetians, who had furnished both ships and troops, got for their share the Peloponnesus, the Isle of Candia, (ancient Crete,) and several cities on the coast of Phrygia. The marquis of Monferrat took Thessaly, and the pope became, for a time, the head of the Eastern, as he was of the Western, church. Of all the numbers who had taken up the cross in this crusade, a very few found their way into the Holy Land, under Simon de Montfort; but they did nothing effectual. The imperial family of the Comnenari was not extinguished in the fall of the Eastern empire. One of them, Alexius, escaped with some ships to Colchis, and founded there, between the sea and Mount Caucasus, a small state, which he called the empire of Trebizond. Another state, dignified likewise with the title of empire, was founded by Theodore Lascarius, who retook Nicæa. Other Greeks formed a league with the Turks and Bulgarians, and with their assistance dethroned the new emperor Baldwin, and, cutting off his legs and arms, exposed him to be devoured by wild beasts.

Notwithstanding the miserable termination of all these religious enterprises, the enthusiastic spirit was still as violent as ever, and a new expedition was fitted out to establish John de Brienne as king of Jerusalem, of which the throne happened now to be vacant. An army of 100,000 excellent troops, French, Hungarians, and Germans, landed at Ptolemais, in Palestine, while Saphadin, sultan of Egypt, the brother of Saladin, had left his dominion to lay waste the Holy Land. It seemed a tempting enterprise for the crusaders to make reprisals upon Egypt, and accordingly they left the Christians in Palestine to defend themselves, and set sail for Damietta, the ancient Pelusium. The siege of this city employed them no less than two years; and after it was taken it was lost by the folly of the pope's legate, who pretended that in right of his master he had a title to regulate the disposition of the army as well as the church. By his orders they were encamped between two branches of the Nile, at the very time when it began its periodical inundation. The sultan of Egypt assisted its operation by a little art, and, by means of canals and sluices, contrived entirely to deluge the Christians on one side, while he burnt their ships on the other. In this extremity they entreated an accommodation, and agreed to restore Damietta and return into Phœnicia, leaving their king, John de Brienne, as an hostage. John, however, soon after got his liberty: and, by a very strange vicissitude of fortune, coming to the assistance of Constantinople during an interregnum after the death of Baldwin, was elected emperor of the East. He gave his daughter in marriage to Frederick II., emperor of Germany, along with his right to the kingdom of Jerusalem. This politic prince was very sensible that nothing was to be made by crusades; he therefore concluded a treaty with the sultan Meladin, by which he secured the right to Jerusalem, Nazareth, and some villages, and agreed to relinquish all the rest.

Such was the state of affairs in the East, and such the small fruit of so much bloodshed, when a very great revolution took place in Asia. Genghis-khan, with his Tartars, broke down from the countries beyond Caucasus, Taurus, and Mount Imaus. They first fell upon the inhabitants of Chorassin, a province of Persia, who, being forced to abandon their own country, precipitated themselves upon Syria, and put all to the sword, Christians, Turks, and Jews indiscriminately. The Christians united to repel these invaders, and the Templars, the Hospitallers, and the Teutonic Knights, (a new order formed by the German pilgrims,) signalized themselves in some desperate efforts of resistance; but the Christians were entirely defeated. They retained still a few places on the sea-coast; but their affairs were, on the whole, in a most wretched situation, when Lewis IX. of France, distinguished by the title of Saint Lewis, prevented for awhile their entire extirpation, by fitting out the last crusade.

Lewis was a prince in every respect formed to render his subjects happy, and to repair, by his political and economical talents, the misfortunes which his country had sustained during the course of a century and a half by those ruinous expeditions to the East. But, unfortunately, in the delirium of a fever, he fancied that he had received a summons from heaven to take up the cross against the infidels ; and neither the return of his reason, the entreaties of his queen, nor the remonstrances of his counsellors could divert him from that fatal project. He employed four years in preparing for the expedition, and set out with his queen, his three brothers, and their wives, and all the knights of France, with a prodigious number of their vassals and attendants. On arriving at Cyprus he was joined by the king of that island, and proceeding to Egypt they began the campaign with expelling the barbarians from Damietta. Here they were reinforced by a new army from France, amounting to 60,000 men, and Melecsala, the sultan of Egypt, thought it his wisest course to sue for peace, which, however was refused him. This denial the Christians had soon abundant reason to repent, for half of their immense army perished by sickness, and the other half was defeated by Almoadin, the son of Melecsala. Lewis himself, with two of his brothers, were taken prisoners, and the third was killed in the engagement. Lewis offered a million of besants in gold for the ransom of himself and his fellow-prisoners; and such was the uncommon generosity of this infidel prince, that he remitted to him a fifth part of the sum. Lewis paid his ransom and returned to his dominions, where, for thirteen years, he employed himself in all the duties of a wise and virtuous prince; but his passion for the crusades returned with double violence. The pope encouraged him by granting him a tenth penny out of the revenues of the clergy for three years; and he set out a second time with nearly the same force as before. But his brother Charles of Anjou, whom the pope had made king of Naples and Sicily, turned the course of his arms to Africa instead of Palestine. Charles's ambition was to seize the dominions of the king of Tunis, and Lewis joined in the enterprise from an earnest desire of converting that prince and his subjects to Christianity; both were unsuccessful in their aims. The Christians were besieged in their camp by the Moors, and the unfortunate Lewis, after losing one of his sons by the plague, fell a victim himself to the same distemper. His brother, the king of Sicily, concluded a peace with the Moors, and some few of the Christian troops who survived that mortal contagion were brought back to Europe. In these two unfortunate expeditions of

Lewis IX., it is computed that there perished 100,000 men 50,000 had perished under Frederic Barbarossa; 300,000 under Philip Augustus and Richard Cœur de Lion; 200,000 in the time of John de Brienne; and 160,000 had before been sacrificed in Asia, besides those that perished in the expedition to Constantinople. Thus, without mentioning a crusade in the North, and that afterwards to be taken notice of against the Albigenses, it is a reasonable computation to estimate that two millions of Europeans, in these expeditions, were buried in the East.

CHAPTER X.

Effects of the Crusades—Rise of Chivalry and Romance.

Several authors have incidentally touched upon the effects produced by the crusades on the government and manners of the European nations; particularly two of the greatest of our English historians, Hume and Robertson, the last of whom has examined that topic, at considerable length, in the Introduction to the History of Charles V. The subject, however, is not, as I apprehend, exhausted. The particular effects which have been touched on by these authors, I shall very briefly recapitulate. Some of them are, as I think, liable to a few objections, and I shall subjoin the notice of such other consequences as I think must have been the natural and certain result of those expeditions.

One immediate consequence of the crusades is generally supposed to have been a refinement of the European manners, and an improvement of the arts imported by the crusaders, from an acquaintance with the countries more polished than their own; yet, the truth is, that we do not find from history, that the period of the crusades was the era of any such actual improvement, either in manners or in the arts. The times immediately succeeding the crusades were, in many respects, rather inferior to those which preceded, than superior. The last crusade was finished in the year 1250: from that time, for above two centuries, there never was a period in which Europe, on the whole, appeared more barbarous and unenlightened; nor was it till after the taking of Constantinople by the Turks, and the utter destruction of the Greek empire, which was in the year 1453, that there was any sensible improvement in the state of the fine arts in Europe. It was then that the Greek artisans, and many men, eminent for their learning, being driven from their country, now occupied by the Turks, resorted to the different kingdoms of Europe, particularly Italy and France; and from that time, we may date with certainty the revival of the arts, and the sensible improvement of the European manners.

One certain effect of the crusades must have been great changes in territorial property throughout the kingdoms of Europe. The nobility and barons who went on those expeditions were obliged to sell their lands to defray their charges. The lands passed into the hands of other proprietors, and their former masters, such of them as ever returned to their country, had expended the whole of their fortunes. This fluctuation of property diminished the weight and influence of the greater barons, and weakened the aristocratical spirit of the feudal system. The lands of a single lord were likewise divided among a number of smaller proprietors; for few individuals were then opulent enough to have purchased entire lordships. This would necessarily diffuse a spirit of independence, and bring men nearer to an equality of property.

In the next place, the towns or boroughs, which were then tied down by a sort of vassalage and clientship to the nobles, began now to purchase their immunity; and, instead of being entirely governed by these nobles, to whom the magistrates were no more than servants and stewards, while they exercised themselves the supreme civil and criminal authority, and imposed what taxes or exactions they thought fit, the towns now acquired a right of choosing their own magistrates, who were responsible to the public; they freed themselves from those arbitrary impositions, and were governed by their own municipal statutes, subordinate to the public laws of the kingdom. Thus the municipal government began, in many of the towns of Europe, to take the place of the feudal.

It is difficult to say whether the church, upon the whole, gained or lost by the crusades. The authority of the popes was certainly increased in the article of an extent of jurisdiction, and their right of conferring kingdoms began now to be less questioned, because it was so customary; but the unsuccessful issue of these enterprises, and their ruinous consequences in depopulating and impoverishing all Christendom, took a strong hold of the minds of men of sense, and thus weakened the papal authority, by exposing the interested and selfish motives which had influenced the see of Rome in preaching up those destructive armaments and expeditions. In another respect, the gain of the church was balanced by its loss. Many of the religious orders and societies acquired considerable territorial opulence by the purchase of the lands of the barons at an easy rate: but this increase of wealth was proportionally diminished by the tax of the tenth penny, which it became customary for the pope to grant to the kings out of the revenue of all the clergy in their dominons.

A very sensible effect of the crusades over the greatest part of Europe was the necessity which the princes of the several countries found themselves to be under, from the scarcity of money, of making an alteration in the coin, and debasing its weight and intrinsic value. This occasioned excessive murmurings among the people, and their resentment was expressed by plundering the Jews, who were at this time the bankers over all Europe, and who it was thought, by amassing prodigious wealth by usury, had robbed and impoverished the different kingdoms in which they resided. Both in England and in France, the Jews were the victims of this false idea, and they were not only stripped of their wealth, but banished from the country.

A few of the maritime cities of Italy were, perhaps, the most substantial gainers by the crusades. Genoa and Pisa enriched themselves in the beginning, by possessing exclusively the trade of furnishing ships to transport the forces to the Levant, and of supplying them, when there, with provisions. Venice came in afterwards for a share of those gains, and showed a more extensive spirit of enterprise, by furnishing troops, and stipulating for a share of the conquered lands. By these means the Venetians acquired the province of Dalmatia, the Peloponnesus, the island of Candia, and several towns on the coast of Asia Minor.

The last particular which I shall mention as a consequence of the holy wars was the perfection of chivalry and of that romantic spirit for adventure, which for some centuries infected all Europe. The real perils which those adventurers encountered were embellished in their narrations, and thence arose a fondness for extravagant stories, and wonderful fictions of the imagination.

On the origin of chivalry, a great deal has been written and conjectured, and many opinions been given, which, though they differ in some particulars, resolve ultimately into the same idea, which is, that this extraordinary institution, or rather system of manners, arose naturally from the state and condition of society in those ages when it was observed to prevail. The government of the Germanic nations, where a vast number of detached tribes were each under the command of an independent chief, and the condition of individuals whose almost constant occupation was war, were a necessary cause of that exclusive regard which was paid to the profession of arms, in comparison with which every other employment was esteemed mean and unimportant. It was customary in many nations, that the first introduction of youth to the occupations of manhood was attended with peculiar ceremonies and distinguished solemnity: and thus, among the German nations, it was extremely natural that the youth should be introduced with particular ceremonies to that military profession in which he was to be engaged for life. The chief of the tribe, under whose banner all his vassals were to fight, bestowed, himself, the sword and armor upon the young soldier, as a mark that, being conferred by him, they were to be used at his command, and for his service alone. When the feudal system became matured, and the vassals themselves had a subordinate train of vassals and dependents, they, in imitation of the chief or overlord, assumed to themselves the power of conferring arms upon their sub-vassals. There is a natural fondness for ceremonies which impress the imagination, and it is probable that, from a few solemnities first used, new solemnities being added from time to time, that extraordinary, complicated, and mysterious pomp at length arose, with which we find the honor of knighthood was conferred about the period of the eleventh century.

The candidate for that honor was previously prepared for it by the most austere fasts. He was obliged to spend a whole night in a church in prayer, to make a solemn and full confession of his sins, to receive the holy eucharist, and to have his body purified by bathing; then he was again introduced into the church, where he presented to the priest a sword, who, giving it his benediction, hung it round the neck of the novice; he again, taking it off, presented it to the knight, or chief, who was to confer the honor upon him; and falling down on his knees, and joining his hands, after solemnly swearing to maintain the cause of religion and chivalry, he received from him the spurs, the halberd, the coat of mail, and the sword. Then the chief, embracing him round the neck, and gently striking him three times with the flat part of his sword upon the shoulder, finished the ceremony by pronouncing these words—"In the name of God, St. Michael, and St. George, I make thee a knight. Be valiant, hardy, and loyal."

The young knight was now entirely possessed with the strong ambition of signalizing himself by some romantic and dangerous adventure. He went forth, if we are to believe literally the chroniclers of those ages, with the determined purpose of provoking to combat some other knight of established renown; and to effect this a pretence was never wanting. He had only to assert boldly that the lady whom it was his happiness to serve and obey, excelled every other female in beauty and in virtue as much as the moon surpassed the stars in splendor, and to insist upon every knight he met making the same acknowledgment.

The high esteem of the female sex we have before remarked to have been characteristic of the Gothic manners. It was remarked by Tacitus, and by Cæsar, of the ancient Germans, and, in the progress of manners from the rudeness of their tribes at the time of these historians to the age of the perfection of the feudal system, it produced at length the high and refined ideas of romantic gallantry. The castles of the barons were in miniature the courts of sovereigns. The constant society of the ladies, who found only in such fortresses a proper security and protection, necessarily encouraged a soft intercourse, which the authority of the baron kept always within the bounds of politeness. The protection of the honor and chastity of the ladies from all insult and outrage became naturally one of the characteristics of an accomplished knight ; and the passion of love, under these circumstances, was necessarily carried to a most romantic height.

Spenser, whose beautiful fictions convey an idea of the true spirit of chivalry, strongly marks this connection of romantic love with the profession of arms :

> "It hath been through all ages ever seen
> That with the praise of arms and chivalry
> The prize of beauty still hath joined been,
> And that for reason's special privity ;
> For either doth on other much rely ;
> For he me seems most fit the fair to serve
> That can her best defend from villany,
> And she most fit his service doth deserve
> That fairest is, and from her faith will never swerve."

To the passion for military glory and romantic love, which distinguish the profession of chivalry, were added very high ideas both of morality and religion : such morality, indeed, and such religion, as we may expect from the rudeness and barbarism of the times. The Gothic knights had the highest pride in redressing wrongs and grievances ; but in this honorable employment the wrongs they committed were often greater than those they redressed ; and in the vindication of the fame or honor of a mistress, a real and most atrocious injury was frequently committed in revenge of one purely ideal. Their religion, too, was of that extraordinary cast, that, though *professedly* superior to all other duties, it always in reality acted a part subordinate to military fame and the honor of the ladies. It is confessed by one of their greatest encomiasts, M. de St. Palaye, that their devotion consisted chiefly in the observance of some external ceremonies, and that the greatest offences might be easily expiated by a penance or a pilgrimage, which furnished an agreeable opportunity for new adventures.

Chivalry, whether it began with the Moors or Normans, did not attain its perfection till the period of the crusades, when a great and interesting object was furnished to those who aspired at military fame. The spirit of adventure and the passion for glory had now a noble field for exertion ; and we have observed accordingly that the most enthusiastic ardor seemed to pervade at once all the European nations. We have already seen how prodigious was the waste of blood in those expeditions, and how few returned to their countries of those immense swarms which poured into the East. But those few who did return found in the admiration and applause of their countrymen a high reward for their labors : their praises were sung by bards and minstrels, and their exploits recorded in a species of composition unknown till this time, the celebrated old Romances. This species of composition was so named from the *Romance* language, in which the first of these works were composed. Latin was the vulgar tongue in France till the beginning of the ninth century; then arose a mixed dialect between the Latin and the Frank tongues, which was termed *Romance*, and which in process of time is now matured into the French language.

Although the most ancient of those compositions, termed romances, treat of the actions of the heroes of chivalry, who existed even some centuries before the period of the crusades, it is very certain that, till the twelfth century, there were none of those works known in Europe. The first works of romantic fiction, which have laid the foundation of all the subsequent romances, were the history of the deeds of the Welsh princes, particularly Arthur, king of the Britons, written, or compiled by Geoffrey of Monmouth, who died in the year 1154; and the fabulous exploits of Charlemagne and his twelve peers, written, as is supposed, by a monk, under the fictitious name of archbishop Turpin, about the same period. At this very time all Europe was engrossed with the second crusade. Godfiey of Bouillon had taken Jerusalem, and the Holy Land was recovered. The attention of the European kingdoms was occupied entirely by those interesting relations which adventurers were daily bringing from the East, of wonderful exploits and extraordinary successes or misfortunes. But the appetite for the marvellous, which was then highly fostered by the ignorance and credulity of the times, was not sufficiently gratified by those relations, exaggerated as we may suppose them to have been. Something more was still required, and the romancer, who, in the relation of contemporary events, found himself too much fettered by known truths, was enabled, by choosing an ancient hero for his theme, to give free scope to his imagination, which, the more wonderful were its chimeras, gave still the higher delight and satisfaction. Eginhart, the contemporary of Charlemagne, and his secretary and biographer, however credulous was the age in which he lived, and however fond of the marvellous, was not at liberty to embellish his narration with colors known by all to be beyond the truth; but the nominal Turpin, in his history of Charlemagne and his twelve peers, who introduced him to view through the medium of three dark centuries, was under no such restraint. Charlemagne is here a very different personage, and the dangers he really underwent in his extensive conquests are nothing to the dreadful perils he and his twelve peers are made to encounter amidst the horrible assaults of dragons and serpents, and the dreadful machinations of giants and enchanters.

The effect of these extraordinary fictions was in those days extremely powerful That there is in the human mind a propensity to relish the description of those chimeras of the imagination has never been denied; and philosophers have endeavored, by a variety of ingenious reasonings, to account for a fact, apparently so singular, as that the mind should take any interest in the description of events or scenes, while, at the same time, we are convinced, from our reason, that they are utterly impossible. The phenomenon may, perhaps, be thus simply accounted for. Every narration or description has, in a smaller degree, the effect of a dramatic representation. We allow ourselves to enter into the situation and feelings of the persons concerned. We adopt for the time their ideas and their character of mind; and as, in order to conceive and to be interested in the feelings of Hamlet, upon the sight of his father's ghost, it is not necessary that the spectator should have a belief in the reality of *ghosts* and *apparitions;* so in the fictions of Geoffrey and of Turpin, of Ariosto and of Tasso, when we see the characters act consistently with the belief of the power of enchantment, and the reality of spirits, giants, and fiery dragons, we adopt for the time their feelings, and are not at all disposed to quarrel with them on the score of absurdity.

But if at this day, under the disadvantage of giving no credit to the reality of these supernatural scenes and objects, we still find ourselves highly interested in such descriptions; how infinitely more powerful must have been their effect in those times when the unenlightened minds of the generality of mankind gave full belief to the power of magic, the agency of spirits, and all the train of "*Gorgons, spectres,* and *chimeras dire!*" That such was the credulity of the times when those romances were written is beyond all question—a credulity, too, which prevailed in times much nearer to the modern: and hence it is not a little wonderful, that some, and those too ingenious critics, should have considered all those fictions as purely allegorical, and as being intended to shadow out real events, or circumstances of genuine manners, and as such attempted to explain them. Dr. Hurd, in his Letters on Chivalry and Romance, (page 28,) says, "We hear much of knights-errant encountering giants, and quelling savages in books of chivalry. These giants were oppressive feudal lords, and every lord was to be met with, like the giant, in his strong-hold or castle. Their dependents, of a lower form, who imitated the violence of their superiors, and had not their castles, but their lurking-places, were the savages of romance. The greater lord was called the giant for his power, the less, a savage for his brutality." It may be asked of Dr. Hurd, what then were the serpents and dragons? and Mons. Mallet, an ingenious Frenchman, will give the answer; for he explains them likewise by the help of allegory. "The serpents and dragons," says he, "which guarded the enchanted castles, were nothing else than the winding walls which surrounded the Gothic fortresses, built on the projecting summits of rocks and precipices. It is pity there were no *cannon* known in those days, when romantic fiction was at its height, otherwise the allegory would have been complete, of the dragons *vomiting fire and voiding stench sulphureous.*" But this idea is altogether a false one: the more ancient romances were neither written with the purpose of conveying an allegorical meaning, nor was there any thought at that time of giving them such interpretation. They were readily received by the general belief in their literal signification; the power of enchantment was then fully credited, and if it is alleged that the authors of those works, who knew that they had spun them out of their own brain, must have been conscious that they were imposing a fiction on the world; I answer, that they believed, as firmly as their readers, that, at least, such events were possible; and in all probability adopted them from traditionary accounts, which they had done nothing more than arrange and embellish.

It will be easily perceived that I speak here only of the more ancient of the old romances. The mode of instruction by allegory came afterwards to be much in use; and when those notions of the power of enchantment began with the wiser sort to lose somewhat of their credit, they still retained the power of strongly impressing the imagination, and captivating the general attention. They were now adopted by the poets as an allegorical vehicle for moral instruction: such at least is the apology by which some of the poets, both of Italy and of our own nation, seem very desirous of excusing themselves for retaining in their works the extravagant fictions of the Gothic ages, though these allegories lie often so deep, and are so little obvious to the reader, as almost always to require a key from the author himself: a circumstance which gives ground for a strong presumption that the purpose of moral instruction was but secondary to the indulgence of the authors' fancy, and the gratification of a taste prevalent in their time, and which probably will always retain a considerable influence. When we read at this day the description of Tasso's enchanted forest, our imagination is involuntarily transported into the region of spirits: we see the demons in the fire—we hear the human groans from the oak, we perceive the blood dropping from its wounded branches—we feel for a time a portion of that horror which possessed the souls of Tancred and Alcastro.* We have no leisure, then, to think of the hidden allegory of that extraordinary fiction, nor to attend to that abstruse and refined moral which Tasso, with much pains, inculcates in his preface—the dangers with which the path of virtue is beset in this evil world, and the constant endeavors of the great enemy of the soul to withdraw the Christian from his duty. Entertainment was the object of those works of fancy, and they attained their aim. Instruction was pretended; but the friends of severe morality knew this to be only a pretence,

* Tasso, Gerusalemme Liberata, canto 13.

and would not admit the excuse. They censured the authors of those compositions with great asperity. Prynne's "Histriomastyx," written in the time of Charles I. of England, and Collier, in the reign of Charles II., were not more severe against the immorality of stage-plays than Ascham, in the reign of queen Elizabeth, against the evil tendency and pernicious consequences of those old romances, performances which he terms "Enchantments of Circe, brought out of Italy to marre men's manners in England."

The taste for the tales of chivalry, and the old romance, seemed indeed to revive in the reign of Elizabeth. She inherited from her father, Henry VIII., a genius for knight-errantry, and was fond of those extraordinary fictions which became once more a prevailing passion. The Arcadia of Sir Philip Sidney and Spenser's Faery Queene, both composed in that reign, are among the last of the classical performances in the spirit of chivalry. That mode of writing, I suspect, is now for ever exploded. Those *speciosa miracu'a* would be no longer tolerable in a modern composition. Fancy is now constrained to ally herself with truth; and the generality even of the vulgar, whose passions are not easily affected unless through the medium either of realities or strong prejudices, would turn away from those compositions which their ancestors read with eager delight, and *trembled while they believed.*

We may congratulate ourselves, no doubt, in the main, upon the victory of reason and good sense over superstitious prejudices; but a good taste with a lively imagination, still charmed with the perusal of those remains of *legendary lore*, will not easily console itself for the dissolution of that ideal world, or venerate the more that increasing philosophic light for having dried up for ever the sources of romantic fiction. As Voltaire himself exclaims:—

"Oh happy times of old, when sure assent
Was given to tales of airy sprites who guard
The household hearth, and earn their due reward
For labors to the careful housewife lent;
Or those kind fays by good Titania sent
To watch the just man's dream, and antedate
Elysium's bliss; such tales at evening fire
To all his listening race the hoary sire,
While mute attention reigned, could well relate,
Or vengeance fell record, of fiend's or demon's hate.

"But these are heard no more. The airy reign
Of Fancy fades away; and all the throng,
That filled creation's void, air, earth, and main,
Of forms ideal cease. To us belong
To trace with searching eye and doubtful ear
Stern Truth, and Science to her dark retreat,
To court coy Wisdom in her cloistered seat,
And Reason's empire own and laws severe.
Error exchanged for Truth, the gain how great!
Ah! Error had her charms—when lost, we own too late."

Such are the natural feelings of one who, though a philosopher, was also a poet. It will however, require genius of a very remarkable order ever to revive among the polished nations of Europe a fervid taste for the romance of chivalry.

CHAPTER XI.

State of the EUROPEAN KINGDOMS towards the End of the Crusades, and in the Age immediately following:—Constantinople recovered by the Greek Emperors—Sicilian Vespers—Crusade against the Albigenses—Rise of the House of Austria—Spirit of the Popedom—Persecution of the Knights Templars—Rise of the Helvetic Republics—Council of Constance.

CONSTANTINOPLE, taken as we have seen by the crusaders, did not remain long in the hands of its Western conquerors. The popes, however, for a while flattered themselves with the disposal of both empires. Peter de Courtenay was crowned at Rome, emperor of Constantinople, and his successor, Baldwin II., acknowledged the pope's superiority, by coming to Rome to solicit the assistance of a crusade, both against the Greeks and against the Mahometans. He solicited to no purpose, and returned to Constantinople only to see it fall into the possession of its ancient masters, the Greek emperors. Michael Paleologus, tutor to the young emperor Lascaris, retook the city; Baldwin fled; and Paleologus imprisoned and put out the eyes of his pupil, and so secured to himself the possession of the empire. He took care, however, to screen himself from vengeance by courting the favor of the pope, and once more reunited the Greeks to the Latin church.

Frederic II., surnamed Barbarossa, was at this time emperor of Germany, and paid homage to the pope for the kingdom of Naples and Sicily, which was possessed by his son Conrad. Conrad, it is said, was poisoned by his unnatural brother, Manfred, who certainly seized on his kingdom, to the exclusion of his nephew, the younger Conradin, whose right it was by inheritance. The holy see was always jealous of the dominion of the German emperors in Italy. Pope Clement IV., who hated the family of Frederic, (the house of Swabia,) and at the same time was desirous of punishing the usurpation of Manfred, gave the investiture of the kingdom of Naples and Sicily to Charles of Anjou, brother of Lewis IX. of France, on condition of his paying a large tribute, and renouncing his right after a limited period of time Charles accepted the condition, and gave battle to Manfred, who was killed in the engagement, and thus Charles became master of Naples and Sicily, while young Conradin, with the aid of his kinsman, the duke of Austria, prepared to vindicate his right to his father's kingdom. The pope armed in support of his vassal, Charles of Anjou. An engagement ensued, in which Conradin and the duke of Austria were totally defeated—they were taken prisoners and condemned as rebels against the supreme authority of the holy church; Charles ordered them to suffer death upon a scaffold. Thus this prince secured his claim to the kingdom of Naples and Sicily, by a deed which filled his new subjects with horror. They submitted, for awhile, with silent indignation to his tyrannical government. The Sicilians at length, to whom the authority of this usurper became every day more intolerable, formed a conspiracy to vindicate their liberty, which terminated in one of the most dreadful massacres ever known in history. In the year 1282, upon Easter Sunday, *at the ringing of the bell for vespers*, it was resolved to put to death every Frenchman through the whole island of Sicily, and the resolution was punctually executed. Even women and infants underwent the general fate, and such was the savage fury of the Sicilians, that the priests assisted in the murder of their brethren, and cut the throats even of their female penitents. Thus the blood of Conradin was amply revenged, and the cruelty of Charles of Anjou signally punished—but these sanguinary proceedings brought new misfortunes on the kingdom of Sicily.

Peter, king of Arragon, who had married the daughter of Manfred, now stepped forth in support of the Sicilians, against Charles of Anjou, and claimed the crown himself in right of his wife. The Sicilians received him with open arms, and the consequence was a ruinous war of several years' duration, which involved this unhappy country in the greatest calamities.

We have mentioned the crusade against the Albigenses, which happened about forty years before this period. It is proper to give a short account of this detestable persecution. The Albigenses were the inhabitants of the Pays de Vaud in Piedmont, and principally of the city of Alby. Some men among them had begun to reason about matters of religion; and in those times, when the abuses of the papal power were very glaring, it was not difficult to persuade the people to shake off a yoke which they found extremely burdensome. These people of Piedmont and Languedoc began to preach up the sacred scriptures as the only rule of conduct, and consequently the exclusion of all papal and ecclesiastical constitutions.* Innocent III. was the first who took measures to repress these dangerous heretics. He sent two

* Many of the Albigenses inclined to the Manichean heresy.—See Mosheim part ii., ch. 5

Cistertian monks, with a commission to try them and excommunicate them, and required the assistance of the temporal lords of the country to deprive them of their estates, and to punish them with the utmost severity. This ecclesiastical commission was the first origin of the horrible tribunal of the Inquisition, which has since been the scourge of the Catholic countries, and particularly of Spain, Portugal, and Italy. Their court was established at Toulouse, which gave such offence and disquiet to the count of Toulouse, that it is said he caused the first inquisitor to be assassinated. The opposition which he showed to the holy see cost him extremely dear. Pope Innocent discharged his subjects from their allegiance, and at length forgave him only on the condition of his giving up several of his castles, and promising to form a crusade himself against his countrymen. The count was compelled to obey, and under the command of Simon de Montfort, this holy campaign was begun. The city of Beziers, which harbored a great number of the heretics, was taken by storm, and all the inhabitants put to the sword; Carcassonne submitted, and implored for mercy, but the inhabitants were all driven out naked, and their goods confiscated. Massacres and public executions followed without number. Those unfortunate wretches died martyrs to their religious opinions, and numbers of them joined in hymns of triumph while they were burning at the stake. The unhappy count, compelled to be a spectator, and even an assistant in those scenes of misery, found means at length to escape, and betook himself to his brother the king of Arragon, whom he persuaded to arm in the cause of humanity. But that prince, whose forces when mustered in the field, it is said, amounted to 100,000, was, according to the incredible narrations of historians, defeated by Simon de Montfort with 1800 men. Simon, this atrocious and bloody villain, was killed soon after by a stroke of a stone, and from that period the crusade, wanting a leader wicked enough to supply his place, began to decline. His son, young de Montfort, was unable to keep the dominions of Languedoc which the pope had settled on his father. He renounced them to Lewis VIII. of France, whose death prevented his taking possession of them, and they were not annexed to the crown of France till the reign of Philip the Bold. The Inquisition, in the meantime, repressed all religious innovations, and the sect of the Albigenses, if it continued secretly to exist, created at least no more disturbance. The effects of this tribunal in quieting men's consciences were so apparent, that pope Innocent IV. established it over all Italy, except in the kingdom of Naples.

The rise and elevation of the illustrious house of Austria was attended with some remarkable circumstances, which strongly mark the spirit of the times. The first prince of the house of Austria, who sat on the imperial throne, was Rodolph, count of

Hapsburg, who was descended from the counts of Tierstiern, noble family of Switzerland. He possessed large patrimonial territories; and the honor he acquired by his military and political abilities induced some of the Swiss cantons to put themselves under his protection. Ottocarus, king of Bohemia, of whose dominions Austria then formed a part, appointed Rodolph his prime minister and steward of his household. On the death of the emperor, Henry II., the electors were so divided in their opinions whom to choose for his successor, that they agreed at length to commit the sole right of nomination to the count Palatine, Lewis, duke of Bavaria. Lewis named for emperor Rodolph of Hapsburg. It may be conceived that it should be somewhat humiliating to the king of Bohemia, who was one of the proudest princes of his time, to find the master of his household elevated to the rank of his sovereign, and as such entitled to exact homage from his dominions of Bohemia. When this demand was made by the heralds of the new emperor, Ottocarus indignantly replied, "Go tell your master that I owe him nothing, for I have paid him his wages." But this imprudent witticism cost him very dear. Rodolph instantly declared war against him, and in one campaign deprived him of Austria, Stiria, and Carniola. The emperor bestowed Austria on his eldest son, and it has ever since remained the patrimonial inheritance of his family. He now acquainted the king of Bohemia that his dignity as emperor positively required that he, the king, should perform homage as his vassal. Ottocarus was obliged to submit: but he required, as a condition, that the homage should be privately performed in the emperor's tent, and before the officers of the empire alone. On the day appointed, he repaired in his robes of state to the camp of the emperor, who chose on that occasion to be clothed in the plainest apparel. When Ottocarus was on his knees before Rodolph, the curtains of the tent were drawn up, and the king of Bohemia was exhibited in that attitude to the whole imperial army. This provoked the king to the highest pitch of indignation. He immediately renounced his allegiance, and declared war against the emperor, in hopes of recovering his dominions of Austria; but in his first battle he was defeated and slain.

Rodolph, like his predecessors of the Swabian line, aimed at the sovereignty of Italy: he wanted power, however, to accomplish this object of ambition, and he contented himself with obtaining sums of money from the principal towns, in token of their allegiance.

The Genoese, the Venetians, and the Pisans, were at this time contributing to the wealth, improvement, and civilization of their country, while the rest of Europe (if we except England under Edward I.) was yet extremely barbarous. A dawning of liberty was, however, beginning to arise in France,—at least we may term it liberty when compared to the ancient servitude. The communities or corporations of cities which we have mentioned as a consequence of the crusades, began, under Philip the Fair of France, to be admitted among the states-general, and by degrees, acquired weight and importance in the nation. Till then, there had been but two orders in the state, the nobility and the clergy. Philip the Fair summoned the third estate to the general assemblies, and established a standing court of judicature, by the name of Parliament; and his successor, Philip the Long, excluded the clergy from assisting in those assemblies, in which, at their first institution they presided. At this time, and long after, the parliament of Paris was nothing else than a supreme court of justice.

It were an object of some importance if we could ascertain what was the precise nature or constitution of the parliament of England at the period of which we now treat; but this is a subject involved in considerable doubt and obscurity.

It is certain that we may regard the Saxon Wittenagemot as the rude model of a parliament; but it is absurd to carry this notion so far as to find in that ancient assembly any thing approaching to the present constitution of England in its three distinct branches of King, Lords, and Commons. We have no good reasons for believing that the commons had in those days a share in the government of any of the European nations, nor till long after that age. If such ideas had existed before the feudal times, that system put an entire stop to them. According to the early feudal ideas, the commons were considered in a very abject and despicable light. Under the first princes of the Norman line, the supreme legislative power of England was lodged in the king and the great council, which was composed of the higher clergy and the barons. The prelates sat both as clergy by ancient usage in all the feudal kingdoms, and likewise by their right of baronage, as holding lands from the king, by the military tenure of furnishing men for his wars. The barons were the immediate vassals of the crown, and the most honorable members of the state. They owed their attendance in the court of their lord as a service, for which they held their possessions; and they were subjected to penalties in case of refusal. The crown had likewise other military vassals, the tenants *in capite*, by knight's service. These were likewise of a very honorable rank, though inferior in power and property to the barons. But though admitted to the general councils, they were not, it is probable, obliged to attendance by any penalty.

So far, there is no doubt as to the members of this general council. The only question is with regard to the commons, or the representatives of counties and boroughs; and this has been keenly agitated by the political parties even of modern times. It is surely enough that we enjoy a high measure of civil liberty at present: let us be grateful for it, and respect that constitution which bestows it on us. Yet there are those who seem to think it an impeachment of their present liberty that their progenitors, eight hundred years ago, could not boast of the same freedom. But history must always shock violent prejudices; and the best informed historians have agreed that the commons were no part of the great council till a long period after the Conquest, and that the military tenants alone of the crown composed that supreme and legislative assembly. All the ancient English historians, when they mention the great council of the nation, call it an assembly of the baronage, nobility, or great men; and none of their expressions can, without the utmost violence, admit of a meaning which will favor the supposition of the commons making any part of that body. But the most certain proof of all arises from the Magna Charta, which enumerates the prelates and immediate tenants of the crown as entitled to a seat in the general council, without the smallest mention of any others; and we have already remarked, in mentioning the particulars contained in the Magna Charta, that most of the stipulations were calculated to enlarge and serve the privileges of the higher orders, with very little regard to the great body of the people. In those times, men were little solicitous to obtain a place in legislative assemblies, and rather regarded their attendance as a burden than a privilege. Besides, by what rule was the people to be assembled? There was no idea of a delegated power in those days, or of the nature of representation: it was a notion too refined for the age. The truth is,—and we shall be convinced of it upon reflection,—that high sentiments of liberty cannot arise in the minds of a barbarous people, but are the cultivated and fostered fruits of refinement and civilization.

Besides this great council of the clergy and barons, the Anglo-Norman kings had their privy council, who were chosen by the king himself among his nobles, to assist him with their advice. It is asserted by Spelman as an undoubted truth, that during the reigns of the first Norman princes, every edict of the king, with the consent of his privy council, had the full force of law. But it is not probable that the barons were so passive as to entrust a power entirely arbitrary and despotic into the hands of the sovereign. All that we may conclude is, that the constitution had not fixed any precise boundaries to the regal authority, and that the prince frequently asserted such powers of prerogative as might be in the main repugnant to strict right, and what his barons might have compelled him to observe. The arbitrary exertions of John are surely no rule for judging of what was then the constitution; for even the reformation by the Magna Charta can be less considered as the conferring of new rights on the barons, than the reestablishment and security of their ancient ones.

The spirit of the popedom, ever arrogant and extending its prerogatives, continued during the thirteenth and fourteenth centuries much the same as we have seen it in the time preceding. Boniface VIII., elected pope in the year 1294, was one of the most assuming prelates that ever filled the pontifical chair; yet he found in Philip the Fair of France, a man determined to humble his pride and arrogance. Philip resolved to make the clergy of his kingdom bear their proportion in furnishing the public supplies, as well as the other orders of the state. The pope resented this as an extreme indignity offered to the church, and issued his pontifical bull commanding all the bishops of France to repair immediately to Rome.* Philip ordered the bull to be thrown into the fire, and strictly prohibited any of his bishops from stirring out of the kingdom. He repaired, however, himself to Rome, and threw the pope into prison; but being soon after obliged to quit Italy, Boniface regained his liberty.

The conduct of Philip in another affair which happened soon after, is not so justifiable as his behavior to the pope.

The Knights Templars, who had their rise in the holy wars, had acquired very great fortunes in those enterprises, and while they lived in splendor and in the most unlimited indulgence of their pleasures, their arrogance and their vices excited a general detestation of their order. The chief cause, however, of the resentment of Philip against this order of knights was probably their being concerned in a sedition, which arose on account of the debasement of the coin of the kingdom. The ostensible grounds of their accusation, and for which they were tried, were certain charges of impiety and idolatry, joined to some indecent practices in the admission of novices into their order. Clement V., who paid Philip implicit deference, issued his bulls to all the princes of Europe, to excite them to extirpate all the knights templars in their dominions, and they were complied with in Spain and in Sicily. They were rejected, indeed, by the English, who sent back the most ample testimony of the piety and good morals of this military order. The consequence, however, was, that in the continental kingdoms, these unfortunate men were put to the most cruel tortures, and finally committed to the flames. This abominable transaction has branded the memory of Philip the Fair with the character of a cruel and detestable tyrant, whatever may have been his wisdom, his spirit, and his political abilities.

Another remarkable event happened at this time, which does more honor to human nature, and is more agreeable to the pen of history to record. This was the revolution of Switzerland, and the rise of the Helvetic republic; the glorious and successful struggle for liberty and independence against tyranny and despotism. It has been mentioned, that Rodolph of Hapsburg, the founder of the house of Austria, possessed, by inheritance, some territories in Switzerland, and that several of the cantons had,

---

* Boniface, in his bull, styling himself, "Dominus totius mundi, tam in temporalibus quam in spiritualibus," Philip thus answered him, "Sciat tua maxima fatuitas, nos in temporalibus alicui non subesse."

from their high opinion of his military and political talents, placed themselves under his protection. The three cantons of Unterwald, Sweitz, and Uri, however, do not seem at any time to have acknowledged a dependence on the house of Austria. Albert, the son and successor of Rodolph, was desirous of subjugating the whole cantons, and erecting them into a principality for one of his children. In this view, he endeavored at first to persuade them to submit voluntarily to his dominion, but finding them tenacious of their liberties, he, with a very injudicious policy, attempted to force them to submission by sending among them viceroys, who exercised every species of the most insolent and tyrannical oppression. They were plundered, taxed, fined, imprisoned, and even put to death without form of law; and in a word, they groaned under all the miseries flowing from despotic power and barbarity. In this miserable situation they had no prospect of relief but in their own courage, and they began secretly to concert measures for delivering them from the tyranny of the Austrian government. Three country gentlemen, whose names were Stauffach, Furst, and Meletald, are said to have been the chiefs of the conspiracy, and to have brought the three cantons of Sweitz, Uri, and Unterwald, to a determined purpose of shaking off the yoke of their oppressors. The story of William Tell has much the air of romance: it is, however, pretty well authenticated. The governor of Uri, a detestable tyrant, is said to have fixed his hat upon a pole in the market-place, with a strict injunction that all who passed should render obeisance to this symbol of dignity. Tell, who refused to pay this homage to the hat, was condemned to be hanged, but received his pardon, on condition of his hitting with an arrow an apple which was placed upon his son's head. The father, fortunately, struck off the apple; but had reserved a second arrow for the governor, in case he had killed his son. This inhuman act of tyranny is said to have been the first alarm to a general revolt of the people, who immediately flew to arms and demolished all the fortresses in the province. Leopold, arch-duke of Austria, marched against the insurgents with 20,000 men. The Swiss fought to the greatest advantage, by keeping to the rocky and inaccessible parts of the country. A small body, of 400 or 500 men, defeated the greatest part of this immense army in the pass of Morgarten: a defile which is said very much to resemble that at Thermopylæ, where the Lacedæmonians fought with less good fortune against the Persians. The rest of the cantons, encouraged by this success, joined the confederacy by degrees. The victory of Morgarten was gained in the year 1315. Bern, which is considered as the principal of the united cantons, did not enter into the alliance till 1352; and it was not till near two centuries after, that the last of the cantons joined the rest, which completed the number thirteen. The Swiss fought with great perseverance, and won their liberty extremely dear. They had no less than sixty pitched battles with the Austrians, and they have retained to this day that independence which they have so well merited.

The thirteen towns, or cantons, which properly constitute the Swiss or Helvetic republic were united by a reciprocal convention, of which the chief article relates to the mutual succors and assistance to be furnished to any of the confederated states as should suffer from foreign attack or violence. The proportion of these succors was minutely stipulated. Another article of the convention stipulated the procedure in accommodating all domestic differences between the several cantons. Each of the cantons was, in all matters that regard not the national confederacy, an independent state. The form of government in the several states was very various. It was in some monarchical, in others aristocratical, and in others again democratical. In the monarchical states, some of the princes of the Germanic body were the sovereigns, as the bishop of Basle, and the abbot of St. Gall. Thus each state had its own form of government, and was regulated by its own particular laws, which it had an unlimited power of framing and of altering, and of modelling its own constitution. All affairs relating to the united confederacy were transacted either by letters or congresses. Letters from foreign powers to the whole confederacy were sent to the town of Zürich, and any proposal or notification from a town or canton, intended for general deliberation, was likewise transmitted thither, from whence it was officially circulated to all the other cantons, who either returned their opinion by letter, or if the matter was doubtful or of great importance, appointed a conference to be held by two deputies from each of the states,—on which occasions a deputy of Zürich sat as president of the assembly.

Thus the whole Helvetic body consisted properly of thirteen distinct, independent, and free republics, united by convention for their mutual security and protection. The Helvetic body, for more than six centuries, supported itself in a respectable state of independence; made war, concluded treaties, modelled its own constitution, enacted laws and ordinances, both in affairs civil and ecclesiastical, and exercised all the various powers of sovereignty. Under the freedom of these republican constitutions, the country of Switzerland came to be wonderfully improved. Where the lands are naturally fertile, and happily situated, they have been cultivated with the utmost skill and success; where nature has denied its advantages, art has amply supplied them. The produce of the country consists in corn, wine, oil, silk, and flax; and of the two last commodities, vast quantities are purchased from other neighboring quarters, which the Swiss employ themselves in manufacturing. The situation of Switzerland, bounded as it is by Germany, Italy, and France, affords great convenience for the sale and dispersion of these manufactures; and there is a communication with the Mediterranean by the river Rhône, and with the German Ocean by the Rhine. Several great lakes afford an inland navigation; and these, and the rivers of the country, the industrious Swiss have turned to the utmost possible advantage. As there is rather a superabundance of population in this country, a great part of the youth were bred to the profession of arms. The art military was there a profitable branch of trade. The republics let out their troops for hire to other nations; and the French, Germans, Spaniards, Sicilians, and the Dutch, found high advantage in the employment of the Swiss mercenaries, who have occasionally constituted the most valuable and best-disciplined part of their armies. It is a remarkable fact, demonstrative both of the populousness of the country and the prevalence of the military profession above all others, that the single canton of Bern, which in extent of territory is not half the size of Yorkshire, was able to bring into the field 100,000 well-disciplined troops at the shortest warning.

The struggles which we have seen so long subsisting between the popes and the emperor, had produced nothing fixed as to the power and prerogatives of each, or as to the great question, who should acknowledge the other's superiority. Henry VII. renewed his claim to Italy, and fought his way to Rome, where he was solemnly crowned, and ordained all the princes of Italy to pay him an annual tribute, styling himself Lord Paramount of the Pope. The pope, as is said, vindicated his rights, by employing a Dominican friar to poison the emperor in the consecrated wafer in which he took the sacrament.

Lewis of Bavaria, whom the pope, John XXII., had deprived and excommunicated, marching likewise to Rome, and holding a general council in the church of St. Peter, solemnly deposed the pontiff and created a new one; but Lewis was called home by the troubles of Germany, and John regained his seat, while the emperor's pope was sent to prison. The papal seat was at this time at Avignon, a city which belonged to the counts of Provence; and it did not return to Rome till the year 1377, when Gregory II., at the request of the citizens of Florence, who judged it might be for their advantage, brought back the residence of the popes to the Vatican.

Under Charles IV., the successor of Lewis of Bavaria, the empire of Germany assumed a more settled form of government than it had hitherto enjoyed. Charles published at Nuremberg that famous imperial constitution, known by the name of The Golden Bull, which was in fact the first fundamental law of the Germanic body. This new constitution, which was made with the utmost possible solemnity, reduced the number of the German electors to seven, whereas, before, all the nobility or lords who were possessors of fiefs, and all the prelates, claimed right to vote in the election of an emperor. The seven electors were the archbishops of Mentz, Treves, and Cologne; the king of Bohemia, the count Palatine, the duke of Saxony, and the margrave of Brandenburg. The golden bull assigned to each of the electors one of the great offices of the crown: the elections were ordered to be made at Frankfort; the emperor to be consecrated at Aix-la-Chapelle by the elector of Cologne; the first diet to be held at Nuremberg; the electorates to be inherited without division by the eldest sons according to the law of primogeniture. The other articles of this celebrated bull regard little else than the pomp of the coronation, and the ceremonial of the court.

Whether the residence of the popes should be at Avignon or at Rome, was a question of no small consequence to the church. It was, in short, a contest whether the clergy of Italy or of France should have the superiority. The French cardinals, at this time the majority of the conclave, being disgusted with the insolence of Urban, who was an Italian, retired to Naples and chose another pope, Clement VII. A short time after, another faction of the cardinals chose a third pope, John XXIII. Meantime the emperor Sigismund judged this division of the holy church to be a very proper occasion for his interfering to decide the dispute, and thus vindicate that imperial authority over the papal see, which had given birth to so many contests. For that purpose he summoned a general council of the church to meet at the city of Constance in Switzerland. Here Sigismund, who had surrounded the council with his army, ordered, in the first place, all the three popes to resign their dignity; and this being complied with, he next made the council elect a fourth person, Martin V., of the family of Colonna.

This important business being ended, Sigismund allowed the council to proceed to their spiritual concerns: and of this nature there were some of the transactions of this celebrated council so remarkable, as to attract the attention of all Europe.

John Huss, the father confessor of queen Sophia of Bavaria, had read some of the books of Wickliffe, who, at this early time, had begun to open the eyes of the people of England to the papal usurpations and the scandalous lives of the pontiffs and their bishops. Wickliffe had gone a step further, and had attacked the doctrine of transubstantiation. Huss did not meddle with these abstruse points, but railed against the ecclesiastical hierarchy, and the disorderly lives of the popes and bishops. He was cited to appear before the council of Constance, and was examined touching the most obnoxious passages of his writings. To deny the hierarchy, and to reproach the conduct and morals of the bishops, were sufficient crimes in the judgment of a council of these bishops, and Huss was condemned to be burnt alive. He might have saved his life by simply declaring that he abjured all his errors. The emperor Sigismund, who wanted to save him, thus reasoned with him:—"What harm can there be," said he, "in any man declaring that he abjures his errors? I am ready this moment to declare that I abjure all my errors;" but John Huss was too sincere to save his life by an equivocation, and he suffered death with heroic courage.

A few months afterwards, Jerome of Prague, the disciple and the friend of John Huss, underwent the same fate with his master. He was a man of superior talents and of great eloquence. The fear of death was at first too powerful, and he signed a recantation of his opinions; but no sooner had he heard how his master had encountered death than he was ashamed to live. He publicly retracted his recantation, preached forth his doctrines, and was condemned to the flames. He made a speech to his judges, which Poggio, the Florentine, who heard it, declares was equal to the finest specimen of Greek or Roman eloquence. "He spoke," says he, "like a Socrates, and walked to the kindled pile with as much serenity as that great philosopher displayed when he drank the poisoned cup."

These executions were attended with consequences to the emperor of which he had little expectation. The succession to the kingdom of Bohemia was opened to him by the death of his brother Winceslaus; but the Bohemians were so exasperated at the fate of their two countrymen, that it cost Sigismund a bloody war of sixteen years' continuance before he acquired the full possession of these dominions.

CHAPTER XII.

History of England in the Thirteenth and Fourteenth Centuries—Deputies from Burghs first called to Parliament—Edward I.—Conquest of Wales—Scotland—Obscurity of its early History—Malcolm Canmore—David I.—Alexander III.—Bruce and Baliol competitors for the Crown—Designs of Edward against Scotland—Sir William Wallace—Battles of Falkirk and Stirling—Death of Wallace—Robert Bruce—Edward II.—Battle of Bannockburn—Edward III.—Battle of Halidown Hill—Invasion of France—The Black Prince—Battle of Cressy—of Durham—of Poictiers—Richard II. —Henry IV.

After the death of John, that wicked and detestable tyrant, we saw his son, the young Henry III., crowned under the auspices of the earl of Pembroke, the protector; and the abdication of Lewis, who found it in vain to persist in his endeavors to possess himself of the kingdom which was now united, to a man, against him. Henry III. had not the vicious disposition of his father, but he was a weak and contemptible prince; fitted to be abused and trampled on by those aspiring barons who had so lately vindicated and extended their rights. Through the whole course of his reign, the kingdom was embroiled in commotions, which proceeded chiefly from that weak and mean policy of Henry in bestowing his offices of trust on foreigners, in order to be a check on the turbulent disposition of the English. These commotions, unimportant in the main in their effects, produced, however, one consequence well deserving observation. Simon Montfort, earl of Leicester, son of that Montfort whom we have lately beheld as the head of the crusade against the Albigenses, encouraged by the weakness of his sovereign, and his own power and popularity, resolved to attempt an innovation in the government, and to wrest the sceptre from the hand of Henry. He called a meeting of the barons, from whom, however, he concealed his particular scheme, and an association was entered into for the redress of public grievances. The king, to appease the growing disorders, summoned a Parliament at Oxford, where he agreed that certain persons of authority—twenty-four barons—should be appointed to digest a new plan of government. At the head of these was Montfort, and their measures contained the first *regular plan* of the British House of Commons. It was ordered that each county should choose four knights, who should examine into the grievances of their respective constituents, and attend at the ensuing parliament to give information of their complaints. These knights of the shires soon exemplified their power against the very persons to whom they owed it. The twenty-four barons, under Leicester, began to overturn the whole arrangement of the offices of government, and to substitute creatures of their own in place of those who had formerly filled them. They delegated to twelve persons, appointed by themselves, the whole powers of parliament, and seemed resolved to continue themselves in office for ever; thus substituting a vile oligarchy in place of the constitution of the kingdom. The knights of the shires, who now perceived their aim, and the aspiring views of their leader, the earl of Leicester, began to show a very laudable spirit. They remonstrated against the continuance of this junto in office; and they called upon the king's eldest son, prince Edward, a youth of noble spirit and most promising abilities, to interpose his authority, and to save England from perdition.

Edward was at this time about twenty-two years of age. He acted with the utmost propriety; and without openly taking the reins from the hands of a father who was unable to hold them, he adopted every measure, apparently under the king's authority, for vindicating his dignity and the interests of the kingdom.

Leicester now began to show the motives of his conduct without reserve. He had raised a formidable army in Wales, assisted by the prince of that province. The citizens of London, with their mayor, Thomas Fitz-Richard, a furious and lawless man, were likewise in his interest. Henry himself, intimidated by this vigorous opposition, meanly acquiesced in all the demands of Leicester. The twenty-four barons were established in office during the life both of the king and prince Edward ; and all the castles and fortresses surrendered into their hands. Prince Edward followed another line of conduct: he summoned the vassals of the crown to arm in the defence of their lord and of the kingdom, and soon collected an army with which he was able to take the field against the rebellious Leicester and his associates, but the impetuosity of his disposition involved him in misfortune. In the battle of Lewes, while he imprudently pursued one wing of the enemy, which he had routed and put to flight, the main body, under the more cool and deliberate Leicester, had cut off the best part of the royal army and taken king Henry prisoner. Edward in his return was surrounded, with his small body of troops, and forced to submit to the conqueror, who now procured a full ratification of all the measures of the confederated barons. Leicester, possessed of the persons of the king and of the prince, in fact ruled the kingdom. In order to confirm his authority, he called a parliament, where, on the part of the people, two knights were summoned from each of the counties, and also deputies from the boroughs, which had hitherto been regarded as too inconsiderable to have a voice in the legislation. This is the first confirmed plan of the English House of Commons.

This parliament, which Leicester, trusting to his popularity and power, expected was to second all his views, did not turn out to be so submissive as he could have wished: many of its members spoke their sentiments with freedom, and urged the reëstablishment of the ancient government of the kingdom, and Leicester was prudent enough to make a merit of what he saw he could not prevent. He released prince Edward from confinement, who no sooner received his liberty than, indignant that ever it had been abridged by a rebellious subject, he raised an army, marched against his enemy, whom he attacked before he was aware of his having taken the field, and Leicester, after a most bloody and obstinate fight of seven hours, was defeated and killed. Henry was now reëstablished in his kingdom by the hands of his gallant son, who had no sooner given peace to England than his enterprising spirit engaged him in the last crusade with Lewis IX., on which expedition he had scarce departed when the weak and pusillanimous Henry died, after a reign of fifty-six years—the longest to be met with in the annals of England, and, but for that one circumstance which we have particularly mentioned, the rise of the House of Commons—the least important.

Prince Edward, now Edward I., and known by the surname of Longshanks, was a monarch of a great and enterprising spirit, a prince whose ambition had no bounds, and who, in the gratification of that ruling passion was not always actuated by the principles of justice and humanity. After signalizing himself in Palestine, and in a very honorable manner giving peace to the Eastern countries, by a truce concluded for ten years with the sultan of Babylon, he was on his way returning home when he received intelligence of his father's death. He succeeded to an undisputed throne; and he found matters in such a situation, the barons so exhausted with their late contentions, and his own character so high on account of the heroic part he had sustained, both at home and abroad, that he might safely have pushed his authority any length; but he was naturally prudent, and though capable of becoming absolute, he satisfied himself with moderate power: he even confirmed the Magna Charta, which, from that time, as being acceded to by one of the boldest and most powerful of the English monarchs, began to be considered as solemnly and unalterably established.

The genius of Edward could not rest without an object of enterprise—he projected the conquest of Wales. Llewellyn, prince of North Wales, had refused to do homage for his dominions, and seemed determined to shake off all submission to the crown of England. The Welsh, who were the remains of the ancient Britons who had escaped the Roman and Saxon conquest,* still preserved their freedom, their own laws, their customs, and their language. Edward determined to subject them entirely to the crown of England; and the refusal of Llewellyn, who had formerly acknowledged his subjection, gave him a favorable pretext. He invaded Wales with an immense army, and cooped up Llewellyn among the mountains of Snowdon, whither he had betaken himself with his troops, as deeming those heights inaccessible to strangers; but *they* were *barren heights*, and the army of Edward prevented all supplies of provisions. The Welsh were, in short, compelled to submit at discretion. Edward dictated the terms of submission, which were, the relinquishment of a large part of the country, the payment of fifty thousand pounds sterling, and a consent of the prince to do homage, and swear fealty to the crown of England; in consideration of which the Welsh were allowed to enjoy their own laws. Some encroachments upon the borders soon invited the Welsh to infringe this treaty, and Edward marched his army into the heart of the country, where, for some time, he met with the most frantic and desperate opposition. At length, a decisive battle, fought in the year 1283, determined for ever the fate of Wales. Llewellyn was killed, and with him expired the government and the distinction of his nation. Wales was soon after formally united to the kingdom of England, and the title of its principality has ever since been borne by the eldest son of the king. Some circum

* See Blackstone's Comment., Introd., § 4.

stances of extreme barbarity marked this conquest upon the part of Edward. The Welsh bards kept alive an heroic spirit of freedom and independence, by rehearsing in their songs the glorious achievements of the ancient Britons: Edward ordered these unhappy minstrels to be massacred wherever they were found.

Mr. Hume, in mentioning this fact, which is well authenticated, admits the inhumanity of Edward's conduct, but seems to justify it on the score of prudence. "The king," says he, "from a barbarous, though not absurd policy, ordered the bards to be put to death." If the death of all that were alive of these unhappy men could have extinguished the profession and talents of a *bard*, or put an end at once to all remembrance of those heroic songs which had been handed down by memory from one generation to another, and which every Welshman had heard from his cradle,—then might the policy of Edward have been a wise one; but as the natural consequence of this inhuman measure in the breasts of the Welsh must have been the perpetuation of those very songs, and an increased abhorrence of their conqueror, and disaffection to his government, we cannot scruple to say that, in this instance, the policy of the king of England was as absurd as it was barbarous. The memory of this event, so inglorious to Edward, is secured for ever by the sublime ode of Gray upon the Death of the Welsh Bards.

The conquest of Wales paved the way for enterprises of more importance, though not attended with such permanent consequences. These were the designs of Edward upon Scotland. That ancient kingdom has made many noble struggles for her liberty and independence, and none more remarkable than against this bold, ambitious, and designing prince. But in order to understand the foundation of those pretences on which Edward founded his claims of sovereignty over this kingdom, it is necessary to take a short view of the history of Scotland previous to the period of which we now treat.

The history of Scotland, before the accession of Malcolm III., surnamed Canmore (i. e. *Great-Head*,) is involved in obscurity and fable.

Malcolm Canmore, after having subdued and put to death the usurper Macbeth, the murderer of his father Duncan, succeeded to the throne of Scotland in the year 1057. He had been aided in the recovery of his kingdom by the English, and was therefore disposed to cultivate a friendship with that nation. But William the Norman having accomplished the conquest of England, Edgar Atheling, the heir of the Saxon line, together with his sister Margaret, took refuge in Scotland; and the reception given them by Malcolm, and his subsequent marriage with the princess Margaret, could not fail to set the two nations at variance. The frequent insurrections of the English nobles in favor of the heir of their former kings—who, destitute of per sonal merit, had nothing but that title to recommend him—produced a succession of hostilities between William the Conqueror and Malcolm, which were equally prejudicial to both kingdoms. In one of these expeditions, in which William advanced pretty far into Scotland, it is alleged that the Scottish monarch, after concluding a truce, did homage to the conqueror for his kingdom of Scotland. A passage in the Saxon Chronicle, which simply says, "that Malcolm agreed with king William of England, and did him homage," was the foundation of a claim of sovereignty over this kingdom by the succeeding monarchs, which involved both nations in much bloodshed. It is foreign to my purpose to enter into critical discussions of controverted points of history. It seems, however, generally allowed that this claim of sovereignty has no solid foundation. It has never been disputed that the crown of England was imperial and independent; though its kings were for many ages the vassals of the French monarchs, and bound to feudal homage for those possessions which they held *in the kingdom of France.* Such likewise was the condition of the monarchs of Scotland—free and independent as kings, but, as possessing English territories, vassals to the crown of England *in those territories.* Malcolm Canmore, above all monarchs, would never have stooped to so mean a submission as that of doing homage for his *kingdom.* He was a prince of high spirit, and of steady and inflexible courage. In the course of a reign of twenty-seven years, he supported the contest with England, under William the Conqueror and his son Rufus, often with great success, and never without honor. To him, and perhaps yet more to the virtues of his queen, the Scottish nation were indebted for that dawning of civilization which is the consequence of wise laws, and a steady administration of government.

The short succeeding reigns of Donald Bane, the brother, and of Duncan II., and Edgar, sons of Malcolm Canmore, scarcely merit notice. On the death of the latter, Alexander I., third son of Canmore, ascended the throne—a prince of high, uncontrollable spirit. He defended most strenuously the independence of the national church against the pretensions of the metropolitan sees of York and Canterbury,— a contest carried on with as much animosity as the more celebrated disputes of the same nature between the emperors and the popedom; and had the independence of his kingdom been at that time called in question, he would have asserted it with equal courage and resolution.

His successor, David I., the youngest of the sons of Malcolm Canmore, was an honor to his country and to monarchy. Though defeated by the English in the great battle of the Standard, he maintained, upon the whole, a very successful war; and, by treaty with Stephen, he secured, as an appanage of his crown the whole earldom of Northumberland. More ambitious, however, of cultivating the arts of peace than of extending the limits of his kingdom, he endeavored to the utmost to repress those barbarous invasions which were equally destructive to his subjects and to their neighbors; and such were the wisdom and excellence of his domestic administration, that Buchannan himself, an historian whose principles are, on the whole, unfavorable to monarchy, has declared his opinion, that a more perfect pattern of a good king is to be found in the reign of David I. of Scotland, than in all the theories of the learned and ingenious. He was succeeded by his grandson, Malcolm IV.

In these reigns there was no pretence made by the English monarchs of a feudal dependency of the kingdom of Scotland. An accidental misfortune, which befell one of the Scottish kings, first encouraged the English to think of bringing this kingdom under dependence. William, surnamed the Lion, the grandson of David I., was taken prisoner at Alnwick; and Henry II., as the price of his liberty, not only extorted from him an exorbitant ransom, and a promise to surrender the places of the greatest strength in his dominions, but compelled him to do homage for his whole kingdom. Richard Cœur de Lion, a prince of more generosity, solemnly renounced this claim, and absolved William from the hard conditions which Henry had imposed. Upon the death of Alexander III., Edward I., availing himself of the situation of affairs in Scotland, revived that absurd claim of sovereignty; and, after a happy period of above a century of peace and good understanding between the nations, began a lengthened series of calamities, bloodshed, and devastation.

As Alexander III. left no male issue, nor any descendant except Margaret, (called the Maid of Norway,) his granddaughter, who did not long survive him, the right of succession devolved to the posterity of David, earl of Huntingdon, third son of David I. Of that line there appeared two illustrious competitors for the crown—Robert Bruce, son of Isabella, second daughter of the earl of Huntingdon; and John Baliol, grandson of Margaret, the earl's eldest daughter. As the rules of succession are *now* understood, the right of Baliol, the grandson of the eldest daughter, was clearly preferable. But in those days the order of succession was not so certainly established, and each competitor had his pretensions supported by a formidable party in the kingdom. To avoid a civil war, which must otherwise have taken place, the candidates agreed to a measure which had very near proved fatal to the independence of the kingdom. They chose Edward I. of England to be umpire of the contest; and this ambitious and artful prince determined to avail himself of the powers thus bestowed on him, and to arrogate to himself the sovereignty of Scotland. He summoned all the Scottish barons to attend him at the castle of Norham, in Northumberland; and having gained some, and intimidated others, he prevailed on the whole assembly to acknowledge Scotland a fief of the English crown, and to swear allegiance to him as their sovereign or liege lord.

He next demanded possession of the kingdom, that he might be able to deliver it to him whose right should be found preferable; and such was the dastardly pusillanimity of all present, whom Edward had intimidated by bringing with him a very formidable army, that this exorbitant demand was likewise complied with, both by the barons and the competitors for the crown. One man alone, worthy of an eternal memorial, Gilbert de Umphraville, earl of Angus, sustained the honor of his country, and peremptorily refused to deliver up those castles which he held from the Scottish kings. Edward, who believed Baliol the least formidable of the competitors, adjudged the question in his favor, and put him in possession of the kingdom, after making him solemnly take the oath of fidelity to himself as *lord paramount*, and subscribe to every condition which he thought proper to require. But the Scots were not long patient under their state of subjection. Edward found himself deceived in the character of Baliol, who determined very soon to get free from that yoke of dependence to which the necessity of circumstances had compelled him to submit. The king of England having summoned him, as a vassal, to answer in his courts to an appeal, at the instance of his Scottish subjects, he, on that occasion, maintained his independence as a sovereign, and soon after, with the consent of his parliament, solemnly renounced the allegiance and fealty which he had sworn to Edward. This renunciation was fatal to Baliol, while it was highly favorable to the political views of Edward. He marched a numerous army immediately into Scotland, to which the distracted state of the country rendered it impossible to oppose an adequate resistance. He carried every thing before him, and the unfortunate Baliol was compelled to implore the mercy of his conqueror, who obliged him to abdicate the throne, and resign the kingdom itself into his hands, and remain a prisoner in England.

In this state of universal despondency arose William Wallace, a man who deserves to be numbered among the heroes of antiquity. With no advantages of birth or fortune, conscious of his personal merits alone, with an invincible spirit, a courage equal to the greatest attempts, and every requisite quality of a consummate general, he undertook to retrieve the honor and the liberties of his country. A few patriots joined him in that glorious attempt, and his confessed superiority of merit bestowed on him the rank of their chief and leader. Taking advantage of an expedition of the English monarch into Flanders, while the government of Scotland had been intrusted to an imperious viceroy, Wallace, with his associates, began hostilities by an assault upon some of the strongest castles which contained English garrisons. Of these they made themselves masters by force or by surprise; and finding from these advantages their numbers daily increasing, they ventured to oppose a regular army of the English, who met them under the command of the viceroy near to Stirling. The stratagem, related by Buchannan, of sawing across the posts of the bridge, over which the English inconsiderately ventured to pass, is of a piece with those many fabulous exploits recorded of Wallace, which are beyond all historical credit. The Scots owed their success in the battle of Stirling to their valor in the field. The English were completely routed; they evacuated the country, and Scotland was once more a free kingdom. William Wallace assumed now the title of governor of Scotland under John Baliol, who still remained a prisoner. But this title which he had so well merited, drew on him the jealousy of the chief nobility, particularly the partisans of Bruce, who meanly continued to rank themselves under the banners of the English tyrant. Edward now returned from the continent, hastened to Scotland at the head of an army of 80,000 men, while the Scots in the interior parts of the country were collecting all their strength to oppose him. But dissensions among their leaders had weakened their patriotic bands, and their numbers were greatly inferior to the enemy. Had they artfully protracted the campaign, instead of hazarding a general engagement, the English, who were then ill supplied with provisions, must, in all probability, have been compelled to an inglorious retreat. But, with imprudent impetuosity, they desired to be led on to action. An engagement ensued at Falkirk, in which the Scots were routed with prodigious loss. Yet even the success of that day was a convincing proof to Edward that it was vain to hope for a complete conquest of the country. The remnant of the Scottish army continued still in the field. The whole country north of the river Forth was hostile to Edward, who, being constantly obliged, during the winter to evacuate the kingdom, found at the beginning of every new campaign, that he had to recommence his labors. At length, highly provoked, and resolutely determined on the entire conquest of the country, Edward concluded peace with his enemies on the continent, in order to bend his whole strength to terminate, as he called it, the rebellion of the Scots. He brought with him an immense army, and penetrating into the northern provinces, he took and garrisoned all the places of strength. Hence, returning southward, the only fortress capable of opposing him was the castle of Stirling, where the Scots were determined to make their last stand for the national liberty. But the event was unsuccessful; they gave way to the immense superiority of the English army, and the chief of the Scottish barons threw down their arms and submitted to the conqueror. A capitulation was signed by Edward, from which William Wallace, and a few of the most resolute of his adherents, were excepted by name. These brave men, now reduced to the condition of fugitives, concealed themselves in remote parts of the country; while Edward, with a policy which must ever be reckoned mean and dastardly, endeavored by high rewards to prompt a discovery of the places of their retreat; and that policy was successful. Wallace was betrayed by Menteith, a vile traitor, who had been in his confidence and friendship. He was given up into the hands of the conqueror; who, with consistent meanness and inhumanity, refined upon the cruelty of his fate by every species of contumely and wanton insult. The deliverer of his country was conducted to London, led in triumph through the streets, and seated on a mock throne in Westminster Hall, his head crowned with laurel. He was arraigned as a traitor to Edward, as having risen in arms against his sovereign, and put to death many of his subjects. "I never was a traitor," said Wallace; "I owe no allegiance to Edward; and I challenge all of you to produce a single instance, in which I have ever acknowledged the king of England to be the *lord paramount*, far less the *sovereign of my country!*" To the rest of the indictment, his having put to death many of the English, he pleaded guilty. Sentence was passed; he was beheaded; his head placed upon a pinnacle of the city; and his body, cut into many portions, was distributed throughout the different cities of Scotland and England. Thus died one of the best of patriots and bravest of men.*

Thus, after a long and obstinate contest, Scotland was a second time reduced under the dominion of Edward—a subjection which,

---

* Lord Hailes, in his "Annals," disputes the fact of Wallace being betrayed by Menteith, and has raised an historical controversy, which his Lordship conducts with no great candor. In his first edition, he asserts the story to rest solely on the authority of Blind Harry. In a note added to his second edition, he is obliged to admit that he has been reminded of another authority, that of Arnold Blair; and he disposes of it by the gratuitous assertion, that the passage referred to is evidently an interpolation of some patriotic and passionate transcriber. The passage is certainly marked both by patriotism and passion; but had Lord Hailes informed his reader that Arnold Blair was a priest, and the domestic chaplain of Wallace, he would have sufficiently accounted for these characteristics, and shown that such an authority was not to be disposed of by a gratuitous allegation. The passage, considered as the lament of a faithful servant over a beloved master, is a striking one, and, as an authority, worth a volume of historical criticism written after the lapse of five centuries. "And here it is to be observed, that these three things concur to immortalize the name of the noble Wallace—his own innocence—the tyranny of Edward—and the treachery of Menteith. Accursed be the day of John Menteith's nativity! —and may his name be blotted out of the book of life! Accursed be the inhuman tyrant that put him to death! while the noble champion of the Scots shall, for the reward of his virtue, have glory without end. Amen!"

But the author of the "Annals," knew well that the treason of Menteith rested yet on another, and also a contemporary authority—that of John Fordun. The eighth chapter of the twelfth book of the Scotichronicon is entitled "De proditione Johannis de Menteth, morte Willelmi Wallace," &c.; and the chapter begins, "Hoc eodem anno nobilis Willelmus Wallace per Dominum Johannem de Menteth, apud Glasgow, nihil mali suspicians, fraudulenter et proditionaliter capitur." This latter part of the Scotichronicon was arranged by Bowyer, from the materials of Fordun; but Bowyer lived but a few years later, and is at least of equal authority. There seems, then, no ground for preferring the *ipse dixit* of Lord Hailes to cotemporary testimony such as this, confirmed by general and continued tradition from that age to the present however, was but of a few months' continuance. Scotland found a second champion and deliverer in Robert Bruce, the grandson of the competitor. His father and grandfather had meanly enlisted themselves among the partisans of the English monarch; and, by their example, this young man too had sworn allegiance, along with most of the barons of the kingdom. But his native magnanimity kindling with his years, his noble spirit could not brook the fallen honors and humiliation of his country. He determined to vindicate its liberty or die in the attempt; and hastily withdrawing himself from the court of Edward, he again set up the standard of war in Scotland. "Better," said he to his partisans, "if Heaven should so decree, that we perish at once like brave men, than drag on with ignominy a life of servitude and oppression."

The circumstances which attended the first operations of Bruce towards the recovery of his country's liberties are variously related by historians. It is certain, however, that the spirit of the nation roused itself at once from its dejection; the English were attacked at the same time on every quarter; they were dispossessed of all the fortresses, and once more entirely driven out of the kingdom. Bruce, in right of the just pretensions of his family, now that Baliol had relinquished all claim in favor of his conqueror, was solemnly crowned king at Scone; while the enraged Edward, hastily advancing with a prodigious army, died at Carlisle, and left the throne of England, with his empty claim to the kingdom of Scotland, to his son Edward II. This prince inherited none of the great qualities of his father; he was a weak and indolent man, but of humane and benevolent affections. The social dispositions, the most amiable which distinguish human nature, are often dangerous ingredients in the character of a prince. Such was the disposition of Edward, that he could not be happy without the society of some mean favorite, to whom he might unbosom every secret of his breast. Piers Gaveston, a young man of beautiful figure and of shining accomplishments, had so fascinated the mind of Edward that he thought no reward equal to his deserts. He bestowed on him the earldom of Cornwall, married him to his own niece, and during a journey he undertook to Paris, to marry the Princess Isabella, left him guardian of the realm. The barons, who could not bear this upstart, determined his ruin. They assembled a tumultuous parliament and a numerous train of armed followers, and compelled the weak Edward to sign a commission delegating the whole authority of government to twelve persons to be chosen by themselves. The king patiently submitted to be stripped of power; but it cost him a severe pang to abandon his favorite to destruction. This, however, he was compelled to do, and Gaveston was thrown into prison, whence endeavoring a short time after to make his escape, he was seized and instantly beheaded. A truce, which had been concluded with

Scotland, in the beginning of the reign of this weak prince, had been infringed on both sides; and Edward now prepared, with an immense army of 100,000 men, to reduce the country to submission, and fulfil the dying request of his father, by making a complete conquest of it. King Robert Bruce met him at Bannockburn, near Stirling, with 30,000 men. By an excellent disposition of the Scottish army, and the signal intrepidity and conduct of the king, the English were totally routed. A prodigious slaughter ensued, and the pursuit continued near 100 miles, till the small remnant of this immense army was entirely driven out of the kingdom. Edward narrowly escaped by flight to Dunbar, whence he was conveyed by sea to his own dominions. This great and decisive victory secured the independence of Scotland, and fixed Robert Bruce firmly upon the throne. It made a deep impression on the minds of the English, and for several years after, no superiority of numbers could induce them to keep the field against their formidable adversaries.

The despicable Edward returned to London, where he had no resource but in the society of a new favorite, one Spenser, who soon became equally odious to the barons and to the queen Isabella. This bad woman, who hated and dishonored her husband, was allowed to go to France, to mediate with her brother Charles the Fair, who threatened to confiscate Edward's continental dominions, unless he came in person to do him homage for them. She found means to get her son young Edward likewise sent over, and then boldly declared that neither should ever return to England till Spenser was banished the kingdom. By these means she gained two advantages: she became popular in England, where Spenser was universally hated; and she enjoyed the company of Mortimer, a young nobleman now the object of her capricious affections, who had escaped from the Tower, where he had been confined for high treason. Isabella, encouraged by her brother, prepared to levy war against her husband. She was seconded by a powerful party in the kingdom; and concluding a match between young Edward and the daughter of the Earl of Hainault and Holland, she procured from that prince a powerful supply of troops. At length she repassed into England, Mortimer, her paramour, being at the head of her troops: while the king fled before them with his favorite Spenser, whose father, an old man of ninety, in vain attempted to defend the castle of Bristol against the rebels. A mutiny of the garrison gave him up into their hands; and such was their inhumanity and savage fury, that after hanging him on a gibbet, they cut his body to pieces and threw it to the dogs. Young Spenser soon after underwent the same fate: he was taken lurking in a convent in Wales, immediately brought out to execution, hanged, and cut to pieces. At length the king, abandoned by his subjects, persecuted by his unnatural queen, and a fugitive in his own kingdom, was taken prisoner, removed to

London, where he was insulted by the populace, confined in the Tower, tried by the parliament, and by a solemn sentence deposed from the throne. The crown was given to his son, who was then only fourteen years of age, and the regency to the queen. Edward did not long remain a prisoner: he is said to have been put to death in a manner shocking to humanity.

The young Edward, kept in bondage by his mother, and her lover, the ambitious Mortimer, had no share of blame in these infamous transactions. The noble spirit of this prince soon shook off the fetters, and amply revenged the death of his father. The queen and Mortimer chose Nottingham Castle, a place of great strength, for their residence. By connivance with the governor, some noblemen, at the king's request, found their way into the favorite's apartment, and carried him off in spite of Isabella's prayers and tears. The parliament immediately condemned him to death, and he instantly underwent the fate he had inflicted on the Spensers. Edward sentenced his mother to perpetual imprisonment, in which she lived for twenty-five years, a miserable monument of criminal and blasted ambition.

Thus freed from the control of usurped authority, the noble spirit of Edward III. began to meditate the most important enterprises. Edward Baliol, whose father, John, had been crowned king of Scotland, applied to the monarch of England to assist him in his pretensions to the kingdom. Some troops were granted, with which Baliol was so far successful as to get himself crowned at Scone; but he was afterwards defeated, and obliged a second time to fly for protection to England. Edward now determined to assist him in person; and marching northward, besieged and took the town of Berwick, when he was opposed, at Halidown Hill, by Sir Archibald Douglas, the Scottish general. Both armies engaged with equal keenness, but Douglas was slain, and the Scots were defeated. Near 30,000 men are said to have fallen in this engagement, among whom were the chief of the Scottish nobility. Edward returned in triumph to England, having fixed Baliol, his vassal and tributary, upon the throne. But the kingdom was as repugnant as ever to the domination of England, and, animated by hopes of assistance from France, renewed hostilities immediately upon Edward's departure.

That monarch prepared now for a new enterprise, which drew after it a train of the most important consequences. The succession to the kingdom of France was then in dispute, and Edward embraced a notion which found great countenance in his ambitious disposition, that he had the best title by inheritance, in right of his mother, the sister of Charles the Fair. Philip of Valois, however, the male heir, had in the meantime taken possession of the throne.*

---

*Philip contended that the Salic law excluded the pretensions of his rival. The English lawyers acknowledged that a female heir was excluded by the

Edward, who wanted but a pretext for an enterprise so suitable to his disposition, styled himself king of France, and prepared immediately for an invasion of that realm. A naval engagement ensued on the coast of Flanders, in which the French lost 230 ships and 30,000 seamen. Edward, landing in France with the chief of the nobility of England, and his son, called, from the color of his armor, the *Black Prince*, then a youth of fifteen years of age, ran a career of the most glorious exploits. The opulent city of Caen in Normandy was taken and plundered, and the English were extending their depredations almost to the gates of Paris, when Philip appeared in their front with an army of 100,000 men. Edward had no more than 30,000, yet notwithstanding this prodigious inequality, he resolved to indulge the ardor of his troops, and come to a decisive battle. They met upon a plain near the village of Cressy, and here ensued one of the most memorable engagements recorded in history. After a most judicious arrangement of his army, Edward and the Prince of Wales received the sacrament with the utmost devotion; and showed, by the calm intrepidity of their conduct, that the resolved alternative was victory or death. This behavior influenced the whole army of the English, who stood to receive the first shock of the enemy with composed and sullen fortitude. A shower of arrows from the English archers began the engagement, which throwing that wing of the French to whom they were opposed into the utmost confusion, the Prince of Wales, taking advantage of their dismay, attacked them with irresistible impetuosity. The king, who commanded a body of reserve, was determined to allow his intrepid son the honor of the day; he kept aloof from the fight, which was maintained on both sides with the most desperate courage.

Some of the nobles, apprehensive for the safety of their prince, despatched a messenger to the king, desiring that a reinforcement might be sent to his relief. Edward first demanded if his son was alive, and being answered in the affirmative, and that he was showing prodigies of valor: "Then tell him," says he, "that the glory of the day shall be *his* alone; let him show himself worthy of the honor of knighthood, with which I have lately invested him." * This speech, reported to the Prince, inspired him with new courage. Alençon, the bravest of the French gen-

---

Salic law on account of the weakness of her sex, but urged that the exclusion went no farther than her own person, and that her son's right was not affected. The question was pleaded in the Court of the Peers of France, and decided in favor of Philip.

* This incident is well told by Froissart. "Then the king said, 'Is my son dead, or hurt, or on the earth felled?' 'No, sir,' quoth the knight, 'but he is hardly matched, wherefore he hath need of your aid.' 'Well,' said the king, 'return to him, and to those that sent you hither, and say to them, that they send no more to me for any adventure that falleth, so long as my son is alive; and also say to them, that they suffer him this day to win his spurs; for if God be pleased, I will this *journée* be his and the honor thereof, and to them that be about him.' "—Lord Berners' Froissart, vol. i., cap. 30.

erals, was slain, and the whole army began to give way to the irresistible fury of the English. Philip, while he exerted every nerve to turn the tide of victory, was compelled to quit the field by one of his own barons, who, seizing his horse by the reins, forced him to abandon the combat. The French were entirely defeated. 30,000 were left dead on the spot. Among these were John, king of Bohemia; Ralph, duke of Lorrain, and a great part of the chief nobility of France. The crest of the king of Bohemia, which was three ostrich feathers, from that day became the arms of the Prince of Wales in commemoration of the signal battle of Cressy, which was fought on the 26th day of August, 1346. This epoch was signalized by one of the most important discoveries that has ever been made, the invention of artillery. Some pieces of cannon, which, it is said, Edward had placed in the front of his army, contributed much to throw the enemy into confusion, and to give victory to the English. This invention, apparently a most destructive one, has certainly, upon the whole, proved beneficial to society. Nations are more upon a level, as less depends upon frantic exertions of courage; and consequently, from a consideration of an equality of strength, the peace of kingdoms is better preserved.—The victory of Cressy was followed by the siege and reduction of Calais, which, from that time, remained for two hundred and ten years in the possession of the English.

While these important proceedings were transacting on the continent, the miseries of war were doubled by one of the most dreadful pestilences recorded in history. Asia and Africa were almost depopulated by it; and in the west of Europe it raged with incredible fury. The Scotch, involved in the common calamity, were yet determined to take advantage of this conjuncture of distress, and while the best of the English troops were on the continent, to make a formidable invasion of that kingdom. David Bruce, then a child, at the head of an army of 50,000 men, invaded and ravaged the north of England to the gates of Durham. The queen, Philippa, a most heroic woman, and worthy to be the wife of Edward, assembled hastily a body of 12,000 men, of which she gave the command to Lord Percy. She animated the army, however, by her own presence, rode through the ranks, and quitted them only in the moment of conflict. The Scots received a fatal overthrow; 15,000 were left dead on the field; and David, their young king, with several of the chief nobility, was carried in triumph to London. In the meantime Philip of Valois died, and was succeeded in the throne of France by his son John. He was a weak, cruel, and tyrannical prince; though his distresses have thrown the most favorable veil upon his character. A truce had been concluded soon after the taking of Calais between Edward and Philip. It was dissolved upon the death of the latter, and hostilities recommenced. The Black

Prince, with an army of 12,000 men, was sent into France, and carried devastation into the heart of the kingdom. John took the field against him with 60,000 men, and advanced towards Poictiers with the design of surrounding and cutting him off at once. The military skill displayed by the prince in the arrangement of his little army was admirable. He contrived to give them the appearance of numbers, while he even diminished them in reality, by placing a considerable body of his troops in ambuscade. The French had to march through a lane to the attack. The Black Prince with one division opposed them on the front, while his main body, divided into two, poured down upon their lengthened flank. The confusion of the enemy was completed by the troops in ambuscade, and this immense army was dispersed and cut to pieces. King John himself, with one of his sons, was taken. The moderation of the Prince of Wales was equal to his heroism. He treated the captive monarch with every distinction due to his rank; he refused to be seated in his presence; and, when he conducted his royal prisoner to London amidst the acclamations of the people, he rode himself on the left hand on a small black palfrey, while John upon the right was mounted on a horse remarkable for his beauty and rich accoutrements. Thus, two monarchs were at the same time prisoners in London, David of Scotland, and John of France.

But whatever had been won in France was successively, and, in a manner, silently lost without the mortification of a defeat. John, who was in the power of the English, could make no treaties which had the force to bind his kingdom. The Dauphin and the states of France carried on the war with great vigor; but, at the same time, so cautiously as not to hazard a general engagement. By this procedure, which was extremely politic, Edward was wearied and harassed into a treaty, in which he consented to renounce all claim to the sovereignty of France; but it was agreed that he should retain possession of Poitou, St. Onge, Perigord, and some of the neighboring districts, together with Calais, and several towns on that quarter. John was sent back to his dominions on promise of a large ransom; but he was without finances, without soldiers, for they refused to obey him, and without credit; yet he had a strong principle of honor, for, being unable to satisfy the conditions of his liberation, he returned to England, surrendered himself once more a prisoner, and died soon after in London.*

Charles, surnamed the Wise, succeeded his father John in the crown of France, and by his excellent political talents, retrieved

* It was a noble maxim of this prince, "That if good faith should be totally forgotten by the rest of mankind, it ought still to find a place in the breast of princes." It has, however, been conjectured, that John's strongest motive for returning to England was a passion he had conceived for the countess of Salisbury, one of the most beautiful women of that age.

the losses and miseries of his country. He quelled a most formidable insurrection of banditti called Malandrins, who were a terror to the whole nation. He even formed them into a body of regular troops, and led them into the kingdom of Castile, against Pedro, surnamed the Cruel, whom his subjects had dethroned, and who, was endeavoring, with the aid of the English, to regain his dominions. This caused a renewal of hostilities between the French and English. The Black Prince marched into Castile, and in conjunction with Pedro, engaged and defeated the French under Henry of Transtamare and Bertrand de Guesclin, one of the most consummate generals of the age. The arms of England again prevailed. The French lost 20,000 men, and Pedro was reinstated in his dominions.

Those glorious exploits which we have related, produced in them no beneficial consequences to England; and the joy of the nation was miserably clouded by seeing the heroic Black Prince return to his country in the last stage of a mortal distemper. This most valiant and accomplished man, whose character had not a single blemish, died, to the unspeakable grief of the nation, in the forty-sixth year of his age. King Edward, who had beheld his decline with all the feelings of a parent for the worthiest of sons, withdrew himself upon his death from all the concerns of government, and died about a year after.

The reign of Edward III., which was of fifty-one years' duration, is on the whole, certainly, one of the most glorious in the annals of England ; nor is it alone the splendor of his foreign victories which has contributed to render the memory of this king great and illustrious. His foreign wars, though most eminently successful, were neither founded in justice, nor productive of any substantial benefit to the nation. But England in his time enjoyed domestic tranquillity. His nobles were overawed by the spirit and valor of their sovereign, and his people attached to him on account of his acts of munificence and his salutary laws. It is judiciously remarked by Robertson, that "conquerors, though usually the bane of human kind, proved often, in those feudal times, the most indulgent of sovereigns. They stood most in need of supplies from their people, and not being able to compel them by force to submit to the necessary impositions, they were obliged to make them some compensation by equitable laws and popular concessions." Edward III. took no steps of moment without consulting his Parliament, and hence that assembly rose into greater consideration during his reign, and acquired a more regular authority than in any former times. Edward confirmed the Magna Charta above twenty times in the course of his reign, and this has been generally considered as a proof of his high regard for the liberties of his people. But it has been judiciously observed by Hume, that these concessions rather give room for a contrary presumption. "If," says he, "the maxims of Edward's reign had not been in general somewhat arbitrary, and if the great charter had not been frequently violated, the parliament would never have applied for those frequent confirmations, which could add no force to a deed regularly observed, and which could serve no other purpose than to prevent the contrary precedents from turning into a rule, and acquiring authority." *

The Prince of Wales had left a son of eleven years of age, who succeeded to the throne of his grandfather, by the name of Richard II. Charles VI. some time after became king of France at the age of twelve, and both these minorities were unhappy for their countries. In England, the three uncles of the king, th dukes of Lancaster, York, and Gloucester, ruled the kingdom with no good understanding between them, and consequently with much disturbance to the nation. Yet Richard himself, when he assumed the reins of government, gave some indications of a vigorous and a happy administration. But this fair prospect was of short continuance. Though a prince of some spirit, he was possessed of a very weak understanding, abandoned to his pleasures, and a slave to unworthy favorites. By their persuasion, and to gratify his revenge as well as his avarice, he confiscated, on a specious pretence of treason, the estate of his uncle, Henry of Lancaster, duke of Hereford, a prince of great resolution and ability, and, by descent from Henry III., of no remote pretensions to the throne of England. While the king was employed in quelling an insurrection in Ireland, Henry of Lancester, who was in high favor with the people, found means to levy a very formidable army: he engaged the earl of Northumberland in his interest, and prevailed on York, then viceroy in the king's absence, to give him no opposition; while, as he pretended, all that he had in view was the recovery of his estate. Richard, on his return from Ireland, found Lancaster at the head of his troops, determined to wrest from him the possession of the crown; his numbers were inconsiderable, and diminished by desertion to his rival. Resistance he saw was vain while the body of the people were his enemies. Lancaster told him he was a novice in the art of government, and that *he* would teach him how to rule the people of England; to which the submissive monarch is said to have replied, "Fair cousin, since it pleases you, it pleases us likewise." Richard, confined in the Tower, was accused of mal-administration, and condemned by parliament, who solemnly deposed him from the throne; he was confined a prisoner in the castle of

* The magnificent castle of Windsor was built by Edward III., and Hume justly remarks, that the method of conducting that work affords a criterion of the condition of the people in that age. Instead of engaging workmen by contract, or for stipulated wages, Edward assessed every county in England to send him a certain number of masons, tilers, and carpenters, as if he had been levying an army.—Ashmole's Hist. of the Garter, p. 129.

Pontefract, and afterwards privately assassinated.* The parliament conferred the crown on Henry of Lancaster, by the title of Henry IV. Thus began the contest between the houses of York and Lancaster, which for several years after involved the kingdom in misery and bloodshed; yet, in the end, contributed to establish and fix the constitution of England.

CHAPTER XIII.

ENGLAND and FRANCE in the FIFTEENTH CENTURY:—England under Henry V.—France under Charles VI.—Battle of Agincourt—Henry V. acquires the Crown of France—Charles VII.—Maid of Orleans—France recovered from the English—The Eastern Empire invaded by the Turks—By the Tartars under Tamerlane—Scanderbeg—Turks under Mahomet the Great take Constantinople—Greek Empire extinguished—Constitution of Turkey—France about the end of the Fifteenth Century—Lewis II.—Charles VIII.—Italy.

A BRANCH of the house of York was yet alive in the heir of the family of Mortimer, a boy of seven years of age. Percy, earl of Northumberland, who had contributed to raise Henry of Lancaster to the crown, had met with some acts of injustice from him, which changed him from a friend into a most implacable enemy. He, with his son Henry Percy, surnamed Hotspur, together with Owen Glendower, a formidable chieftain of Wales, and a large party of the Scots, united their forces with the resolution to elevate Mortimer, as true heir to the crown of England. Henry

* [Such is the account generally given by English historians, who, though they differ as to the manner of his death, give no credit to the rumors which disquieted the mind of Henry IV., of the escape of Richard into Scotland; and the specific account given by the contemporary Scots historians to this effect, has been wholly discredited by English writers. Recent researches, however, confirm the narrative of Bowyer, that Richard II. escaped from Pontefract castle, was discovered in the Western Isles, was honorably treated by Robert III., and, after his death, by the Regent Albany, during a period of no less than eighteen years, and died in Stirling castle, 1419. A Dissertation annexed to the third volume of the History of Scotland, by Mr. Fraser Tytler, not only produces the most unexceptionable testimony to these facts from original public documents, but gives the most probable grounds for believing that Henry IV., notwithstanding the pains which he took to convince his subjects of the death of Richard, was not only well aware of his existence in Scotland, but deeply interested that he should be kept there; in fact, that Richard II. was an hostage in the hands of the ambitious and unnatural Albany, for the secure detention of his sovereign James I., in England; and James, in like manner, an hostage in the hands of Henry IV. and V., for the detention in Scotland of so dangerous a rival to the reigning monarch of England.—See Tytler's History of Scotland vol. iii.—E. 1834.]

met the rebels and their allies at Shrewsbury. Northumberland was detained by sickness, but his place was well supplied by the intrepid Hotspur. He again found a formidable antagonist and rival in prowess in young Henry of Monmouth, the son of the king, who was afterwards the great Henry V. The death of Hotspur, by an unknown hand, decided the fate of the day, and Henry was victorious. Northumberland, commiserated for his age and misfortunes, obtained his pardon. The kingdom regained for a while its quiet, till it was again embroiled by a confederacy, at the head of which was the archbishop of York. This was quelled by the death of its author, who was the first prelate who had been capitally punished in England.—This period has been distinguished as the dawn of the Reformation, and Wickliffe as its morning-star. The efforts of this eminent reformer and his followers to disseminate true religion, and thereby dispel the darkness of popery which prevailed extensively throughout the land, exposed them to many trying conflicts both with the ecclesiastical and secular authorities, and many of his zealous followers suffered an extreme degree of rigor. This reign saw, likewise, the first capital punishments in England on account of religious opinions. Henry died at the early age of forty-six, and left the throne to his gallant son, Henry V., who, in the humiliation of France, brought the kingdom of England to a very high pitch of glory.

The care which Charles V., surnamed the Wise, had taken to retrieve the misfortunes of France, was in a great measure the cause of the ruin of that monarchy. The duke of Anjou, one of the uncles of Charles VI., who governed as regent in the minority of his nephew, not satisfied with embezzling the treasures of the crown, oppressed the people with the most intolerable exactions. Paris, and many other of the principal towns, rose openly in arms, and the king himself set out for Brittany, with the purpose of depriving their oppressor of his power and authority. At this critical period the young monarch was unfortunately seized with a deprivation of his intellects, which broke out in the most dreadful fits of madness. The ignorance of men in those ages attributed this fatal, but natural calamity, to the effects of witchcraft. An Italian lady, the wife of his brother, the duke of Orleans, was accused as the author of his misfortunes, and the suspicion was increased by a very strange accident. In a masquerade at court the king appeared in the garb of a wild man, covered with leaves, which were stuck with pitch upon a close habit of linen, and he led in chains four other satyrs, dressed in the same manner. The duke of Orleans, who held a burning torch, approached accidentally too near these combustible knights; one of the habits took fire, and the four satyrs, who were four of the principal nobility, were burnt to death. The king escaped with life, but was seized with a dreadful fit of frenzy. To relieve him, they sent for a magician from Montpellier, and he became somewhat better. The fact was, his disease had lucid intervals, and in these he sometimes resumed the management of his kingdom—which was of the worst consequence to France, for no measure was ever pursued to an end or with stability. The duke of Burgundy, who hated Orleans, and wanted to secure to himself the whole authority of the kingdom, caused this nobleman, his own nephew, to be assassinated. A party rose in favor of his children, to revenge themselves on Burgundy. The queen, who aimed likewise at the chief administration, had a party who espoused her interest. All France was in commotion, and Henry V. of England could not have chosen a more favorable opportunity for the execution of his ambitious designs.

On pretence of recovering the ancient patrimony of the crown of England, Henry made a descent on Normandy, with an army of 50,000 men. He took the tower of Harfleur, and carried devastation into the country. A contagious distemper arrested his progress, and destroyed three-fourths of his army, and in this deplorable condition, with about 9000 effective troops, he was met by the Constable D'Albret, at the head of 60,000 men. In this situation a retreat was attempted by the English, but they were harassed by the enemy, and compelled to come to an engagement on the plain of Agincourt. On that day the English arms obtained a signal triumph. The French were so confident of success, that they made a proposal to the English about surrendering, and began to treat for the ransom of their prisoners. Henry observed in their immense army the remissness and relaxation which commonly attend a great superiority of numbers. He led on his little band to meet them in order of battle. The French stood for a considerable space of time, and beheld this feeble foe with indignation and contempt. "Come on, my friends," said Henry; "since they scorn to attack us, it is ours to show them the example. Come on, and the blessed Trinity be our protection." The English archers, as usual, began the conflict. Their arrows were a yard in length, and falling as thick as hail upon the main body of the enemy, threw them into great confusion. After the first discharge, the archers seized the sword, and rushing on a body of horse, which were advanced beyond the line, dispersed and drove them back upon the ranks of infantry. A body of English cavalry, in the meantime, sprung from an ambush, and attacked one flank of the army, which was assailed by the foot on the other. Henry, dismounting from his horse, threw himself into the hottest of the engagement, and singly maintained for awhile a combat against several French knights. He was felled to the ground, but owed his life to the intrepidity of a gallant Welshman, who despatched, with his own hand, several of his assailants. Recovering his senses, he was attacked by the duke of Alençon, who cleft with his sword a part of the king's helmet. Alençon, however, was killed in that attempt, and the French were broken, dispersed, and entirely cut to pieces. The number of the slain amounted to 10,000, and 14,000 were taken prisoners. The loss of the English in the victory of Agincourt is said not to have exceeded forty men—a fact bordering upon the incredible.

France was now in the most deplorable situation, but Henry was obliged to return to England for a supply both of men and money. He landed, however, soon after on the continent with an army of 25,000 men, and prepared to strike a decisive blow for the crown of France. The duke of Orleans, as we have mentioned, had been assassinated by the duke of Burgundy. He, in his turn, fell by the treachery of the Dauphin, who was afterwards Charles VII. But his son, to revenge the death of his father, concluded a league at Arras with the monarch of England. With this assistance Henry proceeded in his conquests, was soon master of all Normandy, and advanced to Paris. The court, with their insane monarch, fled to the city of Troye, where Henry, still pursuing, forced on a treaty with the queen-mother and the duke of Burgundy, by which it was stipulated that he should marry Catharine, the daughter of Charles VI., and receive all France as her dowry. It was agreed that the insane monarch should retain, for life, the title of king, while Henry enjoyed the government, to which he was to succeed without dispute upon his death. Such was the tenor of a treaty very glorious for England, but too repugnant to the interests of both kingdoms to be of any long continuance.

In the meantime the Dauphin, aided by a body of 8000 Scots, took advantage of the king's return to England to vindicate his hereditary dominions, which had been thus conferred on a stranger, by those who had no power to dispose of them. He attacked the English army under the duke of Clarence, and gained a complete victory; but the return of Henry changed the face of affairs, and all was submission to this victorious monarch. This, however, was the last term of his glories; an incurable disease attacked his vitals, and he died in the thirty-fourth year of his age, one of the most heroic princes that ever swayed the sceptre of England. The duke of Bedford, brother of Henry V., was declared regent of France, and Henry VI., a child of nine months old, was proclaimed king at Paris and at London.

On this fact of the conquest of France by Henry V., Voltaire makes an observation which deserves attention, as developing the springs of popular opinion:—"If this revolution," says he, "like some others, had been of long duration, and the successors of Henry had maintained what he had won, and been at this day monarchs of France, where would have been the historian who would not have judged their title good? We should not then have been told by Mezerai, that the painful disease, and death of this prince, was a punishment of God, inflicted for his usurpation

Would not the popes have ratified the authority of his successors by apostolic bulls? Would not the people have regarded them as the anointed of the Lord? Where then would have been the authority of this famous Salic law? A chimera for the court wits to exercise their raillery, and a text for the fawning sermons of the courtly preachers! What Frenchman would not have extolled to the skies the great Henry V., the avenger of assassination and the deliverer of France?"

Charles VII., a prince who deserved to inherit his father's throne, recovered it by slow degrees. He had to oppose him the duke of Bedford, who, as regent of France, was master of the power and revenues of the kingdom; and he had against him, likewise, the duke of Burgundy, who was become one of the most formidable princes of Europe. The national resources of the kingdom were so entirely exhausted, that the mark of silver, which in the age of Charlemagne had been valued at half a livre, was now valued at ninety livres. In this distressed situation of France, Charles, availing himself of the superstition of the age, projected an extraordinary scheme for the recovery of his kingdom, by feigning an interposition from Heaven in his favor. A gentleman, of the name of Baudricourt, saw a young servant maid at an inn in Lorraine, whom he immediately conceived to be a fit person for playing a very extraordinary part. She was taught her cue, and made to counterfeit a divine inspiration. They carried her before the king, where the answers that were put in her mouth, and the demeanor which she assumed, convinced every body that she was inspired. Orleans was, at this time, besieged by the English. Joan of Arc, this heroic maid, who had now assumed the dress of a man, undertook to relieve the town and compel the English to abandon the enterprise. She put herself at the head of the French troops, attacked, beat, and dispersed the English, who believed her to be the devil himself, delivered Orleans, and placed the crown upon Charles's head in the church of Rheims. She proceeded for some time in this career of success, till she was at last taken prisoner at Compiegne. The regent Bedford, either in a fit of passion, or to satisfy the revenge of the English, instead of respecting, as he ought to have done, this singular instance of intrepidity in one of her sex, was prompted to behave with meanness and cruelty. She was tried as a heretic and sorceress by an ecclesiastical tribunal, and condemned and burnt at Rouen.*

The arms of Charles gained more advantage by the death of this heroine than, perhaps, they had done by her life; for this piece of cruelty contributed to render the government of the

* This execrable deed was warranted by a solemn sentence of (Cauchon) the bishop of Beauvais, (Martin) the vicar-general of the Inquisition, nine doctors of the Sorbonne, and thirty-five other doctors in theology. Two of these inhuman doctors were afterwards condemned by Charles VII., and suffered the same punishment they had inflicted on this heroic woman.

English extremely odious. Charles was every day making some new conquest, though it cost him fifteen years before he made his entry into Paris, and almost as many more before the English were entirely driven out of France. They retained, in the end, nothing but the town of Calais, and lost all those domains which had belonged to the crown of England by inheritance. Such was the small fruit that remained of the glorious victories of Cressy, Poitiers, and Agincourt. Charles VII. governed his kingdom with great wisdom, and established a better political economy than any monarch of France since the days of Charlemagne.

While the situation of the West of Europe was such as we have described, the ancient and venerable empire of the East was in the last stage of existence. The Turks were daily acquiring strength in Asia Minor, and gradually encroaching upon the frontier of the empire of Constantinople.

Othman, the Turkish sultan, had fixed the seat of his empire at Byrsa, in Bithynia, and his son Orcan advanced to the borders of the Propontis. The Greek emperor, John Cantacuzenus, did not disdain to court an alliance with this prince, by giving him his daughter in marriage. The Turks, in the reign of his successor, John Paleologus, began to think of crossing over into Europe; and, as the Genoese were then in possession of one of the suburbs of Constantinople, they agreed to give this people a large sum of money for the use of their ships to transport them across the Bosphorus. They passed accordingly, and besieged, took, and garrisoned the city of Adrianople, within one hundred and fifty miles of Constantinople, a circumstance most justly alarming to the capital of the East. It was in this situation of affairs that the emperor, John Paleologus, made his application to the pope for relief—a measure sufficiently humiliating; but, on his return to Constantinople, his conduct was still meaner, for he concluded a treaty with the sultan Amurath, not like one crowned head with another, but as a slave with his master; and he gave him, as a hostage, his son Manuel, who actually served in the Turkish army against the Christians. Amurath was succeeded by Bajazet, surnamed the Thunderbolt, who brought the Greek empire to the lowest pitch of debasement. He ordered the emperor to destroy the fortifications of Constantinople, and to admit a Turkish judge into the city to decide all causes between the Turks and Christians. At length he laid siege to it in form; and the capital of the Eastern empire would have fallen at once into the hands of the Turks—had it not owed its preservation for awhile to another race of barbarian invaders. Tamerlane, a prince of the Mongol Tartars, saved Constantinople by attacking Bajazet.

Timurbek, or Tamerlane, was a descendant of Gengis-khan; he was born in Sogdiana, which is now the country of the Usbecks, and was endowed with that enterprising genius, great courage, and unbounded ambition, which distinguished all who have made extensive conquests. He had already subdued Persia, India, and Syria, when the enemies of Bajazet, Mussulmans and Christians, invited him into Asia Minor, as an heroic prince to whom they wished to be indebted for their deliverance. In compliance with this request, very flattering to his ambition, he sent an embassy to Bajazet, requiring him to raise the siege of Constantinople, and give up immediately all his conquests. This message, as may be believed, was treated with scorn and indignation, and Bajazet marched against him with an army whose numbers almost surpass credibility. He engaged him near Ancyra, in Phrygia; his army was cut to pieces; three hundred and forty thousand are said to have fallen in the field, and Bajazet became the prisoner of Tamerlane. It is vulgarly reported, that he inhumanly confined this unhappy monarch in an iron cage, and trod upon his back to mount his horse. But this prince, who was really an heroic character, was never guilty of such meanness or cruelty. The oriental historians affirm, with more truth, that he treated the captive prince with great clemency, and with respect suitable to the rank of which his misfortunes had deprived him.

Tamerlane made Samarcand the capital of his empire, and there received the homage of all the Asiatic princes, and even friendly embassies from several of the sovereigns of Europe. One circumstance, which strongly marks a greatness of character in this Tartar potentate, was his toleration. He believed himself neither in the sect of the Lama nor in the faith of Mahomet; but acknowledged one Supreme Being, without any mixture of superstitious observances; yet he suffered all men, both Mussulmans and idolaters, to exercise their own religious worship; and while he was passing Mount Libanus, he is said to have even assisted, with reverence, at the religious ceremonies of some of the Christian anchorets who dwelt on that mountain. Tamerlane had no learning himself, but he was careful to have his grandchildren instructed by the best preceptors he could procure; and such was the benefit of this example, that his successor, Olugbeg, founded at Samarcand an academy of sciences, where astronomy, considering the barbarism of the times, was brought to a very considerable height. Samarcand is now fallen from the eminence which then distinguished it, and, in the possession of the Usbeck Tartars, has relapsed into its ancient state of barbarism.

The fate of Constantinople was thus retarded for awhile by the victories of Tamerlane; but the Turks, after the death of that prince, resumed their schemes of destroying the empire of the East. The sultan, Amurath II., was a prince of a singular character. No man was better qualified to increase the grandeur of his empire, and no one was so fond of a life of quiet and retirement. He twice resigned the crown, and was twice prevailed on by his bashaws and janizaries to resume it. A most solemn treaty had been concluded, in the year 1444, between him and Ladislaus, king of Poland; and on the faith of this treaty, which gave peace to his dominions, Amurath had devoted his days to retirement and the study of philosophy, leaving the government in the hands of his son Mahomet. Cardinal Julian Cæsarini, the pope's legate, with the concurrence of his master, persuaded the king of Poland that it was necessary to break this treaty, which, being made with Mahometans, could not be binding on Christians, and Ladislaus accordingly invaded the Turkish territories; but he paid dear for his perfidy. The janizaries prevailed on Amurath to return from his solitude. He marched to battle at the head of his army, and, taking the treaty with him in his bosom, solemnly invoked God, the avenger of injustice, to punish this violation of faith, and outrage to the law of nations. The Christians were entirely defeated: the Mahometans triumphed. The king of Poland lost his life, and his head was carried in procession through the ranks of the Turkish army. To complete this signal vengeance, the author and adviser of this unjustifiable act, cardinal Julian, was drowned as he crossed a river, borne down by the weight of an immense treasure, with which he was attempting to make his escape. Amurath retired once more from the cares of empire, and was once more prevailed on to resume his crown. He left his dominions to his son Mahomet II., who inherited his military, if not his philosophic talents; but his designs against the Greek empire, as well as his father's, were retarded, as those of Bajazet had been, by the necessity of defending their own territories against another very powerful invader: This was Scanderbeg.

Scanderbeg, whose real name was John Castriot, inherited from his father the country of Albania, a small part of the kingdom of Epirus. In his infancy, Amurath had seized on Albania, and taken possession of the person of Scanderbeg. He treated him, however, with great clemency, and even educated him as his own child. But this distinction did not satisfy the young Scanderbeg, who secretly determined to regain his independence, and recover his hereditary kingdom. Amurath had entrusted him with the command of a small army, for the purpose of an expedition into Servia; but he was no sooner at the head of these troops than he turned his arms against the sultan. By means of intelligence with his subjects of Albania,—by his military talents, his great activity, and the excellent discipline which he introduced, he was able, with a small army, to maintain his ground, and secure the independence of his native province against the whole of the united force of the Turkish empire.

The revolt of Scanderbeg retarded, but did not put a stop to, the designs against Constantinople. At this time the declining empire of the East was in reality divided between three capitals: one was Constantinople, another was Adrianople, which, about a century before, had been taken, as we have mentioned, by Amurath I., and the third was Trebizond, at the extremity of the

Euxine Sea, which had been the retreat of the family of the Comneni. Constantinople was torn by religious factions, while Mahomet the Great, a youth only twenty-one years of age, son of the philosophic Amurath, formed the plan of extinguishing the empire of the Greeks, and making that illustrious city the capital of the Ottoman power. He laid siege to Constantinople in the year 1453, while the indolent Greeks made a very feeble preparation for defence, trusting to an immense barricade of strong chains, which blocked up the entry to the port, and prevented all access to the enemy's ships. The genius of Mahomet very soon overcame this obstacle. He laid a channel of smooth planks for the length of six miles, resembling the frames which are constructed for the launching of ships. In one night's time he drew eighty galleys out of the water upon these planks, and next morning, to the utter astonishment of the besieged, an entire fleet descended at once into the bosom of their harbor.

The Christian princes of Europe beheld this attack upon the metropolis and bulwark of Christendom with great indifference; they were indeed too much occupied at home to give any indulgence to the spirit of crusading. The emperor, Frederic III., wanted both power and courage for such an enterprise; Poland was under a very bad government; France was slowly recovering from the miseries in which she was involved by the English; and England was torn by domestic dissensions. The Italian princes were at war with each other; and Spain was under a number of separate governments, one half Christian and the other Mahometan. The only succor which Europe lent to the unfortunate Greek empire was a few Genoese ships sent to their aid by the emperor Frederic of Germany. In this situation the city was soon reduced to the necessity of capitulating; but when the articles were in dispute, an imprudent renewal of hostilities, on the part of the Greeks, exposed them to all the fury of the conquerors, who entered the city sword in hand. Constantine, the emperor, was killed in the assault, and Mahomet immediately converted his palace into a seraglio, and the splendid church of Santa Sophia into a Mahometan mosque. Thus ended the empire of the East, in the year 1453, one thousand one hundred and twenty-three years from the building of Constantinople by Constantine the Great.

The Turks, in this important conquest, showed a spirit very opposite to that of barbarians. Most of the churches were preserved entire, and the public exercise of religion allowed as before to all the Christians. Mahomet permitted the conquered Greeks to choose their own patriarch, and even installed him himself by giving him the crosier and ring, and from that time to the present, the Turkish sultans have always elected the patriarch of Constantinople, who is called Œcumenical. The pope, indeed, chooses another, who is styled the Latin Patriarch; and these two pontiffs continue to the present time to be as violently at enmity with each other as ever were the Eastern and the Western churches. Mahomet likewise founded several colleges and schools for philosophy, medicine, and most of the liberal arts and sciences. He was himself an able scholar, skilled in the foreign languages, both European and Asiatic, and was so much a lover of the arts as to entice, by very liberal rewards, several of the greatest proficients in painting and sculpture to come from Italy and reside at Constantinople.

Mahomet the Great pursued his conquests, and soon made himself master of all Greece. He likewise subdued Epirus, after the death of Scanderbeg, and began to meditate the conquest of Italy. The Venetian fleet opposed his progress in that country, and, attacking him in Greece, made themselves masters of the city of Athens. This, however, they were not able long to preserve. Their commerce was always their chief interest, and they were glad to enter into a treaty with the Turks by which they purchased from them the liberty of trading into the Black Sea. The Greeks remained under the dominion of the grand signior in a state of oppression, little short of slavery; they were suffered, however, to retain their religion and their laws. They were allowed, paying a small tribute, to carry on a little commerce, and cultivate their lands. The patriarch's revenues must, at least, have been considerable, as he paid, at his installation, no less than 8000 ducats, one half to the exchequer of the grand signior, and the other to the officers of the Porte. The greatest subjection the Greeks have been under, was in the tribute of children. Every father has been compelled to give one of his sons to serve among the janizaries or in the seraglio, or to pay a sum for his ransom.

The constitution of the Turkish empire is supported by the absolute government of the prince, the extreme celerity with which his mandates are carried into execution, and the despotic authority which he is enabled to exercise in the disposal of the lives and fortunes of all his subjects. Should the sultan be confined to a degree of authority in any shape less absolute than what he enjoys, the constitution of the empire would fall to pieces. It has been even maintained by some authors, as a maxim of state in the Ottoman empire, that the sultan cannot abridge his own power, and that his oaths and promises are always revocable when in any shape restrictive of his authority. Yet the sultan himself swears to observe and to govern according to the law of Mahomet, which, though it touches both matters of religion and of government, the learned doctors among the Turks maintain to be only binding upon the emperor in the articles of the Mussulman faith. Yet by these same doctors the principle of the most implicit obedience to the sultan is held forth to his subjects as a doctrine of religion, rather than a maxim of state.

The contexture of the Turkish government is such a fabric of slavery, that it is almost impossible that any subject of the empire should inherit a free or an ingenuous spirit. The grand signior himself is born of a slave of the seraglio. The viziers are often slaves by birth, and through the whole empire it is hard to find any that derive their origin from ingenuous parents. It is therefore no wonder that the Turks should inherit a disposition fitted for the rule of an absolute master. "Ita quosdam homines," says Grotius, after Aristotle, "novimus natura esse servos, et ita populi quidam eo sunt ingenio, ut regi quam regere norint rectius." *

It is a part of the policy of the empire, that a certain number of young men should be educated in the seraglio, out of whom the sultan chooses his principal officers. But what is a very extraordinary piece of policy, if we may believe Rycaut, it is necessary that these youths should be of Christian parents. The reason he assigns is, that being educated in a different religion they will hate the Christians; but this is a very lame solution of a very inconceivable fact. A better reason, supposing the fact a true one, is afterwards given, when he says, that the Christian slaves, strangers in the empire, will necessarily have fewer connections or dependents on their interest, and be the better disposed to an absolute submission to the will of their master. One thing is certain, that it is a fundamental maxim of the Turkish polity, that the servants of the prince should be such as he can entirely command, and can at any time destroy without danger to himself.

The prime vizier is the first officer of the empire. There are six others, who are called viziers of the bench, who sit as assessors with him in judgment in cases of law, of which he is judge in the last resort over the whole empire. These subordinate viziers, however, never dare to interfere, unless the grand vizier demands their opinion. The power of the grand vizier is absolute over all the subjects of the empire. In the disposal of lives he is limited only in two respects: he cannot take off the head of any of the beglerbegs, or the bashaws, without the imperial signature, nor can he punish any of the janizaries, or of the soldiery, but through the medium of their military commanders.†

Inferior in a civil capacity to the grand vizier are the beglerbegs, who command several provinces, and the bashaws who command one province. The dignity of these officers is merely personal: there is not such a thing in the Ottoman empire as an hereditary office or dignity; and it is esteemed a rule of excel-

* "Thus some nations are slaves by nature, born to be governed, not to govern."

† [The order of the janizaries has been abolished of late years; and many see in that abolition a sure omen of the dissolution of the Turkish empire — 1834. E.]

tent policy to make frequent changes in these offices. Removal, therefore, is often practised without cause of discontent: but as this arbitrary change might convert a friend into a dangerous enemy, there is most commonly a sufficient cause alleged for sending the degraded officer a bowstring along with the order for his dismission.

The revenues of the grand signior consist chiefly in the product of the several countries subject to his dominion. A vast number of vessels arrive annually from Greece, Egypt, Natolia, and the coasts of the Black Sea, which bring all sort of stores that are necessary for the seraglio, for the janizaries, or for the fleet. It appears, from the registers of the empire, that till the year 1683, the revenues of the grand signior's exchequer did not amount to two millions sterling, a sum quite inadequate to the expenditure of the Turkish government and the support of their armies. It is therefore customary for the bashaws, in each province, to have funds assigned them upon the province itself for the maintenance of their troops.

The patrimony of the sultan arises, in a great measure, from the confiscation of the estates of the viziers and bashaws; and when he has occasion to supply his privy purse, it costs him only the condemnation of one of these unfortunate grandees. On the whole, the revenues of the Turkish empire are very inconsiderable. But the absolute power of the sultan supplies that defect, and can execute very great projects at a small expense.

We now return westward, to take a view of the kingdom of France about the end of the fifteenth century.

France, towards the end of this century, began entirely to shake off the feudal government. The only two great fiefs remaining were Burgundy and Brittany. Charles the Bold, duke of Burgundy, was one of the richest and most powerful princes in Europe: but his ambition was the cause of his downfall, the loss of his dominions, and their absolute annexation to the crown of France. His favorite object was the conquest of Switzerland and of Lorraine. The Swiss entirely routed him in two pitched battles in their own country, and when he sought to wreak his resentment on Lorraine, the same Swiss followed him thither, and defeated him in a third engagement, where he lost his life. Lewis XI., by the feudal law, took possession of his dominions of Burgundy as a male fief; while the princess Mary, the duke's daughter, married Maximilian, son of the emperor Frederic III., who thus became sovereign of the Netherlands. This match laid the foundation for many wars between France and the empire.

Lewis XI. was a prince of a very inconsistent character. His reign was a complication of tyrannical acts, of murders, and assassinations, though at the same time, of some wise ordinances with respect to the public police of France. The increase of his dominions by the acquisition of Burgundy, and of Provençe, which was bequeathed to France by the count de la Marche, augmented greatly the power of the crown. The fiefs, as we have said, were now almost totally extinguished. The great nobles had long ago ruined their fortunes by the crusades. The people had emancipated themselves from their jurisdiction, and repaired for justice to the civil magistrate. The parliaments, which we have seen established upon a fixed plan by Philip the Fair, were now composed of lawyers, and acted agreeably to the statutes and usages of the realm; and the king, who possessed the authority of supreme legislator, was endowed with a power of great extent.

It is to Lewis XI., who was a vicious, unprincipled tyrant, that France owed the extension of her commerce, the establishment of posts through the kingdom, and the regular administration of justice.

The count de la Marche, in bequeathing Provençe to Lewis XI., left him likewise the empty title, which he enjoyed himself, of king of the two Sicilies. Lewis was satisfied with the effective donation of Provençe, and thought no more of the Sicilies; but his son, Charles VIII., who was a weak and an imprudent prince, was extremely ambitious of reigning in Italy; accordingly, in the beginning of his reign, he projected, very inconsiderately, the conquest of Naples, an enterprise which, though successful, was in the end fatal to the French: an enterprise remarkable too on this account, that it excited the first idea of that plan which has since been a part of the general policy of Europe, the preservation of a balance of power.

The picture of Italy at this juncture may be drawn in a few words. The papal dominions were not very extensive. The house of Gonzaga was in possession of Mantua, and the little sovereignties of Faenza, Imola, Rimini, Bologna, and Ravenna, had been all usurped from the Holy See during the residence of the popes at Avignon. Modena and Ferrara had likewise an independent sovereign; Piedmont was in possession of the dukes of Savoy; Pisa was subject to the Florentines; and Genoa to the duke of Milan, who was then a very powerful prince. The house of Orleans had mainly attempted to make good their pretensions to the sovereignty of Milan. Francis Sforza, the bastard of a soldier of fortune, had deprived their ancestors of this fine territory, of which the Sforzas became now the hereditary princes. Ludovic Sforza, for his own ambitious ends, was at pains to persuade Charles VIII. to undertake the conquest of Naples.

Florence, at this time, was at a very high pitch of splendor. It had now for above a century been distinguished, no less for its commerce than for its cultivation of the liberal arts. Perhaps here never was a family which deserved better of mankind than hat of the Medici. Cosmo de' Medici, who was born in the year

1389, lived as a private citizen of Florence, without courting rank or titles, though the wealth which he had acquired by commerce might have raised him to a level with the most powerful of the European princes. The use he made of his riches was to relieve the poor, to perform the most splendid acts of public munificence, to embellish and to refine his country, and to promote the cultivation of the sciences and fine arts, by inviting to Florence from every quarter men eminent for their learning and talents. He died distinguished by no diadems nor splendid epithets of honor, but known by that most honorable of human titles, *the Father of his Country*. His reputation, however, gained for his descendants the chief authority in Florence. The dignity of Gonfalonier, which properly signifies Standard-bearer, but came to be the office of the highest authority, was enjoyed by his son and his grandsons; and Peter de' Medici, his great grandson, was in possession of the chief power at Florence, at the time of Charles VIII.'s expedition into Italy.

Charles set out for Italy without taking the proper precautions which the importance of the enterprise required. Roderico Borgia, who ascended the papal throne by the name of Alexander VI., a pontiff whose memory has been deservedly execrated by all historians, had, as well as Ludovico Sforza, the duke of Milan, invited Charles to undertake this expedition. Scarce, however, had he set foot in Italy, when they began to traverse his designs, and joined against him with Alphonso, king of Naples. Charles, incensed at his perfidy, marched immediately to Rome, and besieged the pope in the castle of St. Angelo. Alexander was at length forced to sue for an accommodation; and then, the French monarch, with great devotion, kissed his holiness's feet, and served him with water to wash his hands. Charles now marched his army into the kingdom of Naples. Alphonso, with the most despicable cowardice, fled into Sicily, where he concealed himself in a convent; and his son Ferdinand retreated to the island of Ischia, after discharging the Neapolitans from their allegiance to his family. Charles was now master of Naples; he entered the city in triumph, took the titles of Emperor and Augustus, and after giving a few entertainments to exhibit his magnificence, and imposing some enormous taxes to exemplify his authority, this most impolitic prince returned to France five months after he had left it, thinking his conquest sufficiently secured by leaving it to be defended by three or four thousand men, while almost all Europe had entered into a combination to deprive him of it. Alexander VI., the states of Venice and Milan, the emperor Maximilian, Ferdinand of Arragon, and Isabella of Castile, all joined in a league against Charles, and met him on his return to France with an army of 30,000 men, while he had only 8000. Fortune, or courage, for he was not deficient in this quality, gave him the advantage over this great superiority of numbers. He defeated the confederates, and secured his return into France. But he left in the duchy of Milan one half of his little army. Scarcely had he arrived at Turin, when he received a message from pope Alexander, who commanded him to withdraw his troops from Italy, to yield his pretensions to the kingdom of Naples, and to come and give an account of his conduct at the tribunal of the holy pontiff on pain of excommunication. He chose rather to return to France. In short, the kingdom of Naples was lost in as short a time as it had been won. Gonsalvo of Cordova, a Spanish general, whom Ferdinand of Arragon had sent to the assistance of Frederic, who claimed the crown of Naples from affinity with the last prince, found it a very easy task to drive the French entirely out of Italy. Such had been the sudden and decisive effect of this great confederacy against Charles VIII., that the princes of Europe thence derived a most useful lesson, and from that period considered it as a general law of policy to be always united in a tacit league to prevent the exorbitant increase of the power of any particular state or sovereign. Robertson, in his History of Charles V., asserts that the idea of the preservation of *a balance of power* in Europe has its date from this confederacy against Charles VIII.: and "from this era," says he, "we can trace the progress of that intercourse between nations which has linked the powers of Europe so closely together, and can discern the operations of that provident policy which, during peace, guards against remote and contingent dangers, and which in war has prevented rapid and destructive conquests." But in this instance the elegant historian certainly pays a higher compliment to modern policy than it deserves. The system in question is perhaps more generally understood by the moderns than it was by the ancients; but (as Hume has remarked) the idea of a balance of power is founded so much on common sense and obvious reasoning, that "it is impossible it could altogether have escaped antiquity, where we find in other particulars so many marks of deep penetration and discernment." Xenophon represents one great combination of powers as having directly arisen from a jealousy of the increasing strength of the Medes and Persians. Thucydides assigns a similar origin to the league which was formed against Athens, and which produced the Peloponnesian war. Demosthenes, on the same principle, alarmed the fears of all the Grecian republics, from the increasing power and inordinate ambition of Philip of Macedon. The Grecian history affords many more examples of the same policy. One example only occurs in the Roman history, where this maxim seems to have been understood and put in practice against this all-conquering people. It is that of Hiero, king of Syracuse, who, though in alliance with the Romans, sent assistance to the Carthaginians during the war of the auxiliaries. In the remarks of Polybius on that subject, we find the principle of a balance of power as ably explained as it could be by any modern politician. "He esteemed it necessary," says Polybius, "both in order to retain his dominions in Sicily and to preserve the Roman friendship, that Carthage should be safe, lest by its fall, the remaining power should be able, without opposition, to execute every purpose and undertaking. And here," continues that author, "he acted with great wisdom and prudence: for that is never on any account to be overlooked; nor ought such a force ever to be thrown into one hand, as to incapacitate the neighboring states from defending their rights against it."—Polyb., lib. i., c. lxxxiii. The system of a balance of power is therefore not a policy of modern invention; although we must own that it had not a general influence on the politics of Europe till the above-mentioned period of the confederacy against Charles VIII. This prince died at the age of eight and twenty, and leaving no children, the duke of Orleans succeeded to the crown of France by the title of Lewis XII., and revived, as we shall afterwards see, his pretensions to the kingdom of Naples.

CHAPTER XIV.

Spain, France, Italy, and Britain at the end of the Fifteenth and beginning of the Sixteenth Century—Ferdinand and Isabella—Extinction of the Moors in Spain—Lewis XII. of France invades Italy—Pope Alexander VI.—Julius II.—England—Henry VI.—Civil Wars of York and Lancaster—Margaret of Anjou—Edward IV.—Richard III.—Henry VII.—Union of York and Lancaster—Impostures of Simnel and Warbeck.

A very important revolution, which at this time took place in Spain, now demands our attention to that quarter. The assistance which Pedro the Cruel had received from the Black Prince was of transitory effect. On the departure of Edward, Pedro was again attacked by his enemies, and murdered by his bastard brother, Henry of Transtamarre, who thus secured for himself and his family the throne of Castile.

The voluptuousness of a court is no uncommon prelude to a revolution in the kingdom. Thus it happened under Henry IV. of Castile, a descendant of Henry of Transtamarre. The weakness and debauchery of this monarch incited a faction of his nobles, headed by the archbishop of Toledo, to take the government into their own hands. They accused their own sovereign of impotency, and declared his daughter Joanna, who was the heiress of the kingdom of Castile, an illegitimate child; she was disinherited, and sent out of the kingdom; while the Cortes, or the assembly of the States, obliged Henry to settle the inheritance on his sister Isabella.

The next concern of the associated nobles was to procure for Isabella a proper husband. Her alliance was courted by several princes. Lewis XI. demanded her for his brother, and the king of Arragon for his son Ferdinand. The king of Portugal sought her himself in marriage. The archbishop of Toledo, who headed the conspiracy against Henry, privately brought about the marriage of Isabella to Ferdinand of Arragon. This procedure exasperated the impotent Henry, who determined to rouse himself from his lethargy, and to exert his utmost endeavors to restore his daughter Joanna to her right of inheritance. A civil war was the consequence, which embroiled the whole kingdom. At length, Henry thought it his best policy to affect, at least, to be reconciled to his sister and to her husband Ferdinand, who took care that no future rupture should occasion their title to be disputed. The sudden and painful death of Henry left little doubt that he had been taken off by poison. Alphonso, king of Portugal, took up arms in favor of his niece Joanna, whom he intended to marry; but, after a war of some years' continuance, this unfortunate princess thought it her wisest course to end those disturbances, which she saw were not to be attended with success, by retiring into a monastery.

A wise and vigorous, though a severe, administration characterized the beginning of the reign of Ferdinand and Isabella. Spain was at this time in great disorder—the whole country was a prey to robbers and outlaws. Even the nobility lived by depredation, and defended themselves in their castles against every legal attempt to restrain their violence. The new monarchs of Castile and Arragon determined to repress these enormities. The castles of the piratical nobles were razed to the ground. The office of the Santa Hermandad, or Holy Brotherhood, was instituted for the detection and punishment of murders, thefts, and all atrocious crimes. But amidst these laudable cares, the abominable tribunal of the Inquisition was furnished with such an extent of powers, that, under the pretence of extirpating heresy and impiety, the whole kingdom became a scene of blood and horror. The fortunes and the lives of individuals were entirely at the mercy of the grand inquisitor and his associates. It was never allowed to a criminal to be confronted with his accuser, nor even to be informed of his crime; the sole method of trial was by exposing the unhappy wretch to the most extreme tortures, which either ended his life in agony, or forced a confession of his guilt, which was expiated by committing him to the flames. It is computed, that after the appointment of Torquemada, the inquisitor-general of Spain, there were 6000 persons burnt in the short space of four years.

The ambition of Ferdinand and Isabella was not limited to the possession of Arragon and Castile; the kingdom of the Moors, of Granada, which was all that remained of the Mahometan dominions in Spain, was a very tempting object of enterprise. Granada was at this time rent by intestine divisions; the factions of the Zegris and the Abéncerrāges had reduced that unhappy kingdom to the lowest state of weakness. The romantic exploits of these contending factions are remembered to this day in many beautiful Moorish ballads, and are pompously described in a very extraordinary work, entitled *Historia de las Guerras Civiles de Granada*, a book which contains a curious and authentic picture of a very singular state of society. In the Moorish kingdom of Granada were preserved the last remains of the genuine spirit of chivalry and romantic gallantry, a state of manners which in that work is very happily delineated.

Aboacen, king of Granada, was at this time at war with his nephew, Abo-Abdeli, who attempted to dethrone him. Ferdinand of Arragon supported Abo-Abdeli in order to weaken both parties; and no sooner was he in possession of the throne, by the death of Aboacen, than Ferdinand attacked his former ally with the united forces of Castile and Arragon. The war was tedious, and lasted several years. Isabella accompanied her husband in several of his military expeditions, and attended him when he laid siege to the city of Granada in 1491. After a blockade of eight months, the pusillanimous Abo-Abdeli, who has been called El Rey Chico, or the Little King, meanly capitulated, contrary to the sentiments and urgent remonstrances of above 20,000 of the inhabitants, who offered to defend their native city to the last extremity. The treaty between Abo-Abdeli and Ferdinand secured to the Moors of Granada a small mountainous part of the kingdom, with the enjoyment of their laws and religion. The Moorish prince, execrated by his people, betook himself to this despicable retreat. He is said to have wept when he cast back his eyes to the beautiful plain and city of Granada. "You have reason," said his mother, "to weep like a *woman* for the loss of that kingdom, which you could not defend like a *man*." Thus ended the dominion of the Moors in Spain, about 800 years after its foundation.

Ferdinand, now master of Arragon, Castile, and Granada, from that time took the title of king of Spain. He wanted only Navarre, which, as we shall see, he soon afterwards invaded and took possession of. Immediately after the conquest of Granada, he expelled all the Jews from the kingdom — a most impolitic step, which deprived Spain of about 150,000 inhabitants. The greatest part of these took refuge in Portugal, and carried with them their arts, their industry, and their commerce; the rest sailed over into Africa, where they were still more inhumanly used than in Spain. The Moors of that country are said to have ripped open their bellies, in order to search for the gold which they were supposed to have concealed in their bowels.

We have already seen that the arms of Ferdinand of Spain were successfully employed in driving the French out of Italy, after the fruitless conquest of Naples by Charles VIII. Lewis XII., his successor, was sensible of the necessity of having the pope in his interest when any claims were to be made good against the states of Italy. He courted Alexander VI. likewise, upon another account; he wished to procure a divorce from his wife, the daughter of Lewis XI., and to marry Anne of Brittany, the widow of Charles VIII. Cæsar Borgia, the natural son of pope Alexander, was, like his father, a monster of wickedness. The palace of the popes was stained with murder, adultery, and incest. Alexander was desirous of securing for his son Borgia an independent sovereignty, and he sent him for that purpose as his ambassador into France to make a treaty with Lewis, on the ground of their mutual pretensions. It was stipulated that the king of France should be divorced from his wife, and have the pope's assistance in the invasion of Italy, provided Cæsar Borgia should receive, in return, the dukedom of Valentinois, with the king of Navarre's sister in marriage, and a pension from Lewis of 100,000 livres. Lewis, having put his kingdom in a state of defence, crossed the Alps, and in ten days made himself master of Milan and Genoa. After some unsuccessful struggles made by Ludovico Sforza to regain the dukedom of Milan, that prince was betrayed by the Swiss troops, whom he had hired to protect his dominions, and given up into the hands of the French, among whom he passed his days as a prisoner, though treated both with humanity and respect. Lewis XII., afraid of Ferdinand of Spain, who had dispossessed his predecessor, Charles of the kingdom of Naples, thought it his most advisable measure to compromise matters with the Spanish monarch, and they agreed to divide the Neapolitan dominions between them. Ferdinand had Apulia and Calabria, and Lewis all the rest. Pope Alexander made no scruples of conscience to give his apostolical sanction to this partition, which dispossessed an innocent monarch, his ancient vassal, of all his territories.

But the French were not destined to have any durable possessions in Italy. Ferdinand soon after agreed with pope Alexander to deprive Lewis of his part of the spoils. Gonsalvo de Cordova, who had the distinguished epithet of El Gran Capitano, was commissioned by his master to extirpate the troops of Lewis, as he had done those of Charles VIII. The French, it is true, made a better defence. The duke de Nemours, a descendant of the great Clovis, and the illustrious Bayard, the *chevalier sans peur et sans reproche*, maintained their right to Naples with great military skill, and vied with each other in romantic feats of personal prowess. But the contention was vain. The conduct of the Great Captain was superior to the valor of the French, and Lewis irrecoverably lost his share of the kingdom of Naples. It is worthy of notice, that in this war between the French and Spaniards in Italy, the art of blowing up mines by gunpowder was first practised by one of the Spanish generals.

Alexander VI., in the meantime, and his favorite son Cæsar Borgia, continued to practise every effort of ambitious villany to increase their power and accumulate wealth. The personal estate of the cardinals on their death devolved to the pope, and many an unhappy cardinal died suddenly during this pontificate. Borgia, by force of arms, made himself master of the territories of some of the richest of the Italian nobles. Four of them he invited to a friendly conference, under the most solemn protestations of amicable intentions, and he massacred two of them by ambuscade. Vitelli, one of these wretched victims, is said to have entreated Borgia, his murderer, to ask of the pope, his father, a plenary indulgence for him in the agonies of death. Such is the deplorable weakness of superstition, that can attribute to the most abandoned of men the power of pardoning all offences against the Deity.* Italy was at length delivered of this monster and his son. It is said they had prepared poisoned wine for the entertainment of some wealthy cardinals, and that the pope himself, and his son, drank by mistake of a bottle intended only for his guests. The pope suffered an agonizing death, but Borgia escaped by having himself sewed up in the belly of a mule. He survived, however, but a short time, and reaped no other fruits of his own and his father's accumulated crimes, but the universal abhorrence of mankind. Most of the towns he had seized threw off their allegiance, and pope Julius II. stripped him entirely of his possessions. In fine, Gonsalvo of Cordova sent him prisoner into Spain, where he died in miserable obscurity. It is sufficient to expose the principles of Machiavel to observe, that he holds forth Cæsar Borgia as a perfect pattern to all princes who have the ambition of uncontrolled dominion, and wish to establish their power upon a solid foundation; as if that power was secure which is founded on terror, or that authority were an object of a wise man's ambition, which must be purchased at the expense of universal detestation.

Julius II., the successor of Alexander VI., was a pontiff of great political abilities, of a bold and ambitious character, and consummately skilled in the art of war. It was he who employed Michael Angelo to cast his statue in brass, and when the

* We understand from Burcard, that it was at this time an established custom for every new pope, immediately after his election, and as the first act of his apostolical function, to give a full absolution to all the cardinals of all the crimes they might thereafter commit of whatever nature and degree. Burcard was master of the ceremonies to the pope's chapel from Sixtus IV. to Julius II.—Accounts and Extracts of MSS. in the King of France's Library.

sculptor would have put a book in his hand, "No," said he, "give me a sword, I understand that better than a breviary.' It was his principal aim to drive the French out of Italy; but he chose, in the first place, to make them subservient to his designs of stripping the Venetians of several extensive territories, which had belonged to the Holy See, and which they had laid hold of on the death of Alexander VI. and Cæsar Borgia. This ambitious republic had acquired immense possessions; and most of the sovereigns of Europe had an interest in depriving her of them, to regain what had been their own property. Julius II brought about for this purpose one of the most formidable combinations of the European potentates that had ever been known. The pope, the emperor Maximilian, Ferdinand king of Spain, Lewis XII., the duke of Savoy, and the king of Hungary, held a conference by their ambassadors at Cambray, and determined the destruction of Venice, which they would certainly have accomplished, had the confederacy long subsisted. Lewis of France began the attack, and defeated the Venetian army in the battle of Agnadello. Each of the competitors seized a share of the spoils of the republic. The pope took possession of all Romagna. The emperor seized the province of Friuli, which has ever since continued in the possession of the house of Austria. The Spaniards took Calabria; and pope Julius, now seeing Venice completely humbled, and having secured his own share, determined, if possible, to make himself master of the shares of all the rest. In this laudable view, he entered into a league with that very republic to whom he had been so severe an enemy, and, by the most dexterous policy, prevailed both on them and the Neapolitans, on the Swiss, and even on the English, to assist him in driving the French out of Italy. The enterprising pontiff headed his armies in person. At the siege of Mirandola, with a helmet and cuirass, and sword in hand, he was among the first who entered the breach. The French for awhile kept their ground, from the signal heroism of their generals—the brave Chevalier Bayard, and Gaston de Foix, who won the famous battle of Ravenna at the expense of his own life; but their troops, from the parsimony of Lewis, were ill supplied; their mercenaries deserted, their generals showed their talents only in making fine retreats, and in the end they lost every foot of territory which they had possessed in Italy. The same Swiss, who had sold Ludovico Sforza to the French, now assisted to reëstablish his son Maximilian Sforza in the dukedom of Milan: and the same league, which had been at first concerted against Venice, was, by a strange vicissitude of fortune, directed against France, so as to prove in the end fatal to Lewis XII. While he was driven out of Italy by the pope, the Venetians, and the Swiss—Ferdinand, king of Spain, seized on Navarre, which has ever since been incorporated with the Spanish monarchy. He employed for this purpose the assistance of Henry VIII. of England, by inviting him to send troops into France for the recovery of Guienne, which troops the Spanish king artfully employed in subduing Navarre. Henry VIII. was thus made the dupe of Ferdinand's artful policy; but this monarch, who was then in the vigor of youth, was impatient to show the world that he had no occasion to recur to the aid of allies to humble the French. His successes in France we shall afterwards mention. It is sufficient here to observe, that Lewis XII. was glad to purchase a peace, to marry the sister of Henry VIII., the princess Mary of England, and, instead of receiving a portion, to pay the sum of 100,000 crowns.

Lewis XII., whose want of success in his foreign enterprises may be attributed to his having for his competitors two such consummate politicians as pope Julius II. and Ferdinand, king of Spain, was, in many respects, an excellent prince. He imposed few and moderate taxes, and was peculiarly attentive to the administration of justice through all his provinces. It is much to his honor, that, by some exemplary severities, he repressed that overbearing and rapacious spirit of the soldiery which had subjected the peasants of France to much misery and oppression. He is a prince whose memory is, on these accounts, deservedly respected by his country.

In order to retain a connected idea of our great object, the affairs of Britain, we must now return to the reign of Henry VI., when, under that infant monarch, and by the great political as well as military talents of his competitor, Charles VII. of France, we saw the English lose, by degrees, all their possessions in that kingdom, of which, a few years before, the French had acknowledged the king of England to be sovereign by inheritance.

Henry VI. soon showed himself to be a prince of the most contemptible abilities. In his minority, the jealousy and misunderstanding between his uncle, the duke of Gloucester, regent of the kingdom, and the cardinal of Winchester, his great uncle, who had the care of the king's person and education, embroiled every political measure, lost France, and filled the nation with faction and disorder. The cardinal, to strengthen his own interest, and depress that of his rival, married this shadow of a king to a woman of the most accomplished and manly spirit that, perhaps, ever appeared—Margaret of Anjou, daughter of Regnier, the titular king of Naples and duke of Lorraine. She had the qualities of a heroine, but they were sometimes stained with a cruelty which knew no bounds in the prosecution of her enemies. Gloucester had been averse to her marriage with the king, and her first step was to devote him to destruction. His wife was accused of treason, aggravated by sorcery; a crime which in those days found the readiest belief. A priest and an old woman, her pretended accomplices, were burnt in Smithfield, and the duchess herself was condemned to perpetual imprisonment. The duke of Gloucester was arrested soon after on an accusation of treason, and was next morning found dead in his bed. These outrageous proceedings produced the greatest disgust in the minds of the people against the queen and the cardinal of Winchester, and rendered the king's name, who was supposed at least to countenance these enormities, both odious and despicable. It was the time for a competitor to start forth, and to avail himself of this general disaffection to the prince on the throne. This competitor was Richard, duke of York, a descendant, by the mother's side, from Lionel, who was one of the sons of Edward III., and elder brother to John of Gaunt, from whom the present monarch was descended. Richard, therefore, stood plainly in right of succession before Henry. He bore for his ensign a white rose, while Henry bore a red one; and this circumstance gave the name to the two factions which deluged England in blood. The weakness of Henry VI., and the unpopularity of the government, gave occasion to frequent commotions.

The duke of York secretly fomented these disturbances, and, pretending to espouse the cause of the people, wrote to the king, advising him to dismiss from his person and councils the most obnoxious of his ministers. The easy monarch made partial concessions; while the duke, who found his influence with the people daily increasing, determined to avail himself of his power, and raised an army of 10,000 men. His enterprises were seconded to his wish by the king's illness, who now became subject to periodical fits of madness; and being incapable of maintaining even the appearance of royalty, York was appointed lieutenant and protector of the kingdom. This was a fatal blow to the party which supported the interests of the house of Lancaster, and who were now removed from all dignities and offices. At length the king, as if awaking from his lethargy, or rather roused by the instigation of his spirited wife, was prevailed on to deprive the duke of York of his power, who had by this time annihilated the royal authority. In consequence of this step, York instantly had recourse to arms. Henry was dragged to the battle of St. Alban's, where the party of York gained a complete victory. The king was wounded and taken prisoner, but treated by the victor with great respect and tenderness. He was soon after led in triumph to London; and the duke of York, permitting him still to enjoy the title of king, assumed to himself that of protector, under which he exercised all the real powers of the sovereign.

Margaret of Anjou, whose courage rose from her misfortunes, prepared to avenge the cause of her husband, and to support the regal authority. With the assistance of those nobles who were devoted to the house of Lancaster, she raised a considerable army, and met the troops of York on the borders of Staffordshire. A desertion from that party increased so much the strength of the royal army, that their opponents instantly dispersed, and the duke fled into Ireland, while his cause was secretly maintained in England by Guy, earl of Warwick, a man of great abilities, and of the most undaunted fortitude. By degrees, the activity of this nobleman collected an army sufficient to take the field. Margaret of Anjou had ranged her army at Northampton, determined to fight herself at the head of her troops, while the despicable king remained in his tent, awaiting in great perturbation the issue of the engagement. The royal army was overthrown, and Henry once more made a prisoner, and brought back to London. Margaret fled with precipitation to Wales, and, her manly spirit never deserting her, employed herself in levying a new army for the rescue of her husband, and the reëstablishment of his authority.

Meantime a parliament was summoned at London, where the duke of York openly claimed the crown of England, as the representative of Edward III., to the exclusion of Henry VI., born of a younger branch. It was now for the first time that the House of Lords seemed to enjoy an unbiassed deliberative authority. The cause of Henry and of the duke of York was solemnly debated, each side producing their reasons without fear or control. York, notwithstanding his successes, could not gain a complete victory in parliament. It was decided that Henry should continue to reign for life, and that the duke should succeed him, to the exclusion of the prince of Wales.

Margaret, meantime, had levied an army of 20,000 men ; and meeting the party of York near Wakefield, an engagement ensued, in which her arms were victorious. The duke of York himself was killed in the engagement, and his head, encircled with a paper crown, was, by the king's order, fixed upon the gates of the city of York. The earl of Warwick, however, kept alive the courage of the vanquished, and carried about the pitiful Henry as his prisoner. He met the army of the queen once more at St. Alban's where the royal arms were again victorious. But when Margaret, who had now set her husband at liberty, prepared to enter London in triumph, she found the gates of the city shut against her. Young Edward, the eldest son of the late duke of York, had begun to repair the losses of his party. London had declared in his favor, and proclaimed him king, by the title of Edward IV. Margaret of Anjou, whose greatness of soul was superior to all her misfortunes, retreated to the north of England, where she found means to assemble an army of 60,000 men. Warwick met her at the head of 40,000, at Towton, on the borders of Yorkshire. An engagement ensued; one of the bloodiest and most desperate that is recorded in the English history. Thirty-six thousand men were left dead upon the field : Warwick gained a complete victory, by which the young Edward was fixed upon the throne, and the vanquished Margaret, with her husband and infant son, took refuge in Flanders.

Here she did not long remain. With what slender assistance she could procure on the continent, she landed again in England: again defeated, she fled over to France to her father, Regnier of Anjou, who could afford her nothing but a retreat. Henry was once more made a prisoner, and confined in the Tower of London. Edward IV., now crowned by the hands of Warwick, became ungrateful to his benefactor. The earl had negotiated a match between the young monarch and the princess Bona, of Savoy, the sister of Lewis XI. of France. When the marriage was on the point of conclusion, Edward chanced to fall in love with one of his own subjects, the widow of Sir John Grey, and privately married her; Warwick was justly incensed, and expressing strongly his resentment of the affront, the young king, equally ungrateful and impolitic, banished him from the council, and thus made him his irreconcilable enemy. It was not long before Warwick found an opportunity of revenge. His daughter was married to the duke of Clarence, the king's brother. This prince he seduced from his allegiance, as well as many of the nobles of the York faction, and Warwick now openly stood forth the champion of the house of Lancaster. After various intermediate changes, Edward was deposed from the throne, and Henry VI. once more reinstated by the hands of Warwick, who was now distinguished by the epithet of *the King-maker*. Edward, banished for awhile to the continent, returned to England. The city of London were his friends, and a powerful party in the kingdom espoused his interest. An engagement followed at Barnet, where the party of York was again victorious; and Margaret of Anjou, returning at that time with her son from France, received the dispiriting intelligence that her army was defeated, and her new champion, the brave earl of Warwick, slain in the engagement.

This most intrepid and matchless woman continued with unshaken firmness of mind to struggle against adversity, and once more prepared to strike a decisive blow for the crown of England. This was at Tewkesbury, where she commanded her army in person, and led her son the prince of Wales through the ranks. But all was in vain: victory declared in favor of Edward, and the unhappy mother, separated from her son, was sent a prisoner to the Tower of London. The prince of Wales, a youth of intrepid spirit, being brought into the presence of Edward, and asked, in an insulting manner, how he dared to invade the territories of his sovereign, "I have entered," said he, "the dominions of *my father*, to revenge *his* injuries and redress *my own*." The barbarous Edward is said to have struck him in the face with his gauntlet, while the dukes of Gloucester and Clarence, and others of the attendants, rushed upon the noble youth and stabbed him to the heart with their daggers. The death of Henry was next resolved, and the duke of Gloucester, in the true spirit of butchery, is said to have entered his chamber, and massacred the feeble monarch in cold blood.* Margaret they allowed to live, in hopes of her being ransomed by the king of France; and that monarch in effect paid 50,000 crowns for her freedom. She died a few years afterwards in France—a woman whom, but for some instances of cruelty in the beginning of her career, all Europe must have venerated and admired.

Edward IV., now firmly seated on the throne, abandoned himself to vicious pleasures. His life was passed in a succession of riots and debauchery, and acts of tyranny and cruelty. His brother, the duke of Clarence, taking the part of a friend who had fallen a victim to the king's displeasure, and inveighing severely against the rigor of his sentence, was on that account alone, arraigned and condemned to suffer death. The only favor shown him was to choose the manner of it, and he very whimsically chose to be drowned in a butt of Malmsey. A war was proclaimed against France, but during the preparation for this enterprise, which was highly grateful to the nation, an event no less grateful happened, which was the death of Edward IV., at the age of forty-two, poisoned, as is supposed, by his brother Richard, duke of Gloucester. He left two sons, the eldest Edward V., a boy of thirteen years of age. Gloucester, named Protector of the kingdom, gave orders that the two princes for security, should be lodged in the Tower. Hastings, a friend to the royal family and an enemy to tyranny, had too strongly expressed his concern for their safety, and attachment to their interest. Richard, on a most frivolous pretence of treason, ordered this nobleman to be arrested in the council, and he was instantly led forth to execution. The duke of Buckingham, the slavish instrument of an ambitious tyrant, had wrought upon a mob of the meanest of the populace to declare that they wished Richard, duke of Gloucester, to accept of the crown; this was interpreted to be the voice of the nation. The crafty tyrant, with affected scruples and with much appearance of humility, was at length prevailed on to yield to their desires and to accept the proffered crown. His elevation had been purchased by a series of crimes, and was now to be secured by an act of accumulated horror. Three assassins, by the command of Richard, entered at midnight the apartment of the Tower where the princes lay asleep, and, smothering them in the bed-clothes, buried them in a corner of the building.

* It is but justice to observe, that this atrocious fact has been altogether doubted. The historians of the times, being under the influence of the house of Lancaster, are to be read with much caution; and nothing, after all, is given as evidence of this fact but common fame. Those writers all fix the time of Henry VI.'s death to the 21st of May, 1471. Guthrie, however, has produced from the records undoubted evidence, that he was alive on the 12th of June thereafter; and some historians, even of the Lancaster party, affirm that it was reported at the time, that he died of anguish and grief of mind. It is certain that his body was conveyed to St. Paul's and there exposed to public view, a circumstance which ill agrees with the idea of a private murder.—See Guthrie's History of England, vol. ii., p. 719, 720.

At length after a reign of two tedious years, an avenger of these atrocious crimes appeared in the person of Henry, earl of Richmond, a prince of the lineage of John of Gaunt. Henry was yet very young when he formed the design of dethroning Richard, and of reclaiming England as the patrimony of the house of Lancaster. His first attempt was unsuccessful; and after his party had been twice defeated, he was obliged to return for shelter to Brittany. Thence he was forced by the treachery of the duke of Brittany's minister, who had privately covenanted to deliver him up to Richard. Betaking himself to the province of Anjou, he was aided by Charles VIII. of France, with a small army of 2000 men. With this slender support he landed in England. The Welsh flocked to his standard, and, animated with courage, he ventured to give battle to Richard on the field of Bosworth. Richard III. met him with an army double his numbers; and the event would probably have been unfortunate for Richmond, had not lord Stanley, with a large body of troops, changed sides in the heat of the engagement, and fought against the usurper. This decided the fate of the day; the army of Richard was entirely defeated, and the tyrant himself met with a better death than his crimes and cruelties deserved. Seeing that all was lost, he rushed with desperate fury into the thickest of the enemy, and fell pierced with innumerable wounds. The crown which he wore on his head during the engagement was immediately placed upon the head of the conqueror.

The army of Richmond sang an hymn to God upon the field of battle, and, with the loudest acclamations, proclaimed him as Henry VII. king of England. This auspicious day put an end to the civil wars between the houses of York and Lancaster. Henry, by marrying the princess Elizabeth, daughter of Edward IV., united in his own person the interests and rights of both these families. This excellent prince, who knew how to govern as well as to conquer, was one of the best monarchs that ever reigned in England. The nation, under his wise and politic administration, soon recovered the wounds it had sustained in those unhappy contests. The parliaments which he assembled made the most salutary laws, the people paid their taxes without reluctance, the nobles were kept in due subordination, and that spirit of commercial industry for which the English have been, in these latter ages, justly distinguished, began to make vigorous advances under the reign of Henry VII. The only failing of this prince was an economy, perhaps too rigid, which, in his latter years, degenerated even into avarice; and though his taxes were not oppressive, he left in the treasury, at his death, no less than two millions sterling; a certain proof of two things—the one, that it is possible, without oppressing the people, for all the emergencies of government to be most amply supplied; the other, that the prince's economy can effectually check that dissipation of the public money by corrupt and rapacious officers, which increases both the weakness of the state and the grievances of the people.

The reign of Henry VII. was disturbed for awhile by two very singular enterprises. The earl of Warwick, son of the late duke of Clarence, had been confined by Richard in the Tower, and by his long imprisonment was totally unknown, and unacquainted with the world. One Simon, a priest of Oxford, trained up a young man, Lambert Simnel, the son of a baker, to counterfeit the earl of Warwick's person, and instructed him in the knowledge of all the facts which were necessary to support the imposture. He first made his public appearance in Dublin, where he found many to espouse his cause, and he was there solemnly crowned king of England and Ireland. Thence passing over to England, he ventured to give battle to Henry near Nottingham. Simnel with his tutor, the priest, were both taken prisoners. The priest, who could not be tried by the civil power, was imprisoned for life; and the impostor himself, who was too mean an object for the revenge of Henry, was employed by him as a scullion in his kitchen.

This enterprise was succeeded by another, which was not so easily defeated. The old duchess of Burgundy, sister of Edward IV., and widow of Charles the Bold, who wished by all means to embroil the government of Henry, caused a report to be spread that the young duke of York, who, along with his brother Edward, was hitherto believed to have been smothered in the Tower by Richard III., was still alive—and she soon after produced a young man who assumed his name and character: this was Perkin Warbeck, the son of a Jew broker of Antwerp, a youth of great personal beauty and insinuating address. He found means, for a considerable time, to carry on the deception, and seemed, from his valor and abilities, to be not undeserving of the rank which he assumed. For five years he supported his cause by force of arms, and was aided by a respectable proportion of the English nobility. James IV., king of Scotland, espoused his interest, and gave him in marriage a relation of his own, a daughter of the earl of Huntley. After various changes of fortune, during all which Perkin showed himself to be a man of genius and intrepidity, he was at length abandoned by his followers on the approach of the royal army, which greatly exceeded them in numbers, and forced to deliver himself up to Henry's mercy, who only condemned him to perpetual imprisonment. This, however, was too much for his impatient spirit. He attempted to make his escape, and secretly tampered with the unfortunate Warwick, still a prisoner in the Tower, to raise a new insurrection; the consequence was, that Perkin Warbeck was hanged at Tyburn, and young Warwick, tried by his peers, condemned and beheaded on Tower-hill.

It is necessary to remark, that the real character and pretensions of Perkin Warbeck are, to this day, a subject of uncertainty and of controversy; and upon an examination of the evidence on both sides of the question, there are many now, as there were then, who believe that this young man was, in reality, the son of king Edward IV. Carte, in his History of England, was, I believe, the first who ventured to suggest his doubts with regard to the common notion of Warbeck's being an impostor, and other reasons have since been added by Guthrie, which strongly countenance the supposition that this young man was really the duke of York. Horace Walpole, in his Historic Doubts on the Reign of Richard III., has taken up the same side of the question, as if it had been a new idea started by himself, though the authors I have mentioned have furnished him with the best part of his arguments.

CHAPTER XV.

Scotland from the Middle of the Fourteenth Century to the End of the Reign of James V.—David II.—Robert II., first of the House of Stuart—Robert III. James I., II., III., and IV.—Marriage of James IV. with Margaret, Daughter of Henry VII. founds the hereditary Title of the House of Stuart to the Throne of England—Battle of Flodden—James V.—Ancient Constitution of the Scottish Government.

The feudal aristocracy had attained to a great degree of strength in Scotland in the time of Robert Bruce. In return for the services of the nobles in placing him upon the throne, Robert bestowed on them large grants of the lands of which they had dispossessed the English. Property before this time had been subject to great revolutions in Scotland. Edward I., having forfeited the estates of many of the Scottish barons, granted them to his English subjects. These were expelled by the Scots, who seized their lands. Amidst such frequent changes, many held their possessions by titles extremely defective, and Robert formed on this ground a scheme for checking the growing power and wealth of his nobles. He summoned them to appear, and show by what rights they held their lands. "By this right," said each of them, laying his hand upon his sword; "by the sword we gained them, and by that we will defend them." Robert, apprehensive of the consequences of exasperating this resolute spirit of his nobles, wisely dropped the scheme.

Robert Bruce had a son, David, and a daughter, Margery. In a parliament, which he held at Ayr, in the year 1315, before the birth of his son David, he had solemnly settled the succession to the crown of Scotland, failing heirs of himself, upon his brother, Edward Bruce, and his male issue; on failure of whom, upon his daughter Margery and her heirs. Margery was afterwards married, in her father's lifetime, to Walter, the high steward of Scotland, of which marriage sprang Robert, the first of the house of Stuart who sat upon the Scottish throne, and who succeeded in virtue of this settlement of the crown made by his grandfather, Robert Bruce.

Robert Bruce died in the year 1329, and was succeeded by his son, David Bruce, then an infant. Taking advantage of this minority, Edward Baliol, the son of John, formerly king of Scotland, urged his pretensions to the crown; and, secretly assisted by Edward III. of England, entered the kingdom at the head of an army. He found a considerable number of partisans among the factious barons, and so great, for awhile, was his success, that he was crowned king at Scone, while the young David was conveyed to France, where he received an honorable protection. But matters did not long remain in this situation. The meanness of Edward Baliol, who was contented to acknowledge the sovereignty of Edward III. over his kingdom, deprived him of the affections of the nation. Randolph, earl of Murray, Robert, the steward of Scotland, and Sir William Douglas, roused the Bruce's party to arms, and, with the aid of Philip of Valois, king of France, David was restored to his kingdom; but it was only to sustain a new reverse of fortune. In an invasion of the English territory, the Scots were opposed by a powerful army, which was led into the field by the high-spirited Philippa, the queen of Edward III. The English gained a complete victory at the battle of Durham, and David, as we have formerly seen, was taken prisoner, and conveyed to the Tower of London. It was, soon after, his fortune to find a brother monarch in the same situation, John, king of France, the son of Philip of Valois, whom we have seen taken prisoner by the Black Prince, at the famous battle of Poictiers, and conducted in triumph to London. In this state of captivity David remained for eleven years, when, in consequence of a treaty of amity between the kingdoms, and a large ransom paid by the Scots, their monarch was again restored to his throne. During a reign thus perplexed, whatever had been the inclinations of the sovereign, it is impossible that his kingdom could have derived much benefit from his administration. David died in the year 1370, and, leaving no issue, the crown, according to the destination of his father, Robert, went to the son of his sister Margery, who was Robert, the *high steward* of Scotland.

The reign of this first prince of the house of Stuart exhibits no events which are worthy of commemoration. It passed in a series of unimportant skirmishes and inroads between the Scots and English, the most memorable of which was that which gave occasion to the heroic ballad of "Chevy Chace." But these incursions produced no effect of consequence upon either kingdom. The great barons were, however, gradually increasing their power; and under the reign of the succeeding prince, Robert III., their contests embroiled the nation in perpetual disturbances and outrages, which the weak and easy disposition of the sovereign was utterly incapable to compose or redress. He delegated the reins of government into the hands of his brother, the duke of Albany, —a measure which gave birth to the most flagitious designs in the bosom of the regent. Robert had two sons—the elder, whom he created duke of Rothsay; and the younger, James, who succeeded him in the throne of Scotland. The regent, Albany, found means to render the conduct of his nephew Rothsay, a young man of spirit and promising talents,* so suspected to his father, that he was confined in the castle of Falkland, where Albany starved him to death. The king, too weak to punish a man to whom he had committed the sole administration of the kingdom, sought only now how to preserve his sole surviving child, James, from a similar fate, which there was every reason to expect from the designs of his unnatural uncle. With the intention of conveying him to France, Robert put his son James on board of a vessel, which, unfortunately, was captured on her voyage by an English ship. The prince was brought a prisoner to London, and his father, whose spirit was quite unequal to so severe a misfortune, sunk into a melancholy despondency, and died about a year after.

James I. was, in the year 1405, declared king of Scotland, by an assembly of the states, which, at the same time, continued the duke of Albany in the regency till the prince should be released from his captivity. This was an event which the English were not willing to hasten, and which the duke of Albany was at no pains to procure. James remained a prisoner for eighteen years, during the reigns of Henry IV., V., and VI. He was treated with great honor and respect, and these monarchs made the best amends for their injustice in detaining him a captive, by the care which they bestowed on his education. He was endowed by nature with excellent talents, and he had at the English court opportunities of improvement which he must have wanted at his own. He learned there those maxims of government, which, to the great benefit of his country, (though, in the end, to his own disadvantage,) he reduced into practice when he regained his throne.†

* The character of David, duke of Rothsay, is said to have borne a great similarity to that of his contemporary and rival, young Harry of Monmouth, the son of Henry IV., and afterwards the great Henry V.

† During the regency of Albany, and in the year 1410, the University of St Andrews was founded by Henry Wardlaw, bishop of that see.

At the return of James into Scotland, he found his kingdom plunged in all the disorders and miseries of anarchy. The authority of a sovereign could never be effectually exercised by regents, who, to secure themselves in power, were obliged to pay court to the greater nobility, and countenance them in, or at least overlook all their usurpations; and hence the kingdom was a scene of perpetual contests between the great lords, and of rapine and injustice among all ranks of the state. James determined to repress these enormities, and he began by the gentler methods of statutory enactments. He gained the affections and the confidence of his people by many excellent laws, tending to establish order, tranquillity, and the equal administration of justice. He then prepared to undermine the power of his nobles, by a very equitable requisition, that those who possessed crown lands should exhibit the titles by which they held them. He next prohibited, with the utmost severity, all leagues and combinations among the nobility; and, as offending against this statute, he seized, during the sitting of parliament, on his cousin, the duke of Albany, son of the regent, with two of his sons, and above twenty of the first rank of the nobility. Albany and his sons, with the earl of Lennox, were beheaded:—the rest he pardoned, and received again into favor. An example of this kind struck awe and terror into the whole order of the nobles.

James was adored by his people, who enjoyed unusual happiness and security under his administration; but the nobles, who daily felt some new diminution of their power, were not long disposed to brook these innovations with submission. The earl of March, whose estates had been forfeited for rebellion against Robert III., the father of James, had been restored to his possessions and honors by the regent Albany. James, on pretence that this restitution was unjust and beyond the powers of the regent, procured a sentence of parliament declaring this decree void, and again depriving the earl of his estate and honors. Many of the nobility, who held land by grants from the regent, suspecting that this was a prelude to a similar deprivation, began secretly to take measures for their mutual security. The earl of Athole, the king's uncle, who aspired to the crown, and who was next heir after James and his issue, together with a few desperate men, the friends and followers of those who had been the chief sufferers under the king's administration, formed a conspiracy against his life. He received intelligence of their designs, but his natural intrepidity treated the danger with contempt; and while in the Dominican convent, near Perth, attended by his queen and a very few of the courtiers, he was murdered in the most cruel manner, in the forty-fourth year of his age, and the thirteenth of his reign.*

* A full detail of this most horrible murder is given by Pinkerton, Hist. of Scot., vol. i., from an old chronicle, translated from the Latin by J. Shirley, printed in the Appendix. This chronicle is a singular curiosity. Its date is about 1440.

All historians allow to James the character of a wise, most accomplished, and excellent prince. No sovereign ever more happily united the utmost attention to the cares of government with elegance of taste, and a love of literature and the arts. In his youth he had successfully cultivated the sciences of poetry and music, and his poetical compositions remaining at this day may well vie with those of the English bards, his contemporaries, Chaucer and Gower. It was his misfortune, that his maxims and manners were too refined for the age in which he lived, and the nation which he governed. Buchanan, in his character of this accomplished prince, has indulged a vein of the most eloquent panegyric. "Tanta ingenii celeritas et vigor in eo fuisse dicitur, ut nullam homine ingenuo dignam artem ignoraverat:" and the same author, animadverting upon what some men had, during the lifetime of James, judged to be too rigorous an authority in the sovereign, he concludes with this reflection: "Mors vero ejus declaravit nihil justitia esse popularius: nam qui vivo detractare soliti erant, mortuum flagrantissimo desiderio sunt prosecuti."

James II., an infant of seven years of age, succeeded to the throne of Scotland in the year 1437. In his youth, under the direction of the chancellor Crichton, a man of great abilities, who had stood high in the confidence of his father, sensible of the power and insolence of the nobles, he pursued the same maxims of government, which an impetuous temper, in some instances, prompted him to carry to a blamable as well as a dangerous excess. The earl of Douglas, an ambitious and high-spirited nobleman, had openly aimed at rendering himself independent of his sovereign: he forbade his vassals to acknowledge any authority but his own. He created knights, appointed a privy council, and, in short, assumed every ensign of royalty except the title of king. The chancellor, determined to suppress these aspiring pretensions, decoyed Douglas to an interview in the castle of Edinburgh, and there, while separated from his followers, he was seized and instantly beheaded. This example of barbarous rigor did not deter his successor William, earl of Douglas, from prosecuting the same ambitious plans; and his fate was equally severe, and yet more unjustifiable. In a conference with the young monarch, he was reproached by him with forming connections with the factious nobility which were dangerous to the public peace and government of the kingdom: the king requesting him to dissolve these associations, Douglas peremptorily refused. "If you will not," said the young James, "this shall:" and drawing his dagger, he instantly stabbed him to the heart. This action, unworthy of a prince, was universally condemned by his subjects, and nothing but the intemperate ardor of youth could ever palliate it. The vassals of the earl assembled immediately in arms, and were joined by a great body of the people. A rebellion arose, which threatened the most dangerous consequences: but the succeeding earl of Douglas, if he possessed sufficient spirit, wanted at least the policy to take advantage of those circumstances which, improved by a man of abilities, might have overturned the government. On the eve of an engagement, which must have decided the fate either of the royal party or its ambitious opponents, Douglas imprudently disgusted some of his chief partisans, who, in revenge, immediately joined the banners of their sovereign. Dispirited by this secession, Douglas lost all courage, and disbanding the remainder of his army, left the kingdom, while the vigor and talents of the monarch soon reduced all into order and subjection. James, who now reigned with absolute authority, did not abuse his power. He applied himself to the civilization of his kingdom, and its improvement by the enactment of many excellent laws, but of which the great scope was the undermining of the power of the nobility ; a purpose, it must be acknowledged, extremely promotive of the security and happiness of the people, though it threw the whole power, with very little limitation, into the hands of the sovereign. The truth is, if an absolute government is at any time to be desired, it is in the case of a rude and uncultivated people. Towards a general and speedy civilization, no form of government is equally effectual. It is only when men have arrived at such a degree of refinement and cultivation as to be able to think wisely for themselves, and to see their *own particular* good in the *welfare of the community*, that a mixed government, justly attempered between the prince and people, is capable of retaining the latter in the line of their duty. The prosecution of these plans for the subversion of the feudal aristocracy was interrupted by the sudden death of James, who was killed by the bursting of a cannon at the siege of Roxburgh, in the thirtieth year of his age.

His son and successor, James III., possessed the same inclination to humble the power of his nobles, but he wanted the abilities of his father and grandfather. He expressed his hatred of his grandees by removing them from his councils, while he lavished his favor and confidence on a few mean persons, who had nothing to recommend them but their skill in some of the arts and sciences, which the king himself understood and cultivated. He pursued, at the same time, the plan of his predecessors, by recalling all rights to the crown-land, which had been granted during his minority, and thus, without the support which they had in the affections of their people, he procured to himself the enmity and resentment of his nobles. It was the peculiar misfortune of this prince, that to his own family he owed his greatest distresses and calamities. His brothers, the duke of Albany and the earl of Mar, joined a confederacy of the nobles to deprive him of the throne. Albany concluded a treaty with Edward IV., in which he assumed the title of king of Scotland, and obliged himself, in return for a promise of aid from England, to do homage, and acknowledge Scotland to be dependent on the English crown. He obtained, accordingly, the assistance of a powerful army from Edward; and James, justly afraid of this formidable invasion, was obliged to solicit the aid of those nobles whom he had so long treated with scorn and exasperated by injuries. They repaired indeed to the standard of their prince, but it was with a resolution to revenge their own wrongs instead of his. While encamped at Lander, several of the chief nobility rushed into the king's apartment, in which he sat surrounded with his despicable favorites; dragged them out in spite of the remonstrances and entreaties of their sovereign; and, without any form of trial, seven of them were instantly hanged over a bridge.

The rebellious Albany continued his machinations, which, however, were finally disappointed in their aim by the death of Edward. James III. might now have recovered the affections of his subjects, had he been capable of deriving improvement from experience: but persevering in his attachment to mean favorites, and in his enmity to his nobles, the breach was daily widening between them and their sovereign. At length, openly taking arms, they persuaded or obliged the duke of Rothsay, the king's eldest son, a youth of fifteen, to set himself at their head, and countenance their design of depriving his father of the reins of government. The king took the field, and encountered the rebel army near Bannockburn, the same place where the valiant Bruce so signally defeated the English army under Edward II. The event of the battle was fatal to James: his army was entirely routed, and he himself slain in the pursuit. He fell in the thirty-fifth year of his age, and was succeeded in the throne of Scotland by his son, James IV., then in arms against him; a circumstance which, after the father's death, struck the young sovereign with infinite remorse. He never forgave himself the offence, and wore, during the whole course of his life, an iron chain around his body as a continual penance.

It is worthy of observation, that in this reign of James III. we find the first traces of the English policy of securing an interest in the kingdom of Scotland by means of pecuniary supplies. The English felt severely the weight which Scotland gave by her coöperation to all the designs of France. To counteract this policy, a treaty was entered into for the marriage of James's eldest son (then a boy two years of age) with Cecilia, the youngest daughter of Edward IV., then in the fourth year of her age; and though the marriage was not to be celebrated till a distant period, it was agreed that the princess's portion should begin to be paid immediately, by annual instalments of 2000 marks, (about £19,000 sterling.) By this policy it was judged that the amity of the nation would be completely secured, while England would thus be left at liberty to exert her whole strength against her potent enemy, France.

James IV. possessed every talent of a great and an accomplished prince. He was fond of military glory, of great personal courage, and of romantic generosity. He saw and pursued the true interests of his people; and such was his conduct towards his nobles, that while he maintained the authority of a monarch, he placed that confidence in them as his counsellors, which was returned by every mark of their duty and attachment. An animosity with England, which took place on account of James's affording a generous protection to Perkin Warbeck, whom he believed to be an injured prince, was soon after obliterated and reconciled by a marriage which Henry VII. brought about between the king of Scots and his daughter Margaret; a connection which founded the hereditary title of James VI. to the crown of England. This amity between the kingdoms was, however, unfortunately dissolved in the succeeding reign of Henry VIII. James, instigated by the French, the ancient allies of Scotland, then at war with Henry, and exasperated at the taking of some Scottish ships, and a few other circumstances which his high spirit interpreted into national affronts, much against the opinion of the chief and best of his counsellors, determined on a war with England. He levied an army of 50,000 men; and such was the attachment of his grandees, that the whole body of the Scottish nobility appeared, with all their dependants, under the banners of their sovereign. They entered the county of Northumberland, and were met by the earl of Surrey, in the field of Flodden. The address of the English general in avoiding an engagement till his army was reinforced; while the Scots, wanting provisions, in an enemy's country, and weakened by daily desertions, were reduced at length to a great inferiority of force; and the imprudent heroism of James in quitting a most advantageous post upon an eminence to attack the English, who were marshalled upon the plain—were the causes of a total and miserable defeat of the Scottish army. Five thousand were left dead upon the field of Flodden, among whom was the king himself, and almost the whole nobility of the kingdom. This fatal battle was fought on the 9th of September, 1513. A confused rumor of the event of the engagement reached Edinburgh on the next day; when the magistrates of the capital ordered a proclamation to be made, which has a striking similarity to one which the reader remembers to have been issued by the senate of Rome.

The Scottish proclamation runs in the following words:—"Forasmuch as there is a great rumor newly arisen within this city touching our sovereign lord and his army, of which there is hitherto no certainty, we strictly command that all manner of persons, townsmen within this city, make ready their arms of defence and weapons of war, and that they appear marshalled therewith at the tolling of the common bell, for holding out and defending the city against all who may seek to invade the same. And we also charge and require that all women do repair to their work, and be not seen upon the street clamoring and crying, under pain of banishment; and that the women of better sort do repair to the church, and there offer up their prayers to God for the safety of our sovereign lord and his army."

It is curious to compare this with the decree of the senate, as recorded by Livy, upon the event of the battle of Cannæ, and the Scottish proclamation will not suffer by the comparison; since, w'th the same expression of calm and determined fortitude, there is less of that parade of words, which, by endeavoring to conceal fear often betrays it.

James V., at the death of his father, was an infant of a year old. The regency of the kingdom was conferred on the duke of Albany, grand-uncle to the king, a native of France, and consequently a stranger to the laws, manners, and genius of the people whom he governed. The disaster of Flodden, which had so greatly weakened the Scottish nobility, had not deprived the remnant of that body of their ancient spirit of ambition and independence. This long minority gave them time to recover strength; and some extraordinary exertions of authority in the regent had combined them in a very formidable association against the power of the crown, which James, upon assuming the government, found it an extremely difficult task to moderate and restrain. "We discern in the character of James V.," says Dr. Robertson, "all the features of a great and uncultivated spirit. On the one hand, violent passions, implacable resentment, an immoderate desire of power, and the utmost rage at disappointment. On the other, love to his people, zeal for the punishment of private oppressors, confidence in his favorites, and the most engaging openness and affability of behavior."

Under a monarch of this disposition, had it been possible to restrain the turbulent spirit of a factious nobility, the nation might have arrived at happiness and splendor. But ambition once kindled in the breasts of his nobles, and encroachments attempted on the power of the crown, this high-spirited prince formed, from the beginning of his reign, a deliberate design of humbling and reducing them to subjection. To this purpose his plan was deeper and more systematic than that of any of his predecessors. The church, which was under the influence of the crown, was naturally hostile to the body of the nobles, who were their rivals in wealth and power. With the concurrence of the clergy, whom he knew he could always command, James determined effectually to abase the power of the grandees.* He chose his

* In order to repress the predatory, ferocious, and most tubulent spirit of the northern chieftains, many of whom had exchanged their allegiance to their native prince, for a league of alliance with Henry VIII. of England, James with a bold and magnanimous policy, circumnavigated the greatest part of his dominions, visiting the whole of the coast to the north of the river Forth, and

counsellors from the church, men of consummate abilities, whom he raised to all the offices of trust and confidence. His prime minister was the cardinal Beaton, an ecclesiastic of very superior genius; who concurred with great keenness and satisfaction in the designs of his sovereign. The nobles, removed entirely from all share in the councils of state, and many of them punished with extreme rigor for very slight offences, were restrained only by their own weakness from breaking out into open rebellion. One imprudent measure of the king gave them at length an opportunity of taking a severe, though an ignominious revenge.

Henry VIII., at variance with the see of Rome, and insecure of the affections of his own subjects, wished to strengthen himself by an alliance with the king of Scots ; and for this purpose proposed an interview at York, where a treaty of amity was to be concluded between the two kingdoms. It was certainly the real interest of James to have concurred with these views of the king of England, which would have been of mutual benefit to both ; and he engaged to meet him for that purpose ; but in the meantime, he unfortunately gave ear to the persuasions of his clergy, who, exasperated by the part which Henry had taken against the see of Rome, and apprehensive of a similar plan of reformation to that which was now taking place in England, employed all their credit with the king to prevent this alliance. They succeeded, and James disappointed the promised interview, which necessarily brought on a declaration of war on the part of Henry VIII.

The king of Scots was now obliged to court the aid of that nobility, which it had been the object of his whole reign to mortify and humiliate. An army was raised for the defence of the kingdom ; but the nobles, upon the first opportunity which occurred, gave a striking proof to what length they had carried their disaffection to their prince. The English army, after an inroad upon Scotland, being obliged from scarcity of provisions to retire again beyond the borders, an obvious advantage was offered to the Scots, who, by pursuing them, might have cut them off in their retreat. James gave his orders for that purpose, but the disaffected barons sternly and obstinately refused to advance one step beyond the limits of the kingdom. Stung to the heart with this affront, James, in a transport of rage and indignation, instantly disbanded his army and returned abruptly to his capital. From that moment his temper and disposition underwent a total change. One measure more was wanting on the part of the nobility to complete their base revenge, and to drive their sovereign to frenzy and despair. His ministers had again prevailed on some of the nobles

then bending his course by the islands of Orkney to the Western Islands, attended by an armament of twelve ships completely manned and furnished with heavy artillery,—he awed into submission the rebellious chieftains, and insisted on their delivering into his hands the principal offenders, whom he detained as hostages for the obedience and peaceable subjection of all their followers.

to assemble their followers, and to attempt an inroad on the western border; but the chief command was given to one of the king's favorites, who was to them particularly obnoxious. So great was their resentment, that a general mutiny instantly took place, and a resolution was formed unparalleled in history. The Scottish army, consisting of 10,000 men, surrendered themselves prisoners to a body of 500 of the English without attempting to strike a blow. On the news of this disgraceful event, the spirit of James totally sunk under the tumult of contending passions, and, overcome with melancholy and despair, he died of a broken heart in the thirty-third year of his age, a few days after his queen had been delivered of a daughter, the unfortunate Mary, queen of Scots, a princess, whose eventful life we shall briefly delineate, in treating of the reign of her contemporary, Queen Elizabeth.

I shall here, in the meantime, make some observations on the ancient constitution of the Scottish government. We have hitherto seen the kings of Scotland employed in a constant struggle towards reducing the exorbitant power of the nobles, who, looking back to those barbarous periods when the rude state of the country, with the want of laws and of policy, made them independent sovereigns in their distant provinces, were continually aiming at the same degree of power and authority which had been enjoyed by their ancestors. Their oppressive and tyrannical measures, and the dangers with which the crown was often threatened by those barons who possessed great wealth and a most formidable vassalage, were sufficient motives for those exertions on the part of the sovereign to reduce them to submission and obedience. The welfare of the country required it, the happiness of the people called aloud for the repression of their tyrannical authority, of which there can be no stronger proof than that, in those attempts of the Scottish kings to humble their nobility, the people almost always took the part of their sovereign. It is well observed by Dr. Robertson, that "if these attempts to humiliate their nobility were not attended with success, we ought not for that reason to conclude that they were not conducted with prudence. Accidental events concurred with political causes in rendering the best concerted measures abortive. The assassination of one king, the sudden death of another, and the fatal despair of a third, contributed no less than its own natural strength to preserve the aristocracy from ruin." But, in the meantime, the attempt was laudable, and the consequences were durably beneficial. A new system was formed of many excellent laws, and order and good policy began gradually to take place of anarchy, violence, and rapine.

In the framing of these laws, the king seems to have possessed almost the sole legislative power; the reason of which it is easy to explain. The Scottish parliament, when it first began to take a regular form, which was in the reign of James I., after the exemption of the lesser barons, or landholders, from personal attendance, consisted of three estates; the nobles, or great barons; the ecclesiastics, or dignified clergymen; and the representatives of the boroughs and shires. The churchmen were devoted to the sovereign, who had the nomination of all vacant bishoprics and abbeys, and they equalled in number the body of the nobles; and the influence of the crown was always sufficient to secure a majority among the representatives of the boroughs and counties. Besides, there was one singular part of the Scottish constitution, which furnished an additional source of the crown's influence in parliament. This was the committee termed the Lords of the Articles, whose business it was to prepare and digest all matters which were to be laid before the parliament, and who had the power of approving or rejecting all motions for new laws and ordinances; a very extraordinary court, which, in fact, possessed in itself the essential powers of legislation, of which the parliament was no more than the mouth or vehicle. These lords of the articles were chosen jointly by the three estates, but from the mode of their election were virtually at the king's nomination.* In some instances they seem to have been appointed by the monarchs solely. Certain it is, however, that they were generally obedient and obsequious to their will. Hence the king had the absolute command of parliament, and it is much to the credit of the Scottish monarchs, as proved by the excellence of their laws, that there are very few instances of their abusing this authority.

The kings of Scotland retained themselves a supreme jurisdiction in all causes, civil or criminal, within the kingdom. This jurisdiction they were formerly accustomed to exercise by their privy council; till the year 1425, when, in the reign of James I., a new court was erected, consisting of the chancellor and a certain number of judges chosen by the king out of the three estates of parliament; and to them was transferred the jurisdiction of the

---

* "The lords of the articles were constituted after this manner. The temporal lords chose eight bishops; the bishops elected eight temporal lords. These sixteen named eight commissioners of counties, and eight burgesses; and without the previous consent of those thirty-two persons, no motion could be made in parliament. As the bishops were entirely devoted to the court, it is evident that all the lords of the articles, by necessary consequence, depended on the king's nomination; and the prince, besides one negative, after the bills had passed through parliament, possessed indirectly another before their introduction."—Hume's History of England, vol. vi., p. 428. The lords of the articles appear first in the records of a parliament held at Perth by David II., 1370, under the description of a committee elected "by the consent of the three communities assembled," to treat and deliberate on "certain *special* and *secret* affairs of the king and kingdom before they came to the knowledge of the general council."—4to. Register, f. v. 40. By and by, the whole business of parliament was exclusively conducted by this committee, who being named in the first day of the session, the other members were immediately declared to be at liberty to depart to their respective homes, and often did not assemble till next year, in order to give their ratification to the laws which the committee had framed. See Pinkerton's History of Scotland, vol. i., for an instructive and curious account of the origin, progress, and constitution of the Scottish parliament.

privy council; the king retaining, as a prerogative, his right of judging in all causes which he should think proper to decide himself. This new tribunal was termed the Court of Session. It was new-modelled by James V., and its jurisdiction limited to civil causes; while the cognizance of crimes was committed exclusively to the justiciary, who had anciently a mixed civil and criminal jurisdiction. The court of session in Scotland was, till the middle of the seventeenth century, composed of an equal number of laymen and ecclesiastics: since that time it has consisted entirely of laymen, whose office is the cognizance of civil causes without any portion of that ancient ministerial jurisdiction which belonged to the Scottish privy council. The highest of the officers of the crown was the chancellor of Scotland. He had the direction of all grants from the crown; and all gifts of offices, all writs and precepts in judicial proceedings, received their sanction from him. In the reign of James III., we find the chancellor ranked immediately after the princes of the blood; and in the reign of Charles II., it was declared specially by law, that the chancellor, in virtue of his office, was perpetual president in the Scottish parliament, and in all the public judicatures in the kingdom.

Anciently, indeed, the highest officer of the crown had been the great *justiciar*, or justice-general, for he exercised an universal jurisdiction, both civil and criminal; and, in the absence of the sovereign, acted as viceroy of the kingdom. After the institution, however, of the court of session, and the appointment of a court of criminal judges, this officer seems to have yielded in importance and dignity to the chancellor. Other officers of state likewise, who possessed high powers, were the chamberlain, the seneschal, or high steward, the high constable, and the mareschal. The chamberlain, besides the care of the king's person, had the administration of the finances and the care of the public police. To the high steward belonged the government of the king's household and family. The constable possessed a supreme jurisdiction in all points of honor, and in all matters connected with war, and the mareschal was the king's lieutenant and master of the horse.

The revenues of the sovereigns of Scotland arose from the same sources as those of all other feudal princes. The crown possessed certain lands in demesne, which, in process of time, it may be supposed were continually increasing by forfeitures and escheats. The feudal casualties likewise brought in considerable sums to the royal exchequer. The profits of wardships, reliefs, and marriages of the king's vassals were very great. The king enjoyed the revenues of all vacant bishoprics; he imposed arbitrary fines for crimes and trespasses; and, finally, he was entitled to demand aids and presents from the subject upon various occasions—such as the marriage of a princess, or the knighting of a prince. In short, it is reasonable to imagine that the revenue of the kings of

Scotland was at all times sufficient for the support of the dignity of the crown, and adequate to the wants of the sovereign and the purposes of government.

The era, when the kingdom of Scotland seems to have become of considerable consequence in the political system of Europe, was the reign of James IV., when Francis I. of France found it necessary to engage the Scottish monarch in a war with England, to prevent Henry VIII. from carrying his arms into the continent.

The political principles which the Scots followed with respect to themselves and their neighbors were obvious and simple. Scotland, by its local situation, was connected with too powerful a neighbor, England, whose great and unremitting aim it was to acquire the sovereignty of this country, and to join her weaker sister to herself as an appanage. Scotland was always on her guard. The Scots, conscious of the perpetual aim of their potent neighbors, and spurning the thought of dependence, of course attached themselves to France, the natural enemy of England; an alliance equally courted by the French, as favorable to their own interest. In those days, that attachment was esteemed patriotic and favorable to liberty and independence, while, on the other hand, the Scots who were the partisans of England were justly deemed traitors to their country. From the period of which we now treat, we shall see it become a settled policy with the English monarchs to secure an interest in this country by keeping up a secret faction in the pay of England, whose object was to direct such public measures as were most expedient for that kingdom. To this source we shall find Scotland to have been indebted for the greatest part of her subsequent misfortunes.

CHAPTER XVI.

View of the Progress of Literature and Science in Europe.

For the sake of a connected view of the Scottish history during the reign of the five Jameses, we have anticipated somewhat in the order of time. We return now to the end of the fifteenth century, a period which may be considered as the epoch of the revival of literature in Europe from that long lethargy in which it had continued for above one thousand years. It is important to consider at some length this interesting subject, and to unite in one connected picture a view of the progressive advancement of European literature, and of its state at this remarkable era.

It is generally admitted that the Arabians were the first restorers of literature in Europe, after that extinction which it suffered from the irruption of the barbarous nations, and the fall of the Western empire. About the beginning of the eighth century, this enterprising people, in the course of their Asiatic conquests, found many manuscripts of the ancient Greek authors, which they carefully preserved; and in that dawn of mental improvement which now began to appear at Bagdad, the gratification which the Arabians received from the perusal of those manuscripts was such, that they requested their caliphs to procure from the Constantinopolitan emperors the works of the best Greek writers. These they translated into Arabic; but the authors who chiefly engaged their attention were those who treated of mathematical, metaphysical, and physical knowledge. The Arabians continued to extend their conquests, and to communicate their knowledge to some of the European nations, which at that time were involved in the greatest ignorance. The Arabians, after their conquests with Spain, founded there several universities; and Charlemagne, likewise, whose zealous encouragement of learning we have already remarked, ordered many of their books to be translated from Arabic into Latin, which being circulated over his extensive dominions, soon became familiar to the Western world. In imitation of the Saracens, too, that monarch founded several universities, among which were those of Bologna, Pavia, Osnaburg, and Paris.*

After the example of Charlemagne, the English Alfred, posterior to him about fifty years, introduced among the Anglo-Saxons a taste for literature, of which he himself, a most accomplished character, possessed a remarkable share. He encouraged learning, not only by his own example, but by founding seminaries and rewarding the labors of ingenious men. But these favorable appearances were blasted no less by the ignorance and barbarism of his successors, than by the continual disorders of the kingdom from the Danish incursions; and from the age of Alfred to the Norman conquest, there was in England a long night of the most illiberal ignorance. At the period of the conquest, the Normans brought from the continent, where learning had not suffered the same extinction, a very considerable degree of cultivation, which diffused itself over all the kingdom. The Latin versions of the Greek authors from the Arabic translations were imported into England; and the bishops settled by the conqueror, who were chiefly foreigners, possessed a much greater portion of erudition than their predecessors. The several convents and abbeys began

* The President Hènault questions that opinion which attributes the foundation of the University of Paris to Charlemagne. "It is not attested," says he, "by any contemporary writer. In all probability the first rise of the university was towards the end of the reign of Lewis the Young; but the name itself did not begin to be used till the reign of St. Lewis; so that Peter Lombard may be looked upon as its founder. Then it was that colleges were erected, different from the schools belonging to the chapters," &c.—Hénault, Abr. Chron.

to found libraries; and in all the great monasteries there was an apartment called the *Scriptorium*, where many monks were constantly employed in transcribing books for their library.

However absurd to the eye of reason and philosophy may appear the principle which led to monastic seclusion, the obligations which learning owes to those truly deserving characters who, in ages of barbarism, preserved alive, in their secluded cloisters, the embers of the literary spirit, ought never to be forgotten. The ancient Classics were multiplied by transcripts, to which undoubtedly we owe the preservation of such of the Greek and Roman authors as we now possess entire. Even the original labors of some of those monkish writers are possessed of considerable merit, and evince a zeal for the cultivation of letters which does them the highest honor.

In this period of the dawn of erudition, Britain produced several authors of very considerable eminence; of these, I shall enumerate a few of the most remarkable. Henry of Huntingdon wrote, in not inelegant Latin, Poems on philosophical subjects, several books of Epigrams, and Love Verses. Geoffrey of Monmouth, a most laborious inquirer after British antiquity, was bishop of St. Asaph in the year 1152. We have mentioned formerly his History of the Exploits of Arthur, King of the Britons, as being one of the first works which laid the foundation of romantic history in Europe. John of Salisbury was a most distinguished ornament of this age. His "Polycraticon" is (in the opinion of Mr. Watson) "a very pleasant miscellany, replete with erudition, and a judgment of men and things which properly belongs to a more sensible and reflecting period." William of Malmesbury stands in no mean rank as an historian. His merits have been displayed and much recommended by Lord Littleton, in his "History of Henry II." Giraldus Cambrensis deserves particular regard for the universality of his genius, which embraced a wide circle of history, antiquities, divinity, philosophy, and poetry.

But the most remarkable genius in this age for classical composition, was Josephus Iscanus, or Joseph of Exeter, who has written two Latin epic poems, which might have been read with pleasure even in a more cultivated age.* The one is on the subject of the Trojan war, of which the historical facts are taken from "Dares Phrygius;" the other is entitled "Antiocheis," the War of Antioch, or the Crusade, a subject for the choice of which Voltaire has given great credit to Tasso; although it is not improbable that he adopted the hint from this ancient poem, which in his age might have been entire, though there remains of it now only a small fragment. The poem on the Trojan war, however, is entirely preserved, and has been frequently printed along with "Dares Phrygius" and "Dictys Cretensis."

* Morhofii Polyhicter, i. 4, ii. 10.

But this dawning of literature was soon obscured, not only in Britain, but over all Europe. From the time of the conquest we may compute the era of a good taste in learning to have subsisted for little more than a century. The cultivation of polite literature and of classical composition was then neglected, to make room for the barbarous subtleties of scholastic divinity. The first teachers of this art were Lombard, archbishop of Paris, and Peter Abelard, so celebrated for his amours and misfortunes; men whose extensive erudition qualified them for better undertakings than to confound the common sense of mankind with frivolous and unintelligible speculations. From this period, school divinity was judged to be the only pursuit worthy of the attention of mankind; till the science of the law, from the discovery of the Pandects at Amalphi, introduced subtleties of another kind, which came in for their share of the prize of public estimation. The relish for elegant literature was now entirely lost, and—while the learned were busy disputing in their colleges and cloisters on law and theology—ignorance and barbarism were gradually drawing their gloomy curtain once more over the minds of the rest of mankind.

The only amusement of the common people at this time which deserves the name of literary, was in the old metrical and prose romances, and what had yet much less merit and more absurdity, wild and unintelligible books of prophecies in rhyme. The works of Geoffrey of Monmouth and the fabulous Turpin, with the abundant offspring derived from their stock, were in high estimation in the twelfth and thirteenth centuries.

In the middle of the thirteenth century, however, arose a genius of singular eminence, who, piercing at once through the thickest cloud of ignorance and barbarism, seemed formed to enlighten Europe. This was Roger Bacon, an English Franciscan friar, who in variety and extent of genius is entitled most deservedly to the highest rank in the annals of European literature. He was acquainted with all the ancient languages, and familiar with the works of their best authors. At that time, when every pretender to knowledge drew his creed of science from the works of Aristotle, and servilely adhered to his dogmas and opinions, the genius of Roger Bacon saw the insufficiency of that philosophy; and he began to apply himself with indefatigable industry to that method of investigation by experiment, and by the observation of nature, which was afterwards, at the distance of four centuries, so happily pursued and so strenuously recommended by an illustrious philosopher of the same name, Francis Bacon, Lord Verulam. In the "Opus Majus" of Roger Bacon, he declares that if it had been in his power, he would have burnt the whole works of Aristotle *quia eorum studium non est nisi temporis amissio, et causa erroris, et multiplicatio ignorantiæ.* Accordingly this great man, applying himself to the improvement of philosophy by observation and experiment, distinguished himself by some of the most important discoveries in astronomy, in optics, in chemistry, in medicine, and in mechanics. He observed an error in the calendar with regard to the duration of the solar year, which had been increasing from the time that it was regulated by Julius Cæsar. He proposed a plan for the correction of this error to pope Clement IV., and has treated of it at large in the fourth book of his "Opus Majus." Dr. Jebb, his editor and commentator, is of opinion that this was one of the noblest discoveries ever made by the human mind. In his optical works, he has very plainly described the construction and use of telescopic glasses; an invention which Galileo 400 years afterwards attributed to himself; and, indeed, that great philosopher probably might have made over again for himself the discovery of a secret which, from the days of Roger Bacon to his own, seems to have been wholly forgotten.* These instruments, he informs us, were made of round glasses, some of which had the property of burning at a great distance. One of these immense burning-glasses, he tells us, a friend of his had labored three years in constructing; but that now, by the favor of God, he would soon have it completed. Roger Bacon and his contemporary, Albertus Magnus, a German monk, were the first Europeans, who cultivated chemistry with any success. There is every reason to believe, from the works of Bacon, that the composition and effects of gunpowder were known to him. "In omnem distantiam," says he, "quam volumus, possumus artificialiter componere ignem comburentem, ex sale petræ et aliis." Yet with all this superiority of genius and wonderful extent of knowledge, Roger Bacon firmly believed in the possibility of the transmutation of metals into gold; in an elixir for the prolongation of life; and in the possibility of predicting future events from the aspect of the heavenly bodies; errors which kept their ground many ages after his day, and have had their advocates, in times comparatively modern, among men even of the most superior genius.

In the twelfth and thirteenth centuries, a very general taste for poetical composition began to arise in the south of Europe, from the songs and compositions of the troubadours or Provençal poets. Their name *trobadores*, or inventors, answers nearly enough to the original meaning of the Greek word *poet*, rendered in the old Scotch usage by *maker*. Hitherto the poetical compositions in the vernacular language had been solely metrical romances; and the Latin poets of the preceding ages, we have seen, chiefly confined themselves to epic poetry. The troubadours, or poets of

* The words of Bacon are not at all ambiguous. "Possunt sic figurari perspicua ut longissime posita appareant propinquissima; ita ut ex incredibili distantiâ legeremus literas minutissimas, et numeraremus res quantumcunque parvas. Sic etiam faceremus solem et lunam descendere secundum apparentiam hic inferius.'

Provençe, wrote in their vernacular language, which was a mixed dialect of the French, the Spanish, and Italian, various poems on occasional and familiar subjects. They were the first inventors of the sonnet, which afterwards became so much in fashion among the Italians. They composed likewise pastorals, ballads, and syrventes or pasquinades, in which they satirized both their ecclesiastical and civil governors. But the compositions in which they chiefly excelled, were extempore dialogues on the subject of love, which they treated in a very refined, platonic, and metaphysical strain. In this particular species of composition they had contests of skill, in which two bards strove for the superiority, before judges, who pronounced sentence likewise in verse. Jean de Notre Dame of Aix, in a discourse upon the poetry of Provençe, has enumerated seventy-six troubadours. Among these are the names of emperors, princes, and other illustrious persons—Frederick Barbarossa—Richard Cœur de Lion—Beranger, count of Provençe—and many others. Anselm Fayditt and Geoffrey Rudel are names of great eminence among these ancient bards. The former was one of the minstrels in the suite of Richard I. of England upon his expedition to the Holy Land; the latter was a mad poet, who fell in love with the countess of Tripoli, whom he had never seen, and who, being afterwards blest with a sight of her, dropped down dead for joy. These troubadours, about the end of the twelfth century, established at Aix in Provençe, a tribunal, called the Court of Love. It consisted of ladies and gentlemen of the highest rank, who determined with great solemnity all questions of love and refined gallantry. After their example, similar societies were formed in the neighboring provinces. At Thoulouse particularly, was instituted the gay society of the Seven Troubadours, who held their meetings in a garden, where they discoursed on love and poetry, and read their performances. From a desire of promoting the advancement of their favorite science, they publicly proposed a premium for the best composition, which was a violet of gold. Of the works of these troubadours, there remain many specimens; but few of them can give much pleasure, unless to those of so uncommon a taste as to relish love without passion, and poetry without nature.

The removal of the seat of the popedom from Rome to Avig non, which happened in the year 1309, first introduced the Italian poets to a familiar acquaintance with the compositions of the bards of Provençe. Then arose Dante, Petrarch, and Boccacio, in whose compositions, though of a much higher nature than the songs of the troubadours, a good critic will easily discern an imitation of them.

Dante Alighieri is supposed to have invented a new species of epic poetry by the introduction of angels and devils in place of the heathen deities; yet there is some reason to presume that the Antiochus of Ischanus, were it yet remaining, would deprive

Dante of the merit of originality in that particular. His Divina Comœdia, however, has far higher merits of its own. It shows genius of the very greatest order; and has never been surpassed in *terrible* pathos, or in the picturesque of descriptive power.

The compositions of Petrarch are of a very different nature. His sonnets and canzonets are exquisitely tender. He has celebrated his passion for the beautiful Laura, with the most amazing diversity of sentiment and expression. The sonnets written after the death of Laura, abound with many strokes of that simple pathetic, which is the true expression of heart-felt grief.

The poetical works of Petrarch make but a small part of his writings: as a biographer, a metaphysician, and chiefly as a moralist, he shone remarkably distinguished in the age in which he lived. From his talents, and the high esteem in which he lived with the most eminent characters of his time, he might have made an equal figure in the political as in the literary world. But his favorite taste was studious retirement, and to that and his passion for his beautiful mistress, he sacrificed every prospect of ambition. The life of Petrarch by the Abbé de Sade, though tedious on the whole, abounds with a variety of anecdotes strongly marking the spirit of the times, and particularly the state of Italy under those incessant commotions which arose from the strife between the papal and imperial powers.*

The poetical compositions of Boccacio are very few, and are obscured by the fame of his prose compositions: yet, if nothing more remained of him than a single sonnet which he has written upon the death of Petrarch, it would be sufficient to entitle him to the character of a most elegant and pathetic poet. Boccacio's great work is his Decamerone, a collection of one hundred novels; many of his own invention, and many undoubtedly borrowed, but all artfully written, and those few which are of a serious nature, eminently beautiful and affecting. The jocose tales are many of them loose and indelicate; and what conveys a very extraordinary idea of the manners of the age, they are all feigned to be told in the presence of a company of ladies, who are even made themselves the relaters of some stories grossly indecent.

These authors, Dante, Petrarch, and Boccacio, seemed to have fixed the standard of the Italian language, which, from that early time to the present, has scarcely undergone any variation.

Contemporary with these, familiar with their works, and even personally acquainted with them, was the English Chaucer. Chaucer lived in the reigns of Edward III. and Richard II. He was a man of the world, a courtier, and even a minister, for he had visited France and Italy in a public character. The Abbé

* [A life of Petrarch, more interesting to the general reader, has been given to the public by the author of this work. See an Historical and Critical Essay on the Life and Character of Petrarch, by Lord Woodhouselee.—Editor.]

de Sade, in the Life of Petrarch, relates that these two illustrious poets met together in Italy at the marriage of the duke of Milan's daughter. It is not then surprising that in the poems of Chaucer we should discover an intimate acquaintance with Italian and French literature, or that amidst all the rust of a barbarous language, the verses of Chaucer should have a degree of polish superior to any of the preceding English poets. The continuance of his "Canterbury Tales," is somewhat similar to that of the Decamerone of Boccacio; but the occasion on which we suppose them to have been delivered, is much more happily imagined than that figured by the Italian author.—Boccacio supposes that during the time of the plague at Florence, ten young persons of both sexes retired to a county-house at a little distance from the city, where they passed ten days; and that their chief amusement after dinner was for each to tell a tale. Chaucer, on the other hand, supposes various pilgrims setting out on a journey to the shrine of Thomas à Becket, at Canterbury, to have met at the Tabarde Inn in Southwark, and, as was the custom in those days, to have supped together at the same table; when, relishing each other's company, they agree to travel together next day, and to relieve the fatigue of the journey by telling each a story. Of these tales, many are of extraordinary merit: they evince great knowledge of mankind, and contain many strokes of inimitable humor, while they display a fine imagination, a considerable acquaintance with classical learning, and with the contemporary literature of the French and Italians.

The friend of Chaucer, or, as he terms him, his master, was Gower, a poet of less genius than elegance. His poems, which show a taste improved by an acquaintance with foreign languages and authors, are of a graver cast than those of Chaucer, and are less licentious. He is mentioned by Chaucer with high approbation, under the epithet of the moral Gower.

A few years posterior to these, and hardly inferior even to Chaucer, in the detail of his execution, was the accomplished James I., king of Scotland. This prince's poem of "Christ Kirk of the Green" abounds with genuine humor, fine imagination, and displays great knowledge of human nature.

In this period of the revival of a literary taste in the European kingdoms, Spain likewise began to emerge from ignorance and barbarism, and to produce authors whose works are read even at this day with pleasure. A college of troubadours had, in imitation of those of Provençe, been instituted in the fourteenth century at Barcelona, to which we may naturally attribute the first dawnings of a poetical, joined to a romantic spirit, which has since become, in a manner, characteristic of the nation. In those collections of old Spanish poetry, called *romanceros* and *canzioneros*, are preserved many poetical compositions of this age, which are extremely beautiful. W[illegible] succeeding age for books of chivalry and romance, every body is acquainted from the inimitable satire of Cervantes. And it may be here observed, that this author, who was a most judicious critic, has enumerated and admirably characterized all the best of the Spanish writers, whose works were known in his time, in that chapter where he describes the burning of Don Quixote's library, by the curate and the barber, who rescued from the flames only such books, both poets and prose-writers, as were possessed of real merit. The books of romance and knight-errantry compose the greatest part of that collection. The epic poems which Cervantes enumerates, as the "Araucana" of Ercilla, the "Austriada" of Jurado, and the "Monserrato" of Christoval Virues, were not composed till the beginning of the sixteenth century, when, as we shall see in treating of the literature of that period, Ercilla, Garcilasso de la Vega, Lope de Vega, Mendoza, and Quevedo, carried the several departments of epic, lyric, dramatic, and satirical composition to a height superior to what they had attained at that time in most of the European kingdoms.

But to return to the age of Dante, of Petrarch, and of Chaucer; although poetry at this time seems to have attained a high degree of splendor, it cannot be said that genius greatly displayed itself in any of the other sciences. History had not attained in this, nor in the succeeding age, to much perfection in any of the European nations. The marvellous is predominant in all the historical compositions of these times; yet, there are a few historians who are worthy of particular mention:—Matthew of Westminster, who composed a very tolerable chronicle of events, from the beginning of the world to the fourteenth century; Walsingham, a monk of St. Alban's, who wrote a pretty good history of the reign of Henry VI. of England, and of the civil wars between the houses of York and Lancaster; Everard, the German, who composed the annals of the dukes of Austria; Peter Duysburg, a Teutonic knight, who has left a history of his order, abounding in curious matter, though communicated in a very barbarous style. Among the French, Froissart is a writer not only admirable for liveliness of style, but of considerable authority with respect to the events of the fourteenth century, especially in what regards France, England, the Netherlands, and Scotland; as is likewise Monstrelet, whose chronicle is remarkable for a bold and impartial mode of thinking, and a critical spirit superior to the age in which he lived. Philip de Commines, a worthy follower of Froissart, has happily painted the reigns of Louis XI. and of Charles VIII. Villani and Platina, among the Italians, are historians of very considerable merit; and even Greece, at this time, has furnished historians worthy of notice. Pachimer, John Cantacuzenos, and Chalcondilas, are each of them eminent in the several periods which they commemorate.

The Italians, in the fifteenth century, seem to have enjoyed a high taste for classical learning. Poggio, the Florentine, the secretary of several of the popes, in his researches after the monuments of ancient erudition, discovered the works of Quinctilian, the history of Ammianus Marcellinus, and some of the compositions of Cicero. He wrote himself a history of Florence in the Latin tongue, remarkable both for excellence of matter and eloquence of expression. Laurentius Valla, Philelphus, Marcillus Ficinus, Nicolaus Perotus, Picus Mirandola, Palmerinus, and Angelus Politianus, are all worthy of notice, as uniting justness of historical reflection to a classical style and purity of expression.

But the taste for classical learning was at this time far from being universally diffused. In this respect the English and the French were very far behind the Italians. A curious proof of the scarcity of books in England in the fifteenth century, and of the great impediments to study, is found in the statutes of New College at Oxford. It was ordered by one of those statutes, that no man should occupy a book in the library above one hour, or two at most, that others might not be hindered from the use of the same. The famous library, founded in Oxford by that great patron of literature, Humphrey, duke of Gloucester, contained only 600 volumes. About the commencement of the fourteenth century there were only *four classics* in the royal library at Paris. These were, a copy of some of the writings of Cicero, Ovid, Lucan, and Boëthius. The rest were chiefly books of devotion, many treatises of astrology and medicine, translated from the Arabic into Latin and French; pandects, chronicles, and romances. This library was principally collected by Charles V. of France. When the English became masters of Paris in 1425, the duke of Bedford sent this whole library, which consisted only of 850 volumes, into England, where part of it was probably the groundwork of duke Humphrey's library at Oxford. Even so late as the year 1471, when Louis XI. borrowed the works of the Arabian physician Rhasis, from the faculty of medicine at Paris, he not only deposited, by way of pledge, a great quantity of valuable plate, but was obliged to procure a nobleman to join with him as surety in a deed, by which he bound himself to return it under a considerable forfeiture.

Thus low was the general state of literature during the greater part of the fifteenth century. But a brighter period was now at hand. The latter part of this century was the era of the entire dissolution of the bonds of barbarism. It was then that classical learning began to be universally diffused, and that a genuine taste was revived for polite literature, and for the productions of the fine arts. The dispersion of the Greeks, upon the total fall of the Eastern empire, and the refuge and welcome, which many of the learned and ingenious of that country found among the Italians, effected very soon a surprising change upon the face of all Europe.

The more pleasing philosophy of Plato began to supersede the scholastic subtleties of Aristotle, and the court of Rome became the seat of elegance and urbanity. Nicholas V., about the year 1440, established public rewards for compositions in the learned languages, appointed professors in the sciences, and employed intelligent persons to traverse all Europe, in search of the classic manuscripts buried in the monasteries. Of the succeeding age of Pope Julius II., and his successor Leo X., and of the splendor to which the fine arts then attained, I shall, in its proper place, take particular notice.

The circumstance which, of all others, most conduced to the advancement and universal dissemination of learning at this period, was the admirable invention of the *art of printing*. Printing seems to have been invented about the year 1440, at Strasburg, by John Guttenburg, but considerably improved by John Faust and Peter Schaeffer. This noble invention was, at its first appearance, deemed so extraordinary, that the servants of John Faust, who came to Paris to sell some of his early publications, were accused of magic, and the parliament ordered all their books to be committed to the flames. It must be owned, however, to the honor of Louis XI., that he condemned this decision of the Parisian judges, and ordered the value of the books to be paid to their proprietors. What inestimable advantages has mankind derived from this glorious art! The scanty gleanings that at this day remain to us of the wisdom of the ancients, serve only to make us regret what we feel we have undoubtedly lost of their knowledge beyond the possibility of recovery. But the art of printing gives us security for the perpetuation of the progress of the sciences in all future ages, and for their extensive circulation; a perfect assurance, that amidst all the vicissitudes in the fate of empires, no period of barbarism can ever arrive when any of the useful, or even of the polite arts, can again suffer a total extinction.

In this account of the revival of learning, and of its progress from its first appearance amid the darkness of the barbarous ages to the end of the fifteenth century, dramatic composition, which forms no inconsiderable part of polite literature, must not be forgotten.

The first dramatic representations known in Europe were devotional pieces, acted by the monks, in the churches of their convents, representative of the life and actions of our Savior and of his apostles. In England, these representations were termed *mysteries*, and sometimes *miracles* and *moralities*. They were brought into use about the twelfth century, and continued to be performed in England even to the sixteenth century. There is, in the reign of Henry VIII., a prohibition by the bishop of London, against the performance of any plays or interludes in churches or chapels. Perhaps, at this time, profane stories had begun to take place of the sacred mysteries: it is certain, at least, that these sacred mysteries themselves often contained great absurdities and very gross indecency.*

Profane dramas succeeded the sacred mysteries: they seem to have been known in France at an earlier period than in England; for about the year 1300 we find frequent mention of farçeurs, jongleurs, and "plaisantins, qui divertissaient les compagnies par leur comédies:" and what made a very extraordinary mixture, these farçeurs very often joined sacred and profane history in the same representation. In one of these dramatic pieces which commemorates the scripture story of Balaam, six Jews and six Gentiles are introduced, conversing on the nativity of our Saviour; and among the latter is the poet Virgil, who speaks several monkish verses *in rhyme.*

Dramatic representation in Italy, appears to have been of the same nature, in these periods, with what we have seen it in France and in England. In Spain, where learning and good taste have not since made proportional advances with the rest of Europe, dramatic representation, till the age of Charles V., was confined entirely to such rude and farcical debasements of the scripture histories as we have already mentioned; and even at this day such absurd performances are not entirely disused. But the patronage of Cardinal Ximenes drew forth a few sparks of genius from the general obscurity; although it was not till the end of the sixteenth century that Lope de Vega and Calderon produced those regular compositions for the stage which have stood their ground to the present day, and are confessedly the masterpieces of dramatical composition among the Spaniards.

* In one of them, which is entitled a "Play of the Old and New Testament," Adam and Eve are introduced upon the stage naked, and conversing in very strange terms about their nakedness. Mr. Warton has given a curious account of this play in his History of English Poetry. In some of the first scenes of this play, God is represented creating the world: He breathes life into Adam, leads him into Paradise, and opens his side while sleeping. Adam and Eve appear naked in the garden, and not ashamed, and the Old Serpent enters lamenting his fall. He converses with Eve: she eats of the forbidden fruit: they are cursed by God: the Serpent exit hissing: they are driven from Paradise by the Cherubim, with a flaming sword,—and Adam then appears digging the ground, and Eve spinning.

CHAPTER XVII.

View of the Progress of Commerce in Europe before the Portuguese Discoveries.

THE last chapter shortly delineates the progress of literature in Europe, from the first dawning of knowledge, which we owed to the Arabians, to the end of the fifteenth century, when from the discovery of the art of printing, learning and the sciences underwent at once a most astonishing improvement. The useful arts kept pace with the sciences; and this period, at which we are now arrived, was, in particular, remarkable for the singular advancement of navigation by the Portuguese, and those discoveries which produced the greatest effects upon the commerce of all the European nations. Previous, however, to giving an account of these discoveries, it is necessary to take a connected view of the progress of commerce in Europe, and its state during several of the preceding ages down to this period of its vigorous advancement at the end of the fifteenth century.

Nothing can show in a stronger light the small knowledge which the ancients possessed of the habitable globe, and the very limited communication which subsisted between different regions, than the opinion which universally prevailed of the earth's being uninhabitable, both in the *torrid* and in the *frigid* zones. This belief was not confined to the vulgar and illiterate: even the most learned and best informed of the ancients, and that too, in a very enlightened age, had no better notions of the actual state of the habitable globe. Cicero, in his "Somnium Scipionis," introduces Africanus thus speaking to Scipio the younger:—"You see this earth encompassed or bound in by certain *belts* or *girdles*, of which the two which are most distant and opposite are frozen with perpetual cold. The middle one, and the largest of all, is burnt up with the sun's heat. Two only are habitable; the people in the southern one are antipodes to us and with them we have no communication." Not to mention the poets, as Virgil and Ovid, Pliny the naturalist and Strabo the geographer, have both delivered the same opinion. We may guess from this, how small a portion of the habitable globe was really known to the ancients. From Monsieur D'Anville's very accurate maps of ancient geography, we see that the limits of the whole surface of the earth supposed to be known to the ancients, extend no further than from the tenth degree of north latitude to the seventieth; but, in fact, the greatest part lying even within these boundaries was perhaps only guessed at; nor can we say that the ancients were intimately acquainted with any other regions than what lay between the tropic of Cancer, and the fifty-fifth, or at most the sixtieth degree of north latitude. To the south, in Africa, the researches of the ancients, if we except the voyage of Hanno, did not extend far beyond the provinces which border upon the Mediterranean, and those on the western shore of the Red Sea, or *Sinus Arabicus*. To the north, they were almost totally unacquainted with those extensive countries—Denmark, Sweden, Prussia, Poland, and the immense empire of Russia. Britain was not known to be an island till it was circumnavigated in the reign of the emperor Domitian.

The Ultima Thule is generally believed to have been one of the Shetland Isles. It does not appear that the Phœnicians, Carthaginians, or Greeks, had ever been within the Baltic Sea. The Romans, indeed, penetrated into it, but never ascertained its limits, or knew that it was bounded by the land. Of the continent of Asia, till the time of Alexander the Great, the Greeks and Romans knew little more than what lies between the Persian Gulf and the western coast of the Caspian Sea. Those immense tracts which were termed Scythia and Sarmatia were hardly otherwise known than by name. Even when geography had attained to the highest perfection to which it ever arrived in the ancient world, which was in the second century after the Christian era, when Ptolemy published his description of the globe, the sixty-third degree of latitude bounded the earth to the north; the equinoctial limited it to the south; to the east, all beyond the Ganges, was but conjectural. One fact recorded by Strabo affords a very striking proof of the great ignorance of the ancients with respect to the situation even of those kingdoms with which they had intercourse. When Alexander the Great marched along the banks of the Hydaspes and Acesina, two rivers which fall into the Indus, he observed that there were many crocodiles in those rivers, and that the country produced beans of the same species with those which were common in Egypt. From these circumstances he concluded that he had discovered the source of the Nile, and prepared a fleet to sail down the Hydaspes into Egypt. In Europe, many even of those countries, which lie between the fiftieth and sixtieth parallels of north latitude, were very imperfectly known to the Romans. What are now called the Netherlands are generally supposed to have been then in a great measure uninhabitable, and the face of the country to have been covered with woods and morasses. In the island of Zealand, indeed, the Romans seem to have had some establishment; and particularly in the island of Walcheren; near to the city of Middleburg, there were discovered the remains of a Roman temple dedicated to the new moon, Nehalennia, the protectress of navigation. Britain was frequented by the Romans for the purposes of commerce. Tacitus, who lived in the reign of Nero, mentions the city of London, where he himself had lived for some time, as well frequented by ships and merchants. It is generally thought that the Britons had wrought the *tin*-mines of Cornwall and Devonshire long before the first Roman invasion, and that the Phœnicians, Carthaginians, and the Greeks traded thither for that useful commodity.* Yet in general the commerce and navigation of the ancients was chiefly confined to the limits of the Mediterranean and Euxine Seas. What trade they carried on beyond these limits was extremely inconsiderable. The Constantinopolitan empire, however, which preserved for some centuries the last remains of the Roman power and magnificence, carried on a commerce with the Asiatic nations, far more extensive than had ever been known to the Romans in the days of their universal dominion. The citizens of Constantinople did not confine their trade to the Archipelago, to the Euxine, or even to the Mediterranean. They imported at first the commodities of the East Indies from Alexandria; but afterwards, when Egypt became the conquest of the Arabians, the industry of the Greeks discovered a new channel, by which the productions of India might be conveyed to Constantinople. They were carried up the Indus, as far as that great river is navigable;—thence they were transported by land to the banks of the river Oxus, which then ran directly into the Caspian, although that communication has now for some centuries been cut off by the lake Aral, which is a new formation. From the Caspian Sea they entered the Wolga, and sailing up that river the goods were again carried across the land to the Tanais or Don, whence they descended directly into the Euxine or Black Sea, and thence proceeded without interruption to Constantinople; a singular proof of the ardor and ingenuity of those Greek mer-

* The Romans had a notion, for some time, that Britain abounded in gold and silver mines; and this report, Mr. Melmoth observes, it is probable, first suggested to Cæsar the design of conquering our island. It was soon discovered, however, that these sources of wealth were chimerical. Cicero, taking notice of this circumstance to Atticus, ridicules the poverty and ignorance of our British ancestors; and Dr. Middleton, remarking on that passage, makes the following striking and useful observations: "From their railleries of this kind, one cannot help reflecting on the surprising fate and revolutions of kingdoms; how Rome, once the mistress of the world, the seat of arts, empire, and glory, now lies sunk in sloth, ignorance, and poverty: enslaved to the most cruel, as well as the most contemptible of tyrants—superstition and religious imposture; while this remote country, anciently the jest and contempt of the polite Romans, is become the happy seat of liberty, plenty, and letters, flourishing in all the arts and refinements of civil life; yet running perhaps the same course, which Rome itself had run before it; from virtuous industry to wealth; from wealth to luxury; from luxury to an impatience of discipline, and corruption of morals; till, by a total degeneracy and loss of virtue, being grown ripe for destruction, it falls a prey at last to some hardy oppressor, and, with the loss of liberty losing every thing else that is valuable, sinks again into its original barbarism."—Ad. Att. iv. Middleton's Life of Cicero, ii. 102.

chants, as well as of the powerful influence of the spirit of luxury in the taste for foreign productions.

After the fall of the Roman empire in the west, the disorders of Italy during its successive subjection to the Goths, the Heruli, and the Lombards, and the turbulent state of all the European kingdoms in those ages, allowed little room for commercial intercourse. It was, however, owing to the ravages of some of those barbarous tribes, that a small state arose, which revived the commerce of Europe, and set an example of industry to the neighboring Italian cities, which very speedily raised them to a high degree of wealth and splendor. At the northern extremity of the Adriatic Sea are a number of small islands lying very close together, which originally were frequented only by fishermen. When Attila, king of the Huns, was ravaging Italy, the inhabitants of the district of Venetia took refuge in these islands, and forming themselves into a community, laid the foundation of the illustrious city and state of Venice.* They began soon to equip small fleets, which they sent to all parts of the Mediterranean, and particularly to the coast of Syria and Egypt, whence they brought home spices and other merchandises of the produce of Arabia and India.

The city of Genoa on the opposite coast of Italy, ambitious of sharing with Venice in this lucrative trade, soon became a formidable rival. Florence and Pisa followed the same example, and the northern Italian states were acquiring a great deal of wealth, while Rome and her pontiffs were engaged in those contentions with the emperors which disturbed the peace of a great part of Europe. These commercial states, however, incited by rivalship in trade, were often at war with each other. Venice and Genoa, during almost the space of three centuries, had frequent hostile conflicts. The Venetians, however, came at length to outstrip all their rivals, and advancing as a military as well as a mercantile power, they acquired very considerable territories on the opposite coasts of Illyrium and Dalmatia.

The crusades, as we have formerly remarked, contributed not a little to increase the wealth of the maritime cities of Italy. The merchants employed their ships in transporting stores and provisions for those immense multitudes which flocked to the Holy Land, and they brought back from the coasts of Syria and of Egypt all the commodities of the East. Some of the most enterprising of these Italian merchants bethought themselves of

---

* Venice is an artificial conjunction of upwards of seventy small islands, divided from each other by shallows, or as they are styled *lagunas;* some so close as to be united by bridges, others at such a distance, that there is no communication but by boats. This city is five miles distant from the main land of Italy, and about the same distance from the Lido, a causeway extending almost forty miles, which defends them from the sea, through which there are several openings that admit boats, and one upon the grand canal, well fortified, at Malamoco which may thence be termed the Port of Venice.

establishing manufactures in their own country, in imitation of those of Constantinople. Silk stuffs (which about the time of the emperor Diocletian were so rare in the Roman empire that they were sold for their weight in gold) were at the time of the crusades in pretty general use. Roger, king of Sicily, about the year 1130, carried off from Athens a number of artificers in the silk trade, and established a considerable manufacture in his capital of Palermo, from whence it soon spread over all Italy. The sugar-cane, which is likewise a production of Asia, was about the middle of the twelfth century introduced into Sicily, from whence it was transplanted into the southern provinces of Spain. From Spain it was carried to Madeira and the Canary Islands, and at length made its way to the American Islands, where it is now chiefly cultivated. But in the middle ages it furnished one chief article of the commerce of the Italian states.

During the twelfth and thirteenth centuries, foreign commerce was almost confined to the Italians. It is generally allowed that Venice was the first of the European states that found out the conveniency and great advantage of a national bank for the purposes of trade. The institution of the Bank of Venice is so early as the year 1157; and the other Italian states of Genoa, Florence, and Pisa, soon followed its example. It is said that its original fund was two millions of ducats. The government of Venice, in one of her wars with the Turks, was put to the necessity of making use of the bank's money to defray the necessary charges; and on that occasion the revenues of the state were pledged for the repayment of the loan. After that period, the government very frequently made use of the bank's capital upon any public emergency. This most ancient bank was ever conducted with such fairness and equity, that the *agio*, or premium upon the shares of its proprietors, would have risen to a prodigious height, had it not been enacted by an ordinance of the state that it should never exceed 20 per cent.

While commerce was thus vigorously promoted by the Italian states, it was scarcely known in any of the other nations of Europe. In the principal kingdoms of France, Spain, and Germany, there were fairs or great markets held at stated times, to which traders, or *mercatores*, resorted from different quarters, and thus made a sort of interchange of their several products or manufactures. These mercatores were little better than hawkers or pedlers. In all the different countries of Europe, (as is the case at this day in several of the Tartar governments of Asia,) taxes were wont to be levied upon the persons and goods of travellers when they passed through certain manors, crossed certain bridges, or erected booths in a fair to sell their goods. These different taxes were known in England by the names of *passage*, *pontage*, *lastage*, and *stallage*. Sometimes an enterprising trader purchased from the king, or one of the great barons, an immunity from paying these taxes within a certain territory, by giving either a sum at once, or an annual tribute; and these persons, who were merchants of some note, were distinguished by the title of *free-traders.*

But the adventurous spirit of the Italian merchants soon enticed them to disperse themselves through every kingdom of Europe; and maintaining a correspondence with their own country, they became the factors of all the European nations. In the middle ages, these Italian merchants passed by the general denomination of Lombards. They were allowed to settle in France, in Spain, in Germany, and England, and even enjoyed many privileges above the natives themselves. These Lombards not only acted as merchants for the importation and exchange of commodities, but as bankers or money-dealers; though in this last branch of business they found a heavy restraint in the ideas of the times. The canon law, proceeding upon a strict interpretation of those passages of Scripture which condemn the taking of usury, was adverse to the custom of demanding even the most moderate interest for the use of money; and hence the banking trade of these Lombard merchants, who very naturally thought themselves entitled to a premium for the loan of their money, fell under the censure of the church, and began to be deemed unlawful. They were obliged, therefore, to carry on their business as bankers to great disadvantage. Their bargains were necessarily kept private, and consequently their exactions, being arbitrary, were often most exorbitant and fraudulent.

The share taken by the Jews in the same business of banking was one strong cause why it continued so long to be in disesteem. To trade in money was considered as little else than to cheat, and accordingly we find that many of the princes of Europe looked upon the fortunes amassed by the Jews as a sort of lawful plunder, and made no scruple to despoil them of their property whenever a public emergency required a speedy supply of money. Thus, in England, king John imprisoned the Jews, in order to force a discovery of their wealth; and many of these unfortunate wretches, who would not reveal their treasures, were punished with the loss of their eyes. But these grievances, which would seem apparently calculated to repress the spirit of commerce, contributed in this instance very materially to its advancement. To guard against these tyrannical depredations made on their property, the Jews invented bills of exchange; and commerce became by this means capable of eluding violence and of maintaining every where its ground: for merchants could now convert their effects into paper, and thus easily transport them wherever they thought proper.

The establishment of the Italian or Lombard merchants in the different kingdoms of Europe could not fail to excite somewhat of a spirit of industry, not only in the advancement of commerce, but of domestic manufactures. These manufactures were promoted by the sovereigns by every encouragement which they could bestow. Among the rest, corporations or monopolies of different trades began now to be established, in the view of encouraging manufactures; a policy perhaps necessary in a state of society where industry is very low, and requires every incentive to its promotion, but extremely hurtful where the industrious spirit is generally diffused. The first institution of those corporations or merchant guilds in the European kingdoms seems to have been in the eleventh century. Most authors are of opinion that they were unknown in England till the Norman invasion, and that even in France at that time they were very rare. It is not improbable that both the French and the Normans borrowed these institutions from the free cities of Italy, where, as commerce may be said to have had its origin in modern times, these communities were probably first in use. In process of time, as trading towns increased in number of inhabitants, the retailers and artisans in these towns obtained charters for incorporating their respective callings; that is, for engrossing to themselves, and monopolizing all the manufactures and even trade of the towns, to the exclusion of non-freemen; a grievance which was in later times severely felt and justly complained of.

About the end of the twelfth century the commercial spirit had begun to make some progress towards the north of Europe. The cities upon the Baltic began to equip merchant ships, which traded to the ports of France and of Britain. A small island, named the Isle of Oleron, near the mouth of the river Garonne, was a rendezvous for the Mediterranean ships belonging to the Lombards, and from them the Baltic merchants furnished themselves with all the commodities of the East. The Isle of Oleron was then the property of the English, who used it as a sort of *entrepôt* in their commerce with France, Spain, and the Mediterranean. The laws of Oleron have at this day great force in all the nations of Europe, and are a standard of procedure in all Admiralty courts in maritime and mercantile questions. The merchants of Oleron, for the regulation of their extensive commerce, framed a code of laws in the time of Richard Cœur de Lion; and these were held so equitable that most of the powers of Europe gave them obedience. In the same manner the laws of Wisbury, a considerable commercial town, situated in the island of Gothland, in the Baltic, were a rule of observance for all the mercantile states in the north of Europe.

These northern states continued to prosecute trade with great vigor; and, animated by the example of the Italian cities, Venice, Genoa, Pisa, and Florence, they began to form extensive schemes of commerce, and unite with each other in equipping considerable mercantile fleets. The Baltic Sea was then infested by pirates, who ravaged the coasts. The city of Lubec, on the Baltic, and Hamburg, at the mouth of the Elbe, ambitious of opening a trade with the neighboring towns, and those on the opposite coasts of Norway and Sweden, were obliged to enter into a league of mutual defence for the protection of their ships against these pirates. So great were found to be the advantages of this confederacy, that in a short time it was acceded to by all the towns upon the coast, from the eastern extremity of the Baltic to the mouth of the Rhine. This association was termed the League of the Hanse Towns; and it became soon so formidable in the eyes of the princes and states of Europe, that many of them courted its alliance. It was one of the regulations of the Hanseatic League to admit no city into their confederacy which was not either free and independent, and exercised civil jurisdiction within itself, or, being dependent on any sovereign or prince, should procure from him an oath to preserve their privileges entire: a fine example how much, even in those days, the enjoyment of civil liberty was considered as essential to the prosperity of commerce.

The regulations made in the general council of the Hanseatic Towns, contributed greatly to the advancement of commercial industry over all the north of Europe. As in the trade of the Hanseatic merchants with the southern kingdoms of Europe, it was found necessary to have an intermediate station on the coast, or *entrepôt*, where the merchants of the different kingdoms might have a general resort, the city of Bruges, on the coast of Flanders, was pitched on for that purpose, and there the northern merchants met with those of Lombardy and the South. The commodities of India, and of the East, were exchanged with the produce and manufactures of the north; and every variety of useful merchandise was, by means of the Baltic and the great continental rivers, easily conveyed through most of the kingdoms of Europe.

After the establishment of the great mart of Bruges, the Flemings began to apply their whole industry to the establishment of manufactures, and Baldwin, the young count of Flanders, encouraged this spirit by bestowing privileges and immunities on the merchants and manufacturers. His successors, however, possessed a very different spirit; they recalled these immunities; and the consequence was, that the manufacturers left Flanders and settled in Brabant, where the dukes of that province showed them for some time all manner of favor. This, however, did not long continue. The revocation of their immunities, by some impolitic sovereigns of that province, banished trade and manufactures from Brabant, as it had done from Flanders; and England now began to give them encouragement. But let us look back a little, and shortly mark the progress of the commercial spirit in this island.

We have remarked that the Romans carried on a trade to the coast of Britain. Tacitus mentions *Londinium, copia negotia-*

torum et commeatu maximè celeberrimum. In the year 614, the venerable Bede mentions London as greatly frequented by foreigners, who repaired thither for the purposes of trade. In the time of Canute, the Dane, the Londoners built a wooden bridge across the Thames, a work of prodigious labor, and no small expense. William of Malmesbury, who wrote in the reign of William the Conqueror, mentions London in or about the year 1041, as a noble, populous, and opulent city. In this reign, the Cinque Ports of England, often mentioned in history, obtained their privileges. Camden in his Britannia informs us, that William the Conqueror, regarding the county of Kent as the key of England, appointed the governor of the castle of Dover to be warden of five principal ports on that coast. These were Dover, Hastings, Hythe, Romney, and Sandwich. To these some other ports were afterwards added, and they are now eight in number. They were obliged each to furnish five ships of war, which were to be at all times at the king's command, and in consideration of this service, they enjoyed several valuable privileges and immunities. They were free from the payment of all subsidies. Their inhabitants could not be sued in any courts but those of their own towns. The warden of these ports exercised, within his jurisdiction, the authority of High Admiral. All the eight towns had their members of parliament, and they enjoyed very considerable immunities.

About what time the woollen manufacture began to be cultivated in England, there is no absolute certainty. But we know that so early as the middle of the twelfth century, it was an object of considerable attention. Howell mentions a charter granted in the middle of the twelfth century by Henry II. of England to the weavers of London, incorporating them into a society, and conferring on them various privileges and immunities. It would appear that there was at this time a considerable spirit of manufacture and trade, both in England and in Scotland. Stowe, in his Chronicles, quotes a charter of the same Henry II., in which, for the encouragement of the woollen manufacture, he enacts, that if any cloth shall be made of Spanish or foreign wool, the mayor of London shall see it burnt.

Anderson, in his Chronological History of Commerce, has remarked, that there must at this time have been some considerable trade or source of wealth in Scotland, since we find that country was able to raise so large a sum as 100,000 marks (equal to £300,000 sterling at present) for redeeming William, surnamed the Lion, who, having a dispute with Henry II. of England, concerning the property of a part of Northumberland, was taken prisoner by a stratagem. The one half of this sum was paid down immediately in coin, the other half was to be paid upon time; and the counties of Northumberland, Cumberland, and Huntingdon, which then belonged to the kings of Scotland, were given in pledge for it. The disproportion of wealth between the two kingdoms must not have been so great at that time as in after periods, since we find how difficult it was for England, a few years after the time of which we now speak, to raise but twice as much for the ransom of Richard I., and towards this ransom, William, king of Scotland, generously contributed a considerable sum. Campbell, in his Political Survey, tells us that part of the ransom of Richard I. was raised by a loan of wool; from whence he rightly infers, that before that time it must have been a staple commodity in England, and the statute we have mentioned of Henry II. shows this to have been the fact.

Even in those early periods the woollen manufacture was an object of considerable importance to government. The kings of England drew a very large revenue from the custom upon wool exported, a great part of which was carried to be manufactured in the low countries. By and by, however, the English monarchs became sensible of the superior benefits of encouraging a home manufacture. Some of the foreign merchants and manufacturers were invited to reside in England. Henry III., in the year 1266, granted to the merchants of the Steelyard (who were a set of Hanseatic traders residing in London) several special immunities, particularly that of importing and exporting all merchandise whatever for the payment of only one per cent. Edward III., a prince of great spirit and abilities, amidst all the splendor of his military enterprises, bestowed particular attention on every thing that could contribute to the promotion of the substantial interest of his people. He endeavored to entice the Flemish artisans to settle in his dominions; he enacted a variety of excellent laws for the encouragement of trade, and strenuously promoted the woollen manufacture, which has since become the chief source of wealth of the nation.

From the death of this monarch, the commercial spirit of the English was for many years on the decline. His successor, Richard II., a weak and impolitic prince, was prevailed on by some of the London merchants to revoke those privileges granted by Edward III. to the foreign merchants; and the consequence was, that even the merchants of Britain soon began to perceive the pernicious effects of this revocation to their own trade, and thought it their wisest policy again to petition the king for a restoration of the privileges of foreigners. In the succeeding reigns, the nation being engaged in a war of many years with France, and afterwards embroiled at home by the disorders arising from the hostile contentions of the houses of York and Lancaster, it was a necessary consequence that the spirit of trade must have languished and decayed; nor was it till these latter disorders were appeased by the accession of Henry VII. to the throne, that commerce again began to occupy the national industry, and engage the attention of the legislature, or rather of the sovereign.

We must, however, observe, that in this intermediate space of time, when the commerce of England seems to have been at a stand, or rather to retrograde, the spirit of trade was vigorously promoted among the Scots by that excellent, wise, and politic prince, James I., as fully appears by the acts of the Scottish parliament passed in his reign. James prevented, by statute, the exportation of gold and silver from his kingdom. He obliged foreign merchants to lay out the money they had received for the merchandise they had imported, in the purchase of the commodities of the country. We find, likewise, in his acts of parliament, mention made of the custom on the exportation of herrings, which, even in those early ages, formed a very capital article of trade, and of a duty on the exportation of woollen cloth, which manufacture it would appear the Scots had at this time borrowed from their neighbors of England. It was in the reign of James I. that the city of Glasgow began to show the first indication of that commercial spirit for which she has since been so remarkably distinguished. Glasgow, at this time, was a small village, consisting of little else than the houses of the clergy belonging to the metropolitan church. A merchant, of the name of Elphinston, engaging in the fisheries upon the coast, and accumulating considerable wealth, inspired his fellow citizens with a similar ambition. But the progress of the trade of Glasgow was not rapid. Her situation upon the western coast of the island was extremely disadvantageous, in times when all the trade, as we have seen, lay with the Hanseatic merchants, and the Italians resorting to Oleron, or Bruges. In fact, it was not till after the trade with America and the West Indies was open to Europe, that Glasgow became at all considerable as a commercial town. It was then that she found her situation equally commodious for the western trade, as it had formerly been disadvantageous for the eastern.

Henry VII. of England, attentive to every thing that could conduce to the welfare and prosperity of his kingdom, revived that spirit of commerce, which had languished from the time of Edward III.; he enacted many excellent laws, and particularly those navigation acts, which prohibited the importation of French wines into the kingdom, unless in British or Irish ships. He likewise encouraged the woollen manufacture, by inducing many Flemish workmen to settle in the kingdom, and giving them establishments in Yorkshire, which was the first rise of those great manufacturing towns of Leeds, Wakefield, and Halifax. He concluded likewise commercial treaties with the principal European powers, for the protection of the merchant-shipping; and through the whole of his reign made the advancement of trade a principal concern of his parliaments.

Such was the state of the commerce of the European nations at the time when the Portuguese made those valuable discoveries in navigation, which gave to Europe the trade of the East Indies.

CHAPTER XVIII.

Discoveries of the PORTUGUESE in the Fifteenth Century, and their Effect on the Commerce of Europe.—Madeira discovered—Pope's Bull, granting to the Portuguese the Countries explored by them—They double the Cape of Good Hope—De Gama reaches India—Goa taken—Their Objects opposed by the Venetians—Portuguese sail to China—Establish Macao—Effects on European Commerce—Rise of Antwerp and Amsterdam—Progress of Commerce and Manufactures in England.

As many of the most useful inventions in the arts have been the result of accident, it is not surprising that some even of the most remarkable of these should have been for ages known to mankind before they were called forth, or applied to any purposes of utility. The property of the *magnetic needle*, in turning constantly to the northern pole, was known in Europe as early as the thirteenth century; but it was not till above a century after that any one attempted to apply it to the purposes of navigation. That most ancient nation, the Chinese, are, indeed, said to have known the property of the magnet for a thousand years before us; yet it is believed that till *our* seventeenth century, when European example had reached them, they had never thought of using it in sailing. The English, in the reign of Edward III., are said to have first employed the compass in their ships, but the world owed to the Portuguese the first great experiments of the value of this invention in the advancement of navigation. Till the middle of the fifteenth century, none of the nations of Europe had ventured to sail out of the sight of their coasts. Their vessels were flat-bottomed, and extremely shallow; and, as they followed in their navigation every turning of the coast, which exposed them continually to shifting and contrary winds, it was not unusual that a voyage, which would now be performed in a few months, lasted at that time four or five years. We have already remarked the very limited knowledge which the Greeks and Romans possessed of the habitable globe. The Eastern Ocean was known only by name, and the Atlantic scarcely attempted out of the sight of the coast of Europe. It was supposed that all to the west was an immense extent of ocean. The famous island of Atlantis, which Plato supposed to be situated in this sea, was a chimera of his own, and was generally treated as such. The torrid zone, as we have formerly remarked, was generally believed by the ancients to be uninhabitable from its heat; and this persuasion had pre vented them, in their coasting voyages, from going beyond the northern tropic. The *Periplus* of Hanno is, indeed, an exception; but it is probable that he did not very well know the extent of his own voyage, which is supposed to have reached within five degrees of the line. If the ancients were acquainted with the coast of Africa thus far, it is at least certain, that the moderns, down to the period of the fifteenth century, never attempted to sail beyond the twenty-ninth degree of north latitude; and a promontory, on the African coast, lying in that parallel, was termed Cape Non, as being supposed the utmost limits of the habitable globe to the South.

In the beginning of the fifteenth century, John I., king of Portugal, having sent a considerable armament of ships to attack the Moors settled on the coast of Barbary, a few vessels were despatched, at the same time, with instructions to sail along the western shore of Africa, and to bring an account of the state of the countries beyond Barbary, which, it was supposed, might be incited to coöperate in the design of conquering the Moors.* The vessels sent on this enterprise doubled Cape Non, and proceeded at once one hundred and sixty miles beyond it to another promontory, named Cape Boyador, within two degrees of the tropic of Cancer. But here the mariners, being affrighted by the rugged appearance of the coast, and a very tempestuous sea, returned to Portugal, and got great credit for the boldness of the attempt. Prince Henry, the son of John, king of Portugal, was a young man of great talents, possessed of that ardor which is fitted to patronise and promote every beneficial design, and that enthusiasm which the dangers and difficulties of an enterprise rather inflame than relax. Struck with the success of this first attempt of his countrymen, he endeavored to engage in his service all who were eminent for their skill in navigation, both Portuguese and foreigners. His first effort, however, was with a single ship, which was despatched with instructions to attempt, if possible, the doubling of Cape Boyador.† The mariners, as usual, were afraid to quit

* The Portuguese writers acknowledge that the island of Madeira was discovered by one Masham, an Englishman, who carried thither a lady he had stolen; and, after her death, endeavoring to escape, was taken by the inhabitants of Africa; who, on account of his being overgrown with hair, by living long in a desolate place, sent him as a present to Don Pedro, then king of Castile; and to this Masham's reports they ascribe all their own and the Spaniards' subsequent discoveries.—Campbell's Political Survey, vol. i., p. 52.—Asia de Joan de Barros, decad. 1., lib. 1., cap. iii.—Hakluyt's Translation of D. Ant. Galvano's Discoveries, 4to., p. 2. —Purchase's Pilgrimage, vol. ii., pp. 1671, 1672.

† In this manly and spirited undertaking, it appears that prince Henry had to encounter the inveterate prejudices of his countrymen. "The systematic philosophers," says a well-informed writer, "were alarmed lest their favorite theories should be perverted by the acquisition of real knowledge; the military beheld with impatience the increase of fame that was obtained by a profession they had always considered as inferior to their own; the nobility dreaded opening a source of wealth, which might equalize the ascendency of rank; and the indolent and splenetic argued, that it was presumption to search for a passage to the southern extremity of Africa, which the wisest geographers had pronounced

the coasts, and consequently, encountered numberless difficulties. A squall of wind, however, driving them out to sea, landed them on a small island to the north of Madeira, which they named Porto Santo: thence they returned to Portugal to give an account of their discovery. Three ships were fitted out by prince Henry the subsequent year, which, passing Porto Santo, discovered the island which they denominated Madeira, from its being *covered with wood.* Here they fixed a small colony, and planted slips of the Cyprus vine, and of the sugar-cane from Sicily, for both which productions the island was remarkably favorable. I have formerly observed that it was from this island that the sugar-cane was transplanted to the West Indies, of which it is not a native.

The Portuguese, once accustomed to launch into the open sea, no longer kept to their former timid mode of navigation. In their first voyage after the discovery of Madeira, they passed Cape Boyador, and in the space of a few years, advancing above four hundred leagues to the south, they had discovered the river Senegal, and all the coast between Cape Blanco and Cape Verd; they were now near ten degrees within the torrid zone, and were surprised to find the climate still temperate and agreeable—yet, on passing the river Senegal, and observing the human species to assume a different form, the skin as black as ebony, the woolly hair, and that peculiarity of feature which distinguishes the Negroes, they naturally attributed this to the influence of heat, and began to dread the consequences of a nearer approach to the line. They returned to Portugal with the account of their discoveries, and the common voice of their countrymen dissuaded them from making any further attempts. But the enthusiasm of prince Henry was redoubled by the success of these experiments; and he resolved to employ the operation of a new and very powerful motive to the prosecution of his schemes of discovery. He applied to the pope, Eugene IV., and representing that the chief object of his pious wishes was to spread the knowledge of the Christian religion among those barbarous and idolatrous nations which occupied the greatest part of the continent of Africa, he procured a *bull*, conferring on the Portuguese an exclusive right to all the countries which they had discovered, or might discover, between Cape Non and the continent of India. Ridiculous as such a donation appears to us, it was never doubted at that time that the pope had a right to confer it, and, what is very singular, all the European powers, for a considerable space of time, paid the most implicit deference to the grant, and acknowledged the exclusive title of the Portuguese to almost the whole continent of Africa.

The death of prince Henry imposed a temporary check on

---

to be impracticable. *It was even hinted, as a probable consequence, that the mariners, after passing a certain latitude, would be changed into blacks, and thu retain for ever a disgraceful mark of their temerity.*"—Clarke's Progress of Maritime Discovery.

this spirit of enterprise, which revived, however, about twenty years afterwards, under the reign of John II. of Portugal. The Cape Verd Islands were colonized and planted; and the Portuguese fleets, advancing to the coast of Guinea, returned with a cargo of gold dust, ivory, gums, and other valuable commodities.

This enterprising people, perceiving now that they were to reap a substantial reward for the dangers and difficulties they had encountered, pushed onwards with great vigor to the south. They perceived presently that this immense continent began greatly to contract itself and to bend towards the east, which encouraged a hope that in place of extending (as the ancients supposed) to the south pole, its boundary by the sea was at no great distance. They passed the equator, and, for the first time, saw a new hemisphere, and perceived those stars which mark the southern pole of the earth. The magnet, which had hitherto pointed constantly to the north, it was now expected would have changed its direction and pointed to the south pole; but it still kept invariably to the north. The Portuguese, nevertheless, sailed on with intrepidity, and at length came in sight of the great promontory which forms the extremity of the continent. This cape, of which the projecting rocks seem to pierce into the clouds, was then clad in all its horrors. It was the season of winter, and the ocean was prodigiously tempestuous. The ships of the Portuguese were shattered with a long voyage, and it was deemed utterly impossible in that condition to double the Cabo Tormentoso, or the Cape of Storms. They returned, however, after a voyage of sixteen months, firmly persuaded that they had ascertained the limits of Africa, and that by doubling that cape, which they might expect to perform in a more moderate season, they should find a new and easy passage to India, and thus engross to themselves a commerce which could not fail to be an inexhaustible source of wealth and power.

The promontory was now termed the Cape of Good Hope; and a strong armament was prepared for this new adventure, which presented such flattering prospects to the ambition of the Portuguese. It was in this very interval of time that Columbus, the Genoese, instigated by a similar spirit of adventurous ambition, discovered the islands of Cuba and Hispaniola, and, soon after, the great continent of America; but of this important discovery we shall afterwards particularly treat.

In the year 1479, the Portuguese fleet under Vasco de Gama doubled the Cape of Good Hope. Hitherto every thing bore an appearance of novelty,—a new race of men, black and barbarous, languages totally unknown, and no traces of resemblance to the European manners. Sailing onwards they were delighted to perceive at once the Arabian tongue, and to find a race of men who professed the religion of Mahomet. They now found that they had almost circumnavigated the continent of Africa, and that this immense peninsula was connected with Asia by the narrow Isthmus of Suez. At length, by the aid of Mahometan pilots, passing the mouths of the Arabian and Persian Gulfs, and stretching along the western coast of India, De Gama arrived at Calicut, on the coast of Malabar, after a voyage of 1500 leagues, performed in thirteen months.

Calicut was at that time a city of great wealth and splendor, the residence of one of those *rajahs*,* or petty sovereigns, who then occupied the greatest part of Indostan, and were chiefly tributaries to the Mogul emperors. De Gama formed an alliance with the rajah of Calicut, and returned to Lisbon with some specimens of the wealth and produce of the country. A fleet of thirteen ships was now fitted out with all despatch, and these, performing the voyage with equal good fortune, began to make settlements upon the coast. They found opposition from some of the petty princes, which obliged them to have recourse to arms; and a war once begun was not finished till the Portuguese had achieved the conquest of all the coast of Malabar

The court of Lisbon now appointed as viceroy or governor of the country, Alphonso de Albuquerque, a man of great spirit and resolution. The city of Goa, which belonged to the rajah of the Deccan, was taken by storm, and became now the residence of the Portuguese viceroy, and the capital of all their settlements in India.

While such was the state of affairs in the East, the Venetians, who had hitherto engrossed the whole trade from India, by means of the Red Sea and the port of Alexandria, soon perceived that this most lucrative commerce was on the point of annihilation, and that every advantage of the Indian trade must now be transferred to the Portuguese. Various expedients were thought of to obviate these impending misfortunes. It was the interest of the sultan of Egypt to concur with the Venetians in support of a trade from which he as well as they had derived great benefits. A plan was meditated for some time of cutting through the Isthmus of Suez, and thus joining the Mediterranean and the Red Sea; but the Egyptians were apprehensive that their low and flat country might be drowned altogether in this attempt, and therefore the project was abandoned. It was now proposed that an immense fleet should be equipped on the Red Sea, which should lie in wait for the Portuguese at the mouth of the Gulf, and destroy them on their passage to India. The sultan of Egypt had no wood to build a fleet, but the Venetians sent him the whole materials from Italy to Alexandria, from whence they were transported, with great difficulty and at an immense expense, over land to Suez. Here a fleet was immediately con-

* *Rajah* is evidently from the same original root with the Latin Rex—*Regis* but this is only one of a thousand such coincidences

structed. But Albuquerque, who was aware of the schemes of the confederate powers, had prepared a force sufficient to baffle all their designs. The armaments which came from Egypt, instead of attacking, were obliged to act on the defensive, and were always beaten by the Portuguese squadrons.

Thus the Venetians found themselves excluded from all intercourse with India by the Red Sea; and as the Persian Gulf, though not so commodious, might still have allowed them some communication with the East, the Portuguese could not rest satisfied till they had deprived them of that likewise. The fleet of Albuquerque entered the Gulf, and ravaging all the coasts, concluded by the taking of Ormuz, which, lying at the mouth of the straits, commands the whole sea.

After this expedition, the Portuguese, finding their power firmly established both in the Arabian and Persian Gulfs, began to extend their conquests in the eastern parts of Asia. They took the island of Ceylon, where there is the richest pearl-fishery in the world; made a settlement in Bengal; and sailing eastward, attacked and conquered Malacca, and received a voluntary submission from the kings of Pegu and Siam. Meeting with some Chinese merchants at Malacca, they were prompted to steer their course to China, a country then scarcely at all known to the Europeans. A Venetian, of the name of Marco Polo, had indeed travelled thither by land, about the end of the thirteenth century, and had brought to Europe some vague accounts of that empire, which were so extraordinary as to be regarded as entirely fabulous. Albuquerque, however, having transmitted to Portugal a relation of his voyage thither, and his opinion of the advantage of forming a connection with this remarkable people, a squadron was sent from Lisbon to convey an ambassador to China, in the year 1518. The Portuguese belonging to this fleet were fortunate enough to recommend themselves to the favor of the emperor, by extirpating some pirates who committed depredations on the coasts. In reward of this service the emperor allowed them to build a settlement at Macao, which very soon became a flourishing city, and opened a commerce for them both with China and with the neighboring islands of Japan.

It is astonishing with what rapidity the Portuguese had made these discoveries and conquests. In less than fifty years they became masters of the whole trade of the Eastern Ocean.

Let us now observe the effects of these discoveries, and the consequences of this new route to India, explored by the Portuguese, upon the commerce of Europe.

The Portuguese were very soon possessed of all the Spice Islands, and it is computed that their produce alone brought to Lisbon annually above 200,000 ducats. As the spice trade had been for some centuries the exclusive property of the Venetians, the loss of it was a blow from which they never recovered. After all the attempts which we have seen made to oppose the Portuguese, they made a last effort to retain still somewhat of its benefits, by making a proposal to the court of Lisbon to become the sole purchasers of all the spice annually imported thither, over and above what Portugal itself could consume ; but this proposal was contemptuously rejected. Some writers have expressed their admiration that a state, so powerful as Venice certainly was at this time, did not fit out her own fleets from the Mediterranean, and, pursuing the same route to the Eastern coast, attempt to colonize and to conquer, as well as the Portuguese, and thus indemnify themselves, in some measure, for what they had lost. But, in the first place, they were obliged, in those times, to be constantly watchful of the growing power of the Turks, who were making daily encroachments on their possessions in the Levant. At this very time, too, the formidable league of Cambray, as we have seen, seemed to threaten them at home with total destruction ; but even when in a state of peace they were in no capacity to vie with the Portuguese in this trade by the Cape of Good Hope. The situation of the latter gave them every advantage. The Venetians, besides a much longer navigation, must have been perpetually exposed to the corsairs of Barbary, who then infested the mouth of the Mediterranean.

But though one state suffered remarkably by this great revolution in the trade of India, the effect was, in general, beneficial to the European kingdoms. Commercial industry was roused in every quarter, and not only foreign trade, but domestic manufactures, made a most rapid progress. In the course of the fifteenth century, France, which hitherto had manifested very little of the spirit of commerce, began to be remarkably distinguished for its trade and manufactures. The towns of Lyons, Tours, and Abbeville, and the ports of Marseilles and Bordeaux, now rivalled the most eminent commercial cities of Europe ; and Antwerp and Amsterdam became the great marts of the north. Bruges, which we have seen hitherto the *entrepôt* between the Hanseatic merchants and those of Italy, began now to be on the decline. It revolted against its prince in the year 1480, and the disorders occasioned by civil commotions were extremely hurtful to its trade. The declension of Bruges was the commencement of the splendor of Antwerp and Amsterdam ; but Antwerp had the superiority. The immunities and liberty of conscience enjoyed there induced, at the era of the Reformation, a number of French and German protestants to establish themselves in it. The city was computed at this time to contain above 100,000 inhabitants. The merchants of Bruges, too, resorted thither on the decline of its trade. The sovereigns of the Netherlands likewise had established there fairs for commerce, free of all tolls or customs. These fairs, of which there were two in the year, lasted for six weeks at a time, and were frequented by merchants from every quarter of Europe. After the establishment of this general commercial intercourse, the Portuguese found Antwerp a most convenient *entrepôt* for transmitting the spices and productions of India, for the supply of the northern kingdoms; and this became an additional and very considerable source of its wealth.

Thus the trade of Antwerp exceeded, for some time, that of all the north of Europe, till Philip II., king of Spain, as we shall afterwards see, by the impolitic restrictions and taxes he imposed —and, above all, by restraints on religion, and the establishment of the tribunal of the Inquisition—excited the revolt of the Netherlands, and lost seven provinces, which, uniting into a republic, maintained a respectable independence from that time till the convulsions caused by the *French Revolution;* and by the most vigorous and unremitting industry carried commerce to its utmost height. The Spaniards took Antwerp in the year 1584, and blocked up and destroyed the navigation of the river Scheldt, imagining that they would thus transfer the commerce of that city to some of the other towns of Austrian Flanders, which had continued in their allegiance; but this policy hurt themselves, and turned entirely to the advantage of their enemies, for the trade of Holland, and particularly that of Amsterdam, rose upon the ruins of that of Antwerp. Amsterdam was, even before this time, a commercial town of considerable importance. The decline of the Hanse Towns had transferred thither a great part of the trade of the north. The Hanseatic confederacy had begun to decline from the year 1428. Jealousy had pervaded the different states, and many of them withdrew themselves from the league. Amsterdam profited by this decline of commerce on the Baltic; and upon the demolition of Antwerp became, as we have already said, the greatest commercial city of the North. Inhabiting a country gained almost entirely from the sea, and extremely unfruitful, the Dutch, urged by necessity, by the means of trade alone, and domestic manufactures, attained to a very high degree of wealth and splendor. The country of Holland does not produce what is sufficient to maintain the hundredth part of its inhabitants. The Dutch have no timber nor maritime stores, no coals, no metal, yet their commerce furnished them with every thing. Their granaries were full of corn, even when the harvest failed in the most fertile countries; their naval stores were most abundant, and the populousness of this country, which, in reality, is but a bank of barren sand, exceeded prodigiously that of the most fruitful and most cultivated of the European kingdoms.

The effects of the Portuguese discoveries in diffusing the spirit of commercial industry being thus extensively felt over Europe, it is not to be doubted that the commerce of Britain was likewise sensibly affected; though it is not, perhaps, possible to trace distinctly to that source the increase of the British trade, which was very conspicuous at that period in the growth and enlargement of our domestic manufactures. It is easier to perceive the effect of another cause, which operated at this time most powerfully in several of the European countries, and particularly in Britain. This was the Reformation. The suppression of the convents in Britain, in the reign of Henry VIII., restoring to society many thousands who were formerly dead to every purpose of public utility, and the cutting off all papal exactions, which were a very great drain to the wealth of the kingdom, were obvious consequences of this great revolution of opinions.

Henry VIII. encouraged domestic manufactures by many excellent laws, and the woollen trade, in particular, arose during his reign to a very great height.* It is worthy of notice, that in this reign, likewise, the interest of money was first fixed by law in England. While this continued an arbitrary matter—that is to say, while the prohibitions of the canon law were in full force, which, as we formerly remarked, condemned all interest as illegal and contrary to the express command of scripture—its exaction, being kept secret, was beyond measure exorbitant. Twenty and thirty per cent. were, in the fourteenth century, accounted a moderate rate of usance. Henry VIII., by a statute passed in the year 1546, for the punishment of usury, limitid the legal interest to ten per cent., at which rate it continued till after the reign of queen Elizabeth.

The prodigious increase of the commerce of England since the days of Henry VIII. may be estimated from this particular. The whole rental of England in lands and houses did not then exceed five millions per annum; it was assessed to the property tax, in 1815, at £49,744,622 sterling.† It is not to be denied, that it is to our commerce we owe our domestic manufactures, the increase and variety of our produce, the improvement of our lands, the rise of their value, and consequently the increase of the real wealth of the nation. It is commercial industry that not only doubles the produce of our country, but doubles, trebles, and quadruples the value of that produce. As for example:—the unmanufactured wool of England, of one year's growth, has been computed to be worth six millions sterling; when manufactured, it is supposed to be worth eighteen millions. In former times we have seen that this wool was exported to be manufactured, and, consequently, that foreigners reaped the greatest part

---

* Henry VIII. confined the woollen manufactures to particular towns. In the infancy of manufactures, monopolies act beneficially, by drawing capital and skill to a particular focus, and thus concentrating their operation. That nursing is useful, nay necessary, in childhood, which becomes useless and injurious in maturity.

† Annual value of real property as assessed to the property tax, 1815:—

England	£49,744,622
Wales	2,154,000
Scotland	6,653,000
	£58,551 622

of the profit of this prodigious increase on its value, while our own people remained inactive and unemployed.

Every other manufacture, as well as that of wool, has within these two last centuries greatly increased in Britain; and, in fact, this island may now be said to be the workshop of the world. In the reign of Henry VIII., and even in the golden reign of Elizabeth, our manufactures were chiefly managed by foreigners, among whom alone the necessary skill was to be found. They now give employment to more millions of British subjects than constituted the whole population of these islands even so late as the beginning of the eighteenth century. To the advancement of our manufactures is to be ascribed the rapid growth of our population since the commencement of that century—for, although, in the agricultural districts of the kingdom, we observe also a steady and progressive increase of the number of inhabitants—it is in those districts which have become the seat of manufactures, that we find that prodigious increase to have taken place which has swelled the population of England and Wales to the present enormous amount.*

---

* This may be well illustrated by a comparison of the increase of population in the two counties of Norfolk and Lancashire—the former, that in which the greatest progress has been made in agriculture—the latter, that in which the advancement of manufactures has been the most remarkable. In point of superficial extent these counties are nearly equal, each being about one thirtieth part of all England. In the year 1700, the population of Norfolk considerably exceeded that of Lancashire, the former being about 210,000, the latter about 166,000. In 1831, the population of Norfolk was 390,000 — thus less than double; while the population of Lancashire had risen to 1,335,800, or multiplied somewhat more than eight-fold. This enormous increase of the population of this county may be dated from a much later period, viz., the year 1767, the date of the invention of the *spinning jenny*—or perhaps, more properly, from the year 1781; for, previous to this time, the cotton manufacture of Lancashire was of a domestic nature; those overgrown masses of moral corruption, the crowded manufactories, were unknown; and that noble race of men, the yeomanry of England, still flourished in that county, where now scarcely a trace of them is to be found.

How far this enormous growth of one member is consistent with the wholesome state of the body politic—and to what it will ultimately tend—are, perhaps, the gravest questions in the whole circle of political inquiry.

The reciprocal dependence, which exists between the agricultural and manufacturing prosperity of a kingdom, is a subject of too deep importance to be safely left by the statesman either to the speculations of the political theorist, or to the narrow and short-sighted views engendered by peculiar interests. The tendency of the *political economists* of the present day is to deny the importance of agriculture to a state; and to maintain, that any inadequacy in the food of the people can be best and most cheaply supplied by commerce;—that the applica tion of capital and industry to increase the productiveness of the soil is altogether *unphilosophical;* their *proper* application being to the extension of manufactures, with which the food of the people can be obtained at less expense from foreigners. So says Mr. Macculloch now, and so said Sir Walter Raleigh in the days of Elizabeth. The political sophist of the present day preaches the abandonment of all the inferior lands of England. His illustrious predecessor argued in like manner: "Do not waste money in draining Romney marsh and the fens of Lincolnshire; they produce more value in reeds and sedges than they will ever do in corn; and you can buy corn cheaper than you can raise it." If the argument be good for any thing now, it was equally true in the days of Elizabeth, and the modern political economist must in consistency lament, that in those

CHAPTER XIX.

Charles V. succeeds to the Throne of Spain—Elected Emperor of Germany—Contest with Francis I.—Alliance with Henry VIII—The Constable of Bourbon takes Francis I. Prisoner—Treaty of Madrid—Henry VIII. takes part with Francis—Charles defeats the Turks in Hungary—Defeats Barbarossa in Africa—Francis allies himself with the Turks—War carried on in Italy and France—Death of Francis I.—Rise and History of the Order of Jesuits—Ferdinand of Saxony Head of the Protestant League—Resignation of Charles V.—The Constitution of the German Empire.

WE are now arrived at an era which is distinguished by some of the most remarkable events in the history of mankind:—the aggrandizement of the house of Austria, by the elevation of Charles V. to the imperial throne—a display of the greatest schemes of policy and ambition—the reformation of the Christian religion from the errors of the church of Rome—and the discovery of the Western World. But these interesting subjects demand a separate and an attentive consideration. We begin with a brief delineation of the most remarkable events of the reign of the emperor Charles V.

From the time of the emperor Sigismund, and the memorable transactions that attended the Council of the Church which was

---

early days Lord Bacon should have lent his powerful mind to arrest the prosperity of his country. But how would the case stand now, had the counsels of Sir Walter Raleigh become the fashionable political economy of the succeeding reigns? The marsh lands of Kent, which he would have condemned to the production of reeds and sedges, amount to 82,000 acres of the finest land in England—those of Lincolnshire, equal, or, perhaps, superior in productiveness, to 473,000 acres. Stating their produce at three quarters of wheat per acre, (thus, on such land, allowing for the inferior value of intermediate crops,) they would yield 1,665,000 quarters, being three times the average amount of all the wheat imported annually into Great Britain for the last thirty years.

The wealds of Kent, Surrey, and Sussex contain nearly 1000 square miles, described in the Saxon Chronicles as a wild, unprofitable waste, covered with heath and rushes, which the application of capital and industry has now converted into one of the most beautiful and fertile districts of England. The whole county of Norfolk, in like manner, is the most artificial soil in England. It is little more than one hundred years since half the county was a rabbit warren, and the greater part of the remainder a poor, thin clay. It is now the most uniform in productiveness of any county in England, exporting grain to the value of £1,000,000 sterling; yet is it essentially a very poor soil, which any suspension of the culture bestowed on it would, in a very few years, cast back to its original sterility. And to this the political economists of the present day would consign it; for it corresponds precisely to No. 6, of Mr. Macculloch's scale. Had this theory been acted on for the last three centuries, where would have been the home market for British manufactures? or rather what would British manufactures have been?—EDITOR, 1834.]

assembled at Constance by this emperor—where he enjoyed the proud triumph of degrading three rival popes, and placing a fourth upon the papal chair—the empire of Germany, which was governed for two years with spirit and ability by his son-in-law, Albert II., enjoyed a state of languid tranquillity during the long reign of his successor, Frederic III., surnamed the Peaceable, which was of fifty-three years' duration. The only circumstance that renders this reign at all worthy of notice was the marriage of his eldest son, Maximilian, with Mary, duchess of Burgundy, who brought, as her dowry, the sovereignty of the Netherlands; which, from that time, with the exception of those provinces that revolted, and formed themselves into the Republic of Holland, have continued, till of late, to be part of the patrimonial dominions of the house of Austria. Maximilian, after the death of his father, was elected emperor in the year 1493. This prince, who was an able politician, laid the foundation of the permanent greatness of the German empire, by procuring the enactment of that celebrated constitutional law, which establishes a perpetual peace between the whole of the states composing the Germanic body, which states, before that time, had been at constant variance upon every trivial opposition of interests. Thenceforth, every such contest was to be treated as an act of *rebellion against the empire.* It is easy to see of what vast importance this law was to the solid interests of the Germanic body.

Maximilian had one son, who died before himself, Philip, hereditary lord of the Netherlands, who, marrying Jane, the daughter of Ferdinand and Isabella, acquired the succession to the whole kingdom of Spain as her fortune. He died, however, before this succession opened to his family, which was destined to be the patrimonial crown of his eldest son, the celebrated Charles V.

Charles V. was born at Ghent in the year 1500. He was endowed by nature with a very extensive genius: he possessed acuteness of talents, indefatigable activity, and unbounded ambition; but his policy was of that crafty nature which is inconsistent with real greatness of soul.

He succeeded to the throne of Spain in the year 1516, upon the death of Ferdinand, his maternal grandfather, and was obliged to struggle with great disorders in that monarchy, which had their origin in the antipathy which the Spaniards conceived against their new sovereigns of the house of Austria. A rebellion actually arose upon this account, which was of several years' duration. It was at length happily quelled; and Charles, at peace in his hereditary dominions, preferred his claim to the German empire upon the death of his grandfather, the emperor Maximilian. He had a formidable rival and competitor for that dignity in Francis I., king of France, a monarch five years older than himself, who had already distinguished himself in Italy by the conquest of the

Milanese, in which war he had defeated the army of pope Leo and of the Swiss in the battle of Marignan. Francis, however, from being the enemy, became soon after the ally of pope Leo X., and of the Swiss. He had compelled the emperor Maximilian to restore the territory of Verona to the Venetians, and procured for Leo the duchy of Urbino. Thus the king of France, at the age of twenty-five, was considered as the umpire of Italy, and the most powerful prince in Europe.

The claims of these illustrious competitors for the German empire were, then, very nearly balanced; but the electors, apprehensive for their own liberties, under the government of either of those great monarchs, determined to reject both the candidates, and made offer of the imperial crown to Frederic, duke of Saxony. This prince, however, undazzled by the splendor of so high an object of ambition, rejected the proffered sovereignty with a magnanimity no less singular than great, and strongly urging the policy of preferring the Spanish monarch, procured the election of Charles of Spain.

The two candidates had hitherto conducted their rivalship without enmity, and even with a show of friendship. Francis declared, with his usual vivacity, "that his brother Charles and he were fairly and openly suitors to the same mistress. The most assiduous and fortunate will succeed; and the other," said he, "must rest contented." No sooner, however, was the contest decided, than he found himself unable to practise that moderation he had promised. He could not suppress his indignation at being foiled in the competition, in the face of all Europe, by a youth yet unknown to fame. The spirit of Charles resented this contempt, and from this jealousy, as much as from opposition of interests, arose that emulation between those two great monarchs, which involved them in perpetual hostilities, and kept the greatest part of Europe in commotion.

Charles and Francis had many mutual claims upon each other's dominions. Charles claimed Artois, as sovereign of the Netherlands. Francis prepared to make good his pretensions to Naples and Sicily. Charles had, as emperor, to defend the duchy of Milan; and, as king of Spain, to support his title to Navarre, which his grandfather, Ferdinand, had wrested from the dominion of France. In short, nature, or rather fortune, seem to have decreed that these two princes should be perpetually at war with each other.

Henry VIII. of England had power enough to have held the balance; as the contest at first between these rival princes was so equal, that the weight of England on either side must have given a decided superiority, and entirely overpowered the single party. But Henry, though he had ambition, had not judgment to direct his conduct, which seems to have been influenced solely by the caprice of his own disposition, when he was not absolutely led, as was frequently the case, by his ministers. He was at this time governed by Thomas Wolsey, a man whom he had raised from an obscure station to the dignity of archbishop of York, and chancellor of England, and whom the pope had made a cardinal, and his legate in England. The counsels and the measures of Wolsey had less in view the interests of the nation than his own greatness and unmeasurable ambition. Wolsey, it is plain, could take no side in directing the part to be chosen by Henry between the rival princes, unless what was agreeable to his master, Leo X.; and the fact was, that Leo was as much in doubt what part to take as any of them. Henry, however, was courted by both the rivals, and had address enough, for some time, to flatter each with the prospect of his friendship. Francis contrived to have an interview with him at Calais, where the only object seemed to be an ostentatious display of the magnificence of the two sovereigns. Charles, who had more art, went himself in person to England to pay his court, and Henry, flattered by this condescension of the emperor, conducted him back to Gravelines, and gave him the strongest grounds to hope for an alliance between them.

A great party of the Spaniards, dissatisfied with the absence of their sovereign, broke out into rebellion; and Francis, judging this a favorable opportunity for the recovery of Navarre, invaded that province, and made an entire conquest of it; but the French, elated with this success, imprudently made an attack likewise upon the kingdom of Castile, which united the Spaniards against them, and they were driven out of Navarre almost as soon as they had got possession of it. The emperor, in the meanwhile, attacked France on the quarter of Picardy; and the French, at the same time, were beaten out of the Milanese and Genoa, a misfortune which was chiefly owing to Francis's own extravagance and want of economy. The Swiss troops in his service had deserted for want of pay.

At this juncture died Leo X.; and Charles, that he might have a pope securely in his interest, and one whom he could absolutely manage, caused the triple diadem to be given to his former preceptor, cardinal Adrian. Cardinal Wolsey had expected the papal dignity, but the emperor found means to soothe him with the hopes of soon succeeding Adrian, who was far advanced in life. The policy of Charles appeared now in its utmost extent. The pope was his dependent, Wolsey was his friend, and Henry, of course, was at length induced to declare himself his ally, and to proclaim war against France, under the delusive idea of recovering the former possessions of the English in that kingdom.

A most formidable combination seemed now ready to overwhelm Francis I., under which a monarch of less spirit and abilities than himself must certainly have succumbed at once. The pope, the emperor, the king of England, the archduke Ferdinand—to whom his brother, Charles V., had ceded the German dominions of the house of Austria—were all united against the king of France.

Francis had formerly owed to the great military abilities of the constable of Bourbon the signal victory of Marignan, and the conquest of the Milanese. It was the misfortune and the imprudence of the French monarch to quarrel with this useful subject, at the very time when he most needed his assistance.

An iniquitous decree of the parliament of Paris, by which the constable was deprived of the whole estates belonging to the family of Bourbon, was the cause of an irreconcilable animosity, and of a firm purpose of vengeance now meditated by the constable against the king of France. He immediately offered his services to the emperor; and, like another Coriolanus, with equal valor and ability, and with equal infamy, became the determined enemy of his country. The emperor received him, as may be believed, with open arms; but in the breast of every worthy man his conduct excited that detestation which it merited. Even the Spanish officers themselves abhorred his perfidy. "If the constable of Bourbon," said one of these generals, "should enter my house, I would burn it after his departure, as a place polluted by treason and perfidy." But Charles V. saw this acquisition through the medium of his own interest, and created the constable generalissimo of his armies.

Too much confidence seems to have been the great error of Francis I. While the troops of the emperor were commanded in Italy by Bourbon, by Pescara, and John de' Medicis, all of them generals of consummate ability, they were opposed by the admiral Bonnivet, a man of very moderate talents, with a very inconsiderable army. The French were defeated at Biagrassa, where the most remarkable circumstance was the death of the illustrious Chevalier Bayard, who had distinguished himself not only by his great military prowess, but by a life regulated by the maxims of the strictest honor, and the most romantic generosity. He was termed by his contemporaries, in the language of chivalry, the *Chevalier sans peur et sans reproche.* In his last moments, while the constable of Bourbon, standing by his side, was lamenting his fate, "It is not *I*," said he, "who am an object of commiseration; it is *you*, who are fighting against your king, your country, and your oaths."

The troops of the emperor, under this illustrious renegade, were carrying every thing before them, when Francis himself hastened into Italy, entered the territory of Milan, and, without difficulty, retook the city; but the imprudent Bonnivet thought proper to besiege Pavia, while a great part of the French army had been detached against the kingdom of Navarre. In this divided situation, the imperial troops, infinitely superior in numbers, and most ably commanded, presented themselves in order of battle. Francis disdaining to retreat, a desperate engagement ensued, in which the

French army was entirely cut to pieces, and the king himself (whose life was saved by a French officer in the imperial army) was made the constable of Bourbon's prisoner.

It is, perhaps, the only impeachment against the political talents of Charles V., that he neglected upon this occasion to improve his good fortune. Instead of marching into France and prosecuting his successes with all the advantage which the captivity of the monarch gave him in his designs upon the kingdom, he chose rather to obtain by treaty and stipulation what he ought to have gained by force of arms. He brought Francis to Madrid,—where his resolute spirit declared at first his intention to die in prison, before he would consent to yield any part or dismember his dominions. At length disease and the miseries of confinement got the better of his magnanimity, and he consented to sign the treaty of Madrid, by which he yielded to Charles the duchy of Burgundy, and the empty superiority of Flanders and Artois; and put his two sons into the hands of the emperor as hostages for the performance of these conditions. Scarcely, however, was he at liberty when he formed a league with the pope, who absolved him for his oaths. The states of Burgundy had published a solemn declaration that no king could dispose of their freedom or sell them like slaves : and on these grounds Francis refused to perform the treaty or return to his imprisonment, and Charles consented to ransom his two sons and give up Burgundy for a large sum of money. Thus from these signal events, the battle of Pavia and the captivity of the king of France, the emperor drew no solid advantage whatever. On the contrary, Francis soon found his situation more promising than before, for Henry VIII., till now the ally of Charles, had become jealous of the emperor's increasing greatness, and finding himself less courted as his aid was less needed, determined to throw his influence into the scale of the king of France.

The treaty of Madrid, disregarded from the beginning, was now interrupted by a formal declaration of war on the part of Henry and Francis. Charles in the meantime had lost an opportunity of obtaining the sovereignty of Italy. The constable of Bourbon had defeated the papal army in the interest of Francis, had taken the city of Rome, and made pope Clement VII. his prisoner. But Bourbon himself was killed in the siege; and Charles again lost his advantages. His avarice got the better of his policy, and he set the pope at liberty, as he had done the princes of France, for a large sum of money. Some apology may perhaps be found for Charles in the great variety of important concerns to which he had now to attend—the beginning commotions excited by the Reformation in Germany, the operations of the Turks in Hungary, the different political views of the Italian states, and the formidable alliance between France and

England. Perhaps it was not in this situation possible to push to the utmost any partial advantage.

Charles had concluded the peace of Cambray which set Francis at liberty, and ceded Burgundy, when he set out from Spain to receive the imperial diadem from the hands of the pope. In Italy he assumed the authority of an absolute sovereign. He granted to Francis Sforza the investiture of the Milanese, and to Alexander of Medicis that of Tuscany; and he made the pope restore Modena and Reggio to the duke of Ferrara.

The depredations of the Turks called him into Hungary. It was here that, for the first time, he appeared at the head of his armies; having hitherto fought only by his generals; a circumstance which has been said to mark the character of Charles V. as having been rather that of a politician than a warrior.* He had the glory of compelling Soliman, with an army, as is said, of no less than 300,000 men, to retire before him, and to evacuate the country. This enterprise was succeeded by another still more illustrious. Hayradin Barbarossa, who had been at first a common corsair, seized upon the city of Algiers, and by treachery and violence had dethroned Muley Hassan and usurped the kingdom of Tunis. The dethroned prince applied to the emperor for support, and Charles, ambitious of every opportunity of acquiring glory, embarked immediately for the coast of Africa, with a fleet of five hundred sail and 30,000 men. Barbarossa met him with an army amounting to 50,000. The imperial troops were victorious. Muley Hassan was restored on condition of paying a tribute to the Spanish crown; and 10,000 Christian captives, who had been detained in bondage at Tunis, were instantly set at liberty and returned with the conqueror to Spain. At this time Charles V. surpassed in reputation all the princes of Europe. No potentate since the days of Charlemagne possessed equal abilities with an equal extent of empire : and if we consider what was the state of this empire, how rich, how flourishing, and how populous, we may regard Charles, in his political capacity, as the greatest monarch that had ever existed in Europe.

It was a mean piece of conduct in Francis—yet perhaps his situation made it his best policy—to call in the aid of Soliman and the Turks, to dispossess Charles of the duchy of Milan. It was concerted that the Turks should attack the kingdom of Naples and Hungary, while a French army invaded the Milanese. Barbarossa landed near Tarento, and spread a dreadful alarm through the whole country. But as the French army was not quick enough to coöperate with him, the project miscarried, and the Turks were obliged to withdraw and reëmbark their troops.

* While the spirit of chivalry prevailed in Europe, kings generally headed their armies in person : but this was sometimes attended with very fatal consequences, for the death or captivity of a sovereign often brought his kingdom to the brink of ruin.

The French army in the meantime had passed the Alps, when Charles V. set out from Rome, obliged them again to retreat across the mountains, and entering Provençe, advanced as far as Marseilles, and laid siege to Arles, while another army ravaged Champagne and Picardy. It was on this occasion of the enterprise against the Milanese, that Francis took it into his head to send Charles a challenge to engage him in single combat; staking as a prize Milan on the one part, and Burgundy on the other. The challenge was accepted, but it may be believed that this extraordinary duel was never fought. A short time after, Francis summoned the emperor to appear before the French parliament and defend himself for having violated the treaty of Cambray. The most ridiculous part of this farce was, that Charles, having failed to compeer, was actually sentenced by the parliament of Paris—and the counties of Artois and Flanders were declared confiscated to the crown of France. In consequence of this absurd procedure, Francis actually took possession of some of the towns in Flanders; but both parties were now desirous of an accommodation, and a truce for ten years was entered into at Nice, by which it was agreed that, till the conclusion of a peace, matters should remain in their then existing situation.

An insurrection happening at this time in the city of Ghent on occasion of a demand of subsidies from the Flemish nobles, the emperor was desirous of making a progress to his dominions in the Netherlands. He asked permission of Francis to pass through the kingdom of France, and promised to grant him the investiture of Milan, which seemed all along to have been the highest object of Francis's ambition. The request was cheerfully complied with. Charles, with an hundred attendants, travelled through the dominions of his rival, who gave orders that he should be every where received with all possible marks of magnificent hospitality, and entertained him himself with great pomp during seven days that he stayed in the city of Paris: but Charles, having obtained his purpose, and reduced the rebels of Ghent to submission, thought no more of the promise regarding the Milanese. He left all Europe to make their remarks on the altered appearance which he and his rival now mutually presented to the world—in a word, on the king of France's generous credulity and his own breach of faith. This was sufficient cause for the dissolution of the late treaty of Nice, and accordingly hostilities recommenced with greater animosity than ever. Francis forthwith renewed his alliance with Soliman, and his fleet, under the count D'Enguien, joined with that of the Turks, made an unsuccessful attempt on the town of Nice.

The French were more fortunate in Italy, where they obtained a most complete victory over the Marquis del Vasto, at Cerizoles; but this, like most of their victories in Italy, produced no lasting consequence of any advantage. Francis, meantime, continued to be harassed in his own dominions both by the emperor and by the king of England, who laid siege to Bologne by sea, while Charles advanced into Picardy; and under these circumstances it was not to be expected that the success of the French in Italy could be of any advantage. France in fact seemed now in the utmost danger; and she owed her preservation to the troubles in Germany, which required the emperor's presence to appease them. The reformation was going on there with great spirit. The protestant party were united against Charles, and this circumstance, extremely fortunate for France, obliged the emperor to conclude the treaty of Crepi with Francis I., who, at the same time, purchased a peace with Henry VIII. for £200,000 sterling. This was the last public event which signalized the reign of Francis I., a prince of a manly and heroic spirit, endowed with abilities sufficient to have made his name illustrious and his country great and happy, had it not been his misfortune to struggle, during the greatest part of his reign, against the superior power and greater political abilities of Charles V. Francis died of that distemper which the discovery of the New World had imported into Europe, and which in those days, from the ignorance of any method of cure, was commonly mortal.

About this time was founded the famous order of the Jesuits, a body whose influence, for two centuries, was much greater in Europe than that of any other religious society, and had its operation in some shape or other on most of the political transactions during a long period of time. The founder of this order was an ambitious enthusiast of the name of Ignatius Loyola. He rightly conceived that, in this period, when the papal authority had received a severe shock, by the defection and apostasy of so many nations from the catholic faith, a body of men who should enlist themselves as the professed and devoted servants of the pope, and hold themselves constantly in readiness to execute with fidelity, at all times and in all places, whatever he should enjoin them, would so recommend themselves to his favor, as soon to obtain the preëminence over every other religious association. The Jesuits, therefore, to the three vows of poverty, chastity, and monastic obedience, added a fourth, which was, implicit devotion to the pope. The manifest utility of this institution to the support of the holy see procured them from pope Paul III. an apostolic bull, granting them the most ample privileges. It was soon perceived that, if confined to their cloisters, their utility would be too much circumscribed. They were allowed to mingle in the world, and to take a share in all the active concerns of public life, which it was their duty to influence and direct assiduously towards the great end of establishing the power and authority of the popedom; and this end it must be owned, they most zealously promoted. Under the command of a superior, or general of the order, whose instructions they were bound to receive with implicit submission, they dispersed themselves over the greatest part of the globe. By the most insinuating arts they courted the favor and wrought themselves into the confidence of statesmen, of civil and ecclesiastical governors, and of sovereign princes; and operating on all to the same purpose, and regularly communicating their intelligence to their head, from whom they received their instructions, the whole catholic world was in a manner directed by one great and pervading system of policy, which centred in the establishment of the pope's supreme temporal and spiritual jurisdiction.* The zeal of this order, and the capacity of its members, while thus promoting the great purpose of its institution, could not fail of attaining both immense wealth and great power. As these increased, this society found enemies in all whose authority they undermined, and whose aims they opposed. Books were written without number to expose their artifice and ambition. Their frauds, their vices, and even atrocious crimes, were loudly proclaimed; and it was urged, with great reason, that the doctrines which they taught, and the maxims they inculcated, were equally pernicious to religion, to civil government, and to all the interests of society. The sovereigns of the different catholic kingdoms, by degrees, began to perceive that their power and even personal security was in danger, and the Jesuits were successively expelled from France, from Spain, from Portugal, and from Sicily; and such at length was the influence of the house of Bourbon with the holy see, that the order was entirely suppressed and abolished in 1773.

The life of Charles V. was a scene of constant turmoil and agitation. His aim, it is said, was universal empire; but at the death of Francis, his most formidable rival, he found himself at as great a distance as ever from the object of his wishes. The protestants of Germany entered into a most formidable confederacy in support of their religious liberties, and the joint forces of Charles, of his brother Ferdinand, king of Hungary and Bohemia, and of pope Paul III., whom he was forced to call in to his aid, were scarcely sufficient to oppose them. He defeated them, it is true, in the battle of Mulberg, but the party was neither broken nor dispirited, and through the remainder of the life of Charles continued to give him perpetual vexation. The party of the protestants was headed at this time by one of the greatest char-

* It has been noticed by M. Duclos, (in his voyage en Italie,) as a remarkable fact, that, notwithstanding the great power and influence of this religious association, none of its members ever arrived at the papal dignity. The reasons which he assigns are these:—the jealousy of the cardinals, who dreaded that very power and influence, as conceiving the Jesuits might monopolize that high dignity to their own order; but still more, the deeper policy of the Jesuits themselves, who considered the papal dignity as not the object but only the instrument of their ambition, which aspired at the government of all the kingdoms of Europe, and the popedom among the rest. But this was a government which was to be silently exercised, and which an open assumption of power would have altogether destroyed.

acters of the age, Frederic, duke of Saxony; the same man whose high reputation, as we have before observed, would have procured him the election to the Germanic empire, even against such candidates as Charles V. and Francis I., had not his own modesty expressly declined that elevated station. It is but justice to this most respectable man to relate an anecdote, told by Roger Ascham, preceptor to queen Elizabeth, who, when in Germany, was personally acquainted with him. Duke Frederic was taken prisoner by Charles V. in the battle of Mulberg, and upon a representation of some of his counsellors, that the exemplary punishment of so eminent a man would prove of great service in checking the progress of the Reformation, the emperor, forgetting his own obligations to him, condemned him to be beheaded, on a scaffold, at Wittemberg. The warrant for his execution, signed by the emperor's hand, was sent to duke Frederic the night before, and was delivered to him while he was playing at chess with his cousin the landgrave of Lithenberg. He read it over attentively, and then folding it up, "I perceive," said he, "that I fall a victim to my religion, and that my death is necessary to the emperor's schemes of extinguishing the protestant faith. But God will maintain his own cause. Come, cousin," said he, "take heed to your game;" and then, with the same composure as if he had received a private letter of little importance, he continued to play till he had defeated his antagonist. It is a satisfaction to learn that the emperor, impressed, as is said, by this admirable example of fortitude, gave immediate orders for a recall of the warrant, and ever afterwards treated the elector of Saxony with the highest respect and esteem.*

These disturbances in Germany continued to embroil the emperor during the remainder of his life, and utterly destroyed his peace. It was impossible for him to form his dominions into a well-connected empire. The jealousies that could not fail to subsist between his subjects of different countries, must have been an insuperable bar to such a coalescence, even though his foreign enemies had allowed him sufficient respite to turn his whole attention to the internal police of his kingdoms; but this we have seen was far from being the case. Henry II., the successor of Francis, was an antagonist equally formidable as his father had been, and made more effective encroachments upon the dominions of the empire. In short, the last years of Charles were the most tumultuous and the least successful. The load of

* Ascham sums up the character of this great man in these remarkable words: —"He is a man wise in all his doings, just in all his dealings, lowly to the meanest, princely with the highest, gentle to all. His noble nature thinketh nothing which he dare not speak, and speaketh nothing which he will not do. Him no adversity could ever move, nor policy at any time entice to shrink from God and from his word. The remembrance of him is never out of place, whose worthiness is never to be forgotten"

cares, and the difficulties which surrounded him on every side, at length entirely overpowered him. The vigor of his mind was broken, his animal spirits were exhausted, and, in a state of despondency and melancholy dotage, he abdicated the empire, and renounced the world at the age of fifty-six.

This celebrated resignation, though prompted by dejection of spirit, was conducted with some policy, and with a regard to the interest of those who were to come after him. Charles wished that his son Philip should succeed, not only to his hereditary dominions, but to the empire. He had, however, unluckily, in the earlier part of his life, taken a step which defeated this last purpose. This was the procuring his brother Ferdinand to be elected king of the Romans, which is always regarded as the preparatory step to the empire. Before Charles resigned the imperial crown, he proposed to his brother Ferdinand to resign in his favor, provided he would consent that Philip should be elected king of the Romans. A third person, however, struck in, and disappointed this negotiation. This was the archduke Maximilian, son of Ferdinand, a youth of abilities and ambition, who frustrated all the emperor's schemes for that purpose, and secured the dignity of king of the Romans to himself. The defeat of this darling project entirely broke the spirit of Charles V. After a solemn resignation of his hereditary dominions to his son Philip, he transmitted his resignation of the empire to his brother Ferdinand; and retiring to Spain, he betook himself to the monastery of St. Justus, where he soon after died, bequeathing to mankind a striking lesson of the vanity of human greatness, the madness of ambition, and the total insufficiency of all earthly dignities or possessions to the attainment of substantial or lasting happiness.*

It may not be improper to conclude this brief sketch of the reign of Charles V., with a few observations on the constitution of the German empire.

Till the reign of Maximilian I., the empire of Germany was a prey to all the disorders of the feudal government. Of this the "Golden Bull," published in 1356, affords sufficient evidence, as it proceeds on the supposition of great barbarism of manners. It is true that the Germans, like the Franks, preserved the ancient custom of holding *general diets*, or assemblies of the states; but these meetings were commonly of so short a continuance, and so extremely tumultuous, that they were of very little consequence in establishing wise political regulations. The emperor Wenceslaus had, indeed, in the year 1383, endeavored to give a better form to the empire. He

* Charles V. had no taste for literature, or disposition to patronise the arts and sciences; even the great Erasmus, who had dedicated to him some of his works, complains that he received nothing but barren thanks for the compliment.—Jortin's Life of Erasmus, p. 304.

proclaimed a general peace, but he found it impossible to take proper measures to secure it.

Sigismund made a similar attempt with no better success. But Albert II. was more fortunate. He actually accomplished the conclusion of a general peace between all the branches of the empire; and, with the consent of the assembly of the states, he divided Germany into six circles, or provinces, which were each to have their own diet or assembly. But still the great object was not completely attained: a spirit of jealousy and disunion continued to pervade the Germanic body, and frequent differences of interest, which were followed by hostile conflicts, threw them back into their former anarchy and barbarism.

At length Maximilian I. procured that famous law of the Germanic body, which established a general and a perpetual peace, by prohibiting all hostilities between the different states, under pain of that state which was the aggressor being treated as a common enemy. The *Imperial Chamber* was established to judge and determine all differences. A new division was made of the empire into ten circles, and each of these provinces named a certain number of representatives, or assessors, to take their place in the imperial chamber, and undertook to carry its decrees or judgments into execution, through the whole extent of its territory. The diet held at Augsburg in the year 1500 established likewise an occasional regency, which was to subsist, without interruption, in the intervals of the meetings of the diets. The regency was invested with all the power of the national assembly. The council was composed of twenty ministers, named by the diet, over whom the emperor himself presided. One elector was always obliged to be personally present in the council; the other six sent their representatives.

Although these establishments gave a more regular form to the government, they would not have been adequate to the preservation of the peace of the empire, and the enforcement of the laws, had not the house of Austria acquired, of a sudden, so much power and influence as to establish itself on the imperial throne, and to render its authority more respectable than that of the former emperors. In fact, although the inferior princes, or electors, were accustomed to have recourse to the imperial chamber for a redress of grievances or encroachments, the more powerful chose rather to do themselves justice by force of arms; and, notwithstanding all the wise regulations, the ancient prejudices remained in full force, and the empire was still a prey to the same disorders.

The accession of Charles V. to the empire formed a remarkable era in its constitution. The princes wisely judged that his elevation was attended with danger; but they were short-sighted enough to imagine, that a capitulation would be sufficient to fix bounds to his authoriry. Charles had vast ambition, great resolution, and that *versatility* of character, which could accommodate itself to any conduct most favorable to his political views. But amidst his ambitious projects, he seemed to have overlooked a very material circumstance: that new system of European politics, the motive of preserving a balance of power between the kingdoms of Christendom, which made the princes of the empire find allies and protectors sufficient to resist and defeat all his schemes of absolute dominion. Charles wished to turn to his own advantage that spirit of *religious enthusiasm*, which was kindled in his time, but his extensive territories gave him too many objects of attention, and he could not prosecute any single enterprise with that constancy which was necessary to promote its success. He attained, however, a measure of authority very far superior to that of any of his predecessors, and virtually established his own family on a throne, which the constitution of the empire declared to be elective, and not hereditary.

The successors of Charles, without his talents, wished to pursue the same system of policy, and might, perhaps, have enslaved Germany, had it not been for the aid she received from other European powers. After a series of wars, and a great deal of bloodshed, the peace of Westphalia, in the year 1648, became the foundation of the public law of the empire, and fixed the emperor's prerogatives and the privileges of the states.

The power of electing an emperor was, by the golden bull of Charles IV., (published in 1356,) vested in seven electors, who were likewise appointed to fill the great offices of the empire. These electors were—the archbishop of Mentz, great chancellor of the German empire; the elector of Cologne, great chancellor of the empire in Italy; the elector of Treves, great chancellor of the empire in Gaul; the king of Bohemia; the count Palatine; the duke of Saxony; and the margrave of Brandenburg. An eighth electorate was afterwards created—viz., that of Bavaria; and to these, in 1692, was added a ninth, that of Brunswick-Lunenburg, or Hanover.

All the princes of the empire acknowledged a legislative power to reside in the diet for the enactment of general laws, which regard the whole body of the state. The diet, or general assembly of the empire, was divided into three colleges, the electors, the princes, and the free cities. After the emperor's commissioner communicated his propositions to the diet, they became the subject of the separate deliberation of the electoral college, and that of the princes. When their opinions were uniform, the resolution was carried to the college of the free cities, and if acceded to by them, it became a *placitum* of the empire. If the emperor gave it his approbation, the *placitum* became a *conclusion*, and formed a *law*, which was obligatory upon the whole of the states. If the emperor and the diet were of different opinions, there could be no general law. Thus it was in the power of the emperor to prevent the enactment of any law, however salutary, which may be contrary to his own interest: a power which was not checked, as in the British government, by the sovereign's dependence on the people for his revenue. Agreeably to the same bad policy, the emperor was the sole proposer of all new laws, a further security for his proposing none but what were favorable to his own interests. It was, likewise, in the power of the director of the diet to prevent the execution of the established laws of the empire. Nothing could be communicated to the diet but by the consent of the elector-archbishop of Mentz. All complaints of grievances, or requisitions made by any of the princes to the Germanic body, must receive his approbatory sanction, and he might refuse them at his pleasure.

These great constitutional defects were the more destructive, when it is considered that the Germanic government had for its object to regulate the contending interests of princes who had all the rights of sovereignty—who had their armies, their revenue, and their fortified cities, and a power of contracting defensive alliances with foreign nations, and were sometimes possessed themselves of foreign dominions greatly more considerable than their Germanic territory. The greater that are the sources of division between the parts of an empire, the greater certainly ought to be the prudence and stability of its laws and policy.

CHAPTER XX.

Of the Reformation in Germany and Switzerland, and the Revolution in Denmark and Sweden—Reformation in England under Henry VIII. and his successors—Immediate causes—Sale of Indulgences—Luther attacks the abuses of the Romish Church—Zuinglius—Reformed Religion acknowledged by Decrees of the Senate in Zurich, Berne, and Basle—the Revolution in Denmark and Sweden—Gustavus Vasa—Anabaptists—Origin of the Name of Protestant—Calvin—Origin of the Reformation in England—Henry declares himself Head of the Church—Persecution under Mary—firmly established under Elizabeth.

THE age of Charles V. is the era of great events and important revolutions in the history of Europe. It is the era of the Reformation in religion in Germany, in the northern kingdoms of Denmark and Sweden, and in Britain. It is the era of the discovery of America; and, lastly, it is the period of the highest splendor of the fine arts in Italy and in the south of Europe. Of each of these subjects we shall treat in order, and shall consider first the Reformation, as undoubtedly the most important, both in a moral and in a political point of view.

The splendid court, and the voluptuous taste of pope Leo X. demanded a greater supply of money than what the patrimonial territories of the popedom could easily afford. A project had likewise been set on foot by his predecessor, Julius II., which Leo keenly adopted, and which required a prodigious sum of money to carry it into execution. This was the building of St. Peter's church at Rome; a fabric which it was intended should surpass all the magnificent structures that had ever been reared by the art of man.

For the construction of this noble edifice, and to supply the luxuries of his court, Leo X. had recourse (to use an expression of Voltaire) to one of the keys of St. Peter, to open the coffers of Christians. Under the pretence of a crusade against the Turks, he instituted through all Christendom a sale of indulgences, or releases from the pains of purgatory, which a pious man might purchase for a small sum of money either for himself or for his friends. Public offices were appointed for the sale of them in every town, and they were farmed or leased out to the keepers of taverns and bagnios. Their efficacy was proclaimed by all the preachers, who maintained that the most atrocious offences against religion might be expiated and forgiven by the purchase of a remission. A Dominican friar of the name of Tetzel, a principal agent in this extraordinary and most abominable merchandise, was wont to repeat in his public orations this blasphemous assertion, "That he himself had saved more souls from hell by these indulgences, than St. Peter had converted to Christianity by his preaching."* This flagrant example of impiety and absurdity, could not fail to shock the understandings of the wiser and more rational even of the clergy; and among the rest Martin Luther, an Augustine monk, unable to repress his indignation, ventured, in a sermon which he publicly preached at Wittemberg the 30th of September, 1517, to condemn, in strong terms, this infamous traffic, and plainly to accuse the pope himself as partaker of the guilt of his agents.†

---

* The form of the absolution issued by Tetzel was as follows:—

"I absolve thee from all ecclesiastical censures, and from all thy sins, how enormous soever: and by this plenary indulgence I remit thee all manner of punishment which thou oughtest to suffer in purgatory: And I restore thee to the sacraments of the church, and to that innocence and purity which thou hadst at thy baptism; so as, at death, the gates of hell shall be shut against thee, and the gates of paradise shall be laid open to receive thee. In the name of the Father, and of the Son, and of the Holy Spirit. Amen."—Keith's Hist. of Scotland, Introd., p. 4.

† Mr. Hume, in his history of the reign of Henry VIII., has chosen to derive the opposition of Luther to the doctrine of indulgences, from selfish and interested motives alone. He asserts that the Augustine friars, who had formerly in their hands the exclusive sale of these indulgences, were incensed at being deprived of that lucrative traffic, by the pope's bestowing it upon the Dominicans; and that in revenge for this affront they commissioned Luther, one of their order, to decry the efficacy of these remissions, and thus put a stop to the gain of the Dominicans. But this calumny has been completely refuted: it has been

Luther was a man of undaunted resolution, of a lively imagination, strong sense, and a considerable portion of learning. In the course of his invectives against the commerce of indulgences, he was naturally led to examine the sources of that authority by which they were dispensed. The scandalous vices of the see of Rome were delineated in their strongest colors; and men began to perceive that there could be no merit in the sight of heaven in impoverishing themselves, to furnish supplies for the luxuries, the vanities, and crimes of a selfish and ambitious pontiff. Learning and a general spirit of inquiry were making rapid advances in the kingdoms of Europe. The art of printing had wonderfully disseminated knowledge, and furnished a ready vehicle for submitting all matters of controversy to the judgment of the world at large. The doctrines of Luther, which were at first vented in his sermons, attracted the notice of Frederic, the elector of Saxony, who took him under his protection. Pope Leo, who was informed of his tenets, was at first inclined to pass the matter over without observation, as in truth his holiness had very little inclination to perplex himself with disputes of that kind. It became necessary, however, from the remonstrances of the more zealous part of the clergy, to take some notice of these new propositions of Luther, and to condemn them by a papal bull. The consequence was, that Luther, inflamed with zeal and indignation, no longer kept any measures with the see of Rome. He composed a book, which he entitled "The Babylonish Captivity," in which he applied to the popedom all those flaming characters and dreadful denunciations of divine vengeance contained in Scripture against the impieties and adulteries of *the whore of Babylon*. He inveighed against private masses, that is to say, such as any man could purchase for a small piece of money to be said for his soul, or that of his friend: Transubstantiation he exploded, as neither the doctrine nor the word was to be found in Scripture. Luther indeed acknowledged that the body of our Savior was present in the sacrament of bread and wine, but very reasonably denied that the bread and wine were actually changed into flesh and blood. The Dominicans in Germany ordered this work of Luther's to be burnt by the hand of the public executioner. But the reformer was not intimidated: he, on his part, caused the pope's bull and the decretals to be burnt in the market-place at Wittemberg. He began to be supported by a very formidable party in Germany, and he every day opened some new battery of attack against the tenets of the Romish religion. The vows of the priests and their celibacy were represented as diabolical institutions, in opposition to the direct commands of God Almighty. The refusal of the

---

clearly shown that the fact on which it is founded, viz., that the exclusive right of sale was taken from the Augustines and bestowed on the Dominicans, is false -See *the Translation of Mosheim*, vol. ii., p. 17. 4to. edit.

communion in wine to the people, was treated as a similar piece of impiety, in violation of the express injunctions and example of our Savior. In short, Luther disputed openly every one of the tenets of the Romish church, for which no express authority could be pointed out in the Word of God.

One of the first champions of the see of Rome, who took up his pen against Luther, was Henry VIII., king of England—the person who we shall see became a few years afterwards the most inveterate enemy of the pope's jurisdiction. Henry had been educated in all the subtleties of the schools, and was fond of passing for a man of learning, and an adept in the vain philosophy of the times. He asked leave of Leo to read and to examine the works of Luther, which at that time were prohibited under pain of excommunication; and in a short time he composed a treatise in defence of the seven sacraments, against the attacks of Luther, which was received by pope Leo (who very probably never read it) with the highest approbation. Henry and his successors (in return for this service done to the church) had the title given them of *Defenders of the Faith.*

Meantime the rest of Europe took very little share in these disputes, which were confined almost solely to Germany. Charles V. was obliged to keep on good terms with the pope, who gave him his assistance against the attempts of Francis I. upon Italy. He therefore found it necessary to declare against the tenets of Luther, and he summoned him to attend an imperial diet at Worms, and there give an account of his new doctrines. The reformer appeared and pleaded his cause with great spirit and resolution. It is said, that the pope's nuncio solicited Charles, who had given Luther a safe conduct, to deliver him up to the court of Rome, as his predecessor Sigismund had behaved by John Huss in the like circumstances: but Charles made answer, that *he* did not choose to have cause to blush like Sigismund; and he permitted Luther, though condemned by the council, to avail himself of his protection and escape into Saxony. The elector of Saxony was now his avowed friend and patron. He found his disciples daily increasing: the mass was abolished in the town of Wittemberg, and soon after through all Saxony. The images of the saints were broken to pieces; the convents were shut up; the monks and nuns returned to a life of freedom; and Luther, to enforce his doctrines by his own example, married a nun himself. It should be acknowledged, to the honor of the reformed religion, that those priests who now returned to the world, gave no handle to their adversaries to reproach them with making an improper use of their freedom. So far from it, that the manners of the reformed clergy are universally acknowledged to have exhibited a very striking contrast to the dissolute and scandalous practices which had long prevailed in the monasteries.

The celebrated Erasmus, whose skeptical turn of mind and

strong ironical talent had, before the appearance of Luther, paved the way for his doctrines by many oblique sarcasms against the abuses of the Romish church, has enumerated in one of his works what he esteems to have been capital errors in the measures taken against Luther by the see of Rome. These may be reduced to six articles, as to some of which the judgment of Erasmus is certainly right; in others, perhaps, disputable. The first error was, that the see of Rome permitted those theses about indulgences to be disputed in sermons before the people. 2. That they opposed to Luther only some mendicant friars, who were but so many declaimers and trumpets of slander. 3. Says he, they should have silenced the preachers of both parties, and appointed learned, prudent, and peaceable men, who would have calmly and temperately instructed the people, and recommended unanimity and the love of the gospel. 4. It was a capital error, that neither party would yield or give up the smallest or most trifling article. 5. The cruelties of the catholics against the Lutherans promoted the success of their doctrines. 6. The most effectual means of persuading men of the truth of their religion, would have been to have seriously amended their lives, and showed an example of penitence and real sanctity.* The three last of these articles are, without doubt, most justly a reproach to the catholics, and are perfectly unanswerable; but the others, perhaps, could not be avoided, considering the state of the church at that time and the opinions of mankind. Hence, Bayle has made a very just inference when he concludes that Luther's design could not have found a more favorable juncture.

Switzerland was the first of the European countries that followed the example of Germany. Zuinglius, a priest of Zürich, carried matters even further than Luther, and denied absolutely that the bread and wine in the holy sacrament partook in any degree of the substance of the body and blood of Christ. The authority of this pastor over his native city was very remarkable. He was accused before the senate, and the cause being tried in form, a plurality of voices declared in Zuinglius's favor. The sentence was intimated to the people of Zürich, and in a moment they all declared themselves of the reformed religion. The churches were purified, the images pulled down, and the mass abolished.

Some years after this, the city of Berne determined this cause in a manner still more solemn. The Romish religion was condemned by the senate, after a disputation which lasted two months. The sentence was notified to the whole canton, and

* "There is no better way," says Lord Bacon, "to stop the rise of new sects and schisms, than to reform abuses, compound the lesser differences, proceed mildly from the first; refrain from sanguinary persecutions, and rather to soften and win the principal leaders, by gracing and advancing them, than to enrage them by violence and bitterness."—Bacon's Moral Essays, sect. i., essay xii.

most cheerfully received; and the people of Basle soon after compelled their senate to pronounce a like decree. Five of the smallest cantons in Switzerland were yet zealous adherents to the church of Rome, and took up arms in defence of their faith. An army of protestants was levied in order to convert them, but Zuinglius, at their head, was unfortunately killed and his party defeated. The catholics, who considered him as a detestable heretic, ordered his body to be cut in pieces and burnt to ashes.

Meantime Lutheranism was making its progress towards the north of Europe. Religion was the cause of a very great and important revolution at this time, in the kingdoms of Sweden and Denmark. Sweden, Denmark, and Norway had been united under Margaret of Waldemar, in the year 1397. The Swedes endeavored to break this union, in the year 1452. They rose in rebellion, and unanimously chose their great marshal, Charles Canutson, for their king. They were, however, forced again to submit to the yoke of Denmark. Being again oppressed, they rebelled once more, and elected for themselves a governor, at the time when Christiern II., a most tyrannical prince, was raised to the throne of the united kingdoms. Trollo, the archbishop of Upsal, in Sweden, carried on a correspondence with the tyrant to extinguish the liberties of his native country. The great senate of Sweden deposed him on that account from his episcopal dignity. The prelate had recourse to Leo X., who granted him a bull, laying the kingdom under a sentence of excommunication. The king and his primate, armed with this instrument of vengeance, set out for Stockholm. The affrighted Swedes returned to their allegiance, acknowledged the authority of Christiern, and Trollo was restored to his episcopal functions. Seven hostages were given as a security of the loyalty of the Swedes, and among these was the young Gustavus Vasa, who was destined to be the deliverer of his country. After this accommodation, so favorable to Christiern, the principal senators and nobles were invited by the monarch to an entertainment. Amidst the most unbounded festivity, the archbishop made his entry, the pope's bull in his hand, and in the name of the church demanded satisfaction for the usage he had sustained. The sentence of excommunication was read aloud, and the tyrant Christiern ordered his guards to seize the whole senate and nobility. Ninety-four senators, and an immense number of the nobility and citizens, were put to death without mercy, and the whole city of Stockholm was a scene of carnage. Among those who were the victims to this infernal revenge was Eric Vasa, the father of young Gustavus, and nephew to Charles Canutson. It was the good fortune of this youth to escape from prison; he fled to the mountains of Dalecarlia, where he concealed himself in the disguise of a workman in the mines. By degrees he opened his project to his companions, discovered to them his name and rank, and soon attached to himself a considerable number of adherents. The city of Lubeck furnished them with arms, and he was joined by such numbers, that at length he took the field against the generals of Christiern, gained some advantages, and recovered a considerable part of the country. That inhuman tyrant took a revenge worthy of himself; he caused the mother and sister of Gustavus, whom he had long confined in prison, to be sewed up in a sack and thrown into the sea.

The Danes themselves, irritated by the oppressions of Christiern, determined at length to throw off the yoke. His uncle Frederic, duke of Holstein, headed the insurrection, and Denmark, by the voice of the chief nobility and senators, pronounced a formal sentence of deposition, which they transmitted to Christiern in his palace at Copenhagen. A single magistrate entered his presence, and delivered to him his sentence, which he obeyed like a coward, as he had reigned like a tyrant. He betook himself to Flanders, where he in vain solicited assistance from his father-in-law, the emperor Charles V., to regain his kingdom. The duke of Holstein was elected king of Denmark and Norway; and Gustavus Vasa, the deliverer of his country, was rewarded with the crown of Sweden, which had formerly been held by his grand-uncle, Charles Canutson.

The bull of Leo X., and its bloody consequences, had entirely alienated the minds of the Swedes and Danes from the religion of Rome. Gustavus was a convert to the opinions of Luther, whose tenets had made considerable progress in the northern kingdoms. Frederic, king of Denmark, concurred with him in the design, and they found it no difficult matter to establish the reformed religion in place of the catholic. The clergy were the more easily reconciled to it as the episcopal hierarchy was preserved, though the revenues of the bishops and their ecclesiastical jurisdiction were considerably retrenched. Gustavus Vasa reigned in peace for a long term of years; and, though an absolute monarch, contributed greatly to the happiness and aggrandizement of his kingdom. He was the first who made foreign nations sensible of the weight which Sweden might have in the affairs of Europe, at the time when, as we have seen, European policy was putting on a new face, and when the idea first arose of establishing a balance of power.

While the tenets of Luther were thus rapidly gaining ground in the North, the following fact will convince us, that he arrogated to himself an authority, very little short of that of the pope, in Germany.

Philip, the landgrave of Hesse Cassel, had taken a disgust at his wife, a princess of the house of Saxony, who he alleged was intolerably ugly, and addicted to drunkenness. The secret was, that he had fallen in love with a young lady of the name Saal, whom he wanted to marry. Luther at this time, with five of his followers, was holding a kind of synod at Wittemberg for the regulation of all matters regarding the church. The landgrave presented to him a petition, setting forth his case, in which he at the same time insinuated, that in case Luther and his doctors should refuse him a dispensation of polygamy, he would, perhaps, be obliged to ask it of the pope. The synod were under considerable difficulty. The interest of the landgrave was too formidable to be disregarded, and at the same time to favor him, they must assume to themselves a power of breaking a law of scripture. The temporal consideration was more powerful than the spiritual one. They agreed to give Philip a dispensation for polygamy, and he accordingly married his favorite, even with the consent of his former wife.

The successful example of Luther gave rise to reformers of different kinds, and among the rest two fanatics of Saxony, whose names were Stork and Muncer, pretended to reform both the catholics and the Lutherans. It was their notion that the gospel gave them a warrant for propagating their tenets by force of arms, which they grounded on these words of scripture: "I am come not to send peace, but a sword." They condemned the baptism of infants, and *rebaptized* their disciples when they were *come to the age of manhood*, whence they got the name of Anabaptists. They preached up an universal equality among mankind, and strenuously contended both for religious and civil liberty; but it was their error to be too violent. They had not strength to support their sanguinary notion of converting men by the sword; and after committing some horrible outrages, they were defeated by the regular troops of the empire, and Muncer and several of his associates had their heads cut off upon a scaffold at Mulhausen.

The united power of the emperor and the pope found it no longer possible, however, to stop the progress of the Reformation. The diet of Spires endeavored to accommodate matters by articles of reconciliation between the Lutherans and catholics. Fourteen of the cities of Germany and several of the electors entered a formal *protest* against the articles of the diet of Spires; and from this circumstance, the partisans of the reformed religion became ever after distinguished by the name of Protestants. The protestants gave in to the assembly of Augsburg a confession of their faith, which has become the standard of their doctrines.

The Anabaptists, who were not suppressed by their defeat at Mulhausen, and the fate of their leader and spiritual guide, continued to commit new devastations. They surprised and took possession of the city of Munster, where they preached their doctrines with such effect, that the people, inspired with frenzy, expelled their bishop, and declared that they would have no other governor than God Almighty. Matthias, who was their chief prophet, having been killed in a sally from the town upon the troops of the bishop who had laid siege to it, John Boccold, a journeyman tailor, who had been distinguished by the name of Jack of Leyden, caused himself with great ceremony to be anointed king, and appointed twelve apostles to proclaim his sovereign authority over all the lower Germany. One of his favorite tenets was polygamy, and he set a most illustrious example himself by marrying fourteen wives. One of his wives having expressed some doubt as to his divine mission, Boccold immediately cut off her head, and the thirteen others danced round her body with transports of joy. Munster being closely besieged, this fanatic defended the city obstinately during twelve months: but he fell at length a victim to the treachery of some of his own followers; and his enemies, whom his obstinate courage had much exasperated, put him to death with every circumstance of cruelty. The sect of the Anabaptists was not annihilated; but what is very extraordinary, from being the most sanguinary of all the species of religious enthusiasts, they are become one of the most peaceable and harmless.

In the meantime, while these outrages of the Anabaptists furnished a handle of invective to the generality of the catholics against every kind of innovation in religion, the more rational part of them beheld in the austere but pure and simple manners of the protestant leaders a contrast which was very favorable to the progress of the Reformation. The dispassionate and solemn manner, in which the cities of Switzerland had proceeded, attracted the attention and respect of all Europe. The magistrates of Geneva, after a long and most deliberate discussion in the senate, where every body was at liberty to propose arguments or to answer them, solemnly condemned the Romish religion, and put up that memorable inscription which is still to be seen in the town-house: "*In remembrance of the divine goodness, by which he hath enabled us to shake off the yoke of Antichrist, to abolish superstition, and to recover our liberty.*" The protestants here got the name of Eignots, a corrupted term, signifying *bound by an oath*,* which has since been further corrupted into Huguenots.

John Calvin, vulgarly accounted the founder of the Reformation at Geneva, was not in fact so; matters had taken that turn I have mentioned, and the senate had established the protestant creed, before this reformer made any figure. Calvin, who was a Frenchman, and born at Noyons, was possessed of very good talents, and wrote much better than Luther. He had, likewise, a considerable share of the learning of the times, that is to say, Latin, Greek, and School philosophy; but his disposition was harsh, austere, and tyrannical. On his coming to Geneva, he

* A corruption of the German word *Eid-genossen.*

found the protestant creed extremely agreeable in most points to the notions which he had propagated in his "Institutiones Christianæ;" but he foresaw that articles of faith would not be long in observance without a proper system of ecclesiastical jurisdiction to enforce them; he, therefore, established synods, consistories, and deacons, and prescribed a regular form of praying and of preaching. The magistracy of Geneva gave these ordinances the authority of law; and they were adopted by six of the Swiss cantons, by the protestants of France, and the presbyterians of Scotland. His ablest advocates will find no apology for his persecution of the learned Castalio, whom he caused to be expelled from his country; and far less for the inhumanity of his conduct to Servetus, who, having presumed to controvert some of his tenets, was tied to a stake and burnt alive. These, it must be owned, are no commendable methods of propagating the mild and humane religion of Jesus Christ. The truth is, neither Luther nor Calvin assumed the character of inspired apostles: if they had, their follies and their vices would have belied their pretence; but the scheme of reformation which they proposed, and partially brought about, was unquestionably a good one, whoever had been its founders. It is to be examined by the test of reason, and derives no blemish or dishonor from the men, or even the motives which first gave rise to it. This observation will apply yet in a stronger degree to what I must now proceed to give an account of,—the rise and progress of the Reformation in England.

The origin of the Reformation in England is to be traced to a cause still more remote from the real interests of religion than that which gave rise to the Reformation in Germany.

As early as the middle of the fourteenth century, the learned Wicliffe had begun an attack against many of the abuses in the church of Rome, both in his sermons to the people and in his writings. In order to render the perusal of the scriptures more universal, he translated them into the vernacular tongue, a measure by nc means agreeable to the Romish teachers, whose aim it had ever been to prevent the people at large from any exercise of their own judgment in spiritual matters, that they might more implictly rely on the guidance of the church. The doctrines of Wicliffe had their influence with many men of learning and talents; but they had not an extensive currency with the people. These were taught to stigmatize the followers of Wicliffe by the name of Lollards, a term of reproach and ridicule; but this did not hinder his opinions from making their way by a silent progress among the rational and thinking part of the nation. Such was the state of things at the beginning of the reign of Henry VIII., who was a prince zealously attached from education to the doctrines of the church of Rome; but he was yet more addicted to the unrestrained gratification of nis pas sions, and this, in fact, was one of the minor, though immediate causes of the Reformation in England.

Henry VIII. had been married for above eighteen years to Catharine of Spain, the daughter of Ferdinand and Isabella, and aunt to Charles V., by whom he had three children, one of them then alive, the princess Mary, afterwards queen of England. Henry was a voluptuous prince and fond of women. Among others of his favorites, he conceived a passion for Anne Bullen, the daughter of a private gentleman, who had either the prudence or the address, by resisting his advances, to win so much upon his affections, as to make him form the resolution of raising her to the throne, and displacing queen Catharine: the difficulty was how to obtain a divorce; but an expedient was not long wanting. Catharine had been first married to prince Arthur, the elder brother of Henry VIII., and upon his death was married to Henry, in virtue of a dispensation from pope Julius II. The conscience of Henry began to be extremely alarmed on account of this incestuous connection, which he had now maintained for eighteen years: he, therefore, solicited Clement VII. to annul the dispensation of his predecessor Julius, and to declare his marriage with Catharine to be a violation of divine and human laws. Clement was reduced to a most disagreeable dilemma. It was absolutely necessary for him to be on good terms with the emperor Charles V., yet he was extremely unwilling to incur the resentment or enmity of a prince of Henry's violent disposition. In this situation, he endeavored to gain time by negotiating, temporizing, and settling preliminaries, in hopes that, in the meantime, Henry's passion might cool, and there might be no necessity for so disagreeable a decision; but the pontiff was mistaken; the king of England had the matter most seriously at heart, and was resolved to compass this match with Anne Bullen whatever it might cost him. He applied to the doctors of the Sorbonne at Paris, and the other French universities, for their opinion upon this momentous case, which his agents, by the proper distribution of English gold, found means to secure in his favor. Even the Jewish Rabbis were consulted; and all finally concurred in declaring the marriage with Catharine to be illegal, and that pope Julius had no right to have dispensed with the law of Leviticus. Armed with this authority, Henry, who had his own clergy at his command, prevailed on Cranmer, archbishop of Canterbury, to annul his marriage. The repudiated queen retired from court, and Anne Bullen was advanced to her dignity. It was the negotiation of this divorce, which occasioned the fall of cardinal Wolsey. Henry imputed the pope's hesitation in that affair to Wolsey's disapprobation of the measure. He had, as we have formerly observed, made the cardinal chancellor of England. He now deprived him of that office, and confiscated his whole estate. He relented, however, a short time afterwards: Wolsey was allowed for some time to enjoy his temporal possessions; but the inconstant monarch soon after renewed his prosecutions, and the cardinal being arrested for high treason, disease and anguish of mind put an end to his life. He was succeeded in the office of chancellor by Sir Thomas More, a man of low extraction, but worthy, by his integrity and abilities, of the dignity to which he was raised. He, too, soon after fell a sacrifice to the inhumanity and caprice of his master.

Clement VII., who saw that it was impossible to look for the favor of Henry, resolved, at least, to keep well with the emperor, and for this purpose he immediately issued a bull condemning the sentence of the archbishop of Canterbury. This measure deprived the see of Rome of all authority over the kingdom of England. Henry immediately obliged his clergy to declare *him* head of the church; and his parliament, without hesitation, confirmed this title, and entirely suppressed the pope's authority within his dominions. The first measure which he took in virtue of his supremacy of the national church was the abolition of the monasteries, and the confiscation of their immense riches, which, according to bishop Burnet's calculation, amounted, besides an immense value in plate and jewels, to a yearly revenue of £ 1,600,000. Out of these spoils he founded six new bishoprics, and a college; —rewarded a few of his own servants so largely as to enable them to found what are now some of the wealthiest houses in the British peerage;—and converted the remainder to his own use. It was pity that, in the execution of this measure, which was certainly attended with many substantial political advantages, there should have been so much indulgence of that savage spirit of destruction, which has deprived posterity not only of many of the finest Gothic structures, but of many valuable treasures of learning, which were contained in the libraries belonging to the ancient abbeys and monasteries.

Yet Henry, though he had thus quarrelled with the pope, and despoiled and abolished the monasteries, had not renounced the *religion* of the church of Rome. He still prided himself on his title of Defender of the Faith, and he continued, in every respect, to be a good catholic, except that he chose to be pope in his own kingdom. He was as great an enemy to the tenets of Luther, of Calvin, or of Wicliffe, as he was to the supremacy of the Roman pontiff; and the favorers of the latter, as well as those who espoused the doctrines of the former, were equally the victims of sanguinary persecution. Meantime the passion of the king was cooled for Anne Bullen, and had changed its object. He had fallen in love with Jane Seymour, one of the maids of honor, and he was not ashamed to accuse the queen of adultery upon the most frivolous grounds, which might have been furnished by the conduct of even the most virtuous woman upon earth. Compliments, idly paid to her beauty by some of her courtiers, were construed into proofs of a criminal intercourse. The parliament, with the meanest submission to the will of the tyrant, passed sentence of death, and Anne Bullen was removed from the throne to the scaffold. She left by Henry a daughter, Elizabeth, afterwards queen of England. Henry was *next day* publicly married to Jane Seymour, who, happily for herself, died about a year afterwards. His *fourth* wife was Anne of Cleves, who did not retain his affections above nine months. He represented to his clergy, that at the time he married her he had not given his inward consent; but it is less surprising that a monarch of this character should urge such an excuse, than that his clergy and parliament should sustain it. Anne was divorced, and he married for his *fifth* wife Catharine Howard. It was upon this occasion that Sir Thomas More incurred, as Wolsey had done, the indignation of his sovereign. He disapproved of the match with Catharine: he was accused of heresy and treason, condemned and beheaded. The character of Catharine Howard, which had been rather suspicious *before* her marriage, was soon a sufficient pretext for a new sentence of divorce; yet her crimes, in the eye of Henry, were such as nothing but her blood could expiate, and she, like Anne Bullen, was publicly beheaded. Catharine Parr, the *sixth* in order whom this tyrant advanced to his bed, escaped very narrowly from the fate of her predecessors, for having dared, with too much zeal, to combat some of his religious opinions: she, however, had the good fortune to survive him. The political occurrences of the reign of Henry, as we have seen, regarded chiefly matters of religion. His warlike enterprises we have already taken notice of, in treating of his contemporaries, the emperor Charles V., Francis I. of France, and James V. of Scotland. He died at length, to the relief of his subjects, in the year 1547, in the fifty-sixth year of his age, and left the throne of England to Edward VI., his son by Jane Seymour.

During the reign of Edward VI., the protestant religion prevailed in England, because the sentiments of the prince were favorable to the doctrines of the Reformation; but this period of toleration was short, for Edward, of whom his people had justly conceived great hopes, died at the early age of fifteen. He had, upon his death-bed, conveyed the crown to his cousin, Lady Jane Grey, descended of Henry VII., in prejudice of his sister Mary; but, after a short struggle, which can hardly be called a civil war, the party of Mary prevailed, and the unfortunate Jane fell a victim to the partial affection of her cousin, and the favor of a great body of the people, who wished to see her settled upon a throne which her moderation would rather have declined than accepted. Mary, who inherited the cruel and tyrannical disposition of her father, began her reign by putting to death her cousin Jane, together with her father-in-law and husband. This outset was a prognostic of the temper of her reign, which was one continued scene of bloodshed and persecution. The protestants, who had multiplied exceedingly during the short reign of Edward, were persecuted with the most sanguinary rigor. It was a doctrine of Mary's, as bishop Burnet informs us, that as the souls of heretics are afterwards to be eternally burning in hell, there could be nothing more proper than to imitate the divine vengeance, by burning them on earth. In the course of this reign it is computed that about eight hundred persons were burnt alive in England. Yet this monster of a woman died in peace; with the consideration, no doubt, of having merited eternal happiness as a reward of that zeal she had shown in support of the true religion.*

Mary was succeeded by her sister Elizabeth, the daughter of Anne Bullen—a protestant; and, perhaps, more zealously so, from an abhorrence of the creed of her sister. The bulk of the nation, influenced naturally by the same motives, became in her reign zealous protestants. From that period the religion of England became stationary. The liturgy was settled in its present form, and the hierarchy of protestant archbishops, bishops, priests,

---

* Mary had prepared to employ the same means for the extirpation of heresy from her kingdom of Ireland, but her purpose was defeated by a singular accident. The following account was found among the MSS. of Sir James Ware, copied from the papers of Richard, earl of Cork:—

"Queen Mary having dealt severely with the protestants in England, about the latter end of her reign, signed a commission for to take the same course with them in Ireland; and to execute the same with greater force, she nominates Dr. Cole one of the commissioners. This doctor coming with the commission to Chester, on his journey, the mayor of that city, hearing that her majesty was sending a messenger into Ireland, and he being a churchman, waited on the doctor, who, in discourse with the mayor, taketh out of a cloak-bag a leather box, saying unto him, *Here is a commission that will lash the heretics of Ireland*, (calling the protestants by that title.) The good-woman of the house being well affected to the protestant religion, and also having a brother, named John Edmonds, of the same, then a citizen in Dublin, was much troubled at the doctor's words; but watching her convenient time, while the mayor took his leave, and the doctor complimented him down stairs, she opens the box, takes the commission out, and places in lieu thereof a sheet of paper with a pack of cards wrapped up therein, the knave of clubs being faced uppermost. The doctor coming up to his chamber, suspecting nothing of what had been done, put up the box as formerly. The next day, going to the water-side, wind and weather serving him, he sails towards Ireland, and landed on the 7th of October, 1558, at Dublin. Then coming to the castle, the Lord Fitzwalters being Lord Deputy, sent for him to come before him and the privy-council; who, coming in, after he had made a speech, relating upon what account he came over, he presents the box unto the Lord Deputy, who causing it to be opened, that the secretary might read the commission, there was nothing save a pack of cards, with the knave of clubs uppermost; which not only startled the Lord Deputy and council, but the doctor, who assured them he had a commission, but knew not how it was gone. Then the Lord Deputy made answer—*Let us have another commission, and we will shuffle the cards in the meanwhile.* The doctor, being troubled in his mind, went away, and returned into England; and coming to the court, obtained another commission; but staying for a wind on the water-side, news came to him that the queen was dead; and thus God preserved the protestants of Ire land."

Queen Elizabeth was so delighted with this story, that she sent for Elizabeth Edmonds, and gave her a pension of forty pounds during her life.—See Cox, Hibernia Anglicana, or History of Ireland, vol ii., p. 308.—Harleian Miscellany, No. 79.—Mosheim's Eccles. History, vol. ii., p. 70.

and deacons established as it now continues. The church of England, in her tenets, has chiefly conformed to the Lutheran system of reformation.

The reign of Elizabeth, on many accounts remarkable, we shall by and by consider in a civil point of view. It is sufficient at present to observe, that with regard to religion her administration was mild and moderate. The laws gave their countenance to the established mode of worship, but authorized no persecution of those who peaceably approved themselves good and quiet subjects, whatever were their opinions on controverted points of theology.

Thus the doctrines of the Reformation obtained, as we have seen, in the course of half a century, a permanent footing in Germany and Switzerland, in Denmark and Sweden, and in England. The progress of the Reformation in Scotland we shall afterwards observe in treating of the reign of queen Elizabeth and of Mary queen of Scots. But we have not yet accomplished our plan of a complete delineation of those remarkable occurrences which characterized the reign of Charles V.

CHAPTER XXI.

Discovery of America.—Columbus discovers Cuba—The Caribbees—America—Description of Inhabitants and Productions—Cruelties of the Spaniards—Conquest of Mexico—Discovery of Peru—Administration of the Spaniards—Possessions of other European Nations in America.

Among those great events which distinguished the reign of Charles V. was the conquest of Mexico by Fernando Cortes, and of Peru by the Pizarros. The discovery of the American continent by Columbus was made some years before, in the preceding reign of Ferdinand and Isabella, but we have postponed till now to mention that great event, that we may here delineate the whole in one connected view.

The union of the kingdoms of Castile and Arragon under Ferdinand and Isabella rendered Spain, as we have seen, one of the most powerful monarchies in Europe. The enterprising genius of one man now opened to her a source of wealth, to all appearance inexhaustible.

Christopher Columbus, an obscure individual, but a man of a penetrating genius, struck with the enterprises of the Portuguese, was seized with an irresistible ardor of achieving something that might perpetuate his fame, while, at the same time, it gratified his predominant passion of curiosity, and the love of adventure. He applied first to the state of Genoa, of which he was a subject, and humbly solicited the public aid for assistance to attempt some discoveries in the western seas. He was treated as a visionary by his countrymen; and with the same ill success he made application to the courts of Portugal and of England. He then betook himself to Spain, where, after fruitless solicitation for several years, he at length obtained from Ferdinand and Isabella an armament of three small ships, and the sum of seventeen thousand ducats, for defraying the expenses of his voyage. After a navigation of thirty-three days from the Canary Islands, during which time his crew, despairing of ever obtaining sight of land, repeatedly threatened to throw their admiral overboard, he at length arrived at one of the Bahama Islands, which he named San Salvador; and soon after, he discovered the Islands of Cuba and Hispaniola, which he took possession of in the name of the monarchs of Spain. The inhabitants of those islands, from their distance from the continent, could give him no hopes of those immense discoveries which were to follow; he therefore returned, within the course of seven months, to Spain, bringing with him some of the natives of Hispaniola, some rarities of the country, and some presents in gold. He was received with triumphal honors, and regarded by the Spaniards as something more than human. There was now no difficulty in prevailing with Ferdinand and Isabella to equip a new armament for the prosecution of these discoveries. Columbus sailed a second time with a fleet of seventeen ships, and returned after the discovery of the Caribbee Islands and of Jamaica. But his enemies, jealous of the reputation he had acquired, had prevailed on the court of Spain to send along with his fleet an officer, who, in the character of justiciary, might establish such regulations in the new colonies as were most for the advantage of the Spanish government. This officer, on account of some differences between Columbus and his soldiers, put the admiral in irons on board his own ship, and returned with him a prisoner to Spain. The court, it is true, repaired this affront in the best manner possible. Columbus justified his conduct, and was sent out a third time in the prosecution of new discoveries. It was in this third voyage that he descried the continent, within ten degrees of the equator, towards that part of South America where Carthagena was afterwards built. To this immense continent Amerigo Vespuzio had the honor of giving his name, as he was the first that reported in Europe the intelligence of that discovery; of which, though he only followed the footsteps of Columbus, he arrogated to himself the merit.

The Americans are a tall race of men, of just proportions, and of a strong conformation of limbs. The color of their skin is a reddish brown; their hair is long, lank, and black, extremely coarse, and they have no appearance of beard: a circumstance which is alleged by M. de Pau as a proof of their being a degenerate race of men, but which seems rather to be a clear specific difference. The inhabitants of this immense continent—if we except those of Mexico and Peru, which were comparatively refined and luxurious nations—were tribes of wandering savages, and utterly unacquainted with almost every art of civilized life. They were naked, except a small covering round the middle; their sole occupation was the chase, and when the season of hunting was at an end, the American, if not engaged in war, spent his time in perfect indolence: half the day was consumed in sleep, and the other half in immoderate eating and drinking. The Indians of America were in their disposition grave even to sadness: they held in contempt the levity of manners of the Europeans, and observing great taciturnity themselves, imputed to childishness all idle talk or conversation. Their behavior was modest and respectful, and in their solemn councils their deliberations were carried on with the greatest order and decorum.

In each tribe there was a species of government which was vested in the chief and in the council of the elders, the authority of the former being balanced by the latter, and prevented from becoming despotical. The chief, therefore, was understood no longer to have a right to dominion, than while he used his power with moderation. He had neither guards, nor prisons, nor officers of justice. The concurrence, therefore, of the tribe was essential to every exercise of his authority. The council was composed of the seniors of the tribe, on whom age and long experience were supposed to have conferred a more ample knowledge of the interests of the tribe, and of the powers and strength of its enemies. These elders met in a hut appropriated for the purpose, and here their deliberations were held, and their orators declaimed with great force of language and the most expressive gesticulation. When the council was over, the whole tribe partook of a feast, which was accompanied with warlike dancing and songs, in which they rehearsed the heroic exploits of their deceased forefathers.

To nations living by hunting, and thus ranging over immense tracts of countries, there must frequently happen such interferences between different tribes as to occasion hostile conflicts and even long-continued wars. It was even no unusual thing for a few individuals of a tribe to solicit permission of the chief to undertake an expedition to avenge any injury they had received, and leave being obtained, the war-kettle was set on the fire as a symbol of their intention of devouring their enemies. This dreadful ceremony was held as an invitation to all to assemble themselves who chose to join the expedition.

The mode in which their wars were conducted was various in the different tribes. It does not appear that, in their engagements, they observed any regular disposition or arrangement; but as soon as they met with their enemies, after sending forth a dreadful cry, they fell on with the impetuous fury of wild beasts; when the one party prevailed, it was a rule to pursue their success by an undistinguishing carnage, as long as the enemy gave the smallest resistance. When that was over, they bound and carried off the prisoners, who were reserved for the most cruel and tormenting death. This the captives themselves knew, and were prepared for. They had, however, one chance of life: for, on returning to their village, the victors made offer to each family of a captive for every relation they had lost in the war. This offer they might either accept or reject. If accepted, the captive became a member of the family; if rejected, he was doomed to die under the most excruciating tortures. In these executions, the women would bear their part, and seem actuated by the spirit of furies. What is most remarkable is the fortitude with which these unhappy wretches submitted to their fate. There was a contest between them and their tormentors which should exceed, these in inflicting, or the others in enduring the greatest exacerbations of pain. It is even said that by insults they endeavored to provoke their executioners, and stimulate their fury by telling them of the cruelties they had themselves inflicted on their countrymen. "You are ignorant wretches," said they: "you know nothing of the art of tormenting. Had you seen the tortures which we and our friends exercised over your countrymen, you would confess your inferiority, and despise your own ignorance."

This horrid picture would seem to argue a disposition so hardened, as to allow no tincture of the common feelings of humanity; but the inference would be altogether unjust. The cruelty of the Indians to their enemies is known to have been compatible with the warmest affections to their friends, and with a measure of generosity, benevolence, and humanity almost exceeding belief. The selfish feelings are the fostered growth of luxury and over-civilization. Disinterestedness and generosity are the characteristics of the savage. His life as well as his property are devoted to the service of his friends, and the connections of civilized man are a slender tie when compared with the fervor of attachment manifested by the wild, untutored Indian. Of the strength and ardor of their affections, there can be no proof so strong, as that which arises from their treatment of the dead. Believing in the immortality of the soul, they bury along with the deceased, his bow and his arrows, together with the most splendid ornaments which belonged to him. They attend him to the grave with the deepest demonstrations of sorrow, and those who are his nearest relations retire for a great length of time to their huts, and refuse to take any concern in the active occupations of the tribe. But this is not all:—their concern for the dead is manifested in a manner yet more striking, by a ceremony the most solemn, and the most awfully affecting that imagination can devise. At stated periods s held what is termed the feast of the dead, or the feast of souls, when all the bodies of those who have died since the last ceremony of that kind, are taken out of their graves, and brought together from the greatest distances to one place. A great pit is dug in the ground; and thither, at a certain time, each person, attended by his family and friends, marches in solemn silence, bearing the dead body of a son, a father, or a brother. These are deposited with reverence in the pit, from which each person takes a handful of the earth, which he preserves afterwards with the most religious care. Such a ceremony, though attended with strong marks of a rude and barbarous state of society, is yet characteristic of a people endowed, in no common degree, with strong, with humane, and generous feelings.

The animals of the continent of America, and its vegetable productions, were equally new, and remarkable as its inhabitants, and the horse, the most valuable of our animals, was there totally unknown. The chief vegetable productions, which Europe has thence acquired, are indigo, cocoa, vanilla, and, above all, the quinquina, that inestimable specific in intermitting disorders, which passes under the name of Peruvian bark. The cochineal insect, which furnishes the richest scarlet dye, is likewise a production of the continent of America.

The conduct of the Spaniards towards the inhabitants of these new-discovered countries, and the cruelties exercised by them under their first governors, furnish a subject which it were to be wished, for the honor of humanity, could be for ever veiled in oblivion. Religion and policy were the pretexts for the most outrageous acts of inhumanity. Avarice, which the more it is fed is still the more insatiable, had suggested to some of these rapacious governors, that the inhabitants of the New World had discovered to the Spaniards but a very small proportion of treasures, which were inexhaustible. The missionaries encouraged the idea, and insinuated, at the same time, that the most proper method of obtaining an absolute authority over these new subjects, was to convert them to the doctrines of Christianity, for which purpose the priests were to be furnished with every authority sufficient for the extirpation of idolatry. The favorite instruments of conversion employed in these pious purposes were the rack and the scourge. While some, to escape these miseries, put an end to their life with their own hand, others, flying from their inhuman persecutors into the woods, were there hunted down with dogs, and torn to pieces like wild beasts. In a little time Hispaniola, which contained three millions of inhabitants, and Cuba, that had above six hundred thousand, were absolutely depopulated. Bartholomeo de las Casas, who was witness himself to those barbarities, and an unsuccessful advocate in the cause of humanity, has drawn those enormities in such colors, as to form a picture of horror almost exceeding credibility.

In this situation were the Islands of Cuba and Hispaniola,

within a very few years from their first visitation by the Spaniards. The continent, as we have observed, was at this time no farther known than a little tract in the neighborhood of the Isthmus of Panama. An expedition was now set on foot for extending the conquests of the Spaniards over the immense continent of America. Fernando Cortez, with a fleet of eleven vessels, and six hundred and seventeen men, embarked upon this expedition, and sailed from the Island of Cuba in the year 1519. It was his good fortune to meet with a Spaniard, who had been detained for some years a prisoner upon the continent, and had thus learned the language of the Mexicans. He advanced into the countiy, which he found, beyond his expectation, extremely populous and civilized. The state of Tlascala made some attempts to resist his progress, but the arms of the Spaniards, and the dreadful effect of a few small pieces of artillery, very soon dispersed and reduced them to submission. Cortez, strengthened by an alliance which he formed with these Americans, proceeded towards the empire of Mexico. The city of Mexico, situated in the middle of a lake, was the noblest monument of American industry. The historians of the times have enlarged upon its extent, its riches, and magnificence. The Mexican empire had attained at this time (which was but an hundred and thirty years from its first foundation) to a very high pitch of grandeur. The people were of a warlike and enterprising disposition. The revenues of the monarch were considerable, and his authority unbounded.

Scarce had Cortez appeared upon the frontier, when a sudden consternation seized the whole empire, and paved the way for an easy conquest. The ships, the arms, the dress of the Spaniards made the Americans regard them at first as beings of a superior nature. When Cortez arrived at the city of Mexico, he was received by the prince, Montezuma, with every mark of reverence and submission. A short stay, however, convinced the Mexicans that their invaders were men like themselves. A detached party of the Spaniards, who were on their way from Vera Cruz to Mexico, were attacked, by a secret order from Montezuma: three or four Spaniards were killed, and the emperor ordered their heads to be carried through the provinces, to destroy a belief which then prevailed among them, that the Spaniards were immortal. The measures taken by Cortez, on the intelligence of this event, were singularly characteristic of his intrepid disposition. Attended with fifty Spaniards, he repaired instantly to the palace, and in the presence of the whole court, after sharply reproving Montezuma for this instance of perfidy to those who had behaved as friends and allies, he carried off the monarch prisoner to the Spanish camp. Here, after being obliged to abandon those who had been concerned in the attack at Vera Cruz to the vengeance of their enemies, the emperor himself was put in irons, and confined in a dungeon. The astonished Mexicans submitted to every term which was required of them; they agreed to the payment of an immense tribute of gold and precious stones, part of which Cortez set aside for his master, the king of Spain, and appropriating part to himself, divided the rest among his soldiers.

Meantime, Velasquez, the governor of Cuba, jealous of that success which he was informed had attended the Spanish arms in Mexico, sent an army of eight hundred men to supersede Cortez, and to assume the government of the country. This intrepid man, leaving his conquests to be secured by fourscore of his soldiers, attacked with the rest of his troops the army of Velasquez, defeated them and forced them to submit to his command as their general. At his return to Mexico, he found his Spaniards besieged in their quarters. The Mexicans had attempted to set at liberty their captive monarch, and on the sight of the Spanish army pouring down upon them in immense numbers they attacked them with the most desperate fury. A horrible carnage ensued, which Montezuma himself endeavored to put a stop to by offering himself a mediator between the Spaniards and the Americans. The pusillanimity of this proposal struck his own subjects with the highest indignation, and an enraged Mexican pierced him to the heart with a javelin. A new emperor was instantly created, a man of an heroic character, but who met with a fate still more deplorable than his predecessor. Under the command of this monarch, whose name was Guatimozin, all Mexico was armed against the Spaniards. Day after day, the Mexican armies were defeated. The Spaniards, for the loss of a man or two, generally revenged themselves with the blood of many hundreds. Unsuccessful by land, the Mexicans attempted to bring the Spaniards to a naval engagement. The lake was covered with some thousands of armed boats, the purpose of which was to destroy a small fleet of brigantines, which, with the utmost apprehensions, the Mexicans had seen the Spaniards construct under the walls of their imperial city. This attempt proved equally unsuccessful with all the preceding. Their feeble armament of canoes was dispersed with such loss and slaughter, as convinced the Mexicans that the progress of the Europeans in knowledge and arts rendered their superiority greater on this new element than they had hitherto found it on land. In a following unsuccessful attempt, their emperor Guatimozin fell into the hands of the Spaniards. He was taken, together with his queen, and some of the bravest and most faithful of his grandees, while crossing the lake in a small vessel. He went on board the vessel of the Spanish commander with an air of dignity and composure, betraying neither fear nor surprise, and desired no favor but that the honor of his wife and her females might be spared. The Spanish captain attended but little to him, endeavoring to prevent the escape of the grandees; but Guatimozin desired him not to be anxious about them: "Not one of these brave men will fly," said he, "do not fear it—*they* are come to die at the feet of their sovereign." He was treated at first with humanity, and every persuasive made use of to prompt him to make a discovery of the place where it was supposed he had concealed his treasures; but in vain. It was next tried what torture might produce, and by the command of one of the Spanish captains, the monarch, together with some of his chief officers, were stretched naked upon burning coals. While Guatimozin bore the extremity of torment with more than human fortitude, one of his fellow-sufferers, of weaker constitution, turned his eyes upon his prince and uttered a cry of anguish: "Thinkest thou," said Guatimozin, "that I am laid upon a bed of roses?" Silenced by this reproof, the sufferer stifled his complaints, and expired in an act of obedience to his sovereign. To the honor of Cortez, he was ignorant of this act of shocking inhumanity. He was no sooner apprized of what was doing, than he hastened to rescue his noble captive while life yet remained; he kept him for three years a prisoner, till at last, discovering a formidable conspiracy that was set on foot by the prince for his release, and the destruction of the Spaniards, it was judged a necessary policy to put him to death.

The fate of Guatimozin was the last blow to the power of the Mexicans, and Cortez found himself absolute master of the whole empire.

The Spaniards, some years before this time, had ventured upon the South Seas in search of some new conquests. About the year 1527, Diego d'Almagro and Francis Pizarro, after sailing along the western coast for about three hundred leagues, landed in the empire of Peru with two hundred and fifty foot, sixty horse, and twelve small pieces of cannon. The prince of the country, named Attabalipa, was of a race of sovereigns called the Incas. They possessed an empire greatly more extensive than that of Mexico, and surpassing it in magnificence and in internal riches. The emperor Attabalipa, at the approach of the Spaniards, had drawn up his army near the city of Quito. Pizarro began with offering terms of friendship, which being disregarded, he prepared himself for a hostile assault. A monk advanced in the front of the army, holding in his hand a bible, and told the inca Attabalipa, by means of an interpreter, that it was absolutely necessary for his salvation, that he should believe all that was contained in that book. He then proceeded to set forth the doctrine of the creation, the fall of Adam, the incarnation of our Saviour, the redemption of man, the power of the apostles, and the transmission of their authority by succession to the pope of Rome, concluding with the donation made by this pope to Ferdinand and Isabella, the predecessors of the emperor

Charles V., of all the regions in the New World. In consequence of this clear deduction, he ordered the inca immediately to embrace the Christian faith, acknowledge the pope's supremacy, and the lawful authority of the emperor Charles V. This strange harangue excited equal astonishment and indignation. The inca, however, deigned to take the book from the hands of the priest, and after eagerly looking at its characters, "Is *this*," says he, "your authority? it is silent, it tells *me nothing;*" and with these words he threw it disdainfully upon the ground. The monk instantly summoned the Spaniards to avenge this impious profanation: they rushed upon the Peruvians with the most savage fury, and massacring all before them, till they arrived at the person of the inca, they brought him off a prisoner to their camp, and loaded him with irons. The terror and dejection of the Peruvians were extreme. The inca promised an immense ransom to obtain his liberty, as much gold as would fill one of the palaces. The promise was not performed in its utmost extent, and this disappointment exasperated his conquerors to such a degree, that the unfortunate inca was condemned to the flames, with a promise of a mitigation of his punishment in case he should embrace the Christian religion. The terrors of a cruel death prevailed on Attabalipa to receive the sacrament of baptism; and immediately thereafter he was strangled at a stake. The same punishment was inflicted on several of the Peruvian chiefs, who, from a principle of generous magnanimity, chose rather to suffer death than disclose the treasures of the empire to its inhuman and insatiable invaders.

The courage of the Spaniards, however, and their enterprising genius, was equal to their inhumanity. Diego d' Almagro marched to Cuzco, through an extent of country where he met with continual opposition, and he even penetrated as far as Chili, two degrees south of the tropic of Capricorn. In Cuzco, a civil war broke out between him and his associate, Francis Pizarro, and what is scarcely to be believed, the Peruvians, instead of profiting by these discords to revenge the injuries of their country, divided themselves between the two parties, and fought against each other under the standards of their tyrants. D'Almagro was taken prisoner, and beheaded by order of his rival, Pizarro, who was himself assassinated soon after, by some of the party of his antagonist.

During this civil war were discovered the mines of Potosi, with which the Peruvians themselves had been unacquainted; a source of riches which to this day is not exhausted. The Peruvians were made to work at these mines for the Spaniards, as the real proprietors. Those slaves, who, from constitutional weakness of body, were soon worn out by the dreadful fatigues which they underwent without the smallest remission of their labors, were replaced by negroes from the coast of Africa, who were transported to Peru as asts of burden of a hardier species.

The policy of Spain with regard to her American colonies is explained at large with great accuracy and ingenuity by Robertson. It is sufficient here to give a general idea of it. The establishments of the Spaniards in the New World, though fatal to its ancient inhabitants, were made at a period when that monarchy was capable of forming them to the best advantage. Spain, by the union of its kingdoms under Ferdinand and Isabella, had become a very powerful state. The increase of the dominions of an empire, naturally tends to increase the powers of the monarch; for in every wide-extended empire the government must be simple and the authority absolute, that his resolutions may be taken with promptitude, and pervade the whole with undiminished force.

Such was the power of the Spanish monarchs, when they were called to deliberate concerning the mode of establishing their dominion over the extent of their new territories. With regard to these they found themselves under no constitutional restraint: they issued edicts and laws for modelling the government of these colonies by a mere act of prerogative. This was very far from being the case with regard to the other European nations, the Portuguese, the English, and the French: and the difference was in a great measure owing to the very inconsiderable advantages which these infant colonies promised to their European masters, and which, therefore, were insufficient to make the state watch over them as a valuable object of attention.

The great maxim of the Spanish jurisprudence with regard to America was to hold the acquisitions in that country to be rather vested in the crown than in the state. The papal bull of Alexander VI. bestowed, as an absolute donation upon Ferdinand and Isabella, all the regions that had been, or might be, discovered in the New World. It was natural, therefore, that the sovereign should have the absolute regulation of what had been conferred on him as a right of property. In every thing, therefore, which relates to the government of the Spanish colonies, the will of the sovereign was a law, the revenues his own, and the officers and magistrates in his sole nomination.

Soon after the acquisition of those territories, they were divided by the Spanish monarch into two immense governments, each under the administration of a viceroy, one of whom commanded in Mexico, or New Spain, and the other in the empire of Peru. The inconvenience and hardships which had flowed from the subjection of such immense tracts of country to a governor, whose residence was necessarily at a distance from a great part of the provinces under his jurisdiction, occasioned the establishment of the third viceroy, whose command extends over the whole tract denominated Terra Firma, and the province of Quito. These viceroys possessed the regal prerogatives in their utmost extent. They exercised supreme authority in every department of government, civ and military. By them, or by the king of

Spain, the conduct of civil affairs in the various provinces and districts was committed to magistrates of different orders, who were responsible to the jurisdiction of the viceroy. There were eleven audiences or tribunals for the administration of justice in causes civil and criminal; and in order to check that inconvenience and grievance which might result from the supreme authority of one man pervading every department of the administration, the viceroys were prohibited from interfering in the judicial proceedings of any of these courts of audience, which, on the other hand, were even entitled to examine and take cognizance of his political regulations, in some particular cases in which any question of civil right is involved. The jurisdiction of the audiences, however, was final only in questions where the property in dispute did not exceed 600 pieces of eight, or £825 sterling: should it exceed that sum, their decisions were subject to review, and might be carried, by appeal, before the royal council of the Indies.

In this great council was vested the supreme government of all the Spanish dominions in America. Its jurisdiction extended to every department, ecclesiastical, civil, military, and commercial. All laws and ordinances must receive its approbation. To it each person employed in America, from the viceroy downward, was accountable. From the first institution of this council, it had been the constant object of the catholic monarchs to maintain its authority, and to render it formidable to all the subjects in the New World. For the regulation of commercial affairs, a tribunal was established in Spain, called Casa de la Contratacion, which may be considered both as a board of trade, and as a court of judicature. It regulated the departure of the fleets for the West Indies, the freight and burden of the ships, their equipment and destination. In these departments its decisions were exempted from the review of any court but that of the council of the Indies.

Such are the great outlines of that system of government which Spain established in her American colonies.

The gold and silver mines of that continent were, at first, of no use but to the kings of Spain and to the merchants; but by degrees the circulation of these metals was more equally distributed, and the value of specie diminished all over Europe very nearly in the same proportion. The means by which this circulation was produced are not difficult to be accounted for. The enterprises of Charles V. made a large distribution of the Spanish gold into Germany and Italy. The marriage of his son Philip with queen Mary of England brought a great acquisition of treasure into that country; and the wars of Philip in the Netherlands are said to have cost him above three thousand millions of livres. Notwithstanding likewise the most severe prohibitions of the kings of Spain, precluding all other nations from any share of commerce with Spanish America, a most extensive trade has, from those times down to the present, subsisted between the Spanish ports and most of the kingdoms of Europe, even through the medium of the Spaniards themselves. The fact is, the wants of her colonies in America could not be supplied by her home productions or exports. These must be furnished by other nations, but as it was still through the medium of Spanish merchants, even this violation of their laws contributed, in effect, very considerably to their profit and emolument.

The example of the Spaniards, who were supposed to derive much more substantial advantages from their possessions in the New World than they have actually done, had roused the jealousy of the other European nations, and excited a desire to participate with them in the riches of this immense tract of inhabited country. Under Henry II. of France, the successor of Francis I., a project was set on foot in the year 1557, by the admiral Coligni, to form an establishment upon the coast of Brazil, where the Portuguese had already settled themselves from the beginning of the century. The expedition embarked, but it was torn by intestine divisions, and was soon utterly destroyed by the Portuguese, who possessed themselves of almost the whole of Brazil, one of the richest and most flourishing establishments in all America.

In North America, the Spaniards were already in possession of that peninsula now termed Florida, to which the French likewise pretended a right, from the circumstance of one of their cruizers having touched there much about the same time. To make good these pretensions, Coligni again sent out a colony in the year 1564, which, as the former had been ruined by the Portuguese, was now cut to pieces and annihilated by the Spaniards. The French, some years afterwards, notwithstanding these unsuccessful attempts, fitted out, principally at the charges of a private mercantile company, a small fleet, with which they established a colony in Canada, with a view to a trade of furs. There the city of Quebec was founded in the year 1608, at that time a collection of insignificant huts, and which only since the beginning of the last century has begun to figure among the towns of North America. A few Jesuits, and some protestants whom accident attracted to that country, contributed to the cultivation of this infant colony, which, however, continually suffered from the depredations of the Indians and from the attacks of the English. The French were so completely overpowered, that about the year 1629 they had not a foot of territory upon the continent of America. Cardinal Richelieu, however, at the instigation of those merchants who had suffered by the loss of the Canadian colony, stipulated, in the treaty of Saint Germains, that it should be restored to the French. The country remained for some time in a miserable condition, and was again retaken by the English in the year 1654; since this period it has changed its master no less than six times, and is now in the hands of the British.

The most profitable and important possessions which the French ever acquired in the Western hemisphere were, the half of the island of St. Domingo, Guadaloupe, Martinico, with some of the small islands of the Antilles.

England derived the right to her settlements in North America from the first discovery of the country by Sebastian Cabot, in the reign of Henry VII., about six years after the discovery of South America by Columbus. At that time North America was in general denominated Newfoundland, a name which is only retained by a large island on the coast of Labrador. The first attempt to plant colonies in North America was not till near a century after this period, under the reign of queen Elizabeth, when Sir Walter Raleigh founded the settlement of Virginia, so named in honor of the sovereign. The colony of Nova Scotia was planted some years afterwards by James I.; and New England was not the resort of any British subjects, till the religious dissensions in the beginning of the reign of Charles I. drove many who were disaffected to the worship of the national church, and sought an unrestrained liberty of conscience, to transplant themselves into that province. New York and Pennsylvania were in the hands of the Dutch till they were conquered by the English, in the reign of Charles II., when, in reward of the services of admiral Penn, a gift of the latter was made to his son, the famous William Penn the quaker. He obtained for his followers a valuable charter of privileges, which, reserving the sovereignty to the crown, allowed to the subject the utmost latitude of civil and religious liberty. Maryland was peopled during the reign of Charles I. by English Roman catholics, as New England had been by the puritans; but the bulk of the inhabitants are now protestants. The Carolinas were settled in the reign of Charles II. Georgia was not colonized till the middle of the eighteenth century, in the reign of George II. The Floridas were ceded to Britain by the treatv of peace in 1763.

CHAPTER XXII.

AGE OF LEO X.—State of the Arts under the Goths—Revival in Italy—Cimabue—Academy for Painting instituted at Florence, 1350—Michael Angelo, Raphael, and Leonardo da Vinci—The different Italian Schools—Flemish School—Dutch Statuary and Architecture—Art of Engraving.

IN enumerating those great features in the history of the progress of the human mind, which exhibited themselves at the end of the fifteenth and beginning of the sixteenth centuries, we remarked the high advancement to which the fine arts attained in Europe, in the age of Leo X.

There are periods in which the human genius seems to turn strongly to one particular direction. In one period the reasoning faculty seems chiefly to delight in contemplating its own powers, the nature and operations of the mind; in another, perhaps the imagination reigns predominant, and the general taste is attracted to works of fancy in poetry or romance. In another era the mechanic or the useful arts engross the general attention, and are cultivated with high success; in a fourth, as in the period of which we now treat, the popular taste, delighted with the contemplation of beautiful forms, bestows its chief attention on the fine arts of painting, sculpture, and architecture

The causes which give the bent or direction to the general taste, and consequently operate in the production of artists, or men eminent in the several departments of literature, sciences, and the arts, are not easily ascertained. That a great deal is owing to the operation of moral causes, I believe is certain; but I doubt greatly if they alone are sufficient to account for this remarkable distinction, of eras favorable and unfavorable for particular arts and sciences. By moral causes, I mean such as the following:—the peaceful or happy situation of a country; the genius or taste of a prince, directed to one particular department of science or of art, together with a liberal disposition to encourage those who are eminent in that department; the accidental circumstance of a few illustrious men contributing by their favor to bring artists into observation and repute, and by their example promoting a fashionable relish for their productions. To these we may add, what, perhaps, has no less influence, the aid derived by one artist from the studies of another; and the emulation that naturally takes place among all the professors of an art, where there are one or two of distinguished excellence.

These causes have unquestionably a very great influence in rendering certain periods more or less favorable than others ; and we may observe in general, with regard to the fine arts, that, in order to their advancement, a state of society is required, wherein men can devote more attention to their pleasures than to their wants. The nation which enjoys peace and security, and where a great proportion of the people possess such a degree of wealth as to exempt them from laborious occupation, is the true soil for these arts to grow and flourish ; and where any of the causes before-mentioned join their operation, it is not surprising that, under such advantages, they should attain a very high degree of perfection.

Yet still I am inclined to doubt if even all these, concurring, are sufficient to account for this phenomenon in its full extent. In the first place, we find that history shows many periods where most of these causes, sometimes all, have concurred, yet the effect has not resulted. Princes have inherited a taste for the fine arts, and lavished their rewards upon indifferent artists. Nations have enjoyed peace, and ease, and opulence, and individuals have sought with eagerness the productions of art of other countries and of other ages, because their own age and country was barren. In the next place, we find that, in those golden ages of the arts, the transition from a bad to a good taste, from obscurity to splendor, was so rapid and instantaneous, as not at all to resemble the slow and gradual operation of moral causes. In those ages the torch of genius seems to have dropped at once from heaven, and to have kindled all in a blaze around it.

In the period of ancient history, we have seen that remarkable splendor to which the fine arts arose in the age of Pericles. In modern times the age of Leo X. is an era equally distinguished.

The art of painting lay long buried in the west, under the ruins of the Roman empire. It declined in the latter ages with the universal decay of taste and genius, and needed not an irruption of the Goths to lay it in the dust. The Ostrogoths, who subdued Italy, that people who were barbarians only in name, had they found it in splendor, would have industriously cherished and preserved it, as they did every monument of ancient grandeur or of beauty : but painting and sculpture were never high among the ancient Romans ; and that the taste and genius for the imitative arts underwent a regular and natural decay, we have the strongest proof in examining the series of the coins of the lower empire.

Such of the arts as were found by the Goths, upon the conquest of Italy, were carefully preserved by them. Muratori, in treating of those ages, informs us, that Theodelinda, queen of the Lombards, about the year 592, built a palace, in which she caused paintings to be put up, representing the heroic actions of the Lombards. That paintings were used in the churches under the

Gothic monarchy in Spain, in a very early period, we know from one of the canons of the council of Eliberi, held in the year 305, which prohibits them as idolatrous.

Instead of extinguishing and suppressing, there is even a probability that the Goths were the improvers, if not the actual inventors, of some of the arts dependent on design. A collection of receipts are given by Muratori, from an ancient manuscript, written in the most barbarous Latin,—from which, however, t is evident that the Goths, at that time, possessed a pretty extensive knowledge in the ornamental arts, particularly in that of the composition of mosaic. That they possessed taste and genius I will not pretend to assert. It is even probable that the mechanical knowledge which showed itself in those ages was in the subsequent times greatly diminished. The fine arts are said to have been revived in Italy by artists from Greece; and it seems highly probable that in that country, which had been eminently distinguished by their splendor and perfection, the taste should have been less entirely lost than in any other.

The most common notion is, that, about the end of the thirteenth century, Cimabue, a Florentine, observing the works of two Grecian artists, who had been sent for to paint one of the churches at Florence, began to attempt something of the same kind, and soon conceived that it would not be difficult to surpass such rude performances. His works were the admiration of his time; he had his scholars and his imitators; among these were Ghiotto, Gaddi, Tasi Cavallini, and Stephano Florentino; and the number of artists continued so to increase, that an academy for painting was instituted at Florence in the year 1350.

Still, however, the art was extremely low, and the artists, with great industry, seem to have had no spark of genius. The successors of Cimabue and of Ghiotto seem all to have painted in one manner. Their works are distinguished by a hard and rigid outline, sharp angles of the limbs, and stiff folds in the drapery; a contour, in short, in which there is not the smallest grace or elegance. Such, with little variation or improvement, was the manner of painting for above two centuries. The best artists valued themselves on the most scrupulous and servile imitation of nature, without any capacity of distinguishing her beauties and deformities. In painting a head, it was the highest pitch of excellence that all the wrinkles of the skin should be most distinctly marked, and that the spectator should be able to count every hair on the beard. Such was the state of painting till towards the end of the fifteenth century, when all at once, as if by some supernatural influence, it attained at a single step to the summit of perfection.

Nothing can more clearly demonstrate that the splendor, to which the fine arts all at once attained, at the period of which we now speak, was owing entirely to natural genius, and not to accidental causes, than this circumstance, that though many remains of the finest sculpture of the ancients existed, and were known in Italy for some centuries preceding this era, it was not till this time that they began to serve as models of imitation. Ghiotto, Cimabue, and their scholars, had seen some of the ancient statues, and many antique basso-relievos met the eye in almost every street in Rome; but they had looked on them with the most frigid indifference: the case was, they found in them nothing conformable to their own miserable taste. These works now began to be regarded with other eyes. Michael Angelo, Leonardo da Vinci, and Raphael arose, men animated with the same genius that had formed the Grecian Apelles, Zeuxis, Phidias, Glycon, and Praxiteles.

And the prodigy was not confined to Rome: Florence, Venice, and other cities of Italy, produced in the same period many geniuses, self-taught like them, who left at an infinite distance all that had gone before them in the path of the arts. Nor was that genius even peculiar to Italy: Germany, Flanders, and Switzerland produced in the same age artists whose works are yet the admiration of Europe. Of these we shall speak in their turn, after having shortly characterized the greatest of the Italian masters, and the several schools of which the different merits are distinct and peculiar.

As the most ancient, and not the least remarkable of these, the school of Florence, deserves to be first mentioned. Of this, the first of the great painters was Michael Angelo Buonarotti, born in the year 1474, whose works attracting the notice of pope Julius II., he was called from Florence to Rome, where he has left in the pontifical palace and in the churches some of the most sublime specimens of his art. A most profound intelligence of anatomy, and a skill in design, formed upon the contemplation of the ancient sculptures, characterize the works of Michael Angelo. He understood most perfectly the human figure, but delighted too much to display his knowledge by exhibiting it in forced and violent attitudes. The subjects of his paintings are happily chosen to exhibit the grand, the sublime, and even the terrible; but he is ignorant of the beautiful. The strength with which he characterizes the muscles of the human body, and the violent fore-shortenings of limbs, are suitable to the persons of heroes, demi-gods, and devils, and these he has most happily represented; but his women are as muscular as the ordinary race of men, and his men are too much beyond nature.* Michael Angelo seems to have studied the human body divested of the skin, where the beginning and termination of the muscles are distinctly seen, and their separation marked by strong lines.

---

* The merit of Michael Angelo was never more truly or forcibly expressed than by a Frenchman, the sculptor Falconet, who, after viewing two of his statues, observed—"J'ai vu Michel Ange—il est effrayant."

The paintings of Michael Angelo are models of design; they are drawn with infinite skill, and to a young artist might almost supersede the imitation of the human figure, and the knowledge of anatomy; but they will not supply the place of the antique; for from that fountain Michael Angelo has adopted nothing else but skill and correctness of outline, without aiming at the attainment of grace or beauty; that was reserved for Raphael.

The Roman school owed its origin to Raphael, who was born at Urbino, in the year 1483. He soon departed from the dry manner of his master, Perugino, and formed to himself one peculiarly his own, in which he has wonderfully united almost every excellence of the art. His invention and composition are admirable, his attitudes grand and sublime, his female figures in the highest degree beautiful. He understood the anatomy of the human figure as well as Michael Angelo, but he never offends by a harsh delineation of the muscles. His skill in the *chiaro-oscuro*, or in the effect of light and shade, is beyond that of Michael Angelo, and his coloring very far superior to him. In the action of his figures there is nothing violent and constrained, but all is moderate, simple, and gracefully majestic. Many painters there are, excellent in different departments, and several that, in one single department, may be found to exceed even Raphael; but in that supreme excellence which consists in the union of all the various merits of the art, he stands unrivalled, and far removed from all competition.

In representing female beauty, Raphael has gone beyond every other artist, and even beyond the antique itself. In his Madonnas, in his St. Cecilia, and in his Galatea, imagination cannot reach a finer conformation of features. In painting the Galatea, he says himself in one of his letters, that, unable to find among the most beautiful women that exellence which he aimed at, he made use of a certain divine form or idea, which presented itself to his imagination.*

In his portraits, he seems to have confined himself to the perfect imitation of nature, without desire to raise or embellish, but without that minute and servile accuracy which distinguishes the works in that style of some of the Flemish masters.

The union of all these excellences, which has placed Raphael at the head of all the painters that ever the world produced, was attained by a youth, who never reached the middle period of life. Raphael died at the age of thirty-seven. What may we suppose he would have been had he lived to the age of Titian or Leonardo da Vinci?

The school of Lombardy, or the Venetian school, arose in the same age; of which the most eminent artists were Titian, Giorgione, Correggio, and Parmegiano. Titian, by the strength of

* See Bellori, Descriz. delle imagine da Raff. d'Urbino

genius alone, and with much fewer advantages than Michael Angelo or Raphael, attained to a very high degree of excellence The praise of Titian in painting the human body is, that it is nature itself. In portrait, therefore, he peculiarly excelled, and, above all, in the representation of female beauty. Without an extreme brilliancy, there is such propriety and truth in his coloring, that his naked figures seem animated flesh. His historical pieces are not numerous: perhaps he wanted invention, and did not excel in composition; but in the introduction of a few figures, he often unites the grace and dignity of Raphael. Leo X., who wished to make Rome the centre of all excellence in the fine arts, would have tempted Titian thither with very splendid offers. He was invited at the same time by Francis I. to reside in France, and by Henry VIII. to the court of England. The emperor Charles V. bestowed on him the highest honors and rewards. But Venice was the residence which he chose; and wherever he himself might remain, he knew that his works would find their way over all Europe. To the merit of Titian there can be no higher testimony than that of Michael Angelo, who declared, that had it been his fortune to have studied at Rome or Florence, amid the great masterpieces of antiquity, he would have eclipsed all the painters in the world.

Giorgione, the rival of Titian, of the same school, had he lived, might have attained perhaps to equal reputation, but he died at the age of thirty-three. Titian lived to the age of one hundred.

Of the same Venetian school, and contemporary with these, were Correggio and Parmegiano. The art of coloring, though carried to a great height by Raphael and by Titian, was not brought to perfection. Correggio, in this respect, was superior to all that preceded, perhaps all that have followed him. The effect of light and shade, though often eminently conspicuous in the works of Raphael and of Titian, seems in these painters to be frequently accidental; as in some of their paintings it is not at all striking. But in Correggio it was the result of study, and was always surprising. From this intimate knowledge of the power of colors artfully contrasted, and the effect arising from a judicious distribution of strong lights and shades, the pictures of Correggio are perhaps more generally pleasing than those of any other painter. Divested of these, and considered only in the outline or design, they are not possessed of consummate merit. In that particular, Raphael and Michael Angelo are so infinitely superior as to be beyond all comparison with other painters.

Francesco Parmegiano had so thoroughly adopted the graceful manner of Raphael, that it was said the soul of that great painter had, after his death, found itself a new body. But the figures of Parmegiano, though highly graceful, have often a degree of affectation: *his* is that grace which is the result of study, whereas in

Raphael it is the result of ease and nature. His taste perhaps might have become more chaste and simple as he advanced in years, but he died at the age of thirty-six. These three—the Florentine, the Roman, and the Venetian—are the chief of the Italian schools of painting. The Florentine is distinguished by grandeur and sublimity, and great excellence of design; but a want of grace, of beauty of coloring, and skill in the *chiaro-oscuro*. The character of the Roman is equal excellence of design, a grandeur, tempered with moderation and simplicity, a high degree of grace and elegance, and a superior knowledge, though not an excellence in coloring. The characteristic of the Venetian is the perfection of coloring, and the utmost force of the *chiaro-oscuro*, with an inferiority in every other particular.

These original schools gave birth to many others. To the school of Raphael succeeded that of the Caraccis, which may be termed the second Roman school. The Caraccis were three brothers, all of them eminent in their art, but of whom Annibal was the most excellent. He left many scholars of great reputation, as Guercino, Albano, Lanfranc, Dominechino, and Guido. Guercino distinguished himself by a graceful and very correct design: the airs of his heads are admirable. Albano painted nymphs, goddesses, and Cupids, with great beauty and delicacy, and in a most pleasing style of coloring: the landscape of his pieces is in general extremely fine. Lanfranc painted chiefly in fresco, and with great force and beauty. Dominechino excelled in character and expression, and Guido in strength and sweetness, with which he united a great deal of majesty. His coloring, however, is in general cold and unpleasant, unless in the famous picture of the Aurora, where he has given all the splendor of coloring which the subject required.

In the age of Leo X. the Flemish school likewise produced its masters, who, though in a different style, and very inferior to the Italian, had, like them, taken a very surprising stretch beyond the abilities of their predecessors. Nature was the prototype of the Flemish, and the antique that of the Italians. John Van Eyk, a Fleming, had, about the beginning of the fifteenth century, found out (or at least greatly improved) the manner of tempering the colors with oil instead of water; and this invention, which gave to painting a greater durability, as well as a warmth more approaching to nature, was very soon adopted by the artists of Flanders, of Germany, and of Italy. In Flanders, Heemskirk, Martin Vos, Frans Florus, and Quintin Matsys, were deservedly distinguished. In Germany, Albert Durer raised the reputation of the art of painting, which in that country was till then extremely low. Without the least conception of the beauties of the antique, this artist, by ability in design and skilfulness of composition, has produced some wonderful pieces. In his heads there is something uncommonly excellent; but the bodies of his figures are lean weak, and ungraceful; and we seldom find in any of his works a happy effect of light and shade: yet in this painter there was so much of an original genius, that Raphael himself admired and valued his productions.

Among the Flemish painters, such at least as were so by nation, Rubens has unquestionably attained the highest rank. He studied with perfect intelligence the ancient models, as well as the works of the best of the Italian artists: but such is the force of a natural and constitutional taste, that his figures, though eminently beautiful, are of that style of beauty, which is peculiar to his own country. To the eye of an Italian the female figures of Rubens are too corpulent to be graceful; to us they are less exceptionable, because they approach nearer to that style of figure with which we are accustomed. In point of drawing, intelligence of anatomy, and the use of the muscles, Rubens is supremely excellent.

Switzerland, too, in this remarkable age, produced a painter of uncommon excellence; this was Hans Holbein. The latter pieces of this artist, probably painted after he had seen some of the works of the schools of Italy, are extremely pleasing. Holbein excelled in the knowledge of the *chiaro-oscuro*, and was an able colorist.

England, it would appear, at this time, had begun to manifest a taste in the fine arts. Erasmus, the friend of Holbein, persuaded that painter to travel to England, as the best field of encouragement for his merit. There the painter lived for many years in high favor with Henry VIII. and the chancellor Sir Thomas More. He was a most industrious artist; and there are at this day more of the works of Holbein in Britain, than in any other country of Europe.

Holland had likewise at this time its remarkable painters, of whom the chief merit was a most accurate representation of nature, but without any selection of the beautiful from the deformed; and often with a preference for the low, vulgar, and ludicrous. It is such nature, however, as is suited to the generality of tastes, for there are but a few who have a real feeling for the sublime and beautiful.

With the art of painting, those of sculpture and architecture were likewise revived and brought to high perfection. In sculpture, Michael Angelo stands unrivalled among the moderns. He has produced some works which are even equal to the antique. His statue of Bacchus is so exquisitely formed as to have deceived even Raphael, who judged it to be the work of Phidias or Praxiteles. But of all the sculptors of modern times, no other artist has approached near to the merit of the antique, nor have there been, in that department, an equal number who excelled as in painting. No position certainly can be worse founded than that of the Abbé du Bos, who maintains that to excel in sculpture does not require so great a degree of genius as to be eminent in painting. That this notion is erroneous, there cannot be a stronger proof than the comparative numbers of eminent painters and sculptors. For one capital sculptor in the age of Leo, who was Michael Angelo, there existed ten capital painters.

The age of Leo was, likewise, the era of a good taste in architecture. The Grecian mode of architecture, which for many ages sunk entirely into neglect, while the Gothic was universally prevalent, began gradually to recover about the beginning of the fourteenth century. The Florentines, from their commercial voyages into the Levant, and intercourse with Greece, were the first who reëstablished the Grecian architecture in Italy. The church of St. Miniato, which was built at Florence in the year 1300, showed the first specimen of the renewed architecture of the ancients. The cathedral of Pisa, built soon after, was constructed by Buschetto, a Grecian architect, who introduced into it some entire columns which had been brought from the ruins of some of the ancient temples in Greece. This magnificent building served as a model for many others constructed in Italy about the same time.

From this period, architecture continued slowly advancing for about two centuries, till it was brought to great perfection in the age of Leo. Bramante, who had carefully studied all the best remains of the ancient buildings in Italy, had been chosen by Julius II. to design the plan of St. Peter's church, and upon his plan that immense and noble structure was begun. It was afterwards superintended by different artists of great eminence, by San Gallo, by Raphael, and by Michael Angelo, and varied probably by each of these in many particulars from its original plan.

Verona likewise, remarkable for some of the most entire and noblest monuments of ancient building, particularly its great amphitheatre, produced in this age many excellent architects—Jocondo, who raised several noble buildings for Lewis XII. of France; San Michael, who adorned his native city with some works in the true manner of antiquity, as did likewise Maria Falconetti But all yielded to the universal genius of Michael Angelo, who, equally eminent in all the works of design, painting, sculpture, and architecture, applied himself in the latter part of his life chiefly to architecture The church of St. Peter owes to him its greatest beauty; and as that building is deservedly esteemed one of the most perfect models of architecture in the world, we must thence conclude Michael Angelo to have been one of the greatest architects.

In treating of the state of the fine arts in the age of Leo X., the art of engraving deserves to be particularly taken notice of, as one of the finest of the modern inventions, and of which the first discovery was but a few years prior to the period of which we now treat. The Italians, the Germans, the Flemish, and the Dutch, have all contended for the honor of this invention. The opinion best founded is, that engraving had its origin in Italy. Tomaso Finiguerra, a goldsmith of Florence, about the year 1460, discovered the method of taking off impressions from engraved silver plates with wet paper, which he pressed upon them with a roller. Andrea Mantigna, a painter, bethought himself of multiplying by that means copies of his own designs. From Italy the art travelled into Flanders, where it was first practised by Martin Schoen of Antwerp, of whose works there remain a very few prints, which are the most ancient engravings now known.

His scholar was the celebrated Albert Durer, who far surpassed his master in abilities. He engraved with excellence in copper and in wood, and of his pieces a very great number have reached the present time. Considered as the first efforts of a new art, they have great merit. In some of those prints which he executed on silver and on copper, the engraving is elegant to a great degree. The immediate successors of Albert Durer were Lucas of Leyden, Aldegrave, and Sebald Behem, or Hisbens, who all engraved very much in the manner of Albert. In Italy, at the same time, Parmegiano had begun to etch some of his own beautiful designs, and is, by many, supposed to have been the inventor of the mode of engraving by means of aquafortis, which expresses the design of the artist with much greater freedom and spirit than the labored stroke of the graver, though its lines have less softness and delicacy: a combination of the two is, therefore, most happily employed by the modern artist, and is productive of an excellent effect, especially in landscape. In Italy, likewise, Mark Antonio and Agostino, contemporaries of Parmegiano, were successfully employed in making engravings from the works of Raphael. These engravings were then much sought after, and are yet in request on account of their antiquity; but in point of merit, and as giving an idea of the beauties of the original, they have been infinitely surpassed by the works of posterior engravers.

There is no art whatever, which, from its first discovery, has undergone so rapid an improvement as that of engraving. When we compare the prints of Albert Durer, or of Lucas of Leyden, with those of Goltzius, engraved about seventy years after, the difference is perfectly astonishing. But when we come down about eighty years farther, and examine the prints of Poilly, Audran, and Edelinck, we are ready to acknowledge a proportional improvement. From that time to the present, in some respects the advancement has been equally sensible, though in others not so apparent. It must be readily confessed that the landscapes of Woollet are greatly superior to those of Bolowert, Saddeler, and Bloemart; but it is a little doubtful whether the historical pieces of Strange, of Bartolozzi and Cunego, surpass those of Poilly, Edelinck, and Treij. This superiority has been achieved by Raphael Morghen.

The moderns, who have carried the use of the graver to a very great height, and have confessedly much improved in the art of etching, have now laid aside one mode of engraving practised by the ancient artists, and brought by them to a very great degree of perfection—engraving in wood with different tints, which was performed by different plates. The inventor of this art was Ugo da Carpi, an Italian ; and it was brought to great perfection by Andrea Andreani, of Mantua. The spaces of white and the washes of which the middle tint is composed, give to these prints all the softness of drawing ; and some experiments have been made in the same way with different colors, which give these performances in some degree the effect of painting.

As I shall not have another opportunity of particularly mentioning the arts dependent on design, it would be improper to quit the subject without taking notice of a mode of engraving different from all those I have mentioned, though its invention belongs to a period considerably later than that of which we now treat : I mean the mode of engraving in mezzo-tinto. It was invented by the celebrated prince Rupert, son of the elector Palatine, about the year 1650 ; and the hint was conceived from observing the effect of rust upon a soldier's fusil, in covering the surface of the iron with innumerable small holes at regular distances. Rupert, who was a great mechanical genius and virtuoso, concluded that a contrivance might be found to cover a plate of copper with such a regular ground of holes so closely pierced as to give a black impression, which, if scraped away in proper parts, would leave the rest of the paper white; that thus light and shade might be as finely blended, or as strongly distinguished, as by the pencil in painting. He tried the experiment by means of an indented steel roller, and it succeeded to his wishes. A crenulated chisel is now used to make the rough ground in place of the roller. This art has been brought to very high perfection. Its characteristic is a softness equal to that of the pencil, and it is therefore particularly adapted to portraits ; and nothing except the power of colors can express flesh more naturally, the flowing of hair, the folds of drapery, or the reflection from polished surfaces. Its defect is, that where there is one great mass of shade in the picture, it wants an outline to detach and distinguish the different parts, which are thus almost lost in one entire shade ; but in the blending of light and shade there is no other mode of engraving that approaches to it in excellence.

The age of Leo, though principally distinguished by the perfection of the arts of design, was likewise a period of very considerable literary splendor. Ariosto, Bembo, and Sadolet, divided the favor of Leo and the esteem of the public with Raphael and Michael Angelo. Guicciardini in the same period rivalled the best historians of antiquity, and Machiavel shone equally in history, politics, philosophy, and poetry. But the literary genius of this age will come to be more particularly treated afterwards in giving a connected view of the progress of literature and of the arts an sciences from the beginning of the sixteenth to the end of th seventeenth century.

CHAPTER XXIII.

SURVEY of the STATE of the PRINCIPAL KINGDOMS of ASIA in the SIXTEENTH and SEVENTEENTH CENTURIES: — Selim reduces Egypt — Solyman takes Rhodes—subdues Hungary, Moldavia, and Wallachia—Selim II. takes Cyprus—Battle of Lepanto—Persians under Shah Abbas—Government and Religion—Tartars—India, early Particulars of—Aurungzebe—Brahmins —Divisions of Castes.

THE Turks, we have seen, in the middle of the fifteenth century, subverted the empire of Constantinople, which from that period became the imperial seat of the Ottoman dominion. In treating of that great revolution, I took occasion to offer some considerations on the government and political constitution of the Turkish empire—that great fabric of despotism.

The Turks proceeded to extend their conquests. Mahomet II. subdued a great extent of territory. Selim I. added new conquests. In the year 1515, he made himself master of Syria and Mesopotamia, and undertook the reduction of Egypt, which was then in the possession of the Mamelukes, a race of Circassians who had been masters of that country ever since the last crusade. The arms of Selim put an end to their dominion; but, what is a very extraordinary fact, he allowed the last of the Mameluke kings to govern Egypt in the quality of his bashaw; and these Mamelukes, though nominally under the dominion of the grand signior, continued in reality the sovereigns of the country, acknowledging but a very slender subjection to the Ottoman power.

Solyman, the son of Selim, who is termed Solyman the Magnificent, was a formidable enemy to the Christians and to the Persians. He took the Island of Rhodes in the year 1521. The knights of St. John were at this time in possession of this island, from which they had expelled the Saracens in 1310. They made a noble defence, assisted by the English, Italians, and Spaniards; but after a siege of many months were forced to capitulate. Solyman, a few years afterwards, subdued the greatest part of Hungary, Moldavia, and Wallachia. He failed in his attempt upon Vienna; but turning his arms eastward against the Persians, he made himself master of Bagdad and subdued Georgia. He concluded a treaty of alliance with the

French, which subsisted for two centuries. His son, Selim II., in the year 1571, took the island of Cyprus from the Venetians; and this industrious people were carrying on a brisk trade with the Turks at the very time that they were making this conquest. Genoa, Florence, and Marseilles were rivals with Venice in the trade of Turkey, for the silks and commodities of Asia. It is remarkable that the Christian nations have traded with the Ottoman empire to a very large extent, without its ever having been known that a Turkish vessel came into their ports for the purposes of commerce, in return for the vast fleets which they annually send to those of Turkey. All the trading nations of Christendom have consuls who reside in the seaports on the Levant, and most of them have ambassadors at the Ottoman Porte, while none are sent from thence to *reside* with other nations.

The Venetians, sensibly feeling the loss of Cyprus,—which, besides the advantages of its produce, was a most convenient *entrepôt* for their trade to the Levant—and finding their own force insufficient for its recovery from the Turks, applied to pope Pius V. for the benefit of a crusade. The pope gave them more effectual aid, by waging war himself against the Ottoman empire, and by entering into a league for that purpose both with the Venetians and with Philip II. of Spain, the son and successor of Charles V. Pius, who was a good politician and a great economist, had amassed, in the course of his pontificate, such wealth as to render the holy see a very formidable power. The wealth of Philip II. was considered at that time as inexhaustible. A great armament was immediately fitted out, consisting of two hundred and fifty ships of war, with fifty transports. Don John of Austria, brother of Philip, (a natural son of Charles V.,) was admiral of the fleet. Historians compute that the number of men on board was fifty thousand. The fleet of the Turks, who had not been wanting in their preparations, consisted likewise of two hundred and fifty galleys. These powerful armaments met in the Gulf of Lepanto, near Corinth, and an engagement ensued, more memorable than any naval fight that had happened since the battle of Actium. All the ancient and all the modern weapons of war were used in this sea-fight, which terminated to the honor of the Christians. The Turks lost above one hundred and fifty ships; the number of their slain is said to have been fifteen thousand; and among these was Ali, the admiral of their fleet, whose head was cut off and fixed upon the top of his flag.*

Don John of Austria acquired by this signal victory a very high degree of reputation, which was still heightened by the taking of Tunis, about two years after. But from these successes the Christians, after all, did not derive any lasting advantage; for

* In the battle of Lepanto, Cervantes, as he informs us in his inimitable romance of "Don Quixo:e," lost his left hand by the stroke of a Turkish sabre

Tunis was very soon recovered, and the Ottoman empire was as powerful as before. The Turks, after the death of Selim II., preserved their superiority both in Europe and in Asia. Under Amurath II. they extended the limits of their empire into Hungary on the one side, and into Persia on the other. Mahomet III., the successor of Amurath, began his reign like a monster, by strangling nineteen of his brothers, and drowning twelve of his father's concubines, on the supposition of their being pregnant. Yet this barbarian supported the dignity of the empire and extended its dominions. From his death, which was in the year 1603, the Ottoman power began to decline. The Persians at this period became the predominant power in Asia, under Shah Abbas the Great, a prince who, in all his wars with the Turks, was constantly victorious. He gained from them many of their late acquisitions of territory; and effectually checking that career of success which had for several years attended their arms, he gave great relief to several of the princes of Europe, who at that time were scarcely able to defend their own dominions. Shah Abbas thus involuntarily shielded the European kingdoms from the fury of the Turkish arms, as we have seen that Tamerlane and Gengis-Khan had formerly been, in an indirect manner, the protectors of Constantinople.

Persia, under Shah Abbas, was extremely flourishing. This vast empire had, some time before this period, experienced a revolution, somewhat similar to that which the change of religion produced in Europe. Towards the end of the fifteenth century a new sect was formed by a Persian named Sophi, and his opinions were eagerly embraced by a great part of his countrymen, merely from the circumstance of thus distinguishing themselves from the Turks, whom they hated. The principal difference seems to have been that the reformer Sophi held Ali, the son-in-law of Mahomet, to have been the legitimate successor of the prophet; whereas the Mahometans generally acknowledged Omar the prophet's lieutenant. Sophi fell a martyr to his opinions, for he was assassinated by some of the opposite sect, in the year 1499. His son Ismael maintained his father's doctrines by force of arms; he conquered and converted Armenia, and subdued all Persia, as far as Samarcand; and he left this empire to his descendants, who reigned there peaceably till the revolutions in the last century. The conqueror, Shah Abbas, was the great-grandson of this Ismael Sophi.

The government of Persia is as despotic as that of Turkey; but there seems to be this substantial difference between the state of Turkey and of Persia, that the inhabitants of the latter enjoy their possessions with some security, for the payment of a small tax or land-rent to the government. The kings of Persia receive presents from their subjects, as the grand signior does; and according to Sir John Chardin's account, the king of Persia's new year's gifts amounted in those days to five or six millions of livres.

The crown of Persia is hereditary, with the exclusion of females from the succession; but the sons of a daughter are allowed to inherit the sovereignty. By the laws of Persia the blind are excluded from the throne. Hence it is a customary policy of the reigning prince to put out the eyes of all those of the blood royal of whom he has any jealousy.

The national religion of the Persians, we have said, is the Mahometan, as reformed by Sophi. The slender difference of opinions between them and the Turks is the cause of an aversion much stronger than ever subsisted between the protestants and catholics. If a Persian were washing his hands in a river, he would conceive himself contaminated if he knew that a Turk had bathed in it. There are, however, various sects of Mahometans in Persia; and some of these adopt not a few of the tenets of Christianity. The ancient religion of Zoroaster, too, is yet preserved among the Persian Guebres, who pretend in their temples to have kept alive the sacred fire from the days of the great founder of their religion down to the present time. Of the religion of Zoroaster we formerly gave a full account.

The language of the Persians is extremely beautiful, and peculiarly adapted to poetical composition. Sir William Jones has given to the public several beautiful translations from that language, which display the utmost luxuriance of fancy; and Mr. Richardson, in his curious dissertation on the languages, literature, and manners of the Eastern nations, has given a pretty full account of the learning of the Persians, who seem at one period (from the tenth to the thirteenth century) to have far surpassed in that respect the contemporary nations of Europe. The epic poet Firdousi, in his romantic history of the Persian kings and heroes, rivals Ariosto in luxuriancy of imagination, and is said to equal Homer in the powers of description. The writings of Sadi and of Hafiz, both in prose and in poetry, are to this day in high estimation with those who are conversant in Oriental literature.

The trade of Europe with Persia is carried on by the Gulf of Ormuz, and by the way of Turkey. The chief manufactures of Persia are raw and wrought silks, mohair, camlets, carpets, and leather; for which the English merchants give woollen cloths in exchange. The sovereign of Persia is himself the chief merchant, and he usually employs his Armenian subjects to traffic for his behoof in different quarters of the world. The agents of the king must have the refusal of all merchandise before his subjects are permitted to trade.*

To the north of Persia, that immense tract of country which is called Tartary had from time to time sent forth a succession of

* [The history of Persia has now been made fully and accurately known to Europeans by the writings of General Sir John Malcolm, who died in 1813.—EDITOR.]

conquerors, who carrying every thing before them, produced astonishing revolutions in the continent of Asia. We have formerly taken notice of the subversion of the empire of the caliphs by this race of northern invaders. Mahmoud conquered Persia and a great part of India towards the end of the tenth century; Gengis-Khan marched from the extremity of Tartary in the beginning of the thirteenth century, and subdued India, China, Persia, and Russia. Batoucan, one of the sons of Gengis, ravaged as far as the frontiers of Germany. Of the vast empire of Kapjac, which was the patrimonial inheritance of Batoucan, there remained in the last century no more than Crim Tartary, which till lately was possessed by his descendants under the protection of the Turks. Tamerlane, whose conquests we have already taken notice of, was of the same nation of the Tartars, and of the race of Gengis.

To the north of China were the Mongol and Mantchou Tartars, who made a conquest of this country under Gengis, and who professed that religion, of which we shall presently speak, whose head is the Great Lama. Their territories again are bounded on the west by the empire of Russia. A variety of different hordes of wandering Tartars occupy the country extending from thence to the Caspian Sea. The sultan Baber,* great-grandson of Tamerlane, subdued the whole country that lies between Samarcand, in the territory of the Usbecs, and Agra, one of the capitals of the Mogul empire. At that time, India was divided between four principal nations—the Mahometan Arabians, the ancient Parsees or Guebres, the Tartars of Gengis-Khan and Tamerlane, and, lastly, the real Indians in different castes or tribes.

The wandering Tartars follow at this day the life of the ancient Scythians. In the spring, a large body or horde, amounting perhaps to 10,000, sets out in quest of a settlement for the summer. They drive before them their flocks and herds; and when they come to an inviting spot, they live upon it till all its verdure is eaten up, and till the country supplies no more game for the chase. They exchange cattle with the Russians, the Persians, and the Turks, for money, with which they purchase cloth, silks, stuffs, and apparel for their women. They have the use of fire-arms, which they are very dexterous at making, and it is almost the only mechanical art which they exercise. They disdain every other species of labor, and account no employment to be honorable, unless that of hunting. When a man, from age, is incapable of partaking in the usual occupation of his tribe, it is customary with them, as it is likewise with the Canadian savages, to build him a small hut upon the banks of a river, and, giving him some provisions, leave him to die, without taking any further charge of him.

---

* [The curious Autobiography of Baber has recently been translated into English.—EDITOR.]

The mode of life with the Tartars during the winter season is for each family to burrow itself under ground; and it is said that, for the sake of social intercourse, they have subterraneous passages, cut from one cabin to another, thus forming a sort of invisible town.

The inhabitants of Thibet, which is the most southern part of Tartary, do not follow the same wandering life with their northern brethren.

The religion and government of Thibet form one of the most extraordinary phenomena in the history of mankind. The kingdom of Thibet is governed by a young man personating a living god, who is called the Great Lama, or Dalai Lama. He resides in a pagoda or temple upon a mountain, where he is seen continually sitting in a cross-legged posture, without speaking or moving, except sometimes lifting his hand, when he approves of the addresses of his votaries. He appears to be a young man of a fair complexion, between twenty and thirty years of age. Not only the people of Thibet, but the neighboring princes, resort to the shrine of the lama, and bring thither the most magnificent presents. The lama is both the national god and the sovereign. He appoints deputies under him, the chief of whom is called the Tipa, who manages the temporal affairs of the kingdom, which it is beneath the dignity of the lama ever to attend to. The creation of this prince, or god, is kept a most mysterious secret by the priests. When it is the misfortune of this poor image of divinity and sovereignty to fall sick, or to lose his youthful appearance, he is put to death by the priests, who have always another young man whom they have privately educated and properly trained to supply his place. Thus the religion of the lama is nothing else than an artful contrivance of the priests of Thibet to engross to themselves the sovereignty and absolute government of the country.

To the south of Thibet lie those countries known both in ancient and in modern times by the name of India; though neither that term nor the word Hindoo are proper to the country, but seem to have been given to those regions and their inhabitants by the Persians. In the Sanscrit, or ancient language of India, the country is called Bharata; a name which has not been given to it by any other nation. The earliest accounts which any of the ancient writers have transmitted to us of this country are those of Herodotus, who wrote his history about a century before the time of Alexander the Great; and it is singular that his accounts, though on the whole very meagre and imperfect, represent the character of the people and their manners precisely the same as those of the modern race of Hindoos. He takes notice of their living chiefly on rice, of their putting to death no animals, and clothing themselves with cotton. He informs us that Darius Hystaspes, about the year 508 before Christ, had sent Scylax of

Caryandra to explore the river Indus; but Scylax had not the good fortune to be believed in the accounts which he gave of his journey. By the expedition of Alexander the Great into India, the Greeks received the first authentic accounts of those countries, which border upon the river Indus. It is certain that this great conqueror penetrated into that part of the country, which is now called the Punjab. Here the extreme distress which his army sustained from the monsoons, or periodical rains, which fall in that country at stated seasons of the year, gave rise to an obstinate determination of his troops to proceed no farther. Alexander, therefore, with much mortification, was obliged to fix nere the limits of his conquests. He now embarked on the Hydaspes, which runs into the Indus, and pursuing his course down that great river for above a thousand miles, till it reaches the ocean, and subduing in his progress all the nations on both sides, he must have explored a great tract of the country of India. Of this expedition, his three officers, Ptolemy, Nearchus, and Aristobulus, kept exact journals, from which Arrian informs us that he compiled his history. The particulars given in these accounts relative to the manners of the people accord likewise entirely with all the modern accounts of the manners of the Hindoos.

After the death of Alexander, the Indian conquests of that monarch fell to the share of Seleucus, who made an expedition into the country, and, it is probable, maintained at least a nominal sovereignty over it. From that time, however, for near two centuries, we hear no more of India from any of the Greek writers till the period of Antiochus the Great, who made a short expedition into that country, and asserted a species of dominion over some of the Indian princes, by forcing them to give him presents of money and a number of elephants. The Greek empire of Bactria, it is probable, kept up an intercourse with the Indian countries in its neighborhood; but from those times down to the end of the fifteenth century, no European power had any thought of establishing a dominion in India; the only intercourse, which continued between the predominant powers of antiquity and that country being confined to the purposes of commerce. Egypt, during the time it was governed by the successors of Alexander, possessed exclusively the commerce of India, by means of the Red Sea. When Egypt fell under the dominion of the Romans, the commodities of India continued as usual to be imported to Alexandria, and from thence to Rome. When the seat of the empire was removed to Constantinople, that capital became, of course, the centre of Indian commodities. But it was not only by sea that the Roman empire maintained its communication with India. We perceive from the Geography of Ptolemy, who lived about two hundred years after the Christian era, that the route by land, across the desert, must have been at that time known; and we have, indeed, certain authority for the fact, that when the

Romans had extended their conquests as far as the Euphrates, finding the intercourse established by caravans, which travelled at stated seasons from those provinces to India, they took advantage of that communication to import the Indian merchandise over land.

Thus, then, from the age of Alexander down to the period of the Portuguese discovery of the route to India by the Cape of Good Hope, we have seen that a commercial intercourse had subsisted between that country and Europe, both by sea and land. It is, however, only since the period of that important discovery that the country of India has become familiarly known to us, and all the wonders of the Indian policy and system of manners laid open; which prove that great nation to have been perhaps the most early civilized, or at least, in remote periods, the most refined and enlightened of the nations upon earth.

Long prior, however, to this last period, and as early as the year 1000 after the Christian era, the Mahometans had begun to establish a dominion in India. Mahmoud, a Tartar soldier of fortune, usurping from the Saracens a large part of the kingdom of Bactria, pushed his conquests first into the eastern parts of Persia, and thence into India, establishing the seat of his sovereignty at Gazna, near the source of the river Indus. Thence he pursued his course towards Delhi, ravaging the country in his progress, and signalizing himself by the most ardent zeal for the extirpation of the Hindoo religion. In the year 1194, Mohammed Gori penetrated into India as far as Benares, the great seat of the Hindoo religion and science, to which he showed himself as great an enemy as his predecessor. One of his successors fixed the seat of his empire at Delhi, which continued thenceforth to be the capital of the Mogul princes. The sovereignty founded in India by Mahmoud was overwhelmed in the year 1222 by Gengis-Khan, as was his empire in the succeeding century by Tamerlane, whose posterity at this day nominally fill the throne of the Mogul empire.

The peninsula of India within the Ganges, we have seen, was invaded by the Portuguese in the beginning of the sixteenth century. They made there several establishments, and the viceroy, who resided at Goa, lived with all the splendor of an Asiatic sovereign. The subjects of the Great Mogul purchased from the Portuguese the produce of the Indian Spice Islands.

The Mogul empire was, even in the beginning of the last century, one of the most extensive and most powerful on the face of the globe. It was then governed by Aurengzebe, a man signalized equally by his crimes and by his good fortune. The Mogul Shah Jehan, the father of Aurengzebe, had conferred on his four sons the dignity of viceroys, and given them the command of four principal provinces of the empire. Aurengzebe, the youngest of the sons, formed a conspiracy with one of his brothers to dethrone their father; accordingly the old emperor was seized and imprisoned, and soon after died, as was suspected, by poison. Aurengzebe now found it necessary to get rid of his brother, who was the accomplice of his crime; and he was no sooner removed, than this unnatural parricide openly took arms against his other two brothers, and proving victorious strangled them both in prison. It was the lot of this wretch, who merited a thousand deaths for his crimes, to enjoy a life prolonged to one hundred and three years, crowned with uninterrupted good fortune; to extend the limits of his empire over the whole peninsula of India within the Ganges, and to die one of the most splendid and powerful of the Asiatic monarchs.

The dominion of the Mogul was not absolute over all those countries which composed his empire. When Tamerlane overran India, he allowed many of the petty princes to retain their sovereignties, of which their descendants long continued in possession. These were the rajahs, nabobs or viceroys, who exercised all the prerogatives of kings within their dominions, only paying a tribute to the Great Mogul, as being the successor of Tamerlane their conqueror, and observing the treaties by which their ancestors had recognised his superiority.

The original inhabitants of India are the Hindoos, or Gentoos, who profess the religion of Brama. Their priests or bramins pretend that their god or prophet Brama bequeathed to them a book called the Vedam, which contains his doctrines and institutions; but as this book is written in the Sanscrit, which is now a dead language, and only understood by these priests, they give what interpretation they please to the text of this religious code, and different bramins often extract from it the most opposite doctrines and opinions. Throughout all Hindostan the laws of government, customs, and manners make a part of religion, being all transmitted from Brama, the author of this sacred volume. It is from Brama that the Indians derive their veneration for the three great rivers of their country, the Indus, the Krisna, and the Ganges. To him they ascribe the division of the people into tribes or castes, distinguished from each other by their political and religious principles. This division of the Indian castes is characteristic of a very singular state of society. The four principal castes, or tribes, are the bramins, the soldiers, the husbandmen, and the mechanics. The bramins, as we have already observed, are the priests, who, like the Roman catholic clergy, are some of them devoted to a life of regular discipline, as the different orders of monks; and others, like the secular clergy, mix in the world, and enjoy all the freedom of social life. The military class includes the rajahs on the coast of Coromandel, and the Nairs on the coast of Malabar. There are likewise whole nations, for example the Mahrattas, who follow arms as an hereditary profession, and who are a kind of mercenaries, who serve for pay to any power that chooses to employ them. The husbandmen, like the soldiers, follow invariably the profession of their ancestors, and occupy themselves solely in the cultivation of their lands. The tribe of mechanics is branched out into as many subdivisions as there are trades, and no man is allowed to relinquish the trade of his forefathers, — a very singular system, which, as we formerly mentioned, prevailed likewise among the ancient Egyptians. Besides these four principal classes or tribes, there is a fifth, that of the pariahs, which is the outcast of all the rest. The persons who compose it are employed in the meanest offices of society. They bury the dead; they are the scavengers of the town; and so much is their condition held in detestation, that if any one of this class touches a person belonging to any of the four great castes, or tribes, it is allowable to put him to death upon the spot. All these classes, or castes, are separated from each other by insurmountable barriers; they are not allowed to intermarry, to live, or to eat together, and whoever transgresses these rules is banished as a disgrace to his tribe. It is well observed by the Abbé Raynal, that this artificial arrangement, which is antecedent to the tradition of known records, is a most striking proof of the great antiquity of this nation; since nothing appears more contrary to the natural progress of the social connections, and such an idea could only be the result of a studied plan of legislation, which pre-supposes a great proficiency in civilization and knowledge.

Between the years 1751 and 1760 the English East India Company conquered and obtained possession of the finest provinces of Hindostan—Bengal, Bahar, and part of Orissa, a territory equal in dimensions to the kingdom of France, abounding in manufacturing towns, possessed of an immense population, and yielding a magnificent revenue; and these territories have been constantly and rapidly extending from that period. The East India Company thence has the benefit of the whole trade of India, Arabia, Persia, Thibet, and China; and, with the exception of some settlements ceded to the Dutch, of the whole of Eastern Asia.

CHAPTER XXIV.

China and Japan:—Tartar Revolutions—Posterity of Gengis-Khan finally maintain Possession of the Throne—Pretensions to Antiquity considered.

Proceeding eastward in the Asiatic continent, the next great empire which solicits our attention is that of China. Towards the end of the thirteenth century, the Tartar posterity of Gengis-Khan were possessed of the sovereignty of China, of India, and Persia. The branch of this Tartar family which then reigned in China was termed Yuen: for the conquerors adopted both the name and the manners of the people whom they conquered. The Chinese were at this time a much more polished people than there invaders, who, therefore, very wisely retained their laws and system of government. The consequence was an easy submission upon the part of the Chinese, who, while they were allowed to follow in quiet and security their ordinary method of life, were very indifferent who sat upon the throne. After this conquest there were nine successive emperors of the family of the Tartars, nor was there the least attempt by the Chinese to expel these foreigners. One of the grandsons of Gengis-Khan was, indeed, assassinated in his imperial palace, but it was by one of his own countrymen, a Tartar; and his next heir succeeded to the throne without the smallest opposition.

At length indolence and luxury put an end to this race of monarchs. The ninth emperor in descent from Gengis-Khan abandoned himself to the most effeminate pleasures, and giving up the whole administration to a set of priests, excited at length both the contempt and abhorrence of his subjects. A rebellion was raised by one of the bonzes, and the Tartars were utterly extirpated from China in the year 1357. The Chinese were now governed for two hundred and seventy-six years by their native princes; but at the end of this period a second revolution gave the throne once more to the Tartars. This revolution affords a singular picture of the national character of the Chinese. Some violences committed against the Mantchou Tartars had given high provocation to this warlike people, and they determined to invade the empire. Their attempt was favored by an insurrection in some of the provinces; the Tartars met with very little resistance. The rebel Chinese, headed by a mandarin of the name of Listching, joined themselves to the Tartarian army, and both together took possession of the imperial city of Pekin. The conduct of the Chinese emperor is unparalleled in history: without making the smallest attempt to defend his capital or maintain possession of his throne, he shut himself up in his palace, and commanded forty of his wives to hang themselves in his presence; he then cut off his daughter's head, and ended the catastrophe by hanging himself. The Tartars took possession of Pekin, and their prince Taitsong pursued his conquests till the whole empire submitted to his authority. This, which is the last revolution that China has undergone, happened in the year 1641; since which time the empire has peaceably submitted to the government of the Tartar princes who are now upon the throne, and who, like their predecessors of the race of Gengis-Khan, very wisely maintain the Chinese laws, manners, and customs, without innovation.

The history of this celebrated empire has afforded a most fertile field of historical controversy. While the Chinese annals, which go back for some thousands of years beyond our vulgar era, are, by some authors, esteemed incontrovertible—while the government and political establishment of this empire are vaunted as a most perfect model of an excellent constitution, and the knowledge of the Chinese in the arts and their acquaintance with the sciences are supposed to have preceded, by many ages, the first dawnings of either in the European kingdoms,—there are other authors, no less respectable for the solidity of their judgment and the extent of their information, who are disposed to treat all these accounts as a gross exaggeration and imposture; who consider the boasted antiquity of this great empire, or, at least, the authenticity of its ancient history, as an absurd chimera—the policy and government of China as an establishment meriting no encomium—and the abilities of the Chinese in the arts, and progress in the sciences, even of those which they are supposed to have practised for thousands of years, to be, at this day, extremely low and inconsiderable. Voltaire and the Abbé Raynal are the most distinguished advocates of the hyperbolical antiquity of this singular people; and the fables of the Chinese have received from them a credence which might not have been so readily accorded, had they not afforded to these authors an opportunity of throwing discredit on the Mosaic accounts of the creation and of the deluge.

The empire of China, say these authors, has subsisted in splendor for above four thousand years, without having undergone any material alteration in its laws, manners, language, or even in the mode and fashion of dress. Its history, which is incontestable, being the only one founded on celestial observations, is traced by the most accurate chronology so high as an eclipse calculated two thousand one hundred and fifty-five years before our vulgar era, and verified by the missionaries skilled in mathematics. Father Gaubil has examined a series of thirty-six eclipses of the sun recorded in the books of Confucius, and found only two of them dubious, and two spurious. Thus the Chinese have joined the celestial to the terrestrial history, and proved the one by the other. "In the history of other nations," says Voltaire, "we find a mixture of fable, allegory, and absurdity; but the Chinese have written their history with the *astrolabe* in their hands, and with a simplicity unexampled in that of any other of the Asiatic nations." Every reign of their emperors has been written by a contemporary historian, nor is there any contradiction in their chronology. "With regard to the population of the empire," says Voltaire, "there are in China, by the most accurate computation, one hundred and thirty millions of inhabitants, and of these, not less than sixty millions of men capable of bearing arms. The emperor's ordinary revenue is about fifty-two millions sterling. The country of China is greatly favored by nature, producing every where, and in the utmost abundance, all the European fruits, and many others to which the Europeans are strangers. The Chinese have had a manufacture of glass for two thousand years; they have made paper of the bamboo from time immemorial; and they invented the art of printing in the time of Julius Cæsar. The use of gunpowder they have possessed beyond all memory, but they employed it only in ornamental fireworks."

They have been great observers of the heavens, and proficients in astronomy, from time immemorial. They were acquainted with the compass, but only as a matter of curiosity, not applying it to navigation. "But what the Chinese best understood," says Voltaire, "is morality and the laws; morality they have brought to the highest perfection. Human nature is addicted there, as in other countries, to vice, but is more restrained by the laws. All the poor in this extensive empire are maintained at the expense of government. A certain modesty and decorum softens and tempers the manners of the Chinese, and this gentleness and civility reaches even to the lowest class of the people. In China, the laws not only inflict punishment on criminal actions, but they reward virtue. This morality and this submission to the laws, joined to the worship of a Supreme Being, constitute the religion of China, as professed by the emperor and men of literature. Confutzee, or Confucius, who flourished two thousand three hundred years ago, was the founder of this religion, which consists in being just and beneficent. He has no divine honors paid to himself, but he has such as a man deserves who has given the purest ideas that human nature, unassisted by revelation, can form of the Supreme Being. Yet various sects of idolaters are tolerated in China, as a grosser sort of food is proper for the nourishment of the vulgar."

Such is the picture of this eastern empire drawn by M. de Voltaire and the Abbé Raynal. To show what portion of it belongs to historic truth, and what to the imagination of its authors, we shall consider separately the state of the sciences in China, the state of the arts, the government and laws of this empire, and the progress of the Chinese in religion, philosophy, and morality.

First, with regard to the state of the sciences. "The prodigious antiquity of the Chinese empire," says M. de Voltaire, "is authenticated beyond a doubt by astronomical observations, particularly by a series of eclipses of the sun, going back so far as two thousand one hundred and fifty-five years before our vulgar era." The evidence of this fact of the series of eclipses, it is to be observed, in the first place, rests upon the authority of certain Jesuits, who, travelling as missionaries into that empire, from which it is a piece of national policy to exclude all strangers, were obliged to court and purchase the privilege of residence in the country by the grossest flattery and adulation of the emperor. Some of these, being men of science, were employed to examine and to put in order the astronomical apparatus in the observatory of Pekin, and to teach their learned men the use of those instruments of which they were possessed, but of which they were grossly ignorant. These Jesuits themselves relate that, about the beginning of the last century, the science of astronomy was so low among the Chinese, that some of their mathematicians, having made a false calculation of an eclipse, upon being accused to the emperor, defended themselves by saying, that their whole calendar was erroneous. The Jesuits were hereupon employed to rectify it—a circumstance which gained them no small credit in the empire.

Now let it be supposed that a modern mathematician, having access to the Chinese astronomical observations, should find that most of those eclipses recorded were calculated with accuracy, it may be asked, what, after all, would this prove? Any ordinary mathematician, who can calculate a single eclipse, can calculate backwards a whole series of them for thousands of years. Thus any man who wished to compile a history fictitious from beginning to end, might, while sitting in his closet, in this way authenticate every remarkable event by eclipses and astronomical observations which would stand the strictest scrutiny. Thus every event in the famous history of Arthur and his Round Table, or of the Seven Champions of Christendom, might have its date authenticated by eclipses and astronomical observations, and consequently (according to the argument of M. de Voltaire) be entitled to the credit of a history as incontestable as the annals of China.

But to come to a more particular examination of this boasted knowledge of the Chinese in astronomy, let us attend, in the first place, to a few facts. In the year 1670, the Chinese astronomers had gone so totally wrong in their calculations, that by a false intercalation the year was found to consist of thirteen months. To remedy this error, an imperial edict was issued for the printing of forty-five thousand new almanacs, three thousand of which were distributed in each province of the empire.

For above two hundred years, what is termed the Tribunal of Mathematics in China has been filled, not by native Chinese, but by Mahometans and Jesuits. These are the men who have made all their astronomical calculations, and had the charge of the Chinese observatory. There are, indeed, some nominal professors of astronomy among the Chinese themselves, but these are so grossly ignorant as to adhere with great obstinacy to an ancient opinion, that the earth is of a square figure.

Before the arrival of the Jesuits, it is acknowledged that the Chinese were possessed of astronomical instruments, and *pretended* to make observations on the heavens. The possession of these instruments is urged as an argument of very considerable proficiency in astronomy and mechanics, and the argument is apparently a good one. But let us remark one fact: the latitude of Pekin is thirty-nine degrees, fifty-five minutes, and fifteen seconds —the latitude of Nankin thirty-two degrees, four minutes, and three seconds; yet all the sun-dials and astronomical instruments, both at Pekin and Nankin, are constructed for the latitude of thirty-six degrees: so that it is absolutely impossible that the Chinese could have made a single just observation at either of these capitals of the empire. A very probable conjecture has been formed with regard to the cause of this singularity. The city of Balk in Bactriana (now Bucharia) is situated in the thirty-sixth degree of north latitude. The sciences began to be cultivated in this city by the Greeks; who, having obtained the government of this province, under the successors of Alexander the Great, shook off their dependence, and founded a pretty extensive empire. In the time that China was governed by the first dynasty of the Tartar princes, these instruments, made for the latitude of Balk, were transported to China, and the Chinese at that time acquired some smattering of their use. Hence the origin of one of the most absurd and disgraceful errors, which the Jesuits acknowledge was maintained by all the Chinese astronomers, that the cities of China were all situated in the thirty-sixth degree of latitude. As for longitude, they had not the most distant idea of it; yet these are the people who are said to have cultivated the science of astronomy for four thousand years, and whose history is authenticated, beyond a doubt, by a course of celestial observations begun before the deluge!

The knowledge of the Chinese mandarins has been highly extolled by the admirers of this eastern nation; and much has been said of those rigid examinations which are undergone before the admission into this office and dignity. Supposing this to be a fact, the reason of these scrupulous trials is very obvious. It arises from the nature of the Chinese language and structure of its characters. It would be no difficult matter, in most countries, to be convinced in a few minutes, whether a person is able to read and write. To discover this in China requires a very tedious examination. It is requisite, for instance, that he who is appointed to the office of a mandarin, should be acquainted with ten thousand characters. He must, therefore, be examined on them all before the extent of his knowledge is ascertained; and a still more tedious inquisition is necessary, to know how many of these characters he can write. But all this rigorous examination is in fact a fiction. It is notorious that the office of mandarin is venal in China, as are most other offices; nor is any other qualification necessary than the ability to advance a handsome sum of money.

There is no science more cultivated by the Chinese than that of medicine, yet there is none in which their knowledge is so contemptible. There is not a physician among them who knows any thing of the internal structure of the human body. They determine the nature of all diseases by feeling the pulse, and the most usual cure for any topical affection is searing the parts affected with a hot iron. The foolish belief of an *elixir vitæ* is predominant in China, and is a great object of the researches of their physicians.

The abilities of the Chinese in the arts have been no less vaunted than their progress in the sciences; and we are assured by their panegyrists, that what have been esteemed the most important discoveries of the moderns, have been possessed by them from time immemorial. "The knowledge of gunpowder," says M. de Voltaire, "they have possessed beyond all memory. They invented the art of printing in the time of Julius Cæsar; and glass they have manufactured for above two thousand years." If it is asked, What is the authority of all these assertions? the answer is—The Chinese annals. If it is inquired, How these annals are authenticated? the answer is—By astronomical observations. What is the force of this ultimate proof we have already seen. Yet, on the supposition of these facts being true, perhaps the severest satire on the knowledge of the Chinese in the arts is to allow that they have possessed these discoveries from time immemorial, and then to inquire to what degree of perfection they have carried them. The discovery of gunpowder, either in Europe or in China, must have been accidental. The Europeans, immediately upon this discovery, improved it to the most astonishing purposes, and produced with it the most powerful effects. The Chinese are said to have possessed this discovery for thousands of years—from time immemorial—yet could find no other use for it than to compose artificial fireworks. The use of fire-arms the Chinese learned from the Portuguese, and the form of their muskets is at this day precisely the same that it was in Europe three hundred years ago.

The art of printing is an invention little more than three centuries old in Europe, yet some of those books, which were printed within twenty years of the discovery, display a degree of beauty and accuracy little inferior to the best specimens of modern typography. The Chinese are said to have possessed the knowledge of printing from the time of Julius Cæsar; but at this day they know not the use of movable types; they print from blocks of wood, in which the characters are cut in the manner of sculpture. In this way the materials of a very small book are large enough to occupy a house; and such is the length of time requisite for so laborious a work as the printing of a book, that it seldom happens that the author of a moderate volume lives to see its publication.

The polarity of the loadstone is not a very ancient discovery in Europe; we find it but obscurely hinted at in some of the works of the twelfth century, yet it was not long known before it was applied to the noblest and most important purposes; and navigation undergoing at once the most rapid improvement, an intercourse began to be established between the remotest quarters of the globe. Upon the first visits of the Portuguese and Spaniards to China, this vain and superficial people, whose character it is to maintain a stupid indifference to all foreign improvements, and either to undervalue them or pretend that they are already acquainted with them, informed the Europeans that they were no strangers to the compass, but that they found no use for it.

Glass the Chinese are said to have manufactured for two thousand years; and perhaps the assertion, though incapable of proof, may be true, as it is difficult to suppose that the same people who have long practised the making of porcelain should have been ignorant of the manufacture of glass; but one fact is certain, it was not till the seventeenth century that they attained the art of making it transparent, and even at this day it is in that respect infinitely inferior to that which is made in Europe.

There is great reason to presume that the Chinese have long practised the art of painting; yet, instead of a liberal art, it has ever been with them a mere mechanic drudgery. Their paintings, with a splendor of coloring, and the most minute accuracy of pencilling, have neither grace, beauty, nor justness of proportion. They have not the smallest notion of perspective. Instead of a gracefulness of attitude, the taste of the Chinese painter delights itself with the expression of distortion and deformity. Let us here remark the contrast between these Asiatics and the Grecian artists. In the images of the gods, which it is to be presumed men would always choose to picture according to their most exalted ideas of beauty and majesty, the Greeks have given a character and expression noble almost beyond imagination. The idols of the Chinese are deformed, hideous, and disgusting beyond measure.

The architecture of the Chinese has the quality of lightness united with strength, and a great deal of variety; but it is possessed neither of the elegance and beauty of the Grecian, nor of the majesty of the Gothic.

Among the most remarkable of the works of architecture in China is the great wall built to protect the empire against the inroads of the Tartars. It extends five hundred leagues, and is forty-five feet in height and eighteen in thickness—a most singular monument both of human industry and of human folly. The Tartars, against whom it was meant as a defence, found China equally accessible as before its formation. They were not at pains to attack and make a breach in this rampart, which, from the impossibility of defending such a stretch of fortification, must have been exceedingly easy:—they had only to travel a little to the eastward, to about forty degrees of latitude, where China was totally defenceless. Marco Polo, the Venetian, went, with a troop of Tartars, to Pekin, in the thirteenth century, and returned into Italy, where he died, without ever having heard mention of this great wall; which circumstance has even induced a suspicion that this immense structure has been built since his time.*

Among the few arts which the Chinese must be allowed to have carried to a high pitch of excellence is that of gardening. That beautiful method of embellishing or adorning, without confining or destroying nature, which is but very lately introduced into the gardens of England, was certainly borrowed from the practice of the Chinese. Even to the end of the seventeenth century, there prevailed in our gardens a formal and insipid regularity; and in the gardens of the continent of France, of Italy, and of Holland, there was not till very lately the smallest trace of that simple and picturesque beauty, which results from the natural diversity of hill and dale, or the judicious intermixture of lawn, of shade, of water, and of rock; yet the Chinese have long understood this happy embellishment of nature. If we may believe Sir William Chambers, who has written a very ingenious and amusing dissertation on this subject, the gardening of the Chinese is a science which proposes for its object, not only to amuse the eye, but to interest the passions.

Another art, which the Europeans must not only allow the Chinese to have invented, but to have brought to a greater degree of perfection than any other nation who have attempted to imitate them in it, is the manufacture of porcelain or China ware. The superior excellence of the Chinese porcelain to any that is

* This suspicion, however, is without foundation. It is known, with considerable certainty, that the wall of China was built in the third century before the Christian era.—Duhalde, tome ii., p. 45; De Guignes, tome ii., p. 59; Gibbon's Decline and Fall, &c., chap. xxvi. Marco Polo did not pass through Tartary to Pekin; but after having followed the usual track of the caravans as far to the eastward from Europe as Samarcand and Cashgar, he bent his course to the southeast, across the Ganges, to Bengal, and keeping to the southward of the Thibet mountains, reached the Chinese province of Shensee, passing thence to the capital, without interfering with the line of the great wall.—Staunton's Account of the Embassy to China, 1793, vol. ii., p. 185.

made in Europe seems to consist in the intrinsic superiority of the materials which they employ. In point of beauty, the porcelain of Dresden, that of Sèvres, in France, and that of Derby, in England, are incomparably superior to any thing that China has produced. There is more taste displayed in the form of the utensils; there is a greater beauty and variety in the colors; and the painting is such as the Chinese artists are in no capacity to rival: but the substance of the manufacture itself is inferior, it is more brittle and less capable of enduring a sudden heat: it partakes more of the nature of glass, and is in fact a different substance from the porcelain of China. The European manufacturers have not been able to discover a clay so pure, so white, or so fine in its consistency, as that which the Chinese employ, and they have been obliged to use too much of the flinty and vitreous substances, which make the European porcelain approach more to the nature of enamel.

The government and laws of the Chinese have afforded to their admirers another subject of the most unbounded eulogium.

All authors agree in representing the emperor of China as absolute in the most unlimited sense of the word; but the encomiasts of the Chinese have veiled the despotism of their government under the more flattering appellation of a patriarchal constitution. The emperor, say they, is considered as the father of his people, who regard him as entitled to the same implicit obedience that a parent is entitled to exact from his children. The mandarins, or great officers of state, are the substitutes of the emperor, whose care it is to enforce this obedience: but the patriarchal system pervades the whole, and in all matters that regard not the public interest, or that of the sovereign, every father is judge in his own family, and his power is absolute over his children. With whatever name this extraordinary constitution may be dignified, it is evidently nothing else than a blind and lawless despotism. Let us observe a few particulars upon the authority of Duhalde, Le Comte, and some of the historians of this empire who are most worthy of credit.

There is not a subject of this empire, says Duhalde, Chinese or Tartar, from the meanest peasant to the highest of the grandees, whom the emperor may not, at his pleasure, order to be bastinadoed. This despotic authority runs through every rank of the state, and each is entitled to tyrannise over his inferiors, as he himself is subjected to the tyranny of those who are above him. Upon the suspicion of treason, every viceroy has the power of inflicting capital punishment instantly, and without the necessity of any trial. We know, by our own laws, how extensive is the interpretation of the crime of treason, and may guess how easy it must be for judges, invested with such discretionary powers, to wrest almost every possible crime so as to bring it under that denomination.

There is, it is true, in China a system of written laws, which, it may be supposed, are a fixed rule of conduct for all judges and magistrates in the exercise of their duty: but one circumstance renders these laws of very little avail: this is, that all the courts of judicature in China are supreme. There is no appeal from any sentence to a superior jurisdiction, and consequently no restraint upon judges against the commission of the greatest iniquity and oppression. Nay, in civil causes there are no laws whatever which regulate the decisions of their courts. Every thing is in the breast of the judges, those mandarins whose offices are bought and sold, and consequently supplied often by men equally worthless and ignorant.

There is nothing more barbarous in the prosecution of crimes in China than that custom borrowed from the Scythians, by which all the relations of a criminal, to the ninth degree, are subjected to the same punishment as the offender himself. The husband suffers for the guilt of his wife, the father for that of his children. Where the father is dead, the eldest son is responsible for all the younger, and each for each.

"The religion of China," says M. de Voltaire, "is of two kinds: one which, like a grosser species of food, is very proper for the vulgar, the other professed only by men of sense, the literati, the bonzes, and the emperor. The first is allowed to be the most superstitious and absurd idolatry; the other, natural religion, or the belief of one all-powerful and benevolent Being, whose most acceptable worship is the practice of virtue." It would, I imagine, be not a little difficult to discover a good political reason for this fact—(supposing it to be one) of the Chinese government authorizing two species of religion so totally opposite and contradictory as pure deism and gross idolatry. If the emperor, the bonzes, and the literati judge the worship of one great and benevolent Being to be a more rational system of religion than that idolatry which is practised by the common people, what political reason should prevent them from instructing these likewise in that rational religion, instead of encouraging them in the most absurd and degrading superstition? It will not be pretended that the worship of one Almighty Being is less proper to restrain the people in the path of their duty, or to encourage good morals, than the worship of idols. But the least reflection will convince us that the fact itself is utterly incredible. There may be in China, as there are, perhaps, in all nations, various and very opposite opinions in matters of religion; but that the law or the government should authorize different and the most opposite religions for separate classes of men—one for the mechanics and another for the magistrates—is a statement which would require very strong authority to entitle it to belief. That religion would soon lose its obligation upon the vulgar which they perceived to be universally disregarded by their superiors.

The advocates of the wisdom of the Chinese in matters of religion appeal to evidence in support of their opinion, and tell us that the Chinese are possessed of five canonical books or *kings*, which furnish the clearest proof of a most pure and refined theology, very different from those superstitions which they allow to be entertained and practised by the vulgar. Let us, therefore, on the supposition of these books containing the substance of their theological dogmas, examine a little into their nature and contents.

The first of these canonical books—the oldest and most respectable in point of authority—is the book or table of the Yking. This Yking, which has been held forth as a mysterious receptacle of the most profound knowledge, and is on that account allowed in China to be consulted only by the sect of the learned, is now known to be nothing else than a superstitious and childish device for fortune-telling or divination. It is a table on which there are sixty-four marks or lines, one half short and the other long, placed at regular intervals. The person who consults the Yking for divining some future event takes a number of small pieces of rod, and, throwing them down at random, observes carefully how their accidental position corresponds to the marks on the table, from which, according to certain established rules, he predicts either good or bad fortune. These rules, it is said, were laid down by the great Confucius, the chief of the Chinese philosophers;—a circumstance which does not tend to increase his reputation. The Jesuit missionaries, who could not root out these prejudices, thought it their best policy to turn them to advantage; and in endeavoring to propagate the doctrines of Christianity, they pretended that Confucius had actually predicted the coming of the Messiah by this table of the Yking. This venerable table, or canonical book, is always consulted in the last resort: that is to say, when in cases of difficulty other authorities fail, or are inapplicable, the Chinese philosophers betake themselves to augury or divination.

The next of the canonical books in point of authority is the Chouking, which is a book containing a few sublime truths, scattered amidst a mass of the wildest ravings, on the subjects of philosophy and morality. The Chouking represents *Tien* or God Almighty, as a great spirit, residing in heaven, who created the world and all that it contains; who continually watches over the government of the universe; who delights in virtue and abhors vice; and who penetrates even the secrets of the heart. But the Chouking, amidst these venerable truths, informs man that the surest method of discovering the will of the Supreme Being is, in all cases of difficulty, to consult the augury of the Tortoise. If the grandees, the ministers, and the people should be of one opinion, says the Chouking, and you of another, provided the judgment of the Tortoise is on your side, your counsel will succeed.

Divination, in short, seems to be the ultimatum of the Chinese religion and philosophy. The other three *kings*, or canonical books, are equally absurd with those we have mentioned. There is an abstract of each of them to be found in Duhalde's description of China, a collection which contains the most authentic information as to every thing that regards this empire; as authentic, at least, as can be obtained from the accounts of those Jesuit missionaries, who are not without reason suspected of very great exaggerations.

The morality of the Chinese has been much the subject of encomium, and it must be owned that the writings of some of their philosophers, of which we have many extracts in Duhalde's collection, contain excellent notions of the relative duties of man in every state of society. But how little do the speculative notions, or the precepts of a few philosophers, influence the practice and the manners of a people! If we believe the accounts of authors best worthy of credit, there is not, on the face of the earth, a nation whose public manners are more depraved, nor any people in whose dealings with each other, or with strangers, there is less regard to honesty, to truth, or good faith.

In all the common intercourse of life the morals of the Chinese are beyond measure depraved. Father Amyot, who is in some respects a very high panegyrist of this nation, makes no scruple to declare that all ranks of the people have no other principles of conduct than interest and the fear of punishment. Commerce, which in other countries is carried on upon the basis of a mutual good faith between the parties contracting, proceeds in China upon this presumption, that all men are knaves and cheats. The author of the excellent narrative of Anson's "Voyage round the World" has given a picture of the morals of the Chinese from facts incontestable, because witnessed by the whole of his crew. The imputation of fraud, treachery, and inhumanity he does not confine to the lower classes of the people, for the facts which he mentions show that even the magistrates, officers, and guardians of the laws countenance the chicanery and villany of their inferiors, and partake of their profits.

From this estimate of the genius and character of the Chinese, drawn from an examination of the state of the sciences, of the arts, of the government and laws of their empire, and of their progress in religion, philosophy, and morality, we may conclude, upon the whole, that the Chinese are a very remarkable people; that every thing in China exhibits the traces of an ancient and early-civilized empire; and that in many respects the people merit the praise both of ingenuity and industry. But when the antiquity of this empire is pretended to be carried back for many thousands of years, and its history, during all that period, affirmed to be authenticated by the most incontrovertible evidence; when that people are supposed to have been for thousands of years able proficients in the sciences, of which at this day they are shamefully ignorant; when they are held out as the inventors of arts, of which they have not yet learned the most obvious uses and improvements; when a government and laws are vaunted as supremely excellent, which countenance the greatest enormities, and are insufficient to restrain the worst of crimes; and when that nation is praised for the perfection of its morality, where fraud, injustice, and inhumanity characterize the bulk of the people, and influence both their transactions with strangers and with each other, we must conclude that their panegyrists have wasted their time and talents in drawing a very false and exaggerated picture, which the evidence of a few facts totally discredits, and which, even independent of these opposing facts, could not be supported upon the basis of common probability.

About the middle of the sixteenth century, the Portuguese discovered the Japanese empire, which consists of several islands on the eastern coast of Asia, between thirty and forty degrees of north latitude. These islands form an extensive and even a polished state, which, for about a century and a half, has sequestrated itself from all connection with foreigners, and subsists in peace, tranquillity, and splendor upon its own internal riches. This was not always the case. The character of the Japanese, which was active and enterprising, and at the same time bold, free, and open, led them to encourage the resort of foreigners to their ports, and they formerly equipped fleets of their own, which traded to the neighboring coast of China and the Philippine Islands; but the insatiable ambition of the Europeans and their destructive policy have produced that change which I mention, and have secluded them for ever from any connection with the empire of Japan.

The Spaniards, soon after they obtained the sovereignty of Portugal, availed themselves of the discovery of these islands, and began to carry on an immense trade to the coast of Japan. The Japanese were fond of this intercourse, and the emperor encouraged it; but this favorable disposition was nothing more than an incentive to the ambition of the Spaniards to aim at the absolute sovereignty of the country. For this purpose they began by their usual mode of employing missionaries to convert the idolatrous Japanese to the Christian religion. Legions of priests were sent over, and so zealous were they in their function, that towards the end of the sixteenth century they boasted that the number of their new converts amounted to no less than six hundred thousand. The priests of the country, finding their interest daily decaying, were as zealous to preserve their ancient religion as the missionaries to destroy it. They represented the missionaries to the emperor as incendiaries, who came to sow dissensions in his dominions, and had already set the one half of his subjects at mortal enmity with the other. Political tenets, it may be believed, had mingled themselves with religious notions, and the emperor was very justly apprehensive, that this fervor shown by the Spaniards and Portuguese for the conversion of his subjects was but a preparative to their designs against the empire itself: he found it necessary, in the year 1586, to forbid the exercise of the Christian religion by a public edict, reserving still to the Spaniards and the Portuguese the liberty of a free trade in his dominions The Spaniards were not satisfied. Some cordeliers were sent from the Philippine Islands on an embassy to the emperor, and they began to build a Christian church in his capital city of Meaco. The consequence was they were driven out by force of arms. Still, however, the indulgence of the emperor allowed these foreigners a free trade till the year 1637, when a Spanish ship happened to be taken by the Dutch, near the Cape of Good Hope, on board of which were found letters from a Portuguese officer to the court of Spain, containing the project of a conspiracy, for dethroning and putting to death the emperor of Japan and seizing the government. The Dutch were jealous of the lucrative trade carried on by the Spaniards in this country, and immediately conveyed intelligence of this conspiracy to the court of Japan. The Portuguese officer was seized, and confessed the whole design. He was immediately put to death, and the emperor, in a solemn assembly of his nobles, pronounced an edict, forbidding, on pain of death, any of his subjects leaving the kingdom; and commanding that all the Spaniards and Portuguese should be instantly expelled from Japan; that all Christian converts should be imprisoned, and offering a very high reward for the discovery of any priest or missionary who should remain in his dominions. The Christians actually rose in arms, and were mad enough to attempt resistance, but they were overpowered and expelled to a man. The Dutch themselves, who had done the empire this essential service, shared the same fate with all other foreigners. They were even compelled to assist in carrying the emperor's edict into execution, and to employ the cannon of their own ships in bombarding a fortress, where some of the Spaniards had betaken themselves for shelter. The only favor the Dutch received was a permission to land upon one of the smallest islands of the empire, provided they would agree to take an oath that they were not of the Portuguese religion, and to trample upon the cross in testimony of it. They were then permitted to exchange their commodities with the natives, but were not allowed to fix their own prices, for this must be done by the Japanese. Such, at this day, is all the intercourse the Europeans have with the empire of Japan; with which, till the middle of the last century, they carried on a most lucrative and beneficial commerce.

CHAPTER XXV.

M. Bailly's Theory of the Origin of the Sciences among the Nations of Asia.

From a consideration of the manners, customs, and laws of the Chinese, and a comparison between them and the Egyptians, of whom we formerly treated at large under the period of ancient history, some learned men among the moderns have formed a conjecture that the Chinese were originally a colony of the Egyptians, and they have thus endeavored to account for the striking similarity between them in many particulars of their manners, laws, and attainments in the sciences. But this similarity is not confined to the Egyptians and Chinese. These nations, together with the Indians, the Persians, and the Babylonians, all exhibit some of the most wonderful features of coincidence ; and this circumstance would, therefore, equally conclude for the common origin of all those different nations. This subject opens views of a very curious and interesting nature.

In the Memoirs of the Royal Academy of Sciences at Paris, we find an account of a dissertation read by M. de Mairan, in which that ingenious writer draws a parallel between the Egyptians and Chinese, from which he concludes, as the only means of accounting for their resemblance, that there must formerly have been a communication between these distant nations, and thinks it probable that a band of Egyptians had at some period penetrated into China.

M. de Mairan's parallel consists of the following remarkable instances of similarity, which may be classed under seven distinct heads.

First, the Egyptians and Chinese had the same fixed attachment to their ancient customs and abhorrence of innovations. Secondly, these nations were alike remarkable for the high measure of respect entertained by children to their parents, for the reverence bestowed on old age, and for the veneration they had for the bodies of their deceased ancestors. Thirdly, the Chinese and Egyptians were alike remarkable for their aversion to war, and deficiency in military genius ; and both, in consequence, were frequently subdued by neighboring nations. Fourthly, both were remarkable for the same general knowledge of the arts and sciences, which they carried to a certain point of advancement, but were unable to go farther. Fifthly, the Egyptians had a hieroglyphical language not representative of the language they spoke, but of ideas only. The ancient Chinese had, in like manner, a hieroglyphical language distinct from the characters they used in ordinary writing. The Japanese and the Coreans derived the use of hieroglyphics from them, and employ them at this day. Sixthly, the Egyptians had a solemn festival called the *Feast of the Lights.* The most solemn festival of the Chinese is the *Feast of the Lantern.** And in the seventh and last place, M. de Mairan remarks, that there is a similarity between the features of the Chinese and the ancient Egyptian statues.

A modern hypothesis, of a very ingenious nature, accounts not only for those remarkable circumstances of similiarity between these two nations, but for many wonderful coincidences both in manners and in opinions of the Indians, the Persians, the Chaldeans, and, in short, of almost all the great nations of antiquity. The hypothesis alluded to is that of M. Bailly, author of the "History of the Ancient and Modern Astronomy," and is contained in a series of letters addressed by him to M. de Voltaire, and published under the title of "Lettres sur l'Origine des Sciences et sur celles des Peuples de l'Asie." This theory is not only in itself a beautiful effort of philosophic ingenuity, but the facts by which it is supported tend to throw considerable light on the early state of the arts and sciences among the Asiatic nations.

It is the idea of M. Bailly, that there has been a very ancient people of whom every trace is now extinct; a polished people who had attained to a great degree of perfection in the arts and sciences, and to whom the Chinese, the Persians, the Chaldeans or Babylonians, the Indians, and the Egyptians, in short, all of the most ancient nations to whom historical record extends, were indebted for that measure of knowledge they possessed in those arts and sciences. "If you see," says M. Bailly, "the house of a peasant chiefly composed of the rudest materials, but here and there interspersed with fragments of sculptured stones, or pieces of elegant columns, you must, of necessity, conclude, that these fragments are the remains of a palace, or elegant edifice constructed by an ancient architect of much greater skill and ability than the builder of that cottage." This principle is the foundation of M Bailly's hypothesis.

China exhibits the traces of a perfection in the sciences, to which the present Chinese and their ancestors, for many ages, have been most signally inferior. They are possessed of astronomical instruments which they cannot use, and the use of which they have no desire to be taught. Science we find among the

* The authors of the Modern Universal History most whimsically derive the origin of this festival from the number of lamps which Noah was obliged to make use of in the ark, and make this an argument in support of their hypothesis, that Noah himself visited China, and planted there all those arts and sciences which were known to the antediluvian world.—See Mod. Univ. Hist., vol. viii., p. 352

modern nations is progressive; the present age avails itself of the lights of the past. In China, all science is stationary, and has ever been so. The Chinese are at present, with respect to most of the sciences, like the inhabitants of a country recently discovered by a polished people, who have communicated some of their improvements to them, and left their instruments among them. If Captain Cook had left a quadrant and a telescope at Otaheite, the inhabitants of that island would at present know as much of the use of those instruments as the Chinese do, who have been astronomers for two thousand years. Hence it is reasonable to infer, that the Chinese have no natural genius for those sciences; they, therefore, could not have sprung up among themselves, but must have been imported into that country from a nation which cultivated them with intelligence and success. Fohi is said to have been the instructer of the Chinese. He was, therefore, probably, a foreigner, and brought his knowledge from a refined and scientific nation.

The date of the foundation of Persepolis, by Djemschid, is fixed by M. Bailly 3209 years before the Christian era. The city is recorded to have been founded on the day of the sun's entry into the constellation of the Ram. A people in their infant state, uniting themselves into society, cannot be supposed to be astronomers, or to mark the foundation of their city by the stars. Djemschid was certainly the leader of a colony of a polished people who took possession of a new country, and established there the arts and sciences which they had long cultivated at home. Djemschid was a stranger in Persia, as Fohi was in China.

The commencement of the Babylonian empire is involved in obscurity. We know, however, that the king of a people at that time named Chaldeans, took Babylon 2500 years before the Christian era. The Chaldeans were an enlightened people, and incorporating themselves completely with the conquered nation, assumed their name of Babylonians, as the Tartars, after the conquest of China, termed themselves Chinese. The priests, however, the depositaries of the sciences, kept their ancient appellation of Chaldeans, which thence became synonymous with soothsayers, or wise men. It is certain that the Chaldeans understood the revolution of comets, which was unknown to Hipparchus, to Ptolemy, and even to all the modern world down to the days of Tycho Brahé. Nay, Cassini himself in his youth believed comets to be nothing else than meteors. Is it not natural to conclude, that those Chaldeans who brought this high degree of knowledge to Babylon, were the remains of a most ancient and most enlightened people?

The bramins of India believe in the unity of God, and in the immortality of the soul; but along with these sublime tenets, which pre-suppose an enlightened and reflecting period of society, they hold a variety of the most contemptible and childish doc trines. They derived the former, we must presume, from wise instructers ; the latter have been the result of their own ignorance. We discern in all the fables of their theology the remains of an ancient and a pure system of religious opinions, which has been corrupted by a superstitious and degraded people.

M. Bailly then reasons from the circumstance of certain singular customs and extraordinary traditions prevailing in different nations, that they must have derived them from a common source. The custom of libation to the gods was common with the Tartars and Chinese, as well as with the Greeks and Romans. All the ancient nations had feasts of the same nature with the saturnalia. The tradition of the deluge is signally diffused, and is commemorated among many nations by different religious institutions. The Egyptians held that Mercury had engraven the principles of the sciences upon brazen columns, which resisted the effects of the deluge. The Chinese have the history of Peyrun, a peculiar favorite of the gods, who was preserved in a boat from the general inundation. The Indians have a similar tradition. Vishnou, one of their gods, under the form of a fish, conducted the vessel which saved a remnant of the human species. The same tradition is to be found in the Edda of the Scandinavians : only their deluge, instead of water, is formed by the blood of a giant. The tradition of the golden age, M. Bailly, with an elegant stretch of fancy, supposes to have arisen from the natural regrets expressed by the first colonies of this ancient people, when they recalled to remembrance the happy territory of their nativity, and painted it in the most flattering colors to their children. The fable of the giants attacking heaven is extremely general. The Indians and Siamese have it, as well as the Greeks. The tradition of the Atlantis, a lost continent, is current among the Chinese, and among all the Asiatic nations. Plato did not invent the story, but gave it as an old tradition among the Greeks. The doctrine of the metempsychosis was part of the religion of the Egyptians, of the Bramins, and of the Persians : and the worship of the grand lama, the priest of the god Fo, in Tartary and in China, is founded upon it. Kæmpfer * shows, that the Amida, or Xaca, of the Japanese, the Fo of the Chinese, the Butta of the Indians, the Badhum of the Isle of Ceylon, the Sommona-kodom of Siam, the Sommona-rhutana of Pegu, are all one and the same personage ; a deity, whose sect the same author compares to the plant, termed the Indian fig, which multiplies itself by the ends of the branches becoming roots. But what constitutes the strongest resemblance, and is, indeed, the point of union of all these different religions, is, that they are all founded on one very profound, though erroneous, doctrine, of the two principles, an *universal soul* pervading all nature, and *inert matter* upon which this soul

* Hist. Gen. des Voyages, tom. xl., 265.

exerts its influence. Bailly concludes justly, "A conformity in a true doctrine is not a convincing proof of a mutual understanding or concert; but a conformity in a false doctrine amounts to some thing very near such a proof."

M. Bailly then proceeds to point out many remarkable coincidences in matters respecting the sciences in all those nations we have mentioned. The Egyptians, Chaldeans, Indians, Persians, and Chinese, all placed their temples, and other public buildings, fronting exactly to the east; the buildings themselves standing due east and west. The worship of fire, or of the sun, has been the original worship of that ancient people from whom they borrowed their arts and sciences; and the temples were so placed, that the first rays of the sun might penetrate into the sanctuary. We formerly remarked the exact position of the pyramids of Egypt, with respect to the cardinal points of the horizon, and thence argued that that people must have made a very considerable advancement in astronomy before they were able thus accurately to regulate the position of those great structures. The same argument must be applied to those other nations we have mentioned, who must all have either made the same progress in the science of astronomy, or have been taught a certain rule by that more ancient nation, whom M. Bailly supposes to have been the common instructer of the whole of them.

In like manner, the Chaldeans, Egyptians, Indians, and Chinese, had all the same period of sixty years for regulating their chronology. Whether this number of years was chosen arbitrarily, or there was some reason for pitching upon it, still the coincidence is an additional proof of the general conformity. The same nations divided the circle into three hundred and sixty degrees, and the zodiac into twelve parts. The week was universally divided into seven days; and what is almost astonishing, the Chinese, the Indians, and the Egyptians, designated these days by the names of the planets, ranged precisely in the same order, which order is entirely an arbitrary one, and not dependent either on their magnitudes or distances from the sun. Chance could not have produced such wonderful coincidences.

Bailly, in his ancient astronomy, has shown that the long measures of the ancients had all one common origin. He has proved, that the circumference of the earth, as given by Ptolemy at 180,000 stadia, and by Possidonius at 240,000 stadia; that two others, one cited by Cleomedes at 300,000, and the other by Aristotle at 400,000 stadia; together with a computation made by a Persian author, which brings the circumference of the earth to 8,000 parasangs — are all one and the same measurement, only counted by stadia of different dimensions and by parasangs. He has shown that the Greek stadia, the Roman miles, the schæna of the Persians, the schæna of the Egyptians, the coss and the gau of the Indians, have all an exact and determined proportion to each other; that they all consist of a small measure repeated a certain number of times; and this universal and original measure, M. Bailly proves to be the grand cubit which is preserved upon the Nilometer at Cairo.* All the five measurements of the earth before mentioned coincide with each other, and are the same with the measurement made by the moderns. But from all that we know of the progress of the Greeks, the Chaldeans, Indians, and Chinese, in the sciences, none of these nations were ever capable of making so exact a mensuration. He, therefore, draws the same inference as from all the other instances of agreement we have mentioned.

"These wonderful coincidences," M. Bailly concludes, "can be accounted for only by three suppositions—First, that there was an easy and free communication between all the nations of Asia; or, secondly, that the circumstances of coincidence have so essential a foundation in human nature, and the nature of things, that nations left to themselves could not fail to have hit upon them; or, thirdly, that they have been all derived from one common source."

With regard to the first supposition, this free communication between distant nations, and interchange of ideas, of customs, of arts, and of sciences, never did exist, nor ever could have existed. Human nature in all ages has been the same; and nations in every period of antiquity, as well as at this day, have manifested the strongest attachment to their own opinions, and to their own modes of thinking and of acting. Between many of the nations of Asia there was no possibility of intercourse. Distance and natural obstructions formed insuperable barriers. Many of those ancient nations had a rooted abhorrence of all strangers. The Egyptians were remarkable for this antipathy. The Chinese are known to possess it in its utmost violence at this day. Whence the conformity, then, of opinions or of arts between these two nations, separated too, as they are, by a distance of three thousand leagues?

Secondly: Those circumstances of coincidence are not such as have so essential a foundation in nature, that nations having no intercourse must of themselves have hit upon them: in truth, many of the circumstances we have mentioned have no better foundation than the caprice of imagination, which is infinitely various. Many of those circumstances of coincidence are, as we have seen, so complicated, that an agreement of two nations by mere chance in the same thing would be nothing less than miraculous. Suppose that, in some future age, there should happen in Europe such a revolution as to destroy all the written records of the present time, and to leave nothing but a few scattered fragments, such as remain at present of the writings of the ancients.

* It is twenty and a half French inches

Suppose that, after an interval of many ages, a learned lawyer were to study those fragments, with a view of finding out the state of jurisprudence in Europe in the eighteenth century: he would find a number of similar laws among the Italians, the French, the Germans, &c. What must he thence conclude? He knows that those nations inhabited different countries, were under different governors, and were rivals and enemies to each other. Would it ever enter into his imagination that they had all borrowed from each other those laws which are found to be the same? No, certainly; this would be a weak and an unphilosophical supposition. He would conclude from those resemblances that all those nations had at one period been subdued by a powerful and predominant people, who framed those laws; and that, after a time, those nations, having freed themselves from the yoke of that powerful people, and established severally free governments for themselves, still chose to retain such laws as they had found by experience to be wise and salutary. This we know to be a truth with respect to the nations of Europe. But perhaps, after a period of two thousand years from this time, the certainty of this fact may be lost, and the whole become only a theory. This should be applied to the subject of which we now treat. The historical certainty is lost, the rational theory remains.

Thirdly: The only rational supposition, then, remains; viz., that there must have been a great original nation, now utterly extinct, and of whose history no document remains, who had advanced to a very high degree of perfection in the sciences and arts; who either subdued or sent colonies to the other countries of Asia; who, in fine, were their instructers, and communicated their knowledge and improvements to nations more barbarous than themselves.

It remains to determine where was the residence of this great nation; and M. Bailly has assigned many plausible reasons for placing it about the forty-ninth or fiftieth degrees of north latitude to the north of Tartary, and in the country now known by the name of Siberia. All ancient history is agreed as to the populousness of that region of the earth, and many nations at this day trace their origin from it. The Chinese assign to themselves an origin from that quarter; and so likewise, as we have formerly seen, do the Danes and other Scandinavian nations. The resemblance of the Japanese in feature and bodily figure to the Tartars strongly marks a descent from that great parent stock. It is ingeniously remarked by Bailly, that the production of nitre is more abundant in Tartary and Siberia than in any other region of the earth. Now, nitre is produced solely from animal substances: a proof thence arises of the great population of those countries.

Other facts tend still more strongly to confirm this idea of the local situation of this ancient people. The observations of the rising of the stars collected by Ptolemy must have been made in a climate where the longest day was sixteen hours. This corresponds to the latitude of forty-nine or fifty degrees; but in the age of Ptolemy there was no nation in Europe which understood astronomy and inhabited that latitude. It must, therefore, have been an Asiatic people, inhabiting the northern parts of Tartary, or the southern regions of Siberia.

The *Zendavesta*, or the sacred book containing the religion of Zoroaster, says, that the longest day of summer is double the length of the shortest day of winter; but this applies not to Persia, where Zoroaster lived, but to a climate twenty degrees to the north of Ispahan.

The measure of the circumference of the earth, as recorded by Aristotle — which, it has been already observed, could not have been computed by the Greeks, nor by any of the ancient nations known in Aristotle's time—gives the measurement of a degree precisely corresponding to its real length in the latitude of forty-nine or fifty. The people, therefore, who executed that great enterprise, the exact mensuration of the earth, lived in that latitude.

The pilgrimages of the Indians to the pagod of the *Great Lama* through a vast tract of desert and inhospitable country is a singular fact, and must have had some extraordinary motive. Does it not afford room to conjecture, that the Indian religion must have originated in that quarter, for which they have still so much veneration? An Indian, who was told that the remotest nations of Europe were wont to take long prilgrimages to the distant country of Judæa, would certainly conclude with reason, that that country had been the original seat of an ancient and venerable system of religion.

It affords no solid objection to this hypothesis, that the country which is supposed to have been formerly so cultivated and enlightened is now inhabited by a rude and ignorant people. To have reasoned as to the ancient state of Turkey from its situation and condition at present, we could certainly never suppose that it had been the residence and native country of the polished Greeks.

One question naturally occurs from the consideration of the above arguments for the local situation of this great people. Does the country in those regions of Asia, which lie in the forty-ninth and fiftieth degrees of north latitude, exhibit, at this day, any traces of having been once inhabited by a polished people? Does it show any vestiges of their works? It is fortunate for the hypothesis of M. Bailly, that there are, though not a great many, yet some vestiges of such works. M. Pallas, who, at the command of the empress Catharine of Russia, surveyed most minutely the extensive regions of Siberia, gives information of some discoveries in the neighborhood of the town of Krasnojarsk, upon the banks of the great river Jeniseia, which indicate that that country had been once inhabited by a people who had made very considerable progress in the arts. Krasnojarsk is situated about the fifty-sixth degree of north latitude. There have been ancient mines discovered in that neighborhood, which have been wrought in some former period, of which there is no account or tradition. They find the instruments which have been used in mining, and which are of forms and materials which indicate great antiquity ; huge hammers made of stone, and instruments like pickaxes, and wedges made of copper. In the plains and in the mountains near the river Irtish, in the same latitude, but farther to the west, there are many ancient burying-places, in which they find knives, daggers, and points of arrows made of copper. In other burying-places, near Krasnojarsk, they have found ornaments of copper and gold ; some of them adorned with embossed figures of various animals, elks, reindeers, stags, &c., all of exquisite workmanship. There is a curious circumstance which evidences the prodigious antiquity of those mines we have mentioned. The props, which support the earth in those mines, are now petrified, and this petrifaction contains sometimes copper and gold. So much time, therefore, has elapsed since those props were erected, that nature has gone through the tedious process of forming those metals ; and the same course of time has entirely annihilated every vestige of the stones with which the same men, who dug those mines, must have built their houses : for in a period of society when men are arrived at the art of forming curious works in gold and copper, we must suppose they dwelt in towns, and could rear regular edifices ; but of such towns and edifices not a trace remains.

Such is the ingenious hypothesis of M. Bailly, and thus far his theory has no small share of plausibility : but when he goes on afterwards to find the history of this great nation in the Atlantis of the ancients, described by Plato, and supposes the first population of the earth to have been at the north pole, he is plainly launching into the region of imagination. It is altogether a very amusing specimen of philosophic ingenuity, but is more valuable as specifying many curious facts relative to the manners and attainments of the ancient nations, and as furnishing strong evidence of the common origin of mankind, than as affording any plausible grounds for fixing the locality of this primæval people.

CHAPTER XXVI.

REIGN OF PHILIP II. OF SPAIN—Revolution of the Netherlands, and Establishment of the Republic of Holland:—William of Nassau declared Stadtholder of the United Provinces—Philip acquires the Sovereignty of Portugal—Schemes against England—Defeat of the Armada—Death and Character of Philip II.

FROM our rapid review of the state of the Asiatic kingdoms, we now return to consider the situation of Europe towards the middle of the sixteenth century.

In the time of Philip II. of Spain, the successor of Charles V., the balance of power in Europe was maintained by four great monarchies. Spain sustained its part by the talents of its monarch and his vast resources in point of wealth, derived from the treasures of the new world; France, by its internal strength and situation; Germany, by the power and abilities of many of its princes, who, though jealous of each other, were united for the defence of their country; and England, by the great political genius and wisdom of queen Elizabeth and her ministers. Of these, perhaps, Philip of Spain acted the principal character, though not the most amiable or respectable. He was, in his temper, selfish, gloomy, overbearing, and tyrannical. Yet he possessed great political activity, indefatigable assiduity in the management of public affairs, and a consummate ability in securing his own kingdom from danger by fomenting divisions among all his neighbors. He was at this time sovereign of Spain, of the Milanese, of the two Sicilies, and of all the Netherlands; and his father, Charles V., had left him an army of the best disciplined troops in Europe. He had, likewise, in the beginning of his reign, the whole force of England under his command, from his marriage with queen Mary.

Pope Paul IV., jealous of this exorbitant power, took advantage of the hereditary passion of the French monarchs to establish themselves in Italy, and formed an alliance with Henry II. of France to deprive the Spaniards of some important branches of their huge empire. A war was therefore declared between France and Spain, of which the object and the prize was the sovereignty of Milan and the Sicilies. The Spaniards began their attack on the French on the quarter of Flanders. Philip, with the assistance of 8000 English, engaged the French at St

Quintin, in Picardy, and gained a most complete and glorious victory. The French lost almost the whole of their general officers and the flower of their nobility. This victory was followed by the taking of the town of St. Quintin; but Philip, who had greater abilities in negotiating than in fighting, gave his enemy time to recover strength while he was meditating to secure these important advantages by a peace. The duke of Guise, whom Henry II. had appointed generalissimo of all the forces of his kingdom, recovered for awhile the spirits of the French, by the taking of Calais and the total expulsion of the English, who had now possessed it above 200 years. But in the meantime the troops of Philip gained another battle in the neighborhood of Gravelines, in which count Egmont, the Spanish general, completely defeated the French under the Marshal de Ternis. This appeared to Philip a favorable juncture for making peace with the greatest advantage: the treaty of Chateau Cambrésis was accordingly concluded between Spain and France, in the year 1559, extremely advantageous for Spain, as the French, mortified by their losses, gave up no less than eighty-nine fortified towns in the Low Countries and in Italy. Philip likewise, assuming all the authority of a conqueror, caused the territory of Bouillon to be restored to the bishop of Liege; Montferat to the duke of Mantua; Corsica to the Genoese; and Savoy, Piedmont, and Bresse to the duke of Savoy. Henry II. was likewise, at the same time, obliged to conclude a peace with Elizabeth of England, of which one condition was, the re-delivery of Calais, which Henry agreed to restore within eight years, or to pay five hundred thousand crowns; but Calais was never restored, nor was the money ever paid. Philip cemented this peace by marrying Elizabeth, the daughter of Henry II. This princess, it is said, had been promised in marriage to his son Don Carlos, a circumstance on which some writers have founded a most romantic story of distress, and which is said to have been the cause of that deplorable catastrophe which, as we shall afterwards see, befell both the unfortunate prince and the queen, his mother-in-law.

Philip returned in triumph to Spain, where his active mind, now at ease from foreign disturbances, began to be disquieted on the score of religion, and he laid down a fixed resolution to extirpate every species of heresy from his dominions. The inquisition was invested with all the plenitude of the powers of persecution. It is wonderful how much the spirit of this tyrant coincided with that of his consort, Mary of England; only Mary burnt the protestants at once, and Philip prepared them for that ceremony by racks and tortures. The king of Spain, hearing that there were some heretics in a valley of Piedmont, bordering on the Milanese, sent orders to the governor of Milan to despatch a few troops that way, and concluded his order in two remarkable words, "*ahorcad todos*"—hang them all. Being informed that the same opinions were entertained by some of the inhabitants of Calabria, he ordered one half to be *hanged* and the other *burned:* the consequences of these cruelties were what he did not foresee, the loss of a third part of his dominions.

The Netherlands were an assemblage of seignories or lordships, subject to Philip II. under various titles. Each province had its particular laws and usages, and was under the command of a governor, who had the title of Stadtholder; and no law was enacted, or taxes imposed, without the sanction of the whole states in the district. In the year 1559, Philip conferred the government of Holland, Zealand, Friesland, and Utrecht, on William of Nassau, prince of Orange, who was also a count of the German empire.

The new opinions of Calvin and of Luther, which had made reat progess in the Netherlands, gave Philip much disquiet. He determined to create new bishops, to establish the inquisition with its amplest powers, and, in order to enforce the most implicit submission to his authority, he resolved to abrogate all the ancient laws of the provinces, and give them a political system of his own devising. The report of these innovations created a dreadful alarm, and a meeting was held of the chief lords of the Netherlands, who deputed two of their number to lay their humble remonstrances before the king at Madrid. The effect which this produced was, that the duke of Alva was immediately sent into Flanders to suppress what was termed an unnatural rebellion; but there had been no *rebellion* if this measure had not occasioned one.

William I., prince of Orange, was a man of a haughty, reserved, and resolute turn of mind. He had seen several of the nobility, his friends, the counts Egmont and Horn, with eighteen other gentlemen, beheaded on account of their religion by sentence of the inquisition at Brussels; and the prince himself was sentenced to undergo the same fate, as a Calvinist and heretic. In the prospect of this impending destruction, he conceived the magnanimous resolution of delivering his country from the yoke of its merciless tyrant, and confident that the great body of the people were kept in their allegiance to the Spanish government only from the principle of fear, which would be dissipated on the first dawning of success, he immediately began to collect an army. In a short time, having reduced some of the most important garrisons in Holland and in Zealand, he was solemnly proclaimed Stadtholder of the United Provinces by a general convocation of the states at Dort, who, at the same time, openly threw down the gauntlet of defiance to Philip II. by declaring that the Romish religion should for ever be abolished from these provinces Hostilities began, on the part of Philip, by laying siege to the rebellious city of Haerlem; and the town being at length compelled to surrender, the whole magistrates, all the protestant ministers, and above fifteen hundred of the citizens, were hanged. Philip's viceroy, the duke of Alva, who at this time resigned his government, boasted, that during the period of his administration he had put eighteen thousand persons to death by the hands of the public executioner. His successor followed the same plan which had been prescribed by his tyrannical master. The Spaniards besieged Leyden, which was most resolutely defended by the prince of Orange. The Dutch threw down the dykes which restrained the encroachments of the sea, and the whole country was laid under water; and what was equally singular, as an effort of vigorous perseverance, the Spaniards continued the siege, and attempted to drain off the inundation. But the Dutch compelled them, at length, to abandon the undertaking. The whole seventeen provinces had suffered equally from the harassing of their sovereign; but jealousy of the power of the prince of Orange prevented a general union, and only seven of these asserted their independence.

Philip now sent his brother, the celebrated Don John of Austria, whom we have seen victorious over the Turks at Lepanto, to endeavor to regain the revolted Netherlands; but the attempt was fruitless. The prince of Orange summoning a meeting of the provinces at Utrecht, a treaty of union was formed, which became the foundation of the commonwealth of Holland. It was agreed, by this treaty, that they should defend each other as one body; that they should consult concerning peace and war; establish a legislative authority; regulate the imposition of taxes; and maintain a liberty of conscience in matters of religion. These *Seven United Provinces* were Guelderland, Holland, Zealand, Friesland, Utrecht, Overyssel, and Groningen. They chose William, prince of Orange, to be their head, with the authority of general of their armies, admiral of their fleets, and chief magistrate, by the name of Stadtholder. This famous treaty bears date the 23d January, 1579.

The intelligence of these proceedings exasperated Philip in the most extreme degree. He proscribed the prince of Orange, and set the price of 25,000 crowns upon his head. William, in his answer, which is one of the finest things recorded in history, considers himself as on a level with the king of Spain; impeaches him for injustice, perfidy, and tyranny at the tribunal of all Europe; and declares, for his own part, that though he might imitate the conduct of Philip by proscribing him in his turn, he abhorred the base revenge, and rested his security upon the point of his sword.

Philip, however, compassed his vengeance against the prince of Orange: the reward had its effect, and repeated attempts were made against the life of this illustrious man. At length one Gerard, a native of Franche-compté, put him to death by assassination. Maurice, the son of William, was declared stadtholder in room of his father; and, though only eighteen years of age, showed himself worthy of that important trust, and approved himself one of the ablest generals of his time. His military talents had the noblest field for their exertion, as his antagonist, Alexander, duke of Parma, then lieutenant to Philip in the Netherlands, was deservedly ranked among the greatest captains in Europe. The siege of Antwerp has immortalized his memory as well as that of its brave defenders. After a most heroic resistance, it was at length taken by the duke of Parma, by means of an immense rampart which he raised upon the river Scheld, in the same manner as the city of Tyre had been taken by Alexander the Great.

To protect this infant protestant state, queen Elizabeth sent the stadtholder four thousand men, under the command of the earl of Leicester; and with this timely assistance, and their own internal resources, the Hollanders were enabled to struggle against the force of the most powerful monarch in Europe. They maintained their independency as the ancient Lacedæmonians had done, by simplicity of manners, public frugality, and the most invincible courage. The simplicity of those times, when the Hollanders lived in clusters of small huts upon the banks of their canals, is very different from their present mode of life, when Amsterdam has become one of the richest of the cities of Europe, and the Hague one of the most polished and luxurious.

The government of the United Provinces was a very curious political structure. Of seventeen provinces of the Netherlands, we have seen that seven only recovered their liberty; the rest, under the governance of the duke of Anjou, a man jealous of the prince of Orange, to whom he was greatly inferior in abilities, contented themselves with repining and murmuring at those grievances which had made their neighbors resolutely withdraw their necks from the yoke. They flattered themselves that they could secure their liberty by negotiations; and the court of Madrid, in order to soothe them, gave them a charter, confirming their privi leges, while, at the same time, it was taking effectual measures to prevent all future attempts that might be made to reclaim and vindicate them. The revolted provinces, we have observed, signed their treaty of union on the 23d of January, 1579, and this alliance, which was renewed in 1583, was, by its nature, indissoluble: it was the foundation of the whole structure of the republic. Each of the United Provinces preserved its own laws, its magistrates, its independence, and its sovereignty; but for *national* purposes they were to form one body; and, in order to complete a union of interests, they renounced the right of forming separate alliances, and established a general council, whose business was to regulate the common affairs of the republic, and to convocate the states-general, a meeting which originally was called only twice a year, but which the great variety and importance of their business soon rendered perpetual.

Strictly speaking, each of the towns, which had a right of sending its deputy to the particular assembly of the province, constituted in itself a republic. Excepting those matters which respected the general interest of the states, these towns were governed by their own laws and magistrates, and their senate possessed a supreme legislature and executive authority. But all the towns of the same province were obliged to form a general council to regulate the affairs of the province, and to serve as a bond of union between its several parts. This council possessed a power of deliberating on all matters which respect the interest of the provinces; and the deputies of the towns which formed this council communicated to their constituents intelligence of all those matters which were there to be agitated, and received their instructions, which they were bound to follow. Every thing was decided in the council of the province by the votes of the majority, unless such questions as regard peace and war, the levying of troops, the forming of alliances, and the establishment of general taxes; all which matters required, by the fundamental treaty of union, the unanimous consent of the assembly of the states-general.

The great national council, or the states-general, met in assembly at the Hague, and were composed of the deputies from the seven provinces—Holland sending three, Zealand and Utrecht two, and the others one; and these had their conduct regulated by the instructions which each deputy received from the council of his province. The majority of suffrages was decisive here as in the provincial assemblies, except in those great questions which we have mentioned regarding war and peace, alliances or general taxes, where unanimity was required.

One obvious disadvantage attending such a constitution was, the delays and difficulties that may retard the execution of any public measure, from the necessity which the deputies or representatives, both in the assembly of the states and in the provincial council, were under of consulting their constituents upon all matters that came before them, and being regulated entirely by their direction. Fifty towns, and all the nobles of the province, must deliberate on any piece of business; and each provincial assembly must come to a fixed resolution, so as to instruct its deputy, before the assembly of the states-general was qualified to take the matter under consideration. The faultiness of such a constitution, which deprived a state of all possibility of acting with celerity in emergencies where success, perhaps, depended on celerity, needs no illustration. A government could not long have subsisted where there was so capital and radical an error, had not a contracting principle been applied in the office and power of the stadtholder.

The powers and prerogatives of the stadtholder were very great; he was commander-in-chief both of the sea and land forces, and disposed of all the military employments; he presided over all the courts of justice; he had the power of pardoning criminals, and all sentences were pronounced in his name; he appointed the magistrates of the towns, from a list of a certain number presented by themselves; he gave audience to ambassadors and foreign ministers, and nominated his envoys to foreign states; he was charged with the execution of all the decrees of the provincial assemblies; he was arbiter and supreme judge, without appeal, in all the differences between the provinces, and between the cities and the other members of the state.

The most extensive powers were conferred upon the first stadtholder of the united states, William I., prince of Orange, and they were not abused; on the contrary, they counterbalanced, in his hands, all the defects of this new constitution. Maurice, like his father, used his power as a good citizen, zealous for the honor of his country. His brother, Frederic-Henry, conducted himself on the same principles; but his son, William II., who succeeded to this dignity in the year 1647, was believed to have views not equally beneficial to the republic. Whether it was that the provinces, after having concluded the definite peace of Munster with Spain, thought that they had less occasion for the office of stadtholder, and began to fear the immense power of that magistrate, or that William became more jealous of his authority in proportion as he saw that it was less necessary, it is certain there was no longer the same good understanding between the states and the stadtholder; and had it not been for the death of William, this discordance might have ended fatally for the constitution. The most zealous patriots, to prevent the like apprehensions, took measures at that time for depriving his posthumous son, William III., of the succession to his father's dignities; but the evils resulting from the want of this office were severely felt in that emergency, when in the reign of Louis XIV. the whole power of France and her allies threatened the total annihilation of the republic. The abilities of William III. rendered him worthy to supply his father's place, and he was no sooner established in it than he retrieved the fortunes of his country. In grateful acknowledgment of his services, the United Provinces not only granted that dignity to him for life, but made it hereditary to the heirs-male of his family.

This last was an error equally pernicious with that of abolishing the office altogether; for it is easy to see that those immense powers, though they might be beneficial in the person of a *temporary* magistrate, were extremely dangerous when the office became perpetual and hereditary. It happened, indeed, that William had no children, and the error at his death might again have been remedied, but the patriots a second time pushed matters too far on the opposite side. They revived the laws which proscribed the office of stadtholder, and for above twenty years there was no such magistrate. Guelderland, however, in the year 1722, elected the prince of Orange of the second branch of the house of Nassau; and about twenty years after, when attacked by France, the rest of the states saw the necessity of reviving the office, and the same prince was nominated Stadtholder of the United Provinces. Ever in extremes, and blind to the real nature of their own constitution, the Dutch were now not contented with making this dignity again hereditary; they even made it descendible to daughters. It was decreed by the last deed of election, that the office should never descend to any prince who enjoyed the dignity of king or of elector of the German empire, or who should not be of the protestant religion. It was stated likewise that the stadtholders should be educated, during their minority, in the United Provinces, and that the office should descend to the posterity of the princesses of Orange, *only* in case they have married with the consent of the states, a protestant prince neither king nor elector.

To console Philip for the loss of the Netherlands, he soon after gained the kingdom of Portugal. Muley Mahomet, king of Fez and Morocco, had offered to become Philip's tributary, on condition of obtaining his assistance against Muley Moluc, his uncle, who had expelled him from his kingdom. Philip refused it, and the Moor then solicited the aid of Don Sebastian, the young monarch of Portugal. This prince embarked immediately for Africa, impatient to display his military prowess; but the event was fatal, for in one single engagement both he himself and the two contending kings, Muley Mahomet and Muley Moluc, lost their lives. This Muley Moluc was a prince who, in some circumstances of character, was equal to the greatest heroes of ancient Greece or Rome. There does not exist in history a nobler instance of intrepidity or greatness of soul than what this man exhibited in his dying moments, in that remarkable engagement. Moluc was in full possession of the empire of Morocco at the time when his dominions were invaded by Don Sebastian; but he was fast consuming with a distemper which he knew to be incurable. He prepared, however, for the reception of so formidable an enemy. He was indeed reduced to such weakness of body, that on the day when the last decisive battle was to be fought, he did not expect to live so long as to know the fate of the engagement. He planned himself the order of battle, and being carried on a litter through the ranks, endeavored, by his voice and gesture, to animate his troops to the utmost exertions of courage. Conscious that the fate of his family and of his kingdom depended upon the issue of that day, he gave orders to his principal officers, that if he died during the engagement, they should conceal his death from the army, and that they should from time to time ride up to the litter in which he was carried, under pretence of receiving orders from him as usual. When the battle had continued for some time, Muley Moluc perceived with great anguish of mind that his troops in one quarter began to give way. He was then near his last agonies: but collecting what remained of strength and life, he threw himself out of the litter, rallied his army, and again led them on to the charge. Quite exhausted, he fell down on the field, and being carried back to his litter, he laid his finger on his mouth to enjoin secrecy to his officers who stood around him, and expired a few moments after in that posture.

The victory, dearly purchased by the loss of this heroic man, was complete upon the part of the Moors. The adventurous Don Sebastian was killed in the battle, and was succeeded in the throne of Portugal by his great uncle, Don Henry; but *he* was at that time on the verge of the grave, and survived his predecessor only two years. The competitors for the crown at his decease were, Don Antonio, the prior of Crato, uncle to the last monarch by the father's side; Philip, king of Spain, his uncle by the mother's side; and pope Gregory XIII., on the absurd pretence that one of his predecessors had bestowed the crown on one of the former kings, who engaged to become his feudatory. The right of Philip was supported by 20,000 men. Antonio, the prior of Crato, solicited the aid of queen Elizabeth, who, though she cordially hated Philip, did not at that time find it convenient to declare war against Spain: but the prior obtained very effectual assistance from the French, who lent him 60 ships and 6000 men. The fleet of Philip, however, infinitely superior to that of his competitor, gave him a decided victory. Don Antonio's pretensions were set aside by one naval engagement, and the unfortunate prior betook himself to the court of France, where he passed his days in a state of honorable dependence; while Philip, without opposition from his holiness of Rome, was crowned king of Portugal.

The arms of this powerful monarch, while they were employed in a vigorous but ineffectual struggle to recover his revolted provinces of the Netherlands, were now turned towards another object, —a war with queen Elizabeth, who openly espoused the cause of the Hollanders, and had, besides, by one of her admirals, Sir Francis Drake, taken and plundered some of the Spanish settlements in America. To revenge these injuries, Philip prepared for an invasion of the kingdom of England, and equipped the Invincible Armada, the most formidable naval armament that had ever been raised by any single nation. This immense armament consisted of 150 large ships of war, manned by 20,000 soldiers and upwards of 8000 seamen, besides 2000 galley-slaves, and armed with 3000 pieces of cannon. To coöperate with this prodigious naval force, 30,000 men were to be conveyed in transports from Flanders, and a general insurrection was expected of all the catholics in Britain to depose Elizabeth, and place her cousin, Mary of Scotland, upon the throne of England. The policy and vigor of Elizabeth and her ministers, who had abundant warning of these hostile preparations, were exerted in putting the kingdom into the most formidable state of defence. Lords lieutenants were appointed in each county to muster and arm all who were capable of serving in the field; * and the maritime counties, where a landing was chiefly apprehended, were strengthened by large bodies of troops, drawn from the remote quarters of the kingdom, and every measure adopted which could either guard against a disembarkment or impede the enemy's progress and cut them off, if the landing was actually accomplished. On the 20th of May, 1588, the Spanish fleet, commanded by the duke de Medina Sidonia, set sail from Lisbon, but were forced by stress of weather to put into Corunna, which they did not leave till the 22d of July.

This vast project was dissipated like a summer's cloud. The English met the Invincible Armada with 100 ships of smaller size and 80 fire-ships. The fire-ships attacked them in the night, which threw them into the utmost confusion; an engagement ensued, in which the English were favored by a storm, which drove the Spaniards upon the coast of Zealand; many of their vessels were taken, a great number beaten to pieces upon the rocks and sand-banks, and only 50 ships with about 6000 men of all this prodigious armament returned to Spain. When intelligence of this great national misfortune arrived at Madrid, the behavior of Philip upon that occasion was, it must be owned, truly magnanimous. "*God's holy will be done,*" said he, "*I thought myself a match for the power of England, but I did not pretend to fight against the elements.*" Beautiful, just, and moral is the short reflection of Bentivoglio upon this signal catastrophe. "Such," says he, "was the fate of the memorable armada of Spain,

---

* Arrayed in a military dress, this heroic queen repaired to the camp at Tilbury, and addressed her army in the following most memorable speech:—

"My loving people, we have been persuaded by some that are careful of our safety to take heed how we commit ourselves to armed multitudes, for fear of treachery; but I assure you I do not desire to live to distrust my faithful and loving people. Let tyrants fear; I have always so behaved myself, that, under God, I have placed my chiefest strength and safeguard in the loyal hearts and good will of my subjects. And therefore I am come amongst you at this time, not as for my recreation or sport, but being resolved in the midst and heat of the battle to live or die amongst you all; to lay down for my God, and for my kingdom, and for my people, my honor, and my blood, even in the dust. I know I have but the body of a weak and feeble woman, but I have the heart of a king, and of a king of England too; and think foul scorn that Parma or Spain, or any prince of Europe, should dare to invade the borders of my realms: to which, rather than any dishonor should grow by me, I myself will take up arms; I myself will be your general, judge, and rewarder of your virtues in the field. I know already by your forwardness, that you have deserved rewards and crowns; and we do assure you, on the word of a prince, they shall be duly paid you. In the meantime, my lieutenant-general shall be in my stead, than whom never prince commanded a more noble or worthy subject (the earl of Leicester); not doubting, by your obedience to my general, by your concord in the camp, and your valor in the field, we shall shortly have a famous victory over those enemies of my God, of my kingdom, and of my people."

which threatened the demolition of the power of England : few enterprises were ever more deeply weighed, few preceded by more immense preparations, and none perhaps ever attended with a more unfortunate issue. How vain and fallacious are the best-concerted schemes of man ! Thus often the Divine Providence, in the wisdom of his impenetrable decrees, has determined the fate of an enterprise quite contrary to the presumptuous expectations of human foresight."*

Philip, who had always several projects on foot at the same time, (and perhaps this was the greatest error of his policy,) was meditating at once the invasion and conquest of England, the reduction of the Netherlands, and the dismemberment of the kingdom of France. We have seen the issue of the first of these projects : the second, though not equally disastrous, fell equally short of its aim ; and in the last, he did no more than foment disturbances which civil discord had already excited, and which in the end procured to him no advantage whatever. Every prospect of his ambition in France was demolished by a single stroke, the conversion of Henry IV. to the catholic religion. The character of Philip II. was that of a turbulent and most ambitious spirit : his was a crafty system of policy, in which there was nothing either great or generous. He was a man fitted to harass and embroil Europe, without that soundness of judgment even to turn the distresses which he occasioned to his substantial advantage. In his own kingdoms he was a cruel, a gloomy, and an inhuman tyrant ; in his family, a harsh and suspicious master, a barbarous husband, and an unnatural father. In the last of these characters, he signalized himself by the murder of his queen and of his son, the unfortunate Don Carlos, whose fate, according to the common accounts, is so extraordinary as to wear the air of a romance, though the truth of the principal facts has never been disputed. There is nothing improbable in the circumstance that this unfortunate prince should conceive an involuntary passion for his mother-in-law, a beautiful princess of equal age with himself, or that she, who could have no affection for a husband of Philip's disposition, should feel a similar attachment. Popular belief does justice to these ill-fated lovers in denying that they ever had a more guilty connection. A disappointed female favorite, for whom Carlos had formerly professed a partial affection, is said, from jealousy and revenge, to have discovered to Philip their correspondence. He seized on the prince's papers, among which, it is said, were found some passionate letters from the queen, as well as a treasonable correspondence with the stadtholder to dethrone his father. As these transactions were veiled in the most profound secrecy, which none of the Spanish historians have ever attempted to penetrate, it is not known whether Don Carlos underwent a trial for his

* Bentivoglio Guerra di Fiandra, lib. iv.

crimes, or was put to death by the royal mandate alone. It is said that he had the choice of his death, and that his veins being opened, he died in the bath, while he held in his hand the picture of his mother-in-law Elizabeth. This unhappy princess, then with child by her husband, to whose bed she had never been unfaithful, was soon after poisoned in a medicine which she took by the command of the tyrant himself. These atrocious facts have never, it is true, been verified by authentic evidence; but it is equally true, that these accusations were brought against Philip by the prince of Orange* in the face of all Europe, and that they were never refuted.

CHAPTER XXVII.

State of France in the end of the Sixteenth Century:—Religious Contentions—Conspiracy of Amboise—Death of Francis II.—Charles IX.—Massacre of St. Bartholomew—Henry III.—League of Peronne—Assassination of Henry III.—Henry of Navarre abjures the Protestant Faith, and is crowned in 1594—State of France—Character of Henry IV.—His Assassination in 1610.

While the Spanish monarchy was possessed of so high a degree of power under Philip II. as to alarm all Europe, France was in a declining situation, divided into factions, embroiled with civil wars, and torn to pieces both by its own subjects and the ambitious designs of its neighbors. These distresses arose from religious differences, from the want of good laws, and the maladministration of its sovereigns.

The doctrine of the reformed religion had made considerable progress in some of the provinces of France, and the persecution of the Calvinists had contributed greatly to the propagation of their opinions. The reign of Henry II., and the jealousy of his catholic clergy, had raised such a spirit of persecution, as to drive those unhappy men who would otherwise have been good subjects into an open rebellion.

The death of Henry II., and the accession of Francis II., was the era of those civil commotions which embroiled France for above thirty years, and brought that kingdom to the brink of ruin. The princes of Lorraine, or the family of the Guises, had established themselves in high credit during the two preceding reigns

---

*See Apology or Defence of the Prince of Orange against the Proscription of the King of Spain.

at the court of France. In the reign of Henry II., they had brought about the marriage of the Dauphin, now Francis II., with their niece, Mary queen of Scots, whose mother was a daughter of the duke of Guise. This match gave them such an ascendency over the young Francis, that, in fact, they ruled the kingdom. In this character it may be supposed they had powerful enemies. The two first princes of the blood, Antony of Bourbon, king of Navarre, and his brother Louis, prince of Condé, together with the constable Montmorency, were possessed of a similar ambition to that of the Guises; they were mortified by their arrogance, and were, therefore, their determined enemies. The Guises were zealots in point of religion, and intolerant catholics : the opposite party favored the doctrines of the Reformation, which had now made considerable progress among the French. Ambition, therefore, and religion coöperating together, set the whole kingdom in a flame. A conspiracy was formed by the Huguenots, at the head of whom was the prince of Condé, with the determined purpose of wresting the government out of the hands of the duke of Guise and his family. The Huguenot conspirators agreed to meet upon a certain day at the town of Amboise, and to open the enterprise by the massacre of the Guises, and by seizing the person of the king. It was discovered by one of the conspirators almost at the moment of its execution. Fifteen thousand troops, which the duke of Guise found means to assemble, cut to pieces the forces of the conspirators as they came in detached parties to the place of rendezvous: many of them sacrificed their lives with the most desperate courage; the rest were taken and executed on scaffolds and gibbets.

The tyranny of the Guises, which increased from the demolition of this conspiracy, procured them more enemies than ever; yet so formidable was their power, that for some time it repressed all opposition. The party of the prince of Condé and the Huguenots were forced to dissemble their mortification, and to affect a placid acquiescence in the government of the Guises. The prince of Condé had the imprudence to come to court; he was immediately seized by order of the duke of Guise, brought to trial for his concern in the conspiracy of Amboise, and condemned to be beheaded. His life, however, was saved by the death of the young monarch, Francis II., and the consequent disturbances in the kingdom. Charles IX., (the brother of Francis,) then a boy of ten years of age, was committed to the guardianship of the queen-mother, Catharine de Medicis, on whom the states conferred, likewise, the administration of the kingdom. The court was a scene of faction and division, as well as the kingdom : the queen was equally afraid of the power of the Guises and the Condés ; she was, therefore, obliged to negotiate between the protestants and catholics, and for that purpose appointed a solemn conference at Poissy, to debate on the articles of religion. The pope sent thither his legate to maintain his interest, or rather to crush all disputes, by declaring the assembly illegal as not convened by himself. His remonstrance, however, was disregarded, the conference was held, and the issue was an edict of pacification, by which the protestants were permitted the exercise of their religion through all France, without the walls of the towns. The consequence of this edict was a civil war. The duke of Guise, the head of the catholic party, met with a few protestants upon the borders of Champagne, who, under the sanction of the edict, were assembled in a barn for the purpose of devotion. His servants broke up the meeting, killed about sixty men, and dispersed and wounded the rest. This inhumanity was the signal of an insurrection through the whole kingdom, which was divided between the parties of the prince of Condé and the duke of Guise, the protestants and the catholics.

Philip II., king of Spain, to increase the commotions, sent some thousands of men to the aid of the catholics. The Guises were successful at the battle of Dreux, where the constable Montmorency, who commanded the royal army, and the prince of Condé were both taken prisoners. Guise, after this victory, laid siege to Orleans, where he fell by the hands of an assassin, who accused the heads of the protestant party as having instigated him to the murder, an accusation which was not generally believed, as it touched the admiral de Coligni, one of the chief supporters of that party, whose excellent character put him far above the suspicion of so vile a piece of treachery. A short peace succeeded these disturbances, and Condé was reconciled to the court; but the admiral kept still at the head of a considerable party in the provinces. The king, who had now attained his fourteenth year, had scarcely assumed the reins of government, when the prince of Condé, who had before attempted to take his predecessor, Francis, out of the hands of the Guises at Amboise, made a similar attempt to rescue Charles IX. from the leading-strings of the constable de Montmorency. The war was of consequence renewed; and Condé and Coligni engaging the army of the constable at St. Denis, the catholic party was defeated, and Montmorency killed. The party of the protestants was now increased by the aid of ten thousand Germans from the palatinate; yet the catholics continued the war with increased obstinacy and resolution, and France was a scene of massacre and desolation. The army of the catholics, which, on Montmorency's death, was now commanded by the king's brother, the duke of Anjou, was victorious in its turn. The prince of Condé was killed in a skirmish after the battle of Jarnac, and Coligni now supported alone the party of the Huguenots. A peace, however, was concluded between the two parties; and France had just begun to repair her losses and disasters, when a most infernal scheme was formed by the catholics for the destruction of all the protestants in France, a measure, perhaps, unparalleled in the annals of human nature, and which excited the horror and detestation of all the kingdoms of Europe. This was the massacre of St. Bartholomew.

The plot was laid with a dissimulation equal to the atrociousness of the design. The queen mother, Catharine de Medicis, a most flagitious woman, had always expressed her hatred of the protestant party, though she had at times shown a personal favor for some of its chief supporters. Her son, Charles IX., a coward in his disposition, was a monster of cruelty in his heart. It was concerted between the mother and her son, that the leaders of the protestant party should be brought to court and taken off their guard by extraordinary marks of favor and attention. Charles had given his sister Margaret in marriage to young Henry of Navarre; and he, together with the admiral Coligni and his friends, were entertained at court with every demonstration of kindness and respect. On the 24th of August, 1572, in the night, and at the ringing of the bell for matins, a general massacre was made by the catholics of all the protestants throughout the kingdom of France. The circumstances of this abominable tragedy are too shocking to be narrated in detail. One half of the nation, with the sword in one hand and the crucifix in the other, fell with the fury of wild beasts upon their unarmed and defenceless brethren. The king himself was seen firing with a musket from a window of his palace upon those unhappy wretches who had escaped into the streets naked from their beds, and endeavored to save themselves by flight.* Father Daniel informs us, that when the news of this massacre was brought to Rome, the pope highly commended the zeal of this young monarch, and the exemplary punishment which he had inflicted on the heretics. It was no wonder, then, that the parliament of Paris decreed an annual procession on St. Bartholomew's day to offer up thanks to God, or that such was the savage fury of this nation, blinded by fanaticism, that they were not satisfied even with the death of Coligni, who fell with his brethren in that massacre, but ordered him to be executed afterwards in effigy.

In the midst of these calamities the throne of Poland became vacant, and the duke of Anjou was chosen king by the assembled states of the kingdom. He accepted the honors conferred on him with some reluctance, and had but just taken possession of his kingdom when he was called to that of France, by the sudden death of his brother, the execrable Charles IX. He set out for Paris without hesitation, and left the Poles, indignant at his departure, to choose for themselves another sovereign. France,

* This dreadful massacre was general through the kingdom of France, except in a few of the provinces, which were saved by the humanity and courage of their governors.

at this time, exhibited a very extraordinary scene; a court involved in every species of luxury and debauchery, and a kingdom groaning under all the miseries which two factions could occasion, exasperated against each other beyond hope of reconciliation. Henry III., the new monarch, neither knew how to keep the protestants within due bounds, nor to content the catholics. He had neither abilities to manage his finances, nor to discipline his army. His debaucheries formed an extraordinary contrast to the superstition of his character, and both brought him into universal contempt. The duke of Guise obtained from him the command of his armies, and it was the interest of this prince to increase the confusions of the kingdom, that the court might always stand in need of his assistance.

In the meantime, young Henry of Navarre, brother-in-law to the French monarch, a youth of a noble spirit, who had escaped from the massacre of St. Bartholomew by going to mass with the catholics, had retired to the province of Guienne. The prince of Condé, the head of the protestants, had invited the Germans into Champagne, and their party was joined by the duke of Anjou, the king's brother. The abject monarch, terrified by this association, concluded a treaty with the protestants, which exasperated his catholic subjects, while it served only to give vigor and spirits to the opposite party. It was this treaty which determined the catholics to form themselves into a league, of which the pretext was the defence of religion, of the king, and of the liberty of the state. They pitched upon the duke of Guise for their leader, who equalled his father in abilities, and was a man of yet greater ambition. The league was solemnly signed at Peronne, and acceded to through the whole of the province of Picardy. The other provinces very soon concurred. The king, who now, with some justice, apprehended more danger from *this* association, nominally formed for his defence, than from all the designs of the protestants, thought to perform a masterly stroke of policy by signing the league himself, which he imagined would give him the absolute command of the party. But he was mistaken. He wished for peace that he might have the enjoyment of his pleasures, but the catholic and protestant confederacies waged war against each other, in spite of him. His brother-in-law Henry, the young king of Navarre, commiserating the misfortunes of France, which he probably foresaw would one day be his own kingdom, wrote to Henry III., painted to him in the strongest colors the mischiefs that attended that armed association, and generously offered his fortune and his life for his protection and defence; but Henry III. was weak enough to listen rather to the pope's bull, which stigmatized the king of Navarre and the prince of Condé as heretics. He rejected the offers of his brother-in-law, continued the persecution of the protestants, and thus aided the duke of Guise in his scheme to dispossess him of his kingdom. He saw his error when it was too late, and was obliged to solicit that assistance which he had rejected when offered. He had disgraced himself by acts of the most impolitic cruelty, and, unable to crush the schemes of the duke of Guise by a manly resistance and vigorous exertions of authority, he meanly employed assassins to murder that prince, and his brother, the cardinal of Lorraine, in the castle of Blois. This cruel and dissolute tyrant continued to reign for fifteen years. His kingdom was at length delivered from him by the hand of a fanatic enthusiast. Jacques Clement, a Jacobin monk, actuated by the belief that he was doing an act of consummate piety, insinuated himself into the palace, and stabbed the king with a knife in the belly. The assassin was put to death on the spot by the king's guards, and Henry died in a few days of the wound.

As the succeeding monarch of France had begun before this time to display his illustrious talents, I shall give a short, uninterrupted sketch of his memorable life.

Henry of Navarre, the first of the house of Bourbon who sat on the throne of France, was descended, in a direct male line, from Robert count of Clermont and lord of Bourbon, the sixth son of Louis IX., surnamed Saint Louis. His mother was Jane d'Albret, daughter of Henry d'Albret, king of Navarre. Attached to the party of the Calvinists, she had educated her son in the same principles, and from those talents which he very soon began to display, the party of the Huguenots in France looked up to him as the great support of their interest.. In 1569, being at that time only sixteen years of age, he was declared, at Rochelle, chief of the Huguenot party ; and the prince of Condé, his uncle, with the admiral Coligni, were named to act under him as his lieutenants. They were unsuccessful at the battle of Jarnac, where Condé lost his life, and likewise in the succeeding engagement at Moncontour. In the following year Charles IX. made peace with the protestant party, in the diabolical view of accomplishing by treachery what he found himself unequal to achieve by his arms. To prove the sincerity of his reconciliation with the Huguenot chiefs, he invited young Henry of Navarre to Paris, and bestowed upon him his sister Margaret of Valois in marriage. The party thus lulled asleep, the barbarous monarch attempted, as we have seen, to extinguish them by a single blow, and in the horrible eve of St. Bartholomew about 100,000 fell by the sword. Henry of Navarre, saved from this massacre of his party by declaring himself a catholic, remained, after this event, about three years a prisoner. After the death of Charles IX., having found means to escape to Alençon, in the year 1576, he put himself once more at the head of the protestants. The conduct of the party we have already seen during the reign of Henry III. This monarch, on his death-bed, had acknowledged

Henry of Navarre the lwful heir to the crown. Three sons of Henry II. had now reigned consecutively; and, having no children, Henry of Navarre, descended from Louis IX., was indeed the first prince of the blood, and consequently the nearest in succession to the throne. But he had to combat the formidable opposition of *The League*, who chose for their sovereign the cardinal of Bourbon, Vendôme. The pope was of necessity Henry's enemy; and Philip II. of Spain encouraged his son-in-law, the duke of Savoy to invade Dauphiné and Provençe. Henry had nothing to support him but the justice of his cause, his own courage, and the zeal of his small party. The first successful effort of his arms was at Arques, in the neighborhood of Dieppe, where with 5000 men he defeated the army of the league under the duke of Mayenne, consisting of 25,000 men. His numbers now increased to 10,000, and he defeated Mayenne a second time, in the celebrated battle of Ivry. He pursued his advantages, and marched directly to Paris. This city, which was strongly in the interest of the league, made a most obstinate resistance; but the Parisians would have been compelled by famine to open their gates to Henry, had not Philip II. sent the duke of Parma with a powerful army to their relief. This event deprived him of the fruit of his victories: but he took such well-concerted steps, that his enemies were able to gain no considerable advantages. The nation, aware of the ambitious views of Philip, began to be afraid of falling under a foreign yoke. Henry was made to understand, that the greatest obstacle to the success of his wishes was his religion. His counsellor Rosni, the celebrated duke of Sully, told him in plain terms, that it was necessary for the salvation of France that he should embrace the catholic faith. The disorders of the kingdom could not otherwise have been composed, nor the schemes of the Spanish monarch defeated. Henry yielded to the necessity of circumstances: he made a formal abjuration at St. Denis, and was crowned king, at Chartres, in the year 1594. The city of Paris was chiefly garrisoned by the Spaniards, but the marshal de Brisac, with infinite address, formed an association of the magistrates and principal citizens, and opened to Henry the gates of the town. He made his public entry into the capital of his kingdom almost without the effusion of blood, and he gave a free pardon to all the partisans of the league; ordering, at the same time, the whole foreign troops instantly to evacuate his dominions. Yet Henry was far from being in possession of the whole of the kingdom of France; and he was obliged to have recourse to as many intrigues as battles, in order to recover it by degrees. Almost his whole life was spent in fighting against one chief or another, in negotiating, and even in purchasing, the submission of his enemies; and, at length, in what situation was this kingdom when he recovered it? The revenues of the state were exhausted, the provinces ruined by neglect and by the ravages of the armies, and the country depopulated. France stood in need of a prince like Henry IV., a genius who understood the arts of peace as well as of war, who was capable of searching into the wounds of the state, and knew how to apply the most effectual remedies.

The ambitious Philip had been far from laying aside his views upon the accession of Henry. His armies continued to ravage the provinces. It was, therefore, necessary for Henry to bend his attention in the first place to the extirpation of these invaders. By the indefatigable industry of his counsellor, Sully, and by loans from his subjects, he found means to raise those supplies which were necessary for the support of a regular army. He was successful against the Spaniards, who were forced to conclude with him the peace of Vervins, the only advantageous treaty that France had made since the reign of Philip Augustus.

From that time forward he devoted his whole attention to the improvement of his kingdom, and the advancement of the happiness of his subjects. He disbanded all his superfluous troops; he introduced order and economy into the administration of the finances; he reformed the laws, repressed every species of persecution, and brought about the most difficult of all coalitions—a perfect harmony and good understanding between the protestants and catholics. A spirit of commerce and manufactures, the certain proofs of a wise and equitable government, began to diffuse itself through all the provinces of the kingdom. The cities were enlarged and embellished; the capital decorated with magnificent buildings; and the fine arts encouraged by the munificent patronage of a prince whose taste was equal to his liberality.

Henry, whom the pope in the beginning of his career had anathematized, as an heretic and usurper, was now the darling son of the church, and the highest favorite of the see of Rome. Such was his credit with pope Paul V., that the pontiff chose him as his mediator with the state of Venice, and at the request of one who had been formerly excommunicated himself, took off a sentence of excommunication which he had denounced against that republic.

His great political talents were equalled by his private virtues He was the kindest master, the most affectionate parent, and the warmest friend. His manners were noble without the smallest tincture of severity, and he possessed that engaging affability of behavior, which in him, deriving its origin from a native goodness of heart, was very different from that affected complaisance, the usual courtly engine of acquiring popularity. There was a greatness of soul in this prince, which manifested itself in the whole of his character. That generosity in the forgiveness of injuries, which is ever the attendant of a noble mind, was in him most remarkable. Many of those who, in the earlier period of his life, had taken the most violent part against him, and who, according to the common rules of human conduct, had nothing to expect after he had attained the throne but punishment, or at least disgrace, were astonished to meet not only with entire forgiveness, but even with marks of favor and confidence. He knew how much even the best natures may be perverted by the spirit of faction. He could not harbor resentment against a humbled adversary, and his own good heart informed him, that an enemy forgiven might become the most valuable of friends. It was thus that he won to himself the affections of those nobles, the chief supporters of the league which so violently opposed his succession to the crown. Of all his enemies, the marshal Biron was the only one who suffered a capital punishment; and to him he had three times offered mercy, on the condition of his making a confession of his crimes.*

To form a proper judgment of this most estimable man, it is necessary to read the Memoirs of the duke of Sully, where we see the picture of the greatest and the most amiable of princes delineated by the hand of a faithful servant, a counsellor, and a companion; a friend who was no less acquainted with the public schemes and the motives of his political conduct than with all the circumstances of his private life.† "Should a faithful picture of this illustrious character," says Voltaire, "be drawn in the hearing of a judicious foreigner who had never before been acquainted with his name; and should the narrator conclude that this very man was at length assassinated in the midst of his people, after repeated attempts against his life by persons to whom he had never done the smallest injury, it would be impossible for him to believe it." Whether this atrocious deed arose from the designs of a party, or was the mere suggestion of a distempered brain in the wretch who perpetrated it, is to this day a matter of doubt and uncertainty. The regicide Ravaillac himself protested that he had no accomplices. On the 14th of May, 1610, as Henry, together with the duke d'Epernon, was on his way to the house of Sully, the prime minister, and while the coach was stopped by some

---

* Perefixe relates a little anecdote, which shows that this beautiful feature of Henry's character, the forgiveness of injuries, extended itself to the meanest ranks of his subjects. Being one day in his coach with the marshal d'Estrées, he desired that nobleman to observe one of the life-guards who walked at the coach-door. "That," said he, "is a brave fellow; it was he who wounded me at the battle of Aumale."

† Who is there that can read without emotion the conversation that passed between this great man and his confidant Sully at Monceaux, when Henry attacked with a dangerous illness, thought himself dying. "Mon ami, je n'apprehende nullement la mort, comme vous le savez mieux que personne, m'ayant vû en tant de périls dont je me fusse bien pu exempter; mais je ne nierai point que je n'aie regret de partir de cette vie sans eslever ce royaume en la splendeur que je m'etois proposée, et avoir tésmoigné a mes peuples, en les soulageant et deschargeant de tant de subsides, et les gouvernant amiablement, que je les aimois comme s'ils etoient mes enfans."—Sully, Economies Royales, tom. i., ch. 85.

embarrassment in the street, the king, suddenly turning towards one of the windows, was struck twice into the heart with a knife, and instantly expired. The affliction felt by his subjects on this great national calamity was such as no words can describe. There never, perhaps, existed a sovereign who more merited, or who more entirely possessed, the affections of his people. Henry had lived to the age of fifty-seven, and at the time of his death is said to have been employed in projecting one of the greatest and most extraordinary schemes that ever entered into the head of man.*

CHAPTER XXVIII.

ENGLAND AND SCOTLAND IN THE REIGNS OF ELIZABETH AND MARY, QUEEN OF SCOTS:—Personal Enmity of Elizabeth and Mary—Reformation in Scotland—Regency of Mary of Guise—John Knox—Intervention of England—Confession of Faith ratified by Parliament—Mary arrives in Scotland—Artful Measures of Elizabeth in Scotland—Murder of Rizzio—of Darnley—Forced Abdication of Mary—James VI. proclaimed—Battle of Langsyde—Mary imprisoned in England—Executed, 1587—Ambitious Schemes of the Earl of Essex—Death and Character of Elizabeth.

WHILE France was torn by intestine convulsions, and bleeding under the infernal ravages of a merciless zeal, signalized by the memorable massacre of St. Bartholomew; while the inhabitants of the Netherlands had shaken off the yoke of Spain, and were bravely vindicating their rights and their religion,—the English nation had attained to a high degree of splendor under the government of a great and politic princess. Elizabeth had been educated in the school of adversity: she was a prisoner during the reign of her sister Mary, and had turned that misfortune to the best advantage, by improving her mind in every great and useful accomplishment. It were to be wished she had cultivated likewise the virtues of the heart; and that her policy (which must be allowed to be extremely refined) had breathed somewhat more of the spirit of generosity and humanity.

---

*The project of a perpetual peace. The delineation of this great scheme, which was singularly characteristic of the genius as well as the benevolence of its author, is to be found in the Memoirs of the duke of Sully. Though the preparations were actually begun for carrying it into effect, it must, in all probability, have failed of success, because it took not into account the predominant passions and weaknesses of mankind; and the impossibility of reasoning with nations as with wise individuals.

Elizabeth had, from the beginning of her reign, resolved to establish the protestant religion in her dominions, a measure which the severities of the reign of Mary had rendered not at all difficult. The protestant party had been increasing under persecution ; and no sooner were the queen's inclinations signified to the people, than almost the whole nation became protestants from choice. The very first parliament after her accession passed an act in favor of the reformed religion.

Elizabeth's great object was to secure the affections of her people, and this she most thoroughly accomplished. She may be reckoned among the most respected of the English monarchs ; though there is no question that she stretched the powers of the crown to a greater height, and her government was more arbitrary and despotic than that of any of her successors, whose encroachments on the rights of the subject gave occasion to such dreadful disquiets, and raised a combustion so fatal to the English nation.

The chief minister of Elizabeth in the beginning of her reign was Robert Dudley, son of the duke of Northumberland ; a man whom she seemed to regard from capricious motives, as he was possessed neither of abilities nor virtue. But she was assisted likewise with the counsels of Bacon and of Cecil, men of great capacity and infinite application. They regulated the finances, and directed those political measures with foreign courts that were afterwards followed with so much success.

In this reign of Elizabeth the affairs of Scotland were unhappily but too much interwoven with those of England. Henry VII. had given his daughter Margaret in marriage to James V., king of Scotland, who, dying, left no issue that came to maturity, except Mary, afterwards queen of Scots. This princess was married when very young to Francis, the dauphin, afterwards king of France, who left her a widow at the age of nineteen. As Elizabeth had been declared illegitimate by Henry VIII., in consequence of her mother Anne Bullen's divorce, Mary was persuaded by her ambitious uncle, the duke of Guise, to assume the arms and title of queen of England ; and when the English ambassador at the court of France complained of this injury, he received no satisfaction. This was the foundation of a personal enmity between the rival queens, which subsisted through life, and laid the foundation of a train of misery and misfortune to the queen of Scots.

The reformation in Scotland, though it arose from the most laudable and disinterested motives, was conducted with a spirit of much higher zeal and animosity than in England. The mutual resentment which the protestants and catholics bore to each other in that country was extremely violent. Many of the English preachers, who had fled from the terrors of the persecution under Mary of England, had taken shelter in Scotland. There they propagated their theological tenets, and inspired the greatest part of the kingdom with the utmost horror for the doctrines and worship of the church of Rome. Some of the principal of the Scottish nobility, the earl of Argyle, the earls of Morton, Glencairn, and others, had espoused the doctrines of the Reformation. They entered privately into a bond of association in opposition to the established church; and by their own authority they ordained that prayers in the vulgar tongue should be used in all the parish churches of the kingdom, and that preaching and the interpretation of the Scriptures should be practised in private houses, till God should move the prince to allow a purer system of public worship, under faithful and true ministers. This determined spirit of reformation was much fomented by the furious and most intolerant zeal of the Roman catholics. Hamilton, archbishop of St. Andrews, a sanguinary bigot, made some attempts to pursue the same horrible methods of conversion of which queen Mary of England had set the example; and a priest who had embraced the new religion was, by his orders, burnt at the stake. The consequence was, that the whole nation began to look with detestation and abhorrence upon the worship of the catholics; and the associated lords presented a petition to parliament, in which, after they had premised that they could not communicate with the damnable idolatry and intolerable abuses of the church of Rome, they desired that the laws against heretics should be executed by the civil magistrate alone; that the Scriptures should be the sole rule for judging of heresy; and that prayers should be said in the vulgar tongue.

The queen-regent, Mary of Guise, who, in the government of Scotland, followed the intemperate counsels of her brothers, instead of soothing or opposing by gentle methods this spirit of reformation, summoned the chiefs of the protestant party to attend a council at Stirling, and denounced all those as rebels who failed to appear. This violent and imprudent measure enraged the people, and determined them to oppose the regent's authority by force of arms, and to proceed to extremity against the clergy of the established church.

The celebrated John Knox arrived at this time from Geneva, where he had imbibed the doctrines of Calvin, of which his natural disposition fitted him to be a most zealous and intrepid promoter. This reformer was possessed of a very considerable share of learning, and of uncommon acuteness of understanding. He was a man of rigid virtue, and of a very disinterested spirit; but his maxims (as Dr. Robertson remarks) were too severe, and the impetuosity of his temper was excessive. His eloquence was fitted to rouse and to inflame. His first public appearance was at Perth, where, in a very animated sermon, he wrought up the minds of his audience to such a pitch of fury, that they broke down the walls of the church, overturned the altars, destroyed the images, and almost tore the priests to pieces. The example was contagious, and the same scenes were exhibited in different quarters of the kingdom. The protestant party soon after took up arms. They besieged and took the towns of Perth and Stirling, and thence proceeded, in martial array, to Edinburgh, where they found the people animated with the same zeal, and eagerly flocking to the banner of Reformation. Mary of Guise, sensible of her inability to withstand this increasing torrent, took a very impolitic step. She brought over a French army to subdue her subjects of Scotland; and they, with whom the motive of religious zeal far outweighed every other consideration, solicited the aid and succor of the protestant queen of England. Elizabeth acquiesced with the utmost cheerfulness in this demand, which coincided so well with her own views and interest. She despatched an army and fleet to their assistance. The French and the catholic Scots were defeated, and the party lost its head by the death of the queen-regent. A capitulation ensued, and a treaty was signed at Edinburgh, in which the political talents of Elizabeth appeared in their strongest point of view. It was stipulated that the French should instantly evacuate Scotland; that the king and queen of France and Scotland should give up all pretensions to the crown of England; that further satisfaction should be made to Elizabeth for the injury already done her in that particular; and that the Scots might the more readily accede to these articles, which hitherto seemed to regard the interest of England alone, it was, by way of soothing them, stipulated that none but natives should be put into any office in Scotland. Thus the politic Elizabeth quelled the disorders of that kingdom by the same measure which secured the stability of her own throne, and gave her the highest influence and authority over the Scottish nation.

The reformed religion now happily obtained a full settlement in Scotland. The parliament ratified a confession of faith agreeable to the new doctrines, passed a law against the worship of the mass, and abolished it throughout the kingdom under the most rigorous penalties. The papal jurisdiction was solemnly renounced, and the presbyterian form of discipline was every where adopted in place of the catholic.

Matters were in this situation when the young Mary, upon the death of her mother and her husband Francis, was desirous of returning to Scotland to take possession of her throne. Anxiously wishing to cultivate the friendship of Elizabeth, she had laid aside the arms and titles which had given that queen so much offence, and she now asked leave to pass through England, probably in the view of having a personal interview, which might lay the foundation of a mutual good understanding. This request Elizabeth refused, unless on the condition of Mary's ratifying the whole articles of the late treaty. This was not all; she equipped a fleet to intercept and take her prisoner on her passage. This danger, however, Mary escaped, and landed safely in her own dominions.

Mary was zealously attached to the catholic religion, the faith of her ancestors, and this attachment was the primary cause of the greatest of her misfortunes; she found herself regarded as an enemy by all the protestants, the bulk of her subjects, who, on the other hand, considered her enemy Elizabeth as their patroness and defender. That princess had very early, and before the arrival of Mary in Scotland, taken the most artful measures to secure to herself the management of this kingdom; she had her minister Randolph as a resident in Edinburgh, who had cultivated a perfect good understanding with the earl of Murray, (the bastard-brother of Mary,) the earl of Morton, and the secretary Maitland of Lethington:—and these three were the very persons on whom the young queen, harboring no suspicions, bestowed, upon her first arrival in her kingdom, the utmost confidence. The views of the ambitious Murray aimed at nothing less than his sister's crown; and still, as new obstacles presented themselves in the way of this criminal ambition, his attempts became, in proportion, more daring and more flagitious.

The first obstacle which opposed the ambition of Murray was the queen's marriage with her cousin Henry, lord Darnley, the son of the earl of Lenox, who bore likewise the same relation to the queen of England—a match, therefore, in every view, proper and adequate, as it connected the only contending claims to that kingdom after the death of Elizabeth.

Elizabeth, who had the weakness to be jealous of these pretensions, was not disposed to be pleased with any matrimonial connection which could have been formed by her rival Mary. It was, therefore, with the entire approbation of her minister Randolph, and her secretary Cecil, that the earl of Murray formed his first plot for the removal of Darnley, the imprisonment of Mary, and the taking into his own hands the government of Scotland. A conspiracy was formed by Murray to seize the persons of the queen and Darnley. It was discovered by Mary, who, with the assistance of the earl of Athol, and a few troops hastily collected, compelled the traitor and his associates to retire for awhile till they had raised sufficient force to rise in open rebellion. They were subdued, however, and Murray fled for shelter into the dominions of Elizabeth. A few of the nobility, whom Murray at first had gained over to his treasonable designs, now returned to their allegiance, and publicly avowed that the intention of the conspiracy had been to put Darnley to death, to imprison the queen, and to usurp the government. From this period, the same plan, though checked at first, was unremittingly pursued, till it was at length accomplished.

The consort of Mary made an ill return to her affections; he was a weak man, an abandoned profligate, and addicted to the meanest of vices. Pleased as she had been at first with his person and external accomplishments, it was impossible that her affection should not at length have given place to disgust at a character so worthless and despicable; and Darnley, enraged at her increasing coldness, was taught to believe that he was supplanted in the queen's affections by the arts and insinuations of a favorite—a despicable one indeed—the musician Rizzio, whom Mary had promoted to the office of her secretary. Murray, at this time at a distance, had his friends Morton and Lethington at court, who had cautiously avoided having an active share in the late conspiracy. A parliament was called, in which it was expected that Murray and his associates were to be attainted for treason; but to prevent this blow, and likewise to follow out the main scheme, a new plot was devised by Morton and Lethington, of which the weak and vicious Darnley was made an active instrument. The queen was then far advancd in her pregnancy, when, as she was one evening at supper in a private apartment of her palace, along with the countess of Argyle, while her secretary Rizzio, and some other of her domestics were in waiting, the earl of Morton, with one hundred and sixty men, took possession of the palace; a few ruffians in arms broke into the apartment, Darnley himself showing the way by a private staircase; they overturned the table at which the queen sat, and seizing the secretary Rizzio, who clung for protection to the garments of his mistress, they stabbed him to the heart, and thence dragging him into the ante-chamber, laid him dead with numberless wounds.

The purpose of this shocking outrage was extremely evident. From the queen's situation nothing less was to be expected than an abortion, and probably the death both of the mother and her child; should this not take place, the odium incurred by Darnley, as the ostensible head and promoter of this conspiracy, must at least be the cause of a total and incurable rupture between him and Mary, a justifiable pretence for those meditated schemes against his life, and even a probable presumption of Mary's acquiescence in any attempts to get rid of a man, against whom she had now so much cause of hatred and disgust. Confiding in the plausibility of these appearances, which to the public eye would, at least with the queen's enemies, induce a strong suspicion of her guilt, the murder of Darnley was immediately resolved on, and a very short time after, the house in which he slept was in the middle of the night blown up with gunpowder.

In this murder, planned by Murray, Morton, and Lethington, there is undoubted reason to believe, that the earl of Bothwell was likewise an associate. This nobleman, who had all along shown the greatest appearance of zeal and attachment to the interests of Mary, had from that cause alone, with little personal merit, attained a very great degree of her favor and esteem. The voice of the public imputed to him the murder of Darnley; but the good opinion which the queen had of him, from his former services, and the just grounds she had to fix that crime upon those who were truly its chief authors and contrivers, exempted this nobleman, in her mind, from all suspicion of guilt.

To satisfy the public opinion, however, Bothwell was tried by his peers for the murder of Darnley, and no evidence being brought against him, he was absolved by the verdict of a jury. The queen, who had never believed him guilty, had now, as she thought a perfect assurance of his innocence. He stood high in her favor; and, prompted by ambition, began to aspire at the dangerous honor of obtaining her hand in marriage. These views, being known to Murray and his associates, seemed to afford, at length, a most promising means for accomplishing the ruin of Mary, and throwing into their hands the government of the kingdom. It now, therefore, became their great object to bring about the marriage of Bothwell with the queen; a formal deed, or bond, was for that purpose framed by the earl of Morton and the chief nobility of his party, recommending Bothwell in the strongest terms as the most proper person she could choose for a husband. Mary gave into the snare; she married Bothwell, a measure which is the most indefensible part of her conduct; for, however she might have been persuaded of his innocence, of which this request of her chief nobility was certainly a very strong testimony, yet the public voice still pointed him out as an associate in the murder of her husband; and to marry this man was a measure as indecent as it was ruinous and impolitic.

The plan of Murray, of Morton, and their allies had now succeeded to their utmost wish, and it was unnecessary any longer to keep on the mask. Bothwell, their instrument in the murder of Darnley, had, by their means, become the husband of Mary. They had thus brought about what to the world would be a strong presumption of her being an accomplice in that murder; and the same Morton and his associates, who had signed that infamous bond, asserting Bothwell's innocence, and recommending him in the strongest terms as a suitable husband to their queen, now formed an association, within a few weeks of their marriage, to make them both prisoners in their palace. On receiving intelligence of this design, Bothwell found means to escape over seas to Denmark; but Mary delivered herself without reserve into the hands of her enemies, who immediately confined her, under a strong guard, in the castle of Loch Leven.*

---

* These black deeds, and the whole of this infernal policy, is thus laid open by Camden, a contemporary author, a person under the patronage, and intrusted with the papers of Secretary Cecil himself.

"Murray," he says, who had taken arms because of Mary's match with Darnley, "fled into England; and there being frustrate of all hope of aid, he dealt by letters with Morton, a man of a deep and subtile reach, who was his inward friend, and as it were his right hand; that seeing the marriage could not be annulled, yet, at least, *the love betwixt them as man and wife might, by close contrivances, be dissolved.*—Morton, being a man skilled in kindling discontents, insinuateth himself into the young king's mind by soothing flatteries, and persuadeth him to put on the crown of Scotland, even against the

Morton and the associated lords had now the sole government of the kingdom. They were, however, desirous of giving their authority a legal sanction; and for that purpose a deed was pre-

---

queen's will, and to free himself from the command of a woman. By this counsel he hoped not only to alienate the queen, but also the nobility and commons quite from the king. And to alienate the queen, first he incenseth the king by sundry slanders to the murder of David Rizzio, a Piemontois; lest, he being a subtile fellow, might prevent their designs. Then the more to alienate her, he persuadeth the king to be present himself at the murther. The king, now considering the foulness of the late act, and seeing the queen was very angry, repented him of his rashness, humbly fled with tears and lamentations to her clemency, and craving pardon for his fault, freely confessed, that, through the persuasion of Murray and Morton, he had undertaken the fact. And from that time forward he bore such hatred to Murray (for Morton, Reuven, and the others were fled into England for the murther of David, with Murray's letters of commendation to the earl of Bedford,) that he cast in his mind to make him away. But whereas, through youthful heat, he could neither conceal his thoughts, nor durst execute them (such was his observance towards the queen his wife,) he told her that it would be for the good of the commonwealth and the security of the royal family, if Murray were made away. She, detesting the matter, terrified him with threats from such purposes, hoping again to reconcile them. But he, stomaching the power which the bastard had with the queen his sister, through impatience, communicated the same design to others. When this came to Murray's ears, he, to prevent the same, under color of duty, contriveth more secret plots against the young king's life, using Morton's counsel, though he were absent. These two, above all things, thought it best utterly to alienate the queen's mind from the king, their love being not yet well renewed; and to draw Bothwell into their society, who was lately reconciled to Murray, and was in great grace with the queen; putting him in hope of divorce from his wife, and marriage with the queen as soon as she was a widow. To the performance hereof, and to defend him against all men, they bound themselves under their hands and seals; supposing that if the matter succeeded, they could with one and the same labor make away the king, weaken the queen's reputation amongst the nobility and commons, tread down Bothwell, and draw unto themselves the whole managing of the state. Bothwell, being a wicked-minded man, blinded with ambition, and thereby desperately bold to attempt, soon laid hold on the hope propounded, and lewdly committed the murther; whilst Murray, scarce fifteen hours before, had withdrawn himself farther off to his own house, lest he should come within suspicion; and he might from thence, if need were, relieve the conspirators, and the whole suspicion might light upon the queen. A rumor was forthwith spread all over Britain, laying the fact and fault upon Morton, Murray, and other confederates; they, insulting over the weak sex of the queen, lay it upon her. No sooner was he returned to the court, but he and the conspirators commended Bothwell to the queen for an husband, as most worthy of her love, for the dignity of his house, for his notable service of the English, and his singular fidelity. Now, the confederates' whole care and labor was that Bothwell might be acquitted of the murther of the king. A parliament, therefore, is forthwith summoned for no other cause; and proclamations set forth that such as were suspected of the murther should be apprehended. And whereas Lenox, the murdered king's father, accused Bothwell to be the murtherer of the king, and instantly pressed that he might be brought to his trial before the assembly of the estates began; this also was granted, and Lenox was commanded to appear within twenty days to prosecute the matter against him. Upon which day Bothwell was arraigned and acquitted by sentence of the judges, Morton managing his cause. This business being despatched, the conspirators so wrought the matter, that very many of the nobility assented to the marriage, setting their hands to a writing to that purpose; lest he, being excluded from his promised marriage, should accuse them as contrivers of the whole fact. By means of this marriage with Bothwell, the suspicion grew strong amongst all men, that the queen was privy to the murther of the king, which suspicion the conspirators increased by send ing letters all about; and in secret meetings at Dunkeld, they presently con pared, by which the queen should resign all concern in the government in favor of her son, then an infant a few months old; and agreeing that the affairs of the kingdom should, during the minority of James, be administered by the earl of Murray as regent. This deed the queen at first peremptorily refused to sign, till at length being told that force would be used to compel her to it, she complied with many tears. In consequence of this, the young prince was crowned at Stirling by the name of James VI., and Murray took upon him the government of the kingdom.

A great part of the nation were justly indignant at these proceedings; yet many more were imposed on by the profound artifice with which the conductors of these measures had veiled their designs. The queen, however, being apprized of the favorable dispositions of many of her nobility, and a considerable proportion of her subjects, found means to escape from the place of her confinement; and in a few days she was at the head of an army of six thousand men. The regent, on his part, assembled his forces, and an engagement ensued at Langside, where the queen's army was totally defeated. Mary, with a few attendants, fled with precipitation into the north of England, where she humbly craved the interposition of queen Elizabeth for her aid and protection.

That artful princess, who had all along employed a secret, though a busy hand, in the machinations of the Scottish confederacy, saw her end now accomplished in obtaining the absolute possession of the kingdom of Scotland. She was possessed of the person of the queen; and Murray and his party were devoted to her interest, from the motive of securing themselves in the administration. It was, therefore, no part of the views of queen Elizabeth to assist the queen of Scots, though honor and a concern for her own reputation in the eyes of the world, made it necessary for her to assume the mask of friendship. Mary had requested to be admitted to an interview with her; but this was refused her by Elizabeth, on the pretence that she lay under the foul aspersion of being accessory to the murder of her husband, from which it was necessary that she should first clear herself.

---

spired the deposing of the queen, and the destruction of Bothwell. Yet Murray, that he might seem to be clear from the whole conspiracy, craved leave of the queen to go into France. Scarce was he crossed over out of England, when behold! those which had acquitted Bothwell from the guilt of the murther, and gave them their consent under their hands to the marriage, took arms against him as if they would apprehend him; whereas, indeed, they gave him secret notice to provide for himself by flight; and this to no other purpose, but *lest he, being apprehended, should reveal the whole plot; and that they might allege his flight as an argument to accuse the queen of the murther of the king.* Having next intercepted her, they used her in the most disgraceful and unworthy manner; and clothing her in a vile weed, thrust her into prison at Loch Leven, under the custody of Murray's mother, who, having been James the Fifth his concubine, most malapertly aggravated the calamity of the imprisoned queen, boasting that she was the lawful wife of James the Fifth, and that her son Murray was his lawful issue."—Camden, pp. 88, 91, 94.

Mary, though, as a sister sovereign, she was under no obligation to submit to the jurisdiction of Elizabeth as a judge, yet, lest her silence might be interpreted to her prejudice, agreed to justify her conduct. A conference was appointed for that purpose. The earls of Murray and Morton produced a direct charge against Mary of being accessory to the murder of her husband, which they founded upon certain letters affirmed to be written from the queen to Bothwell, containing plain intimations of her guilt. Mary desired to be indulged with a sight of these letters, and undertook to prove them forgeries; and she very reasonably made that request a preliminary condition to her stating any defence against the charge of her accusers. This request, however, was refused; copies only of the letters were produced; she was not allowed to see or examine the originals, and the conference broke off.* The queen of England dismissed Murray and his associates back to Scotland, and kept Mary a prisoner in close confinement.

Elizabeth's own nobility appear now to have seen through the ungenerous policy of their sovereign, and to have condemned her conduct to the queen of Scots as disgraceful and inhuman. The duke of Norfolk, the first peer of the realm, whom Elizabeth had appointed her chief commissioner for examination of the evidence against Mary, immediately after the breaking up of the conferences, courted her in marriage; a circumstance strongly presumptive of his belief in the innocence of Mary, though the scheme proved fatal to that nobleman, and was very prejudicial to the interests of the queen of Scots. The influence of Norfolk, and his numerous connections among the principal nobility, were of themselves sufficient to excite the jealousy of Elizabeth; he had concealed from her his matrimonial views; and when these were discovered, her fears suggested the most dangerous consequences. Norfolk was committed to the Tower; his friends rose in rebellion for his deliverance. Their attempts were suppressed. Elizabeth restored him to his liberty; but a new insurrection, of which the object was the deliverance of Mary and the accomplishment of her marriage with Norfolk, brought that unfortunate nobleman to the scaffold, and hastened the fate of the Scottish queen.

Mary who it does not appear had as yet any part in those insurrections of which her deliverance was made the object, worn out at length with the miseries of her confinement, and continually apprehensive of a violent and cruel death—which Elizabeth, as

---

* The forgery of these letters and of the sonnets, pretended to be written by Mary to Bothwell, has been proved with an overpowering force of accumulated evidence, by Mr. Goodall, Mr. Tytler, Dr. Stuart, and Mr. Whitaker.—See Goodall's Examination of the History of Queen Mary; Tytler's Inquiry, Historical and Critical, into the Evidence of Mary Queen of Scots; Stuart's History of Scotland; and Whitaker's Mary Queen of Scots vindicated.

it appears from letters under her hand and her secretary's, did not hesitate to prompt her keepers privately to inflict upon her—began now secretly to solicit the aid of foreign princes for her rescue. She had for that purpose her agents at the courts of Spain, of France, in the Low Countries, and in Rome. The catholic party in England espoused her cause; an invasion was projected from abroad; and a conspiracy was formed, of which the objects were the deliverance of Mary, the establishment of the catholic religion, and the assassination of queen Elizabeth. This dangerous conspiracy was detected by the address of the secretary Walsingham, and the principal agents deservedly suffered death. There was undoubted evidence that Mary had intelligence and concern in that part of the design which regarded her own deliverance; and it being thence inferred that she was privy to the scheme of assassination, it was now resolved to bring her to trial as a criminal for that offence.

The greatest difficulty to be overcome on the part of Elizabeth was the plea most forcibly urged by Mary, that she was an independent princess; that she owed no allegiance to Elizabeth, no obedience to her laws, no submission to her tribunals; and that though she might, as a sister sovereign, deign to vindicate her character to the world if she were at liberty, she would never condescend, while forcibly detained a prisoner, to plead for her life at the bar of any court whatever. This difficulty was most artfully removed on the part of Elizabeth. It was urged to Mary by her judges, that she injured her reputation by avoiding a trial, in which her innocence might be proved to the satisfaction of all mankind. This observation so powerfully impressed her, that she forgot the dictates of prudence, and agreed to submit to a tribunal where her condemnation was certain and inevitable. Two of her secretaries, corrupted, as was supposed, for the purpose, swore to certain letters dictated by her, which proved an acquiescence in the whole conspiracy. Mary desired that she might be confronted with her secretaries, who, she affirmed, would not, to her face, persist in a false accusation; but this request was refused: the evidence was held conclusive, and the queen of Scots was condemned to suffer death; a sentence which was executed on the 8th day of February, 1587, in the forty-fifth year of her age, and nineteenth of her captivity in England. Previously to this event, Murray had fallen the victim of the private revenge of one Hamilton of Bothwell-haugh, whom he had injured; Lethington, seized with remorse, took part with his injured sovereign, and poisoned himself in prison, to escape the sentence of his enemies; Morton, for some time regent of the kingdom, and in that capacity the object of universal hatred for his crimes and vices, was finally brought to trial, and suffered death, on a full proof of his concern in the murder of Darnley. Such was the merited reward of their inhuman treasons.

The attention of the English was now called aside from dwelling on this disastrous event by the formidable preparations made by Philip II. of Spain for an invasion of the kingdom. The unsuccessful issue of all these preparations we have already recorded in treating of the reign of that monarch. Of the whole of the invincible armada there returned to Spain only fifty-three shattered ships; and the seamen as well as soldiers who remained, only served, by their accounts, to intimidate their countrymen from attempting to renew so dangerous an enterprise. The English, on the other hand, were incited to make some descents, in their turn, upon the Spanish coasts; and Elizabeth's navy, under the command of those great admirals, Raleigh, Howard, Drake, Cavendish, and Hawkins, began to establish that superiority at sea which Britain ever since has almost uninterruptedly maintained.

Among those who chiefly distinguished themselves in these Spanish expeditions, was the young earl of Essex, a nobleman of great courage, fond of glory, and of a most enterprising disposition. He possessed no less the talents of a warrior than of a finished courtier; yet his impetuosity was apt to exceed the bounds of prudence. He was haughty, and utterly impatient of advice or control. Elizabeth, then almost sixty years of age, was smitten with the personal charms of this accomplished youth; for it was peculiar to the queen, that though she had always rejected a husband, she was passionately fond of having a lover. The flattery of her courtiers had pursuaded her that, though wrinkled and even deformed, she was yet young and beautiful;* and she was not sensible of any disparity of choosing Essex for her partner in all the masks at court. Dudley, earl of Leicester, had died some time before. The death of Lord Burleigh, which happened soon after Essex came into favor, left him without a rival, not only in the queen's affections, but in the direction of her councils. The brilliant station which he now occupied, and still more the haughtiness of his temper, procured him many enemies; while the openness and unreservedness of his disposition gave these enemies every advantage. A rebellion had been for many years ferment-

* A curious proof how desirous Elizabeth was of the praise of beauty exists in a proclamation issued by her in 1563, in the thirty-third year of her age, and fifth of her reign, which sets forth, that, from the great desire which all ranks of people have shown to have portraits of her majesty, there have been a great number of pictures made "which do not sufficiently express the natural representation of her majesty's person, favor, or grace, but for the most part have erred therein;—And for that her majesty perceiveth that a great number of her loving subjects are much grieved, and take great offence with the errors and deformities already committed by sundry persons in this behalf;—Therefore she straitly charges all manner of persons to forbear from painting, graving, printing, or making any portrait of her majesty, or from showing or publishing such as are apparently deformed, until some perfect pattern or example shall be made by some coning person, which shall be approved by her," &c. &c. This proclamation is published in the Archaiologia of the London Society of Antiquaries, vol. ii., p. 169, from the original draught in the handwriting of Secretary Cecil.

ing in Ireland, and the earl of Tyrone, who headed the malcontents, had committed infinite devastations to that country, and threatened with his party to shake off all dependence on the crown of England. Essex was deputed to quell these disorders; he was, however, unsuccessful, and procured nothing further than a cessation of hostilities. His enemies at court took occasion from this miscarriage to undermine him in the favor of the queen—a purpose to which he himself contributed by hastily throwing up his command, and returning without leave to England. He trusted, it is probable, to the empire he had obtained over the queen's affections, which was indeed so great, that in spite of the highest dissatisfaction at his conduct, he was soon as much in her good graces as ever. But this impetuous and incautious man lost himself at length irretrievably by some personal reflections which he unguardedly threw out against his royal mistress. It was told her that his affection was all grimace, and that he had frequently declared that he thought the queen as deformed in her mind as she was crooked in her body. She now considered Essex as entirely unworthy of her esteem, and permitted his enemies to drive him to those extremities to which the impetuosity of his own disposition continually prompted him. Among other wild projects, he had concerted with some of his friends to beset the palace, to take possession of the queen's person, and forcibly compel her to remove from her councils all who were disagreeable or obnoxious to him; a scheme which one can hardly suppose to have proceeded from a brain that was not distempered. It was the fortune of Elizabeth's government, that all the machinations of her enemies were frustrated by a timely discovery. The queen's favor would, perhaps, have been still extended to him, but for another attempt equally treasonable, and yet more extravagant in its nature. This was to raise the city of London; and at the head of the citizens, with whom he believed himself extremely popular, to attain an absolute authority in the kingdom, and the removal of all his enemies. But he was deceived in the notion of his own popularity—he was opposed by the citizens—and being attacked in the streets, was compelled to retreat for shelter into his own house. His case was now desperate: he maintained a siege in his house against the queen's troops, and was at length compelled to surrender himself at discretion. He was tried by his peers, found guilty, and condemned to death as a traitor. The queen, with real reluctance, signed the warrant for his execution; and he was privately beheaded in the Tower, in the thirty-fifth year of his age.

From the death of Essex, the queen, now in the seventieth year of her age, seemed to lose all enjoyment of life. She fell into profound melancholy; she reflected then with remorse on some past actions of her reign, and was at times under the most violent emotions of anguish and despair. Her constitution, enfeebled by age, very soon fell a victim to her mental disquietude; and perceiving her end approaching, she declared that the succession to the crown of England should devolve to her immediate heir, James VI. of Scotland. She died on the 24th of March, 1603, after a reign of forty-five years. There are few personages in history who have been more exposed to the calumny of enemies and the adulation of friends than queen Elizabeth. It is probable that her character varied considerably in the different periods of her life; yet, upon the whole, it is not difficult to pronounce an uniform judgment with regard to the conduct of this illustrious princess. The vigor of her mind, her magnanimity, her penetration, vigilance, and address, certainly merited the highest praises. She was frugal without avarice, enterprising without temerity, and of an active temper; yet free from turbulency and vain ambition.

On the other hand, as a queen, she was rigid to her people, imperious to her courtiers, insincere in her professions, and often a hypocrite in her public measures; as a woman, she was suspicious, jealous, and cruel. She was intemperate in her anger, insatiable in her desire of admiration, and, with all her excellent sense, continually the dupe of flattery.

Few sovereigns succeeded to the throne of England in more difficult circumstances, and none ever conducted the government with more uniform success and felicity; but, in fact, there never was a sovereign who carried the notions of prerogative higher than queen Elizabeth, or had so thorough a disregard for the people's liberties. Those engines of arbitrary power, which, in the hands of her successors, excited that indignant spirit of the people which ended at length in the destruction of the constitution, were employed by this politic queen without the smallest murmur on the part of her subjects. The tyranny of the courts of Star-chamber, and of High Commission, which we shall see the cause of those violent ferments in the time of Charles I., was most patiently submitted to under Elizabeth. The tone of the queen to her parliaments was, "I discharge you from presuming to meddle with affairs of state, which are matters above your comprehension." So distant was the condition of the subject in those so much vaunted days of queen Elizabeth from that degree of liberty which we at present enjoy—a consideration, this, which ought to produce at least a respect for that improved constitution which has secured to us that valuable blessing, a patriotic desire to preserve this constitution inviolate, and to maintain its equal balance, distant alike from the tyrannical encroachments of arbitrary power, and the insatiable claims of democratic faction.

CHAPTER XXIX.

GREAT BRITAIN in the Reigns of JAMES I. and CHARLES I.—Accession of James VI. of Scotland to the Throne of England—Change of popular Feeling on the Rights of the Subject—Gunpowder Plot—His unworthy Favorites—Pacific Reign—Death—Charles I.—Differences with his first Parliament—Petition of Rights—Religious Innovations attempted in England and Scotland augment the Discontents—The National Covenant—Proceedings of Charles's last Parliament—Impeachment and Execution of Strafford—Bill passed declaring Parliament perpetual—Catholic Rebellion in Ireland made a Pretext for the Parliament's levying an Army—Bench of Bishops impeached and imprisoned—King impeaches five Members of the House of Commons—Civil War—Solemn League and Covenant—Scots coöperate with Parliament—Cromwell—Battle of Naseby—Cromwell turns the Army against the Parliament—Trial and Execution of Charles—Reflections.

UPON the death of Elizabeth, the crown of England passed with great tranquillity to her successor, James VI., king of Scotland, whose right united whatever descent, bequest, or parliamentary sanction could confer. If James mounted the throne with the entire approbation and even affection of his English subjects, it is certain that he did not long preserve them. He was unpopular from his manners, which were pedantic and austere, from his preference to his Scottish courtiers, and still more so from his high notions of an uncontrollable prerogative, which he was continually sounding in the ears of his subjects, both in his parliamentary speeches and in the works which he published,—a bad policy, which, giving occasion to men to examine into the ground of those pretensions, served only to expose their weakness. The vigor of Elizabeth's government scarce left room to scrutinize its foundation, but her successor was fond of such disputes, and was never so happy as when engaged in a learned argument upon the *divine right* of kings. About this period, the minds of men throughout all Europe seem to have undergone a very perceptible revolution. The study of letters began to be generally cultivated. Philosophy led to speculative reasonings on laws, on government, on religion, and on politics. In England, especially, which, in point of science, possessed a higher reputation at this period than any of the European kingdoms, these studies had a sensible influence on the current of public opinion. The love of liberty, which is inherent in all ingenuous nations, acquired new force, and began to furnish more extensive views of the rights of the subject than had prevailed in any former period of the constitution.

James, though of no mean capacity, was yet so blinded by self-conceit, and by the prejudices of education, that he failed to perceive this revolution, so dangerous to absolute or despotic power.* His reign was, therefore, a silent but a continued struggle between the prerogative of the crown and the rights of the people. The seeds were sown of that spirit of resistance, which, though it did not break out in his time into acts of violence, proved afterwards fatal to his successor.

Domestic events were such as chiefly signalized the reign of James I. He was scarcely seated on the throne, when he became the object of at least an alleged conspiracy, in which lord Cobham, lord Grey, and Sir Walter Raleigh were associated. Cobham and Grey were pardoned. Raleigh underwent a trial, which, though the issue declared him guilty, leaves the mind in a state of absolute skepticism with regard to the reality of this conspiracy, or of his concern in it. Raleigh's sentence was suspended for the course of fifteen years, during most of which time he was confined in the Tower, where he employed himself in the composition of his History of the World, a work excellent in point of style, and in many branches valuable in point of matter. In the last year of his life he received the king's commission of admiral to undertake an expedition for the discovery of some rich mines in Guiana. This, which, if not law, humanity at least ought to have interpreted into a pardon of his offence, was however not so understood by the monarch, whose heart had no great portion of the generous feelings. Raleigh's expedition was unsuccessful; the court of Spain complained of an attack which he had made upon one of their settlements. James wished to be at peace with Spain, and Raleigh at his return was ordered to be beheaded on his former sentence.

In the second year of this reign was framed another plot of a more dangerous nature, and one of the most infernal that ever entered into the human breast to conceive—the *Gunpowder Treason.* The circumstances of this conspiracy, which had for its object to cut off at one blow the king and the whole body of the parliament, are so generally known as to need no detail. It had originated from the disgust and disappointment of the catholics, who, on the accession of James, the son of a catholic, had formed to themselves illusive hopes of the establishment of their

* "It appears," says Hume, "from the speeches and proclamations of James I., and the whole train of that prince's actions, as well as his son's, that he regarded the English government as a simple monarchy, and never imagined that any considerable part of his subjects entertained a contrary idea. This opinion made those monarchs discover their pretensions, without preparing any force to support them; and even without reserve or disguise, which are always employed by those who enter upon any new project, or endeavor to innovate in any government. The flattery of courtiers further confirmed their prejudices; and above all, that of the clergy, who, from several passages of Scripture, and these wrested too, had erected a regular and avowed system of arbitrary power. —Essay on the Protestant Succession.

religion. It was discovered from a circumstance of private friendship; for, strange as it may appear, such hellish designs are not always incompatible with a degree of the social and benevolent affections. The conduct of the king in the punishment of this conspiracy was an instance of moderation, if not humanity. The majority of his people would have gladly seen an utter extinction of all the catholics in the kingdom. But James confined the vengeance of the laws to those only who were actually engaged in the plot—a measure which was by a great part of his subjects construed into his own tacit inclination to favor the popish superstitions—an idea, of which the absurdity was yet greater than its illiberality.

It was perhaps the small share which James had of the affections of his people that produced his attachment to particular favorites. Robert Carr, whom he created earl of Somerset, had no other pretensions to recommend him but a graceful person and a good address. He was a weak and an unprincipled man. He fell from the king's favor on conviction of his being guilty of a crime for which he should have suffered an ignominious death—the murder of Sir Thomas Overbury. Somerset had married the countess of Essex—a most debauched woman, who, to accomplish this marriage, had procured a divorce from the earl of Essex, in which she had found a chief obstacle in Sir Thomas Overbury, a confidant of Somerset. This flagitious woman now prevailed on her husband, Somerset, to have Overbury removed by poison, which they accomplished in a most barbarous manner, by feeding him daily for some months with poisoned victuals, while confined, through the means of Somerset, in the Tower. For this murder, Somerset and his countess were condemned to suffer death, but they both received the king's pardon.* His place was supplied by George Villiers, afterwards duke of Buckingham, on whom the king, in the space of a few years, lavished all possible honors: yet this man was devoid of every talent of a minister; he was headstrong in his passions, imprudent, impolitic, and capricious. He was distinguished by a romantic spirit, which led him into the most extravagant excesses; and the indulgence of his favorite passions had their influence even upon the public measures of the nation. He projected an absurd expedition of Charles, the prince of Wales, into Spain, on a visit, in disguise, to the Infanta, the daughter of Philip IV., who had been proposed to him as a desirable match. Their adventures on this expedition have more the air of romance than of history; but Buckingham was the hero of the piece. He filled all Madrid with his intrigues,

* State Trials, vol. i.; and Sir Fulke Greville's Five Years of King James, in the Harleian Miscellany, vol. vii. Mallet, in his Life of Bacon, takes up the calumnious report, which was spread by some of the king's enemies, that James was privy to the murder of Overbury; but the circumstances of presumption which he mentions are quite inconclusive.

his amours, serenades, challenges, and jealousies. He insulted the prime minister Olivarez by openly making love to his wife, as he did afterwards, with still more folly and insolence, to the queen of France; in short, the projected match with the Infanta seemed to be the least object of Buckingham's journey, and it accordingly was never concluded.

The pacific inclinations of James I., though they contributed in the main to the happiness of his subjects, were unfavorable to the glory and honor of the nation. James had some talents which would have qualified him to shine in a private station; but he had none of the distinguishing virtues of a monarch. His conduct towards his son-in-law, the elector palatine, then dispossessed of his dominions by the emperor Ferdinand II., has been generally and most justly censured as mean, dastardly, and inglorious. The whole nation would have gladly armed in defence of the fugitive prince, and repeated addresses were made by parliament to incite James to make a vigorous effort in his behalf. He was at length compelled to send a feeble armament to the continent without sufficient preparations for its support. Famine and a pestilential distemper cut off one half of the troops, and the other were too weak to be of any service. This was the only attempt towards a military expedition during the reign of James I., who soon after died in the fifty-ninth year of his age, after he had swayed the sceptre of England for twenty-two years, and that of Scotland from his cradle.

We have briefly taken notice of some of those maxims of government adopted during the reign of Elizabeth and her predecessors—the high stretches of the prerogative of the crown, and that tone of despotic authority used by the sovereign to the parliament, which seemed by the general consent of the nation to be then understood as agreeable to the constitution of England. But this was a false idea: the actual government and the constitution are two things extremely different. The rights of the subject, though long forgotten and neglected, were not extinguished: they were overlooked during the wars with France, and the civil commotions between the houses of York and Lancaster; they were overpowered under the artful and splendid despotism of the house of Tudor; but under the first sovereign of the house of Stuart, the nation began gradually to awake from its lethargy; a few threw back their eyes to the ancient charters of freedom, to which the impolitic discourses of the prince had called their attention; and in the reign of his son we shall now see that spirit completely roused, which was not to be satisfied with the attainment of more than ancient liberty—a spirit highly laudable in its first exertions, but fatal and even deplorable afterwards in its immediate consequences.

It may be allowed, on an impartial estimate of the character and personal qualities of Charles I., that had the nation in his reign entertained no higher ideas of the liberty of the subject, or of the powers of parliament, than those which prevailed during the two preceding centuries, this prince would have reigned with high popularity. It was his misfortune to fill the throne of England at the period of this remarkable crisis in the public opinions, and to be educated in the highest notions of the powers of the crown at the time when those usurped powers were justly doomed to come to an end. It was his misfortune, too, that with many good dispositions, and a very large share of mental endowments, he wanted that political prudence which should have taught him to yield to the necessity of the times, and that it was wiser to abandon a little of that power which he conceived to be his right, than, by obstinately maintaining it to its utmost extent, to risk an entire deprivation of it.

Charles disagreed with his first parliament. He was ambitious of sending an effectual aid to his brother-in-law, the elector palatine — a measure which parliament in the preceding reign had most strongly prompted. But this parliament repressed his ardor by voting a supply totally inadequate to its purposes. The honor of the king was engaged to his foreign allies; he was resolved to carry on the war; and dissolving the parliament, he betook himself to the expedient, often employed by his predecessors, of issuing warrants under the privy seal for borrowing money of the subject. The first military expedition was unsuccessful, and a new parliament, to whom Charles made application for new supplies, was yet less complying than the former. His minister, the duke of Buckingham, was impeached upon pretences extremely frivolous; the prosecution was dropped; and Charles, while he heaped fresh honors upon his favorite, revenged himself for this supposed insult by imprisoning two of the members of the House of Commons.

Thus the quarrel began between the king and parliament. These causes of dissension were trifling at first, but daily receiving addition from new offences, they grew into confirmed disgust on both sides.

Unable to obtain supplies from parliament, Charles was frequently compelled to the measure of raising money by loans from the subject; but what made this measure an intolerable grievance, was, that soldiers were billeted on such as refused to lend, and some were even imprisoned on that account alone. These arbitrary proceedings justly excited universal discontent, and the ill humor of the nation was further increased by a war against France at Buckingham's instigation, which ended in a fruitless attempt upon Rochelle. The parliament, again dissolved, made way for a new House of Commons, animated with the same spirit as their predecessors. They began seriously to reform the constitution. It was immediately voted, that all methods of raising money without consent of parliament were illegal—that it was a violation of the people's liberties to billet soldiers on them, or to compel them to loans by imprisonment. A solemn deed entitled *A Petition of Right*, was framed and digested, of which the objects were to abolish these loans, and all taxes raised without consent of parliament, as well as the arbitrary practice of billeting soldiers, and martial law. The bill passed the two houses of parliament, and was at length with some difficulty assented to by the king, who was naturally much mortified at this violent retrenchment of what, from the example of his predecessors, he esteemed the established prerogative of the crown.

The Commons, who had thus far proceeded in the great design of vindicating the liberties of the people, began now to carry their scrutiny into every part of the government. One great cause of discontent was removed by the death of the duke of Buckingham, who was stabbed by an Irish fanatic. But grievances of a more serious nature still remained to be redressed. The duty of *tonnage* and *poundage*, a small tax on each ton of wine and pound of commodities, was one of the methods of levying money, which Charles believed a part of the crown's prerogative, and at the same time not directly contrary to the Petition of Right, as, though it stood on the footing of an original parliamentary grant, it had often been continued from one reign to another without being renewed by parliament. It was easy to see, that though the king himself and the partisans of the crown might in reality satisfy their consciences that in levying this duty there was no breach of the late concessions made by the Petition of Right, it was sufficient to afford a very strong handle to the opposite party to complain of a violation of that statute.

Charles, continuing to levy those exceptionable duties of tonnage and poundage, had proceeded so far as to imprison one of the members of the House on his refusal to pay them. This imprudent violence threw the Commons into the most outrageous ferment, which the king found no other means of effectually quelling but by a new dissolution of the parliament, which he did now with a firm determination of calling no more such assemblies till he should perceive the symptoms of a more compliant disposition.

To avoid the occasion of new supplies, Charles made peace with France and Spain; but money was requisite for the support of government, and he now found it necessary to continue to levy the duties of tonnage and poundage, together with the tax on ship-money, an assessment on the whole counties for victualling and supporting the navy; and high fines were imposed for various offences, without any judicial trial, by the sole authority of the court of Star-chamber. It is true that all these exertions of power were sanctioned by former custom, and now in a manner authorized by absolute necessity; yet there is not a doubt that they were unconstitutional: it was, therefore, with a most laudable spirit that John Hampden, a member of the House of Commons, refused to pay the tax of ship-money, and brought the question to a trial before the Exchequer Chamber, where, in the opinion of most men, it was decided with great partiality in favor of the crown; a decision, indeed, which gave Charles grounds for persevering in it as a legal measure; but his real interest suffered essentially by that judgment, which increased the party of the discontented, and taught men to believe and affirm that the fountains of justice were corrupted, and that the law would now give its sanction to any measures, however arbitrary or unconstitutional.

These motives of discontent were further increased by the fervor of religious enthusiasm. The king, by the advice of Laud, archbishop of Canterbury, a prelate of great indiscretion, had relaxed the penalaties against catholics, or allowed them to be commuted for pecuniary fines. Laud had likewise introduced into the church-discipline some insignificant changes, such as re-placing the communion-table at the east end of the church, and the priests using an embroidered vestment—circumstances which were represented as a certain prelude to the entire re-introduction of the superstitions of Rome.

It was extremely imprudent in Charles to venture at this time, likewise, upon religious innovations with his subjects of Scotland. James had, with some success, established in that country a hierarchy on the pattern of the English church, and Charles wanted to complete the work of his father, by resting discipline upon a regular system of canons, and modelling the public worship by the forms of a liturgy. These designs were extremely odious to the Scots, and they met with the reception which might have been expected. The bishop of Edinburgh, beginning to read the service in the cathedral-church, was assaulted with the most furious rage, and narrowly escaped being torn in pieces by the populace. The tumult spread through the whole kingdom, and the heads of the presbyterian party, assembling themselves in the capital, subscribed the famous bond called the *National Covenant*, by which, after a formal renunciation of the abominations of popery, they bound themselves by a solemn oath to resist all religious innovations, and to defend to the utmost the glory of God, and the honor of their king and country. The consequences of this association, which was eagerly subscribed by all ranks and conditions of the people, were extremely alarming; and Charles, perceiving he had gone too far, offered to suspend the use of the liturgy, provided matters were put on the same footing as before, and the Scots would retract their covenant. But they replied that they would sooner renounce their baptism; and summoning a general assembly at Glasgow, they, with great deliberation, not only annulled the liturgy and canons, but utterly abolished the episcopal hierarchy, which, for above thirty years, had quietly subsisted in the kingdom.

To maintain this violent procedure, it was very soon perceived that there would be a necessity of having recourse to arms, and the Scots commenced hostilities by seizing and fortifying the most important places of strength in the kingdom. To quell these disorders in Scotland, Charles, much against his inclination, found it absolutely necessary again to assemble his parliament. But this assembly, after an interruption of eleven years, seemed to meet with the same spirit as that which had occasioned their dissolution. Instead of supplies, the king heard of nothing but the grievances of *tonnage* and *poundage* and the *ship-money*, and violent complaints against the arbitrary jurisdiction of the *Star-Chamber*. With a blind precipitation, Charles dissolved this parliament as he had done the preceding—a measure which he ought to have foreseen might well increase, but could never contribute to remove, the discontents of the people. The Scots, in the meantime, having penetrated into the heart of England, and still professing great duty and loyalty, while they were committing the most determined acts of hostility, the king saw himself once more reduced to the necessity of calling a new parliament, his *fifth* and *last*.

The time was come when those disputes, which for many years had been violently fermenting in the nation, had attained their utmost crisis. Charles now saw, when it was too late, that the orrent was irresistible, and he resolved to give it way. This parliament began, like all the others, by bringing forward a complicated catalogue of grievances. The tonnage and poundage was aimed at among the first; a bill was prepared, expressly granting this duty for the period only of two months; and fixing, in the strongest and most positive terms, the right of parliament alone to bestow it. It was passed by the king without hesitation. Monopolies of every kind were abolished; and all who were concerned in them, as well as in levying the ship-money, were fined as delinquents. A bill was brought in for the regular summoning of parliament every third year: this bill, a most important concession, likewise received the royal assent. Encouraged by these successful experiments of their power, a heavier blow was yet meditated against the sovereign, in the impeachment of his favorite minister, the earl of Strafford. By a concurrence of accidents, this nobleman labored under the odium of all the three nations of the British empire. The Scots regarded him as the adviser of all the measures obnoxious to that country; the Irish, whom he had governed as lord lieutenant, had found him extremely arbitrary; and, with the English, at least the parliamentary leaders, it was sufficient cause of hatred that, having begun public life as an assertor of the popular claims, he had in maturer age become the chief friend and counsellor of the king.

Strafford was impeached; for against an unpopular minister it is easy to form articles of impeachment. Laud, the archbishop of Canterbury, was, in like manner, arraigned for treason, and both committed prisoners to the Tower. The great and fundamental charge against them, which was compounded of an infinite number of articles of offence, was the design, which the Commons supposed to have been formed by their counsel and advice, of subverting the laws and constitution of the kingdom, and introducing arbitrary and unlimited authority.

Strafford was brought to trial; he defended himself with great ability. The charge upon the whole was certainly relevant; but though it was apparent he had acted with great intemperance and indiscretion, nothing was proved which was sufficient to justify a penal conclusion. His enemies now found it necessary to attempt a new mode of prosecution, and this was the most unjustifiable part of their procedure. A bill of attainder was brought into the House of Commons, in which the principal proof adduced of Strafford's guilt was a scrap of paper in the handwriting of Sir Henry Vane, consisting of notes taken of a debate in the privy council on the subject of the war against the Scots, in which Strafford was said to have urged the king to go on to levy the ship-money, and to have hinted that he was now absolved from all rules of government. Six counsellors, together with Vane, had been present at this debate. Four of these declared that they recollected no such expressions of Strafford's; the other two could give no evidence, as one had left the country and the other was a state-prisoner. Vane's evidence, therefore, stood single and unsupported; yet a majority of the Commons passed the bill of attainder; and the Peers, intimidated by these violent and desperate measures, which made every man tremble for his own safety, choosing most of them to absent themselves from parliament, the bill was likewise, by a slender majority, carried through the upper house.

It remained now to obtain the royal assent. The populace flocked in thousands around the palace, crying loud for justice. Alarms were spread through the city of popish conspiracies, invasions, and insurrections. Open threats were uttered of the vengeance of God and man against all who protected or opposed the punishment of the guilty. The king's servants declined giving counsel or advice. The queen, terrified with these violent and increasing tumults, pressed him, with tears, to satisfy the demands of the people. Strafford himself (a singular instance of generosity and greatness of mind) wrote to him, entreating that, for the sake of public peace and to compose these fatal misunderstandings between the king and people, his life might be made a sacrifice.

Charles, after a conflict too severe for his fortitude, granted a commission to four noblemen to give the royal assent to the bill of attainder—a step which, to the last moment of his life, he never forgave himself. The Commons, taking advantage of the agony of his mind on this trying occasion, which left no room for just or cool reflection, laid hold of that opportunity to obtain his assent to a bill which rendered the parliament perpetual, which declared that they should not be dissolved, prorogued, or adjourned without their own consent. Strafford was beheaded on Tower Hill.

Thus the present parliament discovered a design which the preceding had either never fully entertained, or most carefully disguised. Hitherto most of the proceedings of the Commons had the sanction of a real regard for the interests of the kingdom, and a patriotic endeavor to fix the constitution on the firm basis of the liberties of the subject. The arbitrary measures of the crown had been, with great propriety, opposed; and a most beneficial effect had ensued of limiting an excessive and dangerous prerogative which, in some of the former reigns, had been so enlarged as in fact to render the sovereign absolute and independent of his parliament. In this reign, by a laudable and vigorous resistance, the Commons had obtained such concessions from the crown as fixed the constitution nearly upon the same equal principles on which it stands at this day: so far they had acted the part of patriots and friends to their country; but from this period their designs are not reducible to the same laudable principle. The last bill of the Commons had rendered the parliament perpetual—a measure which, in fact, annihilated the English constitution, by destroying that just equilibrium upon which its existence depends; and we shall now see the consequences of that decisive step, the plan pursued to its final accomplishment in the total extinction of the monarchical government.

Ireland, during these transactions, exhibited a scene of horror and bloodshed. The Irish Roman catholics had judged these turbulent times a fit season for asserting the independency of their country, and shaking off the English yoke. From a detestable abuse of the two best of motives, *religion* and *liberty*, they were incited to one of the most horrible attempts recorded in the annals of history. They conspired to assassinate, in one day, all the protestants in Ireland, and the design was hardly surmised in England till above forty thousand had been put to the sword.

To extinguish this dreadful rebellion, the king solicited the aid of the parliament, and committed to them the charge of the war. They immediately laid hold of that offer, which they interpreted in its most ample sense, as implying a transference to them of the whole military and executive power of the crown. Troops were levied with the utmost industry and alacrity, arms provided, and all military stores furnished from the royal magazines; a measure which served two most important purposes, to disarm the king and to arm themselves. The Irish rebellion, the ostensible motive, was but slightly attended to, while schemes of much more consequence were in agitation at home. There was nothing now required but a cause for an open rupture, and that was not long wanting.

The Commons found a considerable opposition to the extreme violence of their measures from the House of Peers. It was therefore necessary that some course should be taken to bring *them* to a more perfect acquiescence. Some of the bishops having presented a formal complaint to parliament that the insults of the populace endangered their lives, and protested against all proceedings in the upper house which might be held in their absence, the Commons framed an impeachment of the whole bench of bishops, as endeavoring to subvert the constitution of parliament, and they were all committed to custody.

These measures had the effect for which, it is presumable, they were intended. The patience of Charles was entirely exhausted, and he was impelled to a violent exertion of authority. The attorney-general, by the king's command, impeached five members of the house of Commons, among whom were John Hampden, Pym, and Holles, the chiefs of the popular party. A serjeant being sent, without effect, to demand them of the Commons, the king, to the surprise of every body, went in person to the House to seize them. They had notice of his intention, and had withdrawn. The Commons justly proclaimed this attempt a breach of privilege. The streets reëchoed with the clamors of the populace, and a general insurrection was prognosticated. The king acknowledged his error by a humiliating message to the House; but the submission was as ineffectual as the violence had been imprudent.

The spirits of the people were now wound up to their highest pitch. War was the last resource; and the signal was soon given for its commencement by a new bill of the Commons, naming the governors and lieutenants of all the fortified places, and making them responsible for their conduct to the parliament alone. The next step was to assume the whole *legislative power*, which was done by a new vote, making it a breach of privilege to dispute the law of the land declared by the Lords and Commons.

Counter-manifestos were now published on the part of the king and of the parliament. It is remarkable that in one of those upon the part of the king, the constitution is represented as a mixture of three forms of government—the monarchical, aristocratical, and democratical; an idea which, perhaps, Charles, in his high notions of an arbitrary prerogative, would not have admitted in the beginning of his reign, and which now, by a strange vicissitude of opinions, was virtually denied by his parliament, who assumed to *themselves, independent of the king*, the whole legislative and executive authority of government.

The royal cause was supported by almost all the nobility, a great portion of the men of landed property, all the mem ners of the church of England, and all the catholics of the kingdom. The parliament had on their side the city of London, and the inhabitants of most of the great towns. I will not enter into a minute detail of this calamitous civil war. The first military operations were favorable to the king; he was aided by his nephew, prince Rupert, son of the unfortunate elector palatine. The parliamentarians were defeated in the battles of Worcester and Edgehill. The queen, who inherited a considerable portion of the spirit of her father, the great Henry IV. of France, brought to the aid of her husband, money, troops, arms, artillery, and ammunition, from the continent. She had raised money even by the sale of her own jewels and effects. The first campaign, on the whole, was favorable to the royalists; though they were defeated in the battle of Newbury, in which Charles lost one of his best counsellors and ablest partisans, Lucius Cary, viscount Falkland, a man of superior talents, and whose virtues were equal to his abilities. He had formerly, with the most laudable zeal for the interests of the subject, stood foremost in all attacks on the high prerogative of the crown; but he wished to reform, not to destroy, the constitution; and, with the same noble ardor with which he had resisted the first tyrannical exertions of the monarch, he now supported Charles in those limited powers which yet remained to him: he pursued the straight and onward path, equally remote from either extreme—a beautiful model of the most exalted and virtuous patriotism.

To strengthen their cause by the active assistance of the Scots, the parliament, of whom the greatest part were inclined to the presbyterian form of discipline, now expressed their desire for ecclesiastical reformation and the abolition of the hierarchy. Commissioners were appointed to treat with the king to adopt the Scottish mode of ecclesiastical worship, and others despatched to Scotland with powers to enter into a strict confederacy in the articles of religion and politics. The Solemn League and Covenant was framed at Edinburgh, in which both parties bound themselves, by oath, to extirpate popery, prelacy, and profane ceremonies, and to reform the two kingdoms according to the Word of God, and on the model of the purest churches; to maintain the privileges of king and parliament, and to bring to justice all incendiaries and malignants. In consequence of this confederacy, 20,000 Scots took the field, and marched into England to coöperate with the parliamentary forces.

The celebrated Oliver Cromwell, who had hitherto made no figure, began now to distinguish himself. A sect had lately sprung up, who termed themselves Independents. They held the presbyterians in as great abhorrence as those of the church of England. They pretended to immediate inspiration from heaven; rejected all ecclesiastical establishments; disdained all creeds and systems of belief; and, despising every distinction of governors and governed, held all men, king, nobility, and commons, to be upon a level of equality. Of this sect, Cromwell was one of the chief leaders. He was a person of a rude and uncultivated, but very superior genius; a man whose peculiar dexterity lay in discovering the characters, and taking advantage of the weaknesses of mankind. He was in religion at once an enthusiast and a hypocrite; in political matters, both a leveller and a tyrant; and in common life, cautious, subtle, and circumspect, at the same time that he was daring and impetuous. With these qualities, Oliver Cromwell acquired such superiority as to attain the command of the parliament and of the kingdom.

By the interest of Cromwell and his party, Sir Thomas Fairfax was chosen general of the parliamentary forces—a man over whom he had an absolute ascendency, and under whom he himself immediately took the command of a regiment of horse.

The royal cause, in the meantime, had met with some success in Scotland from the great military abilities of the marquis of Montrose; but matters in England wore a different aspect. The royal army was totally defeated in the battle of Naseby. This victory was decisive. With the shattered remains of his troops, the king retired to Oxford, and on the point of being besieged, while he lay between the Scots and English armies, he came to the resolution of putting himself into the hands of the Scots, who, he still flattered himself, as his countrymen, had yet some regard for his person and authority; but here he was disappointed. Equally inveterate and inflamed, and at this time dependent upon the English for indemnifying them in the charges of the war, they made no scruple to deliver up Charles to the parliament, who cheerfully paid all their demands of arrears.

The war was now at an end; but the views of Cromwell were only in their first opening. The parliament, who had no further occasion for the army, now thought of disbanding them; but Cromwell and the troops had no such inclination. The king was in the hands of the commissioners of parliament, and Cromwell, without waiting for the general's orders, despatched a party of 500 horse, who seized the king's person, and brought him safe to the army. The parliament was thrown into the utmost consternation, which was redoubled when they beheld Cromwell, now chosen general, march to within a few miles of the city of London. His design was not long ambiguous. He caused eleven members of the House of Commons, the chiefs of the presbyterian party, to be impeached for high treason; and afterwards entering the city, where all was uproar and confusion, he ordered the lord mayor and the chief magistrates to prison. The speakers of the two houses surrendered, and put themselves under the army's protection. The parliament was now at their mercy, and they had in their hands the king and the whole authority of the government.

The king, who now saw the spirit of the army directed so strenuously against his enemies, began to believe himself in the hands of his friends; but he was miserably deceived. Cromwell had determined the destruction both of king and parliament. The eyes of Charles were soon opened to his situation. Rumors were artfully propagated of designs against his life, of which the intention was to force him to attempt an escape from his confinement. They had the desired effect; he found means to escape from Hampton Court, and to fly to the Isle of Wight, where he was forthwith detained a close prisoner.

Here a negotiation was begun between the king and the parliament, which, from the concessions made by Charles, had, at first, every appearance of terminating this state of anarchy. He agreed to resign to the parliament the power over the militia and army, and the right of raising money for their support. He agreed to abolish episcopacy; and that for three years the presbyterian form of worship should take place; after which, a lasting plan should be settled by the advice of parliament. He resigned the disposal of all the offices of state, and the power of creating peers without consent of parliament. In short, he acquiesced in all their demands; two articles only excepted; to give up his friends to punishment, and to abandon his own religious principles.

After a debate of three days, the parliament, of whom a great majority were now most sincerely desirous of an accommodation, passed a vote, by which it was declared that the king's concessions were a reasonable foundation for the House to proceed upon in the settlement of the kingdom. The vote was no sooner heard, than Cromwell marched into London, surrounded the House of Commons, and suffering none to enter but his own party, excluded about two hundred of the members. Thus there remained about sixty of the Independent party, sure and unanimous in their intended measures. The vote agreeing to the king's concessions was now rescinded, and another passed, declaring it treason in a king to levy war against his parliament, and appointing a high court of justice to take trial of *Charles's treason.* This vote being sent up to the House of Lords, was rejected without a dissenting voice. But this mockery of a parliament was not thus to be stopped in their career. The next vote was that the Commons of England have the supreme authority of the nation, independent of either king or peers. Cromwell himself was ashamed of the glaring illegality of these proceedings, and apologized for his conduct by declaring that he had a divine impulse that the king had been abandoned by heaven.

Thus sixty fanatical Independents, who had the assurance to term themselves the Commons of England, and to arrogate the supreme authority of the nation, prepared a spectacle for the astonishment of all Europe. The king was brought to trial

With great dignity of demeanor, and with high propriety, he refused to ratify the authority of this illegal tribunal, by answering to those charges of which he was accused, but offered to vindicate publicly his conduct to his subjects and to the world. A few witnesses being called, who swore to his having appeared in arms against the forces of the parliament, sentence was passed, condemning him to be beheaded. Without regard to the remonstrances of France, of Holland, and of now repenting Scotland, or to the judgment formed of these proceedings by all the European nations, this sentence was carried into effect, and Charles fell by the stroke of an executioner on the 30th day of January, 1649.

From this event, the fate of Charles I., two questions naturally arise: the one, whether it is in any case lawful for the subject to carry resistance so far as to employ the sword against the sovereign, or to bring him to justice as a delinquent; the other, whether, in the particular case of Charles, his subjects were justifiable in that procedure.

As to the first question, I hold the principle of *resistance* to be inherent in all government; because it is consonant to human nature, and results from the nature of government itself. Government is founded either on *superior force*, which subjects every thing to the despotic will of the governor, or it is founded on a *compact*, *express* or *tacit*, by which the subject consents to be ruled, and the prince to rule, according to certain laws and regulations. In the former case of a government founded on force, resistance is implied in the very idea of such a constitution; and force is lawfully employed to dissolve a connection which owed its existence to force. In the case of a government subsisting by an express or tacit agreement between the prince and subjects, while the prince maintains his part of the contract by a strict adherence to those rules by which it is stipulated that he is to govern, resistance is unlawful and rebellious; where he violates those rules, resistance is legal and justifiable. In all governments, therefore, the principle of resistance is naturally inherent; and if that is allowed, I see nothing that can, or that ought, to limit it in degree, till its purpose is accomplished.

With regard to the second question, whether, in the case of Charles, the subjects were justifiable in carrying their resistance so far as to put the sovereign to death, neither, do I apprehend it difficult to form a precise opinion. The narrative I have given of the transactions of this reign leads to a conclusion, which is equally remote from either extreme, equally condemnatory of the opinions of the bigoted supporters of arbitrary power, and the furious partisans of the rights of the people. The many violations of the constitution by Charles I., (whether he understood them to be such or not is nothing to the purpose,) unquestionably justified that resistance on the part of the people, which at length produced its effect in obtaining such concessions from the sovereign as afforded the utmost possible liberty to the subject, consistent with the idea of a limited monarchy. But from the moment that end was attained, resistance ceased to be lawful. It could have nothing else for its object than the destruction of the constitution. In the case of Charles, the sovereign, taught by severe experience that the people had rights, which, when arbitrarily infringed, they had strength to vindicate, at length not only gave them back their own, but yielded so much of his lawful and constitutional authority as to leave himself little more than the name and shadow of royalty. To insist on a further abasement was illegal and inhuman; to push revenge the length of a *capital punishment* was a degree of criminality for which there is not an adequate term of blame.

Such are the reflections which would naturally arise on this subject in an impartial breast, upon the supposition that Charles I. had been brought to trial and condemned to death by the authority of the *people of England*, or a fair representation of them in parliament. But let it not be forgotten *who* were those that took upon them to act in the name of the people of England, and what was the nature of that parliament which authorized his trial and condemnation—a handful of fanatics, who, after expelling two hundred of the members of parliament, the people's lawful representatives, annulling a vote of the house which agreed to the king's concessions, passing another vote which declared the House of Peers a useless branch of the constitution, assumed to themselves the whole legislative and executive authority of government. The perversion of that man's understanding must be deplorable indeed, who, professing himself an advocate for the rights of mankind, holds *these* to be laudable exertions of virtue and of patriotism.

CHAPTER XXX.

Commonwealth of England, Reigns of Charles II. and James II. —Charles II. acknowledged King in Scotland and Ireland—Marquis of Montrose—Cromwell defeats the Scots at Dunbar—Battle of Worcester—Navigation Act—Cromwell dissolves the Parliament by Violence, and puts an End to the Rupublic—Barebones's Parliament—Cromwell named Lord Protector—His successful Administration—Death—Richard his Son resigns the Protectorate—the Rump Parliament—Disunion in the Council of Officers—General Monk—Charles II. proclaimed—Profuse and voluptuous Reign—War with Holland and France—Plague and Fire of London—Treaty of Aix-la-Chapelle—Alarms of Popery—Titus Oates—Bill excluding the Duke of York from the Crown—Habeas Corpus Act—Distinction of Whig and Tory first used—Conspiracy of Russell, Sidney, and Monmouth—Death of Charles—James II.—Monmouth beheaded—Violent Measures of James excite the Disgust of all Parties—William, Prince of Orange—James escapes to the Continent—Crown settled on the Prince and Princess of Orange—Declaration fixing the Constitution.

That select assembly of sixty or seventy fanatical Independents, which styled itself a parliament, having passed a vote which abolished the House of Peers as a useless part of the constitution, began to think of framing some rules and forms for the administration of the government; and the more disinterested friends to liberty were soothed for some time with their favorite system, a republic. The Scots, however, of whom the great majority had yet an attachment to monarchy, and who had sufficient reason for being disgusted at the conduct of the Independents to the English Presbyterians, determined to acknowledge the son of the late monarch for their lawful sovereign, and with the consent of parliament they proclaimed Charles II. king; but on the express condition of his subscribing the Solemn League and Covenant. Ireland recognised him without any conditions.

The Scots, while they were thus inviting Charles to take possession of one of his paternal kingdoms, gave an example of that cruel and detestable fanatic spirit, which, to their shame, they seem to have possessed at this time above every other nation. James Graham, marquis of Montrose, a man whose heroism and singular endowments of mind would have rendered him an honor to any age or nation, had, in the latter years of the late monarch, distinguished himself in many successful attempts, both in Scotland and in England, in favor of the royal cause. After the king's captivity, when the war was at an end, he had, at his sovereign's command, laid down his arms and retired into France. Upon the king's death, with the aid of some foreign troops, he landed in the north of Scotland, with the purpose of reducing the party of the Covenanters, and establishing the authority of Charles II. upon a constitutional basis, independent of those servile conditions which that party was desirous of imposing on him. He expected to be joined by a large party of the Highlanders, but he found the whole country fatigued with the recent disorders, and much indisposed to renew hostilities. In the meantime he was suddenly attacked by a large body of the Covenanters, and, taken by surprise with an inferior force, he was defeated and made prisoner. His fate was attended with every circumstance of insolence and cruelty, which distinguishes revenge in the meanest of souls. He died upon a gibbet, and his limbs were distributed through the principal cities of the kingdom. This was *he* whom one of the most penetrating judges of character (the cardinal de Retz, who intimately knew him) declares to have been one of those heroes of whom there are no longer any remains in the world, and who are only to be met with in the narratives of ancient history.

Meantime Charles, who had no other resource, betook himself to Scotland, and was obliged, however unwillingly, to accede to every condition that was proposed to him. Fairfax, general of the parliament, had resigned all command of the army, and Cromwell, who was now commander-in-chief, after a successful expedition into Ireland to quell the party of the royalists in that country, marched with 16,000 men into Scotland, against his old friends and allies the Covenanters, who, now that Charles had subscribed to their terms, had become his firm adherents. They were much superior to Cromwell's army in number of their troops, but were as much inferior in point of discipline. They were defeated at Dunbar in a decisive engagement; and Charles, soon after retreating into England in hopes to unite the royalists in that country in his favor, Cromwell immediately followed, and attacking the royal army at Worcester, then extremely inconsiderable in their numbers, cut them entirely to pieces. Charles fled in disguise through the western counties of England, continually pursued, encountering for above forty days a most romantic series of dangers and difficulties, and often relying for safety on the meanest peasants, whose fidelity he found unshaken, notwithstanding the immense rewards which were offered for his discovery. At length he found a vessel which conveyed him to the coast of France.

Cromwell in the meantime returned in triumph to London. The republican parliament began now to make their government truly respectable, by the greatness of those designs which they formed, and the vigor with which they pursued them. A scheme was proposed to the states of Holland upon the death of the stadtholder, William II., for an union and coalition between the two republics. It was not relished by the Dutch, who were better pleased to maintain their own independence; and the parliament of England, piqued at their refusal, immediately declared war against them. The *navigation act* was passed, which prohibited all foreigners from importing into England in their ships any commodity which was not the growth or manufacture of their own country; an act which struck heavily against the Dutch, because their country produces few commodities; and their commerce consists chiefly in being the factors of other nations. This statute was in another way beneficial to the English, by obliging them to cultivate maritime commerce, from which they have derived the greatest part of their national wealth. In this war, which was most ably maintained on both sides—under Blake, the English admiral, and Van Tromp and de Ruyter, admirals of the Hollanders—the English, on the whole, had a clear superiority; the Dutch were cut off entirely from the commerce of the Channel; their fisheries were totally suspended, and above sixteen hundred of their ships fell into the hands of the English.

The parliament, glorying in these successes, which were so much to the honor of the Republic, began to find themselves independent of Cromwell and the army, and determined on a reduction of the land forces, which, while they found themselves so powerful at sea, were only an unnecessary burden upon the nation. This measure, which would have been fatal to the ambition of Cromwell, was prevented by him in a most extraordinary manner. Many circumstances had of late been observed, which discovered the selfish aims of this ambitious man; yet so great was his influence with the army that he readily found agents to coöperate with him in every scheme which he proposed.

Calling a council of his officers, a remonstrance was framed, to be presented to the parliament, reminding them that it was averse to the spirit of a democracy that any set of magistrates should be perpetual, and desiring that they might immediately think of dissolving, after issuing writs for the election of a new parliament. This application, it may be imagined, met with a sharp reply, which was nothing more than what Cromwell wished and expected. Before the smallest hint had transpired of his design, he now presented himself with three hundred soldiers at the door of the House of Commons. Leaving his guards without, he took his seat for some time and listened to their debates; then rising hastily up: "I judge," said he, "this parliament to be ripe for dissolution, (taking one of the members by the cloak.) *You*," said he, "are a whoremaster; (to another) you are a drunkard, and (to a third) you are an extortioner. The Lord hath done with you, get you gone, you are no longer a parliament." Then stamping with his foot, which was a signal for the soldiers to enter, "*Here*," said he, pointing to the mace which lay on the table, "take away that fool's bauble;" then ordering the soldiers to drive all the members out of the house, he locked the door himself, put the key into his pocket, and went home to his lodgings in Whitehall. Thus, by one of the boldest actions recorded in history, the famous Republic of England, which had subsisted four years and three months, was annihilated in one moment. This measure, which has drawn upon Oliver Cromwell the execrations of the violent partisans of liberty, as it dispelled that fine delusion of a patriotic motive, to which they would gladly have attributed the extinction of monarchy in the person of Charles, was regarded by the friends of the constitution with high satisfaction; and they now made the most flattering comments on the necessary instability and fundamental weakness of all systems of government which owe their existence to force and violence.

Yet Cromwell, thus become absolute master of the whole power, civil and military, of the three kingdoms, thought it necessary to leave the nation some shadow, some phantom of liberty. It was proper that there should be the appearance of a parliament; and he therefore, by the advice of his council of officers, summoned one hundred and twenty-eight persons from the different towns and counties of England, five from Scotland, and six from Ireland, to assemble at Westminster, with power to exercise legislative authority for fifteen months. These, who were chiefly a set of low fanatical mechanics, anabaptists and independents, were in scorn denominated by the people Barebones's Parliament, from the name of one of their most violent and active members, Praisegod Barebones, a leather-seller. This assembly, whose shameful ignorance, meanness, and absurdity of conduct rendered them useless and contemptible both to Cromwell and the nation, voluntarily dissolved themselves by a vote after a session of five months. A few of the members who dissented from this measure continuing to occupy the House of Commons, Cromwell sent one of his officers to turn them out. This officer, a colonel White, entering the house, demanded what they were doing there: the chairman answered, "They were seeking the Lord." "Then," said White, "you may go elsewhere, for to my certain knowledge the Lord has not been here these many years;" so saying, he turned them out of doors. Thus the supreme power became now vested in the council of officers. These, who were at Cromwell's absolute disposal, nominated him Lord Protector of the three kingdoms. He was installed in the palace of Whitehall, declared to hold his office for life, and an instrument was prepared, granting to him the right of making peace, war, and alliances, and authorizing a standing army to be kept up of 30,000 men for the support of government. He was obliged by the same instrument to assemble a parliament every three years. Thus the nation found that, after all their struggles, they had only exchanged one master for another, and in point of real freedom, it was confessed by the partisans of the revolution themselves, that this change was nothing for the better.

The administration of Cromwell was arbitrary, vigorous, and

spirited; the nation was loaded with enormous taxes; but the national character was high and respectable. He finished the war with Holland, and compelled the Dutch to yield to the English the honor of the flag, besides obliging them to pay to the East India Company £85,000 as a compensation for their losses The glory of the English arms at sea was nobly sustained by Blake—a zealous republican indeed, and consequently an enemy of all usurped power—but a man who loved his country, and knew that his duty called him to maintain its interest whatever might be the state of the government.

Yet amidst these successes abroad, the protector found his situation at home extremely uneasy. His parliaments were refractory, and he was often obliged to have recourse to the violent method of excluding, by a guard at the door, such of the members as he knew to be disaffected to him. At length, by using every art to influence the elections, and to fill the house with his sure friends, he got one parliament so perfectly to his mind, that a vote was proposed and passed for investing the protector with the dignity of *king*, and a committee was appointed to confer with him on that subject, and overcome any scruples which he might have on that score. But Cromwell's scruples were not violent; * he had other objections than what proceeded from his

* It appears, from a very curious conversation, which took place *four* years before this vote of the parliament, between Cromwell and Whitelocke, (reported by the latter in his Memorials,) that Cromwell was most earnestly desirous of the title of king; and that, although he put that desire chiefly on the ground of uniting the discordant councils and controlling the factions of the parliamentary leaders, it was chiefly the motive of his own personal safety, and the security of his usurped power, that in reality influenced him to desire that title and dignity. The following is a short part of that most extraordinary conversation. Cromwell takes Whitelocke aside, and begins by complimenting him highly, both on his wisdom and abilities, and on his firm attachment and fidelity to himself. Then he pictures, in strong words, the instability of that power which their party had, with so much labor and expense of blood, acquired; that the army was divided into factions, and hostile to the parliament; and that the latter seemed to have no other aim than to engross for their own members all offices of honor or profit; while, being the supreme power, they were under no control and liable to no account. "In short," adds Cromwell, "there is no hope of a good settlement, but, on the contrary, a great deal of fear, that what the Lord hath done so graciously for them and us will be all again destroyed: we all forget God, and God will forget us and give us up to confusion; and these men will help it on if they be suffered to proceed in their ways: some course must be thought on to curb and restrain them, *or we shall be ruined by them.*

"Whitelocke.—We ourselves have acknowledged them the supreme power, and taken our commissions and authority from them; and how to restrain and curb them after this, it will be hard to find out a way for it.

"Cromwell.—*What if a man should take upon him to be king?*

"Whitelocke.—I think that remedy would be worse than the disease.

"Cromwell.—Why think you so?

"Whitelocke.—As to your own person, the title of king would be of no advantage, because you have the full kingly power in you already, concerning the militia, as you are general. As to the nomination of civil officers, those whom you think fittest are seldom refused, and although you have no negative voice in the passing of laws, yet what you dislike will not easily be carried and the taxes are already settled, and in you power to dispose the money raised. As to foreign affairs, though the ceremonial application be to the parliament, yet own inclinations. He dreaded the resentment of the army. A majority of the officers had signed a remonstrance against this measure; and it was reported that many of them had entered into an engagement to put him to death if ever he should accept the crown. Even his own family, his son-in-law and brother-in-law, entreated him to refuse that dangerous offer, and threatened to resign their commissions and withdraw themselves from his service. At length Cromwell, with much reluctance, was obliged to refuse that dignity which he most anxiously desired, and had taken such uncommon measures to attain.* To console him for his mortifying disappointment, the parliament confirmed his title of protector, to which they added a perpetual revenue, and the right of appointing his successor. They gave him authority likewise to name a house of peers, and he issued writs to sixty members, among whom were five or six of the old nobility, some gentlemen of family and fortune, and the rest

---

the expectation of good or bad success is from your Excellency; and particular solicitations of foreign ministers are made to you only. So that I apprehend, indeed, less envy and danger and pomp, but not less power and real opportunities of doing good in your being general than would be if you had assumed the title of king.

"Cromwell.—I have heard some of your profession observe, that he who is actually king, (whether by election or by descent,) yet being once king, all acts done by him as king are lawful and justifiable, as by any king who hath the crown by inheritance from his forefathers; and that by an act of parliament in Henry VII.'s time, it is safer for those who act under a king, be his title what it will, than for those who act under any other power. And surely the power of a king is so great and high, and so universally understood and reverenced by the people of this nation, that the title of it might not only indemnify, in a great measure, those that act under it, but likewise be of great use and advantage in such times as these to curb the insolences of those whom the present powers cannot control."

Whitelocke replies, that whatever truth there may be in this in general, the assumption of this title by Cromwell would be attended with danger both to himself and his friends; that he would lose the favor of the whole of the republican party; and, as the question would come simply to be whether Stuart or Cromwell should be king, a new civil war would follow, and the great majority would side with the ancient line. Finally, he proposes that Cromwell should make a treaty with Charles, and secure for himself as high a station as he chose, while such bounds might be set to the monarchical authority as would be best for the nation's liberties. In conclusion Whitelocke adds, that Cromwell seemed displeased with this counsel, and that his carriage towards him was altered from that time, and he not long after found an opportunity to send him out of the way by an honorable employment, that he might be no obstacle to his ambitious designs.—Whitelocke Memorials, Anno 1652.

* The following ancedote, which rests on the authority of Harry Neville, one of the council of state, is found in the life of that author. "Cromwell having a design to set up himself, and bring the crown upon his own head, sent for some of the chief city divines, as if he made it a matter of conscience to be determined by their advice. Among these was the leading Mr. Calamy, who very boldly opposed the project of Cromwell's single government, and offered to prove it both unlawful and impracticable. Cromwell answered readily upon the first head of unlawful, and appealed to the safety of the nation being the supreme law. 'But,' says he, 'pray Mr. Calamy, why impracticable?' He replied, 'Oh, it is against the voice of the nation: there will be nine in ten against you.' 'Very well,' says Cromwell; 'but what if I should disarm the nine, and put the sword in the tenth man's hand—would not that do the business?'"

officers who had risen from the meanest professions. But none of the old nobility would deign to accept of a seat in this motley assembly: and by naming so many of his friends to sit in the upper house, the protector found he had lost the majority in the House of Commons, which now began to dispute and oppose all his measures. Enraged at his disappointment, he hastily dissolved this parliament, as he had done several of the preceding.

At length, a prey to disquietude and chagrin, and haunted by continual fears of attempts against his life,* the tumult of his mind gradually preyed upon a strong bodily constitution, and brought on a mortal disease, of which he died, on the 3d of September, 1658.

He had nominated his son Richard to succeed him in the protectorate, a man in every respect opposite to his father; of no genius, ability, or judgment; and possessed of mild and humane dispositions. He was, from the beginning of his government, the sport of factions. He was unable either to command respect from the army, or compliance from the parliament. Some of the principal officers, among whom was his own brother-in-law, Fleetwood, formed cabals against his authority, and went so far as to demand, in an imperious manner, that he would dissolve his parliament, and trust solely to his council of officers. Richard had the weakness to comply with their request, and he dismissed that assembly which was the sole support of his pitiful authority. He found now that he was virtually dethroned, and he soon after signed his demission in form. His brother Henry, who was lord-lieutenant of Ireland, a man of the same pacific dispositions, soon after imitated his example, and resigned his government; and thus fell at once into their original obscurity the family of the Cromwells, which had raised itself to a height above that of the sovereigns of their country. The council of officers were now possessed of the supreme power; but wishing to show some respect to the remains of a constitution, they collected together as many as could be found of that nominal parliament which had tried and put the king to death. This assembly, grown now both odious

---

*The situation of Cromwell some time before his death was extremely disquieting. The lawfulness of putting to death a tyrant was a doctrine that he himself had done his utmost to inculcate; his inordinate ambition preventing him from foreseeing its necessary application to his own usurped authority. A very able pamphlet was published, entitled "Killing no Murder," in which the author propounded three questions for discussion: viz., 1. Whether the Lord Protector was a tyrant? 2. If he be, whether it is lawful to do justice upon him without solemnity; that is, to kill him? 3. If it be lawful, whether it is likely to prove profitable to the Commonwealth? all which questions were resolved in the affirmative, and the conclusion was enforced with uncommon powers of eloquence and of argument. This book was written by captain Titus, under the feigned name of William Allen. Cromwell was deeply impressed by this performance; he saw the increasing discontents of the nation, the growing disaffection of the army, and even an alienation of his own kindred and relations. His mind became tortured with anxiety, and a fever of the spirits ensued, which terminated his life.

and contemptible, was termed by the people the "Rump Parliament." Its measures giving offence to the council of officers who assembled it, they very speedily dissolved it.

It is scarcely possible to conceive the disorder and anarchy that at this time prevailed universally in the nation. The government of Cromwell, vigorous and spirited as it was, had been in the main very prejudicial to the solid interests of the kingdom. The national taxes during his administration had, one year with another, amounted to twelve millions sterling; a sum to which never any thing nearly equal had been hitherto raised by the crown. His expenses for spies and secret intelligence are estimated at no less than £60,000 sterling a year. He left upon the nation above two millions of debt, though he found in the treasury above £500,000, and in stores to the amount of £700,000. The army, which was the main support of his government, and which amounted to 60,000, sometimes 80,000 men, kept in constant pay, was a most expensive drain to the revenue. Upon the death of the protector, the sole authority of government was in the hands of this standing army, of which the principal leaders began to aim, each for himself, at playing the same part which had raised Cromwell to the supreme power. Matters ran so high, that nothing less than a new civil war was apprehended, and the nation looked forward with despair to a series of calamities which seemed to have no end. In this state of affairs it is not to be wondered at that the great bulk of the people began earnestly to desire the restoration of their ancient form of government.

George Monk, one of Cromwell's generals, commanded at this time the army in Scotland, and by means of that authority he secretly planned the restoration of the exiled monarch, for which he found the most favorable dispositions in the nation. The tyranny of the council of officers becoming every day more intolerable, Monk marched his army into England, and declared that it was his resolution to compose the disorders of the kingdom, by bringing about the election of a free parliament. This measure, which the republican party knew to be equivalent to calling back the king, was most violently opposed; but Monk was seconded by the nation, and even the army began to abandon their republican leaders. After every attempt to excite a new civil war, which was their last resource, they were obliged to agree to the proposed measure, and a free parliament was assembled. Here matters did not long remain doubtful, an envoy from Charles having presented a declaration, by which he promised a full indemnity to all his former opponents, with the exception of such as the parliament should name, besides full liberty of conscience; and payment to the troops of all their arrears. The message was received with transports of joy, and Charles II. was proclaimed king, amidst the universal acclamations of his people, on the 29th of May, 1660.

This period of the Restoration was the proper time to have settled the respective rights of the crown and people upon a fixed and permanent basis, and it was proposed in parliament by some of the wisest and most politic of its members; but the great majority were so impatient, that they could not bear the thoughts of a lengthened negotiation, and blindly chose to repose implicit confidence on their sovereign's good dispositions.

The parliament settled on the crown a revenue of twelve hundred thousand pounds. The troops were paid and discharged, and only five thousand men, with some garrisons, were retained, as a standing military force. Eleven regicides, excepted by parliament from the general indemnity, were tried and brought to justice; and these men died with the intrepidity and constancy of martyrs.

The reign of Charles II. was the era of gaiety and splendor, but not of honor to the nation. Never was there a more sudden revolution in the manners of a court than what took place upon the Restoration. Instead of that savage gloom, the consequence of fanaticism, and a rude austerity of manners, the new monarch diffused around him an air of ease and merriment, a taste for show and magnificence, and all that relish for luxury and voluptuousness which distinguished the court of France at the same period. But the French monarch, Louis XIV., amidst all his relish for luxury and magnificence, was influenced by the prevailing passion of aggrandizing his kingdom and studying the national glory as well as his private pleasures. Charles, on the contrary, voluptuous and prodigal, carried to such a height his love of pleasure as materially to interfere with the cares of government. From a total want of economy, his expenses constantly exceeded his revenue; he was ever dependent on, and begging from his parliaments, and was obliged to recur to expedients dishonorable to the nation to supply the private wants of the crown. After dissipating the portion of his wife, Catharine of Portugal, and 200,000 crowns which had been given him by France, he sold Dunkirk, in the second year of his reign, to Louis XIV., for £400,000 sterling; a transaction no less displeasing to the English than agreeable to the French, to whom that place was a most important acquisition.

A new war was kindled between England and the Dutch, principally from their being rivals in maritime commerce. The House of Commons was desirous of a war, and Charles undertook it, after they had granted him a subsidy larger than had ever been voted, amounting to two millions and a half sterling. By the vigor and prudent foresight of the grand pensionary, John de Witt, the Dutch were in a most formidable state of defence. The English fleet, consisting of one hundred and forty-four sail, was commanded by the king's brother, James duke of York, and under him by prince Rupert and the earl of Sandwich. Louis XIV., then engaged in a defensive alliance with the states, determined to take an active part for their support, and England was now involved in a war both with France and Holland. After several desperate but indecisive engagements, England began to perceive that this war promised nothing but expense and bloodshed. A plague, which was then raging in London, consumed above 100,000 of its inhabitants: * a most dreadful fire, happening almost at the same time, had reduced almost the whole of the city to ashes; and amidst so many calamities it was not wonderful that the war-like ardor of the nation should be considerably abated. A negotiation was carried on at Breda, and a peace was concluded between the belligerent powers in 1667. By the treaty of Breda, New York was secured to the English, the Isle of Polerone, in the East Indies, to the Dutch, and Acadia, in North America, to the French.

An unsuccessful war is in England constantly attended with strong marks of the public odium to those who are believed to have been its advisers and conductors. The chancellor Clarendon, a man equally respectable for his virtue and integrity as for his eminent abilities, had at this time fallen under the popular displeasure, as being the king's first minister. It is certain that he had disapproved of the Dutch war, but he had advised the sale of Dunkirk, which was a measure still more odious. He was impeached in the House of Commons for treason, and condemned to perpetual exile. He passed the remainder of his life in France, which he dedicated to the composition of his History of the Civil Wars of England, a work which will live for ever.

England, scarcely reconciled to the Dutch, now formed with them, in conjunction with Sweden, a triple alliance to oppose the successes of Louis XIV. against the Spanish monarchy in the Low Countries; and the consequence of this triple alliance was an effectual stop to the victorious career of the French monarch, and the conclusion of the treaty of Aix-la-Chapelle, in the year 1668.

The domestic administration of Charles II. was far from being tranquil. It was his misfortune to be guided by very bad counsellors. His connections with France had been extremely disagreeable to the nation; his schemes of absolute government, the favorable disposition he showed to the catholics, and his allowing himself to be much influenced by the advice of his brother, the duke of York, who was avowedly of that religion,—all these circumstances concurred to furnish grounds for complaint and dissatisfaction. The terrors of popery were now revived, and the loudest complaints resounded from all quarters of the kingdom. A bill was brought into parliament for imposing a test oath on all

* See Account of the Ejected Clergy annexed to the Life of Baxter, by Calamy, vol. iii., pp. 33, 34; where there is a progressive account of the increase and decrease of this dreadful distemper from week to week, during the year 1665

who should enjoy any public office. They were obliged to take the sacrament in the established church, and to abjure the doctrine of transubstantiation; and, in consequence of this new law, to which the king was obliged to give his consent, his brother James, duke of York, lost his office of high admiral.*

But these concessions did not quiet the general fears and dis contents. A worthless impostor, one Titus Oates, who had more than once changed his religion, now set the whole nation in a ferment, by the discovery of a pretended plot of the catholics. He asserted that the pope, claiming the sovereignty of England, had entrusted the exercise of his power to the Jesuits, who had already got patents for the principal offices of the kingdom; that fifty Jesuits had undertaken that the king should be assassinated, and the crown bestowed on the duke of York, who, if he declined it, was likewise to be murdered; that the Jesuits, who it was supposed had already almost reduced London to ashes in the late dreadful fire, had planned another fire and massacre, with which they intended to begin the execution of their project.

These most extraordinary chimeras received, however, some countenance from circumstances. The duke of York's secretary was seized, and among his papers a variety of letters being found between him and the king of France's confessor and the pope's nuncio, which proved nothing else but a very indiscreet zeal for the Romish religion, it was easy to put such constructions on this correspondence as to strengthen Oates's story of the conspiracy. The informer received the thanks of parliament, with a pension of £1200 sterling, a reward which was sufficient to incite another villain, one Bedloe, to act the same part, and to add yet more circumstances of horror to this conspiracy, of which his narrative tallied in the main with that of Oates.† The popular frenzy was inflamed to the highest pitch; the parliament partook of the general madness, and a new test was proposed, by which popery

* It is a curious fact, that *test-oaths* are as old as the times of the ancient Athenians. Stobæus informs us, that there was a particular law at Athens, obliging every citizen, before his admission to any public office, to take an oath, "that he would defend the altars, and conform himself to the religious rites of his country.'

† The following fact shows how much these most astonishing prejudices had affected the minds even of those whose rank in life, education, and professional habits ought to have more peculiarly removed them from the influence of such impostures. It is given on the authority of Mr. Hooke, the Roman historian. "Lord Chief Justice Scroggs, hearing the testimony of Oates concerning a consultation among the papists in London, at which Oates swore *he was present* himself, disproved, in the fullest manner, by several persons who came over from France for the purpose, and who all swore to their *having seen Oates at St. Omer's on the very day he pretended to have been in London;* to one of them, who, on cross-examination, said 'he was certain Oates was at St. Omer's on that day, if he could believe his own senses;' replied, 'that all papists were taught not to believe their senses;' and so set aside the testimony of all the witnesses who had sworn to that fact"

was declared to be idolatry, and all members who refused this declaration were excluded from both houses. It was but by a majority of two voices that the duke of York was exempted from this test, who intreated, with tears in his eyes, that he might be allowed to exercise his religion in private. The queen was even accused of having intelligence of this conspiracy, of which the object was to murder her husband and remove herself from the throne.

Amidst these inquietudes the king's disgust was further increased by the accusation of the treasurer Danby, on the score of his having sold a peace to France. This was a direct attack upon the king himself, as it stood proved by his hand-writing, that Danby's letters in this negotiation were written by his order. To prevent these dangerous scrutinies, Charles thought it his most prudent measure to dissolve the parliament.

A second parliament went even farther than the first. The treasurer was impeached and committed to prison; and a bill passed the House of Commons for excluding the duke of York from the succession, as being a professed catholic. The famous act of *Habeas Corpus* was likewise the work of this parliament; one of the chief securities of English liberty. By this excellent statute, the nature of which we shall hereafter more fully consider, it is prohibited to send any one to a prison beyond seas: no judge, under severe penalties, must refuse a prisoner a writ of *habeas corpus*, by which the gaoler is directed to produce in court the body of the prisoner, and to certify the cause of his detainer and imprisonment;—every prisoner must be indicted the first term after his commitment, and brought to trial in the subsequent term. A law of this kind, so favorable to the liberty of the subject, takes place in no government except that of Britain, and even of itself is a sufficient argument of the superiority of our constitution to that of all other governments.

The spirit of faction among the people was, however, daily increasing. The parties of *Whig* and *Tory* now became first known by these epithets. The former were the opposers of the crown against the latter, who were its partisans; and as in most popular factions, each party had on its side a great deal of right and a great deal of wrong, most of the tory faction would have gone the length of supporting the monarch in the most arbitrary stretches of despotic power; and most of the whigs would gladly have stripped him of all power whatever. But between these two extremes is the line of moderation, a course easy to be seen, but very difficult to be steered; almost impossible to be kept in actions, and extremely difficult even in opinions; for the moderate man must make his account to be a favorite with neither party, but to be often obnoxious to both; and he must be endowed with that strength of mind as to find in his own conscience, and in the approbation of a few, a recompense to balance the entire loss of popular applause.

The party of the *Whigs* seemed predominant in the next parliament, and vengeance was taken on several of the unfortunate catholics, on suspicion of concern in the popish plot. Among these was the viscount Stafford, an old and venerable peer, who was condemned and executed upon the testimony of Titus Oates and two of his infamous and perjured associates. In the subsequent reign this wicked impostor was convicted of perjury, and condemned to the pillory and perpetual imprisonment, from which he was not released till after the revolution, when his signal services and sufferings were rewarded with a considerable pension.

The king, harassed by this parliament to give his consent to the bill excluding his brother from the throne, had no other expedient but to dissolve them, and he found their successors in the next parliament to be equally violent. To pacify them, he proposed that the duke of York should be banished for life, retaining after his accession only the title of king, while the next heir should govern the kingdom as regent; but this expedient was rejected, and the consequence was a dissolution likewise of this parliament, which was the last that Charles II. assembled.

He now began to adopt an economical system, and to retrench the expenses of the crown. He found his friends increasing in proportion, and was enabled to extend his authority; but still the great cause of dissatisfaction remained: the duke of York was at the bottom of all the measures of government, and his counsels encouraged Charles in his natural propensity to despotism. A conspiracy formed by Shaftesbury, and in which lord Russell, Algernon Sidney, and the duke of Monmouth, the king's natural son, were concerned, might have overturned the government, had not Shaftesbury, provoked at some unforeseen delays, retired in disgust to Holland. The rest were discovered and betrayed by one of the associates. Russell and Sidney suffered death with great fortitude, and gloried in being the martyrs of the cause of liberty. Monmouth was pardoned, but afterwards, retracting his confession, was obliged to fly from court.

The discovery of this conspiracy strengthened the power of the crown, and Charles continued to rule till his death, with an almost absolute degree of authority. The duke of York, without taking the test, resumed his office of high-admiral, and was now tacitly acknowledged by the nation as the successor to the throne. Charles died in the year 1685, in the fifty-fifth year of his age, and twenty-fifth of his reign; and the duke of York, accordingly, succeeded by the title of James II.

This short and inglorious reign, distinguished by nothing but a series of the most absurd and blind efforts of intemperate zeal, and arbitrary exertions for establishing a despotic authority in the crown, does not merit a long detail.* James was the instrument of his own misfortunes, and ran headlong to destruction. In a government where the people have a determined share of power, and a capacity of legally resisting every measure which they apprehend to be to their disadvantage, every attempt to change, in opposition to their general desire, the religion or civil constitution of the country, must be impracticable. The Roman catholics in England were not at this time one-hundredth part of the nation. How absurd, then, (as Sir William Temple told his sovereign,)—how contrary to common sense was it, to imagine that one part should govern ninety-nine who were of opposite sentiments and opinions! Yet James was weak enough to make that absurd and desperate attempt. The nobility of the kingdom, by natural right the counsellors of the sovereign, were obliged to give place to a set of Romish priests, who directed all his measures; and James, as if he was determined to neglect nothing which might tend to his own destruction, began his reign by levying without the authority of parliament all the taxes which had been raised by his predecessor: he showed a further contempt of the constitution and of all national feeling by going openly to mass, and though in his first parliament, he solemnly promised to observe the laws and to maintain the protestant religion, he, at the same time, hinted in pretty strong terms, that if he found them at all refractory or backward in granting such supplies as he should require, he could easily dispense with calling any more such assemblies. It was not a little surprising that he found this parliament disposed to receive meekly this first specimen of his despotic disposition, and to grant him all that he required of them.

The duke of Monmouth having entered into a new rebellion, the parliament declared him guilty of high treason, and voted a large sum of money for quelling this insurrection. Monmouth was defeated, made prisoner, and beheaded, and the nation now discovered one particular of the king's disposition with which they had hitherto been unacquainted—a great degree of cruelty and inhumanity. Vast numbers of those unhappy prisoners, who were taken after the defeat of Monmouth, were hanged without any form of trial; and the execrable Judge Jeffreys filled the kingdom with daily executions under the sanction of justice.

---

* At the beginning of this reign an excellent address was presented to James by the Quakers.

"These are to testify to thee our sorrow for our friend Charles, whom we hope thou wilt follow in every thing that is good. We hear that thou art not of the religion of the land any more than we; and, therefore, may reasonably expect that thou wilt give us the same liberty that thou takest thyself.

"We hope that in this and all things else thou wilt promote the good of thy people, which will oblige us to pray that thy reign over us may be long and prosperous."

It had been happy for the new sovereign had he attended to the equity of this requisition, and to the wisdom of the advice which it conveyed.

Many of these trials were attended with the mos iniquitous procedure; but all applications to the king for pardon were checked by a declaration, that he had promised to forgive none who should be legally condemned. "When the bench is under the direction of the cabinet, trials are conspiracies, and executions are murders."*

The Commons seemed possessed with a spirit of the most abject slavery; the king was proceeding fast to invade every branch of the constitution, and met from them with no resistance; the House of Peers, however, taking upon them to examine the dispensation given from taking the test oath, James, who could no longer bear even the shadow of opposition, immediately prorogued the parliament.

This intemperate procedure raised a general alarm; but the king's imprudence knew no bounds, and went on from one exasperating measure to another. The bishop of London was suspended from his ecclesiastical function, for refusing to censure a clergyman who had preached against the doctrines of the church of Rome. Six other bishops, having refused to publish the king's equally fraudulent as illegal *declaration for liberty of conscience*, were immediately committed to prison. James sent an ambassador to the pope, though all correspondence with Rome was by law treasonable, and he received the pope's nuncio in London, who published pastoral injunctions, and consecrated several Romish bishops. A catholic president was appointed by the king to Magdalen college, Oxford, and on its refusal to admit him, the whole members were expelled except two who complied. In short, the king's intentions were not at all disguised; and the Roman Catholics began openly to boast that a very little time would see their religion fully established.

James had three children, the princess Mary, who was married to William, prince of Orange, the stadtholder of the United Provinces; Anne, married to prince George of Denmark; and James, an infant, born in the year 1687. The prince of Orange, who, from the time of his father-in-law's accession, began to look towards the crown of England, had kept on good terms with James till the event of the prince of Wales's birth, which was a disappointment to his hopes of succession. He now began to think of securing it by force of arms, to which the misconduct of the king and the discontents of the people gave him the most flattering invitation. While he was employed on the continent in secretly making vigorous preparations for war, his agents and emissaries secured him a great number of adherents in England. The king had disgusted all parties. The whigs who lamented the loss of the national liberty, and the tories who trembled for

* Ralph's History of England, pref.

the danger of the established church, all joined in a hearty detestation of the measures of the crown.

One singular circumstance was the infatuation of the king, and his total blindness to the progress of those measures both at home and on the continent which were preparing his immediate downfall. When Louis XIV. apprized him of his danger, and offered to send him the aid of a fleet, and to make a diversion in his favor by invading the United Provinces, he refused the offer, and would not give credit to the information.

At length the prince of Orange set sail with a fleet of five hundred ships and fourteen thousand men. He landed in England on the 15th of November, 1688, having sent before him a manifesto, in which he declared his intentions of saving the kingdom from destruction, vindicating the national liberty, and procuring the election of a free parliament. He was received with general satisfaction. The chief of the nobility and officers hastened to join him. James found himself abandoned by his people, by his ministers, his favorites, and even by his children. In a state of despair and distraction, he formed the dastardly resolution of escaping into France, and he sent off beforehand the queen and the infant prince. Following them himself, he was taken by the populace at Feversham and brought back to London. But the prince of Orange, to facilitate his escape, sent him under a slight guard to Rochester, from whence he soon found an opportunity of conveying himself to the continent.

The parliament was now summoned, but met simply as a *Convention*, not having the authority of the king's convocation. The Commons declared, that James having attempted to overturn the constitution of the kingdom by breaking the original contract between the king and people, and having, by the advice of Jesuits and other wicked persons, violated the fundamental laws and withdrawn himself out of the kingdom, had abdicated the government, and that the throne was thereby vacant. This vote, the terms of which, rather than the subtance of it, occasioned some debate in the House of Peers, was at last passed by a considerable majority.

The most important question remained : how was the government to be settled ? A variety of different opinions ultimately resolved into two distinct proposals : either that a regent should be appointed, or the crown settled upon the king's eldest daughter Mary, the princess of Orange, and in case of her issue failing, upon the princess Anne. The stadtholder, while these matters were in agitation, conducted himself with infinite prudence and good policy. He entered into no intrigues with either of the houses of parliament, but during their whole deliberations preserved a total silence. At length, when it was resolved that the crown should be settled in the way of one of these alternatives, he assembled some of the chief nobility, and announced that, having been invited into the kingdom to restore its liberties, he had now happily effected that purpose; that it behooved not him to interfere in the determinations of the legislature with regard to the settlement of the crown; but that, being informed as to the two alternatives which were proposed, he thought it his duty to declare that in executing either of these plans he could give no assistance; that he was determined to decline the office of a regent, and that he would rather remain a private person than enjoy a crown which must depend upon the life of another.

The sister princesses themselves seconded these views of the stadtholder; and the principal parties being thus agreed, a bill was proposed and passed by the convention, settling the crown on the prince and princess of Orange—the former to have the sole administration of the government; the princess Anne to succeed after their death; her posterity after those of the princess of Orange, but before those of the prince by any other wife.

To this settlement of the crown the convention added a declaration, fixing the nature of the constitution with respect to the rights of the subject and the royal prerogative. Of this declaration the following are the most essential articles. The king cannot suspend the laws nor the execution of them without the consent of parliament. He can neither erect an ecclesiastical nor any other tribunal by his own sole act. He cannot levy money without a parliamentary grant, nor beyond the terms for which it shall be granted. It is declared the right of the subjects to petition the crown, for which they can neither be imprisoned nor prosecuted. Protestant subjects may keep such arms for their defence as are allowed by law. No standing army can be kept up in time of peace but by consent of parliament. The elections of members of parliament must be free and uninfluenced, and there must be a freedom of parliamentary debate. Excessive bails, exorbitant fines, and too severe punishments are prohibited. The juries on trials for high treason must be members of the communities; and to remedy abuses, it is necessary that parliaments be frequently assembled. A new form was published instead of the old oath of supremacy, which declares that no prince, prelate, state, or foreign sovereign, hath, or ought to have, any jurisdiction, power, superiority, preëminence, or authority, ecclesiastical or spiritual, in the kingdom.

In Scotland the revolution was not, as in England, effected by a coalition of the whigs and tories. There was an entire separation of these opposite parties. A convention was summoned at Edinburgh, where the tories, finding themselves greatly inferior in numbers, withdrew from the assembly, which then proceeded to pass a decisive vote that James, by mal-administration and abuse of power, had forfeited all title to the crown; they therefore made a tender of the royal dignity to the prince and princess of Orange.

Such was the final settlement of the British government at the great era of the revolution of 1688.

CHAPTER XXXI.

ON THE CONSTITUTION OF ENGLAND: —Historical Sketch of, up to the Revolution—The Legislative Power—Constitution of the House of Commons—House of Peers—the Executive Power—Powers of the Crown now limited—Habeas Corpus Act—Trial by Jury—Liberty of the Press.

IT has been customary for our political writers, in order to give the greater weight to their theories of government; to trace the origin of the British constitution to a most remote period of antiquity. The opinion of Montesquieu is well known, who derives our constitution from the woods of Germany, and finds among those rude nations in their military assemblies the model of the British parliament; but if every assembly of a people is the model of a parliament, I see no reason why we may not derive it as well from the Spartans, the Athenians, or Romans, as from the Germans. Its antiquity is sufficiently remote if we can trace our constitution even as far back as the Norman conquest.

The Anglo-Saxon Wittenagemot, as has been observed, contained, indeed, the rude model of a parliament; at least of a great council: for there are no grounds for believing that there was any thing in that assembly approaching to a representation of the people.

William the Conqueror subverted the ancient fabric of the Saxon government; he dismissed the former occupiers of lands to distribute them among his Normans; and he established at once a system best suited to maintain his own power—the feudal government, till then unknown in Britain. In the continental nations of Europe, the feudal system arose by slow degrees. The authority of the crown was limited by the power of the barons, and the king had scarcely any thing more than a nominal superiority over his nobles. It was very different in England: the feudal system was introduced at once, by a monarch whose power was absolute. He totally extinguished the ancient liberties of the people; he divided England into 60,215 military fiefs, all held of the crown, the possessors of which were obliged, under pain of forfeiture, to take up arms and repair to his standard on the first signal. The feudal system in France was only a number of parts, without any reciprocal adherence: in England it was a compound of parts, united by the strongest ties—where the regal authority, by its immense weight, consolidated the whole into one compact, indissoluble body; and from that remarkable difference we may account for the great difference of their constitutions. In France, the several provinces had no principle of union. The people found themselves oppressed by the great feudal lords, and often raised insurrections, and made frequent struggles for freedom; but these struggles, being partial, were of no consequence to the general liberty of the kingdom. In England, again, *all* found themselves oppressed by the enormous weight of the crown. It was a common grievance, and broke out at times into a violent struggle for the general liberty. It was the excessive power of the crown that in England produced at length the liberty of the people, because it gave rise to a spirit of union among the people in all their efforts to resist it.

The forest laws were a grievance felt by the whole nation; both by the barons and their vassals. William the Conqueror reserved to himself the exclusive privilege of killing game throughout all England, and enacted the severest penalties against all who should attempt it without his permission. The suppression, or rather mitigation of these penalties, was one of the articles of the *Charta de Forestâ*, which the barons and their vassals afterwards obtained by force of arms. "*Nullus de cetero amittat vitam vel membra pro venatione nostrâ.*" (Charta de Forestâ, cap. 10.) In these struggles they began to scrutinize into the foundations of authority, and to open their eyes to the natural rights of mankind.

Henry I. was forced to give way a little to this rising spirit, and to mitigate those laws which lay heaviest on the general liberty. Under Henry II. liberty took still a greater stretch, and the people obtained the privilege of trial by juries, one of the most valuable parts of the English constitution. John, imprudently, oppressed this spirit, and sought to check it in its infancy. We know the consequence—a general confederacy of all ranks and orders of men, which at length forced the sovereign into those valuable concessions, the *Charta de Forestâ* and *Magna Charta*, which, had they but been scrupulously observed, the English would have been from that time a free people. The *Magna Charta*, however, observed or not observed, was always a code which certified the people of what were really their rights, and what they were entitled to vindicate.

The next memorable era in the growth of the English constitution was the reign of Henry III., when the deputies of the towns and boroughs were first admitted into parliament. It was always the chief object of his successor, Edward I., to ingratiate himself with his subjects; and requiring large subsidies for his great enterprises against Wales and Scotland, he took the new method of obtaining *from* the consent of the people, what his predecessors had endeavored to exact *by* their own power This, therefore, is the era of the origin of the House of Commons. Edward confirmed the great charter no less than eleven times in the course of his reign,—a certain proof to what lengths the people had attained in the assertion of their liberties; he likewise enacted one statute, which, next to the *Magna Charta*, may be considered as the great foundation of the rights of the people: "That no tax should be raised, or impost levied, without the consent of Lords and Commons."

Thus matters continued gradually advancing; and the scale of the people was daily acquiring an increase of weight, during the reigns of Edward II., Edward III., and Henry IV.; but the subsequent reigns were not so favorable. The wars against France, and the contests between the houses of York and Lancaster, so embroiled the nation, that the people had not leisure to think of grievances from the power of the crown, while their lives and fortunes were otherwise at stake; and when Henry VII. mounted the throne, the people, wearied out by calamities and longing for repose, abhorred even the idea of resistance. The nobility, almost exterminated, had no strength; and the people, who in their struggles with the crown had had nobles for their leaders, were now afraid to form any opposition. During the government of the house of Tudor the royal prerogative was gradually enlarging itself, and the people became accustomed to all compliances; comforting themselves with the thought that if the sovereign had the right of demanding, they had the right of granting, and consequently, if they chose, might still refuse. But the crown, even had they refused, had opened to itself collateral channels of supplies, and was, in fact, very soon independent of parliament in every article, unless in the framing of new laws. The authority of the Star-chamber and High Commission under the two last Henrys, and under Mary and Elizabeth, supplied in most respects to the sovereign the place of a parliament, and was always at his command. The talents of Elizabeth, and the respectable figure then made by the nation in all public measures against foreign powers, blinded the people to such exertions of authority as would in these days appear the height of tyranny. The nation then seemed drowned in the most supine indifference to domestic liberty; and the people, like the subjects of an absolute monarchy (which England, at that time, truly was in almost every sense,) had confined all their ideas to the power, dignity, and splendor of the crown.

But the succeeding prince awakened them from that inglorious lethargy. The former monarchs had marched in silence from one step to another, till they arrived at the height of despotism. James I. imprudently proclaimed his title and right to that authority—he was at no pains to disguise it; and the people, who had been for some time accustomed to be ruled like slaves, could not bear to be told that they were so. A spirit of opposition, which confined itself to complaints under this reign, began in the next to break out into active efforts. To abase the power of the crown was resolutely determined. The commons felt their weight, they knew what were their legal privileges, and they followed, at first, the most constitutional methods to vindicate them. Charles I. was ignorant of the dangers which surrounded him, and, led away by a very natural motive to maintain the power of his predecessors, he was imprudent enough to exert with rigor an authority which he wanted ultimate resources to support. At length, sensible of his own weakness, and perhaps at length conscious that the claims of the people were founded in justice, he signed the petition of rights, a grant more favorable to the liberties of the subject than the *Magna Charta*. The constitution, freed from all those despotic restraints, with which it had been fettered by the house of Tudor, was now fixed on a basis more favorable to the people's liberties than had ever been known in the annals of the nation. Public discontent was now entirely removed—but selfish ambition remained unsatisfied. A few men who had all along made patriotism a cloak for their views of private interest, regretted the prospect of that harmonious coalition which promised now to take place between the king and people. Trifles were sufficient pretext for new discontent; the storm was blown up afresh, and continued with increasing violence till the regal authority was utterly extinguished.

"It was a curious spectacle," says Montesquieu, "to behold the vain efforts of the English to establish among themselves democracy." Subjected, at first, to the power of the principal leaders of the long parliament, they saw that power expire only to pass, without bounds, into the hands of a protector; they saw it afterwards parcelled out among a set of officers of a standing army; and shifting on and on from one kind of subjection to another, they were at length convinced, that to endeavor to establish liberty in a great nation, by making the *people* interfere in the common business of government, is of all attempts the most chimerical; that the *authority of all*, with which men are amused, is in reality no more than the authority of *a few powerful individuals*, who divide the republic among them. They were obliged at last to return to the best of all constitutions, a limited monarchy.

New struggles, under the reign of Charles II., paved the way for new limitations. The Habeas Corpus Act was established, the great security of personal freedom. The constitution had begun again to take a form, when it was invaded by his successor, James, in so violent a manner, as to invite a foreign aid for its support. The consequence was the revolution, a new settlement of the succession to the crown, and a new and solemn contract between the king and people; the principal articles of which we have already seen:—the abolition of the power of taxation without the consent of parliament; the abolition of the crown's dispensing power; the abolition of a standing army in time of peace; the subject's right of petitioning the crown; the freedom of parliamentary debate; and to these we may add the liberty of the press, which was established a few years afterwards.

The revolution, therefore, is the era of the final settlement of the English constitution. It was, before that, fluctuating and uncertain; at best, the people only guessed at the extent of their rights; they were now defined and positively ascertained.

Let us now consider that constitution under two distinct heads—the legislative and executive power, the last of which involves the prerogative of the crown.

The capital principle of the English constitution, on which all others depend, is, that the legislative power belongs to parliament alone; that is, the power of making laws, of abrogating them or of changing them. The constituent parts of parliament are, the king, lords, and commons. The House of Commons is composed of the deputies of the different counties, the deputies of the principal towns, and of the two English universities. These, in all amounted to five hundred and thirteen members; and to these were added, on the union with Scotland, forty-five representatives from that kingdom, and, since the union with Ireland, one hundred from that country.* The Commons are elected by the freeholders, by authority of the king's writ, under the great seal, directed to the sheriffs of the counties. Every member of the House of Commons, though elected by one particular district or borough, is understood to serve for the whole realm; for the purpose of his being elected is not for the benefit of any particular division of the country, but for the good of the whole. His office is to advise his sovereign (in terms of the writ of summons) *de communi consilio super negotiis quibusdam arduis et urgentibus, regem, statum et defensionem regni Angliæ, et ecclesiæ Anglicanæ concernentibus.* And therefore he is not bound to consult with, or take the advice of his constituents, upon any particular point, unless, as Sir William Blackstone rightly observes, he thinks t proper or prudent to do so. Under any other view of the duties of a representative, the House of Commons would cease to be a deliberative assembly. If, in the affairs of common life, twenty individuals agreed to meet for the purpose of discussing some point of common interest, and each should come to the

* The numbers of the House of Commons, as it now stands under the Reform Act of 1831, are five hundred representatives for England and Wales, fifty-three for Scotland, and one hundred and five for Ireland,—total six hundred and fifty-eight.—EDITOR.

meeting bound by an oath to maintain his individual opinion, to what purpose should they meet at all ? *

The House of Lords or Peers is composed of the lords spiritual, who are the archbishops of Canterbury and York, with the twenty four bishops of England; and the lords temporal, or dukes, marquises, earls, viscounts, and barons of that kingdom. To these, since the unions, are added sixteen peers, delegated by the body of the Scottish nobility, and twenty-eight temporal and four spiritual lords, to represent the peerage and prelacy of Ireland.† The lord chancellor is the president of the House of Peers; the speaker is the president of the House of Commons. The king is the third component part of parliament. It is he alone who can convoke it, and he only can dissolve or prorogue it. The moment the parlia

* Among those things which the spirit of faction has at all times principally chosen to lay hold of as objectionable under the British constitution, is, the state of popular representation; which has been strongly held forth as incompatible with justness and with the equal rights of the subject. A very great majority of the people, it is said, have no elective voice in choice of the members of the House of Commons, and are, therefore, unrepresented in parliament. But these objectors ought to consider, first, that the great matter of importance is not that each individual of the public should have a voice in choosing a member of parliament. The point of importance is, that each individual should feel that the community is regulated by equal, wise, and salutary laws, of which all the members of the state alike reap the benefit, and the mode by which that end is best attained is the wisest. Secondly, they should consider that the right of voting for a member of parliament is a *public trust*, and as trusty a civil office as any other in the state. Now all public offices or trusts being constituted only for the general good, it is proper that they should be conferred under such conditions and limitations as that general good may require. The general sense of the British nation has ever been, that it would be most destructive to allow all individuals without distinction an elective voice in the nomination of members of parliament, as such a system would lead to every species of corruption, profligacy, and disorder. The nation has, therefore, wisely limited the elective franchise to those who possess certain qualifications deemed necessary to the proper exercise of it. The chief of these is a certain measure of property sufficient to place its possessor above a state of absolute dependence and servility, and to give him an interest in the common good of the state. When, therefore, the nation has fixed the terms on which this public trust ought to be conferred, and that not capriciously, but upon a wise and reasonable consideration of the general good, no man who finds himself destitute of such qualifications has any ground to complain of injustice that is done to him. He has only thereby an incitement to exert himself laudably to place himself beyond the line of exclusion.

† The distinction of ranks and honor is of most essential benefit in the state, as furnishing a reward for public services, at once captivating to the ambition of individuals, and without imposing a burden on the community. The laudable emulation thence excited gives life and vigor to the community, and prompts individuals to distinguish themselves in every way by which they can render service to their country. A body of nobility, moreover, is a grand support both of the rights of the crown and of the people, by furnishing a control upon the encroachments of either of these powers. It is highly expedient too, and indeed necessary for this end, that they should form a separate and independent branch of the legislature. If blended in one house with the commons, their influence would be nothing; and the weight of the people would carry every thing before it, to the abolition of a mixed form of government. Of this, the French revolution has furnished a striking proof; as to that circumstance alone, the assembling of the nobles and their voting in one mass with the *tiers état*, (a measure planned for the very end which followed, and weakly or traitorously consented to by Neckar,) was owing the utter demolition of the kingly government, and all the anarchical measures and misery that ensued.

ment is dissolved, it ceases to exist: a prorogation only suspends its power during a limited time.

The limited duration of parliament secures its purity and its independence; and the renewal and change of members in that branch which is nominated by the people, prevents those dangers that might arise from the hereditary constitution of the other branches. Strict laws are in force to prevent disorders at elections; and it is wisely provided that even the death of the sovereign shall afford no room for commotions or occasion embarrassment in the public business; for in the eye of law the throne is never vacant; but from the moment of the king's death, is supposed to be filled by his heir. Further, on the death of any king or queen, "the parliament in being shall continue for six months, unless sooner prorogued or dissolved by the successor. If the parliament be at the time of the king's death separated by adjournment or prorogation, it shall notwithstanding assemble immediately; and if no parliament is then in being, the members of the last parliament shall assemble and be again a parliament." *Blackstone*, b. i., ch. 2. "In like manner, the privy council shall continue for six months after the demise of the crown, unless sooner determined by the successor." *Ibid.*, b. i., ch. 5. The judges, by an act of parliament passed in the reign of George III., hold their offices for life; and all the great officers of state, and in general all officers civil or military throughout the whole British empire, continue in office for six months after the king's demise, unless removed by the successor.

Each of the houses of parliament has a negative on any proposition made by the other, and the king has a negative on both.

All measures respecting government, all questions regarding public affairs, all propositions for the public good, may take their rise indifferently in either house, and become the subject of deliberation; with this exception, that all bills for granting money must have their beginning in the House of Commons, and can admit of no change or alteration in the House of Lords, who must either simply receive or simply reject them.* All other questions or propo-

* The reason usually given generally for this jealousy of the commons with respect to money bills, is, that the supplies are raised on the body of the people, and therefore it is proper that they alone should have the right of taxing themselves: a reason which would be good, only in the case that the commons taxed none but themselves. The true reason, according to Sir W. Blackstone, arises from the spirit of the constitution. The lords being a permanent hereditary body, created at pleasure by the king, are supposed more liable to be influenced by the crown, and when once influenced, to continue so, than the commons, who are a temporary elective body, freely nominated by the people. It would, therefore, be extremely dangerous to give the lords any power of framing new taxes for the subject: it is sufficient that they have a power of rejecting, if they think the commons too lavish or improvident in their grants. Under the description of money bills are included all grants by which any money is to be raised for any purpose, or by any mode whatever, from the subject; either for the exigencies of government, and collected from the kingdom in general, as the land-tax; or for private benefit, and collected in any particular district, as by turnpikes, parish rates, and the like. Blackstone, b. i., ch. 2.

sitions which are passed in the affirmative in either of the houses, are next transmitted for the consideration of the other, where, if rejected, the measure is at an end; if passed, nothing else is required but the royal assent. If that is refused, the bill remains without force or effect; if granted, it is an established law, which cannot be repealed but by the united will of all the three constituent parts of parliament.*

The executive power of the government is lodged in the crown. The king is charged with the execution of the laws, and supplied with necessary powers for that purpose. In the exercise of this duty, however, the king is no more than the first magistrate, and his conduct must be regulated by the laws of the realm equally with that of his subjects.

In that capacity, the first branch of his office is the administration of justice. He is the chief of all courts of judicature, of which the judges are only his substitutes. He by his law officers is the prosecutor in all high crimes and offences; and he has the power of pardoning or remitting the execution of all sentences.

In the second place, the king is the fountain of all honor; and the distributor of titles and dignities, as well as the disposer of the offices of state.

In the third place, he is the superintendent of commerce; he has the prerogative of regulating weights and measures, and the sole power of coining money.

In the fourth place, he is the head of the church; he names the archbishops and bishops, and can alone convoke the assembly of the clergy, and dissolve and prorogue them.

In the fifth place, he is commander-in-chief of all the sea and land forces; he alone can levy troops, equip fleets, and name all officers by sea and land.

In the sixth place, he has the power of declaring war and making peace, of contracting alliances, and sending and receiving ambassadors.

And lastly, the king is above the reach of all courts of law, and is not personally responsible to any judicature for his conduct in the administration of government.

From this enumeration of the powers of the sovereign, at first sight, a stranger might almost conclude that the king of England was an absolute monarch. He has not only a negative on all the proceedings of the legislative assemblies, but can summon or dismiss them at his will, and the whole executive power of the

* It is to be remarked, however, that it is an established part of the constitution of parliament, "That whatever matter arises concerning either house of parliament, ought to be examined, discussed, and adjudged in that house to which it relates, and not elsewhere." Hence, for instance, the lords will not suffer the commons to interfere in settling the election of a peer of Scotland; the commons will not allow the lords to judge of the election of a burgess; nor will either house permit the subordinate courts of law to examine the merits of either case Blackstone, b. i., ch. 2.

state centres in him alone. But let us now seriously attend to the manner in which these powers and prerogatives of the crown are limited; and here we shall discern the wisdom, the beauty, and singular excellence of the British constitution.

1. The king is entirely dependent on parliament for all subsidies; the revenues of the crown are a mere trifle. The king can levy armies and equip fleets, but without the aid of parliament he cannot maintain them. He bestows offices, but without parliament he cannot pay salaries. He declares war, but without parliament he cannot carry it on. De Lolme has well compared the powers of the king of England to a ship completely equipped, but from which the parliament can at pleasure drain off the water and leave it aground.

Such is the weight in the scale of parliament against the powers of the crown; a weight so entirely preponderating, that parliament itself has moderated the exercise of its prerogatives, by an established usage of granting at the commencement of every reign a settled revenue upon the prince for life, a provision sufficient to support the dignity of the crown without putting it in his power greatly to abridge the liberties of the people; and a provision which being at an end with the life of the sovereign, and requiring a new grant for every successor, puts it in the power of parliament to remedy all abuses and encroachments at the beginning of every reign, and thus bring the constitution back to its first principles. In short, there is in the British constitution a power of periodical reformation, which is an effectual check to its ever being corrupted by encroachments from the crown. The sovereigns of Britain do not now succeed to the powers and prerogatives of their predecessors. The constitution is, or may be, fixed at the beginning of every reign: because, except the name of king, the sovereign has neither power nor dignity, till the parliament vote his revenue and subsidies; which they can withhold till every abuse is remedied, and all former encroachments retrenched and put a stop to.

But still further is the power of the sovereign subject to continual limitation. The king can never reign without a parliament. By an act of Charles II. he must assemble a parliament at least once in three years, and, in order that the election of members may be made with due deliberation, the writs must be issued forty days before the meeting of parliament.

The king is the head of the church; but he cannot alter the established religion, nor call individuals to account for their religious opinions; and ecclesiastical regulations must be made by the assembly of the clergy.

The king is the first magistrate: but he cannot interfere with the courts of judicature in the administration of justice: he can assist at no trials, civil or criminal, and any person may demand the king's name and authority to prosecute crimes.

He has the privilege of coining money; but he cannot alter the standard either in weight or alloy.

He has the power of pardoning offences, but he cannot exempt the offenders from making a compensation to the parties injured, if it is demanded.

The king has the military power. The sea-forces he can raise, disband, and regulate at pleasure, because they cannot be turned against the liberties of the people; but the land forces he cannot raise without the consent of parliament. A standing body of troops is, indeed, established by parliament; but the funds for their payment are never granted for more than a year. The Mutiny Act, by which alone they are regulated, must be renewed from year to year.

The king, in the last place, is above the reach of all courts of law; but his *ministers*, his indispensable instruments, are answerable for all the measures of government. All misapplications of the public money, all ruinous and improper expeditions, all abuses of power are chargeable to *their* account; and the Commons, the guardians of the constitution, have a right to impeach them at the bar of the House of Lords. A minister impeached for misconduct cannot plead in excuse the commands of the sovereign, nor will it avail him, pleading guilty to the charge, to produce the royal pardon. He must suffer as the author of those measures of which he was the instrument: a noble and most effectual antidote against the evils of misgovernment!

The laws, which thus effectually limit the power of the crown, secure likewise the freedom of parliament. The freedom of debate cannot be questioned, or any member called to account on that score, in any court or place out of parliament.

To these observations I shall add a few remarks on three striking peculiarities of the English constitution in favor of the liberties of the subject: the *Habeas Corpus Act*, *Trial by Jury*, and the *Liberty of the Press*.

The methods which the laws of England formerly established to remedy unjust imprisonment, were what are termed writs of *main-prize*, *de odio et atia*, and *de homine replegiando*, which were orders to the sheriffs of the counties, to inquire into the causes of the prisoner's confinement, and, according to the circumstances of his case, either simply to discharge him or admit him to bail. But these methods are now tacitly abolished by the habeas corpus, which is a writ issuing from the court of King's Bench, whose effects extend over all England, by which the king requires the person who holds any of his subjects in custody, immediately to carry him before the judge, to certify the date of his confinement and the cause of it, and to abide the judge's decree whether he shall detain him or set him at liberty. Of this beneficial statute there were frequent evasions which from time to time called forth various amendments. The last and most effectual of all was by the act of Habeas, which, as we have observed, passed in the thirtieth year of Charles II., and which has cut off every source of oppression and every handle of evasion.

The principal articles of this act are, in the first place, to fix the different terms for bringing a prisoner, in proportion to the distance of the place of his confinement: the longest term is twenty days. In the second place, the officer or keeper must, within six hours, deliver to the prisoner, on his demand, a copy of the warrant of his commitment, under the penalty of one hundred pounds, and being disabled to hold his office. In the third place, no person once delivered by a writ of habeas corpus shall be recommitted for the same offence, under the penalty of £500 sterling. Fourthly, every person committed for treason or felony shall, if he require it, in the first week of the next term, or the first day of the next session, be indicted in that term or session, or else admitted to bail. If acquitted, or not indicted, he shall be discharged. Fifthly, any of the twelve judges, or the lord chancellor, refusing a writ of habeas, shall forfeit £500. In the last place, no subject of England shall be sent prisoner to Scotland, Ireland, Jersey, Guernsey, or any place beyond the seas, under penalty to the party committing, and to all who assist or advise, of forfeiting £500, to be recovered with treble costs, being disabled from holding any office, being imprisoned for life, forfeiting his whole estate for life, and being incapable of the king's pardon. Such is the nature of the habeas corpus, a most invaluable security for the personal liberty of the subject, a security which is enjoyed under no government on the face of the earth but our own.

It must be observed that the habeas corpus being an English law, and prior to the treaty of union, does not extend to Scotland. The liberty of the subject, however, is almost as effectually guarded in that country as in England; though there the term of imprisonment before trial may, indeed, be of longer duration. By the Scottish statute 1701, cap. 6, no person can be imprisoned in order to trial for any crime without a warrant in writing expressing the cause, and proceeding on a signed information, unless in the case of indignities done to judges, riots, and some other offences mentioned in the statute. Every prisoner committed to gaol for crimes not capital, is entitled to a release on finding bail, according to his circumstances; and for the relief of those who are unable to find bail, any prisoner may apply to the criminal judge requiring that his trial may be brought on without unnecessary delays. The judge, within twenty-four hours of such application, must issue letters directed to messengers for intimating to the prosecutor that he may fix a diet for the prisoner's trial within sixty days after the intimation, under the pains of wrongous imprisonment. Still further, and that there may be no unnecessary or oppressive protraction of a trial after it is once begun, the prisoner is entitled to insist for his liberty, if his trial is not concluded within forty days, if before the supreme criminal court, and within thirty if before any other. This privilege is competent to be pleaded in all cases, except in the crime of forgery. Thus the natives of Scotland seem to be nearly on a par with those of England, in that most inestimable of all blessings, personal liberty.

The only exception to the general liberty of the subject, under the British government, is the power of impressing seamen by the king's commission for the supply of the navy. This power has at all times been reluctantly submitted to, and much complained against as an infringement of the rights of the subject. But *salus populi est suprema lex*. If it is absolutely necessary for the preservation of the state, on occasion of sudden danger from an enemy, that the navy should be instantly and effectually armed, that circumstance at once demonstrates the legality of the practice. Moreover, as the subjection to this hazard is known by all who engage in the profession of a seaman, their entry into the profession is a tacit consent to whatever is necessarily attendant upon it. It has been very clearly shown by Sir Michael Foster, that this practice, and the granting of powers to the admiralty for that purpose, is of very ancient date, and has been uniformly continued to the present time, so as now to be understood as a part of the common law of the land.

Another of the highest privileges of a British subject is the trial of all crimes by jury. The preliminaries to trial are different in England and in Scotland. The number of jurors are different; twelve in England and fifteen in Scotland. Unanimity of opinion is required in the former, a majority of voices is decisive in the latter. In both modes of trial it is the privilege of the criminal to be judged by the impartial verdict of his peers. The prisoner has even a share in the choice of his jury, for the law has allowed him the right of challenging or objecting to such as he may think exceptionable. In England the prisoner may challenge peremptorily, that is, without showing any cause, twenty jurors successively. The witnesses upon the trial deliver their evidence in presence of the prisoner, who is allowed to question them, and to produce witnesses in his own behalf. In cases of treason, the accused person may challenge successively thirty-five jurors; he may have two counsel to assist him on his trial; and no treason, unless actual attempt upon the life of the king, can be prosecuted after three years from the offence. The opinions of the judges in summing up the evidence have no weight but such as the jury choose to give to them, and their verdict ought to proceed entirely on their own belief and conviction. Lord chief-justice Hale has, in his History of the Common Law of England, summed up, in a very few words, the duty and powers of a jury. "The jury, in their recess, are to consider their evidence; to weigh the credibility of the witnesses, and force and efficacy of their testimonies: they are not bound to the rules of civil law, to have two witnesses to prove every fact, unless it be in cases of treason; nor to reject one witness because he is single, or always to believe two witnesses, if the probability of the fact does upon other circumstances reasonably encounter them. It may fall out that a jury, upon their own knowledge, may know a thing to be false which a witness has sworn to be true; or may know a witness to be incompetent or incredible though nothing be objected against him, and may give their verdict accordingly."

The effect of the verdict of a jury is final and positive. If the prisoner is acquitted, he is instantly set at liberty, and cannot on any pretence be tried again for the same crime. If found guilty, the judge must pronounce sentence according to the law. But this law must contain a positive enactment with regard to the special crime which was brought before the jury; for, in crimes, no constructive extension of laws can be admitted. The spirit of our laws considers the impunity of an offender as a very small matter in comparison with the dangers that would result from such extension.

The last particular I shall take notice of, and what is in fact the guardian of the British constitution, is the *liberty of the press.*

To supply the unavoidable deficiency of all legislative provisions, to prevent the silent deviations of magistrates from their duty (transgressions the more dangerous that no punishment can reach them); and to be a constant check upon the minutest departments of the constitution, as a pendulum regulates the equable motion of all the wheels of a clock,—there is one power in the British government whose exertions are constant and unremitting, a just regulator of the whole parts of that nice and complicated machine. This is the power which every individual has of expressing his opinion of the whole conduct of government, without reserve, by word or writing—a power which is so regulated, however, as to insure all the benefit of the ancient censorship without its mischiefs. The censorial tribunal at Rome was entirely arbitrary, which repressed all freedom of judgment in the public; or, at least, rendered it of no consequence, since the regulation of government was supremely lodged in the breasts of a few men, with whom that judgment could have no effect. But a British subject has the right of free judgment on all public measures, of remonstrating to his governors, of carrying his complaint and his appeal to the public by means of the press, of submitting to the general opinion the views and principles of these governors expressed in parliament; and thus, by openly examining and scrutinizing their whole conduct, to furnish the most powerful restraint against every species of malversation. It is peculiar to the British government, that there is no person so high in administration, as not to feel the weight of public opinion. The loss of popular favor to a states man will furnish such opposition to his measures as to gall and imbitter every hour of his life. Even the taunts, the curses, or the hissings of the vulgar, there is no man whatever that can long support with any degree of tranquillity; and when he considers, that not only his present fame is at stake, but also his memory, to the latest posterity, by means of the press, he will soon find that he is irresistibly and most powerfully restrained within the bounds of his duty.

The notoriety of the whole proceedings of government by means of the press, and the perfect knowledge which is diffused through the nation of all that is said and done in parliament, is attended, moreover, with the beneficial effect of purifying, from time to time, the legislative assembly. As the votes and political sentiments of the members are always known, and every county or borough has its eye on the conduct of its representatives, the House of Commons may undergo a gradual purgation from successive vacancies, or be purified at once at the commencement of every new parliament.

Yet this inestimable privilege of British subjects, without certain limitations, would, instead of good, be productive of the greatest mischiefs. Were any man at liberty to wound the vitals of the government under which he lives, by an open attack upon the fundamental doctrines of civil subordination, and the respect due to the established laws of the land; were he at liberty to loosen the bonds of civil society, by combating the first principles of all religion; or were he suffered with impunity to injure the reputation, life, or property of his neighbor, by false and malicious accusations, there would be *no government;* and liberty itself would perish, because it would have no safeguard or protection. The liberty of the press in Britain consists, then, in *this*, that there is no examination or censure of writings *before* they are published; the press is open to every thing; but *after* publication, such writings as offend in the particulars I have mentioned, are subject to the penalties of the law, awarded on the verdict of a jury. The impartial public are thus ultimately the judges of the tendency of all writings addressed to themselves; and it is equally wise and consistent with the spirit of that liberty, that all authors should stand or fall by their determination.

Such is the British constitution; a system of government blending in the most beautiful manner the three forms of monarchy, aristocracy, and democracy—a system, of which the wisest of the ancients seem only to have had indistinct dreams; which Tacitus * considered as a fine chimera, too perfect to be reduced into practice; and which, independent of any theoretical plans—the result of the speculations of philosophical politicians, has insensibly arisen from the chain of events, and the concurrence of circum-

* Ann. lib. iv.

stances, to a very high degree of perfection. Absolute perfection is not to be predicated of any human institution. It is sufficient to say, that under its influence the condition of society, whatever fluctuations it must from the constitution of our nature be liable to, has been such as to answer all the wishes of the good, the virtuous, and the industrious part of the community; and that its restraints have proved grievous to those alone on whom restraint is necessary.

The constitution of Great Britain is in its nature improvable in various parts of its structure; but with what caution these improvements ought to be undertaken, the past history of our own country, and the more recent experience of a neighboring kingdom, affords the most instructive warning. It is liable to dangerous invasion, both from the sovereign and from the people. The former may for awhile impair its excellence and cloud its lustre; but the latter is alone competent to destroy its existence.

CHAPTER XXXII.

History of France under Louis XIII., and of Spain and Portugal under Philip III. and IV.—Mary de Medicis Regent—Siege of Rochelle—Cardinal Richelieu—Death of Louis XIII.—Spain—Philip III.—Philip IV.—Degraded state of Spain—Portugal throws off the Spanish Yoke—Constitution of Portugal—Constitution of Spain.

The wise, equitable, and vigorous administration of Henry IV. had raised the kingdom of France from the lowest pitch of misery and anarchy to peace, dignity, and prosperity. Upon his death, all these advantages were lost at once. Mary de Medicis, his widow, a woman of a weak mind, but of ungovernable passions, and of a domineering, insolent character, had been appointed regent in the minority of her son Louis XIII. Her restless and ambitious spirit embroiled both the court and the nation in factions; and in endeavoring to secure to her interest the nobility, whom it was not possible ever firmly to unite among themselves, she squandered away the public money. The kingdom lost all its weight abroad, and relapsed into the same disorders at home, which we have seen in the times of Francis II., of Charles IX., and of Henry III. Mary de Medicis disgusted the French, in the first place, by her partiality to her countrymen, the Italians. Concini, a Florentine, a high favorite of the queen regent, was advanced to the dignity of a marshal of France; a sufficient reason for rendering the queen and her minister odious to the nobility and to the kingdom. The Maréchal d'Ancre, for such was the title he assumed, trusted too much to the favor of his mistress, and to that appearance of power which was its consequence. The nobility combined against him, and he was assassinated in a most inhuman manner in the palace of the Louvre. The populace, in that spirit of savage cruelty, which in all scenes of disorder seems to be characteristic of that nation, are said actually to have torn his heart from his body and devoured it. The vengeance of the nobility did not stop with the death of the minister. The queen herself was a sufferer as well as her favorite. Her guards were removed, she was hurried from Paris, and confined in the castle of Blois, where she was kept a prisoner for two years, till she was released by the duke d'Epernon, to whom she had originally been indebted for her appointment to the regency of the kingdom.

In this conjuncture every thing was involved in anarchy and confusion. The queen-mother was actually at war with her own son, the whole nation divided into parties, and the government of France in the lowest state of weakness and inefficacy.

The genius of the great Richelieu, then a young man, effected a reconciliation for a time between the contending factions, and he obtained, as a reward for this piece of service, the dignity of a cardinal, at the queen's solicitation. But this calm was of short continuance. The factious nobility began to excite new disturbances, which Louis XIII., who was now of age, had neither the discretion nor the ability to compose. These commotions were increased by religious differences, for the protestants, who had enjoyed an unmolested tranquillity under Henry IV., and for a while under the minority of Louis, were now exposed to fresh persecutions. They were obliged to take up arms; and a political and a religious war raged with equal violence at the same time. The king, amidst these commotions, was obliged alternately to bribe his own servants, and to negotiate with his rebel nobility.

While public affairs were in this situation, Mary de Medicis had the address to bring the new favorite Richelieu into the council, against the inclination of the king and his favorite counsellors; and in a very short time this great politician completely gained the confidence of his royal master, and signally displayed his splendid abilities in quieting all disorders, and raising the French monarchy to a very high pitch of splendor.

The cardinal de Richelieu entered on his administration with that vigorous activity which marks a bold and daring spirit. A fleet was necessary for the reduction of Rochelle, where the Calvinists, who then suffered great persecution, were attempting to imitate the example of the Hollanders, and throw off their subjection to the crown of France The cardinal found it impossible to fit out an armament with that celerity which was necessary, and he concluded a bargain with the Dutch to furnish a fleet for subduing their protestant brethren. An opportunity thus offered of making money—the Dutch had no scruple on the score of conscience; and they fought for the catholic religion as keenly as they had done half a century before for the protestant.

It was necessary, however, that the nation should be able to carry on its wars without having recourse to the aid of foreigners, and Richelieu gave peace to the protestants, that he might be in a capacity of attending to the most material interests of the kingdom, its strength and internal prosperity.

At this time three ministers, equally powerful, regulated the general policy of all Europe; Olivarez in Spain, Buckingham in England, and Richelieu in France. Of these, Buckingham was reckoned the worst politician, as he studied more his own private passions than the grandeur of his country, which is the true source of ambition in a politic minister. An intrigue of Buckingham's with Louis's queen, Anne of Austria, which gave high umbrage to the court of France, is supposed to have been the real cause of a war with England. That minister prevailed on his sovereign to light up the contention between the protestants and catholics in France, by sending a force to the aid of the Calvinists of Rochelle. But the design was not so speedily executed as to escape the vigilance of cardinal de Richelieu, who, at the head of a considerable body of men, obliged Buckingham, with the loss of half his armament, to return to England.

The Rochellers, however, held out the town with the most obstinate resolution against the troops of the cardinal, who was obliged to employ every resource of policy, as well as of war, for their reduction. In this siege, which lasted for the course of a whole year, the cardinal commanded in person. It was found impossible to take the town while it continued open to the English fleet. An immense mole was therefore constructed in the sea to prevent the approach of the English shipping. Th expedient succeeded, and Rochelle at length was obliged to surrender. It was stripped of its privileges, and the catholic religion established in place of the protestant; though the Calvinists were allowed the private exercise of their worship. The rest of the protestant towns of France were treated in the same manner as Rochelle; their fortifications were thrown down, and they were deprived of every privilege that might be dangerous to the state. Thus the protestant party in France a very numerous body of men, were disarmed and crushed for ever. Neither the Swiss nor the Dutch were so powerful as the French protestants, at the time that these nations erected themselves into independent sovereignties. Geneva, though a very inconsiderable state, asserted its liberty and maintained it. Yet the Calvinists of France were quite overpowered, and the reason was, that they were scattered through all the provinces: it was impossible to unite them, and they were attacked by superior numbers, and by disciplined troops.

Louis XIII., though a monarch of a weak frame of mind, had somewhat of a military disposition. He entered into the schemes of Richelieu for the aggrandizement of France, and fought at the head of his armies, both in his own kingdom and in Italy. Richelieu was a man whose genius was truly astonishing. He was negotiating at one time *with all* and *against most* of the sovereigns of Europe. His principal aim was to humble the house of Austria; he wanted to establish a duke of Mantua independent of the king of Spain; he proposed to harass the Austrian dominions in Flanders, and had prevailed with Gustavus Adolphus, the king of Sweden, to make a descent upon Germany. But while these great schemes were in agitation, a formidable cabal at court was secretly undermining his power. Gaston, duke of Orleans, the king's brother, detested the cardinal de Richelieu; Mary de Medicis was jealous of that very power which she had contributed to raise; and most of the nobility were his secret enemies. This illustrious man, whose intrepidity was equal to all situations, suppressed these cabals in a manner which astonished all Europe. The maréchal de Marillac, one of the nobles who was most obnoxious to him, was arrested at the head of an army, and condemned and executed for treason. The duke of Orleans, the king's brother, apprehensive of a similar fate, quitted the kingdom; and the queen-mother, Mary de Medicis, removed from all concern in the government, ended her career of ambition in voluntary exile at Brussels.

The duke of Orleans, however, flattered himself with the idea of being the avenger of the royal family. He was supported by the duke de Montmorenci, who raised at his own expense an army of several thousand men. The king's army, or rather that of the cardinal, came to an engagement with him, which terminated all the hopes of Orleans and his adherents. Montmorenci was taken prisoner, condemned and executed for treason, and the duke, after making all submissions, thought himself extremely happy to be allowed to quit the kingdom and retire to Brussels, to keep his mother company. The most surprising circumstance in the whole of these transactions is, that cardinal de Richelieu found himself able to make such exertions of the most despotic power while *the nation* were his enemies. He surmounted all opposition; and while the genius of most men, even of great abilities, would have found it sufficient occupation to wage war against those cabals and factions which were continually meditating his downfall, this extraordinary man not only completely foiled the schemes of his enemies, but found means to raise the kingdom of France to a most flourishing condition at home, while he extended her glory and influence over all Europe. While he was making open war against the house of Austria in

Germany, Italy, and Spain, he was at this very time employing his thoughts in the establishment of the *French Academy*. He held meetings in his palace of the most celebrated literary geniuses of the age; he cultivated the *belles lettres* with success, and composed himself some dramatic pieces, which were exhibited on the French theatre.

The war against Austria, however, did not succeed to his wishes, till the duke of Weimar gained at length a complete victory, in which he took prisoners four of the imperial generals; and till the Spanish branch of the house of Austria was stripped of Portugal by the revolution in that kingdom, and dispossessed likewise of Catalonia by an open rebellion in the year 1640.

Louis XIII., who, though a prince of a gloomy disposition, had his favorites among the court ladies, was weak enough sometimes to listen to those reports which they were fond of circulating to the prejudice of the cardinal de Richelieu. The queen herself, Anne of Austria, had been so imprudent as to signify her aversion to him. Richelieu laid his hands upon her father confessor; ordered the queen's papers to be seized, on the pretence of a correspondence with the enemies of the state; and Anne of Austria had very nearly undergone the same fate with Mary de Medicis. The king himself had sometimes hastily expressed his indignation at the violent conduct of his minister. A favorite of the king, the young marquis de Cinque Mars, encouraged by these expressions, which he took for a certain presage of the downfall of Richelieu, entered into a conspiracy with Gaston, duke of Orleans, and the duke de Bouillon, against the cardinal's life. The plot was discovered; Cinque Mars was put to death, the duke de Bouillon had his estate confiscated, and Gaston, after making an humble submission, consented to remain a prisoner at the castle of Blois. The detection of this conspiracy was the last scene of the life of cardinal de Richelieu, as well as that of Louis XIII., who survived him but a few months.

The administration of cardinal de Richelieu, though stained with factions, with civil war, and with daily executions, was, on the whole, extremely glorious for the kingdom.

France, in his time, was opulent at home; her finances were in good order; and she was most respectable abroad. There appeared at this time likewise the dawn of that good taste which led to such distinguished splendor in the succeeding age of Louis XIV.

SPAIN.

From the period of the death of Philip II., the Spanish monarchy visibly declined in its influence abroad — though, at the same time, the authority of its sovereigns, or the power of the prince over the subject, was daily increasing. The government, absolute as it was, was ill administered. There was no regulation or system of supplies for the exigencies of the state. So great was the neglect and the disorder of the revenues during the reign of Philip III., that in the war which still continued with the United Provinces, he had not money to pay his troops. His naval forces were inferior to those of Holland and Zealand, and they stripped him of the Molucca Islands and of Amboyna in the East Indies, while, at the same time, his armies in the Netherlands could make no impression on the power of this infant republic. He was obliged, in fine, to conclude a truce with Holland for twelve years, to leave the Dutch in possession of all they had acquired, to promise them a free trade to the East Indies, and to restore to the house of Nassau its estates situated within the dominions of the Spanish monarchy.

It is impossible to fathom the reasons of a policy so very destructive as that which was embraced by Philip III. in this juncture of national weakness. The Moors, who had still subsisted in Spain from the period of the conquest of Grenada, and were a peaceable, an useful, and a most industrious race of subjects, were computed to amount at this time to six or seven hundred thousand. Some trifling insurrections, occasioned by the persecutions of the inquisition, attracted the notice of the sovereign, who, with the most indiscreet, impolitic, and destructive zeal, decreed, that all the Moors should be expelled from the kingdom of Spain. Two years were spent by Philip in transporting the most industrious part of his subjects out of the kingdom, and in depopulating his dominions. A few of these wretched exiles betook themselves to France; the rest, and the greatest part, returned to Africa, their ancient country. Spain became an immense body without vigor or motion. The court of Philip III was a chaos of intrigues, like that of Louis XIII. The monarch was governed by the duke of Lerma; but the confusion in which every thing was involved, at length drove *him* from his station of a minister. The disorders increased under Philip IV., who was ruled by Olivarez, as his father had been by Lerma. It is a curious fact, that the best information we have of the court intrigues during these reigns, and of the character of the prime ministers, Lerma and Olivarez, is to be found in a book of romance, the *Adventures of Gil Blas*, written by M. le Sage, who, in treating occasionally of state affairs, has interspersed a great deal of genuine history. We may observe, at the same time, that the account which the same author has given of the state of literature in Spain is extremely just, and that his picture of the manners of the people is in general very faithful.

Spain, during the reign of Philip IV., was as impotent abroad as she was miserable at home. Every species of commerce was repressed by the most exorbitant taxes. The Flemish manufactures supplied the whole kingdom, for the Spaniards had neither arts of their own, nor industry. In short, notwithstanding her immense territories, and those prodigious sources of wealth which she possessed in America, Spain was so exhausted, that the ministry under Philip IV. found themselves reduced to the necessity of coining money of copper, to which they gave the value of silver. This reign was one continued series of losses and defeats. The Dutch, at the expiration of the truce, made themselves masters of Brazil. The province of Artois was invaded by the French, and Catalonia, jealous of her privileges, which the crown had encroached upon, revolted and threw herself into the arms of France.

The revolt of Catalonia was the signal for another of much more importance. Portugal, at this very period, shook off the yoke of Spain, and recovered her former independence as a kingdom. No revolution was ever effected with more speed or with more facility. The imprudent and impolitic administration of Olivarez had alienated the minds of the Portuguese from all allegiance to the Spanish crown.

John, duke of Braganza, who was descended from the ancient race of the Portuguese monarchs, had at this time the command of the army. Instigated by the ambition of his duchess, a woman of great spirit, and seeing the disposition of the nation completely favorable to his views, he caused himself to be proclaimed king in the city of Lisbon; and this example of the capital was immediately followed all over the kingdom, and in all the Portuguese settlements abroad. Portugal, from that era, became an independent sovereignty, after having been for sixty years an appanage or dependency of the kingdom of Spain.

The government of Portugal approaches to an absolute monarchy. Nominally, indeed, in most important articles which regard the liberty of the subject, the consent of the states is necessary; these, however, are but rarely convoked. The ordinary business of the government is conducted entirely by the king and his council of state, which is appointed by himself. The revenue of the crown arises from its domains, the duties on exports and imports, the taxes, and, formerly, from a stated proportion of the gold imported from the Brazils. Commerce and manufactures are in a very low state in Portugal; their trade, being conducted with no enlarged views or liberal policy, is of little solid advantage to the country; and with a soil and climate equal to any in Europe, the agriculture of the kingdom is greatly neglected.

This period, between the reign of Philip II. and the end of the reign of Philip IV., though it saw the diminution of the Spanish greatness in point of power, was the era of its highest lustre in point of literary genius. The entertainments of the stage were far superior to those of any other European nation; and the Spaniards likewise carried poetical composition, romance, and even history, to a considerable degree of perfection. The mechanic and the useful arts were, however, in a very rude state. The

Spaniards, during these reigns, had very few of the refined pleasures of life, but in return they were free from those miseries which fell to the lot of their neighbors. While France and England exhibited a painful scene of faction, civil war, and bloodshed, the Spaniards passed their days in indolent and tranquil insignificance.

It is somewhat curious to remark, that at the time when, in all the rest of the European nations, the scale of the people was acquiring weight against the power of the sovereign, the reverse was the case in Spain. The kingdom, from being once elective, had for some ages become hereditary; but it was not till the reign of Charles V. that the king of Spain became an absolute prince.

There is no question that Spain was once an elective kingdom. In treating formerly of the manners of the Gothic nations, we took notice, that during the reign of the *Visigoth* princes in Spain, these sovereigns were always chosen by the *proceres* or nobles; although at the same time this assembly of the *proceres* generally paid the greatest regard to the family of the last prince, or to the person whom he, upon his death-bed, had designed as his successor. This, it must be allowed, is a very near approach to hereditary succession, and through length of time commonly changes into that constitution. Accordingly, for many centuries past, there appears not the least trace of an elective monarchy in Spain; the crown devolving always, of course, without any form or ceremony, on the nearest in blood to the last prince. The kings of Spain have sometimes limited the succession to certain families, ranks, and persons; of which the first instance was that of Philip III., in the year 1619, and the second, of Philip V., in 1713.

The power of the king was formerly limited by the cortes, or parliament of the kingdom. These, which formerly, especially in Castile, had great prerogatives, and were a powerful restraint upon the authority of the sovereign, were in a manner annihilated by Charles V., who deprived the nobles and the prelates of their seat in those assemblies; allowing only a convention of the deputies or agents of the towns, who have very little power, and are absolutely at the devotion of the sovereign.

The king of Spain now governs with the advice of his cabinet council, the *Consejo Real*, who are the secretary of state, and three or four of the principal nobility, with whom he chooses to consult upon the affairs of government. There is no body or department in the constitution which is entitled to restrain or regulate the will of the sovereign, who is therefore an absolute prince.

CHAPTER XXXIII.

GERMANY FROM THE ABDICATION OF CHARLES V. TO THE PEACE OF WESTPHALIA.—Ferdinand I.—Thirty Years' War—Ferdinand II.—Palatinate laid waste—Gustavus Adolphus—Ferdinand III.—Peace of Westphalia.

AT the time when France was in a very flourishing situation under Henry IV., England, under Elizabeth, and Spain extremely formidable under Philip II., the empire of Germany made by no means so respectable a figure. Since the abdication of Charles V. till the reign of Leopold, it had no influence whatever in Italy. The contrary pretensions of the emperors to nominate the popes, and those of the pontiffs to confer the imperial dignity, were insensibly fallen into oblivion. Germany was a republic of princes over whom the emperor presided, and these princes, having constant interferences of interest, generally maintained a civil war, which was fomented by the three contending sects of religion, the Catholics, Lutherans, and Calvinists. Yet the political fabric of the empire, amidst all its disturbances, remained unshaken.

Ferdinand I. endeavored to unite the three religious sects, and to effect a harmony between the princes of the empire: but the attempt was vain. Maximilian II. was less absolute than Ferdinand, and could still less bring about such a coalition; and his successor, Rodolph II., was yet inferior to him in the necessary talents of a sovereign. He was fonder of philosophical researches than of the cares of the empire, and spent that time with Tycho Brahé, the astronomer, which would have been more profitably employed in opposing the measures of Henry IV., a prince, who, had he reigned but a few years longer, would in all probability have annihilated, or at least very greatly abridged, the power of the house of Austria. The religious dissensions continued daily to increase in virulence and animosity, and at length the catholic and protestant leagues plunged Germany into *a civil war of thirty years' continuance*, and reduced that empire to the greatest extremity of national distress. Upon the death of Matthias, the successor of Rodolph, Ferdinand, archduke of Gratz, was elected emperor. He was a zealous catholic, and the protestants of Bohemia, who had suffered under the government of Matthias, were apprehensive of still greater restraint under Ferdinand They determined, therefore, to be governed by a prince of their own persuasion; and they accordingly conferred the crown of

Bohemia on the elector palatine, who had married the daughter of James I., king of England. This prince encountered a series of misfortunes. The emperor Ferdinand put him under the ban of the empire, engaged a small army at Prague, and took from him both his crown and his electorate; he fled into Silesia, and thence successively into Holland, to England, and to France. His father-in-law James refused him the smallest assistance, contrary to the importunities of the whole English nation, and to his own personal glory, as he would thus have become the head of the protestant cause in Europe. It was evidently the interest likewise of Louis XIII. to hinder the princes of Germany from being oppressed, and to check the increasing power of the emperor. Yet the elector palatine was refused aid from that quarter also. The emperor Ferdinand, in a diet held at Ratisbon, declared him fallen from all his estates and dignities, and bestowed his electorate on Maximilian of Bavaria.

The protestant party, now almost overpowered, chose Christian IV., king of Denmark, to be their chief, but his armies were successively defeated by the imperial generals. The party of the catholics were carrying all before them, and every thing seemed to promise that Ferdinand would become absolute through the whole of Germany, and succeed in that scheme, which he seemed to meditate, of entirely abolishing the protestant religion in the empire. But this miserable prospect, both of political and of religious thraldom, was dissolved by the great Gustavus Adolphus, who, being invited by the protestant princes of Germany to espouse the cause of the reformed religion, was induced to assist them, not only as being himself of that persuasion, but as it was of consequence to his own kingdom of Sweden, to prevent the emperor from obtaining a firm footing upon the Baltic.

Gustavus entered Germany, and drove the imperial army out of Pomerania. He attacked the celebrated general Tilly, and entirely defeated him at Leipsic. The whole country submitted to him, from the banks of the Elbe to the Rhine. He marched triumphant through the whole of Germany, while the emperor Ferdinand, fallen at once from all his proud pretensions, was reduced so low as to solicit the pope to publish a crusade against the protestants. On their part all was in a train of success, and the elector palatine was on the verge of being restored to his crown and electorate, when the heroic Gustavus, in the midst of his victories, was killed in the battle of Lutzen. The elector palatine, oppressed with infirmities and misfortunes, died of a broken heart. It was the son of this elector, the gallant prince Rupert, who, together with his brother Maurice, distinguished themselves in the civil wars of England in support of the royal cause, during the reign of their uncle Charles I.

After the death of Gustavus, the war, on the part of the protestants, was carried on by the Swedish generals; and Oxen stiern, the chancellor of Sweden, succeeded his master Gustavus, as head of the protestant interest. Cardinal de Richelieu at the same time declared war against the two branches of the house of Austria, which were attacked at once by France, Sweden, Holland, and Savoy. Under these distressing circumstances died the emperor Ferdinand II., during the whole of whose reign the empire had been subjected to all the miseries of foreign war and of civil commotions.

The Austrian power continued still to decline under his son Ferdinand III. The Swedes gained a footing in the empire; and the French supported the protestant princes with troops and with money. At length Ferdinand III., heartily tired of an unsuccessful war, concluded the peace of Westphalia in the year 1648. In virtue of this celebrated treaty, the Swedes and the French were become the legislators of Germany: the dispute between the emperor and the princes of the empire, which had subsisted for seven hundred years, was finally decided. Germany became a great aristocracy, composed of a monarch, electors, princes, and imperial towns. The Germans were now obliged to pay five millions of rix-dollars to the Swedes, for the aid they had received from them. The kings of Sweden became princes of the empire, and acquired Pomerania with a considerable part of the imperial territories. The king of France was made landgrave of Alsace, and the palatine family was restored to all its rights, except the upper palatinate, which remained with the elector of Bavaria. Above a hundred and forty restitutions were decreed and complied with; and, what was of the greatest importance, the religious dissensions were finally put an end to. The three religions—the Catholic, the Lutheran, and the Calvinist, were equally established. The imperial chamber was composed of twenty-four protestant members, and twenty-six catholic, and the emperor was obliged to admit of six protestants, even in his aulic council at Vienna.*

---

* What is termed the peace of Westphalia consisted, in fact, of two treaties; the one made at Osnaburg, 16th August, 1648, between the Germans and Swedes; the other, in the same year (25th October,) at Munster, between the Germans and the French. The capital proviso is contained in the eighth article of the Treaty of Osnaburg; which, therefore, we shall here transcribe.

"For preventing any disputes that hereafter may arise in the political state, all and every one of the electors, princes, and states of the Roman empire, ought to be so confirmed by virtue of this treaty, in their ancient rights, prerogatives, freedom and privileges, in the free exercise of their territorial rights, in matters ecclesiastical and political in their dominions, in their rights of regality, and in the possession of all these together, that no person may have it in his power to give them actual molestation, on any pretence whatsoever. They shall, without any contradiction, enjoy the privilege of suffrage in all deliberations concerning the right of the empire, particularly when laws are to be made or interpreted, war to be declared, contributions to be imposed, levies of troops to be made, and their quarters regulated; new fortresses to be erected, in the name of the public, in the territories of the states, or garrisons to be placed in the old ones; as also when any treaties of peace or alliance are to be concluded, or any other affairs of that nature to be treated; none of these, or others of the like kind, shall be undertaken or permitted without the suffrage and free consent of all the states

The peace of Westphalia was the preservation of the German empire, which was otherwise tending headlong to ruin. A war of thirty years' continuance had desolated the country, and destroyed some of the most opulent and flourishing of the towns. The quarrels between the protestant and catholic princes must have terminated only by the entire destruction of one party or of the other. Industry was at a stand, agriculture neglected, commerce and manufactures totally annihilated. This salutary peace settled all disputes, and fixed the contending religions, which were the cause of them, upon an unalterable basis: and from that time Germany, gradually recovering from her wounds and misfortunes, at length became a great, a powerful, and a polished nation.

CHAPTER XXXIV.

France under Louis XIV.—Anne of Austria Regent—Cardinal Mazarin—Condé—Turenne—War of the Fronde—Cardinal de Retz—Treaty of the Pyrenees and of Oliva—Christina, Queen of Sweden—Peace of Breda—Wars in Flanders—Triple Alliance—Sabatei Sevi—Louis attacks Holland—Death of Turenne—Peace of Minequar—Revocation of the Edict of Nantes—Louis continues the War in Germany—Peace of Ryswick—Spanish Succession—Prince Eugene—War with England—Marlborough—Battle of Blenheim—Gibraltar taken by the English—Battle of Ramillies—Louis' Schemes in favor of the Stuarts—Successors of the Allies—Battle of Malplaquet—Humiliation of Louis—Battle of Villa Vitiosa restores Philip to the Throne of Spain—Peace of Utrecht, 1713—Peace of Radstadt—Constitution of France under the Monarchy.

Louis XIII. had, by his will, appointed a council of regency for the queen, Anne of Austria; but the parliament of Paris, at her desire, annulled the will, and gave her the full administration of the kingdom during her son's minority. Cardinal Mazarin, an Italian of great address, who had gained upon the favor of the queen, soon rose to the office of prime minister, with all the power of his predecessor Richelieu. The Spaniards, judging the minority of the king and the change of the ministry to be a

---

of the empire, assembled in the diet. They shall, above all things, have the perpetual right of making alliances between themselves and foreigners for their own preservation and security; provided, nevertheless, that such alliances are not directed against the emperor and empire, against the public peace, or against the present transaction in particular; and that they do not in any ways infringe the oath which they have all taken to the emperor and empire."

favorable crisis for an attack upon France, marched an army into Champagne, and besieged Rocroi; but they met with a severe check from the young duke d'Enghien, afterwards the great Condé; and this victory gained by the French at Rocroi paved the way for a series of triumphs. Condé pursued his success; he took from the Spaniards the strong city of Thionville, in Luxembourg, and thence marching into Germany, attacked the imperial forces, and signally defeated them at Fribourg, after a battle which lasted three days. The maréchal Turenne, his competitor for glory, was not at this time so successful. He was defeated by the imperialists at Mariendhal, in Franconia; but Condé, soon after joining his forces to those of the marshal, revenged this disaster by a signal victory at Nordlingen. The details of wars are foreign to our purpose. The peace of Westphalia composed, as we have already observed, the differences between France and the empire. But at this very time a civil war was kindled in Paris, of which the object was the removal of the cardinal Mazarin. The fortune and the power of this minister naturally excited envy, and gave rise to cabals to pull him down; and the maladministration of the finances, the distresses of the state, and the oppression of the people, by a variety of new taxes, were sufficient to render these discontents universal. The parliament, which saw edicts pronounced for taxes, without being, as usual, confirmed by them, expressed an open and violent disapprobation of Mazarin's measures. The coadjutor to the archbishop of Paris, (afterwards the cardinal de Retz,) a man of an impetuous temper, and at the same time of an artful and intriguing character, kindled these discontents into a civil war, to which they gave the name of the Fronde. This, it is believed, is the sole instance of a national rebellion, which had no higher aim than the removal of an unpopular minister. The prince of Conti, brother of the great Condé, the dukes of Longueville, Beaufort, Vendôme, and Bouillon, headed the rebels; and the queen-regent, together with the royal family, removed the court to St. Germain, with a design to besiege the city of Paris and reduce the parliament to submission.

The gay humor of the French, that spirit of levity which turns every thing into ridicule, was never more conspicuous than in this war; a strong contrast to the temper that characterized those civil commotions, which almost, at this very time, had drowned England in blood. The grievances of the English prompted to a serious, a gloomy, and a desperate resistance, which embroiled the whole nation, and ended in the destruction of the constitution. The grievances of the French kindled the civil war of the Fronde, but afforded to this volatile people nothing more than the occasion of an agreeable confusion, and a fit subject for lampoons and ballads. The Parisians marched out to attack the royal army, adorned with plumes of feathers and fine nosegays ; and when the regiment of the coadjutor de Retz, who was nominal archbishop of Corinth, was defeated by the royalists, they called this engagement the first epistle to the Corinthians. The women had as active a share in these proceedings as the men ; and the duchess of Longueville actually prevailed on the great Turenne to leave the king's party, and revolt with his army to that of the rebels. A seeming reconciliation took place for some time, and the court returned to Paris ; but the violence of Mazarin, who put the prince of Condé and his brother Conti, with the duke of Longueville, under arrest, threw every thing again into disorder. The parliament, provoked at these indignities, passed sentence of perpetual banishment on Mazarin, who left the kingdom ; though, by his authority with the queen-regent, he ruled at a distance as absolutely as if he had been at court.

Louis, however, became of age in the year 1652, and the face of affairs was entirely changed. The cardinal de Retz, the chief author of the disturbances, was imprisoned. Gaston, duke of Orleans, the king's uncle, who had been incessantly concerned in all state cabals, was banished ; and a perfect calm succeeded the tumults of the Fronde. Mazarin again returned to court, and enjoyed a degree of authority as high as ever.

Condé had carried his rebellion to a greater height than any of the other partisans. He had joined the Spaniards ; and he now, in conjunction with the archduke Leopold, laid siege to the town of Arras ; but Turenne marched against him, forced him to raise the siege, and left him nothing but the honor of making a good retreat. On the other hand, Turenne, who had besieged Valenciennes, was compelled to raise the siege by Condé and the Spaniards. With the aid of the English, Turenne now laid siege to Dunkirk. The Spaniards, in fine, lost that important place, which France, according to agreement with Cromwell, ceded to the English, and which, as we have already seen, was sold back to the French during the reign of Charles II. Along with Dunkirk, the Spaniards were deprived of several of their strongest towns in Flanders, and, mortified by their losses, concluded in the year 659, the celebrated treaty of the Pyrenees.

The principal article of this treaty, besides the cession of several towns on both sides, was, that Louis XIV. should marry the infanta of Spain — with a portion of two millions five hundred thousand livres — in consideration of which, that princess should renounce all rights which she might eventually have to the crown of Spain.

Thus the war was ended in the south of Europe by the treaty of the Pyrenees, and peace was restored to the north in the year following, by the treaty of Oliva.

About this time Christina, queen of Sweden, the daughter of the great Gustavus Adolphus, attracted the attention of all Europe by her voluntary retirement from the cares of government, at the age of twenty-seven. Christina was fond of literature and the fine arts, and to that passion she sacrificed both her crown and her religion. The court of Sweden, while she reigned, instead of statesmen and politicians, was filled with philosophers and learned men: the cares of government were neglected. She spent her whole time in literary conversations, in the study of the learned languages, or in her cabinet of medals, statues, and pictures. It was not extraordinary that a woman of this disposition should wish to retire from the cares of government, that she might dedicate her whole time to her favorite studies.

The states of Sweden solicited her to marry Charles Gustavus, her cousin. She declined the proposal; but gratified the inclinations of the kingdom by naming him for her successor, and, at a solemn assembly of the states, in the year 1654, she made a formal resignation of the government in his favor. She set out immediately, in man's apparel, for Rome; but soon after left that city for Paris, which she ever afterwards distinguished as her principal place of residence. The conduct of this singular woman has been variously judged of: she herself thought it glorious—and her panegyrist Voltaire holds it forth as much to her honor—that she preferred living with men who could *think*, to the government of a people without literature. But how much nobler would it have been for this philosophic queen to have bestowed her attention on the introduction among her subjects of those sciences which tend to the good of mankind! It was an evidence of a little soul, to reproach those with ignorance, or barbarism, whom it should have been her study, as it was her duty, to have cultivated and improved. It was not, therefore, surprising that a woman, whose conduct was evidently regulated more by caprice than by a sound understanding, should repent of the step she had taken, and wish to resume that government she had abdicated. Upon the death of her cousin Charles X., she solicited the government from the states of Sweden, without success; and, mortified with the disappointment, she went back to Rome, where she died in the year 1689. The example of Christina, it would appear, had been contagious: for a very short time after her resignation, John Casimir, king of Poland, abdicated his throne, and retired to the Abbey of St. Germain, near Paris, where he passed the remainder of his days but the conduct of Casimir was more justifiable than that of Christina: he was of a weak constitution, and far advanced in life. He had been educated a churchman and a man of letters, and though naturally disinclined to the cares of royalty, he sustained the dignity of his kingdom during a pretty long reign, both as an able legislator and as a warrior. He shook off the burden, only when age and want of health unfitted him to support it with honor and advantage.

Meantime Louis XIV. began to display some proofs of a genius which, till now, from the circumstance of a very faulty education, had lain entirely concealed. Mazarin had died in the year 1661, with the honor of having brought about the peace of Westphalia and the treaty of the Pyrenees; and Louis, whom he had hitherto led about as a child, assumed himself the reins of government. He had borne the yoke of Mazarin with great impatience, and, in some instances, had shown that impetuosity of temper which strongly characterized his disposition. Upon occasion of a meeting of the parliament of Paris, where some of the royal edicts were called in question, Louis, then a boy of sixteen years of age, entered the hall of parliament in boots, with a whip in his hand; and, confident of the powers of an absolute prince, told them, with an air of high authority, that he was acquainted with the audacity of their procedure, and would take care to restrain them within the bounds of their just prerogatives. Upon the death of Mazarin, the first acts of the administration of Louis were rather violent than politic. An idle dispute about precedency had happened in London between the Spanish and French ambassadors. Louis immediately ordered the Spanish ambassador at Paris to quit the kingdom, and recalled his own from the court of Spain. Philip IV. was threatened with a renewal of the war, unless a proper submission should be made, and an acknowledgment of the precedency of France, to which that monarch was obliged to consent. A similar affront offered to the French ambassador at Rome was followed by a yet more humiliating satisfaction. The pope was obliged to beg pardon by his legate, and a pillar was erected at Rome to perpetuate the affront and the reparation.

It must be acknowledged that there was something very great and noble in the extent and variety of those measures which Louis pursued for the aggrandizement, the splendor, and the real advantage of his kingdom. He purchased Dunkirk from the English, and strengthened it with immense fortifications. At one and the same time he despatched an army to the aid of the emperor Leopold against the Turks; another to the assistance of the king of Portugal against Spain; and a fleet to the aid of the Dutch against the English. Charles II., for the gratification of his people, had undertaken this war against the Dutch, which, after it had been for some time prosecuted with no advantage to the nation, oppressed, at that time, with the dreadful calamity of the fire of London and the miseries of the plague, was concluded by the peace of Breda, in the year 1667.

From the time of Henry IV., the finances of France had been in a very ruinous condition. The abilities of the great financier Colbert now put matters upon a better footing. He granted protections to trade, established free ports, founded an East India company, and set on foot a variety of useful manufactures in the kingdom. He reduced the interest of money to five per cent. With the assistance afforded him by this able minister, Louis XIV.

was in a condition to undertake a great variety of the most splendid and beneficial projects. The construction of the canal of Languedoc, which joins the bay of Biscay to the Mediterranean; the paving of the principal cities throughout the kingdom; the establishment of a regular internal police; the foundation of the Academy of Belles Lettres and Inscriptions, as well as the Academy of Sciences, are all illustrious monuments of the genius and abilities of Louis XIV.

Philip IV., king of Spain, died in the year 1665, and Louis (though by the treaty of the Pyrenees he had renounced all claim to any part of the Spanish dominions in the right of his wife) now formed a design of seizing Flanders and Franche-Comté. The pretence was, that the money which was stipulated as the queen's portion had never been paid. He made his claim in due form, which was rejected by the queen-regent of Spain, and Louis immediately marched at the head of an army, with marshal Turenne, into Flanders, where most of the towns surrendered at his approach. The city of Lisle, though strongly fortified, held out only nine days.

After this expedition, terminated with equal celerity and success, Louis returned to enjoy the pleasures and applauses of his court. Yet, in the midst of luxury and festivity, he had secretly planned another stroke against the Spanish dominions; and all at once, before the smallest hint of his intentions had transpired, he set out with the prince of Condé and his son, the duke d'Enghien, with an army, for the reduction of Franche-Comté. In three weeks, he had subdued the whole province, and returned victorious to Paris. These exploits, thus superficially related, would incline us to believe that Louis XIV., a youth at this time of the age of twenty-two, promised to rival in military glory the Cæsars and Alexanders of antiquity; but, should we examine them in detail, we shall find no such heroism of character. In the reduction of Flanders and Franche-Comté, the glory of the conquest was due to Turenne and the engineer Vauban. The monarch of France lived in his camp as much at ease and in as much luxury as in his palace at Versailles. He thought it imprudent to hazard the safety of his royal person at the head of his troops, but kept an elegant court in his tent, where his general officers communicated to him from time to time the operations of the campaign.

Meantime, however, these successes alarmed the rest of Europe A triple alliance was formed between England, Holland, and Sweden, to oblige Louis to make peace with Spain, and to relinquish all claim of territory in right of his queen. This alliance put a stop to the progress of the French monarch. The union of these powers was too formidable to be opposed; and a treaty was signed at Aix-la-Chapelle, by which Louis, though he kept part of Flanders, restored Franche-Comté, and confirmed the treaty of the Pyrenees.

After the treaty of Aix-la-Chapelle, France continued to increase equally in strength and in splendor. Her commerce grew with her navy. Colbert and Louvois labored with indefatigable industry in the finances and police, and that kingdom became an object of admiration as well as jealousy to foreigners. The active genius of Louis would not suffer him to rest without a foreign enterprise. The Turks had invaded the island of Candia, (the ancient Crete,) one of the principal possessions of Venice; and Louis sent thither an armament of 7000 men to the aid of the Venetians. That assistance, however, came too late, and Candia was taken by the Turks under the grand vizier Cuprogli.

A singular affair, which happened at this time in Turkey, excited considerable disturbances in that empire, and brought great confusion upon the Jews in the face of all Europe: this was the detection of the impostor Sabatei Sevi, who pretended to be the Messiah. The Jews at this time confidently expected the coming of the Messiah; as it was supposed that the mystic number 666, which is found in the book of the Revelations, implied that their great deliverer was to appear on earth in the year 1666. Sabatei, who was an enthusiast of considerable talents and address, took advantage of this opinion, and began to preach and perform miracles. Smyrna and Damascus, where he first appeared, were thrown into great confusion. He made converts without number. The Jews every where left off trade, and refused to pay their debts. Sabatei made a progress through the Turkish empire, followed by immense multitudes of converts. He arrived at Constantinople, and was immediately thrown into prison. The sultan, Mahomet IV., went himself to see him, and immediately proposed to him either to turn Mahometan or be impaled alive. Sabatei wisely chose the former. He now pretended that he had been commissioned by God to substitute the Mahometan for the Jewish religion; but he sunk into contempt; and the Jews who had been his disciples became the objects of scorn and derision in all the European nations.

To return: the aid sent by Louis to the Venetians against the Turks arrived too late: other projects now occupied the monarch of France. Irritated at the Dutch, who, by means of the triple alliance, had checked his designs against the dominions of Spain, Louis now meditated the conquest of Holland, and he took every measure necessary for so great an enterprise. England, Sweden, and the emperor, entered into his views, and formed an alliance to annihilate this republic, which at this time was internally embroiled by civil factions. The grand pensionary, John de Wit, and his brother Cornelius, from an ardent desire of vindicating the liberty of their country, which was in danger from the exorbitant power of the stadtholder, had procured the abolition of that office after the death of William II. His son, William III., naturally aspired to the attainment of his father's dignities, and had formed a powerful party among the states. At this era of division, the great John de Wit, able politician as he was, had attended more to the internal peace and happiness of his country than to the securing her from foreign danger. The marine of Holland was formidable, but the land forces were in a very poor condition.

Upon the first intimation of Louis's design, the command of the fleet was given to the admiral de Ruyter, and that of the land forces to the prince of Orange. Louis marched into Holland at the head of a prodigious army. In three months, the provinces of Utrecht, Overyssel, and Gueldres were entirely subdued; and the French advanced almost to the gates of Amsterdam. Holland was reduced to the very brink of destruction; and it was seriously proposed to transport the wealth of Amsterdam and its inhabitants to the East Indian colony of Batavia. At the desire of John de Wit, however, a requisition was made for peace ; but the terms prescribed by Louis—viz., the destruction of their forts, the giving up all their possessions beyond the Rhine, and abolishing the protestant religion, were conditions to which it was not possible to accede. In this desperate situation, the prince of Orange, in whom the nation reposed the utmost confidence, was at length created stadtholder, and became the principal support of the state. As a last resource, the Dutch broke down the dykes, and letting in the sea upon the level country, threw the whole under water. To this measure, and still more to an alliance which was forming for their protection with Denmark and the elector of Brandenburg, the Dutch owed their rescue from destruction. Louis was content for the present with the glory he had achieved by the conquest of the three provinces of Gueldres, Overyssel and Utrecht. It was impossible for him however to keep them: they were ransomed by the Dutch; and the French monarch, satisfied with the honors of the campaign, returned with great pomp to Paris, where he built the triumphal gate of St. Denis.

The prince of Orange, in the meantime, to revenge the injuries which his country had sustained, exerted his influence with all the powers of Europe. He prevailed with both branches of the house of Austria to join against France, and found means likewise to draw off the English from her alliance. The emperor sent his general Montecucculi with 20,000 men, and the elector of Brandenburg marched 25,000 to the assistance of the Hollanders. Marshal Turenne commanded an army of 20,000 French upon the Rhine. With these he beat the imperialists, and carried havoc and desolation into the palatinate ; but in the prosecution of his successes he was killed by a cannon-ball near Sasbach.* After

* The fine speech of St. Hilaire (the lieutenant-general of artillery) is well known. The same bullet which killed Turenne carried off his arm ; and his son lamenting his misfortune with tears, "Weep not for me," said St. Hilaire : "for that great man we ought all to weep ; " "Paroles comparables," says Voltaire "à tout ce que l'histoire a consacré de plus héroïque ; et le plus digne éloge de

the death of Turenne, Condé, with 45,000 men, attacked the prince of Orange near Mons, in a most desperate engagement, where the victory at last remained doubtful. A singular enterprise was attempted by marshal Luxemburg. He marched an army of 12,000 men upon skates, from Utrecht, to attack the Hague; but the project was unfortunately defeated by the coming on of a thaw before they had reached the Hague, which obliged them to return without any effect. In the meantime, marshal du Quesne had three naval engagements with De Ruyter, in all of which the event was undecided.

After various and alternate successes by sea and land, a peace was at length concluded at Nimeguen, in year 1678, much to the honor of France. Franche-Comté was given up by the Spaniards, and it has ever since been annexed to the French dominions. Spain likewise surrendered to them almost all the conquered towns in the Netherlands.

During the continuance of this peace, Louis XIV. did not make a prudent use of his good fortune. He still kept up his troops, and, by corrupting the magistrates of Strasburg, found means to seize upon that important city, which exasperated the emperor to such a degree, as almost to rekindle the war. The elector of Brandenburg, however, prevented the union of the Germanic body, and Louis retained his conquest. This most ambitious monarch was in the meanwhile secretly stirring up the Turks to coöperate with the Hungarians in invading the imperial dominions on the quarter of Hungary. The Hungarians were at this time in arms against the court of Vienna, to vindicate their privileges, which the emperor had encroached upon. The allied forces marched up to the gates of Vienna, and laid siege to the city, which was on the point of falling into the hands of the Turks, had not John Sobieski, king of Poland, most seasonably come to its relief. It is almost incredible that the emperor, who had meanly abandoned the city, and fled to Passau, should, at his return to his capital, insist on receiving a submissive homage from the very man to whom he owed the preservation of his dominion. It was not at all surprising that a proposal so absurd should be treated by John Sobieski with suitable disdain.

His intrigues having failed in this quarter, Louis now turned his arms towards Flanders, and his northern frontiers, and while he amused the emperor and the Spaniards in negotiations, he seized upon Courtrai, took and demolished the fortifications of Treves, and made himself master of the whole principality of Luxemburg;

Turenne." Turenne was indeed a singular character. Every endowment of nature, and every acquirement of education necessary to form the character of a consummate general, seemed to centre in him. His intrepid and enterprising mind was ever under the guidance of a vigorous and penetrating judgment: he never fought for fame, but always with that judicious caution which, though it may lessen the splendor of an enterprise, ensures its success.

and having secured these important advantages, he concluded his negotiations by a truce for twenty years. Louis next projected the reduction of the piratical states of Barbary, and received the submission of Algiers, which was soon followed by that of Tunis and Tripoli. Genoa, which had offended by selling ammunition to the pirates, and building ships for the Spanish navy, was bombarded—one half of this magnificent city was reduced to ashes, and the doge and principal senators were sent to Paris to deprecate the vengeance of Louis.

Theological controversies next engaged his attention, and after a tedious contention with the church of Rome, originating between the Jesuits and Janesenists, Louis now formed a very impolitic project for the extirpation of Calvinism from his dominions. Colbert had protected the Calvinists, from a conviction that they were as useful as any other subjects; but at the death of that able statesman, the most rigorous measures were adopted and pursued. The edict of Nantes had been passed in the reign of Henry IV., giving the protestants liberty of conscience; and had been confirmed by Louis XIII., under certain restrictions with regard to public worship. Louis *revoked the edict:* the whole Huguenot churches were demolished, the ministers banished, and, what was a refinement of persecution, the protestants were at the same time prohibited, under the severest penalties, from quitting the kingdom. That prohibition, however, was ineffectual, and above 500,000 people made their escape out of France, and, carrying with them all their property, found a welcome asylum in Germany, Switzerland,* Holland, and England. By this most impolitic measure, France sustained a very severe loss, not only in the article of population, but in commerce and manufactures.

It was much about the same time that a similar excess of intolerant zeal produced, as we have already seen, the fall of the house of Stuart from the throne of Great Britain.

In the year 1692 a remarkable division arose in the empire of Germany, on occasion of the creation of a ninth electorate in favor of the duke of Brunswick-Lunenburg-Hanover. The emperor had given him the investiture; but the princes protested, and would have had recourse to arms, if Leopold had not suspended the creation. It continued to be a subject of dissension till the year 1708, when the states gave their consent to the investiture of the duke of Brunswick, who soon after became king of Great Britain by the title of George I.

---

* Voltaire affirms, that "there are not less than a thousand families of French refugees settled at Geneva, and to these that city, which formerly was only considerable as a school of theology, owes its industry, its manufactures, and its consequent opulence. The Genevese at present are in a capacity of lending to the king of France a sum from which they draw an annual interest of five millions of livres." Fragment sur là Révocation de l'Edit de Nantes.—Voltaire, Œuvres. t. xxvi., 4to.

In the meantime Louis carried on the war in Germany, with his son, the dauphin, at the head of his armies. The cities of Heidelburg, Mentz, Philipsburg, Spires, were taken, and the palatinate was ravaged with fire and sword. Marshal Luxemburg, successful in the Low Countries, defeated king William in the celebrated battles of Steenkirk and Nerwinden, in the year 1692 and 1693. Marshal de Noailles was at the same time victorious in Spain. This period, in short, seems to have been the crisis of the greatness and splendor of Louis XIV., the ultimate boundary of his vast successes.

However flattering these brilliant triumphs had been to the pride of the nation, Louis, who was a very able politician, began at length to perceive that his ambitious views were attended with no solid advantage. The variety and extent of his military enterprises had been attended with a prodigious waste of treasure. He had lost the ablest of his ministers, Colbert; and that excellent arrangement of the finances, which, during his administration, afforded his master the most abundant supplies for the accomplishment of his great designs, had been much relaxed under the management of his successors. Louis, in short, thought it his most advisable plan to conclude the peace of Ryswick, in the year 1697, of which the conditions, though proposed by himself, were extremely humiliating after such a career of glory. He restored to Spain all that she had lost by the war in Flanders, and all his conquests near the Pyrenees. He restored several towns to the emperor, and the territory of Lorraine to its duke, and finally he acknowledged the prince of Orange king of England. It has been pretended that these concessions were made with a political view, to pave the way for his succession to the crown of Spain, as Charles II. of Spain was then dying, and Louis pretended a title as grandson of Philip III., notwithstanding his mother's renunciation of all right to that crown. But this refined piece of policy is now certainly known to have been all a fiction. The true secret of the humiliating peace of Ryswick was the exhausted state of France, the enormous expenses of the war, the disorder of the finances, and the murmurs of the people at the increase of taxes for supplying the monarch's various and expensive schemes.

The succession to the kingdom of Spain was, it is true, a subject of great political intrigue. The emperor and the king of France were the natural competitors: while king William of England, apprehensive of such an increase of power, proposed a treaty of partition with France and Holland, by which Spain and all her possessions in America were to be secured to the elector of Bavaria, the two Sicilies to the Dauphin, and the duchy of Milan to the emperor's second son. This division of his kingdom in his own lifetime naturally irritated the Spanish monarch to a high degree. It occasioned great cabals at the court of Madrid; and Charles II., at length, rather choosing to make a settlement himself of his dominions than to allow them to be disposed of by others, bequeathed, by his will, the whole monarchy to the duke of Anjou, the Dauphin's second son; and failing the younger branches of the family of France, to the archduke Charles, the youngest son of the emperor, but upon condition that the empire and Spain should never be united under the same sovereign. He died soon after. Whether Louis XIV. ought to have agreed to the partition treaty, or accepted the will of the king of Spain, has been disputed by the French politicians, and was seriously deliberated by Louis himself. By the partition treaty, the crown of the two Sicilies and Lorraine would have been added to his dominions, and he might have reckoned upon the assistance of England and Holland against the emperor. By accepting the legacy of the kingdom, he exposed himself to a general war for the establishment of his grandson. The last of the measures, however, he chose; and contrary to all expectation, instead of a general war breaking out, the whole powers of Europe remained for some time in perfect tranquillity. The duke of Anjou, by the name of Philip V., took possession of his crown, and was acknowledged by the pope, the duke of Savoy, the state of Venice, the northern potentates, and even by Portugal, England, and Holland. These two last powers, however, England and Holland, considered the Spanish dominions in Italy in a different point of view, and they entered into an alliance with the emperor to detach them from the principal inheritance. This occasioned a war in Italy, in which prince Eugene commanded the imperial army. This illustrious man was son of the count de Soissons of the house of Savoy, governor of Champagne. In his youth having met with some mortifications at the court of France, he went into the emperor's service, who was then at war with the Turks. Louis, who treated him with disdain, did not at that time foresee that this young man would one day humble his pride, and shake the foundations of his empire.

In the year 1701, James II. of England died at the castle of St. Germains, and Louis was imprudent enough to exasperate the English by recognising the title of king in his son. The consequence was, that England resolved to prosecute a war against France with the utmost rigor. The death of king William, which happened in the year following, it was hoped by the French might have been a favorable circumstance, and it was expected that the political system would have been in some measure changed by the accession of queen Anne. But there was no alteration; the duke of Marlborough, at that time commander-in-chief of the forces of England, confirmed the Dutch in the league formed against France, and a war was declared which brought that kingdom to the lowest ebb of misfortune.

Louis XIV., now in the decline of life, was unable to give

that attention to state affairs which he had shown in the vigor of his administration. Military discipline had languished after the death of Luvois and Turenne, and neither the domestic government, the army, nor the state of the nation were correspondent to the former successful years of this reign. The army of the enemy, on the contrary, was commanded by Marlborough and prince Eugene, who, with great extent both of political and military genius, had the treasures of England and of Holland at their disposal. France had to combat their united forces; and to increase the mortification of Louis, the duke of Savoy changed sides, and sold himself to the emperor. Portugal, likewise declared against France, and every endeavor was used to dethrone Philip V., and to place the emperor's son upon the throne of Spain. Marshal Villars had, however, with considerable success, opposed the arms of the imperialists, when he was most imprudently recalled for the pitiful purpose of extinguishing an insurrection of some fanatics in one of the provinces. The duke of Marlborough, in the meantime, was carrying every thing before him. He took the towns of Venlo, Ruremond, and Liege, and in the following campaign defeated marshals Tallard and Marin, together with the elector of Bavaria, in the celebrated battle of Blenheim or Hochstet. The French army, which consisted of 60,000 men, were completely routed: 12,000 were killed on the field, and 14,000 taken prisoners. Prince Eugene shared the honor of this day with Marlborough. He arrived with his army while the English were in the heat of the engagement, and by this seasonable reinforcement contributed to the victory. The emperor, who by this day's success became master of the electorate of Bavaria, conferred upon the duke of Marlborough the dignity of a prince of the empire, along with the territory of Mindelheim.

The Spanish branch of the house of Bourbon was in the meantime in a state yet more wretched than its parent stock England and Holland were uniting their utmost efforts in favor of the emperor's son, the archduke Charles. The English, by sudden enterprise, took possession of the fort of Gibraltar, which they have kept since that time. It had been in vain battered by the cannon of their fleet, and was at length taken by a few boats stealing unperceived under the Mole, which was scaled by the English sailors, while the Spaniards watched only the operations of the ships of war. In six weeks, the English, pursuing their successes, subdued the whole provinces of Catalonia and Valencia.

In Flanders, marshal Villeroy had flattered himself that he would yet retrieve the honor of the arms of France, and was impatient till he measured his strength with Marlborough in the field of Ramillies; but the event of this battle was yet more disgraceful to the French, and honorable to the English general, than that of Blenheim. In one half hour, the French were totally routed, and 20,000 men left dead upon the field. The consequence of this defeat was the loss of almost all Spanish Flanders.

A short gleam of success attended, however, at this time the arms of Louis XIV. in Italy.

The duke of Vendôme had the honor of defeating prince Eugene at the battle of Cassano, and of forcing that general to retreat into the country of Trent. He was pursuing his successes when he was most imprudently recalled, to replace marshall Villeroy, in the Low Countries; and his successor in Italy, far inferior to the trust reposed in him, furnished a counterpart to his conduct by a series of errors, of losses, and misfortunes. The French were defeated at Turin, and the whole country was abandoned to the emperor; while in the meantime, his son, the archduke, was proclaimed at Madrid; and Philip V., on the point of losing his kingdom, had thoughts of evacuating Spain altogether, and establishing his dominion in America. This desperate resolution, however, was changed upon the victory of Almanza, where the duke of Berwick, the natural son of James II., defeated the imperialists with their allies, and restored the spirits of the desponding monarch.

The aged Louis, encouraged by this prospect of success, though harassed in so many quarters, had yet spirit enough to think of another ambitious enterprise. This was the establishment of the pretender James upon the throne of Britain. A fleet was fitted out, which was to land him in Scotland, where it was supposed he would meet with partisans sufficient among his countrymen to insure the success of his cause. But the enterprise was unsuccessful; the squadron appeared upon the coast, but England, being apprized of the project, had made every preparation, and even recalled twelve battalions from Flanders for the protection of the kingdom. James, without landing, returned to France, to wait a more favorable opportunity for the prosecution of his designs.

Misfortunes were now accumulating fast upon the head of Louis XIV. Prince Eugene and Marlborough defeated the French army at Oudenarde, and made themselves masters of Lisle, Ghent, and Brussels. In Spain, Philip V. was daily losing ground, and the party of the archduke daily increasing. The emperor Joseph had even obliged the pope, Clement XI., to acknowledge the archduke king of Spain. The English took Sardinia and Minorca; and the house of Bourbon, both in France and Spain, seemed hastening to its ruin.

The general voice of the kingdom of France was now for peace; and the once haughty Louis, now miserably humbled, sent his minister to negotiate in person at the Hague, where he met with the most mortifying treatment from Marlborough,

Eugene, and the grand pensionary Heinsius. They demanded nothing less, as a condition of peace, than that the king of France should undertake, at his own charges, to dethrone his grandson Philip, and even limited him to the space of two months for the fulfilling of this condition. The spirit of the aged Louis broke out into the most just indignation at this inhuman and dishonorable proposal. "Since," says he, "I must die fighting, it shall be with mine enemies, and not with my children." He prepared, therefore, for a resolute continuance of that war which was only to involve him in fresh misfortunes.

Marlborough and Eugene prosecuted their conquests in Flanders; and the battle of Malplaquet, though attended with greater loss to the allies, was a defeat upon the part of the French, and a new misfortune to the kingdom. Eight thousand of their best troops fell in this engagement, and the consequence was that Louis now found himself reduced to the necessity of entreating conditions equally humiliating with those which had been so arrogantly proposed to him. He offered to extend the Dutch frontier so as to comprehend Lisle and Tournay; to restore Strasburg and Brisac; to fill up the harbor of Dunkirk; to acknowledge the archduke as king of Spain; and to give no assistance to Philip V. With the same inhumanity these offers were rejected, and peace refused, unless upon the condition of his actually dethroning his grandson with his own arms.

At this time the public misery of the kingdom excited universal despair: the army of the archduke had defeated the forces of Philip at Saragossa; and Spain, in the meantime, was invaded by Portugal; when affairs in that quarter most unexpectedly took a sudden turn for the better. Louis, amid all his distresses, had sent the duke of Vendôme to their assistance, and this able general revived the drooping spirits of the nation. An extraordinary exertion was made, and a formidable army was soon in the field, to which the Portuguese and English found themselves perfectly unequal. The victory at Villa Vitiosa restored Philip V. to his capital of Madrid, and put an end to the pretensions of the archduke, who soon after was gratified with the attainment of a higher object of ambition, the succession to the empire by the death of his brother Joseph. Thus Spain was restored to perfect quiet; and France, not long after, obtained that peace which she so earnestly longed for, and so much stood in need of.

A few successes of the French in retaking some of the towns in Flanders would never have produced this beneficial effect, had it not been for the domestic differences of the English and the influence of the court intrigues. The faction of the whigs, of which Marlborough was the head, had begun gradually to lose their influence at court, principally from this cause, that queen Anne was disgusted with the imperious and haughty behavior of the duchess of Marlborough, who had arrogated to herself the authority and influence of a prime minister. The duchess was disgraced; the ministry was changed; the tories came into power, and it was resolved to make a peace with France. This peace was concluded at Utrecht, in several separate treaties, in the course of the year 1713. It was stipulated, in the first place, that Philip, king of Spain, should renounce all claim that he ever might have to the kingdom of France; and that his brother, the duke of Berri, should, in like manner, renounce all right to the crown of Spain. The Dutch obtained a considerable frontier, the emperor eight provinces of Spanish Flanders, and had his right secured to the kingdom of Naples and Sardinia; the duke of Savoy got the island of Sicily, with the title of king; the English gained, upon the part of Spain, Gibraltar and Minorca; and France yielded to them the settlements of Hudson's Bay, Newfoundland, and Acadia. Besides these acquisitions in territory, the English insisted for and obtained the demolition of the harbor of Dunkirk, with all its fortifications. All that France obtained, which she had not then in her possession, was the restitution of Lisle and a few small towns in Flanders. She did not even for awhile obtain a complete peace; for the obstinacy of prince Eugene had prevented the emperor from acceding to the treaty of Utrecht, and the war was continued upon the Rhine till the successes of marshal Villars forced the emperor and his general at length into conditions; and in the year following a peace was concluded at Radstadt, between Villars and Eugene.

Louis did not long survive the pacification of his empire. He died, on the 1st of September, 1715, in the seventy-eighth year of his age. He preserved to the last that courage which characterizes a vigorous mind. The last words which he uttered, as reported by Madame Maintenon, who heard them, were the dictates equally of a wise and a magnanimous spirit; he called to him his grandson the dauphin, who stood by his bed-side, and holding him between his arms gave him his blessing; and said to him, "My son, you are going to be a great king; be always a good Christian. Do not follow my example with regard to war; endeavor to live in peace with your neighbors. Render to God what you owe to Him; follow always the most moderate counsels: endeavor to reduce the taxes, and thus do that which I have unhappily not been able to do. Take notice, my son: these are my last words, and let them sink deep into your mind—remember that kings die like other men." Such was the end of Louis XIV. The misfortunes of the nation, the enormous expense of an unsuccessful war, and the oppression of those taxes which were necessary to support it, had lessened this great man in the affections of his subjects, who ought not to have overlooked those lasting advantages which they had derived from his government in point of arts and sciences, in the advancement of literature, and all that contributes to heighten the enjoyments of social life.

THE CONSTITUTION OF FRANCE UNDER THE MONARCHY.

To understand the history of France, some acquaintance with its further monarchical constitution, as it existed previous to the Revolution, is necessary to the reader of history. The ancient constitution under the first and second races of its kings, and the political institutions of Clovis and Charlemagne, have already been noticed; and in tracing the history of the kingdom, those changes which gradually took place, and insensibly substituted the monarchical for the aristocratical form of its government, have been adverted to; but of these a short recapitulation is necessary to bring the subject into one view.

Under the first or the Merovingian race of the kings of France, we have seen that the royal prerogative was extremely inconsiderable. The general assemblies of the nation, the Champs de Mai and the Champs de Mars, which met annually at stated seasons, possessed the right of electing the kings, of providing them a certain revenue, and of enacting laws for the regulation of the whole community. Under the second or Carlovingian race, the power and authority which the vast abilities of Charlemagne had added to the crown dwindled entirely away in the hands of his weak posterity; and the national assemblies possessed a prerogative and jurisdiction almost as extensive as in the time of his predecessors. But, under the third race of monarchs, termed the Capetian, the constitution had so far changed, that the national assemblies had lost their legislative authority, or at least entirely relinquished the exercise of it. From that period their jurisdiction extended no further than to the imposition of new taxes, the determination of questions respecting a disputed succession to the crown, appointing a regency during the minority of a monarch, and sometimes presenting an humble remonstrance to the sovereign, in the name of the subject, against any measures of the crown which were felt as national grievances. The kings now began gradually to assume the power of legislation, which towards the end of the fourteenth century was considered as a right which resided wholly in the crown. The power of taxation immediately followed; nor does it appear that the first exercise of these rights by the crown without consent of the national assemblies, was attended with the smallest murmur on the part of the people, and these assemblies, now completely stripped of all their valuable powers, were very seldom convoked, and at length entirely laid aside.

Another power, however, insensibly arose, which in some measure supplied their place, in imposing a small restraint and limitation on the amplitude of the regal prerogative; I speak of the French parliaments—and particularly the parliament of Paris. During the feudal government, the parliament of Paris was nothing more than the king's court, to which he committed the supreme administration of justice within his own domains, as well as the power of deciding with respect to all cases brought before it, by appeal from the courts of the barons. As this court was commonly supplied with judges of great ability, and the forms of procedure were better regulated than those of the provincial jurisdictions of the kingdom, of all of which the judges were likewise in the king's nomination, the parliament of Paris gradually acquired a degree of reputation, dignity, and respect superior to the provincial parliaments. The kings of France, when they first began to assume the legislative power, that they might the better reconcile the minds of the people to this new exertion of prerogative, produced their edicts and ordinances in the parliament of Paris, that they might be approved and registered there before they were published and declared to be of authority through the kingdom. The monarchs were likewise accustomed to consult with this court with respect to the most arduous affairs of government, and frequently regulated their conduct by its advice in declaring war, making peace, or in other matters of public concern. Thus by degrees the nation began to look upon the parliament of Paris as the supreme depositary of the laws of the kingdom, and as a body which divided in some respects the powers of sovereignty with the monarch, and was a check upon any violent abuse or exorbitant stretch of his authority: and the parliament, availing itself of this general belief, and naturally disposed to extend its own powers and prerogatives, at various times made a bold stand for the liberties of the people, ventured to question the right of the monarch to lay on arbitrary impositions, and frequently refused to verify and register his edicts.

Yet, strictly speaking, the parliament of Paris must be considered as having usurped these powers, to which, from the original constitution of that assembly, they had no legal right. In fact, they were nothing more than a supreme court of justice; they were in no shape the representatives of the people. They were a set of judges nominated by the king, paid by him, and removable by him at pleasure from their office. The practice of registering and verifying the royal edicts in this court was, as we have already observed, introduced by the monarchs to reconcile the people to that change of the constitution which gave the king the sole legislative authority. We know for certain that when this practice first began, the parliament acted as a mere official instrument, and never pretended to refuse to register or give their sanction to any edict which was presented to them. Even after the lapse of above two centuries, since they first assumed the right of questioning and refusing to verify the royal edicts, they possessed in reality no power to maintain and defend this privilege

When the parliament refused to give its sanction to any of the royal edicts, the king had only to repair in person to the hall where they were assembled, and command the edict to be read, verified, and registered; and the order of the sovereign must have been obeyed; for it was one of the fundamental laws of the French monarchy that, in the presence of the king, the function of every magistrate is suspended for the time.

Yet even these powers of the parliament of Paris, though they could thus be defeated by the sovereign, were no inconsiderable restraint upon his authority. They effectually prevented that authority from degenerating into absolute despotism, at least, by opposing every encroachment of the crown, and by giving the alarm to the nation when any measure was attempted to be carried into execution which would have proved a serious grievance. The parliament of Paris was frequently broken for a contumacious resistance to the will of the monarch, and its members driven into banishment; but it happened in general that the measure which had been the cause of their resistance was abandoned by the prince, and the nation was thus delivered from a grievance against which otherwise they could have had no redress.

The constitution of the provincial parliaments, which were twelve in number, was in every respect the same with that of the parliament of Paris. It was necessary that the king's edicts should be registered by them before they became of general force. They were the chief courts of justice in the province, and some of them acted likewise in a ministerial capacity, as the parliaments of Burgundy, Brittany, Dauphiné, Provençe, Languedoc, and French Flanders, who, when the king thought fit to raise a new tax or assessment upon the province, settled the proportions payable by individuals, and directed the mode of levying it.

The king of France was then to be considered as an absolute prince, but whose authority was at the same time considerably restrained by the consuetudinary regulations of the kingdom, and could not easily become entirely despotic or tyrannical. The crown was hereditary, but it could not pass to a female—nor to a natural son, though legitimated; and it was settled by a royal edict in 1717, that upon the total failure of the line of Bourbon, the crown should be elective, the choice lying in the states of the kingdom, clergy, nobility, and citizens.

The royal revenue was computed to be about three hundred millions of livres, or twelve millions three hundred thousand pounds sterling; but it must necessarily have varied considerably according to the pleasure of the monarch, for it consisted of two separate funds, one of which was fixed, and the other arbitrary. The fixed or ordinary revenue of the crown comprehended the royal domains, or the king's patrimonial lands, lordships, and forests; the duty on wine, called the *aids;* the duty on salt, called the *gabelle;* the land-tax, or *taille;* the *capitation*, or poll-tax;

and the gift of the clergy, who, so late as the year 1753, purchased away their ancient tax of the twentieth penny, by obliging themselves to pay a yearly sum of twelve millions of livres, or five hundred thousand pounds sterling. The extraordinary or arbitrary revenue of the crown consisted in such other taxes as the monarch thought proper to impose, and the money arising from the sale of offices, which was a very large fund. Most of those duties we have mentioned were leased out to the farmers-general of the revenue, who paid a settled sum to the crown, and appointed their under-farmers and receivers.*

With respect to the ecclesiastical constitution of France, the Gallican church, though catholic, and acknowledging the pope as supreme head in matters spiritual, had greatly limited his power within the kingdom. The declaration of the assembly of the clergy of France, signed in the year 1682, bears that the sovereign power in all temporal matters is in no shape subject to the power of the pope, which extends only to matters relative to salvation; that no temporal power can be deposed by the pope, nor subjects absolved from their allegiance to their lawful prince by his authority; that the pope himself is subject to the general councils of the church, which are to be obeyed in preference to his mandates; that the canons which are enacted by those general councils are the supreme rule of obedience in all matters ecclesiastical; and that the judgment of the pope in matters of faith is not infallible, unless it is supported by the assent of the catholic church, declared in a general council. In consequence of these regulations, neither the sovereign, his officers nor magistrates, were subject to any church discipline, either inflicted by the bishops or by the pope himself. The pope had no other jurisdiction in France than such as the king was pleased to grant him. No appeals were competent to the see of Rome, unless in a very few ecclesiastical cases, specially defined: no subject could be summoned to Rome; no legate from the pope could act in France without the royal licence; nor could the pope levy any money from the kingdom unless those small fees and imposts which are decreed to be payable to the see of Rome by the Concordat, a decree of a general council of the catholic church. The ecclesiastical power in France was, in fact, subordinate to the civil; for in all church matters where there was any suspicion of an abuse or an unjust sentence, it was competent to appeal from the ecclesiastical courts to the parliaments, where the matter was determined as a civil cause.

* The history of the French finances may be best understood from the following books:—a small work published in 1599, under the administration of Sully, entitled "Recueil des Réglemens, Edicts, Ordonnances, et Observations sur le faict des Finances;" and the "Comptes Rendus des Finances du Royaume sous Henri IV., Louis XIII., et Louis XIV.," by M. Mallet, printed at London in 1789, which contains an introduction of great merit, inquiring into the origin of the several taxes, and the ancient management of the revenue.

CHAPTER XXXV.

PETER THE GREAT, CZAR OF MUSCOVY, AND CHARLES XII. OF SWEDEN·—Origin of the Russian Empire—Siberia conquered—Rapid extension in Asia—Peter the Great—Forms the first small Body of regular Troops—Equips a Fleet—Travels in Search of Knowledge—Returns to Russia—His vast Innovations—Charles XII. of Sweden—Confederacy against—Defeats the Russians in the Battle of Narva—Invades Poland—Takes Warsaw and Cracow—Places Stanislaus on the Throne—Invades the Ukraine—Is defeated at Pultowa—Taken Prisoner by the Turks—Returns to his Dominions—Killed at Frederickshal—Character—Peter the Great puts his Son to Death—Death of Peter—Internal Improvements of his Empire.

DURING the latter part of the reign of Louis XIV., two most illustrious characters had begun to figure in the north of Europe—Peter the Great, czar of Muscovy, and Charles XII., king of Sweden. To the vast empire of Russia we have hitherto paid no attention, because, till now, it was quite uncivilized, and had scarcely any connection with the European kingdoms. Its early history is still very obscure. Till the middle of the fifteenth century, the Russians were an unconnected multitude of wandering tribes, professing different religions, and most of them yet idolaters. A sovereign, or duke of Russia, paid a tribute to the Tartars of furs and cattle, to restrain their depredations. Ivan Vassilov'ch, a spirited chief, rescued them from this subjection. About the middle of the fifteenth century he increased his dominions by the accession of Novogorod and of the territory of Moscow, which he took from the Lithuanians ; and from that period, the Russian czars or princes began to assume the splendor and dignity of sovereigns, but their dominions were barbarous and uncultivated. It was not till the year 1645, when Alexis Michaelowitz succeeded to the throne, that the first code of Russian laws was published, and some attempts were made to introduce that civilization which was afterwards so happily accomplished by his son, Peter the Great. The limits of the empire at this time, too, did not comprehend one third of what is now subject to the dominion of the sovereigns of Russia.

Till about the end of the sixteenth century, the dominions of Russia were bounded by the river Wolga to the east, that is to say,—they extended no farther than the limits of Europe. At that time a Cossack chief of the name of Jermack, who followed the profession of a robber, and was the leader of a gang of banditti, was the means of adding to the Russian empire all that immense tract of country known by the name of Siberia. He had long infested the Russian borders by his depredations, till at last being taken prisoner with the greatest part of his followers, and condemned to suffer death, he threw himself upon the clemency of the czar, and offered, on condition of receiving a pardon, to point out an easy conquest of an immense extent of empire unknown to the Russians. His offer was accepted, the czar approved of the expedition, and Jermack set out as the general of a regular army for the conquest of Siberia, then in the hands of the Tartars. This expedition was attended with all the success that could be wished. The Tartars fled before the Russians; but venturing at length to make a stand, a general and decisive battle was fought near the city of Tobolsky, where the Tartars were entirely defeated, and their king, with the whole of the royal family, was sent in chains to Moscow. They were, however, very honorably treated, and the son of the last prince had an assignment of territory of a large extent given him in Russia, which is at this day, or has very lately been, enjoyed by his family, together with the title of Sibersky Czarovitz, or prince of Siberia. The Russians continued to extend their conquests to the east with great rapidity, and in half a century found themselves confined only by the eastern limits of the Asiatic continent.

The czar Alexis Michaelowitz, who first introduced a regular system of laws among the Russians, paved the way for that civilization which his son Peter afterwards accomplished. Alexis left three sons, Phædor, Ivan, and Peter, and a daughter Sophia. Phædor succeeded his father, but died young in the year 1682, leaving the crown to his youngest brother Peter, then only two years of age, in exclusion of the elder Ivan, a man of no capacity; but the princess Sophia had that capacity which her brother wanted. She committed some dreadful excesses to obtain the government of the empire, and carried the point so as to cause herself to be associated with her brothers in the regency; but this did not satisfy her. She aimed at an exclusive possession of the sovereignty, and for that purpose formed a conspiracy against the life of Peter, which terminated in her own ruin. The young Peter assembled some troops, severely punished the conspirators, confined Sophia in a monastery, and, leaving only an empty title to his brother Ivan, made himself master of the empire in the year 1689.

The rudeness and imperfection of Peter's education, and some early habits of intemperance and debauchery, did not prevent him from very soon exhibiting proofs of that genius by which he was so remarkably characterized. An acquaintance with a young foreigner of the name of Le Fort, by birth a Swiss, and a man of penetrating genius, infused those first ideas of improvement into the mind of the czar, and gave birth to a variety of designs for the cultivation and refinement of his people. The first objects of his attention were the army and the marine. The Strelitzes, a body of militia consisting of about thirty thousand men, like the Turkish Janizaries, had frequently embroiled the empire by their seditions. Peter determined to abolish entirely this dangerous body, and for that purpose began with the formation of a regiment, which, by degrees, he increased to the number of twelve thousand men. To set an example of subordination to his nobility, he served himself in the quality of a private soldier; thence advancing gradually to the rank of captain and general officer. In the formation of this first body of regular troops, he owed a great deal to the assistance of an able person, of the name of Gordon. He, at the same time, with the help of foreign workmen, constructed a small fleet, and resolved to make an early experiment of his power, by laying siege to Azoph, then a Turkish settlement, at the head of the Black Sea, upon the mouth of the Don or Tanais. The enterprise was successful; he defeated the Turkish fleet, and made himself master of Azoph—upon the reduction of which he celebrated a triumph at his return to Moscow.

The genius of Peter was soon sensible, that it was not at home he was to learn those arts which were necessary for the cultivation of his empire. He resolved, therefore, to travel in search of knowledge through the different countries of Europe, and thence to bring home whatever might be of use or importance towards the prosecution of his great design. He named three ambassadors, Le Fort, and two of his nobility, who were to be the ostensible characters at the several courts which he intended to visit, while he himself appeared as a private man in their suite. He began his journey by Livonia, and from thence, passing through Germany, took up his residence for some time in Holland, where he applied himself, with the assiduity even of a common mechanic, to the acquisition of those useful arts in which his country was most deficient. He studied the art of ship-building by working in the docks with his own hands. He lived with the ship-carpenters, clothed himself like them, and confined himself to the same diet and the same hours of labor. To the practice of these arts, he joined the knowledge of their theory by studying with great attention the principles of mathematics and mechanics. He attended the lectures given at Amsterdam in natural philosophy, and the schools of anatomy and surgery; in short, he labored with unremitting industry to acquire a knowledge of all the useful arts and sciences. Russia, indeed, was very late in being civilized; but as the civilization of this empire was not owing, as in other nations, to a gradual progress of society, but was effected at once by the genius of a single man, who introduced the arts and sciences among them in their highest perfection; it has hence happened, that the Russians have made more progress in a century, than any other nation seems ever to have done in double, or even treble the space of time. Ship-building, at the period in question, had been brought to greater perfection in England, than in any other nation in Europe. Thither Peter went, in the year 1693, still as a private man, in the suite of his ambassadors. He was there employed, as he had been in Holland, in the constant observation and acquirement of every thing that might tend to the improvement of his empire. The founding of cannon; the art of printing; of paper-making; the construction of clocks and watches; every thing attracted his attention. During his residence, both in Holland and in England, he engaged several ingenious artists to accompany him at his return to his own dominions. He cultivated a particular acquaintance with Mr. Ferguson, an excellent geometrician, and Mr. Perry, not less eminent as an engineer. The former he employed in the institution of the Marine Academy at Petersburg, and the latter in the construction of navigable canals, and many noble bridges in various parts of his dominions.

Meantime the absence of the czar had given occasion to some disturbances in the empire. The spirit of innovation, which he had already shown, and the further fruits expected from his foreign travels, gave great disgust to a barbarous people wedded to their ancient manners. The ambition of Sophia fomented these disquiets, and the Strelitzes had determined to place that princess upon the throne. At this important juncture Peter returned to Russia; he found it necessary to make a most severe exertion of his power; and he took that opportunity of entirely annihilating that dangerous body of the Strelitzes, who by this revolt furnished him with a just pretext. They had marched in arms to Moscow. The regular troops of the czar, headed by Gordon, and another foreign officer, attacked and totally defeated them; a vast number was slain; their leaders who were taken prisoners were broken upon the wheel; two thousand were hanged upon the walls of Moscow and on the side of the high roads, and the rest banished with their wives and children into the wilds of Siberia. Thus the whole of this formidable body was destroyed, and their name abolished for ever. The astonished Russians beheld this dreadful example with silent terror, which paved the way for an easy submission to all those innovations which the czar afterwards made in the constitution, police, laws, and customs of his empire.

He now levied regular regiments upon the German model; taught the soldiers a different form of exercise, gave them new arms, and a commodious uniform. The sons of the *boyars*, or nobility of Russia, before arriving at the rank of officers, were now obliged to rise step by step from the rank of common soldiers, and the same became the law of his marine promotions. He established a new system of the finances, and introduced a thorough reformation into the church, suppressing the dignity of patriarch, which had frequently struggled for an authority superior to the crown. He took from the bishops all civil and criminal jurisdiction, and established a new set of ecclesiastical canons and regulations; one of the most useful of which was, that no man or woman should embrace a monastic life before the age of fifty.

While this truly great genius was thus employed in new modelling the most extensive, and polishing and refining the most barbarous empire in the world, a competitor was arising, who was to dispute with him the dominion of the North, and who rivalled the fame of the most celebrated conquerors of antiquity. This was Charles XII., king of Sweden.

This monarch had succeeded his father in the year 1697, when only fifteen years of age. The most striking feature of his disposition at that time was a most impetuous, haughty temper. He was averse to all manner of study, and, consequently, had very little of the benefits of education; yet the situation of his kingdom very soon unveiled his talents and temperament.

Three powerful enemies joined in a league to oppress him. Sweden was then in possession of the territories of Estonia and Livonia; and Charles XI., his father, had violated the privileges of the Livonians, which they had asserted by a deputation, at the head of which was a nobleman of the name of Patkul, who had incensed the monarch by too bold a remonstrance in favor of the liberties of his country; he was condemned to death, but he escaped, and denounced a signal vengeance against the king of Sweden; he found means to persuade Augustus, king of Poland, and the czar, Peter, that they had now an opportunity of recovering, during the weakness of that monarchy, all the provinces they had formerly lost. They were joined by Frederick IV., king of Denmark, and it was not doubted that Sweden would fall a victim to so formidable an alliance.

It was the opinion of Charles's counsellors that a negotiation should be set on foot, to avert the impending ruin; but the king himself instantly gave orders to prepare for war. "I shall attack the first," said he, "who declares against me, and by defeating him I hope to intimidate the rest." From that time Charles dedicated his life to a series of fatigues and dangers, and enjoyed not a moment of ease or relaxation.

The king of Denmark began by the attack of Holstein, while the king of Poland poured down upon Livonia, and the Russians upon Ingria. Charles XII. immediately landed upon the island of Zealand, on which is situated Copenhagen, and carried on his military operations with such vigor, that the capital of Denmark was on the point of being taken. Frederick thought himself happy to save his kingdom by purchasing a peace, and indemnifying the duke of Holstein. Charles, now impatient to be revenged on the czar, hastened into Ingria with an army of nine thousand men. The Russians, to the number of sixty thousand, had laid siege to Narva; the Swedes attacked them in their intrenchments; a signal defeat ensued, and thirty thousand were taken prisoners, together with their whole baggage and artillery. Such was the first campaign of Charles XII., who was then only in the seventeenth year of his age.

The reflection of Peter the Great upon this occasion was extremely noble: "We must make our account," said he, "that the Swedes will long continue superior to us; but they will teach us at last to conquer them;" and the event justified his prediction.

Meantime Charles determined to make the king of Poland feel his power, as he had done his brothers of Denmark and Russia; he reduced Courland, crossed Lithuania, and penetrated into the heart of his dominions. He might have conquered the country; but to have maintained it in subjection would have required such a military force to be constantly kept up as Charles could not afford. He, therefore, adopted another plan. This was to depose the present monarch, Augustus, and place another upon the throne. His designs were seconded by the miserable state of Poland, from the constitution of its government. The people were under the most absolute slavery to their nobles; and these, independent of the crown, were constantly at war with each other; the state had no principle of union, but was subject to all the abuses of the ancient Gothic governments; and to add to these, the primate of the kingdom, cardinal Rajouski, secretly meditated a revolution, and entered immediately into the views of the king of Sweden. Charles, with little difficulty, made himself master of Warsaw in the year 1702. Augustus was then at Cracow; and being resolved to come to an action, was defeated at Clissaw, by an army which was only half his number. Cracow was taken, and the whole country gave way to the conqueror. The perfidious primate, in an assembly of the states at Warsaw, now openly took part against the king his master; and in the year 1704 the throne of Poland was declared vacant. The victorious Charles signified to the states of the kingdom his desire that Stanislaus Leckzinski, a young nobleman of Posnania, should be elected king. The electors made some hesitation on account of his youth. "If I am not mistaken," said Charles, "he is as old as I am." It is almost needless to add, that Leckzinski was elected king of Poland.

Meantime the arms of the czar had been victorious in Ingria—he had reduced all that province to subjection: but in Poland he was quite unfortunate in his design to reëstablish the dethroned Augustus. In that country the Russians were every where defeated. Charles was lord of the whole kingdom, and likewise of Saxony, which he laid under very heavy contributions. Augustus was driven to despair, and secretly sued for peace. The conditions prescribed by Charles were, that he should renounce his crown, acknowledge king Stanislaus, and deliver up Patkul the Livonian, who was then with him in the quality of ambassador from the czar. To these terms Augustus shamefully sub mitted. Charles even obliged him to write a complimentary letter to Stanislaus, wishing him joy upon his accession to the throne. The unfortunate Patkul was given up to the king of Sweden, who, with great inhumanity, and even the highest injustice, condemned him to be broken alive upon the wheel. This action is the greatest stain upon the memory of Charles, who ought to have respected that unhappy man for the very circumstance which was his offence—a noble interposition in behalf of the liberties of his country. Still more ought he to have respected the sacred character which he bore of the czar's ambassador.

Charles now concluded a peace with Augustus, who retired to his electoral dominions of Saxony, and Stanislaus was seated on the throne of Poland, when the czar was very near causing the election of a third sovereign to that kingdom. A diet was actually held for that purpose, when a negotiation was set on foot by the French minister in Saxony to reconcile the Swedes and Russians. Charles abruptly broke off all treaty, by bluntly declaring that he would negotiate with the czar in his capital of Moscow; a piece of presumption to which, when reported to Peter the Great, that monarch replied, "My brother Charles wants to play the part of Alexander, but he shall not find in me a Darius."

This period was, in fact, the crisis of the good fortune of Charles XII., and from this time we view him scarcely in any other light than that of an impetuous and obstinate madman.

At the head of 45,000 men he entered Lithuania, and carrying every thing before him, was in the way of making good his promise of a visit to the capital of Moscow. But instead of pursuing this direct route, he turned southward into the Ukraine, the country of the Cossacks, situated between Little Tartary, Poland, and Muscovy. This country he expected soon to subdue, and then to fall upon the capital of Russia. An old chief of the Cossacks, a traitor to his sovereign the czar, had inspired Charles with this fatal resolution, by promising to join him with an army, and to furnish him with all necessary supplies. Charles advanced; but the Cossacks were disobedient to their chief, and refused to depart from their allegiance. The Swedes began to be in want of provisions, and a reinforcement expected from Livonia was cut off by the czar's army. In this desperate situation, the Swedes, in the depth of winter, were making their way through the country of an enemy, exposed to daily attacks, and in want of every necessary supply. Under all these disadvantages, however, Charles crossed the whole country of the Ukraine, and laid siege to Pultowa, from whence he expected to pursue his march to Moscow, and to overturn the imperial throne of Russia. But the famous battle of Pultowa put an end to all his hopes. The two monarchs equally signalized their courage and abilities, but the czar was victorious. 9000 Swedes were killed on the field, and 14,000 taken prisoners, with a loss upon the part of the Russians of only 1300 men. Charles, a fugitive, with a few followers, crossed the river Dneiper, and sought an asylum in the dominions of the grand seignior.

The czar now made haste to restore Augustus to the throne of Poland. He entered into a league with that prince, the king of Denmark, and the elector of Brandenburg, the first *king* of Prussia; and making the best profits of his victory, he made himself master of Finland and Livonia.

Let us now mark the conduct of Charles. In Sweden, where it was not known whether their king was dead or alive, the regency had thoughts of capitulating with the czar. When Charles heard of this proposal, he wrote to the senate that he would send them one of his boots to govern them. With his feeble train of followers, who amounted only to 1800 men, he formed a small camp near Bender, from whence he endeavored to prevail with the court of Constantinople to arm in his favor against the Russians. Many successive negotiations were employed for that purpose, and as often defeated by the viziers of the grand seignior, who had no inclination to embroil their country in a war against so formidable an empire. At length the ministers of Charles prevailed; and the Turks, according to a practice not unfrequent among them, began hostilities by imprisoning the Russian ambassador. The czar hastened his preparations; and, deceived by the governor of Moldavia, as Charles had been before by the chief of the Cossacks, he advanced into that country in expectation of a revolt in his favor, where he found every thing, instead of friendly, wearing the appearance of the most determined hostility. The Ottoman army, amounting, as is said, to above 200,000 men, surrounded him, and cut off all communication with his expected reinforcements of troops and provisions. In this desperate situation, he was at length reduced to the necessity of capitulating with the sultan's grand vizier.

When Charles heard of this capitulation, which put an end to his hopes of aid against the Russians, his rage amounted to frenzy. He had kept himself during three years and a half in his camp at Bender, in expectation of that declaration of war which he had at last obtained; and he now saw in an instant a peace concluded, which left him, in a manner, a prisoner with the Turks, without the hope of changing his situation for the better. The grand seignior had, with much generosity, defrayed the whole expenses which Charles had incurred while in his dominions, which, from the uncommon profusion of that prince, were excessive. He now, with the same generosity, offered him a large sum, with an escort of troops to conduct him safely to his own dominions. This offer Charles rejected with the utmost disdain; and he now conceived a resolution, desperate almost beyond credibility. It was to no purpose that he was assured by the officers of the grand seignior that if he delayed to depart from their dominions, he would be compelled by military force. He braved the whole power of the Ottoman empire, and declared his determined purpose to defend his little camp to the last drop of his blood. His own officers employed supplications, remonstrances, and at length menaces, to make him depart from this frantic design. Charles was inflexible; and the slender remains of his army, who, by desertions, were now reduced to 300 men, were determined not to abandon their sovereign. They fortified the camp in the best manner possible. The Turkish general, astonished at so daring a resolution, gave them three days to deliberate whether to die or capitulate. At the end of the third day the Swedes were as resolute as ever. The attack was begun, and the intrenchments, invested at once on every quarter, were broken in an instant. A small house within the camp became the citadel and last resort of Charles and his intrepid Swedes. Their number was now reduced to a very few, whom personal regard attached to their sovereign. They did not fail, however, to remonstrate with him against the madness of his resolution; and in consulting how to sustain a siege in this last retreat, there was but one man who declared a positive opinion that the place might be defended. This was his majesty's cook. "Then, Sir," says the king, "I name you my chief engineer." They now proceeded to barricade the doors and windows, and kept up an incessant fire from within upon the whole Turkish army. The besiegers, exasperated at length at the numbers killed by this handful of madmen, threw fire upon the roof of the house, which in a moment was all in flames. It was now necessary to quit their post: a desperate sally was made; and this handful of Swedes, armed with their swords and pistols, were cutting their passage through an army of several thousand men, when Charles, entangled with his spurs, and accidentally falling to the ground, was surrounded by a body of janizaries. In short, the whole troop, after making an incredible carnage, were seized and taken prisoners. An attempt of this kind is only to be paralleled in the romances of knight-errantry.

This obstinacy and infatuation was the occasion of the loss of Charles's dominions in Germany, and almost of his kingdom of Sweden. The czar, king Augustus, the king of Denmark, and the elector of Hanover, entered into an alliance, and wrested from him all the conquests formerly gained by Gustavus Adolphus.

Charles, now a prisoner near Adrianople, was at length willing to return to his own dominions, and desired the grand seignior's permission for what he before so obstinately refused. After having remained above five years in Turkey, he set out in the beginning of October; 1714. Dismissing his Turkish escort on the frontiers, and parting even from his own people, he travelled in disguise, with two of his officers, through the whole of Germany. He arrived at length at Stralsund in Pomerania, one of the most important of his towns upon the Baltic. He knew the designs of Denmark and Prussia to attack this city, and he prepared for a vigorous defence. An incident is recorded of this siege which strongly marks the character of Charles. The town was bombarded, and a shell penetrated the roof of his house, and fell into the apartment where he was dictating his dispatches. The secretary, terrified out of his senses, having let fall his pen—"Go on," said the king, gravely; "what has the bombshell to do with the letter which I am dictating?" The city, however, was taken, and Charles obliged to escape in a small bark to Carlescroon, where he passed the winter. At this time he had not seen his capital of Stockholm for fifteen years. In this situation, in which any other monarch would have thought of providing as well as possible for the security of what remained of his kingdom, Charles projected to wrest the kingdom of Norway from Denmark. He invaded that country with an army of 20,000 men; but having failed to provide for their subsistence, he was obliged very soon to abandon the enterprise. He had at this time for his prime minister the baron de Gortz, a native of Franconia, a man of an artful, active, and very comprehensive genius. His fertile head had projected an immense revolution, of which the first step was to conclude a peace and alliance with the czar. George I., king of England, had purchased Bremen and Verden, with their dependencies, from the king of Denmark. Gortz's plan was not only to deprive George of these provinces, but to set the pretender James upon the throne of England. The czar, who was to be secured in all his conquests, readily joined in the scheme; and the Swedish minister at the court of London was promoting the conspiracy among the jacobites of England, when the plot was discovered by intercepted letters. Charles, however, and the czar continued their negotiations, and matters, notwithstanding this discovery, would probably have been brought to an issue by an open declaration of war on their parts against England, but for one fatal event, which broke all their measures. The king of Sweden, in the prosecution of his views against Norway, had laid siege to Frederickschal in the middle of winter. Walking on the parapet of one of his batteries, and in conversation with his engineer, he was struck on the head by a cannon ball, and instantly expired.

His character, in a few words, is well summed up by Voltaire. "He carried all the virtues of a hero to that excess that they became as dangerous as their opposite vices. The obstinacy of his resolution occasioned all his misfortunes in the Ukraine, and kept him five years in Turkey. His liberality degenerating into profusion ruined his kingdom of Sweden. His courage pushed to temerity was the occasion of his death. His justice often amounted to cruelty; and in the last years of his life the maintenance of his authority approached to tyranny. His many great qualities, of which a single one might have immortalized another prince, were the ruin of his country. He never was the first to attack, but he was not always as prudent as he was implacable in his revenge. He was the first who had the ambition to be a conqueror without the desire of aggrandizing his dominions. He wished to gain empires only to give them away. His passion for glory, for war, and for revenge, prevented his being a good politician, a quality, without which there can be no great conqueror. Before he gave battle, and after he gained a victory, he was all modesty; after a defeat he was all resolution, rigid to others as to himself; counting for nothing the fatigues or the lives of his subjects any more than his own. He was, in short, a singular man rather than a great one; a character more to be admired than imitated. His life ought to teach kings how much a pacific government is superior to the acquisition of the greatest glory."

The kingdom of Sweden gained by the death of Charles. She recovered her liberty by the abolition of the arbitrary power of her sovereigns, and new-modelled the form of her government His sister succeeded him in the throne, and raised to it her husband Frederick the landegrave of Hesse Cassel.

The following was the form prescribed for the Swedish government in future. The legislative authority was to be in the diet, which consisted of a certain number of deputies chosen by the nobles, the clergy and the burgesses, and even the peasantry. The executive power was properly in the senate, composed of sixteen persons, where the king presided, and had only the casting vote in certain cases. It was the diet which named to vacancies in the senate, by presenting three subjects for the king to choose one. The principal employments, both civil and military, were filled up by the senate from the king's recommendation. The diet was appointed to be held every three years, in the month of January. If it were not assembled at the usual time, every thing done in the interval was declared to be null. They could not declare war without the king's consent. When assembled they could neither conclude peace, truce, nor alliance, without his consent. All laws and ordinances were appointed to be published in the name of the king: but if he absented himself, or delayed his signature too long, the senate were empowered to supply the want of it and sign for him. On ascending the throne, he must take the oath of government before the diet, and was to be declared an enemy of the states, and *ipso facto* deprived of the throne, in case he violated his engagements.

When the new government was established, the great plans of the baron de Gortz were of necessity laid aside. He was adjudged a traitor to his country, for having projected a dangerous war when the nation was exhausted and ruined; and he lost his nead for the bad counsels he had given to his late sovereign The states of Sweden concluded a peace with the king c England, to whom, as sovereign of Hanover, they ceded for a sum of money the duchies of Bremen and Verden. They likewise made peace with Denmark, and soon after with the czar, who kept all the provinces he had won.

Peter the Great, ever intent on projects of real utility, was at this time preparing for an expedition into Persia, with the design of securing the command of the Caspian Sea, and thus bringing the commerce of Persia, and a part of India, into Russia. In 1722, he had gained three provinces of the Persian empire, by concession of the Sophi, to secure his protection against an usurper. Peter was at this time far advanced in life, and was without a child. His only son, Alexis Petrowitz, he had put to death some time before, in a very tragical manner. This youth would have undone all the works of his father. He was a barbarian by nature. He had declared himself an enemy to all improvement and innovation, and consumed his life in the practice of the meanest debaucheries. His father, seeing his disposition to be incorrigible, had ordered him to go into a monastery. The son corresponded with others disaffected as himself. He was at length arrested and condemned by the voice of one hundred and forty judges, to suffer death as a traitor.

Peter the Great died in the year 1724, and was succeeded by the czarina Catharine, formerly a young Livonian captive, whom he had taken in his first expedition into those provinces, and who certainly possessed merit equal to the station to which she was raised.

Besides these various establishments, which we have already taken notice of as made by this illustrious man, in the beginning of his reign, he had during the course of it accomplished a variety of the most useful designs. A court of police was erected at St. Petersburg, a city which he had reared from a despicable collection of fisherman's huts to be one of the most magnificent towns in Europe. This court of police extended its jurisdiction over the whole provinces of the empire, regulating every thing which regarded the maintenance of good order, watching over the improvement of trades and manufactures, and fixing the laws of commerce. The public laws of the empire were promulgated in a printed code. The courts of justice which were formerly filled with the nobility, without any trial of their capacity, or previous education requisite for that office, were supplied by Peter with judges of approved knowledge, education, and integrity. In ecclesiastical matters, instead of the office of Patriarch, which he had very early abolished, he instituted a perpetual synod of twelve members, over whom he himself occasionally presided; and to this tribunal was allotted the supreme ecclesiastical jurisdiction.

With respect to the government, or political constitution, of the empire of Russia, it must be considered as an absolute monarchy. Peter the Great, being the founder of a new constitution, was sovereign without limitation. His will was law. He aimed, however, at setting some bounds to the power of his successors; and in that view he instituted a senate, which, like the parliament of Paris, should possess the power of ratifying or giving authority to the acts of the sovereign; but, in fact, there has ever been so strict a conformity between the will of the prince and the decrees of this assembly, that the imperial power, instead of being abridged, seems rather to have been strengthened by it.

Such is a brief sketch of the rise of this extraordinary power, which the singular genius of one man was able to rear from the most unpromising materials. By the influence of his single mind, an obscure and barbarous people, almost unknown to history,—without arts; without laws; under no regular organization of government; occupying a thinly-peopled and ill-cultivated country; possessed, in fact, of no political existence,—have, within the course of a single century, overleaped all the intermediate steps of progressive civilization, and mounted at once to the highest rank among the powers of Europe.

CHAPTER XXXVI.

VIEW of the PROGRESS of SCIENCE and LITERATURE in EUROPE, from the END of the FIFTEENTH to the END of the SEVENTEENTH CENTURY:—Progress of Philosophy—Lord Bacon—Experimental Philosophy—Descartes—Galileo—Kepler—Logarithms—Circulation of the Blood—Royal Society of London Instituted—Sir Isaac Newton—Locke—Progress of Literature—Epic Poetry—Ariosto—Tasso—Milton—Lyric Poetry—Drama—English and French History.

As one of the most useful objects of the study of history is to mark the progress of the human mind in those sciences and arts which either contribute to the great purposes of public utility, or conduce to the rational enjoyments of social life, we have endeavored, through the course of this work, to exhibit, from time to time, a progressive picture of the state of the sciences and of literature. A former chapter on this subject embraced a very comprehensive period, from the revival of literature in Europe, to the end of the fifteenth century.

We have there observed how much literature was indebted to the discovery of the art of printing for its advancement and dissemination. Classical learning, the art of criticism, poetry and history, among the sciences, began from that time to make a rapid progress in most of the kingdoms of Europe. It was not so, however, with philosophy, and the more abstract sciences; and the reason was obvious; the remains of ancient learning are to this day the models of a good taste in the "Belles Lettres," and the knowledge of the classical authors, poets, and historians, was no sooner revived, and their works disseminated, than they were successfully imitated by the moderns. In philosophy, on the contrary, the light which was borrowed from the works of the ancients served only to mislead and bewilder. The philosophy of Aristotle, which then had possession of the schools, or even the more pleasing systems of Plato, which began to be opposed to his scholastic subtleties, were fetters upon all real improvement in philosophical researches. It was not till these were removed, till all the rubbish of the ancient philosophy was entirely cleared away, that men began to perceive, that, to understand the laws of nature, it was necessary to observe her phenomena, and to study her works; and that all systems and theories antecedent to such study were idle and absurd chimeras. We formerly remarked the commendable attempt which was made by our countryman, Roger Bacon, so early as the middle of the thirteenth century, to undermine the fabric of the Aristotelian philosophy, and to substitute experiment and observation for system and conjecture; but his attempt was ineffectual. There is nothing so difficult to be removed as dogmatism and pedantry. Conviction is a severe mortification of pride to a man who values himself upon his wisdom; besides, the philosophy of Aristotle had at this time become a part of the tenets of the church, and it was reckoned equally impious to combat any of the doctrines of that philosopher as to attack the fundamental articles of the Christian faith.

The learning of the schools continued then to reign triumphant, even down to the middle of the sixteenth century, when it received, at least in England, a mortal blow from a second philosopher of the same name, Francis Bacon, lord Verulam, who flourished in the latter part of the reign of Elizabeth, and was afterwards chancellor of England under James I. When we consider the vast variety of researches to which this great man has turned his attention, employed alternately in the study of nature, of the operations of the mind, of the sciences of morals, politics, and economics, we must allow him the praise of the most universal genius that any age has produced. But when, on an acquaintance with these works, we discern the amazing views which he has opened; the just estimate he has formed of the knowledge of the preceding ages in every one of the sciences, the immense catalogue which he has given of the desiderata still to be known in each department, and the methods he has pointed out for prosecuting discoveries, and attaining that improvement of knowledge, we regard the intellect of Bacon as that of a superior being. In his treatise *de Augmentis Scientiarum*, and the *Novum Organum*, he enforces the necessity of experiment to the knowledge of nature. He exposes the absurdity of forming systems and theories antecedent to the recording of facts. He points out the numberless errors thence arising; and thus having purged philosophy of all its mystical and unintelligible jargon of terms, categories, essences, and universals, he points out the sure method of reasoning from experiment, so as to attain the knowledge of general laws.

Although the works of Bacon began to open the eyes of the learned world, and to unmask the futility of those researches in which philosophers had hitherto employed themselves, they produced this effect only by very slow degrees. In the continental kingdoms of Europe the Aristotelian philosophy maintained its ground, even down to the seventeenth century. Gassendi, a native of Provençe, about the year 1640, had ventured, with great caution, to dispute some of the principles of that philosophy, and without availing himself of the works of Bacon, attempted to revive the atomic system of Epicurus; but he had very few followers.

Descartes, soon after, proposed his system of the world; in which, though he condemns the common practice of laying down vague conjectures for principles, he himself did nothing better. He sets out upon this principle, that in order to form the universe, nothing else was requisite but matter and motion: that extension is the essence of all bodies, and space being extended as well as matter, there is no difference between space and matter, consequently there is no void or vacuum in nature. He divides this homogeneous mass of space and matter into angular parts of a cubical form, leaving no interstices between them. "To these cubes," says he, "the Author of Nature gave a rotatory motion round their axes, and likewise an impulse forwards, which drives them round the sun as a centre." From the attrition of the parts in this rotation, he supposes the planets to be formed. This strange romance of the Vortices of Descartes struck at first by its novelty, and, in fact, seemed to explain several of the phenomena of nature. He gained a great number of disciples, and more admirers; and such is the dogmatism of opinion, that even after a complete detection of the errors of the Cartesian system, and the publication of the Newtonian philosophy, that of Descartes continued to have its advocates in France till the middle of the present century.

The Copernican system of the planets, which is now universally received, had been proposed long before the age of Descartes, and was adopted by him as the groundwork of his philosophy. Copernicus gave this system to the world in the year 1553. It was solemnly condemned by the Inquisition in the year 1615; at the very time when many new experiments and discoveries had concurred to establish its absolute certainty.

In the year 1609, Galileo constructed telescopes. We have formerly observed, that in the *Opus Majus* of Roger Bacon, there are plain intimations that the effect of a combination of convex glasses in approaching and magnifying distant objects, was known to that ingenious man : but there is reason to believe that after his time the invention was lost nor was it recovered till about four hundred years afterwards by Galileo. In the year 1610 Galileo, with a telescope which magnified the object thirty-six times, discovered the satellites of Jupiter, and their motion, the horned phases of the planet Venus, the extremities of the ring of Saturn, and the spots in the sun's disc, which showed its motion round its axis. For these discoveries, which tended to confirm the Copernican heresy, Galileo was thrown into prison by the inquisition, and forced to purchase his liberty by retracting his opinions.

Kepler, much about the same time, that is, towards the beginning of the seventeenth century, added to these discoveries the knowledge of the laws which regulate the motions of the planets. Copernicus and Tycho Brahé believed that they moved in a circular orbit round the sun. Kepler demonstrated that they move in ellipses, of which the sun forms one of the foci ; that their motion is slower in their aphelion than in their perihelion ; that is, slower when at a distance from the sun than when nearer—in such a proportion, that a ray or line drawn from the planet to the sun, would, in the course of the planet's revolution, pass over equal spaces in equal times. He discovered likewise the analogy between the distances of the several planets from the sun, and their periodical revolutions ; and he found the great law that regulates the planets, that the squares of their periodical times was in the same proportion as the cubes of their mean distances from the sun.

The age of Kepler and Galileo was the era of great discoveries n the arts and sc ences. The invention of the telescope gave rise to a thousand experiments by means of glasses ; and the science of optics received great improvements. The new discoveries in astronomy led to improvements in navigation ; and geometry, of course, made rapid advances towards perfection. The science of algebra, which Europe is said to have owed to the Arabians as well as the numeral ciphers, contributed greatly to abridge the labor of calculation ; as did still more the invention of logarithms, discovered in the year 1614, by Napier of Merchiston. The improvement of mechanics kept pace with the advancement of geometry ; and the science of natural philosophy was successfully cultivated in all its branches. The Torricellian experiment, made about the year 1640, determined the height of the atmosphere. Experiments upon the oscillations of pendulums, which were found always to preserve an equal time, though the spaces described were unequal, suggested the idea of applying the pendulum to regulate the motions of a clock ; and the observation that adding to its weight adds nothing to the celerity of its motion led to the conclusion that the velocity with which a body gravitates to the centre is not in proportion to its weight. Galileo had discovered the laws which determine this velocity.

The ardor of prosecuting discoveries extended itself through the whole of the sciences. In the year 1616, Dr. Harvey made the great discovery of the circulation of the blood: at least he was the first who brought direct demonstration of the truth of that theory, which before his time had been only a matter of conjecture to some of the ablest anatomists. Hippocrates speaks of the *usual motion* of the blood, but had no idea of a constant and regular circulation. Servetus, about the middle of the sixteenth century, had remarked that the whole mass of blood passes through the lungs by the pulmonary artery and veins; but the discovery of the complete circulation of this fluid, passing from the heart by the arteries to every part of the body, and thence returning to the heart by the veins, is due to Harvey alone.

About the middle of the seventeenth century, the spirit of sound philosophy was vigorously promoted in England by the institution of the Royal Society. Some time after the civil wars, a few learned men, particularly Mr. Boyle, Dr. Wilkins, Mr. Evelyn, Dr. Wallis, and Dr. Wren, held private meetings for the sake of philosophical conversation. Cowley, the poet, had proposed in his works a very ingenious plan for a philosophical society, the idea of which he had probably borrowed from lord Bacon's *House of Solomon*, described in his fanciful work of the *New Atalantis*. This plan of Cowley's contributed to the institution of a regular society by those gentlemen we have mentioned, which soon attracted the notice of Charles II., who granted to them his letters patent, and declared himself the founder and patron of the Royal Society of London. Experimental philosophy and natural history were the objects which deservedly engrossed their principal attention. The former of these Mr. Boyle prosecuted with great ingenuity and with the most successful industry. The world owed to him many valuable discoveries in chemistry, in mechanics, and in natural philosophy. He is distinguished by the invention of, or at least a great improvement in, the air-pump, and the experiments made *in vacuo*, which have thrown light upon almost every branch of the study of nature. To Mr. Evelyn, one of the first and most respectable members of the Royal Society, the world owes many ingenious works on agriculture, gardening, architecture, and sculpture. His excellent treatise, entitled *Sylva*, on the culture of trees, was read as one of the first discourses delivered before this society, and contributed to introduce a laudable and forward spirit in that most valuable of improvements through the whole of the island. In short, that emulation which characterizes all new institutions, gave rise to many ingenious treatises on a variety of branches of experimental philosophy and the study of nature.

Foreign nations began now to imitate the English in the foundation of similar societies for the improvement of philosophy. The Academia del Cimento at Florence, was established by the cardinal Leopold de Medicis, about the year 1655. Eleven years afterwards, in the year 1666, Louis XIV., at the request of several of the French *literati*, founded the Royal Academy of Sciences. Colbert invited Cassini from Italy, and Huygens from Holland, to reside in Paris, and bestowed on them very liberal pensions. Soon after, the Royal Observatory of Paris was built at the king's expense, and Picard and Cassini employed themselves in the construction of a meridian line. Picard was employed, in the year 1670, by the French Academy, to measure a degree of the meridian, which he found to be 57,060 French toises; and thence he made the first computation which approached to certainty of the size of the earth. Some of those great discoveries we have mentioned, and particularly that of the laws of the planetary motions laid down by Kepler, and the optical experiments of Galileo, paved the way for the immortal Newton.

This great man, whose genius far outshone all who have gone before him in the path of philosophy, and who has, perhaps exhausted the most important discoveries of the laws of nature, so as not to leave to posterity the possibility of eclipsing his fame, had, it is certain, made the greatest of his discoveries before he had attained the age of twenty-four. Before that early period of life he had discovered the theory of universal gravitation. Dr. Pemberton, who has given an excellent view of his philosophy, informs us that Newton, as he sat one day alone in a garden, fell into a reverie or speculation on the power of gravity. It occurred to him, that as this power is not found sensibly to diminish at the remotest distance to which we can ascend from the centre of the earth, for instance, at the top of the highest mountains, it was not unreasonable to suppose that it might extend much farther than was usually thought. Why not (said he to himself) as high as the moon? and if so, her motion must be influenced by it. Perhaps it is that which retains her in her orbit! However, though the power of gravity is not sensibly weakened in the little change of distance at which we can place ourselves from the centre of the earth, yet it is very possible that so high as the moon this power may differ much in strength from what it is here. To make an estimate what might be the degree of the diminution, he considered with himself that if the moon be retained in her orbit by the force of gravity, no doubt the primary planets are carried round the sun by the like power; and by comparing the periods of the several planets with their distances from the sun, he found that if any power like gravity held them in their courses, its strength must decrease in the duplicate proportion of the increase of distance. Supposing, therefore, the power of gravity, when extended to the moon, to decrease in the same proportion, he computed whether that force would be sufficient to keep the moon in her orbit, and he found it would be sufficient. Newton had now the satisfaction to perceive that this inquiry, which an accidental thought had given rise to, led to the discovery of an universal law of nature, which solved the most striking of her phenomena. It is thus that genius proceeds, step by step, from the simplest principles to the most sublime conclusions.

Newton, amidst many other discoveries, is immortalized by his theory of "Light and Colors." He analyzed the composition of light by means of the prism, and found that the smallest ray into which it can be separated is a compound substance, or *fasciculus*, consisting of several elementary rays distinct from each other, each tinged with a particular color, and incapable of being further altered after this separation. He perceived that these colored rays could not possibly be separated from each other—if their nature were not such, that in passing through the same medium they were refracted under different angles. This, together with the principle of the different reflexibility of different rays, is the fundamental discovery of Sir Isaac Newton in optics, from whence he has deduced the most important conclusions.

While natural philosophy was thus advancing by the efforts of the genius of Newton, his contemporary, Locke, exalted metaphysics into a rational science. The method which Bacon has proposed for the study of nature, Mr. Locke has ingeniously applied to the study of the mind. It was not Locke's view or intention to form a plausible theory of the human understanding, as many metaphysicians had done before him. He wished to examine the mind as an anatomist does the body, and faithfully to record his observations. For this purpose he observes the visible signs of the first operations of the mind in an infant; he follows its progress up to maturity of reason; he compares these signs and this progress with the manifestations of the reasoning faculty in animals; and finding that from practice or experience, according as man or the animal advances in life, there is a gradual increase in the number of ideas, as well as an improvement in combining and modifying them, he very naturally draws this inference, that there are no innate ideas in the mind, but that they are all communicated to it gradually, either from the impressions of external objects, or by reflecting on these impressions; a conclusion which has very unjustly drawn upon Mr. Locke the imputation of skepticism in religion, as if it took away any argument for the existence of a God to maintain, that the mind did not intuitively perceive that truth, or to maintain that no such idea existed in the mind of an infant of a year old, but was the result of an improvement of reason. The truth is, the piety of Locke was one of the most remarkable features of his character.

LITERATURE.

The beginning of the sixteenth century, the pontificate of Julius II. and Leo X., was an era no less remarkable for the cultivation of the fine arts of painting, sculpture, and architecture, than for the higher species of poetical composition. Trissino, an Italian, was the first of the moderns who composed an epic poem in the language of his country. Trissino chose for his subject the delivery of Italy from the Goths by Belisarius under the emperor Justinian. The subject was well chosen; and the poem, though very moderate in point of execution, had great success from the novelty of the attempt. The greatest fault of Trissino is that he copies Homer too closely in his descriptions, imitating even that which is generally esteemed a defect in the great father of epic poetry, his extreme minuteness in describing trivial particulars.

The Portuguese Camoens followed next; a poet possessed of much greater powers than Trissino. He had attended Vasco de Gama in the first voyage of the Portuguese to India by the Cape of Good Hope; and this great enterprise he celebrated in his poem called the "Lusiad," a great part of which he composed while upon the voyage,—a work, though irregular, abounding in poetical fire, and displaying the finest imagination. It has undergone many translations into the other languages of Europe, and is known in England by the able one of Mr. Mickle.

Towards the end of the sixteenth century, Spain likewise produced an epic poem of no inconsiderable merit, the "Araucana" of Don Alonzo Ercilla. What is remarkable in this poem is, that the author himself is the hero of it. Ercilla, who was a young man of talents and of an enterprising spirit, embarked for the province of Chili in South America. Upon the intelligence of a revolt of some of the natives against his sovereign, Philip II. of Spain, he raised a few troops, and carried on a long war with the inhabitants of Araucana, whom at length he reduced to submission, and this war is the subject of his poem. It is a very irregular composition, but displays many strokes of true genius.

A work had some time before this (about the middle of the sixteenth century) appeared in Italy, which engrossed the attention of all the literary world. This was the "Orlando Furioso" of Ariosto, an epic poem, which, with a total disregard of all the rules of this species of composition, without plan, without probability, without morality or decency, has the most captivating charms to all who are possessed of the smallest degree of genuine taste. Orlando is the hero of the piece, and he is mad. Eight books are consumed before the hero is introduced, and his first appearance is in bed desiring to sleep. His great purpose is to find his mistress Angelica; but his search of her is interrupted by so many adventures of other knights and damsels, each of them pursuing some separate object, few of which have any necessary relation to the great action of the piece, that it becomes almost impossible to peruse this poem with any degree of connection between the parts. We are amused with a number of delightful stories, told with wonderful power of fancy and poetical genius; but in order to pursue any tale to an end, the reader must hunt for it through a dozen of books, for it is often cut short in the most interesting part, and resumed at the distance of five or six cantos, as abruptly as it had been broken off. There is no good moral in the adventures of the mad Orlando, and the scenes which the poet describes are often most grossly indecent; yet, with all its faults, the work of Ariosto will maintain its ground for ever, as furnishing a strange, irregular, but very high degree of pleasure.*

Tasso is much more of a regular genius than Ariosto; and in his poem of the *Gierusalemme Liberata* sometimes soars to a pitch of the sublime equal to the finest flights of Homer or of Virgil. He is peculiarly excellent in the delineation of his characters; but the episodes which he introduces have too little connection with the principal action; as that, for instance, of Olinda and Sophronia, in the beginning of the poem, which, though a most beautiful episode, conduces nothing to the main design. It is now generally allowed that Boileau and Addison have much undervalued the merit of Tasso, when, in contrasting him with Virgil, they speak of the tinsel ornaments of his poem compared with the gold of the other. Tasso, though not on the whole so correct a poet as Virgil, has his strokes of the sublime—his golden passages—which will stand the test of the severest criticism. In point of fancy and imagination, no poet has gone beyond him: witness the description of his enchanted forest; nor have we any where more beautiful examples of the true pathetic.

From the date of the Gierusalemme Liberata of Tasso, the genius of epic poetry seems to have lain asleep for above a century, till the days of Milton; with the exception only of the Fairy Queen of Spenser, which has many detached passages abounding in beauties, but, as an intricate and protracted allegory, is dry and tedious upon the whole. The merits of the Paradise Lost have been so admirably illustrated by Addison in the Spec-

---

* Ariosto was a man of learning, and wrote admirably in the Latin tongue. Cardinal Bembo wished to persuade him to compose in that language, as being more universally intelligible than the Italian. "I would rather," said Ariosto, "be the first of the Italian writers than the second of the Latin." A delicate compliment to the person to whom he spoke; but, at the same time, a strong evidence of the high estimation in which he rated his own abilities.

He had an elegant villa at Ferrarà, but of small extent; and on the front of his house was this apposite inscription :—

Parva, sed apta mihi, sed nulli obnoxia, sed non
Sordida, parta meo sed tamen ære, domus.

To a friend who expressed his surprise, that he who had described so many stately and magnificent palaces in his Orlando, had built for himself so poor a fabric, he replied with laconic wit, "It is much easier to join words than stone

tator, and the work itself, as well as his criticism, are so generally known, that it becomes entirely unnecessary in this place to bestow much time in characterizing it. Compared with the great epic poems of antiquity, the Iliad, the Odyssey, and the Æneid, the Paradise Lost has more examples of the true sublime than are to be found in all those compositions put together. At the same time, if examined by critical rules, it is not so perfect a work as any one of them; and there are greater instances of a mediocrity, and even sinking in composition, than are to be found in any of those ancient poems, unless in the sixth book, which is almost one continued specimen of the sublime. It is but seldom that the poet sustains himself for a single page without degenerating into bombast, false wit, or obscurity. The neglect of the merit of Milton during his own life is sufficiently known. Hume, in his History of England, mentions an anecdote which strongly marks the small regard that was had for this great poet, even by that party to whose service he had devoted his talents. Whitelocke, in his Memorials, talks of *one Milton, a blind man, who was employed in translating a treaty with Sweden into Latin!*

Lyric poetry during the sixteenth century was cultivated in many of the European kingdoms, but with no high success. The smaller poems, or Rhymes of Ariosto and of Tasso, have little tincture of that genius which shines in their greater compositions. They have servilely trod in the steps of Petrarch, and seem to have thought that lyric poetry admitted of no other species of composition than a sonnet or a canzonette in praise of a mistress. The only one among the Italians who truly merits the denomination of a lyric poet seems to be Chiabrera, in whose odes there is a wonderful brilliancy of imagination, and even a great portion of grandeur and the true sublime. It was an illustrious mark of honor which the town of Savona, his native city, paid to the merit of this great poet, in declaring him perpetually exempted from all public taxes. Such were the rewards with which the Greeks and Romans were wont to distinguish literary genius.

The genius of the French, in the sixteenth century, seems not more adapted to lyric poetry than that of the Italians. The French poets, Ronsard and Bellary, imitated the Italian sonnets of Petrarch, with all his false wit, but without his passion. Marot, however, in a few of his little tales, displays that *naïveté* and easy humor in which he was afterwards so successfully rivalled by La Fontaine; but the French language was yet extremely harsh and unharmonious. It was not till the end of the sixteenth, and beginning of the seventeenth century, that the French versification received a considerable degree of polish from the compositions of Racan and Malherbe. Some of the odes of Malherbe have all the ease of Horace, as well as his incidental strokes of the sublime. Towards the end of the seventeenth century this species of poetry was cultivated in France, with high success, by La Farre, by Chapelle, and Bachaumont by Chaulieu and Gresset, in whose compositions, besides infinite ease and spirit, we find a certain epigrammatic turn of wit, of which the compositions of the preceding age afford no example.

The English language was even later than the French in attaining that smoothness and harmony which is essential to lyric poetry. In the compositions of the sixteenth century, of Spenser, of the earl of Surrey, of Sir John Harrington, and Sir Philip Sidney, we often find poetical imagery and great force of expression; but an entire ignorance of harmony and the power of numbers. The lyric pieces of Shakspeare himself bear but few traces of his great genius; nor from that time is there any sensible improvement in the English poetry for nearly half a century, till the time of Cowley and of Waller. The merit of Cowley has been variously estimated; but I believe, in general, rather undervalued. In his poems there is a redundancy of wit, and in his Pindaric odes particularly, too great irregularity and often obscurity; yet many of his poetical pieces, where the subject itself restrained these faults, display the highest beauties. The elegy on the death of Mr. Harvey is extremely natural and pathetic. It is not a little extraordinary that neither Dr. Hurd, who has given to the public a very judicious selection of the works of Cowley, nor Dr. Johnson in his Life of this poet, should have mentioned one little piece, which it would pernaps be difficult to parallel for poetical beauties in any language:—this is a lyric ode, introduced in the third book of the Davideis, as sung by David under the window of his mistress, beginning "Awake, awake, my lyre." I am much mistaken if this is not one of the best specimens of lyric composition that ever was written. The fame of Cowley does not rest alone upon his poetical writings. His prose essays are uncommonly excellent, and exhibit a natural and pleasing picture of himself, a very amiable and accomplished character.

The verse of Waller is more polished and harmonious than that of any of the preceding or contemporary poets; but his compositions have a great deal of that quaintness and trifling witticism which was in fashion in his age, and he possesses no genius either for the sublime or the pathetic.

In the end of the seventeenth century, lyric poetry in England was carried to its highest perfection by Dryden. The ode on St. Cecilia's Day has never since been equalled; and it may even be pronounced equal to the best lyric compositions of antiquity. The genius of Dryden, as a poet, was universal. As a satirist, he has the keenness without the indelicacy of Horace or Juvenal. In this species of composition, his Mackflecknoe and Absalom and Achitophel have never been surpassed. He excels Boileau in this respect, that the satire of the French poet is too general, and therefore falls short of its great purpose, which is to amend. The author who makes mankind in general the subject of his censure or of his ridicule will do no good as a reformer. Dryden, as a fabulist, displays a very happy turn for the poetical narrative, and though the subjects of his fables are not his own, they are in general well chosen. The merit of his dramatic pieces, though considerable, is not very high. He certainly possessed that invention which is the first quality of a dramatic poet; but he is very deficient in the expression of passion, and in his finest scenes we are inclined more to admire the art of the poet than to participate in the feelings of his characters.

In a former chapter upon the revival of European literature, we noticed the very rude state of dramatic poetry in Europe, even so late as the end of the fifteenth century. It was not till the end of the sixteenth, that this species of composition began to furnish any thing like a rational entertainment. It was then that Lope de Vega in Spain, and Shakspeare in England, produced those incomparable pieces which, at this day, are the delight of their countrymen. The Spaniard possessed an inventive genius, equally fertile with that of the English poet; he had more learning, and went beyond him even in the rapidity of his compositions. His dramatic pieces amount to above 300, and he was often known to finish a play within four-and-twenty-hours. It is not surprising that we should find numberless defects, great absurdities, and continual irregularity in the conduct of those hasty productions; but in most of them we discern the marks of a great and comprehensive genius, an inexhausted fund of imagination, and infinite knowledge of human nature.

The merits of Shakspeare have often been analyzed, and are familiar to every person of taste. He cannot be measured by the rules of criticism—he understood them not, and has totally disregarded them; but this very circumstance has given room for those beauties of unconfined nature and astonishing ebullitions of genius which delight and surprise in his productions, and which the rules of the drama would have much confined and repressed. I know not whether there is not something, even in the very absurdities of Shakspeare, which tends, by contrast, to exalt the lustre of his beauties and to elevate his strokes of the sublime. It is certain that dramatic poetry in England has not improved as it became more refined, and as our poets, in imitation of the French, became scrupulous observers of the unities. The old English drama, with all its irregularities, is incomparably superior to the modern, both in the nice delineation of character and in the natural expression of the passions. In the plays of Shakspeare, of Beaumont and Fletcher, and of Massinger, every person is a highly-finished picture. We not only see the importance of each character to conduce to the plot, but, taking any character by itself, we have pleasure in contemplating it. Like a good paint ing, we admire not only the composition and the whole of the group, but if we confine our attention to a single figure, we find it beautifully drawn and highly finished. Most of the modern plays fall infinitely short in this respect. The persons taken singly are nothing—they have no strong features to distinguish them. A modern dramatic writer will paint a virtuous man or a vicious man; but he gives him nothing but the general marks of the character: you admire or you detest his actions, and you hear him speaking either good moral sentiments or purposes of villany; but examine this hero or this villain, he wants *particular features;* he cannot be described; he resembles those masks or vizards, which were worn by the Greek and Roman comedians, of which one was painted to express each of the passions, and the same mask was constantly worn as often as the same passion was to be represented.

In the modern plays, too, a correctness of language, a harmony of numbers, and a brilliancy of metaphor, have come in place of that natural warmth, that unforced and passionate expression, which eminently distinguished the old dramatic compositions. The tragi-comedy (I do not mean where there are two distinct plots, which is a very unnatural species of composition, but where there is a mixture in the same plot of serious and ludicrous personages) seems now to be laid aside by our dramatic writers, deterred, as it would appear, by the censure of Addison; yet, with great deference to so judicious a critic, I cannot help thinking that his opinion would deprive us of a very rational source of pleasure. We may appeal to the example of some of the finest plays in our language whether the introducing a comic scene has a bad effect, even when succeeding or succeeded by another of the deepest distress. Where the comic characters have their business in the tragic plot, and the whole tends to one interesting event, as there is nothing but what is consonant to nature in such mixture of characters, so there is nothing which shocks our feelings. It is not unnatural that clownish servants should jest while their master is in affliction; and a short scene of this kind, exhibited as it were in passing on to the serious parts, instead of violating our feelings, has the effect perhaps of heightening our pathetic emotions, by the sudden, strong, and unexpected contrast of happiness and misery. The old dramatic writers perhaps went to an extreme, and sacrificed too much to the taste of a populace delighted with ribaldry and buffoonery; but *they* certainly err as much on the other side who have banished all association of the comic and the tragic in the same composition.

To those who are admirers of a strict conformity to dramatic rules, we would recommend the compositions of the French stage towards the middle of the last century. If dramatic poetry is to be considered as an exhibition of the characters of mankind, which some very good critics have defined it to be, the French drama, in this respect, at least their tragedy, must be allowed to be much inferior to the English. If considered as an artificial composition, recommending virtue by example, and exposing vice, we acknowledge the drama of the French to have better attained those important ends. In the dramatic compositions of either nation, we find there is room for the introduction both of sublime and of pathetic sentiments; but in the French drama we admire the art of the poet, who describes a feeling, while in the English we sympathize with the character who expresses it.

Till the middle of the seventeenth century, dramatic poetry among the French was extremely low. Pierre Corneille is allowed to have brought it at once to the highest pitch of excellence which it has ever attained. We cannot say that Corneille has not availed himself of the compositions in other languages; for besides that the correct regularity of his pieces demonstrates a thorough acquaintance with the rules of the drama, he has borrowed some of his plots both from the Greek tragedians and some of the dramatic writers of Spain. Yet a proof that the genius of Corneille was more original than the effects of study, is, that his earliest pieces, written in his youth, are better than those which were the fruit of his maturer years and more cultivated judgment. Of thirty-three pieces, there are no more than six or seven which still keep possession of the French stage, and will probably maintain their ground for ever. The tragedy of the Cid, Rodogune, Cinna, Polyeucte, Les Horaces, have never yet been surpassed by any dramatic writers among the French. The Menteur of Corneille shows that his genius could adapt itself equally to comedy and to tragedy. This great poet enjoyed already a very high reputation, when Racine appeared, to dispute with him the palm of dramatic composition. Corneille, with more of the sublime of poetry, had less acquaintance with the tender passions. It is here that the *forte* of Racine lay. The pathetic of Britannicus is superior to any thing that Corneille has attempted in the same style. Athalie is full of grandeur and dignity of sentiment, and the comedy of the Plaideurs shows that the genius of Racine was as universal as that of his great competitor.

But the palm of French comedy was reserved for Molière. It may perhaps be said of the comedies of Molière, that they are the only examples of that species of composition which have actually produced a sensible effect in reforming the manners of the age. The French physicians in his time were precisely what he represents them—illiterate, mysterious, and ignorant quacks. The women of fashion were overrun with a pedantic affectation of learning; and the French nobility affected that arrogant and supercilious demeanor which demands respect from the consideration of birth or fortune, without the possession of a single laudable or valuable quality. The keen but delicate satire of Molière produced a very sensible reformation; and the latter part of the reign of Louis XIV. was as entirely free from the quackery of physic, the pedantry of the ladies, and the absurd pride of the nobility, as the commencement of it was marked by those characteristics.

The last eminent dramatic writer among the French who distinguished the seventeenth century was Crebillon, who is the only one of the French poets of the stage, if we except Voltaire, who has drawn his images of the sublime from the source of terror. In tragedy he had before him the models of Corneille and Racine, but his genius was original, and he disdained to imitate. His pieces are, therefore, deficient in that correctness, or that polish in the structure of the verses, which is the fruit of study and of imitation; but he must be a tasteless critic, who, in reading the tragedy of Radamiste et Zénobie, or of Atrée et Thyeste, feels his passions so disengaged as to attend to the irregulairty of a verse or the harshness of a cadence. Let us observe, too, to the honor of Crebillon, that in all his pieces virtue and morality are powerfully inculcated—a characteristic to distinguish him from a worthless son, the younger Crebillon, who, in a variety of licentious novels, has prostituted excellent talents in the service of vice.

With the mention of the principal historians who adorned the sixteenth and seventeenth centuries, I close this hasty sketch of European literature.

In France we find, as historians of that period, De Thou and Davila. The History of the president De Thou, comprehending the annals of his own time, from 1545 to 1607, is written with great judgment and impartiality. He wrote in Latin, and his style, with considerable purity, has an uncommon degree of force and elevation. Davila, an Italian, has no other title to be classed among the French historians than having long resided in France, and written of the affairs of that kingdom. His History of the Civil Wars of France, from the death of Henry II. to the peace of Vervins, in 1598, and the establishment of Henry IV. upon the throne, is written in excellent Italian, and, if considered as the composition of a partisan, is marked by no common degree of candor and impartiality.

In Italy, Machiavel, in the beginning of the sixteenth century, composed his History of Florence, a work classical in point of style, though not always to be depended on in point of fact. Bentivoglio, in his History of the Civil Wars of Flanders, has united great political knowledge with perspicuity of narration and force of language. He is often wonderfully eloquent. As a model of the perfect historical style, we cannot recommend a finer example than Bentivoglio's introduction to the work we have mentioned.

Among the English historians, Sir Walter Raleigh possesses a purity of language remarkable for the times in which he lived:

for the age of James I. was distinguished by a false and vicious taste in writing. But his chief excellence is his judicious selection of facts. His History of the World, though a work of great judgment and perspicuity, is yet in point of style rather beneath that dignity of expression which is required in historical composition.

Clarendon has great natural powers; no author possessed more acuteness in discerning characters, or a happier talent in delineating them. He is an author who is looked upon as a party writer, as every writer must be who gives the history of a period distinguished by the violence of party, and who relates transactions in which he himself was actively concerned. But Clarendon was a man of virtue and probity: he never wilfully misleads; and if we cannot implicitly assent to his political creed, we respect his talents and revere his integrity.

At this period of the history of the world, the department of Universal History may be said to terminate. It would certainly be desirable that any work on so comprehensive a subject should include the widest range in point of time, and even embrace the events of the present age; but many circumstances conspire to render this difficult in a work on general history, and almost impossible in the form and for the purpose for which this work was composed, viz., as a course of lectures delivered from an academical chair in the University of Edinburgh. The quantity of important matter which accumulates as we reach the more recent periods—the interest which attaches itself to innumerable events, less from their actual importance, than from their connection with the feelings and passions of the present day—conspire to render the materials of recent history of a magnitude so disproportioned to those which form the narrative of more distant periods, that no discrimination could suffice to condense them within the requisite compass. It is the lapse of time alone that settles the relative importance of such materials; that throws into the shade or blots out from the canvass, those details which, however interesting they may seem to the actors, are of no real value to posterity; and leaves the great picture of human affairs charged with such features only as deserve a lasting memorial, and preserve their importance long after their immediate interest has ceased to enhance it.

It is not, therefore, in a work on General History that the student must expect to obtain a knowledge of his own times, or of those which immediately precede them; but the general views which he may here receive of the history of former ages, and that method and arrangement which he will here find pursued, will enable him to prosecute his historical studies with more real benefit to himself, and with less risk of being led astray by the partial and often contradictory statements of contemporary annalists.

INDEX

TO THE

UNIVERSAL HISTORY

INDEX.

The numerals before the Arabic Figures refer to the different Volumes.

www.ingramcontent.com/pod-product-compliance
Lightning Source LLC
LaVergne TN
LVHW021306110826
845150LV00003B/493

* 9 7 8 1 4 2 5 5 5 9 7 7 9 *